BEGINNER TO PRO

D1188979

murach's
visual basic
6

Ed Koop

Anne Prince

Joel Murach

MIKE MURACH & ASSOCIATES, INC.

2560 West Shaw Lane, Suite 101 • Fresno, CA 93711-2765

Writers:	Ed Koop
	Anne Prince
	Joel Murach
Cover design:	Zylka Design
Production:	Tom Murach

Other books in this series

Visual Basic 5 by Ed Koop and Anne Prince

Access 97 by Anne Prince and Joel Murach

Printed in the United States of America.

10 9 8 7 6 5 4 3
ISBN: 1-890774-04-9

Library of Congress Cataloging-in-Publication Data

Koop, Edward.
    Murach's Visual Basic 6 : beginner to pro / Ed Koop, Anne Prince,
Joel Murach.
              p.   cm.
  ISBN 1-890774-04-9
  1. Microsoft Visual BASIC.   2. BASIC (Computer program language)
I. Prince, Anne. II. Murach, Joel, 1968- . III. Title.
IV. Title: Visual Basic 6.
QA76.73.B3K66   1999
005.26'8--dc21   99-13011
                                            CIP

Contents

Introduction   xiii

Section 1   The basics of Visual Basic programming

Chapter 1   Introduction to Visual Basic programming   3
Chapter 2   Visual Basic coding essentials   47
Chapter 3   How to work with forms and controls   103
Chapter 4   How to test and debug an application   139

Section 2   The essentials of database programming

Chapter 5   Introduction to database applications   171
Chapter 6   Introduction to database programming   207
Chapter 7   How to build bound forms with ADO   253
Chapter 8   How to build unbound forms with ADO   289
Chapter 9   How to use the Data Environment Designer to build forms   335
Chapter 10   How to use the Data Report Designer to develop reports   373
Chapter 11   How to use the Data View window to work with databases   403

Section 3   Other development skills

Chapter 12   How to enhance the user interface   435
Chapter 13   How to use class modules and ActiveX components   475
Chapter 14   How to develop an application for the Internet   519
Chapter 15   How to distribute an application   543

Appendixes

Appendix A   How to download or create the Access databases   581
Appendix B   The specifications for the SQL Server databases   597
Appendix C   Special considerations for users of the Learning Edition   603
Index   607

Expanded contents

Section 1 The basics of Visual Basic programming

Chapter 1 Introduction to Visual Basic programming

How to build a user interface 4
An introduction to forms and controls 4
How to start a new project 6
How to work with the IDE 8
How to add controls to a form 10
How to set properties 12
Common properties for forms and controls 14
The property settings for the Calculate Investment form 16
How to save a project and its forms 18
How to test a form 18
Exercise set 1-1: Build the user interface 20

How to write the code for an interface 22
How an application responds to events 22
How to code an event procedure 24
How to code a general procedure 26
How to refer to properties and methods 28
How to use functions 30
How to get help information 32
How to test and debug an application 34
Exercise set 1-2: Write the code 36

An enhanced version of the Calculate Investment form 38
How the enhanced interface works 38
The property settings for the new controls 38
The code for the enhanced application 40
How to print the code for an application 42
How to create an EXE file for an application 42
Exercise set 1-3: Enhance the application 44

Chapter 2 Visual Basic coding essentials

Basic coding skills 48
How to use continuation characters and comments 48
How to use the Edit toolbar 50
How to create a standard module 52
How to code with a readable style 54
Exercise set 2-1: Experiment with coding techniques 56

How to work with variables and constants 58
How to declare variables 58
How to control the scope of variables 60
How to assign values to variables 62
How to create user-defined constants 64
How to use Visual Basic constants 64

How to code arithmetic expressions 66
How to code conditional expressions 68
How to work with arrays 70
Exercise set 2-2: Use variables and constants 72

Visual Basic statements **74**
How to code If statements 74
How to code Select Case statements 76
How to code For…Next statements 78
How to code Do…Loop statements 80
How to code On Error statements 82
How to code With statements 84
A summary of other Visual Basic statements 86
Exercise set 2-3: Use some new statements 88

Procedures and functions **90**
How to code and call a Sub procedure 90
How to code and call a Function procedure 92
A summary of the Visual Basic functions 94
How to use the MsgBox function 96
A parsing routine that uses eight different functions 98
Exercise set 2-4: Create and use functions 100

Chapter 3 How to work with forms and controls

Basic skills for working with forms **104**
How to add a form to a project 104
How to change the startup form 106
How to use the Project Explorer 108
How to use the Form Layout window 110
Exercise set 3-1: Add a new form to the project 112

Basic skills for working with controls **114**
The controls in the standard Toolbox 114
How to work with option buttons and check boxes 116
How to work with combo boxes and list boxes 118
How to add controls to the Toolbox 120
How to use a masked edit box 122
How to use the Validate event 122
How to use the Object Browser 124
Exercise set 3-2: Add controls to the new form 126

How to develop a multiple-document interface **128**
The difference between single-document and multiple-document
interfaces 128
How to create the parent and child forms 130
How to add menus to a form 132
How to write code that works with child forms 134
Exercise set 3-3: Create a multiple-document interface 136

Chapter 4 How to test and debug an application

Basic debugging skills **140**
How to set the options for debugging 140

How to work in break mode 142
How to use breakpoints 144
How to control the execution of an application 146
Exercise set 4-1: Use break mode and step through code 148

How to use the debugging windows **150**
How to use the Immediate window to work with values 150
How to use the Locals window to monitor variables 152
How to use the Call Stack to monitor called procedures 154
How to use the Watch window to monitor expressions 156
When and how to use the Quick Watch feature 156
Exercise set 4-2: Use the debugging windows 158

Other debugging techniques **160**
How to create a routine that handles specific types of trappable errors 160
How to test an error-handling routine 162
How to use compiler directives with debugging statements 164
Exercise set 4-3: Code and test an error-handling routine 166

Section 2 The essentials of database programming

Chapter 5 Introduction to database applications

Introduction to multi-user database applications **172**
The hardware components of a multi-user system 172
The software components of a typical multi-user database application 174

How a relational database is organized **176**
How a table is organized 176
How the tables in a database are related 178
How the fields in a table are defined 180

**How to use SQL to work with the data
in a relational database** **182**
How to query a single table 182
How to join data from two or more tables 184
How to modify the data in a table 186
How to use views, stored procedures, and triggers 188

**How a DBMS provides for referential integrity,
security, and locking** **190**
How referential integrity works 190
How data security works 192
How locking works 194

Data access options and implementations **196**
Common data access options 196
Common data access implementations 198

Client/Server implementations **200**
Multi-tier systems and ActiveX components 200
Enterprise systems 202
Internet and intranet applications 204

Chapter 6   Introduction to database programming

Basic skills for building bound forms 208
How to use an ADO data control to process data 208
ADO data control and bound control properties 210
Cursor options 212
Locking options 214
How to build the connection string for an ADO data control 216
Property settings for the bound Vendors form 218
Code for the bound Vendors form 218
Exercise set 6-1: Build a bound form 220

How to work with ActiveX data objects 222
The ActiveX Data Object model 222
Common ADO properties and methods 224
Techniques for working with ADO objects through code 226
Exercise set 6-2: Enhance the bound form 228

Basic skills for building unbound forms 230
How the unbound version of the Vendors form works 230
How to process data without using a data control 232
How to open a connection to a database 234
How to open a recordset 236
How to use a control array 238
Code for the unbound Vendors form 240
Exercise set 6-3: Build an unbound form 250

Chapter 7   How to build bound forms with ADO

How to work with bound controls 254
Two forms that use bound controls 254
How to work with the DataList and DataCombo controls 256
How to work with the DataGrid control 258
How to set the properties for a DataGrid control 260
Property settings for the controls on the Vendors form 262
Why this application uses client-side cursors 264
Exercise 7-1: Build the Vendors form 266

Coding techniques for bound forms 268
How to use some common events for an ADO data control 268
How to use the MoveComplete event of an ADO data control 270
How to use the Error event of an ADO data control 272
The code for the standard module of the Vendors application 274
The code for the Vendors form 274
Bugs that occur when using a Jet database 276
Exercise set 7-2: Write the code for the Vendors form 278

The property settings and code for the New Vendor form 280
The property settings for the New Vendor form 280
The code for the New Vendor form 282
More about bugs that occur when using a Jet database 284
Exercise set 7-3: Build the New Vendor form 286

Chapter 8 How to build unbound forms with ADO

How to work with unbound controls 290

Three forms that use unbound controls 290

How to work with the ListBox and ComboBox controls 292

How to work with the MSFlexGrid control 294

Property settings for the controls on the Vendors form 296

Exercise set 8-1: Build the Vendors form 298

Coding techniques for unbound forms 300

How to work with Command objects 300

How to work with stored procedures that contain parameters 302

How to check for ADO and OLE DB provider errors 304

How to work with Connection and Recordset events 306

How to use transaction processing 308

How to create a connection string using a login form 310

The code for the standard module of the Vendors application 312

The code for the Vendors form 312

Exercise set 8-2: Write the code for the standard module
and Vendors form 320

**The property settings and code for the Login
and New Vendor forms** 322

The property settings for the Login and New Vendor forms 322

The code for the Login form 324

The code for the New Vendor form 326

Exercise set 8-3: Build the New Vendor and Login forms 332

**Chapter 9 How to use the Data Environment Designer
to build forms**

Basic skills for working with the Data Environment Designer ... 336

How to work with the Data Environment Designer 336

How to edit or create a Connection object 338

How to create a Command object 340

How to build a bound form from a Command object 342

How to change the mapping defaults 344

How to use Data Environment objects in code 346

Exercise set 9-1: Develop a bound form 348

Other skills for working with Command objects 350

How to use the Query Designer to create a query 350

How to use the Advanced tab to set Command properties 352

How to use the Relation tab to define a parent-child relationship 354

How to use the Grouping tab to define record groups 356

How to use the Aggregates tab to define aggregate fields 358

How to use the Parameters tab for queries that use parameters 360

Exercise set 9-2: Create the Command objects for a new project 362

An enhanced Vendors application 364

The enhanced Vendors form 364

The properties for the data-bound controls 366

The code for the Vendors application 368

Exercise set 9-3: Build an enhanced Vendors form 370

Chapter 10   How to use the Data Report Designer to develop reports

Basic skills for developing a data report 374
How to create a data report from a DataEnvironment object 374
How to work in the Data Report window 376
How to add predefined fields to a report 378
How to format, preview, and print a report 380
Exercise set 10-1: Create a simple data report 382

How to add grouping and totals to a data report 384
How to create groups based on any field in a report 384
How to create groups based on hierarchical relationships 386
How to add functions to a report 388
Exercise set 10-2: Create a report with grouping and totals 390

How to use code to work with a data report 392
How to preview or print a data report 392
How to create a form that opens reports 394
How to modify a report at run-time 396
How to create a data report without a DataEnvironment object 398
Exercise set 10-3: Create a form for printing reports 400
Exercise set 10-4: Modify a report at run-time 401

Chapter 11   How to use the Data View window to work with databases

Introduction to the Data View window 404
Basic skills for working in the Data View window 404
How to create a data link 406
Exercise set 11-1: Create a data link and view database objects 408

How to work with tables 410
How to create or modify a table 410
How to work with constraints, relationships, indexes, and keys 412
How to add or change table data 414
Exercise set 11-2: Modify the data and design of a table 416

How to work with other database objects 418
How to create or modify a database diagram 418
How to create or modify a view 420
How to create a query 422
How to create or modify a stored procedure 424
How to create or modify a trigger 426
Exercise set 11-3: Create a database diagram and other database objects ... 428

Section 3   Other development skills

Chapter 12   How to enhance the user interface

An introduction to user interfaces 436
Single-document and multiple-document interfaces 436
Splash forms and startup forms 438

How to start an application with a splash form 440
Two quick ways to add help information 442
Exercise set 12-1: Start an MDI interface 444

How to add menus, toolbars, and status bars 446
How to create menus 446
How to create a toolbar using a PictureBox control
and command buttons 448
How to create a toolbar using Toolbar and ImageList controls 450
How to create a status bar 452
How to use code to work with menus, toolbars, and status bars 454
Exercise set 12-2: Enhance the interface 456

How to use the Microsoft Help Workshop 458
An overview of the Microsoft Help Workshop 458
How to create a topic file 460
How to create a contents file 462
How to map a help topic to a numeric value 464
How to compile and test the help project 466
How to use a help file in a Visual Basic application 468
Exercise set 12-3: Add help information 470

Chapter 13   How to use class modules and ActiveX components

How to create and use class modules 476
An overview of class modules 476
How to use the properties and methods of a class object............................. 478
How to create a class module 480
How to define class properties 482
How to define class methods.. 484
How to define and use class events 486
The code for the Book Order class module 488
The code for the Book Order form module 490
Exercise set 13-1: Create the Book Order application 492

An enhanced version of the Book Order application 494
How the enhanced application works 494
The code for the enhanced class module 496
The code for the enhanced form module 500
Exercise set 13-2: Enhance the Book Order application 502

How to create and use ActiveX components 504
An overview of ActiveX components 504
How an application communicates with ActiveX components..................... 506
A general procedure for creating and testing an ActiveX component 508
How to create an ActiveX project 510
How to set the properties for an ActiveX project 512
How to use ActiveX components 514

The benefits of using class modules 516
Exercise set 13-3: Create and use an ActiveX component 517

Chapter 14   How to develop an application for the Internet

An introduction to building Internet applications 520
An introduction to Internet applications 520
The two types of Internet applications you can build with Visual Basic 522
Features and requirements of DHTML and IIS applications 524

Basic skills for building a DHTML application 526
An overview of DHTML applications 526
How to use the DHTML Page Designer 528
How to develop the code for a DHTML application 530
How to test and build a DHTML application 530

Basic skills for building an IIS application 532
An overview of IIS applications 532
How to create an HTML page 534
How to use the Webclass Designer 536
How to develop the code for an IIS application 538
How to use webclass tags to display data on an HTML page 540
How to test and build an IIS application 540

Chapter 15   How to distribute an application

An introduction to the Package and Deployment Wizard 544
How the Package and Deployment Wizard works 544
How to install the Package and Deployment Wizard 546
How to start the Package and Deployment Wizard 546
How to work with the Package and Deployment Wizard 548

How to distribute an application 550
Step 1: Create the package 550
Step 2: Deploy the package 558
Step 3: Run the setup program to install the application 562
Exercise set 15-1: Install the Accounts Payable application 564

Other deployment issues 566
How to work with scripts 566
How to handle missing dependency information 568
How to create a dependency file for an ActiveX component or control 570
How to create an installation CD 570
A summary of the files in the Package and Support folders 572
How to deploy Internet applications 574
Exercise set 15-2: Install the Book Orders application 576

Introduction

In chapter 1 of this book, you'll learn how to develop a substantial Visual Basic application. By the time you finish the first four chapters, you'll know how to develop, test, and debug applications with multiple-document interfaces. *No other VB book gets you started that fast.*

In section 2 of this book, you'll learn how to develop database applications the way the best professionals do. At the same time, you'll learn how to use the best new features of Visual Basic 6 for developing those applications. *No other VB book teaches you so much about database programming and the new Visual Basic 6 features.*

In the last section of this book, you'll master other skills that a professional programmer needs, like how to distribute an application and how to create and use ActiveX components as you develop systems. *No other VB book prepares you so thoroughly for working as a Visual Basic programmer in industry...or for mastering new VB skills on your own.*

5 ways this book differs from all the others

- Section 1 of this book is a short course in Visual Basic programming, and section 2 is a complete course in database programming. To develop the same skills that you'll gain in these two sections, you'd have to buy both a beginner's book and a database programming book from most competing publishers. And you wouldn't learn as much.

- To help you learn more easily, this book presents 12 complete, real-world, business applications, including all of the Visual Basic code. In our experience, working with complete applications like these is the best way to learn. That's because you see all of the relationships between the objects, properties, methods, events, and Visual Basic code that an application requires. And yet, no other book takes this approach to Visual Basic training.

- To insure your success, all of the programming chapters include exercise sets that guide you through the development of the applications...but only after you've learned the skills you need for doing the exercises. In contrast, most other books introduce new skills and information within their exercise sets. We believe that's an ineffective way to teach, and that's one more reason why you'll learn faster and better when you use this book.

- As you page through this book, you'll see that all of the essential skills are presented in the figures, or illustrations, on the odd-numbered pages, while the text on the facing pages gives the perspective that you need for using the skills (as one of our authors puts it, the illustrations contain all the information he used to have to highlight in his texts when he was in school). We've been experimenting with this presentation method for about four years; it works better than any other we've ever used; and you won't find anything like it anywhere else.

- After you use this book to learn Visual Basic programming, it becomes the best reference guide you've ever used. Why? Because all of the crucial information is presented in the figures under headings that clearly identify the information chunks. This not only means that you can find what you're looking for faster, but also that you read less to get the information you need.

Who this book is for

This book works best if you have programming experience with another language, if you're upgrading to VB6 from an earlier version, or if you've already read a beginning VB book. If you're completely new to VB, section 1 is a fast-paced introduction. If you're upgrading or you've read another VB book, section 1 is a great review of the critical VB skills.

On the other hand, this book can also work well if you have no programming experience at all, as long as you're comfortable with the accelerated pace (we've found that people who are good at math and science have no trouble with the programming notation, even when it's new to them). You do have to be familiar with the Windows 95 or 98 interface, but that just means that you've used one or more Windows programs like Word or Excel.

What this book does

Since the trick to learning Visual Basic is seeing how all of the parts of an application fit together, chapter 1 of this book introduces you to the parts: the objects that you work with; the properties, methods, and events of the objects; and the Visual Basic code that lets you work with the properties and methods whenever a specific event occurs. Once you understand these relationships, your learning will progress quite rapidly because you'll understand the underlying concepts of an event-driven language and its object orientation.

After this introduction, chapter 2 presents the coding details of the Visual Basic language, chapter 3 presents more of the skills you need for working with form and control objects, and chapter 4 presents the features that help you test and debug a program. By the time you complete this first section, you'll have the conceptual understanding and hands-on skills that you need for developing, testing, and debugging an application that doesn't require the use of a database.

But 90% of all Visual Basic applications *do* retrieve and update the data in a database. That's why section 2 teaches you how to develop database applications. In chapter 5, you'll learn the concepts and terms that let you understand how those applications work. In chapters 6, 7, and 8, you'll learn how to build those applications with ADO, which is the preferred access method for Visual Basic 6. And in chapters 9, 10, and 11, you'll learn how to use three of the new features of Visual Basic 6: the Data Environment Designer for Rapid Application Development (RAD), the Data Report Designer for preparing reports, and the Data View Window for modifying and enhancing a SQL Server or Oracle database. When you finish this section, you'll have the skills of an entry-level database programmer in industry.

Then, section 3 presents some ways to produce even more professional applications. In particular, chapter 12 shows you how to enhance the user interface for an application by adding a startup form, a splash screen, menus, toolbars, and help. Chapter 13 shows you how to create objects of your own as well as ActiveX components. Chapter 14 introduces you to the complexities of writing an application for the Internet. And chapter 15 shows you how to distribute a finished application to the clients of a system.

What edition of Visual Basic 6 do you need

If you're familiar with Visual Basic, you know that it's available in three different editions: the Learning Edition, which costs around $100; the Professional Edition, which costs around $500; and the Enterprise Edition, which costs more than $1000. As you might guess, if you have the Professional or Enterprise edition, you can do everything that's presented in this book.

The good news for readers with a limited budget, though, is that you can learn most of the essential skills that are presented in this book with just the Learning Edition. The primary exceptions are chapters 9, 10, and 11, which show you how to use the new database tools, and chapter 14, which shows you how to develop web applications. These features aren't included in the Learning Edition.

Beyond that, you'll find that the Learning Edition doesn't support one of the controls presented in chapter 3, one of the ADO methods presented in chapters 7 and 8, and the creation of ActiveX components as presented in chapter 13. For a complete summary of these limitations and the ways to work around them, please refer to appendix C.

Web site items that can help you learn more quickly

To do the exercise sets for the chapters in sections 2 and 3, you're going to need two databases. You can set up Access versions of those databases on your system in just a few minutes by downloading them from our web site at *www.murach.com*. Or, if you don't have Internet access, you can create the databases on your own. For more information about either alternative, please refer to appendix A.

If you're in a school or training environment, you may have access to a SQL Server version of these databases on a network server. In that case, you can refer to appendix B to get the database specifications. This appendix should also be useful to the administrator who's responsible for converting the downloaded Access databases to SQL Server.

Beyond that, you can download the 12 applications that are presented in this book, including both SQL Server and Access versions of the database applications. Then, you can compare our applications with the ones you develop in the exercises. To download these applications, go to the Downloads portion of our web site (*www.murach.com/downloads*).

Access 2000 and SQL Server 7.0 considerations

When we wrote this book, Access 2000 and SQL Server 7.0 hadn't been released. Once they were released, though, we tested the 12 applications in this book using both those products. Since we expected these products to be upward-compatible, we were surprised to discover two minor problems.

One of the problems is caused by ADO 2.1, which is the version that you get with SQL Server 7.0. The other is caused by the Jet 4.0 OLE DB provider, which you get with Access 2000. You can find the details about these problems on pages 269 and 330.

Support materials for trainers and instructors

If you're a trainer or instructor who would like to use this book as the basis for a course, a complete set of instructional materials is available for it. They consist of behavioral objectives, short-answer tests, PowerPoint slides for classroom presentations, and student projects that have the students apply what they've learned to new applications. Taken together, this book and the instructional materials make a powerful teaching package.

To find out more, please visit the "Instructor Info" section of our web site at *www.murach.com*, call us at 1-800-221-5528, or e-mail me at *mike@murach.com* and ask about the Instructor's Guide for *Murach's Visual Basic 6*.

Please let me know how this book works for you

From the start, our goal has been to teach you Visual Basic more quickly and more thoroughly than any other book…and to give you both the know-how and the confidence you need to develop applications in the corporate world.

If you have any comments about this book when you finish it, I'd enjoy hearing from you. I'd especially like to know if this book lived up to your expectations. To reply, you can e-mail me at *mike@murach.com* or send your comments to our street address. We always appreciate it, too, if you post your comments at the online bookseller sites (the good comments, anyway!).

Thanks for buying this book. Thanks for reading it. And good luck with your Visual Basic programming.

Mike Murach, Publisher

Section 1

The basics of Visual Basic programming

The fastest way to learn Visual Basic programming is to do it, and that's the approach that the chapters in this section take. So in chapter 1, you'll learn how to develop a substantial Visual Basic application. When you're done, you'll know how to build a user interface and how to add the code to it that makes it work the way you want it to.

Then, chapter 2 presents the coding essentials that you'll use in the Visual Basic applications that you develop. Chapter 3 shows you how to develop a user interface that uses more forms and controls. And chapter 4 shows you how to use the Visual Basic features that help you test and debug an application. By the time you finish these chapters, you'll have developed an application that consists of three forms in a Multiple Document Interface. You'll have the essential skills that you need for working with every application you develop. And you'll have a clear view of what Visual Basic programming is and what you have to do to become proficient at it.

To make sure that you're successful as you develop, test, and debug the applications in each of these chapters, exercise sets are interspersed throughout the text. These exercises guide you through the development and enhancement of the applications; they encourage you to try new techniques; and they are an essential part of the learning process.

1

Introduction to Visual Basic programming

Although most programming books start with an introductory chapter or two, the quickest and best way to *learn* Visual Basic programming is to *do* Visual Basic programming. That's why this chapter shows you how to develop a substantial Visual Basic application without any preface or preamble. When you turn the page, you'll start learning how to build the user interface for the application. And before long, you'll start to experience the excitement of Visual Basic programming.

To make sure that you're able to successfully develop the application that's illustrated in the text, three exercise sets within this chapter guide you through its development. If you have extensive programming experience, you may want to develop the application without the guidance of the exercise sets. But otherwise, doing the exercises will help you learn faster and more thoroughly.

How to build a user interface **4**
An introduction to forms and controls 4
How to start a new project 6
How to work with the IDE 8
How to add controls to a form 10
How to set properties 12
Common properties for forms and controls 14
The property settings for the Calculate Investment form 16
How to save a project and its forms 18
How to test a form 18
Exercise set 1-1: Build the user interface 20

How to write the code for an interface **22**
How an application responds to events 22
How to code an event procedure 24
How to code a general procedure 26
How to refer to properties and methods 28
How to use functions 30
How to get help information 32
How to test and debug an application 34
Exercise set 1-2: Write the code 36

An enhanced version of the Calculate Investment form .. **38**
How the enhanced interface works 38
The property settings for the new controls 38
The code for the enhanced application 40
How to print the code for an application 42
How to create an EXE file for an application 42
Exercise set 1-3: Enhance the application 44

Perspective **46**

How to build a user interface

When you develop a Visual Basic application, you start by designing a user interface. To do that, you add controls like text boxes and command buttons to a form. Then, you set the properties for the form and its controls. After you get that interface working right, you can write the Visual Basic code that makes the interface do what the user wants.

An introduction to forms and controls

Figure 1-1 shows a simple user interface for a Visual Basic application that does investment calculations. This is the interface for the application that you'll develop in this chapter. It consists of a single *form*. As you can see, this form is similar to a window in any other Windows applications with a Close button in its upper right corner. In a more complicated application, the user interface may require two or more forms as you will see in chapter 3.

To complete the user interface, *controls* are added to each form. These controls let the user interact with the application. When you use the application in this figure, for example, you can enter values into the *text boxes* and you can execute commands by clicking on the *command buttons*. Other common controls are *option buttons, labels*, *check boxes, combo boxes,* and *list boxes*.

Forms and controls are two types of *objects* that you'll work with as you develop Visual Basic applications, and each of these objects has its own *properties*, *methods*, and *events*. In this chapter, you'll learn how to use some of these properties, methods, and events as you develop the application for the user interface shown in this figure.

A typical Visual Basic form

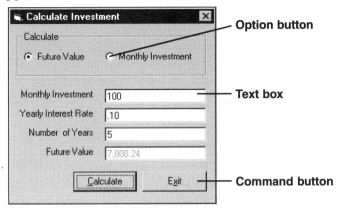

Concepts

- *Forms* provide the basis of the user interface for a Visual Basic application.

- *Controls* are added to a form so it provides the data and actions that are required. Some of the most common controls are *command buttons, text boxes, labels, option buttons, check boxes, list boxes,* and *combo boxes*, but many others are also available.

- Forms and controls are two types of *objects* that you work with in Visual Basic.

- An object has *properties, methods,* and *events.* You can set the properties of an object to control how the object looks and acts. You can invoke the methods of an object to perform actions on the object. And you can write code that responds to the events that happen to an object.

Figure 1-1   An introduction to forms and controls

How to start a new project

In Visual Basic, the applications that you develop are called *projects*. To start a new project, you use the New Project dialog box shown in figure 1-2. This is the dialog box that's displayed when you start Visual Basic, but a similar dialog box is displayed when you choose the New command in the File menu.

For most projects, you'll use the Standard EXE option to start a project that can be used to create an *executable file*, or *EXE*, that can be run from any machine that uses Windows 95, Windows 98, or Windows NT. When you select this option, Visual Basic starts a new project and displays a new form for it as shown in the next figure.

If you want to open an existing project right after you start Visual Basic, you can use the Existing and Recent tabs of the New Project dialog box. If, for example, you click on the Recent tab, you'll see a list of the projects that you worked on most recently. Then, you can double-click on the project you want to open. If the project you want isn't available on the Recent tab, you can click on the Existing tab to see a dialog box that's similar to the Open dialog box used in most Windows programs.

After you start Visual Basic and work on one project, you can start another new project by using the New command in the File menu. In this case, only the New tab is shown in the dialog box. Similarly, you can open an old project by using the Open command in the File menu, which shows only the Existing and Recent tabs in the Open dialog box.

The dialog box that's displayed when you start Visual Basic

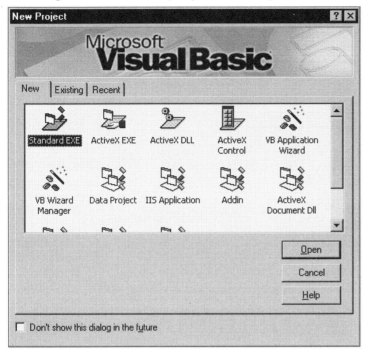

Operation

- Visual Basic lets you create several different types of projects. Most of the time, though, you choose the Standard EXE option to create a standard project.

- When you start Visual Basic, the New Project dialog box lets you open a new project, an existing project, or one that you worked on recently.

- After you've worked on one project, you can use the New command in the File menu to start another project or the Open command to open an existing project.

Figure 1-2   How to start a new project

How to work with the IDE

Figure 1-3 presents the Visual Basic application window. Since you use this window to perform all phases of application development, it is known as the *Integrated Development Environment*, or *IDE*. Like other Windows programs, Visual Basic provides menus and toolbars that you can use to perform its various operations. You can also right-click at appropriate places to get shortcut menus that provide context-sensitive commands.

To develop a form in Visual Basic, you work in the *Form window*. When you start a new project, a single blank form is displayed in this window. Then, you can use the *Toolbox* and the *Properties window* to develop this form. And if you add more forms to the project, you can use the *Project Explorer* to manage the forms.

By default, the Toolbox, Properties window, and Project Explorer are docked on the sides of the application window. However, they can also float in the middle of the application window. If you spend a little time experimenting with the skills described in this figure, you shouldn't have any trouble displaying, hiding, positioning, and resizing any of the windows in the IDE.

If you're familiar with other Windows applications, you should recognize some of the buttons in the Standard toolbar like the Open, Save, Cut, Copy, and Paste buttons. These buttons work much as they do in any other Windows application. If you place the mouse pointer over one of the toolbar buttons, you should see a ToolTip that gives its function. That will help you find the buttons for displaying the toolbar, Properties window, or Project Explorer.

The IDE for a new project

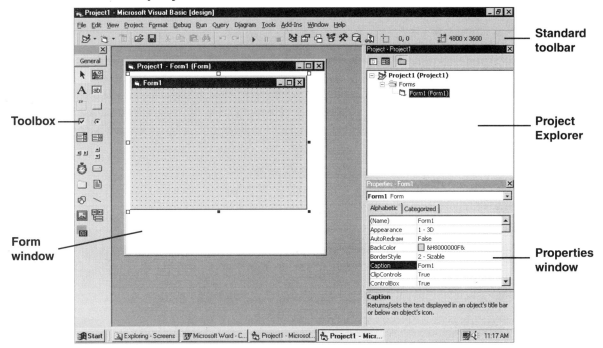

How to work with the Form window

- To select the form, click on it. Then, to change the size of the form, drag one of the handles that appear around it.
- To maximize or minimize the Form window, click on the Maximize and Minimize buttons.

How to work with the Toolbox, Project Explorer, and Properties windows

- To display one of these windows, you can click on the appropriate toolbar button or select the appropriate command from the View menu.
- To hide one of these windows, click on the Close button in the upper right corner of the window.
- To dock a floating window, drag it by the title bar to the edge of the window. To undock a docked window, drag it by the title bar away from the edge of the window. You can also dock or undock a window by double-clicking on the window's title bar.
- To size a window, position the mouse over the edge of the window until it becomes a double-arrow and then drag the edge of the window.

How to use shortcut menus

- When you right-click on a window or an object in a window, a context-sensitive shortcut menu is displayed. Then, you can select the command you want from that menu.

Figure 1-3   How to work with the IDE

How to add controls to a form

Figure 1-4 shows how you can use the Toolbox to add controls to a form. As you can see, one way to do that is to click on the control in the Toolbox, then click and drag in the form to place and size the control. In this figure, for example, a command button is being added to the form. You can also double-click on a control in the Toolbox to add a control in the center of the form.

After you add controls to a form, you often need to size and position them. If you experiment with the skills described in this figure, you shouldn't have any trouble working with one control at a time. Working with more than one control at a time, however, can take some practice.

Let's say, for example, that you have four text box controls on your form and you want to make them all the same size with the same alignment. First, you need to select all four text box controls. To do that, you can hold down the Shift key and click on the four controls. In this case, the last control you select will be highlighted by handles that look different than the others. Then, you can use the commands in the Format menu to give the other three text boxes the same height, width, and alignment as the highlighted control.

A form after some controls have been added to it

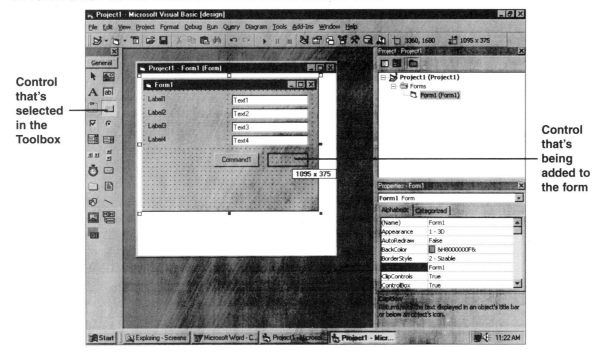

Control that's selected in the Toolbox

Control that's being added to the form

Operation

- To add a control to a form, click on the control in the Toolbox. Then, click in the form where you want to place the control and drag the pointer on the form to size the control. (You don't just drag the control from the Toolbox to the form.)

- You can also add a control by double-clicking on it, which places the control in the middle of the form. Then, you can move and size it.

- To select a control, click on it. To move a control, drag it. To size a selected control, drag one of its handles.

- To select more than one control, hold down the Shift key and click on the controls you want to select. You can also select more than one control by clicking on a blank spot on the form and then dragging around the controls you want to select. Notice that one of the selected controls is highlighted by handles that look different from the others.

- To align or size a group of selected controls relative to the highlighted control, use the Align or Size command in the Format menu. You can also drag one of the selected controls to move all of the selected controls to a new location.

Figure 1-4   How to add controls to a form

How to set properties

As you design a form, you set some of the *properties* for the form and its controls. That way, the form and its controls will look and work the way you want them to when the form is initially displayed.

To work with the properties of a form or control, you work in the Properties window as shown in figure 1-5. To display the properties for a specific form or control, you click on that object to select it. Then, when you click on a property in the Properties window, a brief description of that property is given at the bottom of the window. To change that property, you change the entry to the right of the property name.

To display properties alphabetically or by category, you can click on the appropriate tab at the top of the Properties window. At first, you may want to use the Categorized tab because it gives you an idea of what the different properties do. Once you get the hang of working with properties, though, you'll probably find the properties you're looking for faster by using the Alphabetic tab.

As you work with properties, you'll find that most properties are set correctly by default. In addition, many properties such as Height and Width are set interactively as you size and position the form and its controls in the Form window. As a result, you usually only need to change a few properties for each object. In particular, you usually need to change the Name and Caption properties that are described in the next figure.

A form after the properties have been set

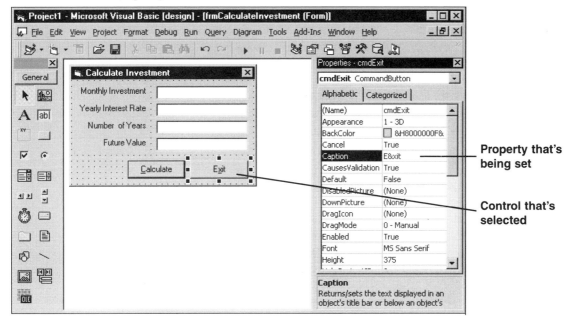

Property that's being set

Control that's selected

Operation

- In the Properties window, the properties for the selected object are displayed. To display the properties for another object, click on the object in the Form window. You can also select an object from the drop-down list at the top of the Properties window.

- To change a property, enter a value into its text box or select a value from its drop-down list if it has one. If a button with an ellipsis (…) appears at the right side of a property's text box, you can click on it to get help setting the property.

- When you click on a property in the Properties window, a brief explanation of the property appears at the bottom of the window. For more information, press F1 to display the help information for the property.

Figure 1-5   How to set properties

Common properties for forms and controls

Figure 1-6 shows 17 common properties for forms and controls. The first three properties apply to forms and controls, the next six properties apply only to forms, and the last eight properties apply to some common controls. Note, however, that some of these control properties only apply to certain types of controls. That's because different types of controls have different properties.

When you set the Name property for an object, you can use lowercase letters at the start of the object name to identify the object type. For example, the *cmd* in *cmdExit* means that the object is a command button. Although you're not required to use prefixes like this when you name objects, the prefixes make your code easier to read and understand.

When you set the Caption property for some objects, such as command buttons, you can use an ampersand (&) to create shortcut keys. If, for example, you enter *E&xit* for the Caption property of a command button, *Exit* will appear on the command button. Later on, when the application is in use, the user will be able to activate that command button by pressing Alt+x.

As you work with other properties, you'll find that you can often set them by selecting a value from a drop-down list. For example, you can select a True or False value for the Visible property of an object. Occasionally, though, you have to enter a number or text value for a property like 1 or 2 for the TabIndex property.

General properties

Property	Example	Description
Name	cmdExit	Sets the name that you use to refer to the object when you write the code for the application. You can use a three-letter prefix at the beginning of the name to identify the type of object.
Caption	E&xit	Sets the text that identifies a form or control. For some controls, you can type an ampersand (&) to underline the next letter. Then, the user can press Alt plus the underlined letter to activate the control.
Visible	True	Determines whether an object is displayed or hidden.

Form properties

Property	Example	Description
BorderStyle	2 – Sizable	Sets the border style for the form. This affects both the appearance and function of the form.
ControlBox	True	Determines whether a control box will be displayed in the upper left corner of the form.
MaxButton	True	Determines whether a Maximize button will be displayed on the form.
MinButton	True	Determines whether a Minimize button will be displayed on the form.
ShowInTaskbar	True	Determines whether a button representing the form will be shown in the Windows taskbar when the form is run.
StartupPosition	2 – CenterScreen	Determines how the form will be positioned on the screen when it is run.

Control properties

Property	Example	Description
Alignment	0 – Left Justify	Sets the justification for the text within some controls such as labels and text boxes.
Cancel	True	Determines whether the control will be activated when the user presses the Esc key.
Default	True	Determines whether the control will be activated when the user presses the Enter key.
Enabled	True	Determines whether the control will be enabled or disabled.
Locked	False	Determines whether the data in some types of controls such as text boxes and combo boxes can be edited.
TabIndex	0	Sets the order in which the controls receive the focus when the user presses the Tab key. Enter 0 for the first control, 1 for the second control, and so on.
TabStop	True	Determines whether the control will accept the focus when the user presses the Tab key to move from one control to another.
Text		Sets the text that's contained in some types of controls such as text boxes and combo boxes.

Figure 1-6   Common properties for forms and controls

The property settings for the Calculate Investment form

Figure 1-7 shows a form after some controls have been added to it and the properties for the form and the controls have been set. As you can see, you only need to change four properties for the form and two or three properties for the controls to get the interface to look the way you want it to. In addition, four properties (Name, Caption, Alignment, and Text) account for all but a few of the settings.

Since the form is designed so it's the right size for the controls that it contains, you can set the BorderStyle property to Fixed Single. Then, the user won't be able to change the size of the form by dragging the edge of the form. In addition, setting the BorderStyle property to Fixed Single automatically sets the MaxButton and MinButton properties for the form to False so the form won't contain Maximize or Minimize buttons. As you get used to working with controls, you'll find that it's common for a change in one property setting to affect other related property settings.

The only property you may need to set that isn't in this summary is the TabIndex property. This property is used to determine which control will receive the focus next when the user presses the Tab key. By default, the tab order is set to the order in which the controls were added to the form. To change this order, you can enter 0 for the TabIndex property of the first control that you want the user to tab to, 1 for the second control, and so on. As you make these entries, Visual Basic automatically adjusts the remaining numbers.

Please note that the Default property for the cmdCalculate button should be set to True. That means that this button will be activated when the user presses the Enter key on the keyboard. In this case, Visual Basic places a dark outline around this button to show that it is the default. Similarly, the Cancel property for the cmdExit button should be set to True. That means that this button will be activated when the user presses the Esc key, just as though the user clicked on this button.

The form for the Calculate Investment application

The property settings for the form

Default name	Property	Setting
Form1	Name	frmCalculateInvestment
	BorderStyle	1 - Fixed Single
	Caption	Calculate Investment
	StartUpPosition	2 - CenterScreen

The property settings for the controls

Default name	Property	Setting
Label1	Caption	Monthly Investment
	Alignment	1 – Right Justify
Label2	Caption	Yearly Interest Rate
	Alignment	1 – Right Justify
Label3	Caption	Number of Years
	Alignment	1 – Right Justify
Label4	Caption	Future Value
	Alignment	1 – Right Justify
Text1	Name	txtMonthlyInvestment
	Text	(empty)
Text2	Name	txtInterestRate
	Text	(empty)
Text3	Name	txtYears
	Text	(empty)
Text4	Name	txtFutureValue
	Text	(empty)
	Enabled	False
Command1	Name	cmdCalculate
	Caption	&Calculate
	Default	True
Command2	Name	cmdExit
	Caption	E&xit
	Cancel	True

Figure 1-7   The property settings for the Calculate Investment form

How to save a project and its forms

When you use Visual Basic, you work with a project file and one or more form files. To save changes to your project file and all form files, you can click on the Save Project button in the toolbar. The first time you click on this button, Visual Basic prompts you with dialog boxes like the ones shown in figure 1-8. The first dialog box is used to save the form file while the second dialog box is used to save the project file. When you complete these dialog boxes, Visual Basic automatically adds the *frm* extension for form files and the *vbp* extension for project files.

Most of the time, you'll want to save all the files for a project in their own folder. In this figure, for example, you can see that both the project file and the form file are being saved in a folder called Chapter 1. That makes it easier for you to manage the files for a project.

If you've entered a Name property for the form, Visual Basic displays that name in the Save As dialog box for the form. Since that's usually the name you want, it makes sense to set the Name property before you save the form. In this figure, for example, the form file is being saved as frmCalculateInvestment. On the other hand, the project file is being saved as Financial Calculations because the project will eventually contain another form that performs a different type of financial calculation. After you've saved a project and its forms, you can see the names you've used in the Project Explorer window.

How to test a project

When your project contains only one form, you can test that form by clicking on the Start button in the toolbar or by pressing F5 as summarized in figure 1-8. Then, the form will run in its own window. As you would expect, you can stop this form from running by clicking on the Close button in the upper right corner. You can also stop it by clicking on the End button in the Standard toolbar of Visual Basic.

The dialog boxes for saving the form and project files

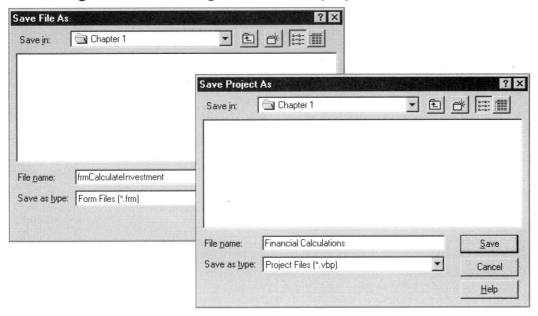

How to save a project and its forms

- To save a project and its forms for the first time, click on the Save Project button in the toolbar. Visual Basic then asks you to provide a name for each form as well as a name for the entire project.

- Once saved, you can click on the Save Project button to save the updated versions of the forms and project at any time. Or, to save the changes to the current form only, you can press Ctrl+S.

- If Visual SourceSafe has been installed on your PC, a dialog box may ask whether you want the project added to SourceSafe the first time you save a project. If so, click on the No button since SourceSafe is designed for version control when two or more people are working on the same project.

How to test a project

- To start a project, click on the Start button in the toolbar or press F5. When the project consists of only one form, this starts that form.

- When a form is running, you can stop it by clicking on the form's Close button or by switching to Visual Basic and clicking on the End button in the toolbar.

Figure 1-8   How to save and test a project

Exercise set 1-1: Build the user interface

This exercise set guides you through the process of creating a user interface. As you work, you'll see how easy this is when you use Visual Basic. Then, in exercise set 1-2, you'll add the code that makes the interface work the way you want it to. And in exercise set 1-3, you'll enhance both the form and the code to make it work even better.

Start a new project

1.   Start Visual Basic and begin a Standard EXE project.

2.   If necessary, use the toolbar buttons to open the Toolbox, Project Explorer, and Properties window and click on the Close button of the Form Layout window. Then, arrange the IDE as shown in figure 1-3 and experiment with the techniques presented in that figure.

Add controls to the new form

3.   Use the techniques in figure 1-4 to add controls to the form with approximately the same sizes and locations as this:

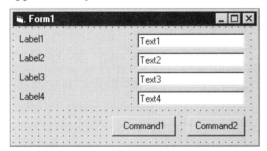

4.   Use the mouse to size and position the top label control as shown above. Next, select all of the label controls by holding down the Shift key as you click on them. Then, use the commands in the Format menu to size and align them the same as the top label control. Repeat this process with the text boxes and command buttons.

5.   Use the Properties window to set the properties for the form and its controls as shown in figure 1-7. Also, check the TabIndex properties to make sure the ones for the four text boxes and two command buttons are numbered from 0 through 5. When you're done, your form should look something like this:

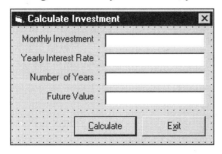

Save and test the form

6. Click on the Save Project button in the Standard toolbar to save the project and its forms in their own folder. In the first dialog box, click on the Create New Folder button and create a new folder for your project named Chapter 1 Financial. Then, save the form file as frmCalculateInvestment and the project file as Financial Calculations in this folder. If a dialog box asks whether you want to add this project to SourceSafe, click on the No button. When you're done, note that the project and form names have been added to the Project Explorer.

7. Click on the Start button in the toolbar or press F5 to run the form. When you do, the Calculate Investment form will run like this:

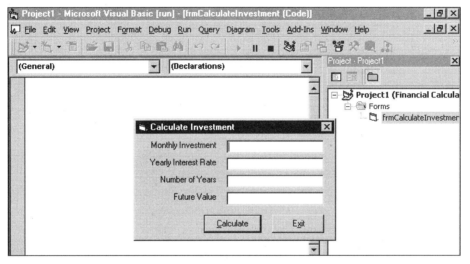

8. Experiment with the Calculate Investment form to see what it can do. When you enter text into the text boxes, notice how the text is aligned and formatted. When you press the Tab key, notice how the focus moves from one control to the other (but if the focus stops on the Future Value text box, you haven't set its Enabled property to False). When you click on the command button, notice how it indents and then pops back out just like any other Windows command button. Notice that the Calculate button has a dark outline around it to show that it is the default button (if it doesn't, you haven't set its Default property to True). As you can see, you've already accomplished a lot without writing a single line of code.

9. If you notice that some of the properties are set incorrectly, click on the Close button in the upper right corner of the form to close the form. Then, make the necessary changes, and run the form again. This time, click on the End button in Visual Basic's Standard toolbar to close the window for the form. When you're satisfied that the form is working right, save all the changes you made by clicking on the Save Project button in the toolbar.

Exit from Visual Basic

10. Exit Visual Basic by clicking on the Close button in the upper right corner of the Visual Basic window.

How to write the code for an interface

After you build a user interface that consists of forms and controls, you write the code that makes this interface work the way you want it to. This is the programming part of application development. The language that you use for this programming is called Visual Basic (VB). A variation of this language called Visual Basic for Applications (VBA) can be used with other Windows applications like Access and Excel.

How an application responds to events

Visual Basic applications are *event-driven*. That means that they work by responding to the events that occur on objects. To respond to an event, you write code in the form of an *event procedure* as illustrated in figure 1-9. This figure shows the event procedure that's executed when the user clicks on the Exit command button on the Calculate Investment form. Between the Sub and End Sub statements that start and end the procedure, the Unload statement unloads the form.

The most common event for most controls is the Click event. This event occurs when the user clicks on an object with the mouse. In addition, three other common events are described in this figure. Note, however, that most objects have many more events that the application can respond to. For example, events occur when the user positions the mouse over an object or when the user presses or releases a key.

Note also that not all events are started by user actions. For instance, the GotFocus and LostFocus events can occur when the user moves the focus to or from a control, but they can also occur when the Visual Basic code moves the focus to or from a control. Similarly, the Unload and Load events occur when the Unload and Load statements are executed, not by a user action.

Event: The user clicks on the Exit button.

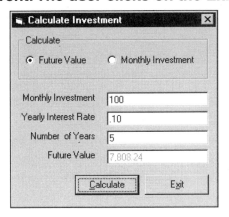

Response: The procedure for the Click event of the Exit button is executed.

```
Private Sub cmdExit_Click()
    Unload frmCalculateInvestment
End Sub
```

Common control events

Event	Occurs when ...
Click	...the user clicks on the control.
DblClick	...the user double-clicks on the control.
GotFocus	...the focus is moved to the control.
LostFocus	...the focus is moved from the control.

Common form events

Event	Occurs when...
Load	...the form is loaded but before it is displayed.
Unload	...the form is unloaded.

Concepts

- Windows programs work by responding to *events* that occur on objects. To tell your project how to respond to an event, you code an *event procedure*.

- An event can be an action initiated by the user like the Click event, or it can be an action initiated by program code like the Load or Unload event.

Figure 1-9   How an application responds to events

How to code an event procedure

To write code, you work in the *Code window* shown in figure 1-10. In this window, you can code *event procedures* for any object and event in an application. As you'll soon see, you also use this window to code other types of procedures.

From the Form window, you can start an event procedure by double-clicking on an object. Then, Visual Basic opens the Code window and generates the Sub and End Sub statements for the default event of the object. In this figure, for example, you can see the statements that are generated when you double-click on the Calculate command button. Then, you can write the code for the procedure between these statements.

Once you're in the Code window, you can start other event procedures by selecting the object and event from the drop-down lists at the top of the window. When you choose an object, you'll see that Visual Basic selects the default event for that object and adds a Sub and End Sub statement for that event procedure to the Code window. If that's not the event you want, you can choose a different event from the drop-down list so the correct Sub and End Sub statements are added to the Code window. Then, you can delete the Sub and End Sub statements that you don't want.

When you write code that's associated with a form, the code is stored in a *form module*. In this figure, for example, the title bar of the Code window shows that the procedure belongs to the form module for the Calculate Investment form. In the next chapter, you'll learn that you can also write procedures that are stored in *standard modules*. These procedures can then be used by the procedures in other modules.

The keyword *Private* in the Sub statement in this figure means that this procedure is a *private procedure* so it can't be called from other modules in the application (although this application doesn't have any). In the next chapter, though, you'll learn how to code *public procedures* that can be called from more than one module.

The third word in the Sub statement in this figure consists of an object name, an underscore, and an event name: cmdCalculate_Click. This is the name of the event procedure and that's how the names of event procedures are formed. The parentheses that follow this name indicate that no *arguments* can be passed to the procedure, which is the way most event procedures are coded.

The Code window with the start of an event procedure in it

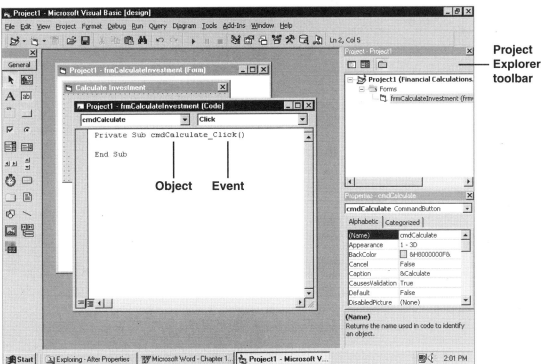

Project Explorer toolbar

Operation

- You use the Code window whenever you write a procedure for an application.
- To display the Code window and start an event procedure for the default event, double-click on the form or control that you want to write the procedure for. Or, to start an event procedure from the Code window, choose the object and event from the drop-down lists at the top of the window. In either case, Visual Basic generates the Sub and End Sub statements for the procedure so you can write the code between those statements.
- You can also code a procedure by typing the Sub statement directly into the Code window. When you complete that statement, Visual Basic automatically drops down two lines and adds the End Sub statement.
- The name of an event procedure consists of the object name, an underscore, and the event name. For example, the procedure named cmdCalculate_Click is for the Click event of the cmdCalculate button.

Three ways to switch between the Form and Code windows

- Click on the View Object or View Code buttons in the Project Explorer toolbar.
- Use the Windows menu to switch between open windows.
- Press Ctrl+F6 or Ctrl+Shift+F6 to move to the next or previous window.

Figure 1-10   How to code an event procedure

How to code a general procedure

In contrast to an event procedure, a *general procedure* doesn't respond to an event. Instead, it is *called* by an event procedure or another general procedure. In figure 1-11, for example, the event procedure for the Click event of the Calculate button consists of a single statement that calls the general procedure named CalculateFutureValue.

You normally code a general procedure when its code needs to be used by more than one procedure. That way, you don't have to repeat the code in each of the procedures that require it. You'll see this illustrated later on in this chapter.

One way to start the coding of a general procedure is to use the Add Procedure command in the Tools menu to display the dialog box in this figure. Here, you can type the name of the general procedure and select the Sub type and the Private scope. Then, when you click on the OK button, the Sub and End Sub statements are generated in the Code window.

Another way to start a general procedure is to type the Sub statement directly into the Code window. When you complete that statement, Visual Basic automatically adds the End Sub statement so you can enter the procedure code between these statements.

The Add Procedure dialog box for a private Sub procedure

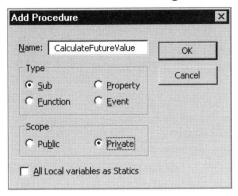

An event procedure that calls a general procedure

```
Private Sub cmdCalculate_Click()
    CalculateFutureValue ————————————————————— Procedure name
End Sub
```

A general procedure that's called by the event procedure above

```
Private Sub CalculateFutureValue() ——————————— Procedure name
    If Val(txtMonthlyInvestment) > 0 _
        And Val(txtInterestRate) > 0 _
        And Val(txtYears) > 0 Then
    txtFutureValue = _
        FV(txtInterestRate / 12, _
            txtYears * 12, txtMonthlyInvestment, 0, 1) * -1
    Else
        MsgBox "Invalid data. Please check all entries."
    End If
End Sub
```

Operation

- To code a general procedure, you can select the Add Procedure command from the Tools menu to display the Add Procedure dialog box. When you complete this dialog box, Visual Basic generates the Sub and End Sub statements so you can write the code for the procedure between those statements.

- You can also code a general procedure by typing it directly into the Code window.

- The settings in the Add Procedure dialog box above will start a *private Sub procedure*. In the next chapter, you'll learn more about that type of procedure as well as *public* and *Function procedures*.

Figure 1-11   How to code a general procedure

How to refer to properties and methods

As you enter the code for a procedure, you often need to refer to the properties and methods of objects. To do that, you type the name of the object, a period (also known as a *dot operator*, or *dot*), and the name of the property or method.

To make this easier for you, Visual Basic provides the Auto List Members feature shown in figure 1-12. After you type an object name and a dot, this feature displays a list of the properties and methods that are available for that object. Then, you can highlight the entry you want by typing the first few letters of its name, and you can complete the entry by pressing the Tab key.

To give you some idea of how properties and methods are used in code, this figure shows two examples of each. In the first example for properties, code is used to set an object's property to False. This code changes the initial value for that property that was set in the Properties window. In the second example, the value in the Text property of a text box object is tested to see whether it's greater than zero. In this case, the property name is omitted so the default property is used, which happens to be the Text property.

In the first example for methods, code is used to set the focus on a text box object. This in turn starts the SetFocus event, which can be used to start an event procedure. In the second example, code is used to hide a form. This is something you may want to do when the application consists of more than one form.

In practice, the property name is often omitted when the programmer wants to refer to the default property of an object. Although this shortens the code, it can also make it more difficult to understand because you have to remember what the default property is. For common objects, like text boxes, labels, and option buttons, though, you should remember what the default properties are so this isn't a problem.

A completion list that displays the properties and methods of an object

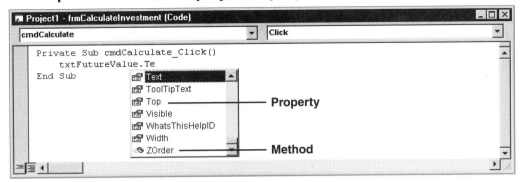

Statements that refer to properties

`cmdCalculate.Enabled = False`	Assigns the value "False" to the Enabled property of the command button named cmdCalculate so the button is disabled.
`If txtYears > 0 Then`	Tests the Text property of a text box named txtYears to see if it's greater than zero. Because no property is specified, the default property (Text) is assumed.

Statements that refer to methods

`txtMonthlyInvestment.SetFocus`	Uses the SetFocus method to move the focus to the text box named txtMonthlyInvestment.
`frmCalculateInvestment.Hide`	Uses the Hide method to hide the form named frmCalculateInvestment.

The default properties of some common objects

Object type	Default property
Text box	Text
Label	Caption
Option button	Value

Operation

- To insert the correct property or method into your code, type the first few letters of the property or method and press the Tab key when the correct one is highlighted.
- Visual Basic will only display a completion list like the one shown above when the Auto List Members feature is on. To turn this feature on, select the Options command from the Tools menu, click on the Editor tab of the Options dialog box, and check the Auto List Members check box.

Figure 1-12   How to refer to properties and methods

How to use functions

To make it easy for you to do a variety of calculations and other common operations, Visual Basic provides many built-in *functions*. The FV function, for example, calculates the future value of a periodic investment. As a result, it can be used to do the calculation required by the Calculate Investment form.

When you use a function, you need to supply one or more *arguments* that provide the values that are required by the function. For the FV function, for example, you need to at least supply the interest rate, the number of periodic payments, and the amount of the periodic payments. In addition, this function provides for two optional arguments that affect the result that's returned to the program by the function.

Here again, Visual Basic provides some help as you enter the arguments of a function as shown in figure 1-13. After you type the function name (in this case, FV) and an opening parenthesis, the Auto Quick Info feature gives you information about the function's arguments with optional arguments in brackets. Then, when you type the comma that's required after each argument, the next argument is boldfaced so you know where you are in the argument list. If you want to leave an optional argument at its default value, you just type a comma to move to the next argument in the list. When you complete the function by typing the closing parenthesis, Visual Basic may adjust some of the spacing before or after commas so you don't have to worry about that.

As you enter the arguments for a function like the FV function, you need to make sure that they are based on the same time period. If, for example, the periodic investment amount is for each month, then the interest rates and number of periods have to represent monthly values. To compensate for the way these values are entered into the controls of the form, you can code arithmetic expressions as shown in this figure. Here, since the investment amounts are monthly, the yearly interest rate is divided by 12 (txtInterestRate / 12) and the number of years is multiplied by 12 (txtYears * 12).

For some functions, the information supplied by the Auto Quick Info feature is all you need for entering the arguments. For other functions, though, you'll need to use the Help feature to get more information about what the arguments are. For the FV function, for example, you'll probably need to refer to the help information before you'll understand its fourth and fifth arguments. You'll also need to refer to the help information to figure out why it returns a negative value, which forces you to multiply it by -1 in order to get a positive result.

In the complete statement shown in this figure, the completed function is shaded. Here, you can see that the Text properties (the defaults) of three text boxes are supplied as the first three arguments, and the last two arguments are 0 and 1. The value returned by this function is then multiplied by -1, and this result is placed in the Text property of the Future Value text box.

The syntax for a function that accepts five arguments

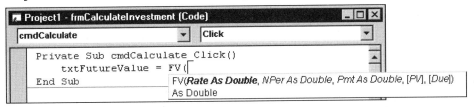

The same function after the first argument has been entered

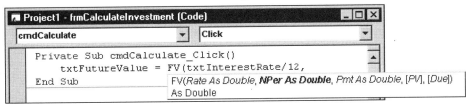

The complete statement

```
txtFutureValue = FV(txtInterestRate / 12, txtYears * 12, _
                    txtMonthlyInvestment, 0, 1) * -1
```

Description

- In general, a *function* returns a value to a procedure based on the *arguments* that are sent to it. In the example above, the FV function returns its value to the Text property of the object named txtFutureValue.

Operation

- After you type the name of the function and a space or an opening parenthesis, the syntax for the function is displayed as shown above. Optional arguments in this syntax summary are enclosed in brackets [ ].

- As you enter the arguments for a function, Visual Basic boldfaces the current argument. To move to the next argument, type a comma.

- To get help information about the arguments for a function, press the F1 key while you're entering it.

- An argument can be an arithmetic expression as illustrated by the first argument in the example above: txtInterestRate / 12. This means that the argument will be the value in the text box named txtInterestRate divided by 12.

- Information about arguments will only be displayed when the Auto Quick Info feature is on. To turn this feature on, select the Options command from the Tools menu, click on the Editor tab, and check the Auto Quick Info box.

Figure 1-13   How to use functions

How to get help information

Visual Basic 6 does not use the standard Help feature that's used with other Windows programs. Instead, it uses a Help feature that's used with the Microsoft Developer Network, or MSDN. As you can see in figure 1-14, this Help feature uses the MSDN browser to navigate through the help information.

When you're working in the Code window or the Form window, the quickest way to get help information is to press F1 while the insertion point is in a word or an object is selected. This starts the MSDN browser. If the Help feature recognizes that word or object, this also displays its help information in the right pane of the browser. In this figure, for example, you can see the help information for the FV function.

Another way to access the MSDN browser is to select the Contents, Index, or Search command from the Help menu. You can also access this browser by pressing F1 when the insertion point isn't in a word that the Help feature recognizes. In either case, you can use the Contents, Index, or Search tab on the left pane to display the information you need in the right pane.

If you've used the Help features for other Windows programs, of course, you shouldn't have any trouble using this one, although it's so cumbersome that you may not like it. Otherwise, a few minutes of experimentation should get you comfortable with the use of this feature.

If you have a modem on your PC, you can use the MSDN browser to get help information from Microsoft's web site. One problem with this, though, is that once you install this browser your PC may try to connect to the Internet whenever you start your PC. This is a known problem that will be eventually be corrected, but it is nonetheless annoying.

The MSDN browser with the help information for the FV function

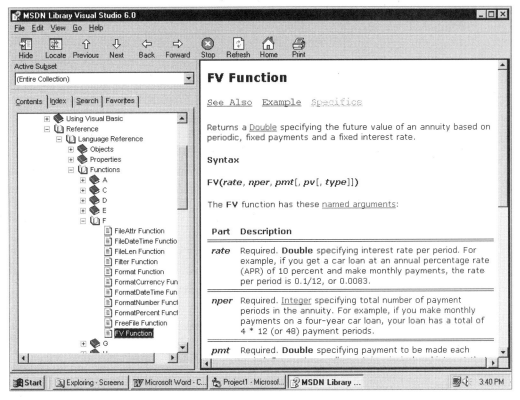

Description

- To display context-sensitive help information, position the insertion point in a keyword in the Code window or select an object in the Form window. Then, press F1. If the Help feature recognizes the keyword or object, the MSDN browser shown above will display the context-sensitive information.

- A second way to get help information is to select the Contents, Index, or Search commands from the Help menu. Then, you can use the Contents, Index, and Search tabs on the left pane of the MSDN browser to display help information in the right pane.

- Once you've used the MSDN browser to display a help topic, you can use the buttons in its toolbar to navigate through help topics and to print help topics. You can also click on underlined words to display more help information.

- If you have an Internet connection, you can use the MSDN browser to get information from Microsoft's web site.

- Depending on how you installed Visual Basic, the Help feature may require that you place one of the Visual Basic CD ROMs in your drive.

Figure 1-14   How to get help information

How to test and debug an application

When you develop a Visual Basic application, it's a good practice to test and debug the code each time you add a new procedure or a few related procedures. Figure 1-15 shows how. Then, when you're sure that those procedures work correctly, you code a few more procedures.

As you enter the code for a procedure and before you test it, Visual Basic checks the syntax for each statement and displays a dialog box when it detects an error. This type of error is illustrated by the first dialog box in this figure, and it is called a *compile error*. You correct this type of error as you enter the code. Can you spot the cause of the compile error in this example? (There's no comma between the second and third arguments.)

When you're ready to test the new procedures that you've added to the application, you can run the program by pressing the F5 key or clicking on the Start button in the Standard toolbar. Visual Basic then compiles and tests the application one statement at a time. If it detects an error when it compiles a statement, a dialog box for a compile-time error is displayed. If it detects an error when it runs the compiled statement, a dialog box for a *run-time error* is displayed. This type of error is illustrated by the second dialog box in this figure.

When you click on the Debug button in the dialog box for some types of run-time errors, Visual Basic switches you to the Code window and highlights the statement that couldn't be executed. This helps you figure out what the problem is so you can correct it.

All too frequently, though, the message in the dialog box is little or no help; the help information that you can get by clicking on the Help button doesn't help either; and the statement that's highlighted isn't really the statement that needs to be corrected. Beyond that, many programming errors are *logical errors* that don't show up as run-time errors. As a result, you have to find and correct those errors when you realize that the program isn't working the way it's supposed to. Fortunately, Visual Basic provides a variety of other features for debugging an application, and you can learn how to use them in chapter 4.

A dialog box for a compile-time error

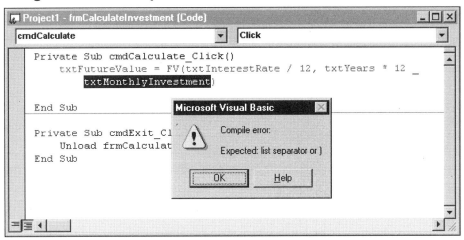

A dialog box for a run-time error

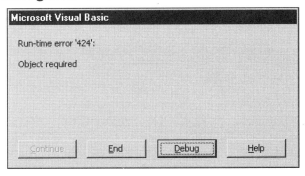

Description

- When a *compile error* is detected, a dialog box like the first one above is displayed. Then, you can click on the OK button to return to the Code window and fix the error.

- When a *run-time error* is detected, a dialog box like the second one above is displayed. This means that the statement compiled okay, but an error occurred when the statement was executed. Then, if you click on the Debug button, you are switched to the statement that caused the error. Or, if you click on the End button, the project will be stopped and you will be returned to the IDE.

Figure 1-15   How to test and debug an application

Exercise set 1-2: Write the code

In the last exercise set, you created the user interface for the Calculate Investment form. In this one, you will write the code for that form.

Open the project

1. Start Visual Basic and open the Financial Calculations project by double-clicking on the project name in the Recent tab of the New Project dialog box.

2. If necessary, use the Project Explorer to display the Calculate Investment form in the Form window. To do that, double-click on the Forms folder to open it, then double-click on the form name.

Code and test the event procedures

3. Double-click on the Exit command button to enter the Code window. This generates the Sub and End Sub statements for the Click event of this object. Then, you can enter the Unload statement between those statements so the entire procedure looks like this:

```
Private Sub cmdExit_Click()
    Unload frmCalculateInvestment
End Sub
```

4. From the Code window, pull down the Object list and select the Calculate command button (cmdCalculate). This generates the Sub and End Sub statements for the Click event of this object. Then, you can enter the FV function between those statements so the entire procedure looks like this:

```
Private Sub cmdCalculate_Click()
    txtFutureValue = FV(txtInterestRate / 12, txtYears * 12, _
        txtMonthlyInvestment) * -1
End Sub
```

    Note here that the underscore character is used to continue the argument list from one line to the next. To get a compile error, though, omit or delete the underscore so you can see the type of message that you get. Note also that this function is multiplied by -1 so it will return a positive value.

5. Press F5 to test the application. Next, to see if the calculation works, enter numeric values in the text boxes and click on the Calculate button or press the Enter key to activate it. Assuming that the calculation does work, click on the Exit button or press the Escape key to end the program. If either of these procedures doesn't work right, of course, you need to find the bugs, correct them, and test the application again.

6. Press F5 to test the application again. This time, enter xx in the Years box or leave one of the fields blank. Then, click on the Calculate button, which will cause a run-time error. This shows that the code for this application needs to be enhanced so it checks for invalid data and advises the user accordingly. You'll learn how to do that when you return to the text. For now, though, click on the End button in Visual Basic's Standard toolbar to end the program.

Use a general procedure for the calculation

7. Select the Add Procedure command from the Tools menu. Then, enter CalculateFutureValue in the Name box, click on the Private button, and click on the OK button. This generates the Sub and End Sub statements for a general procedure.

    Next, highlight the two lines of code in the cmdCalculate_Click procedure; cut them to the clipboard by using Ctrl+X or the Cut button in the toolbar; move the cursor to the blank line in the CalculateFutureValue procedure, and paste the statements into that procedure by using Ctrl+V or the Paste button in the toolbar. At this point, the entire procedure should look like this:

    ```
    Private Sub CalculateFutureValue()
        txtFutureValue = FV(txtInterestRate / 12, txtYears * 12, _
            txtMonthlyInvestment) * -1
    End Sub
    ```

8. Enter one statement in the procedure for the Click event of the Calculate button so it looks like this:

    ```
    Private Sub cmdCalculate_Click()
        CalculateFutureValue
    End Sub
    ```

9. Press F5 to test the program. If you've done everything right, the form should work the way it did before…as long as you enter valid numeric data into its text boxes. If it doesn't, you need to debug the code and test it again.

Get help information and add arguments to the FV function

10. When you return to the Code window, move the insertion point into the function name FV and press F1. This should open a Help window that tells you more about that function. Study this information to see if you can figure out what the fourth and fifth arguments do (that's not easy, is it?). With the Help window still open, modify the FV arguments so the fifth argument is 1, which means that the investment amount is deposited at the start, not the end, of each month. At this point, the function should look like this (and it will return slightly different results when executed):

    ```
    txtFutureValue = FV(txtInterestRate / 12, txtYears * 12, _
            txtMonthlyInvestment, , 1) * -1
    ```

    (Here, the fourth argument is omitted, which is indicated by the two commas in succession, so it's left at its default value.)

11. Return to the Help window and experiment with the Contents and Index tabs to get other information that may interest you. If you want to print a topic, click on the Print button in the toolbar. Then, close the Help window.

Save the project and exit from Visual Basic

12. Click on the Save button to save the project and its form. Then, click on the Close button in the upper right corner to exit from Visual Basic.

An enhanced version of the Calculate Investment form

In the remaining pages of this chapter, you'll learn how the Calculate Investment form can be enhanced so it does more and works better. First, you'll see how you can add three controls to it so it does two calculations instead of one. Second, you'll learn how to add code to it that checks to make sure that the users enter valid data and warns them when they don't. Last, you'll learn a quick way to create an executable file that can be distributed to the users of the application.

How the enhanced interface works

Figure 1-16 shows the enhanced user interface for this application. When the user clicks on the Future Value option button, the form calculates the future value of an investment based on the entries in the first three text boxes. When the user clicks on the Monthly Investment option button, the form calculates the monthly investment that is needed to attain a specific future value based on the entries in the last three text boxes.

The property settings for the new controls

Figure 1-16 also shows the property settings for the three controls that have been added to the form. Here, the Value property for the first option is set to True so it will be selected when the application starts. In addition, since the TabIndex properties for the text boxes and command buttons use the first six index values (0 through 5), the option buttons should use the next two values (6 and 7).

Two versions of the enhanced Calculate Investment form

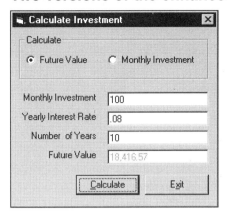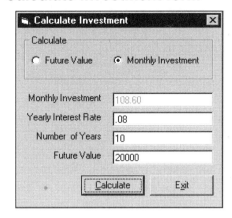

The property settings for the new controls

Default name	Property	Setting
Frame1	Caption	Calculate
Option1	Name	optFutureValue
	Caption	Future Value
	TabIndex	6
	Value	True
Option2	Name	optMonthlyInvestment
	Caption	Monthly Investment
	TabIndex	7

Operation

- When you click on one option button within a frame, it is turned on and the others are turned off. To make this work correctly, though, you have to add the frame to the form before you put the option buttons within the frame. If option buttons aren't placed within a frame, two or more can be on at the same time.

- For this application, if you click on the Future Value option button, the Future Value text box should be disabled and the form should be used to calculate the future value. If you click on the Monthly Investment option button, the Monthly Investment text box should be disabled and the form should calculate the monthly investment amount. This means that you have to change the enabled properties of the appropriate text boxes whenever the user clicks on an option button.

Figure 1-16   The form and property settings for the enhanced interface

The code for the enhanced application

Figure 1-17 presents the code for all of the procedures in the enhanced application except the procedure for the Click event of the Exit button, which doesn't need to be changed. If you study this code, you'll see that it includes event procedures for the Click events of the two option buttons and the Calculate command button. It uses three general procedures that are called by the event procedures. And it uses the SetFocus method of two different text boxes to move the focus to them. This is the first use of *methods* that you've seen in this book, but by no means the last.

If you have much programming experience, you should be able to understand this code without much trouble. If you don't, the explanations that follow should help. To some extent, though, you won't understand the code until you read the next chapter, which presents the Visual Basic coding essentials in more detail.

The first procedure is executed when the user clicks on the Future Value option button. This procedure disables the Future Value text box, enables the Monthly Investment text box, and calls a general procedure that clears both of these text boxes. Then, it uses the SetFocus method to move the focus to the Monthly Investment text box.

The second procedure is executed when the user clicks on the Monthly Investment option button. This procedure contains four statements that are similar to the four statements used by the first event procedure.

The third procedure is the general procedure that's called by the first two procedures. This procedure clears the Monthly Investment text box and the Future Value text box by moving an empty text string into them. This type of text string is represented by two quotation marks in succession.

The fourth procedure is executed when the user clicks on the Calculate command button. It uses an If statement to call one general procedure if the FutureValue option button is selected and another general procedure if the other option button is selected.

The fifth procedure is a general procedure that performs the future value calculation. It uses an If statement to check that valid numeric values have been entered into the three enabled text boxes. To do that, it uses three Val functions, which extract the numeric values from these controls (if there are any). Then, if all three values are greater than zero, this procedure uses the FV function to perform the calculation and assign the resulting value to the Future Value text box. But if the values aren't valid, this procedure performs a MsgBox function that displays a dialog box with a message that warns the user about the invalid data and lets the user continue.

To display the result of the FV function with only two decimal places, the fifth procedure has the FV function within a FormatNumber function. In other words, one function is nested within another function. In this case, the outer set of parentheses contains the arguments for the FormatNumber function, while the inner set contains the arguments for the FV function.

The code for the enhanced application

```
Private Sub optFutureValue_Click()
    txtFutureValue.Enabled = False
    txtMonthlyInvestment.Enabled = True
    ClearTextBoxes
    txtMonthlyInvestment.SetFocus
End Sub

Private Sub optMonthlyInvestment_Click()
    txtFutureValue.Enabled = True
    txtMonthlyInvestment.Enabled = False
    ClearTextBoxes
    txtInterestRate.SetFocus
End Sub

Private Sub ClearTextBoxes()
    txtMonthlyInvestment = ""
    txtFutureValue = ""
End Sub

Private Sub cmdCalculate_Click()
    If optFutureValue = True Then
        CalculateFutureValue
    Else
        CalculateMonthlyInvestment
    End If
End Sub

Private Sub CalculateFutureValue()
    If Val(txtMonthlyInvestment) > 0 _
        And Val(txtInterestRate) > 0 _
        And Val(txtYears) > 0 Then
    txtFutureValue = _
        FormatNumber(FV(txtInterestRate / 12, _
            txtYears * 12, txtMonthlyInvestment, 0, 1) * -1)
    Else
        MsgBox "Invalid data. Please check all entries."
    End If
End Sub

Private Sub CalculateMonthlyInvestment()
    If Val(txtFutureValue) > 0 _
        And Val(txtInterestRate) > 0 _
        And Val(txtYears) > 0 Then
    txtMonthlyInvestment = _
        FormatNumber(Pmt(txtInterestRate / 12, _
            txtYears * 12, 0, txtFutureValue, 1) * -1)
    Else
        MsgBox "Invalid data. Please check all entries."
    End If
End Sub
```

Figure 1-17   The code for the enhanced application

Like the fifth procedure, the sixth procedure is a general procedure that performs a calculation after it checks for valid entries. It uses the Pmt function within the FormatNumber function and assigns the result to the Monthly Investment text box.

How to print the code for an application

If you want to print the code for an application, you can use the Print command in the File menu. The dialog box for this command lets you print the code for the module that you're currently working on or for the entire project. After you print the code, you can lay the pages side by side so you can review the procedures without jumping from one to another in the Code window. This often comes in handy when you're debugging an application.

How to create an EXE file for an application

Once the application works the way you want it to, you can create an *executable* file, or *EXE*, for the application. Then, you can run the application from any computer that's running under Windows 95, Windows 98, or Windows NT.

To create an executable file, you select the Make projectname.exe command from the File menu, which displays the dialog box shown in figure 1-18. Then, you choose the folder that you want to save the file in and click on the OK button. If you choose the Desktop folder, this puts an icon on your desktop that can be used to start the application.

When you start the application, it runs independently, just like any other Windows program. In this figure, for example, you can see the application running on the desktop. But if you check the taskbar, you can see that Visual Basic isn't running.

For simple applications, that's all you need to do to create an executable file that can be distributed to users. For more complex applications, though, you need to create a setup program that properly installs the application and its components on each user's system. You can learn how to do that in chapter 15.

The dialog box for the Make command in the File menu

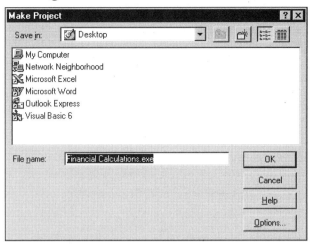

The application as it runs on a desktop

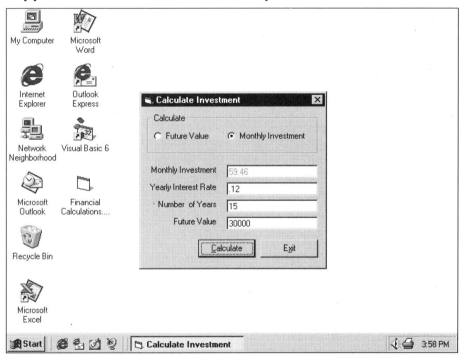

Note

- You can save an EXE file in any folder that you choose. When you save an EXE file in the Desktop folder, it is also displayed as an icon on the desktop as shown above. To delete both the icon and the EXE file, right-click on the icon and select the Delete command.

Figure 1-18   How to create an EXE file for an application

Exercise set 1-3: Enhance the application

In this exercise set, you'll enhance the application that you created in the last two exercise sets.

Open the project

1. Start Visual Basic and open the Financial Calculations project you created in the previous exercise sets.

Enhance the interface

2. Display the Calculate Investment form in the Form window, select the form, and resize it so it is taller. Then, press Ctrl+A to select all of the controls on the form and drag the controls toward the bottom of the form so you create some space at the top of the form.

3. Add the frame control at the top of the form as shown in figure 1-16. Then, add the two option buttons within this frame. Notice that each option button includes room for a caption.

4. Set the properties for the controls as summarized in figure 1-16. If necessary, adjust the sizing and positioning of the controls. When you're done, the form should look like the one in this figure.

5. Press F5 to test the form. Click on each option button to make sure that one is turned off when the other is turned on. If they don't work right, you probably need to delete the frame and option buttons from the form and add them again, this time making sure to add the frame first and the option buttons within the frame. When you're done testing the interface, click on the Exit button to stop the application.

Enhance and test the code

6. Double click on the Future Value option button to enter the Code window and generate the Sub and End Sub statements for its Click event. Enter the code for the Future Value option button as shown in figure 1-17.

7. Select the Monthly Investment option button from the Object list in the Code window. This should generate the Sub and End Sub statements for the Click event for that option button. Next, use copy-and-paste techniques to copy the statements from the event procedure for the Future Value option button to the new procedure. Then, modify this code so it looks like the code in figure 1-17.

8. Enter the ClearTextBoxes procedure directly into the Code window by typing:

    ```
    Private Sub ClearTextBoxes
    ```

    When you press the Enter key, Visual Basic will add the parentheses after the Sub statement and add the End Sub statement. Then, you can code the rest of this procedure as shown in figure 1-17.

9. Select the CalculateFutureValue procedure from the Procedure list in the Code window to move to that procedure. Then, modify this procedure so it looks like the one in figure 1-17 and be sure to add the FormatNumber function around the FV function. If you get compile errors as you enter the code, be sure that the parentheses and underscores are coded correctly.

10. Press F5 to test the application. At this point, the future value calculation should work and the result should be displayed with only two decimal places. In addition, a dialog box should be displayed when you enter invalid data in one of the text boxes. When you click on the Monthly Investment button, though, the calculation shouldn't work, although the appropriate text boxes should be enabled, disabled, and cleared. If anything isn't working right, of course, you need to exit from the form, fix the bugs, and test again.

11. Code the CalculateMonthlyInvestment procedure as shown in figure 1-17. After you enter the Sub and End Sub statements, you can copy the CalculateFutureValue procedure and paste it between the Sub and End Sub statements. Then, you can modify the code as necessary.

12. Modify the event procedure for the Click event of the Calculate command button so it uses an If statement as shown in figure 1-17.

13. Test the application again. This time everything should work. If you encounter any errors, of course, you must fix them and test again. When you've got the application working right, use the Print command in the File menu to print the code. Then, note that the procedures aren't in any logical sequence.

Make and run an executable file

14. Now that the application works the way you want it to, you can create an executable file for it. To do that, select the Make Financial Calculations.exe command from the File menu. In the resulting dialog box, keep clicking on the Up One Level button until you're at the Desktop folder. Then, click on the OK button to save the executable file on your desktop.

15. Click on the Save Project button in the toolbar to save the changes to the project and the form. Then, exit from Visual Basic and minimize all of the other application windows. When you're done, you should see an icon for the executable file on the desktop.

16. Double-click on the Financial Calculations icon to run the project. Use the application and you'll see that it works just the way it did when Visual Basic was running. Now, though, the executable application can be run from any PC that uses Windows 95, 98, or NT.

17. If you want to delete this application from your desktop, you can right-click on its icon and select Delete from the resulting shortcut menu. This also deletes the EXE file from the Desktop folder.

Congratulations! You've come a long way in just 45 pages.

Perspective

If you've developed the application that's presented in this chapter, you've learned a lot. You know how to get around the IDE. You know how to build an interface that consists of forms and controls. You know how to write the code that makes the interface work the way you want it to. You know what objects, properties, methods, and events are, and you've used them in your code. You've got a pretty good idea of how to develop, test, and debug an application. Above all, you've developed a working application that is by no means trivial to prove that you've learned something.

On the other hand, you've also got a lot to learn. So in chapter 2, you'll learn more about the Visual Basic language itself. That will give you more confidence when you're writing code. In chapter 3, you'll learn how to use several more controls and two or more forms in a single application. That will help you design more elaborate user interfaces. And in chapter 4, you'll learn the testing and debugging skills that you need as your applications become more complicated.

Terms you should know

form	Project Explorer
control	event-driven
text box	Code window
command button	event procedure
option button	form module
object	private procedure
property	general procedure
method	calling a procedure
event	dot operator
project	dot
Integrated Development	function
Environment (IDE)	argument
Form window	compile error
Toolbox	run-time error
Properties window	logical error
	executable file (EXE)

2

Visual Basic coding essentials

In the last chapter, you were introduced to some of the statements in the Visual Basic language like the If and Unload statements. To become a proficient Visual Basic programmer, though, you need to master this language. As a result, this chapter presents the coding essentials that you need for all of the

Basic coding skills **48**
How to use continuation characters and comments 48
How to use the Edit toolbar 50
How to create a standard module 52
How to code with a readable style 54
Exercise set 2-1: Experiment with coding techniques 56

How to work with variables and constants **58**
How to declare variables 58
How to control the scope of variables 60
How to assign values to variables 62
How to create user-defined constants 64
How to use Visual Basic constants 64
How to code arithmetic expressions 66
How to code conditional expressions 68
How to work with arrays 70
Exercise set 2-2: Use variables and constants 72

Visual Basic statements **74**
How to code If statements 74
How to code Select Case statements 76
How to code For...Next statements 78
How to code Do...Loop statements 80
How to code On Error statements 82
How to code With statements 84
A summary of other Visual Basic statements 86
Exercise set 2-3: Use some new statements 88

Procedures and functions **90**
How to code and call a Sub procedure 90
How to code and call a Function procedure 92
A summary of the Visual Basic functions 94
How to use the MsgBox function 96
A parsing routine that uses eight different functions 98
Exercise set 2-4: Create and use functions 100

Perspective **102**

applications you develop. It also presents the skills you need for learning how to use other statements and functions of the language on your own.

If you have much programming experience, you should be able to read this lengthy chapter quickly, then refer back to it whenever you need to know specific coding details. But even if you don't have much experience or if you're a beginning programmer, you may want to read this chapter quickly and refer back to it as needed. As you will see, no one can remember all of the details of this language.

To make sure that you learn the coding essentials, you should do the exercise sets in this chapter. They will give you hands-on experience with the critical skills. In addition, you may want to experiment with some of the Visual Basic statements and functions on your own.

Basic coding skills

To start, this chapter reviews some of the coding skills that you were introduced to in chapter 1. In addition, it presents some new skills and guidelines that can help you write code that's easy to understand and maintain.

How to use continuation characters and comments

Figure 2-1 shows how you can use a *continuation character* to continue a Visual Basic statement on the next line. To do that, just type a space followed by an underscore (_) at the end of the line. In the first coding example, you can see that these characters are used to continue the If statement to a second and third line. You can also see that these characters are used to continue the FV function to a second and third line.

This figure also shows several ways to add a *comment* to a block of code. To do that, you just type an apostrophe followed by the text for the comment. In the first coding example, you can see one comment that describes what the If statement that follows is doing and another comment that describes what the FV function that follows is doing. In the second coding example, you can see a comment coded to the right of a line of code. In the third coding example, you can see a comment block that could be included at the top of a procedure. When you review the code of others, you will often find comments interspersed throughout the code to help document what the code is doing.

Comments can also be useful when you're writing and testing code. If, for example, you don't want to delete a line of code but you want to test a procedure without running that line of code, you can type an apostrophe before the line to convert it to a comment. This is sometimes referred to as *commenting out* a line of code. Later, you can restore the line of code by removing the apostrophe.

A procedure that uses continuation characters and comments

```
Private Sub CalculateFutureValue()
    ' Check input values to make sure they're > zero
    If Val(txtMonthlyInvestment) > 0 _
            And Val(txtInterestRate) > 0 _
            And Val(txtYears) > 0 Then
    ' Use the FV function to calculate future value
    ' The fifth argument (1) means that payments
    '     are made at the start of a month
        txtFutureValue.Text = _
            FormatNumber(FV(txtInterestRate / 12, _
                txtYears * 12, txtMonthlyInvestment.Text, 0, 1) * -1)
    Else
        MsgBox "Invalid data. Please check all entries."
    End If
End Sub
```

A comment coded to the right of a line

```
txtFutureValue.Enabled = False ' Disable this text box
```

A comment block coded at the start of a procedure

```
' ===========================================================
' Date:    12/1/98
' Author:  Ed Koop
' Purpose: Check input values and calculate future value
' ===========================================================
```

How to continue a statement

- Type the *continuation character*, which is a space followed by an underscore, at the end of the line you want to continue.

How to code a comment

- Type an apostrophe (') followed by the comment. A comment can be coded to the right of a statement or on a line with no statement. However, a comment can't be coded to the right of a continuation character.

- You can also code a comment by typing the keyword Rem (short for Remark) followed by a space and the comment, but it's easier to use the apostrophe.

Figure 2-1   How to use continuation characters and comments

How to use the Edit toolbar

Figure 2-2 shows how you can use the Edit toolbar to work with code. If you experiment with this toolbar, you'll find that its buttons provide some useful functions for working with comments and indentation and for moving between procedures.

In particular, you can use the Edit toolbar to modify several lines of code at once. In this figure, for example, you can see how to use the Edit toolbar to add and remove comments from a block of code. To do that, you select the lines of code and click on the Comment Block button or the Uncomment Block button. Similarly, you can use the Indent and Outdent buttons to adjust the indentation for selected lines of code.

You can also use the Edit toolbar to work with *bookmarks*. After you use the Toggle Bookmark button to mark lines of code, you can easily move between the marked lines of code by using the Next and Previous Bookmark buttons. Although you usually don't need bookmarks when you're working with short modules like the one presented in the last chapter, bookmarks can be helpful when you're working with modules that contain more than a few pages of code.

If you experiment with the other buttons on the Edit toolbar, you'll find that they can help you display the same information that's provided by the Auto Quick Info and Auto List Members features described in the last chapter. As a result, you only need to use these buttons if these features aren't on.

A Code window with the Edit toolbar displayed

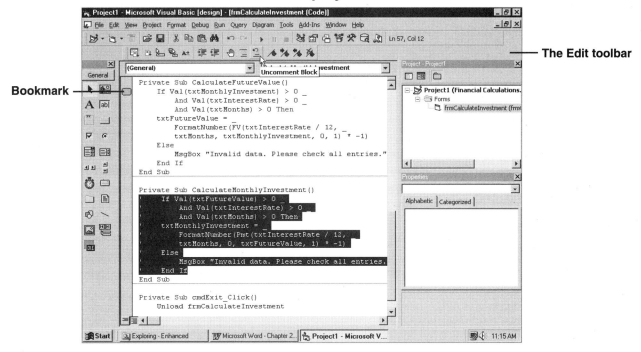

Bookmark

The Edit toolbar

Operation

- To display or hide the Edit toolbar, right-click in the toolbar area and choose Edit from the shortcut menu.

- To add and remove comments from several lines of code at once, select the lines of code and click on the Comment Block or Uncomment Block buttons.

- To adjust the indentation of several lines of code at once, select the lines of code and click on the Indent or Outdent buttons.

- You can use *bookmarks* to quickly move between lines of code. To set or remove a single bookmark, move the insertion point into a line of code and click on the Toggle Bookmark button. To move between bookmarks, use the Next Bookmark and Previous Bookmark buttons. To remove all bookmarks, click on the Clear All Bookmarks button.

Figure 2-2   How to use the Edit toolbar

How to create a standard module

In the last chapter, you learned how to create a *form module*. That's a module that contains all of the procedures that are related to a form. If a project contains more than one form, it has one form module for each form.

In addition, a project can contain one or more *standard modules*. This type of module is used for procedures or variables that are used by more than one form module. If, for example, a project consists of two form modules that require the use of a procedure named ParseText, that procedure should be stored in a standard module.

To create a standard module, you use the Add Module dialog box as shown in figure 2-3. To display this dialog box, you select the Add Module command from the Project menu or from the shortcut menu that's displayed when you right-click on the Project Explorer.

Although a standard module typically contains code that's used by more than one form module, it can also contain a Sub procedure that's executed when the project starts. For that to work, this procedure must be named Main. Then, you can have this procedure run when the project starts by setting the Startup Object property of the project to Sub Main as shown in this figure.

The dialog box for the Add Module command in the Project menu

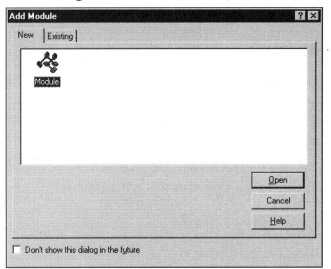

The dialog box for the Project Properties command in the Project menu

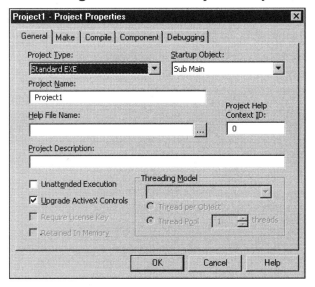

Operation

- Use the Add Module command in the Project menu to add a *standard module* to your project. Once added, the module will appear in the Modules folder of the Project Explorer. To save and name the new module, press Ctrl+S and complete the dialog box that appears.
- If you want the project to start by running a procedure named Main in the standard module, use the Project Properties command in the Project menu to change the Startup Object.

Figure 2-3   How to create a standard module

How to code with a readable style

When you compile and run an application, Visual Basic makes sure that your code follows all of its rules. But even if it does, your code may still be difficult to understand if you don't adhere to some practical coding guidelines like the ones presented in figure 2-4. If you follow guidelines like these, it will be easier for you and others to understand, debug, and maintain your code.

To make your code easier to read and understand, we recommend that you group all the variable and constant declarations at the start of a procedure so they're easy to find (you'll start learning about variables and constants in the next figure). We also recommend that you use indentation to show the structure of the statements that you use and that you write your code in a straightforward way that someone else will be able to follow.

To create names that are easy to interpret, you should start the names of objects and variables with standard prefixes and use long, meaningful names. In this coding example, three-character prefixes are used for controls and single character prefixes are used for variables. In contrast, the procedure name for a general Sub procedure shouldn't have a prefix, and its name should start with a verb to indicate what the procedure does.

Even though many people recommend the use of comments and many programmers sprinkle their code with comments, our last recommendation is to avoid their use. The trouble with comments is that they may not accurately represent what the code does. That often happens when a programmer changes the code, but not the comments that were written for it. Then, it's even harder to understand the code, because the comments are misleading. Besides that, if you follow our other naming and coding guidelines, your code should be easy to understand without comments. That's why we recommend that you use comments only to describe blocks of code that are unusually hard to understand.

Now that you know our guidelines, you can modify and expand them to create your own. If you're working on a team project, what's important is that everyone on the team first agree on a set of coding guidelines...and then follow them.

A procedure that's coded with a readable style

```
Private Sub CalculateFutureValue()
    Dim iMonths As Integer
    Dim fInterestRate As Single
    Dim cFutureValue As Currency
    Dim iIndex As Integer
    If Val(txtMonthlyInvestment) > 0 _
            And Val(txtInterestRate) > 0 _
            And Val(txtYears) > 0 Then
        iMonths = Val(txtYears) * 12
        fInterestRate = Val(txtInterestRate) / 12
        cFutureValue = 0
        iIndex = 1
        Do Until iIndex > iMonths
            cFutureValue = (cFutureValue + _
                txtMonthlyInvestment) _
                * (1 + fInterestRate)
            iIndex = iIndex + 1
        Loop
        txtFutureValue = cFutureValue
    End If
End Sub
```

The variable and constant declarations should be at the start of the procedure

Indentation should be used to make the code easier to read

Coding recommendations

- Group related variable and constant declarations, and code all declarations at the start of the procedure.
- Use indentation to make the code easier to understand.
- Write the code in a straightforward way, not a clever or cryptic way.

Naming recommendations

- Start the names of objects, variables, and constants with standard prefixes.
- Use meaningful names after the prefixes, even though that usually means long names.
- Use consistent names. Don't, for example, use curFutureValue to refer to a variable and txtFV to refer to a text box control when both are used for the future value of an investment.
- Start the names of general Sub procedures with a verb (as in CalculateFutureValue), but omit the verb in the names of Function procedures (as in FutureValue).

Comment recommendations

- Use comments only when the code is difficult to understand. Then, make sure that the comments are correct and up-to-date.

Notes

- Indentation, capitalization, and spacing have no effect on the operation of the code.
- As you enter code, Visual Basic may adjust the capitalization and spacing.

Figure 2-4   How to code with a readable style

Exercise set 2-1: Experiment with coding techniques

In this exercise set, you'll experiment with comments, the Edit toolbar, and a standard module.

Open the project

1. Open the Financial Calculations project that you created in chapter 1.

Use comments and the Edit toolbar

2. Open the Code window for the form and add a comment block at the start of the two calculation procedures to describe what they're doing. If you like, add other comments to the procedures in this form module. Then, press F5 to run the project and see that these comments have no effect on its operation.

3. Right-click in the toolbar area and click on Edit to display the Edit toolbar. If it's floating, drag its title bar to the toolbar area and release it. If it isn't floating, click in the area between two buttons and drag it to a floating position. Then, position the Edit toolbar where you want it to be displayed.

4. Use the Edit toolbar to comment out the lines in the CalculateFutureValue procedure that are indicated here:

```
'       If Val(txtMonthlyInvestment) > 0 _
'           And Val(txtInterestRate) > 0 _
'           And Val(txtYears) > 0 Then
        txtFutureValue = _
            FormatNumber(FV(txtInterestRate / 12, _
                txtYears * 12, txtMonthlyInvestment, 0, 1) * - 1)
'       Else
'           MsgBox "Invalid data. Please check all entries."
'       End If
```

To do that, you can drag the mouse through the lines you want to comment out, then click on the Comment Block button. Note that the uncommented code that remains is a valid statement because all parts of the If...Else statement have been commented out.

5. Run the project to make sure that it still works...as long as you enter valid numeric data in the text boxes.

6. Use the toolbar button to uncomment the lines that you commented out in step 4.

Use a standard module

7. Use the Add Module command in the Project menu to add a standard module to the project. Next, press Ctrl+S and save the module with the name Standard Module. You should now be able to see this module in the Modules folder of the Project Explorer.

8. Code this procedure in the standard module that you've just created:

```
Private Sub Main()
    MsgBox "Welcome to the Calculate Investment form"
    frmCalculateInvestment.Show
End Sub
```

This displays a message box and then uses the Show method of the Calculate Investment form to display that form.

9. Use the Project Properties command in the Project menu to change the Startup Object to Sub Main. This means that the Main procedure that you wrote in step 8 will be executed when the project is started. Now, press F5 to run the project. Once you respond to the message box, the Calculate Investment form should be displayed.

Use bookmarks and indentation

10. Use the Edit toolbar to set one bookmark in the Main procedure of the standard module. Next, switch to the Code window for the Calculate Investment form by clicking on the form name in the Project Explorer and then clicking on the Code button at the top of the Project Explorer. Then, set a second bookmark in the first procedure in this module and set a third bookmark in the CalculateFutureValue procedure. Now that the bookmarks have been set, use the other toolbar buttons to switch from one procedure to another. After you've experimented with that, use the appropriate toolbar button to clear all of the bookmarks.

11. Review the code in the two modules of this project to see whether you can make it more readable by applying some of the guidelines in figure 2-4. If you want to change the indentation of any of the lines, use the buttons in the Edit toolbar.

Clean up and save the project

12. Delete the Main procedure in the standard module. Then, use the Project Properties dialog box to change the Startup Object back to the Calculate Investment form. The application should now work the way it did when you started this exercise set.

13. Save the project and keep it open if you're going to continue with this chapter.

How to work with variables and constants

Variables are used to store data that changes as a procedure runs. In contrast, *constants* are used to store data that doesn't change. Although you can define your own constants, you can also use constants that are built into the Visual Basic language.

How to declare variables

When you declare a *variable*, you assign one of the eleven Visual Basic *data types* to it. These data types are summarized in figure 2-5. For instance, the *string* data type is used for any alphanumeric or text characters. The *Boolean* data type is used for either of two values: True, which is actually a value of +1 or -1, and False, which is actually a value of zero. And the Date data type is used to store a value that represents both the date and time.

The next five data types in this table are for numeric variables. When you choose one of these, you should make sure that it's appropriate for the size and type of number that the variable must hold. If the variable doesn't require decimal places, for example, you use either the Integer or Long data type. For dollar values with two decimal places, you use the Currency data type. And for values with more than two decimal places, you use the Single or Double data type depending on how many significant digits you need to carry. These data types use E notation for storing extremely large or small numbers.

If you declare a variable without specifying a data type, the Variant data type is used as the default. This data type can hold either a number or a string, depending on the context that the variable is used in. In general, though, it's better to specify one of the other data types because that uses less system resources and usually results in code that's easier to understand.

When you declare a variable, it is given one of the initial values that's summarized in this figure. In particular, variable-length string variables are initialized to *zero-length strings* ("") while numeric variables are initialized to zero (0). A Variant variable, on the other hand, is initialized to Empty. This means it has no beginning value but is treated as zero in a numeric context or as a zero-length string in a string context.

To declare a variable, you use the syntax in this figure. To start, you type one of four keywords, which you'll learn more about in the next figure. Then, you type a name for the variable starting with a one- or three-character prefix, followed by the word *As*, followed by the data type for the variable.

If you look at the first two examples in this figure, you can see how the Dim keyword is used to declare various types of string variables. In the first example, a string variable named sErrorMessage is declared. In the second example, a string variable named sUserName is declared with a fixed length of 25 characters. Then, if the string stored in this variable has less the 25 characters, trailing spaces will be added to the string. In the third example, you can see how two variables can be declared in a single statement.

Data types and recommended prefixes

Data type	Prefix	Data type description
String	str or s	Any characters
Boolean	bln or b	True (a value of +1 or -1) or false (a value of 0)
Date	dtm or d	Date and time with the date stored as the number of days since December 30, 1899, and the time stored as the fractional portion of 24 hours (for example, a value of 1.5 represents January 1, 1900 at 12:00 noon.
Integer	int or i	Integer from –32,768 to +32,767
Long	lng or l	Integer from –2 billion to +2 billion
Currency	cur or c	Number with four decimal places
Single	sng or f	Single-precision, floating-point number with approximately 7 significant digits
Double	dbl or p	Double-precision, floating-point number with approximately 14 significant digits
Byte	byt or t	Positive integer value from 0 to 255 in binary format
Object	obj or o	Address that refers to an object
Variant	vnt or v	Either string or numeric data (the default)

Initial values for variables

Data type	Initial value
Variable-length strings	A zero-length string ("")
Fixed-length strings	All zeros ("000")
All numeric types	Zero (0)
Boolean	False
Variants	Empty

The syntax for declaring a variable

```
Dim|Private|Public|Static varname [As type]
```

Typical variable declarations

```
Dim sErrorMessage As String
Dim sUserName As String * 25
Dim iIndex As Integer, fInterestRate As Single
Private bAddMode As Boolean
Public iUserStatus As Integer
Static iRunningValue As Integer
```

Note

If you omit the data type when you declare a variable, the Variant data type is assumed. However, you should avoid using this data type.

Figure 2-5   How to declare variables

How to control the scope of variables

Figure 2-6 shows how you can use the Dim, Private, and Public keywords to control the *scope* of a variable. In general, you should define your variables so they have the smallest possible scope. By limiting the scope of your variables, you simplify your code and reduce the likelihood of errors.

If you need to use a variable only within a single procedure, you should declare the variable within that procedure using the Dim keyword. A variable that's declared within a procedure is called a *procedure-level variable* or a *local variable*.

If you need to use a variable in more than one procedure, you can declare it in the Declarations section at the start of a module using the Dim, Private, or Public keyword. If you use Dim or Private, the variable is available only to the procedures within the module and is called a *module-level variable*. (Dim is the same as Private when coded in the Declarations section.) If you use the Public keyword, the variable is available to the procedures in all the modules in the application and is called a *global variable*.

You typically declare global variables in a standard module. Then, those variables are created when the application starts and are available throughout the execution of the application. In contrast, if you declare a global variable in a form module, it isn't created until the form is loaded.

To clearly show the scope of a variable, you can add a one-letter prefix to the variable name as described at the bottom of this figure. For example, the *m* in the *mf* prefix used in this figure indicates that the variable is a module-level variable while the *f* indicates that the variable is a floating-point number.

If you use the Static keyword when you define a variable, you define a special type of local variable. Unlike other local variables, a Static variable isn't restored to its initial value each time the procedure that it's in is executed. As a result, you can use a Static variable to keep cumulative totals or results like a count of the number of times that a procedure was executed during a user session.

A module-level variable in the Declarations section

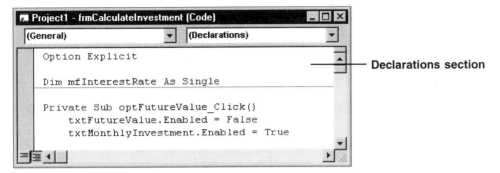

Declarations section

Keywords

Keyword	Meaning
Dim	The variable is available only within the procedure or module that declares it. When declared within a procedure, it's known as a *procedure-level variable* or a *local variable*. When declared within the Declarations section at the start of a module, it's known as a *module-level variable*.
Private	Private can only be coded in the Declarations section of a module. It means that the variable is available only to the procedures within the module that declares it.
Public	Public can only be coded in the Declarations section of a module. It means that the variable is available to the procedures in all of the modules in the project. This is known as a *global variable*.
Static	The variable is available only within the procedure that declares it (a local variable), but it retains its value from one execution of the procedure to another.

Extra prefix letter to indicate the scope

Scope	Prefix	Example
Procedure	None	blnSwitch or bSwitch
Module	m	mintIndex or miIndex
Global	g	gblnSwitch or gbSwitch

Figure 2-6   How to control the scope of variables

How to assign values to variables

Once you declare variables, you can assign values to them as shown in figure 2-7. To do that, you use a Let statement, but the keyword Let is optional and usually omitted. As a result, you just code an equal sign after the variable name followed by an expression for the value. This type of statement is also known as an *assignment statement.*

The first five examples in this figure show how to assign values to string variables. The first example shows that you must enclose characters in quotes when you assign them to a string variable. The next four examples show how you can use the ampersand (&) to *concatenate* strings. In the second example, two strings in text boxes are concatenated with a space in between. In the third example, "Form Name: " is concatenated with the Caption property of a form. And in the fourth example, you can see how you can use a Visual Basic constant (vbCrLf) to include a line break in a string (you'll learn more about these constants in the next figure).

The last example for strings shows that you can use the same variable on both sides of the equal sign in an assignment statement. Here, "to exit from this form" is concatenated with whatever the variable sMessage originally contained, and the result is stored back into sMessage. If, for example, sMessage starts with a value of "Are you sure you want," its new value is "Are you sure you want to exit from this form?"

The next four examples show how to assign values to numeric variables. If you've used a spreadsheet application like Excel before, you shouldn't have much trouble understanding these examples. They use the standard arithmetic operators and functions that will be described in more detail in a moment. Here again, the last example shows that you can use the same variable name on both sides of the equal sign. If, for example, iIndex starts with a value of 2, it has a value of 3 after this statement is executed.

The last three examples show how to assign values to variables for dates and Boolean values. To assign a date to a date variable, you can code the date within number signs (#) or quotes. Then, the string date is converted to the correct numeric value before it is stored in the variable. To assign a value to a Boolean variable, you can use the True and False keywords to represent the Boolean values of 0 for false and +1 or -1 for true.

Whenever you use variables, you should make sure that the Option Explicit statement is coded at the start of the module. Then, you have to declare a variable before you can assign a value to it. In contrast, if the Option Explicit statement isn't coded, a variable is "implicitly" declared as a Variant data type whenever you use a new variable name to the left of the equal sign in an assignment statement. As a result, a simple misspelling of a variable name can lead to the implicit declaration of a new variable and debugging problems later on. Fortunately, the Option Explicit statement is automatically entered into each new module if you turn on the Require Variable Declaration option…so make sure this option is on.

Typical assignment statements for variables

Strings

```
sMessage1 = "Invalid data entry."

sName = txtFirstName & " " & txtLastName

sFormName = "Form Name: " & frmCalculateInvestment.Caption

sMessage = "Are you sure you want" & vbCrLf & _
           "to exit this form?"

sMessage = sMessage & " to exit from this form?"
```

Numbers

```
iMonths = Val(txtYears) * 12

cSalesTax = cProductTotal * .0775

cIncreasePct = (cThisYTD - cLastYTD) / cLastYTD * 100

iIndex = iIndex + 1
```

Dates and Boolean values

```
dYear2000 = #January 1, 2000#

dYear2000 = "January 1, 2000"

bNewCustomerSwitch = True
```

Notes

- To identify strings, enclose them in quotes.
- To *concatenate* strings, use the ampersand (&). Although you can also use a plus sign (+) to concatenate two strings, this can cause confusion since the plus sign is also used for arithmetic operations.
- To identify dates, enclose them in pound signs (#) or quotes.
- You can use the True and False keywords to specify the Boolean values 0 (for false) and −1 or +1 (for true).

The Option Explicit statement

- The Option Explicit statement should be coded in the Declarations section of each module in an application so that all variables must be declared explicitly.
- The Option Explicit statement is entered automatically in each module when the Require Variable Declaration option is on. To turn this option on, choose Options from the Tools menu and click on the Editor tab.

Figure 2-7   How to assign values to variables

How to create user-defined constants

Once you understand how to declare variables and assign values to them, you shouldn't have any problem declaring a constant as shown in figure 2-8. As you can see, you declare a constant and assign a value to it in the same statement. To begin, you use the keyword Const to declare the constant. Then, you use the equal sign followed by an expression to supply a value for each constant. In addition, you can use the Private and Public keywords to determine the scope of the constant, just as you do for variables.

How to use Visual Basic constants

Besides the constants you define, you can use any of the dozens of constants that are defined by Visual Basic. The names of these constants all start with the prefix *vb*, and figure 2-8 presents a few of the most common ones. When you use one of the Visual Basic constants, your code becomes easier to read because you substitute a meaningful name for a cryptic number.

The syntax for declaring a constant

```
[Private|Public] Const constname [As type] = expression
```

Typical declarations for user-defined constants

```
Private Const iMonths As Integer = 60
Public Const gfInterestRate As Single = .125 / 12
```

Some of the built-in constants that can be used in string variables

Constant	Equivalent	Description
vbCr	Chr(13)	Carriage return character
vbLf	Chr(10)	Linefeed character
vbCrLf	Chr(13) + Chr(10)	Carriage return and linefeed combination
vbTab	Chr(9)	Tab character

Some of the built-in constants for key codes

Constant	Value	Description
vbKeyEscape	0x1B	Esc key
vbKeyReturn	0xD	Enter key
vbKeyF1	0x70	F1 key
vbKeyF2	0x71	F2 key

Typical uses of the Visual Basic constants

- To check the parameters that are passed to event procedures
- To check the response codes that are returned by functions
- To set a property for a form or control

How to find the constants that you need

- Use the Help feature to get information for a function or event. This information usually includes a summary of the related constants.
- Use the Contents tab of the Help feature in this sequence: Visual Basic Documentation, Reference, Language Reference, Constants.

Figure 2-8   How to work with constants

How to code arithmetic expressions

Figure 2-9 presents examples and rules for coding *arithmetic expressions*. As you code these expressions, you use *arithmetic operators* like +, -, *, and / as well as the caret (^) for exponentiation ("raising to a power of"), the backslash (\) for integer division, and the word *Mod* to get the remainder of an integer division.

To evaluate an arithmetic expression that doesn't include parentheses, Visual Basic performs the operations from left to right based on the *order of precedence*. This order says that all the exponentiation is done first; followed by the evaluation of minus signs before variables (called *negation*); followed by multiplication and division; and so on. Since most arithmetic expressions are relatively short, it's usually not difficult to understand how an expression will be evaluated.

If there's any chance for confusion, though, you should use parentheses to specify how you want an expression evaluated. Then, the expressions in the innermost sets of parentheses are evaluated first, followed by the expressions in outer sets of parentheses. When all of the expressions in parentheses have been evaluated, the evaluation continues using the normal order of precedence on a left to right basis.

If you apply the evaluation rules to the expressions in the examples, you should understand how the results will be derived. In the second example, the variable named sglRadius is squared (raised to the power of 2) and then multipled by 3.1416. In the fourth example, the first variable is divided by the second variable and the result is the remainder of this division operation. In the last example, the expression in the first set of inner parentheses is divided by the expression in the second set of inner parentheses; then, that result is raised to the power of .5, which is the same as taking the square root of it.

Arithmetic expressions

```
cThisYearSales - cLastYearSales
3.1416 * sglRadius ^ 2
(cThisYTD - cLastYTD) / cLastYTD * 100
iDividendValue Mod iDivisorValue
((cUnitSales * 50) / (cUnitCost * .15)) ^ .5
```

Order of precedence for arithmetic expressions

1. Exponentiation (^)
2. Minus sign before a value (negation)
3. Multiplication and division (* or /)
4. Integer division (\)
5. Mod operation (remainder of integer division)
6. Addition and subtraction (+ or -)

Use of parentheses

- Use parentheses whenever there's any doubt about the sequence in which the operations will be performed. Then, the operations in the inner sets of parentheses are done first, followed by the operations in the outer sets of parentheses.

Figure 2-9   How to code arithmetic expressions

How to code conditional expressions

Figure 2-10 shows how to code *conditional expressions*. These expressions evaluate to either True or False, and you can use these expressions in If statements and other Visual Basic statements. As you code these expressions, you can use *relational operators* like =, <, and > as well as *logical operators* like Not, And, and Or.

To evaluate a conditional expression, Visual Basic performs the operations from left to right based on the order of precedence. If you review this order, you can see that arithmetic operations are done first followed by relational operations and logical operations. Although you can use six logical operators with Visual Basic, the ones you'll use the most are Not, And, and Or, and they're summarized at the bottom of this figure.

The first example in this figure tests a variable named sSwitch to see if it contains a value of Yes. If it does, the expression is true; otherwise, the expression is false. Similarly, if the Boolean variable in the second example has a value of True, the conditional expression is true; otherwise, it's false. The third conditional expression is just another way of coding the second example. In other words, if the condition is just a Boolean variable (or a Boolean property), Visual Basic assumes that the condition is true if that variable is equal to True.

In the second last example, you can see that two or more And operators can be coded in an expression with little chance for confusion. But when you mix two or more logical operators, you usually need to use parentheses to clarify how the expression should be evaluated. This is illustrated by the last example (if you remove the parentheses, can you tell what the evaluation will be?).

An If statement that tests a conditional expression

```
If cMonthlyInvestment > 0 Then
```

Conditional expressions

```
sSwitch = "Yes"
bNewCustomer = True
bNewCustomer
iValue = 1
iValue Not > 99
cMonthlyInvestment > 0 And fInterestRate > 0 And iMonths > 0
cThisYTD > cLastYTD Or (cLastYTD <= 0 And cThisYTD >= 1000)
```

Order of precedence for conditional expressions

1. All arithmetic operations in the usual order of precedence

2. Relational operations (=, <>, >=, >, <=, <)

3. Logical operations in this order: Not, And, Or, Xor, Eqv, Imp

Summary of common logical operators

Operator	Description
Not	Reverses the value of the expression.
And	Connects two or more expressions. If both expressions are true, the entire expression is true.
Or	Connects two or more expressions. If either expression is true, the entire expression is true.

Use of parentheses

- Use parentheses whenever there's any doubt about the sequence in which the operations will be performed. Then, the operations in the inner sets of parentheses are done first, followed by the operations in the outer sets of parentheses.

Figure 2-10   How to code conditional expressions

How to work with arrays

Figure 2-11 presents what you need to know whenever you need to use an *array*. When you declare a *one-dimensional array*, you define a variable as usual, but you also specify the number of occurrences that you want to provide for. For instance, the first Dim statement example in this figure provides for ten occurrences (from 0 through 9) of a variable named intValue.

Then, to refer to any one of the values in this array, you use the variable name followed by an *index* value like this:

```
intValue(7)
```

This refers to the eighth value in this array; intValue(0) refers to the first value; and intValue(9) refers to the last value.

The second Dim statement example in this figure shows another way to declare a one-dimensional array that provides for ten occurrences. In this case, though, you can use index values from 1 through 10 to refer to the values in the array.

The third Dim statement example declares a *two-dimensional array*. You can think of this type of array as a matrix or table that consists of rows and columns. Then, the first number in the declaration gives the number of columns and the second number gives the number of rows. As a result, this Dim statement defines an array that provides for 25 values. Then, to refer to the items in this array, you use an index with two values as in:

```
intValue(1, 3)
```

This refers to the fourth value in the second column, because the index ranges are from 0 through 4.

Similarly, the fourth Dim statement example in this figure declares an array with 5 columns and 5 rows. In this case, though, the index ranges are from 1 through 5.

So there's no confusion about what the ranges of index values are, this figure also shows how to assign values to all of the occurrences of a one-dimensional and a two-dimensional array. In practice, though, you normally use a For...Next loop to add values to an array. You'll learn how to do that later in this chapter.

Typical array declarations

```
Dim intValue (9) As Integer          'Index values are 0-9
Dim intValue (1 To 10) As Integer    'Index values are 1-10
Dim intValue (4, 4) As Integer       'A two-dimensional array
Dim intValue (1 To 5, 1 To 5)        'Another two-dimensional array
```

Code that puts 10 interest rates into a one-dimensional array

```
Dim cRate (1 To 10) As Single
cRate(1) = .01
cRate(2) = .02
cRate(3) = .03
cRate(4) = .04
cRate(5) = .05
cRate(6) = .06
cRate(7) = .07
cRate(8) = .08
cRate(9) = .09
cRate(10) = .10
```

Code that puts 10 interest rates into a two-dimensional array

```
Dim cRate (1, 4) As Single
cRate(0, 0) = .04
cRate(0, 1) = .05
cRate(0, 2) = .06
cRate(0, 3) = .07
cRate(0, 4) = .08
cRate(1, 0) = .045
cRate(1, 1) = .055
cRate(1, 2) = .065
cRate(1, 3) = .075
cRate(1, 4) = .085
```

Description

- To refer to any of the values in an array, you use an *index*. For a one-dimensional array, this is the number in parentheses that follows the array name. For a two-dimensional array, this is two numbers in parentheses that are separated by a comma.

- In practice, you often use a For...Next loop to load an array as illustrated later in this chapter.

Figure 2-11   How to work with arrays

Exercise set 2-2: Use variables and constants

In this exercise set, you'll modify the Financial Calculations project so it uses one variable, one user-defined constant, and one built-in constant.

Open the project

1. If it's not already open, open the Financial Calculations project you worked on in exercise set 2-1.

Declare a variable and set an option

2. Open the Code window for the Calculate Investment form and move the insertion point to the top of the Code window. Is an Option Explicit statement there? If not, enter one. Then, pull down the Tools menu, select the Options command, click on the Editor tab, check the Require Variable Declaration box, and close the dialog box. Now, all new modules will include the Option Explicit statement.

3. After the Option Explicit statement, enter a Dim statement that declares a Single variable that will be used for interest rate. When you're done, your code should like this:

```
Option Explicit
Dim fInterestRate As Single
```

Use the variable in two procedures

4. Move to the CalculateFutureValue procedure, and enter this assignment statement right after the Then keyword in the If statement:

```
fInterestRate = txtInterestRate / 12
```

5. Modify the code for the FV function so it uses this variable. When you're done, the new statement and changes should look like this:

```
fInterestRate = txtInterestRate / 12
txtFutureValue = _
    FormatNumber(FV(fInterestRate, _
        txtYears * 12, txtMonthlyInvestment, 0, 1) * -1)
```

6. Highlight the assignment statement you entered in step 4 and press Ctrl+C to copy it to the clipboard. Move to the CalculateMonthlyInvestment procedure and press Ctrl+V to paste the assignment statement for the Interest Rate variable into this procedure right after the Then keyword in the If statement. Then, modify the code for the Pmt function so it uses this variable.

7. Press F5 to run the project and test both calculations. They should work the same as they did before. If you encounter any errors, fix them before you move on. When you're done, return to the Code window.

8. Move the Dim statement for fInterestRate from the Declarations section to the start of the CalculateFutureValue procedure. Then, test the project. This time, the CalculateMonthlyInvestment procedure shouldn't work because the variable has local scope.

9. Return to the Code window and copy the Dim statement for the variable to the start of the CalculateMonthlyInvestment procedure. Note that the same variable name can be used in two different procedures because both have local scope. Now, test the project to make sure that it works correctly.

Declare a constant

10. Switch to the Form window for the Calculate Investment form. Select the Future Value text box and use the Properties window to change the BackColor property to the ToolTip setting (or the setting of your choice). Then, select the value for this setting and copy it to the clipboard.

11. Switch to the Code window, move to the Declarations section, and declare a string constant by typing "Const msHighlight As String = ". Then, press Ctrl+V to paste the value for the background color from the clipboard. When you're done, the declaration for the constant should look something like this:

```
Const msHighlight As String = &H80000018
```

Use the constant in two procedures

12. Move to the event procedure for the Click event of the Future Value option button. Then, add these two statements:

```
txtFutureValue.BackColor = msHighlight
txtMonthlyInvestment.BackColor = vbWhite
```

    The first statement uses the constant you just declared while the second statement uses the Visual Basic constant for the color white.

13. Copy the two statements you just added to the event procedure for the Click event of the Monthly Investment option button. Then, switch the constants for the two statements to reverse the background colors.

14. Test the project to make sure that it works as it did before, but with background colors that clearly indicate which boxes contain the results of the calculations. If you encounter any errors, fix them before you move on.

15. Switch to the Code window for the standard module that you created in exercise set 2-1. If it isn't already there, type an Option Explicit statement at the start of this module. Next, move the constant declaration from the form module to the standard module. Then, test the project and click on the option button for Monthly Investment. The application should fail at this point because the constant isn't available to the Click procedure for that button.

16. To correct this, add the keyword Public to the start of this declaration. Next, change the constant name to *gs*Highlight because its scope is now global. Then, change the prefix in the two references to this constant. Last, test the project to make sure that it still works right.

Save the project

17. Save the project and keep it open if you're going to continue with this chapter.

Visual Basic statements

In chapter 1, you were introduced to just two Visual Basic statements: the If and Unload statements. Now, you'll learn more about those statements as well as the other essential Visual Basic statements.

How to code If statements

Figure 2-12 presents the syntax of the Visual Basic If statement. If the conditional expression that's coded after the word If is true, the statements after the word Then are executed. Otherwise, the statements after the word Else are executed.

As you can see, the one-line If statement doesn't end with the words End If because the end of the statement is indicated by the end of the line. In contrast, the block If statement must end with the words End If. The block If also provides for ElseIf clauses, which let you code a series of conditions and statements to be executed when a condition is true.

The first example in this figure shows how you can use an If statement without an Else or ElseIf clause. In this case, if the value in a text box is less than or equal to zero, an error message is displayed.

The second and third coding examples show how to use Else and ElseIf clauses. In the third example, the values in a variable named iQuantity are tested and appropriate values are assigned to a variable named fDiscount. If none of the conditions in the ElseIf clauses are true, though, the final Else clause is executed and an error message is displayed.

The last example in this figure shows how one If statement can be nested within another If statement. This is referred to as a *nested If statement* or *nested If statements*, and you can nest If statements many levels deep. In this example, one If statement is nested within the Then portion of another If statement, but an If statement can also be nested in the Else portion.

When you code nested If statements, you must make sure that you end the inner statement with the words End If before you continue the coding of the outer statement. Otherwise, Visual Basic will display an error message as you code. This automatic checking helps you code error-free If statements.

The syntax of the one-line If statement

```
If condition Then statements [Else statements]
```

The syntax of the block If statement

```
If condition Then
    statements
[ElseIf condition-n Then
    statements] ...
[Else
    statements]
End If
```

An If...Then statement without an Else clause

```
If Val(txtMonthlyInvestment) <= 0 Then
    MsgBox "You must enter a positive number in this text box."
End If
```

A simple If...Then...Else statement

```
If optFutureValue Then
    CalculateFutureValue
Else
    CalculateMonthlyInvestment
End If
```

An If statement with ElseIf clauses

```
If iQuantity = 1 Or iQuantity = 2 Then
    fDiscount = 0
ElseIf iQuantity >= 3 And iQuantity <= 9 Then
    fDiscount = .1
ElseIf iQuantity >= 10 And iQuantity <= 24 Then
    fDiscount = .2
ElseIf iQuantity >= 25 Then
    fDiscount = .3
Else
    MsgBox "Invalid quantity."
End If
```

Nested If statements

```
If Val(txtInterestRate) > 0 And Val(txtYears) > 0 Then
    If optFutureValue And Val(txtMonthlyInvestment) > 0 Then
        CalculateFutureValue
    ElseIf optMonthlyInvestment And Val(txtFutureValue) > 0 Then
        CalculateMonthlyInvestment
    Else
        MsgBox "Invalid data. Please check all entries."
    End If
Else
    MsgBox "Invalid data. Please check all entries."
End If
```

Figure 2-12   How to code If statements

How to code Select Case statements

Figure 2-13 shows the syntax for the Select Case statement and two of the ways this statement can be used. In the first example, the test expression is just an integer variable that can range from 0 through 3. Based on the value in this variable, the Show method is used to display one of four different forms.

In the second example in this figure, the test expression is an integer variable named iQuantity. Then, if iQuantity has a value of 1 or 2, fDiscount is set to zero. If the quantity is from 3 to 9, the discount is .1. If the quantity is from 10 to 24, the discount is .2. If the quantity is greater than or equal to 25, the discount is .3. And if none of these conditions is true (Else), an error message is displayed. Note the variety of ways that these values can be specified in a Select Case statement.

The benefit of using the Select Case statement is that your code is usually easier to read and understand than it is when you use nested If statements. To appreciate that benefit, compare the second example in this figure to the third example in the previous figure. Although the results are identical, which is easier to understand?

The syntax of the Select Case statement

```
Select Case testexpression
    [Case expressionlist
        statements] ...
    [Case Else
        statements]
End Select
```

A Select Case statement that tests a variable named iIndex

```
Select Case iIndex
    Case 0
        frmVendors.Show
    Case 1
        frmInvoices.Show
    Case 2
        frmPayments.Show
    Case 3
        frmCredits.Show
    Case Else
        MsgBox "Invalid index number."
End Select
```

A Select Case statement that sets discount percentages

```
Select Case iQuantity
    Case 1, 2
        fDiscount = .0
    Case 3 To 9
        fDiscount = .1
    Case 10 To 24
        fDiscount = .2
    Case Is >= 25
        fDiscount = .3
    Case Else
        MsgBox "Invalid Quantity"
End Select
```

How to code the expression list

Syntax	Meaning
To	Specifies a range of values.
Is	Precedes a conditional expression.

Figure 2-13   How to code Select Case statements

How to code For...Next statements

Figure 2-14 presents the syntax for the two versions of the For...Next statement, which is used to implement *For...Next loops*. The first version lets you repeat a series of statements for each value of an index or other variable. By default, the value of the index or variable is incremented by one each time the loop is completed. If you want to increment the index or variable by a value other than one, though, you can include the Step clause on this statement.

The second version of the For...Next statement lets you repeat a series of statements for each element in a group. For example, you could repeat the statements for each Control object in a Controls collection.

The first example in this figure shows how you can use a For...Next statement to add the numbers 1 through 10 to an array. The key to understanding this code is realizing that iIndex is incremented by one for each For...Next loop. Although the second example works the same way, it's incremented by 2 so the numbers 2, 4, 6, 8, and 10 are assigned to the second, fourth, sixth, eighth, and tenth items in the array.

The third example shows how you can use a For...Next statement to perform a future value calculation like the one that's performed by the FV function. As you can see, this example uses three variables. The iIndex variable counts the number of loops, the iMonths variable sets the total number of loops, and the cFutureValue variable stores the dollar amount for the calculation. For each For...Next loop, the arithmetic expression on the right side of the equal sign adds the monthly investment amount to the future value variable and multiplies that value by one plus the monthly interest rate. Then, this value is assigned to the future value variable on the left side of the equal sign.

The fourth and fifth examples show how you can use a For Each...Next statement to work with all of the objects in a collection. In the fourth example, the For...Next loop executes once for each control on the current form (which is referred to by the Me keyword). As a result, every control on the form is enabled. In the fourth example, a special type of If statement is used to check if the type of object is a command button. As a result, every command button on the form is enabled.

The syntax of a For...Next statement

```
For counter = start To end [Step step]
    statements
Next [counter]
```

The syntax of a For Each...Next statement

```
For Each element In group
    statements
Next [element]
```

A For...Next statement that puts the numbers 1 through 10 in an array

```
Dim iIndex As Integer, iArray (1 To 10) As Integer
For iIndex = 1 To 10
    iArray (iIndex) = iIndex
Next iIndex
```

A For...Next statement that puts the numbers 2, 4, 6, 8, and 10 into array items 2, 4, 6, 8, and 10

```
Dim iIndex As Integer, iArray (1 To 10) As Integer
For iIndex = 2 To 10 Step 2
    iArray (iIndex) = iIndex
Next iIndex
```

A For...Next statement that calculates a future value

```
Dim iIndex As Integer
Dim iMonths As Integer
Dim cFutureValue As Currency
iMonths = txtYears * 12
For iIndex = 1 To iMonths
    cFutureValue = (cFutureValue + txtMonthlyInvestment) * _
                   (1 + txtInterestRate / 12)
Next iIndex
```

A For Each...Next statement that enables all controls on a form

```
Dim oControl As Control
For Each oControl In Me.Controls
    oControl.Enabled = True
Next oControl
```

A For Each...Next statement that enables all command buttons on a form

```
Dim oControl As Control
For Each oControl In Me.Controls
    If TypeOf oControl Is CommandButton Then
        oControl.Enabled = True
    End If
Next oControl
```

Figure 2-14   How to code For...Next statements

How to code Do...Loop statements

Figure 2-15 shows how you can use Do...Loop statements to create *Do loops* that perform the same types of repetitive processing as For...Next loops. If you compare the Do loops shown in this figure with the For...Next loops shown in the last figure, though, you'll see that For...Next loops generally lead to simpler code that's easier to understand. As a result, you'll probably use For...Next loops more than Do loops. However, it's worth taking a moment to see how Do loops work.

The syntax at the top of the figure shows two versions of the Do...Loop statement. In the first version, the condition is tested before the series of statements is executed. In the second version, the condition is tested after the series of statements is executed. This means that the loop will be executed at least one time.

The examples of Do loops show how you can use both versions of the statement to calculate a future value. Before the loop begins, you must assign a value of 1 to the iIndex variable. Otherwise, the initial value of 0 will be used and an extra loop will be counted. Once the loop begins, you must include a statement like this

```
iIndex = iIndex + 1
```

to manually increment the iIndex variable. Here, a value of 1 is added to the current value of the variable for each loop. When the value of this variable becomes greater than the value of the iMonths variable, the Do loop ends.

The syntax for the Do statement with the test first

```
Do [{While|Until} condition]
    statements
Loop
```

The syntax for the Do statement with the test last

```
Do
    statements
Loop [{While|Until} condition]
```

A Do loop with the test first that calculates future value

```
Dim iIndex As Integer
Dim iMonths As Integer
Dim cFutureValue As Currency
iMonths = txtYears * 12
iIndex = 1
Do Until iIndex > iMonths
    cFutureValue = (cFutureValue + txtMonthlyInvestment) * _
                   (1 + txtInterestRate / 12)
    iIndex = iIndex + 1
Loop
```

A Do loop with the test last that calculates future value

```
Dim iIndex As Integer
Dim iMonths As Integer
Dim cFutureValue As Currency
iMonths = txtYears * 12
iIndex = 1
Do
    cFutureValue = (cFutureValue + txtMonthlyInvestment) * _
                   (1 + txtInterestRate / 12)
    iIndex = iIndex + 1
Loop While iIndex <= iMonths
```

Figure 2-15   How to code Do statements

How to code On Error statements

If one of the statements in a procedure can't be executed while an application is running, a run-time error occurs. If, for example, your application tries to divide a variable by zero or multiply a variable by a non-numeric value, a run-time error occurs. Then, if your code doesn't handle the error, the application ends. To describe this, we say "the application failed" or "crashed" or "blew up."

Since you don't ever want your applications to crash while they're being used, you should always include code that handles the errors that might occur while your application is running. This code can be referred to as *error handling* or *error trapping* code because it *traps* the errors that occur. Often, this type of code makes up a large portion of the code for a procedure.

To trap the errors that occur, you use the On Error statement that's summarized in figure 2-16. To see how it works, it's probably best to start with the example that's shown. Here, the On Error statement is the first statement in the procedure. It says that the system should go to the *label* named ErrorHandler if an error occurs while any of the unshaded statements that follow are executed. After the unshaded statements, you can see the Exit Sub statement that's executed if no error occurs. It says to return to the procedure that called this one.

After the Exit Sub statement, you can see the ErrorHandler label that the On Error statement branches to if an error does occur. Note that a label like this must end with a colon. Note also that the code that follows this label is only executed when an error occurs...thanks to the Exit Sub statement. If that statement weren't there, the code would "fall through" to the MsgBox function, even though no error occurred, which isn't what you want.

After the ErrorHandler label, you can see the code that's executed when an error does occur. Here, a MsgBox function is used to display the Number and Description properties of an Err object. Visual Basic sets these properties whenever a *trappable error* occurs. After the user responds to the message box, the End Sub statement says that the application should return to the procedure that called this one.

The message box in this figure shows the error number and description for an error that occurs when one of the arguments for the FV function is non-numeric. Often, though, this type of message isn't meaningful to the user of the application. As a result, it's often better to develop your own error messages rather than use the description in the Err object.

Although many error-handling routines end with an End Sub statement, you can also end a routine with a Resume statement. This statement can be used to return to the statement that caused the error (Resume), the first statement after the statement that caused the error (Resume Next), or the statement identified by another label that you code within the procedure (Resume *label*). You can use one of these alternatives when the error-handling routine corrects the error or provides a way for the user to correct an entry error.

The statements for error handling

Syntax	Meaning
On Error GoTo *label*	If an error occurs in one of the statements that follow, go to the line identified by the label.
On Error Resume Next	If an error occurs in one of the statements that follow, resume processing with the first statement after the statement that caused the error.
On Error GoTo 0	Disable the error-handling code.
Resume	Use this in an error-handling routine to resume processing with the statement that caused the error.
Resume Next	Use this in an error-handling routine to resume processing with the first statement after the one that caused the error.
Resume *label*	Use this in an error-handling routine to resume processing at the line identified by the label.
Exit Sub	Exit from the Sub procedure and return to the procedure that called it.

A procedure that contains an error-handling routine

```
Private Sub cmdCalculate_Click()
On Error GoTo ErrorHandler
    txtFutureValue.Text = _
        FormatNumber(FV(txtInterestRate / 12, _
            txtYears * 12, txtMonthlyInvestment.Text, 0, 1) * -1)
    Exit Sub
ErrorHandler:
    MsgBox "Error Number: " & Err.Number & vbCrLf _
        & "Error Description: " & Err.Description
End Sub
```

A message box displayed by the error-handling code

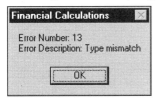

The Err object

- When a trappable error occurs in Visual Basic, you can use the properties of an object named Err to get information about the error. Two of the most useful properties are Err.Number, which gives the number of the error, and Err.Description, which gives a description of the error.

Figure 2-16   How to code On Error statements

If you don't want to perform any special processing when an error occurs, you can use the Resume Next format of the On Error statement. You can also use the GoTo 0 format of the On Error statement to disable the error-handling routine. Although these formats can be useful while you're developing an application, you usually don't use them in a finished application.

How to code With statements

The With statement doesn't provide any new capabilities. Its purpose is to let you write code without repeating the name of a specific object. This can save you some typing, and it can make your code easier to read.

In figure 2-17, you can see the syntax for this statement and two coding examples. The first example shows code that sets two properties and uses a method without using a With statement. In this case, the object name (txtMonthlyInvestment) is repeated in all three lines of code. In contrast, the second example shows how this duplication of the object name can be eliminated by using the With statement.

In this example, the With statement just eliminates two repetitions of the object name so it doesn't save you much typing. When you create routines that require many repetitions of an object name, though, the With statement can significantly reduce coding and make your code easier to read. You'll see this illustrated in section 2 of this book.

The syntax of the With statement

```
With object
    statements
End With
```

Three lines of code without a With statement

```
txtMonthlyInvestment.Enabled = True
txtMonthlyInvestment.BackColor = vbWhite
txtMonthlyInvestment.SetFocus
```

The same code with a With statement

```
With txtMonthlyInvestment
    .Enabled = True
    .BackColor = vbWhite
    .SetFocus
End With
```

Figure 2-17   How to code With statements

A summary of other Visual Basic statements

Although you've just been introduced to the Visual Basic statements that you'll use most of the time, you should know that there are many others. Some of these are summarized in figure 2-18. As you can see, there are statements for loading and unloading forms, for working with strings, for processing the records in sequential and ISAM files, and for controlling application execution, as well as some miscellaneous statements.

To learn more about the Visual Basic statements, you can use the Help feature. In particular, you can use the Language Reference section of the Help feature to display an alphabetical list of the statements available in Visual Basic. For the applications presented in this book, though, you'll only need to use the statements that have already been presented.

Statements for working with forms	
Load	Loads a form into memory.
Unload	Unloads a form from memory.

Statements for working with string variables	
Lset	Left aligns a string within a string variable.
Mid	Replaces a specified number of characters in a string variable with characters from another string.
Rset	Right aligns a string within a string variable.

Statements for file processing	
Open	Opens a file.
Close	Closes a file.
Get	Reads a record from a file.
Put	Writes to a disk file.
Seek	Positions a file for the next read or write operation.
Lock	Locks a range of records in a file.
Unlock	Unlocks a range of records in a file.

Statements for controlling program execution	
End	Terminates program execution immediately and releases all resources.
Stop	Sets a breakpoint in the code that suspends execution.
Exit	Provides a way to prematurely exit from a Do loop, For loop, Sub procedure, or function when used in these forms: Exit Do, Exit For, Exit Sub, or Exit Function.

Miscellaneous statements	
Beep	Sounds a tone through the computer's speaker.
Type	Lets you define a new data type that contains one or more elements. Often used to define the fields within the records of a file.

How to use the Help feature to find the statements that you need

- You can use the Contents tab to get an alphabetical list of statements. To do that, open the Visual Basic Documentation folder, the Reference folder, the Language Reference folder, and Functions folder, and then each letter folder.

Figure 2-18   A summary of other Visual Basic statements

Exercise set 2-3: Use some new statements

In this exercise set, you'll modify the code for the Calculate Investment form so it uses a For…Next statement, an On Error statement, and a nested If statement.

Open the project

1. If it's not already open, open the Financial Calculations project you worked on in exercise set 2-2.

Use a For…Next Loop to calculate the future value

2. Move to the code for the CalculateFutureValue procedure, and delete all the code between the Sub and End Sub statements except this Dim statement:

```
Dim fInterestRate As Single
```

Then, enter this code between the Dim and End Sub statements:

```
Dim iMonths As Integer
Dim cMonthlyInvestment As Currency
Dim cFutureValue As Currency
Dim iIndex As Integer
fInterestRate = txtInterestRate / 12
iMonths = txtYears * 12
cMonthlyInvestment = txtMonthlyInvestment
For iIndex = 1 To iMonths
    cFutureValue = (cFutureValue + cMonthlyInvestment) * _
                    (1 + fInterestRate)
Next iIndex
txtFutureValue = FormatNumber(cFutureValue)
```

3. Press F5 to run the project. Then, test it with valid data and also with invalid data (try entering x as the monthly investment). Although it should work with valid data, it should blow up when you enter invalid data. If it doesn't work with valid data, fix any errors before you continue.

Add error processing to this procedure

4. After the Dim statements in the CalculateFutureValue procedure, enter an On Error statement like this:

```
On Error GoTo ErrorHandler
```

5. Just before the End Sub statement, add the ErrorHandler label and a MsgBox function like this:

```
ErrorHandler:
    MsgBox "Error Number: " & Err.Number & vbCrLf _
        & "Error Description: " & Err.Description
```

6. Press F5 to run the project, enter some valid data for a future value calculation, and click on the Calculate button. Note that even though the calculation works correctly, the message box is displayed. Why? Because there is no Exit Sub statement that tells Visual Basic when to exit from the procedure.

7. To fix this, exit from the Calculate Investment form, return to the Code window, and add an Exit Sub statement before the ErrorHandler label. Then, test the project again with both valid and invalid data. This time it should work correctly. If it doesn't, find the errors and fix them.

Use a nested If statement for error handling

8. Move to the cmdCalculate_Click procedure and modify it so it uses this nested If statement:

```
If Val(txtInterestRate) > 0 And Val(txtYears) > 0 Then
    If optFutureValue And Val(txtMonthlyInvestment) > 0 Then
        CalculateFutureValue
    ElseIf optMonthlyInvestment And Val(txtFutureValue) > 0 Then
        CalculateMonthlyInvestment
    Else
        MsgBox "Invalid data. Please check all entries."
    End If
Else
    MsgBox "Invalid data. Please check all entries."
End If
```

With this code, invalid entries are caught before the calculation procedures are called. As a result, those procedures don't need to check the entries to make sure they are valid.

9. Move to the CalculateMonthlyInvestment procedure and comment out the parts of the If statement including the MsgBox function in the Else clause.

10. Test the project to make sure that an appropriate error message is displayed whenever you enter invalid data. To do that, enter x in the Monthly Investment text box and click on the Calculate button. When you do, you should get the message box you created in step 8. Then, enter 1000 in the three text boxes for a future value calculation and click on the Calculate button. When you do, you should get the message box you created in step 5. If the application doesn't work like this, find and fix any errors before you continue.

11. Delete the lines that you commented out in step 9. Then, test the project one last time to make sure that it still works.

Save the project

12. Save the project and keep it open if you're going to continue with this chapter.

Procedures and functions

In the application for chapter 1, you coded and called general procedures, and you used four Visual Basic functions. Now, you'll learn more about coding general procedures, you'll learn how to code your own functions, and you'll learn more about the functions that are a part of the Visual Basic language.

How to code and call a Sub procedure

Figure 2-19 shows the syntax for coding and calling a *Sub procedure*. The syntax for the Sub statement shows that all Sub procedures must include three parts: (1) the Sub and End Sub statements, (2) a procedure name, and (3) a set of parentheses after the name. Within these parentheses, an argument list is optional. You only need to code it if one or more arguments need to be passed to the procedure.

In addition, you can use the Private and Public keywords to set the scope of the procedure. When you use the Private keyword, a Sub procedure can be called only by another procedure in the same module. When you use the Public keyword, the procedure can be called by any procedure in any of the modules of the project.

In the syntax for the Call statement, you can see that the Call keyword is optional, and most programmers omit this word. Then, if the called procedure requires arguments, the arguments are coded without parentheses after the procedure name. In contrast, if you code the word Call, you must code the arguments within parentheses.

The first two coding examples show Sub and Call statements for a procedure that doesn't include any arguments. The next two code examples, however, show the Sub and Call statements for a procedure that requires four arguments. In the Sub statement for the procedure that requires four arguments, you can see that four values are expected when the procedure is called. Then, in the Call statement that calls this procedure, you can see that four variables are passed to the called procedure in the same sequence and with the same data types specified in the Sub statement for the procedure.

By default, the arguments that are passed to a Sub procedure are passed by reference, which means that the address of the argument, not its value, is passed. When you pass an argument by reference, the procedure has access to the actual variable and can change its value. If you don't want a procedure to change the value of the variable, though, you can pass it by value. Then, a copy of the variable is passed so if the procedure changes that value, it doesn't affect the value of the variable used by the calling procedure.

To pass an argument by value, you use the ByVal keyword in the Sub statement like this:

```
ByVal Months As Integer
```

To pass an argument by reference, which you'll do most of the time, you can either omit the ByVal keyword or use the ByRef keyword.

The syntax of the Sub and End Sub statements

```
[Private|Public] Sub name([argumentlist])
    statements
End Sub
```

The syntax of the Call statement

```
[Call] name[(argumentlist)]
```

A Sub statement with no arguments

```
Private Sub CalculateFutureValue()
```

A Call statement with no arguments

```
CalculateFutureValue
```

A procedure named CalculateFutureValue that requires four arguments

```
Private Sub CalculateFutureValue(Months As Integer, _
        InterestRate As Single, _
        MonthlyInvestment As Currency, _
        FutureValue As Currency)
    Dim iIndex As Integer
    For iIndex = 1 To Months
        FutureValue = (FutureValue + MonthlyInvestment) _
            * (1 + InterestRate)
    Next iIndex
End Sub
```

The code that calls the CalculateFutureValue procedure

```
iMonths = txtYears * 12
fInterestRate = txtInterestRate / 12
cMonthlyInvestment = txtMonthlyInvestment
CalculateFutureValue iMonths, fInterestRate, _
    cMonthlyInvestment, cFutureValue
txtFutureValue = cFutureValue
```

A Sub statement with one argument that is passed by value

```
Private Sub CalculateNewRate (ByVal OldRate As Single)
```

Notes

- If you omit the keyword Call, which is the norm, you can code the arguments without using parentheses. If you include the word Call, you must code the arguments in parentheses.

- By default, the arguments that are passed to a Sub procedure are passed *by reference*. Then, the called procedure can modify the value in the calling procedure.

- When an argument is passed *by value*, a copy of the variable is passed to the called procedure. Then, if the called procedure modifies the value, the value in the calling procedure isn't changed. To pass an argument by value, you use the ByVal keyword.

Figure 2-19   How to code and call a Sub procedure

By passing arguments from one procedure to another, you limit the scope of the variables that are used. For instance, all of the variables in both the called procedure and the calling procedure in this example are local variables. The alternative is to code the variables as global or module-level variables so the variables don't have to be passed from one procedure to another. Although that works okay in a small application that requires just a few variables, it becomes difficult to keep track of the variables when an application requires dozens of variables. Then, passing arguments from one procedure to another actually makes your procedures easier to understand and debug. In addition, your application will use fewer system resources.

How to code and call a Function procedure

Figure 2-20 presents the syntax for coding and calling a *Function procedure* (or just *function*). The main difference between a Sub procedure and a function is that a function returns a value to the calling procedure. To specify the value to be returned, you assign it to the function name within the function. To specify the type of data to be returned, you include the As type clause on the Function statement.

After the syntax summaries, you can see code that creates and calls a function. This function requires three arguments and returns the future value of an investment. Since this function is called within an assignment statement, the future value that's calculated by the function is assigned to the Future Value text box.

If you compare this function with the Sub procedure in the preceding figure, you can see how similar the function and procedure are. In fact, both accomplish the same purpose. In general, though, you should use a function when you need a calculated value returned, and you should use a Sub procedure for other purposes.

The syntax of the Function and End Function statements

```
[Private|Public] Function name([argumentlist]) [As type]
    statements
    name = expression
End Function
```

The syntax of the Call statement

```
[Call] name[(argumentlist)]
```

A function named FutureValue that requires three arguments

```
Private Function FutureValue(Months As Integer, _
                InterestRate As Single, _
                MonthlyInvestment As Currency) _
                As Currency
    Dim iIndex As Integer
    For iIndex = 1 To Months
        FutureValue = (FutureValue + MonthlyInvestment) _
            * (1 + InterestRate)
    Next iIndex
End Function
```

A procedure that calls the FutureValue function

```
Public Sub CalculateFutureValue()
    Dim iMonths As Integer
    Dim fInterestRate As Single
    Dim cMonthlyInvestment As Currency
    iMonths = txtYears * 12
    fInterestRate = txtInterestRate / 12
    cMonthlyInvestment = txtMonthlyInvestment
    txtFutureValue = FutureValue(iMonths, _
        fInterestRate, cMonthlyInvestment)
End Sub
```

Notes

- If you use the keyword Call to call a function, the return value is discarded. Normally, though, you need to use the return value so you omit the word Call.

- You can use the ByVal keyword when you define an argument for a function just as you can for a Sub procedure. The default, however, is to pass the value by reference.

Figure 2-20   How to code and call a Function procedure

A summary of the Visual Basic functions

Before you create a new function, you should check whether Visual Basic provides a built-in function that you can use. Figure 2-21, for example, summarizes some of the functions that Visual Basic provides. In particular, Visual Basic provides most of the functions that you're likely to need for working with dates and strings and for performing math and financial calculations.

In the exercise sets for chapter 1, you used the Val, FormatNumber, MsgBox, FV, and Pmt functions. Since the skills for working with these functions are the same as the skills for working with other functions, you shouldn't have much trouble using the functions you need for specific purposes…once you find them. To do that, it's usually best to use the Index tab of the Help window to search for a type of function like "string functions" or "financial functions." The alternative is to use the Contents tab to get an alphabetic listing of the functions, which is a time consuming and tedious way to find the function that you need.

In the next two figures, you'll learn more about nine of the functions in this summary. First, you'll learn more about the MsgBox function since it has some peculiarities that you won't find in other functions. Then, you'll see how you can use some of the string functions to extract the words from a text string.

Some of the date and time functions

Function	Description
Date	Returns the current date.
Now	Returns the current date and time.
Time	Returns the current time.
DateValue	Receives a date string and returns a date numeric value.

Some of the string functions

Function	Description
InStr	Returns the position of the first occurrence of one string within another.
Left	Returns a specific number of characters from the start of a string.
Len	Returns the length of a string.
LTrim	Removes spaces from the start of a string.
Mid	Returns a specific number of characters from a string starting from a specific location in the string.
Right	Returns a specific number of characters from a string starting from the right.

Some of the math and finance functions

Function	Description
Int	Returns the integer portion of a number.
Val	Returns the number contained in a string as a numeric value.
Rnd	Returns the next random number as a decimal fraction between 0 and 1.
FV	Calculates the future value of a periodic payment amount.
SLN	Calculates a straight-line depreciation amount.
SYD	Calculates a sum-of-years' digits depreciation amount.

The immediate If function

Function	Description
IIf	Evaluates a conditional expression and returns one value if the expression is true and another value if the expression is false.

Two dialog box functions

Function	Description
MsgBox	Displays a message in a dialog box, waits for the user to click a button, and returns an integer indicating which button the user clicked.
InputBox	Displays a message in a dialog box, waits for the user to enter text or click a button, and returns a string that contains what the user entered.

How to use the Help feature to find the functions that you need

- Use the Index tab to look for functions by type as in "financial functions" or "string functions."
- You can also use the Contents tab to get an alphabetical list of functions. To do that, open the Visual Basic Documentation folder, the Reference folder, the Language Reference folder, and Functions folder, and then each letter. Although this gives you access to the information for each function, this isn't an efficient way to find it.

Figure 2-21   How to use Visual Basic functions

How to use the MsgBox function

Figure 2-22 shows how to use the MsgBox function to display a dialog box and check the response from a user. Since this is one of the most useful Visual Basic functions, you'll want to thoroughly understand how to use it.

The syntax at the top of the figure shows that the MsgBox function can use three arguments. Although the first argument is the only one that's required, you can use the second argument to control how the command buttons in the dialog box are displayed, and you can use the third argument to specify a title for the dialog box. When you specify a value for the second argument, the MsgBox function returns a value that indicates which command button was clicked. Then, you can use that value to determine the processing that's performed next.

The first coding example in this figure shows how to code a simple message box that doesn't return a value. Here, only the first argument is coded, and the argument is coded after a space instead of within parentheses. In this case, Visual Basic uses the default options for the other two arguments. As a result, just an OK button is displayed in the message box, and the name of the application is displayed in the title bar.

The second example shows how to code a message box that returns a value. The second argument for this MsgBox function includes two Visual Basic constants to indicate (1) that the dialog box should contain both Yes and No buttons and (2) that the first button (Yes) should be the default. That means that the user can press the Enter key to select the Yes button instead of clicking on it. Notice that a plus sign (+) combines the two constants. That's because the constants represent numeric values that are added together to determine the value of the buttons argument. The third argument for this MsgBox function sets "Confirm Exit" as the title of the dialog box.

In this example, the MsgBox function is coded in the Unload event procedure for a form. This event occurs when the Unload statement is executed by another procedure. Note that this Unload procedure provides for an integer argument named Cancel. If this argument is set to True by the procedure, the Unload event is cancelled.

In the code for this Unload procedure, you can see that the MsgBox function is coded within an If statement. Then, if the value returned by the function is equal to the Visual Basic constant named vbNo, it means that the user responded by clicking on the No button. In that case, the Cancel argument for the Unload procedure is set to True so the Unload operation isn't performed.

The syntax of the MsgBox function

```
MsgBox(prompt[, buttons][, title])
```

A MsgBox function that doesn't return a value

```
MsgBox "Invalid data. Please check all entries."
```

A MsgBox function that returns a value

```
Private Sub Form_Unload(Cancel As Integer)
    If MsgBox("Are you sure you want to exit?", _
        vbYesNo + vbDefaultButton1, "Confirm Exit") = vbNo Then
        Cancel = True
    End If
End Sub
```

Some of the Visual Basic constants for the buttons argument

Constant	Value	Description
vbOKOnly	0	Display OK button only.
vbOKCancel	1	Display OK and Cancel buttons.
vbAbortRetryIgnore	2	Display Abort, Retry, and Ignore buttons.
vbYesNoCancel	3	Display Yes, No, and Cancel buttons.
vbYesNo	4	Display Yes and No buttons.
vbRetryCancel	5	Display Retry and Cancel buttons.
vbCritical	16	Display Critical Message icon.
vbInformation	64	Display Information Message icon.
vbDefaultButton1	0	First button is default.
vbDefaultButton2	256	Second button is default.
vbDefaultButton3	512	Third button is default.

Some of the Visual Basic constants for return values

Constant	Value	Description
vbOK	1	User chose the OK button.
vbCancel	2	User chose the Cancel button.
vbAbort	3	User chose the Abort button.
vbRetry	4	User chose the Retry button.
vbIgnore	5	User chose the Ignore button.
vbYes	6	User chose the Yes button.
vbNo	7	User chose the No button.

Figure 2-22   How to use the MsgBox function

A parsing routine that uses eight different functions

To conclude this chapter, figure 2-23 presents a parsing routine that illustrates the use of six string functions, an InputBox function, and a MsgBox function. These functions are shaded so you can easily spot them. In addition, this routine illustrates the use of a Do loop, nested If statements, and a standard module (since the InputBox and MsgBox functions provide for the input and output, the project doesn't require a form).

The purpose of a parsing routine is to divide a string of characters into the words that are contained within the string. This type of routine is often used in business applications to divide the name field into first, middle, and last name or to divide an address field into city, state, and zip code. That way, the user can enter the full name or address line into a single text box, while the code does the work of breaking the name or address into parts. For instance, the name entered in the InputBox for this figure is parsed into first name, middle initial, and last name.

If you study this code, I hope that you'll be able to figure out how it works without any help. That will show that you've learned a lot in this chapter. If you do the exercise set that follows, you can experiment with this code, get help information for the functions, and so on. As a result, I'm only going to point out a few highlights and let you figure out everything else on your own.

The InputBox function displays the InputBox shown at the top of this figure and receives whatever data the user enters. Then, after the parsing routine divides the user entry into words, the MsgBox function displays the words with one word per line. To keep this routine simple, the assumption is that the user will only enter from one to three words. If, however, the user clicks on the OK button without entering any text, the routine shouldn't do any parsing and the application should end.

After this routine gets the text from the InputBox, the LTrim, InStr, Left, Mid, Right, and Len functions are used to parse the text. This code is complicated by the fact that it has to work whether the user enters one, two, or three words. That's why the nested If statements are needed.

In practice, a routine like this is often more complicated because you can't make the assumption that the user will enter one, two, or three words. Also, a routine like this is likely to be coded as a function so it can be copied into other applications and used by other programmers whenever they need to parse text.

InputBox with string entry

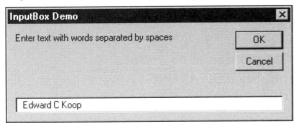

MsgBox with parsed words

A routine that uses eight different functions as it parses a string into words

```
Option Explicit
Dim msText As String

Sub Main()
    msText = " "
    Do Until msText = ""
        Call ParseText
    Loop
    End
End Sub

Sub ParseText()
    Dim iBlankPosition1 As Integer
    Dim iBlankPosition2 As Integer
    Dim sWord1 As String
    Dim sWord2 As String
    Dim sWord3 As String
    msText = InputBox("Enter text with words separated by spaces", _
        "InputBox Demo")
    If msText = "" Then Exit Sub
    msText = LTrim(msText)
    iBlankPosition1 = InStr(msText, " ")
    If iBlankPosition1 = 0 Then
        sWord1 = msText
    Else
        sWord1 = Left(msText, iBlankPosition1 - 1)
        iBlankPosition2 = InStr(iBlankPosition1 + 1, msText, " ")
        If iBlankPosition2 = 0 Then
            sWord2 = Right(msText, Len(msText) - iBlankPosition1)
        Else
            sWord2 = Mid(msText, iBlankPosition1 + 1, _
                        iBlankPosition2 - iBlankPosition1 - 1)
            sWord3 = Right(msText, Len(msText) - iBlankPosition2)
        End If
    End If
    MsgBox sWord1 & vbCrLf & sWord2 & vbCrLf & sWord3, , "Parsed Words"
End Sub
```

Figure 2-23   A routine that illustrates the use of eight functions

Exercise set 2-4: Create and use functions

In this exercise set, you'll get a response from a MsgBox function, create a function that receives three arguments, and create a project that parses text entered into an InputBox.

Open the project

1. If it's not already open, open the Financial Calculations project you worked on in exercise set 2-3.

Use the value returned by a MsgBox function

2. Open the Code window for the Calculate Investment form. Then, start a new procedure for the Unload event of the form. To do that, select Form from the Object list at the top of the window and select Unload from the Event list.

3. Between the Sub and End Sub statements, enter an If statement that uses the value returned by a MsgBox function as shown in figure 2-22.

4. Test the project, and click on the Exit button to see how this works. In this case, clicking on the No button should cancel the Unload event and return you to the form while clicking on the Yes button should unload the form and return you to the Code window.

Create a function that requires three arguments

5. Use the Add Procedure command from the Tools menu to create the Function and End Function statements for a private function named FutureValue. Move the insertion point between the parentheses at the end of the function and enter three arguments for the function as shown in figure 2-20. Then, enter "As Currency" after the parentheses.

6. Between the Function and End Function statements, enter the code that's shown in figure 2-20. To save typing, you can move the Dim statement for the iIndex variable and the For…Next loop from the CalculateFutureValue procedure. Then, you can modify the For…Next loop so it uses the variable names defined in the Function statement. To do that, all you need to do is to delete the prefixes for the variables.

7. Navigate to the CalculateFutureValue procedure. If you haven't already moved it out of the procedure, delete the Dim statement for the iIndex variable and the For…Next loop. Then, modify the assignment statement for the Future Value text box so it uses the FutureValue function you just created. When you're done, the assignment statement should look like this:

```
txtFutureValue = FutureValue(iMonths, _
        fInterestRate, cMonthlyInvestment)
```

Since you no longer need the cFutureValue variable, you can also delete the Dim statement for that variable from this procedure.

8. Test the project to make sure that it works. When it does, you've created a custom function that gets the same results as the FV function.

9. Move the FutureValue function to the standard module. Then, test the project. When you do, you should get an error since the function was originally defined as a private function. To correct this, change the keyword in the Function statement from Private to Public. Then, test the project again to make sure it works correctly.

Save and close the current project and start a new one

10. Click on the Save Project button to save the current project.

11. Use the New command in the File menu to start a new Standard EXE project. This should automatically close the old project.

12. Use the Add Module command in the Project menu to add a standard module to the new project. Next, right-click on the form shown in the Project Explorer, and choose the Remove command to remove that form from the project.

13. Click on the Save Project button in the toolbar and use the Save File As dialog box to create a new folder called Chapter 2 Parsing. Then, save the files for the standard module and the project in this folder with the names Standard Module and Parse Text.

Use seven other functions

14. Open the Code window for the standard module. In the Declarations section, enter the Dim statement for the msText variable as shown in figure 2-23. If necessary, enter the Option Explicit statement as well. Then, enter the entire Main procedure.

15. Start the ParseText procedure in figure 2-23 by entering the Sub and End Sub statements for the procedure, the five Dim statements, the assignment statement, the one-line If statement after that, and the MsgBox function at the end of this procedure. Then, test the procedure. At this point, the procedure should end if you just press the Enter key when the InputBox is displayed (no entry), and the MsgBox should be displayed if you enter one or more characters before pressing the Enter key. If it doesn't work this way, find the errors and fix them.

16. Enter the rest of the code in figure 2-23 into the ParseText procedure. Then, test the project. At this point, the project should parse the entered text into from one to three words. If it doesn't, you need to debug it.

Save the project and exit from Visual Basic

17. Click on the Save Project button to save the current project. Then, click on the Close button in the upper right corner to exit from Visual Basic.

Perspective

The goal of this chapter has been to improve your knowledge of the syntax, statements, and functions of the Visual Basic language. If you have much programming experience, you should now see that Visual Basic is much like other languages that you've used. If you haven't had much programming experience, you should definitely do the exercise sets to make sure you get started right with this language.

Once you're confident that you know how to use the Visual Basic language, you're ready to go on to the next chapters in this section. In chapter 3, you'll learn how to use more of the objects, properties, methods, and events that are also a part of the Visual Basic language. In chapter 4, you'll learn more about testing and debugging an application. As you will see, some of the debugging statements will also help you better understand how the Visual Basic statements work.

Terms you should know

continuation character	arithmetic operator
comment	order of precedence
commenting out	negation
bookmark	conditional expression
form module	relational operator
standard module	logical operator
variable	array
constant	one-dimensional array
data type	index
string data type	two-dimensional array
Boolean data type	nested If statements
zero-length string	For...Next loop
scope	Do loop
procedure-level variable	error handling
local variable	error trapping
module-level variable	trappable error
global variable	label
assignment statement	Sub procedure
concatenate	Function procedure
arithmetic expression	function

3

How to work with forms and controls

In chapter 1, you learned how to work with a project that consisted of one form that used five different types of controls. Now, you'll learn how to work with projects that use more than one form. You'll also learn how to use several new controls including one that isn't in the starting Toolbox. When you finish this chapter, you'll have the skills that you need for developing multi-form applications that use a variety of controls.

Basic skills for working with forms **104**
How to add a form to a project 104
How to change the startup form 106
How to use the Project Explorer 108
How to use the Form Layout window 110
Exercise set 3-1: Add a new form to the project 112

Basic skills for working with controls **114**
The controls in the standard Toolbox 114
How to work with option buttons and check boxes 116
How to work with combo boxes and list boxes 118
How to add controls to the Toolbox 120
How to use a masked edit box 122
How to use the Validate event 122
How to use the Object Browser 124
Exercise set 3-2: Add controls to the new form 126

How to develop a multiple-document interface **128**
The difference between single-document
and multiple-document interfaces 128
How to create the parent and child forms 130
How to add menus to a form 132
How to write code that works with child forms 134
Exercise set 3-3: Create a multiple-document interface 136

Perspective **138**

Basic skills for working with forms

To develop an application that uses more than one form, you need a few new skills. So those are the skills you'll learn next.

How to add a form to a project

When you start a new project, a single blank form is started for you. Then, to add another form to a project, you use the Add Form dialog box shown in figure 3-1. To add a new blank form to the project, which is what you'll do most of the time, you choose the Form icon in the New tab and click on the Open button.

Note, however, that the New tab also offers icons for special types of forms. If you choose one of these, a new form is started with some controls already on it. If, for example, you choose the Dialog icon, the form contains OK and Cancel buttons with some of their properties already set the way you might want them. Since this can save you a few minutes, you may want to use a few of these form options as you enhance the user interface for an application as described in chapter 12.

If you want to add an existing form to a project, you can use the Existing tab of the Add Form dialog box. This can be useful if you want to use the same form in two different projects or if you want to create a form that's similar to an existing form. Before you modify an existing form, though, you must save the form with a new name or in a new folder. Otherwise, the changes you make will be applied to the original form.

The Add Form dialog box

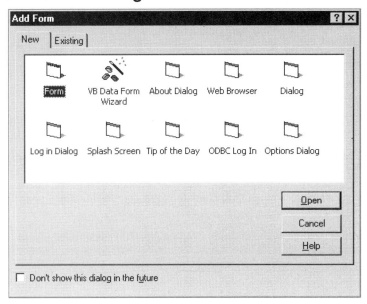

Operation

- To access the Add Form dialog box, select the Add Form command from the Project menu or select New and then Form from the shortcut menu for the Project Explorer. Or, click on the Add Form button in the Standard toolbar (if this isn't the second button from the left, click on the arrow to the right of that button and select Form).

- To create a blank form, select the Form option from the New tab of the Add Form dialog box and click on the Open button.

- To create a form that has some controls on it with properties already set, choose one of the other options in the New tab. This can be useful when you're enhancing the user interface (see chapter 12).

- To copy an existing form into a project, click on the Existing tab of the Add Form dialog box and choose the form that you want to copy. Before you modify the form, though, save it with a new name or in a new folder. Otherwise, the modifications will be made to the original form.

Figure 3-1   How to add a form to a project

How to change the startup form

By default, the first form that's added to a project is the form that will be displayed when you start the application. If that's not what you want, you can change the Startup Object property of the project as shown in figure 3-2. To change that object to another form, for example, you just select the form name from the drop-down list for the Startup Object.

If you want to execute code before a form is displayed, you can code a Sub procedure named Main in any standard module in the project. Then, to execute this procedure when the application starts, choose the Sub Main option for the Startup Object property.

To illustrate, the code example in this figure shows a Sub procedure named Main that uses the InputBox function to check for a password. If the user enters the correct password, Visual Basic uses the Show method of a form to display the form. Otherwise, Visual Basic displays a message box that informs the user that the password is incorrect. As a result, the application won't start unless the user enters the correct password.

The Project Properties dialog box

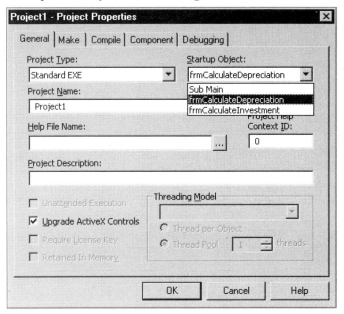

A Sub Main procedure in a standard module

```
Private Sub Main()
    If InputBox("Enter Password") = "Green" Then
        frmCalculateInvestment.Show
    Else
        MsgBox "Incorrect Password"
    End If
End Sub
```

Operation

- To access the Project Properties dialog box, select the *projectname* Properties command from the Project menu.

- To change the form that's displayed when the project starts, select the form that you want from the Startup Object combo box.

- To run code when the project starts, select the Sub Main option from the Startup Object combo box. Then, add a standard module to the project, create a Sub procedure named Main in this module, and add the code to this procedure.

Figure 3-2   How to change the startup form

How to use the Project Explorer

When a project contains more than one form, you can use the Project Explorer to open and switch between the Form and Code windows of the project. Figure 3-3 shows how. In this example, the project consists of two forms and a standard module. As a result, you can open three different Code windows (one for each form module and one for the standard module) as well as two Form windows (one for each form).

If you take a few minutes to experiment with the Project Explorer, you shouldn't have much trouble using it. In fact, many elements of the interface are similar to the interface for the Windows Explorer. For example, you can expand or collapse a folder by clicking on the plus (+) or minus sign (-) to the left of the folder.

The fastest way to open or switch to the Form window for a form is to double-click on its form name. In contrast, the fastest way to open or switch to a Code window depends on the type of Code window. For a standard module, you can double-click on the module name. For a form module, you need to click on the form name to select it and then click on the View Code button at the top of the Project Explorer. Another way to move from one open window to another is to use the Window menu.

When a project contains many forms, you'll sometimes need to remove a form from the project. To do that, you can right-click on the form and select the Remove command from the resulting menu. Although this removes the form from the project, it doesn't delete the file for the form. To delete the file, you need to use the Windows Explorer.

A project with two forms and a standard module

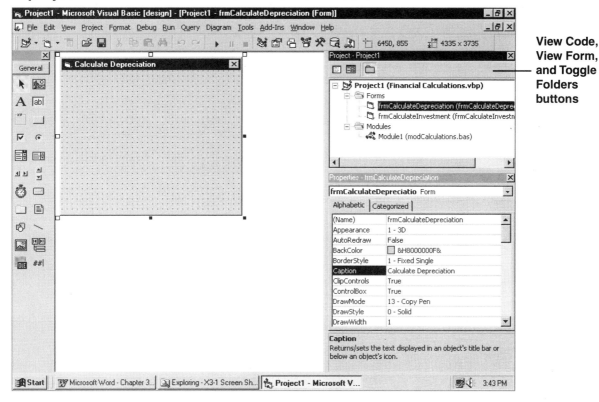

View Code, View Form, and Toggle Folders buttons

Operation

- To open or switch to a Form or Code window, click on the form or module name to select it. Then, click on the View Form or View Code button at the top of the Project Explorer. You can also open or display a Form window by double-clicking on a form name, and you can open or display a Code window by double-clicking on a module name.

- To expand or collapse a folder, click on the plus (+) or minus (-) sign to the left of the folder.

- To display or hide the Forms and Modules folders, click on the Toggle Folders button at the top of the Project Explorer.

- To remove a form from a project, right-click on the form and select the Remove command from the resulting shortcut menu. You can also click on the form to select it and then select the Remove command from the Project menu. Note, however, that removing a form from a project doesn't delete the file from your computer. This works the same way for modules.

- Two other ways to switch from one open Form or Code window to another are (1) to use the Window menu and (2) to press the shortcut keys Ctrl+F6 (to move to the next window) and Ctrl+Shift+F6 (to move to the previous window).

Figure 3-3   How to use the Project Explorer

How to use the Form Layout window

In chapter 1, you learned how to center a form on the screen when it is started by setting the StartUpPosition property for the form. Now, you'll learn how to use the Form Layout window to manually set the startup position for a form. This is useful when a project contains more than one form. In figure 3-4, for example, you can see how two forms can be positioned so they don't overlap.

When you first display the Form Layout window, Visual Basic doesn't display any forms in the window. After you run the project, though, the forms that have open Form windows are displayed and you can add forms to or remove forms from the Form Layout window by opening or closing their Form windows. Once the forms are displayed in the Form Layout window, you can position them by dragging them.

Since your users may be running their computers at a lower screen resolutions than the one you're using, their monitors may not have as much room to display the forms of an application. As a result, you need to take screen resolution into account when you design forms and set the startup position for a form. In general, it's a good idea to position your forms so they'll be displayed properly with the lowest resolution, which today is usually 640 by 480.

To display resolution guides for lower resolutions than the one you're using, you can right-click on the Form Layout window and select the Resolution Guides command from the shortcut menu. In this figure, for example, the monitor's resolution is 800 by 600, but the resolution guides in the Form Layout window clearly show how much space is available with a resolution of 640 by 480.

Two forms displayed in the Form Layout window.

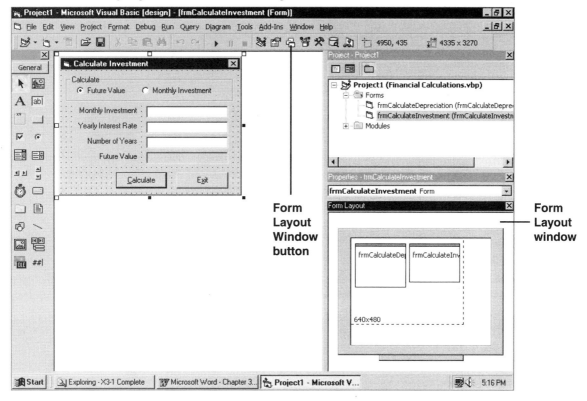

Form Layout Window button

Form Layout window

Operation

- To display the Form Layout window, click on the Form Layout Window button in the toolbar.

- To display the forms in the Form Layout window, use the Project Explorer to open the Form window for each form you want to display. Then, run the project. After that, you can add a form to the Form Layout window by opening the form's Form window or remove a form from the Form Layout window by closing the form's Form window.

- To adjust the position of a form that's displayed in the Form Layout window, position the mouse over the representation of the form until it turns into a four-pointed arrow. Then, drag the form to the location you want. When you do, the StartUpPosition property for the form will be set to Manual and the Top and Left properties for the form will automatically be adjusted.

- To display resolution guides for monitors with lower resolutions than your monitor's, right-click on the Form Layout window and select the Resolution Guides command from the shortcut menu.

- To reset the StartUpPosition property for a form, right-click on the form in the Form Layout window, select Startup Position from the shortcut menu, and select the property setting from the submenu.

Figure 3-4   How to use the Form Layout window

Exercise set 3-1: Add a new form to the project

In this exercise set, you'll add a new form to the Financial Calculations project you developed in the first two chapters, and you'll use some of the skills for working with a project that contains more than one form.

Open the project

1. Start Visual Basic and open the Financial Calculations project you created in chapter 1 and modified in chapter 2.

Add a form to the project

2. Select the Add Form command from the Project menu to display the Add Form dialog box. Then, choose the Form option from the New tab to add a blank form to the project.

3. Set these properties for the new form:

Property	Setting
Name	frmCalculateDepreciation
Caption	Calculate Depreciation
BorderStyle	1 – Fixed Single

4. Click on the Save Project toolbar button to access the Save File As dialog box. Navigate to the folder that contains the rest of the files for the Financial Calculations project, and click on the Save button to save the file as frmCalculateDepreciation.

5. Press F5 to run the project and see that the Calculate Investment form is displayed, but the Calculate Depreciation form isn't. Then, click on the Exit button to return to Visual Basic.

Change the startup form for the project

6. Select the Project1 Properties command from the Project menu to access the Project Properties dialog box. Then, select the new Calculate Depreciation form from the Startup Object combo box.

7. Press F5 to run the project. This time the Calculate Depreciation form should be displayed. Click on its Close button to return to Visual Basic.

Switch between forms and modules

8. Use the Project Explorer to open the Form and Code windows for both forms and to open the Code window for the standard module.

9. Use the Window menu to switch between the five open windows. Then, press Ctrl+F6 and Ctrl+Shift+F6 to cycle through the open windows.

10. Switch to the Form window for the Calculate Investment form. If this window isn't already maximized, click on its Maximize button to maximize it. Then, select the Calculate and Exit command buttons by clicking on them while holding down the Shift key, and copy these buttons to the clipboard by pressing Ctrl+C.

11. Switch to the Form window for the Calculate Depreciation form. Then, paste the Calculate and Exit command buttons on the form by pressing Ctrl+V, and position the buttons by dragging them to the bottom of the form. If you use the Properties window to look at the properties for either of these buttons, you'll see that all properties are set as they were on the other form.

12. Double-click on the form background of the Calculate Depreciation form to switch to the Code window for the form and to generate the Sub and End Sub statements for the Load event of the form. Then, enter this code between the Sub and End Sub statements:

```
frmCalculateInvestment.Show
```

13. Press F5 to run the application. Now, both forms should be displayed on your screen and each form should have a button in the Windows taskbar. Use the taskbar to switch between the two forms. Then, close both forms.

Size and position the forms

14. Close the Properties window by clicking on its Close button. Then, open the Form Layout window by clicking on the Form Layout Window button in the toolbar. If necessary, size the Form Layout window so it's displayed as shown in figure 3-4. Notice that the Form Layout window doesn't display any forms.

15. Press F5 to run the project. Then, close both forms to return to Visual Basic. Now, the Form Layout window should display both forms.

16. Drag the forms in the Form Layout window so they're positioned as shown in figure 3-4. If you're using a monitor with a higher resolution than 640 by 480, use the shortcut menu for the Form Layout window to display the resolution guides and reposition the form windows within the guides.

17. Press F5 to run the project. Now, Visual Basic should display both forms as they were positioned in the Form Layout window. Then, click on the Close buttons to stop both forms from running.

Clean up and save the project

18. Click on the Close button for the Form Layout window to close this window. Then, click on the Properties Window button in the toolbar to display the Properties window.

19. Save the project and keep it open if you're going to continue with this chapter.

Basic skills for working with controls

In chapter 1, you learned how to use five of the controls in the standard Toolbox. Now, you'll learn how to use more of these controls as well as some controls that aren't in that Toolbox.

The controls in the standard Toolbox

Figure 3-5 summarizes the controls that are available in the standard Toolbox. In chapter 1, you learned how to use labels, text boxes, frames, and command buttons. In the next two figures, you'll learn how to use option buttons, check boxes, combo boxes, and list boxes.

If you need to use some of the other controls in the standard Toolbox, you should be able to figure out how to use them on your own. Since most of these controls are standard controls that you've used in other Windows applications, you can probably guess what they do. For example, the DriveListBox, DirListBox, and FileListBox controls are controls that can be used to select a file.

Note, however, that the two scroll bar controls are not used to navigate up or down as you might think. Instead, they're used to select a value. When you use these controls, you use the Min and Max properties to set a minimum value and a maximum value. Then, the user can select a value between these two values by dragging the box on the scroll bar.

If you need to add a graphic image to a form, you can use the PictureBox or Image control. Then, you can use the Picture property for either of these controls to select the graphic that you want to display. These controls support most standard image formats including bitmap (.bmp), metafile (.wmf), icon (.ico), jpeg (.jpg), and gif (.gif) files. Since the Image control requires fewer system resources than the PictureBox control, you should use it whenever possible.

However, the PictureBox control provides more functionality than the Image control. First, it is a *container control* that can contain other controls. For example, a picture box can contain several Image controls. Second, the PictureBox control has many more properties, methods, and events that you can use.

If you want to run blocks of code at specific time intervals, you can use the Timer control. Since this control isn't displayed when you run the application, you can place it anywhere on your form. Then, you can set its Interval property and write an event procedure that responds to its Timer event (the only event for this control).

If you want to insert an object from another program into a form, you can use an *OLE (Object Linking and Embedding)* control to embed the object. For example, you can embed an object from an application like Microsoft Word into your application. Then, when you run the application, you can access the functionality of Word from the Visual Basic application.

Control	Name	Description
	PictureBox	Displays a container that can hold other controls or a graphic.
	Label	Displays descriptive information.
	TextBox	Lets the user enter or modify a value.
	Frame	Groups controls or defines areas of a form.
	CommandButton	Performs an operation when clicked.
	CheckBox	Turns an option on or off.
	OptionButton	Turns an option on or off. If two or more of these buttons are in a frame, turning one button on turns the others off.
	ComboBox	Lets the user enter a value or select an item from a list.
	ListBox	Displays a list that the user can select from.
	HScrollBar	Increases or decreases a value.
	VScrollBar	Increases or decreases a value.
	Timer	Executes code at a specified interval.
	DriveListBox	Lets the user select a disk drive from a drop-down list.
	DirListBox	Lets the user select a directory from a list.
	FileListBox	Lets the user select a file from a list.
	Shape	Displays one of five types of geometric shapes including rectangles, squares, and circles.
	Line	Displays a line.
	Image	Displays a graphic.
	Data	Lets the user navigate the records in a recordset.
	OLE	Contains an OLE object.

Figure 3-5   The controls in the standard Toolbox

How to work with option buttons and check boxes

Figure 3-6 shows you how to work with option buttons and check boxes. The main difference is that option buttons within the same frame are mutually exclusive while check boxes operate independently. In other words, when you place option buttons within a frame and the user selects one of the buttons, all of the other buttons are automatically turned off. In contrast, when the user selects a check box, that has no effect upon the other check boxes on the form, even when they're within a frame control.

When you place an option button or a check box on a form, you use the Name property to name the control, the Caption property to set the caption for the control, and the Value property to set the default value for the control. As you can see, you can set the Value property of an option button to True or False and the Value property of a check box to Checked, Unchecked, or Grayed.

The two code examples in this figure show how you can use the Value property in code. In the first example, the Value property of an option button is used as the condition in an If statement:

```
If optFutureValue Then
```

Here, both the property name and the comparison is omitted, but this is equivalent to:

```
If optFutureValue.Value = True Then
```

This is a shorthand that Visual Basic accepts and that's commonly used by Visual Basic programmers.

Similarly, chkDue is used as the fifth argument for the Pmt function. Then, if the Due check box isn't checked, a value of 0 is used for the fifth argument. If it is checked, a value of 1 is used for this argument. You may remember from chapter 1 that this argument determines whether the payments are applied at the end or the start of each month.

A form that contains two option buttons and a check box

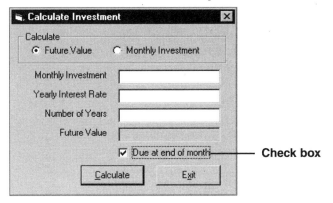

Check box

The Value property (default property)

Option buttons	Check boxes
True	0 – Unchecked
False	1 – Checked
	2 – Grayed

Code that uses the option buttons

```
If optFutureValue Then
    CalculateFutureValue
Else
    CalculateMonthlyInvestment
End If
```

Code that uses the check box

```
txtMonthlyInvestment = _
        FormatNumber(Pmt(mfInterestRate, _
            txtYears * 12, 0, txtFutureValue, chkDue) * -1)
```

Figure 3-6   How to work with option buttons and check boxes

How to work with combo boxes and list boxes

Figure 3-7 shows you how to work with combo boxes and list boxes. In the form at the top of this figure, a combo box lets the user select a number that represents the life of an asset and a list box displays the depreciation amount for each year of the asset's life. To use this form, the user enters the initial cost of the asset and the final value of the asset (which is often zero) in the text boxes. Then, the user selects the life of the asset from the drop-down list of the combo box or enters the number of years into that box. Last, the user clicks on the Calculate button to display the year and depreciation amounts in the list box.

When you use a combo box or list box, you use the AddItem method to load the items into the control. For instance, the first coding example in this figure shows how you can use a For...Next loop to load the combo box named cboLife with the numbers 1 through 40. In this case, the code is in the Load event procedure for the Form so the combo box is loaded when the form is loaded. After that, the user can select a value from the combo box and other procedures can use that value. You can see, for example, that cboLife is used as the third argument for the SYD function in second coding example in this figure. This means that the value in its default property (Text) is used for this argument.

The second coding example shows how you can load a list box when the Click event of the Calculate button occurs. This example begins by invoking the Clear method to clear all items from the list box. Then, a For...Next loop uses the SYD function to load the list box. Although this code may look confusing, it's easy to understand if you break it down. For each year in the asset's life (i), the AddItem method is used to add a string to the list box. This string starts with the year followed by a colon and some spaces

```
lstDepreciation.AddItem ("Year " & i & ":    " &
```

followed by the value derived from the SYD function

```
SYD(mskInitialCost, mskFinalValue, cboLife, i)
```

after the FormatCurrency function is used to format the result.

Note in both of these examples that the letter *i* is used as the name of the variable that determines how many times the For...Next loops are executed, instead of a longer name like iIndex. This is a common programming practice when a procedure requires only one index variable.

When you work with list boxes and combo boxes, you should be aware that the Change and Click events are the most common events for a combo box and its Text property contains the value in its text box. In contrast, the Click and DblClick events are the most common events for a list box and its Text property contains the value of the item that is selected by clicking or double-clicking. If, for example, you click on an item in a list box, the value of that item is stored in the Text property of the list box.

A form that contains a combo box and a list box

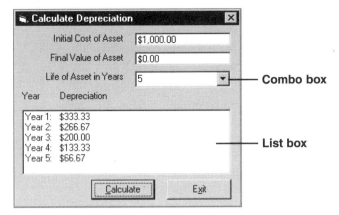

Common methods

Method	Description
AddItem	Adds an item to a list box or combo box.
RemoveItem	Removes an item from a list box or combo box.
Clear	Removes all items from a list box or combo box.

Code that loads a combo box with the integers from 1 through 40

```
Private Sub Form_Load()
    Dim i As Integer
    For i = 1 To 40
        cboLife.AddItem i
    Next i
End Sub
```

Code that clears and loads a list box

```
Private Sub cmdCalculate_Click()
    Dim i As Integer
    lstDepreciation.Clear
    For i = 1 To cboLife
        lstDepreciation.AddItem ("Year " & i & ":    " _
            & FormatCurrency(SYD(mskInitialCost, _
                mskFinalValue, cboLife, i)))
    Next i
End Sub
```

Note

- The Text property is the default property for combo boxes and list boxes.

Figure 3-7   How to work with combo boxes and list boxes

How to add controls to the Toolbox

When you start a new project, the Toolbox contains the standard controls shown in figure 3-5. However, Visual Basic provides a variety of other controls that you can use in your applications. To add any of those controls to the Toolbox, you can use the techniques that are summarized in figure 3-8.

The Controls tab of the Components dialog box lists all of the controls that can be added to a project. Although many controls come with Visual Basic, you can also purchase controls from other vendors. In either case, you can add a control to the Toolbox by checking the box for the control. Then, the new control is added to the bottom of the Toolbox. (If you can't see the new control because there are too many controls in the Toolbox, drag the edge of the Toolbox to enlarge it.)

By default, the Toolbox contains a single tab named General. If you add controls to the Toolbox, however, you may want to place them on a separate tab. To create a new tab, right-click on the Toolbox, select the Add Tab command from the menu that's displayed, and enter a name for the tab. Then, the tab appears as a button at the bottom of the Toolbox, and you can display the tab by clicking on that button. To add a control to the tab, just drag the control to it.

The Components dialog box

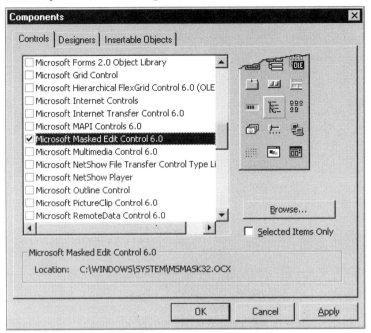

Description

- To access this dialog box, select the Components command from the Project menu.
- To add a control to the Toolbox, click on its check box to select it. To remove a control from the Toolbox, click on its check box to deselect it.
- Some of the options in the Controls tab add more than one control to the Toolbox. The Microsoft Data Bound List Controls 6.0 option, for example, adds both a data-bound combo box (DBCombo) and a data-bound list box (DBList).
- When you add a control to the Toolbox, it's added to the tab that's currently displayed. By default, the Toolbox contains a single tab named General. To add another tab, use the Add Tab command in the shortcut menu for the Toolbox. Then, you can drag controls from one tab to another.

Figure 3-8 How to add controls to the Toolbox

How to use a masked edit box

If you look back to figure 3-7, you can see that the values in the first two text boxes use the currency format. Although you can accomplish this by applying the FormatCurrency function to the data in a normal text box, using a masked edit box like the one in figure 3-9 usually works better. That's because the Format property of this control lets you format the data that's displayed. In addition, its Mask property lets you restrict the data that the user can enter into the control.

Since the masked edit box isn't displayed in the Toolbox by default, you need to use the procedure in the last figure to add the Microsoft Masked Edit Control 6.0 to the Toolbox. Then, you can use standard techniques to add the control to the form and to work with the control. In fact, if you don't specify a Format property or a Mask property, working with masked edit boxes is almost identical to working with text boxes.

To set the Format property for a masked edit box, you select the format that you want from the drop-down list. In this figure, for example, the format for standard currency is being selected. If you experiment with the formats that are available, you shouldn't have much trouble finding the formats that you need for numbers, dates, and times. If you need to, though, you can enter your own custom format.

To set the Mask property, you design an *input mask* that controls what the user can enter. Within the mask, the pound sign (#) represents digits, the question mark (?) represents letters, and the ampersand (&) represents digits or letters. If, for example, the mask is *####*, the user can enter a maximum of four digits into the box. Although these three mask characters will be adequate for most of the input masks that you design, other characters are available for more complex input masks. For more information about these characters, use the Help feature to look up the Mask property.

How to use the Validate event

With Visual Basic 6, the Validate event occurs when the focus leaves a control like a text box and the control that receives the focus has its CausesValidation property on (this property is on by default). Then, the code for this event procedure can check the data in the box to make sure that it's valid. This is illustrated by the procedure at the bottom of figure 3-9. As you can see, the Sub statement for a Validate event procedure contains a Cancel argument. If this argument is set to True, the procedure ends and the focus is returned to the control that's being validated.

In this example, the procedure is executed when the Validate event occurs for a masked edit box. This procedure then checks to see whether the value in its Text property is less than or equal to zero. If it is, the Cancel argument is set to True, a message is displayed, and the focus is returned to the masked edit box. Otherwise, the application continues without any interruption. This is an easy way to validate the data that a user enters.

A masked edit box and its Format property

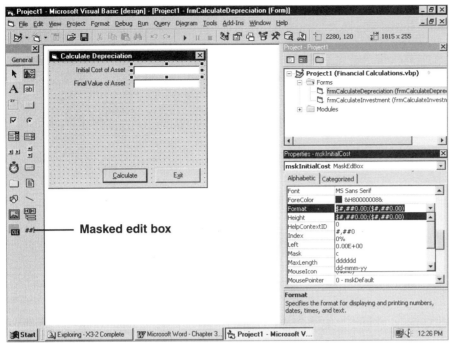

Masked edit box

Common properties

Property	Description
Format	Lets you select a format that determines how the data will be formatted after it is entered into the box.
Mask	Lets you define an *input mask* that restricts the data that the user can enter to the characters defined in the mask.

Typical input masks

Mask	Mask when run	Typical entry	Entry requirements
(###) ###-####	(___) ___-____	(555) 384-2384	10 digits
(###) &&&-&&&&	(___) ___-____	(800) TAG-2000	3 digits, then 7 letters or digits
##/##/##	__/__/__	12/25/98	6 digits
##-???-##	__-___-__	12-Dec-98	2 digits, 3 letters, and 2 digits

The Validate event procedure for a masked edit box

```
Private Sub mskInitialCost_Validate(Cancel As Boolean)
    If Val(mskInitialCost) <= 0 Then
        MsgBox "You must enter a positive number."
        Cancel = True
    End If
End Sub
```

Figure 3-9   How to use a masked edit box and the Validate event

How to use the Object Browser

Since Visual Basic provides so many different controls, it's impossible to remember the properties, methods, and events for working with all of them. Fortunately, though, you can use the Object Browser to quickly view all of the properties, methods, and events for an object. In figure 3-10, for example, you can see some of the properties, methods, and events for a masked edit box. You can also use this browser to get information about available constants like the MenuAccelConstants that are in the Classes list.

By default, the Object Browser displays the objects in the *class libraries* (collections of objects) that are available to your project. However, you can narrow the types of objects that are displayed by choosing a specific class library from the Project/Library list at the top of the Object Browser window. For example, there's a class library for Visual Basic objects and a class library for the MSMask objects (if you add the masked edit box to the Toolbox). The current project is also included in this list so you can look just at its objects and modules.

When you select a class library, all of the objects in that library are displayed in the Classes list. Then, you can click on one of those objects to display its properties, methods, and events in the Members list. In addition, a brief description of the object is displayed in the Details pane at the bottom of the window.

In the Members list, the icon to the left of a member tells whether it's a method, property, or event. If you click on a member, an explanation of that member is displayed in the Details pane. Then, to get more information about that member, you can press F1.

By default, the items in the Classes and Members list are sorted alphabetically as shown in this figure. However, you can sort the members by type by right-clicking in one of the lists and choosing the Group Members command from the shortcut menu that's displayed.

The Object Browser with the MaskEdBox control selected

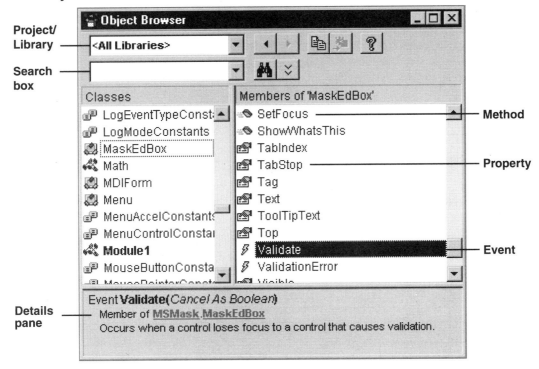

Description

- The Object Browser lets you display the objects, properties, methods, and events that are available to your application. It also lets you display available constants.

- To display the Object Browser, select the Object Browser command from the View menu or click on the Object Browser toolbar button.

- To restrict the objects displayed in the Object Browser, select a *class library* or the current project from the Project/Library drop-down list.

- To display the members for an object, select it from the Classes list.

- To group the items in the Classes and Members lists by type instead of alphabetically, right-click on the Object Browser and select the Group Members command from the resulting shortcut menu.

- To search for an item, enter some text in the Search box and click on the Search button. Then, the Show/Hide Search Results button will let you display or hide the results of the search.

- To get additional help about the selected item, click on the Help button or press F1.

Note

- The icon before each member in the Members list indicates whether it is a method, property, event, or constant.

Figure 3-10   How to use the Object Browser

Exercise set 3-2: Add controls to the new form

In this exercise set, you'll add some controls to the Calculate Depreciation form you created in the last exercise set. Then, you'll set the properties for these controls and write the code behind the form.

If you're using the Learning Edition of Visual Basic 6, you'll discover that the masked edit control isn't available with this edition when you do step 2. As a result, you'll have to use text boxes instead of masked edit boxes as you do this exercise set. This will mean that the data in the top two boxes of the form won't be displayed with the currency format.

Open the project
1.   If it's not already open, open the Financial Calculations project you worked on in the last exercise set.

Add controls to the form
2.   Select the Components command from the Project menu to display the Components dialog box. Then, check the Microsoft Masked Edit Control 6.0 in the Controls tab and click on the OK button. When you do, the MaskEdBox control should be added to the Toolbox.

3.   Use the Toolbox to add five label controls, two masked edit controls, one combo box control, and one list box control to the form. Then, resize and position the controls and the form so they look approximately like this:

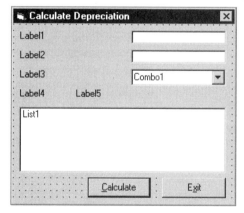

Set the properties for the controls
4.   Use the Properties window to set the Caption and Alignment properties for the labels so the form looks like it does in figure 3-7.

5. Set these properties for the masked edit boxes, the combo box, and the list box:

Default name	Property	Setting
MaskEdBox1	Name	mskInitialCost
	Format	$#,##0.00;($#,##0.00)
MaskEdBox2	Name	mskFinalValue
	Format	$#,##0.00;($#,##0.00)
Combo1	Name	cboLife
	Text	5
List1	Name	lstDepreciation
	TabStop	False

6. Press F5 to run the application. This should display both forms. Next, enter values in the two masked edit controls, and notice how the values are formatted. Then, click on the Close buttons for both forms to stop the application and return to Visual Basic.

Add the code behind the form

7. Double-click on the Exit button to switch to the Code window and generate the Sub and End Sub statements for the Click event of this button. Then, add an Unload statement like the one you created in chapter 1 so the form will be closed when the user clicks on the Exit button.

8. Navigate to the Sub and End Sub statements for the Load event of the Form. Then, add the For...Next loop that's shown in figure 3-7 so the combo box will be loaded with the numbers 1 through 40 when the form is loaded.

9. Begin the Sub and End Sub statements for the Click event of the Calculate button. Then, add the code that's shown in figure 3-7 so the depreciation amounts for each year will be added to the list box when the user clicks on the Calculate button.

10. Add procedures for the Validate events of the two masked edit boxes. These procedures should check the entries in these boxes for validity as shown in figure 3-9. The initial cost entry should be greater than zero, and the final value of the asset should be either zero or greater than zero. You'll also need to change the CausesValidation property of the Exit command button to False. If you don't, you won't be able to exit from the form without entering valid values in the masked edit boxes.

11. Press F5 to test the application. To test the Calculate Depreciation form, first enter some valid values and click on the Calculate button to make sure that works correctly. Then, enter some invalid values to make sure that appropriate error messages are displayed. If you find any errors, fix them and test again. When you've got the form working right, click on the Exit buttons to close the forms and end the application.

Save the project

12. Save the project and exit from Visual Basic.

How to develop a multiple-document interface

So far in this book, you've been working with Visual Basic's default interface, the single-document interface. Now, you'll learn how to use a multiple-document interface. As you'll see, this is the type of interface that's used with Microsoft Office applications such as Microsoft Word and Microsoft Excel.

The difference between single-document and multiple-document interfaces

Figure 3-11 shows the primary user interfaces when applied to the Financial Calculations application. The first interface is known as the *single-document interface*, or *SDI*, while the second one is known as the *multiple-document interface,* or *MDI*.

In a single-document interface, each form runs in its own application window, and this window is usually shown in the Windows 95/98 taskbar. Then, you can click on the buttons in the taskbar to switch between the open forms. When you use this interface, each form can have its own menus and toolbars.

In a multiple-document interface, a container form called a *parent form* contains one or more *child forms*. Then, the menus and toolbars on the parent form contain the commands that let you open and view forms, and you can use its Window menu to switch between the open forms. When you close the parent form of an MDI application, all of the child forms are closed and the application ends. The main advantage of a multiple-document interface is that the parent form keeps all of the child forms organized and provides a central location for storing the objects that are common to the entire application such as menus and toolbars.

Incidentally, you can also develop an *explorer-style interface* with Visual Basic 6. In this type of interface, a single window is split into two panes, and the Windows Explorer is an example of this type of interface. Then, you can use the left pane to navigate between different parts of the application, and you can use the right pane to work with the application. This type of interface, however, isn't presented in this book.

Single-document interface (SDI)

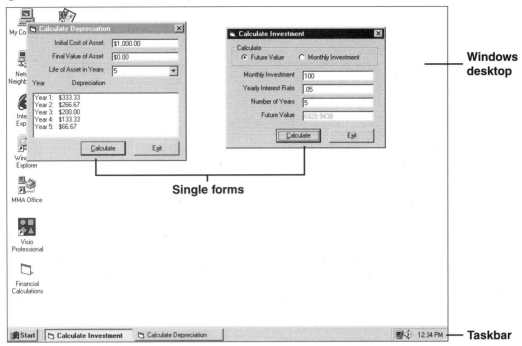

Multiple-document interface (MDI)

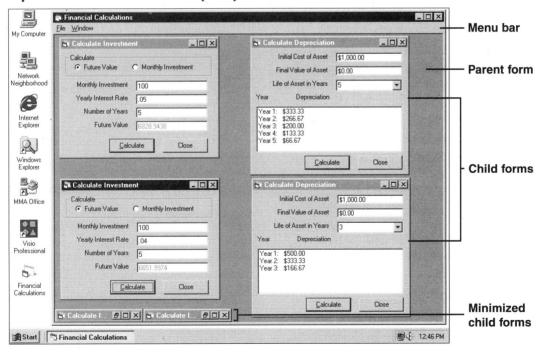

Figure 3-11   Single-document and multiple-document interfaces

How to create the parent and child forms

In figure 3-12, you can see the design view of the parent form for the Financial Calculations form that's shown in the previous figure. This parent form contains a menu bar that includes a File menu and a Window menu. In the next figure, you'll learn how to create menus like these.

To create a parent form, you use the Add MDI Form command in the Project menu; you can't just change an existing form to an MDI form. Then, you set the properties for the form just as you would for any other form. If, for example, you always want the form maximized when it is displayed, you can set the WindowState property to Maximized.

To create a child form, you just set the MDIChild property of the form to True. After that, the child form will always be displayed within the interior of the parent form. To make sure that a child form is always sized appropriately for the interior of the form, you usually set the BorderStyle property to Single Fixed so the form can't be resized. If you look at the Project Explorer window, you can see that Visual Basic uses different icons for the parent form and the child forms for a project.

When you unload the parent form, all of the child forms are unloaded first. If one of the child forms has a task in progress, though, this can cause problems. If, for example, a user has used a child form to make changes to a database but hasn't saved the changes, the child form shouldn't be unloaded without asking the user whether the changes should be saved. To provide for situations like this, you can code a procedure for the QueryUnload event of each child form. Then, if you set the Cancel argument to True, the Unload events for all of the forms are cancelled.

Incidentally, when you use MDI, you can use forms that are neither parent nor child forms. These forms are usually *modal forms*, which means that they have to be closed before the application can continue. To display a modal form, you use the show method with 1 as the argument as in this example:

```
frmAboutAP.Show 1
```

In contrast, a form that doesn't have to be closed before the application continues is called a *modeless form*, and all the forms that you've used so far are modeless. In chapters 7, 8, and 12, you'll see how modal forms are used in some typical applications.

An application with one parent form and two child forms

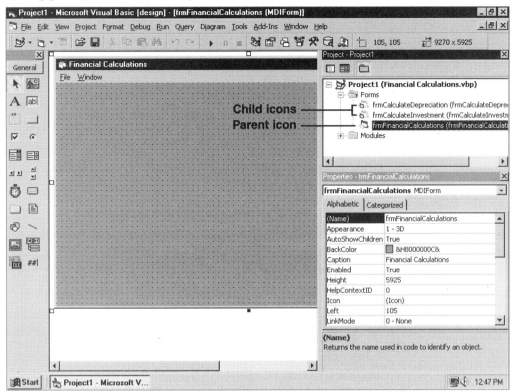

Description

- To create the parent form, pull down the Project menu and select the Add MDI Form command.
- To create a child form, set the MDIChild property for a form to True.
- When you unload the parent form, all child forms are automatically unloaded. When you load a child form, the parent form is automatically loaded.

Figure 3-12   How to create parent and child forms

How to add menus to a form

Figure 3-13 shows how to use the Menu Editor dialog box to create the menus for a form. Since each form can have its own menus, the first step is to display the form you want to work with. Then, you open the Menu Editor dialog box by clicking on its toolbar button.

Within the Menu Editor dialog box, you use the Caption and Name boxes to set those properties for each menu object. Then, you can use the arrow buttons to change the level of indentation for each object, which identifies it as a menu title, menu command, or submenu. You can also provide a shortcut key for each menu object. When you're done with an object, you click on the Next button.

The check boxes for each menu object correspond to the properties of the object. If, for example, you remove the check from the Visible check box, that menu object won't be displayed when the application starts. Similarly, if you remove the check from the Enabled check box, the menu object won't be enabled. And if you add a check to the Checked box, a check mark will appear before the menu object. These, of course, are only the starting properties for a menu object, and you can use code to change these properties while an application is running.

When you create the menus for a form, you should try to follow the conventions that are used by other Windows applications. For instance, you'll want to keep the File menu on the far left (at the top of the Menu Editor list), the Help menu on the far right (at the bottom), and the other menus in a consistent sequence between the File and Help menus. Similarly, if a menu command leads to a dialog box, you should include an ellipsis (…) at the end of the Caption property for the object. You should also use *mnu* as the prefix for the menu objects.

After you use the Menu Editor dialog box to add the menus to a form, the menu bar appears on your form in the Form window, and you can pull down its menus to make sure they're set up right. Then, to provide the code for a menu object, you can click on the object, which switches you to the Code window and starts the Click event for the menu object. In the next figure, you can see some typical code for these events.

The Menu Editor dialog box with two menus and four commands

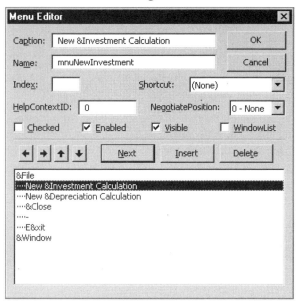

The File menu that results from the dialog box shown above

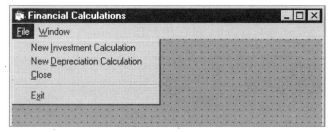

Operation

- To access the Menu Editor dialog box, display the form and click on the Menu Editor button in the toolbar.

- The Caption and Name properties are required for all menu objects, and *mnu* is commonly used as the prefix for the name of a menu object.

- To display a separator bar between menu commands, enter a single hyphen (-) in the Caption property (and still enter a Name property).

- Click on the arrow buttons to indent menu objects or move them up or down.

- Click on the Next, Insert, and Delete buttons to move to the next menu object, to insert a menu object, or to delete a menu object.

- By default, the Checked, Enabled, and Visible check boxes are set correctly for most menu objects.

- Check the WindowList box if you want to add a list of open child forms to a Window menu.

Figure 3-13   How to add menus to a form

How to write code that works with child forms

Figure 3-14 shows some special techniques that you can use to write code that works with child forms. In particular, it shows how you can create more than one *instance* of a child form. In addition, it shows how you can use the ActiveForm property and the Me keyword to refer to these child forms.

In the first coding example, you can see the code that's executed when the user selects the New Investment Calculation command from the File menu. Here, the procedure begins by declaring a variable. Although this variable is similar to the variables you learned about in the last chapter, it uses the New keyword to create a new object. As a result, this type of variable is called an *object variable*. In this case, the Dim statement tells Visual Basic to create a variable called frmForm for a new Calculate Investment form. Then, the SetFocus method is used to display the new object and move the focus to it (although you could also use the Show method to display the object).

When you use an object variable for a form, you can't always refer to it by its name since there may be more than one instance of it. Instead, you need to use the ActiveForm property of the MDIForm object. In the second coding example, you can see how the ActiveForm property is used with the Unload statement when the user selects the Close command from the File menu. Since the MDIForm object will always be active when you select the Close command from the File menu, you don't need to include the name of the MDI form before the ActiveForm property.

In the third coding example, you can see how Me is used with the Unload statement when the user clicks on the Close command button for one of the child forms. Here, the Me keyword unloads the form that contains the button that has been clicked.

A multiple-document interface with two instances of a form

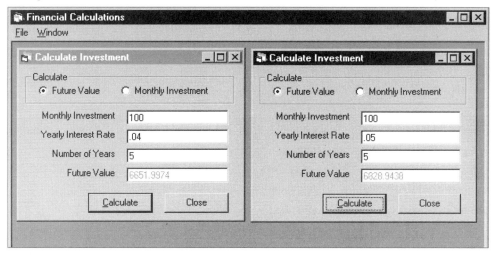

Code that creates a new instance of a child form

```
Private Sub mnuNewInvestment_Click()
    Dim frmForm As New frmCalculateInvestment
    frmForm.SetFocus
End Sub
```

Code that uses the ActiveForm property to refer to the active child form

```
Private Sub mnuClose_Click()
    Unload ActiveForm
End Sub
```

Code that uses the Me keyword to unload an instance of a child form

```
Private Sub cmdClose_Click()
    Unload Me
End Sub
```

Figure 3-14   How to write code that works with child forms

Exercise set 3-3: Create a multiple-document interface

In this exercise set, you'll create a multiple-document interface for the Calculate Investment and Calculate Depreciation forms.

Use the Windows Explorer to make a copy of the project

1. Start the Windows Explorer and navigate to the folder that contains your Visual Basic files. Then, use the Windows Explorer to make a copy of the folder and rename the folder "Chapter 3 MDI."

2. From the Windows Explorer, double-click on the Financial Calculations project file in the Chapter 3 MDI folder to start Visual Basic and open the project.

Add the parent form to the project

3. Use the Add MDI Form command in the Project menu to add an MDI form to the project.

4. Use the Properties window to set the Name property for the new form to frmFinancialCalculations, the Caption property to Financial Calculations, and the WindowState property to Maximized. Then, drag the bottom right corner of the Financial Calculations form so it takes approximately 75% of the space on your screen.

5. Click on the Save Project button to access the Save File As dialog box, and save the form file as frmFinancialCalculations in the folder that you created in step 1.

Convert the existing forms to child forms

6. In the Project Explorer, double-click on the Calculate Depreciation form to display it. Next, use the Properties window to set the MDIChild property to True. When you do, notice how the icon that's displayed in the Project Explorer changes. Then, set the MaxButton and MinButton properties for the form to True.

7. Click on the Exit command button to select it. Next, use the Properties window to change its Name to cmdClose and its Caption to Close. Then, double-click on the Close button to access the Click event for this button and enter "Unload Me" between the Sub and End Sub statements. When you're done with that, delete the Click event procedure for the old Exit command button.

8. Repeat steps 6 and 7 for the Calculate Investment form.

9. Press F5 to run the application. When it starts, both child forms should be displayed within the Financial Calculations form. Experiment with the Maximize, Minimize, and Restore buttons for the child forms. Then, click on the Close button of the parent form. This should unload both child forms along with the parent form.

10. Switch to the Code window for the Calculate Depreciation form, navigate to its Load event procedure, and delete the line that displays the Calculate Investment form.

Add menus to the parent form

11. In the Project Explorer, double-click on the Financial Calculations form to display its Form window. Then, click on the Menu Editor button in the toolbar to display the Menu Editor dialog box, and use this dialog box to add File and Window menus like the ones shown in figure 3-13. For the four commands on the File menu, use these names: mnuNewInvestment, mnuNewDepreciation, mnuClose, and mnuExit. For the Window menu, be sure to select the WindowList check box. When you're done, click on the OK button to return to the Financial Calculations form.

Add the code for the parent form

12. Select the New Investment Calculation command from the File menu. When you do, Visual Basic will switch to the Code window and generate the Sub and End Sub statements for the Click event of this command. Then, enter the code for this command between these statements as shown in figure 3-14.

13. Select mnuNewDepreciation from the Object list of the Code window to generate the Sub and End Sub statements for the Click event of this command. Then, copy the code you entered in step 12 into this new procedure, but substitute frmCalculateDepreciation for frmCalculateInvestment.

14. Select mnuClose from the Object list of the Code window to generate the Sub and End Sub statements for the Click event of this command. Then, enter this code in this procedure:

```
On Error GoTo ExitSub
    Unload ActiveForm
ExitSub:
    Exit Sub
```

In this case, you need to add the error-handling code in case the user selects the Close command when no forms are open.

15. Select mnuExit from the Object list of the Code window to generate the Sub and End Sub statements for the Click event of this command. Then, enter an Unload Me statement in this procedure.

16. Press F5 to test the application. Then, use the commands on the File menu to create multiple instances of the two child forms. To switch from one window to another, use the Windows menu. When you're done testing the application, select the Exit command from the File menu to exit from the parent form.

17. If you test carefully, you will find that the Validate event for a masked edit control on the Calculate Depreciation form no longer returns the focus to the control with the invalid data. This is a Visual Basic bug, but you can fix it by using the SetFocus method to set the focus as in: mskInitialCost.SetFocus.

Save the project and exit from Visual Basic

18. Click on the Save Project button to save the project and its forms. Then, exit from Visual Basic.

Perspective

Now that you've completed this chapter, you should have all the skills that you need for developing applications that require two or more forms. In addition, you should know how to use eight of the 20 controls in the standard Toolbox as well as the masked edit box control. Even better, you should now be able to figure out how to use most of the other controls in the standard Toolbox. If, for example, you want to add an Image or Timer control to a form, you should be able to get it to work the way you want it to without much trouble.

In the remaining chapters of this book, you're going to learn more about using forms and controls. In chapters 6 and 7, for example, you're going to learn how to use some of the controls for working with the data in databases. And in chapter 12, you're going to learn how to create some of the special forms that you need for enhancing the user interface of an application. So by the time you complete this book, you'll have all the skills that you need for working with forms and controls.

Terms you should know

container control
Object Linking and Embedding (OLE)
input mask
class library
single-document interface (SDI)
multiple-document interface (MDI)
parent form
child form
explorer-style interface
modal form
modeless form
instance
object variable

4

How to test and debug an application

If you've done much programming, you know that testing and debugging an application is both difficult and time-consuming. Fortunately, though, Visual Basic provides some excellent tools for finding errors. In this chapter, you'll learn how to use those tools.

Basic debugging skills **140**
How to set the options for debugging 140
How to work in break mode 142
How to use breakpoints 144
How to control the execution of an application 146
Exercise set 4-1: Use break mode and step through code 148

How to use the debugging windows **150**
How to use the Immediate window to work with values 150
How to use the Locals window to monitor variables 152
How to use the Call Stack to monitor called procedures 154
How to use the Watch window to monitor expressions 156
When and how to use the Quick Watch feature 156
Exercise set 4-2: Use the debugging windows 158

Other debugging techniques **160**
How to create a routine that handles specific types of trappable errors 160
How to test an error-handling routine 162
How to use compiler directives with debugging statements 164
Exercise set 4-3: Code and test an error-handling routine 166

Perspective **168**

Basic debugging skills

Before you begin debugging, you can set the options that control how Visual Basic handles errors. Then, you can use the basic debugging skills to find and fix most types of errors.

How to set the options for debugging

In chapter 1, you learned how to handle *compile errors* and *run-time errors*. You also learned that some types of errors let you enter *break mode*, a special mode that lets you fix coding errors without having to cancel the execution of the application. In a moment, you'll learn more about working with break mode. But first, figure 4-1 summarizes the options that control the way Visual Basic identifies and deals with errors.

By default, the Break in Class Module option is on. This means that Visual Basic will enter break mode for any error if an On Error statement hasn't been coded to handle the error. Although this option will work for most of the applications you develop, you can change to one of the other Break options whenever that's appropriate. If you choose the Break on All Errors option, Visual Basic will enter break mode for all errors even if an error handler is active. If you choose the Break on Unhandled Errors option, Visual Basic will enter break mode for unhandled errors, but not within class modules. (For more information about class modules, please read chapter 13.)

Incidentally, the Break option you choose is saved from one Visual Basic session to another. So if you want to change this option just for the current session, use the Toggle command in the shortcut menu for the Code window.

Another option you need to be familiar with is the Compile On Demand option. If this option is selected, as it is by default, the Visual Basic statements are compiled as they're executed. But if this option isn't selected, every module in the project is compiled before the application is executed. Because this can cause unnecessary problems as you're developing an application, you'll want to make sure that the Compile On Demand option is on until you're ready to test the entire application.

By default, the Auto Syntax Check and Auto Data Tips options are on, and that's usually what you want. If the Auto Syntax Check option is off, Visual Basic won't display compile errors as you enter code in the Code window. Then, compile errors won't be displayed until you run the application. If the Auto Data Tips option is off, you won't be able to display data tips when your application enters break mode.

The General tab of the Options dialog box

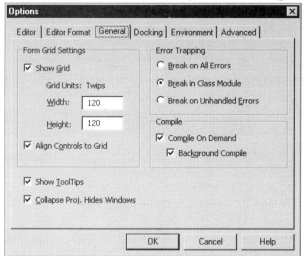

The General tab

Option	Description
Break on All Errors	Causes the project to enter break mode any time an error occurs.
Break in Class Module	Causes the project to enter break mode if no error handler is active. If the error occurs in a class module, the project breaks at the line of code that caused the error.
Break on Unhandled Errors	Causes the project to enter break mode if no error handler is active. If the error occurs in a class module, the project breaks at the line of code that referenced the class module.
Compile On Demand	Compiles the project as it executes.
Background Compile	Finishes compiling the project during any idle time as the project executes.

The Editor tab

Option	Description
Auto Syntax Check	Checks the syntax of statements as you enter them in the Code window.
Auto Data Tips	Displays the value of a variable or property in break mode when the mouse pointer is positioned over the variable or property.

Notes

- To display the dialog box shown above, choose the Options command from the Tools menu.
- To change the three Break options for all future Visual Basic sessions, use the Options dialog box shown above. To change these options for the current session only, right-click in the Code window and select the option you want from the Toggle submenu.

Figure 4-1   How to set the options for debugging

How to work in break mode

When a run-time error occurs, Visual Basic displays a dialog box that indicates what type of error has occurred. From this dialog box, you can enter break mode by clicking on the Debug button. You can also enter break mode by clicking the OK button for some types of compile errors and by using some of the techniques described later in this chapter. In break mode, the Code window is displayed and the statement that caused the error is highlighted as shown in figure 4-2.

If you can determine the cause of an error, you can make the appropriate change in the Code window while the application is in break mode. Then, if you press F5 or click on the Continue button, the statement that caused the error is executed again so you can see immediately if the change you made corrected the problem.

In many cases, though, you need to do more than change code to correct a problem. For example, you may need to change the value of a property or variable to determine if that's what caused the problem. Or, you may need to rerun lines of code that have already been executed. To perform these functions, you can use the debugging tools that are presented in this chapter, and many of these tools are available from the Debug toolbar shown in this figure.

Although you can change the code any way you want to when an application is in break mode, you can't always continue executing the application from the point where the error occurred. That's because some coding changes can't be applied while the application is executing. For example, the data type of a variable can't be changed once it's declared. So if you try to make this type of change, Visual Basic displays a dialog box indicating that the project will be reset. Then, if you accept the change from this dialog box, Visual Basic ends the execution of the application. Or, if you cancel the change, the change is reversed and you are returned to break mode where you can continue debugging the application.

How an application looks in break mode

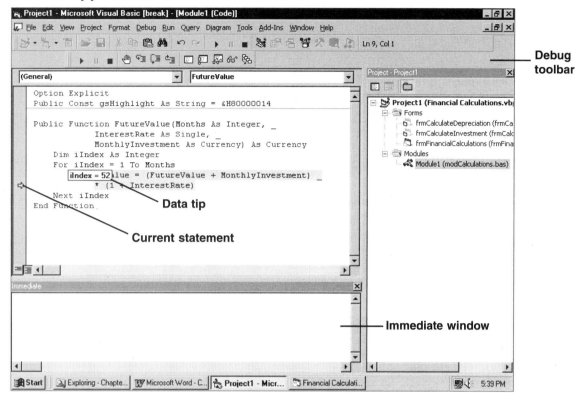

Data tip

Current statement

Debug toolbar

Immediate window

Description

- When a run-time error occurs, Visual Basic displays a dialog box for the error. To enter break mode, click on the Debug button. You can also enter break mode by clicking on the OK button for some types of compile errors.

- In *break mode*, Visual Basic displays the Code window and highlights the statement that caused the error. By default, it also displays the Immediate window, which you'll learn about in figure 4-5.

- To display a *data tip*, position the mouse pointer over the code for a variable or property as shown above.

- To display the Debug toolbar, right-click in the toolbar area and select Debug from the shortcut menu.

- To change code, click in the Code window and enter new code. Then, to continue running the program, press F5 or Click on the Continue button in the Standard or Debug toolbar.

- To exit break mode, click on the End button in the Standard or Debug toolbar.

Figure 4-2   How to work in break mode

How to use breakpoints

Although you can enter break mode when you encounter an error, you can also set a *breakpoint* to enter break mode at the statement of your choice. To set a breakpoint, you use the techniques presented in figure 4-3. Then, when you run the application, it will enter break mode when it reaches the breakpoint but before the statement at the breakpoint is executed.

For some applications, you may want to set more than one breakpoint. You can set them either before you begin the execution of an application or while the application is in break mode. Then, when the application is run, it will stop at the first breakpoint and you can use the debugging tools described in this chapter to check the state of the application. When you're ready to continue, you can press F5 or click on the Continue button to move to the next breakpoint, or you can use the Step commands described in the next figure.

Once you set a breakpoint, it remains active until you remove it or close the project. To remove a breakpoint, you use the same techniques that you use to set a breakpoint. And to remove all of the breakpoints in an application at once, you use the Clear All Breakpoints command in the Debug menu.

A breakpoint in a Code window

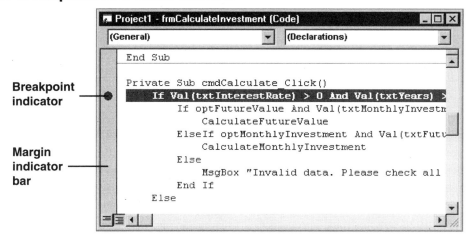

Breakpoint indicator ────

Margin indicator bar ────

Description

- You can use *breakpoints* to suspend the execution of an application. You can set a breakpoint before you run an application or while the application is in break mode.

- To set a breakpoint, click in the margin indicator bar to the left of the statement where you want the breakpoint. You can also set a breakpoint by pressing F9 or clicking on the Toggle Breakpoint button in the Debug toolbar. To remove a breakpoint, use the same techniques.

- You can set a breakpoint only on a line that contains an executable statement. You cannot set breakpoints on blank lines, comments, or declarative statements.

- When your application encounters a breakpoint, it enters break mode before it executes the statement that contains the breakpoint. To continue executing the application, you can press F5 or click on the Continue button.

Figure 4-3   How to use breakpoints

How to control the execution of an application

Figure 4-4 presents the commands that you can use to control the execution of an application. As you can see, some of these commands are in the Run menu and others are in the Debug menu. The Start, Break, and End commands are not only available from the Run menu, but also from both the Standard and the Debug toolbar.

To execute one statement of an application at a time, you use the Step Into command. Then, the application enters break mode before each statement is executed so you can test the values of properties and variables and perform other debugging functions. Similarly, the Step Over command executes one statement at a time, except that the statements in a called procedure are executed without interruption (they are "stepped over"). You can use either of these commands to start application execution or to restart execution when an application is in break mode.

If you use the Step Into command to enter a procedure, you can use the Step Out command to execute the remaining statements in the procedure without interruption. After that, the application enters break mode before the next statement in the calling procedure is executed.

To skip over code that you know is working properly, you can use the Run To Cursor or Set Next Statement command. You can also use the Set Next Statement command to rerun lines of code that were executed before an error occurred. And if you've been working in the Code window and have forgotten where the next statement to be executed is, you can use the Show Next Statement command to move to it.

The commands for controlling application execution

Menu	Command	Toolbar	Function
Run	Start/Continue	▶	Start or continue execution of the application.
	Break	‖	Suspend execution of the application.
	End	■	End execution of the application.
	Restart		Restart the entire application.
Debug	Step Into	⤵≡	Execute one statement at a time.
	Step Over	⤳≡	Execute one statement at a time except for called procedures.
	Step Out	⤴≡	Execute the remaining lines in the current procedure.
	Run to Cursor		Execute the application until it reaches the statement that contains the insertion point.
	Set Next Statement		Set the statement that contains the insertion point as the next statement to be executed.
	Show Next Statement		Display the next statement to be executed.

Description

- If you use the Step Into or Step Over command to start the execution of an application, Visual Basic will enter break mode before it executes the first statement in the application. If you use the Run to Cursor command, Visual Basic will enter break mode when it reaches the statement that contains the insertion point. In either case, Visual Basic will highlight the current statement in the Code window.

- Once the application enters break mode, you can use the Step Into, Step Over, Step Out, and Run To Cursor commands to execute one or more statements and return to break mode.

- To alter the normal execution sequence of the application, you can use the Set Next Statement command. Just place the insertion point in the statement you want to execute next, issue this command, and click on the Continue button to continue application execution.

- Another way to enter break mode during the execution of an application is to use the Break command. This is useful when you need to stop the execution of an application that's caught in a loop. To issue the Break command, you can press Ctrl+Break, or you can switch to the Visual Basic window and click on the Break button.

Figure 4-4   How to control the execution of an application

Exercise set 4-1: Use break mode and step through code

In this exercise set, you'll experiment with break mode, and you'll step through the code for the future value calculation.

Open the project and change the startup form

1. Start Visual Basic and open the MDI version of the Financial Calculations project that you created in chapter 3.

2. Select the Properties command from the Project menu and use the Startup Object combo box to select the Calculate Investment form.

3. Use the Options command in the Tools menu to make sure that the Auto Syntax Check and Auto Data Tips options are on. You may also want to check some of the other options to make sure that they're set appropriately.

Change some debugging options and enter break mode

4. Open the Code window for the Calculate Investment form. Then, right-click in the Code window, select the Toggle submenu, and select the Break On All Errors command. That way, Visual Basic will ignore any error-handling routines for this Visual Basic session.

5. Run the project. When you do, the Calculate Investment form should be displayed within the Financial Calculations form. Then, enter 100 in the first three text boxes, and click on the Calculate button. When you do, Visual Basic should display a dialog box that indicates that you have encountered a run-time error.

6. Click on the Debug button to enter break mode so Visual Basic displays the FutureValue function in the standard module with the statement that caused the error highlighted. Then, position the insertion point over each of the variables in the procedure to check its current value. Note that the FutureValue variable is too big to fit in the Currency data type.

7. Use the taskbar to switch to the Financial Calculations application. Notice that you can't edit any of the values in the text boxes and that the command buttons don't work. Then, use the taskbar to switch back to Visual Basic, and click on the End button to exit from break mode. This should close the Financial Calculations window and return you to the Code window.

8. Right-click in the Code window, select the Toggle submenu, and select the Break In Class Module command. That way, Visual Basic will use any error-handling procedures that are in place.

9. Run the project, enter 100 for the first three text boxes, and click on the Calculate button. Note that the error-handling routine for the CalculateInvestment procedure displays a message box and Visual Basic doesn't enter break mode. Then, click on the OK button to close this message box, and click on the Close button for the Financial Calculations form to close the form and return to Visual Basic.

Step through the future value calculation with invalid data

10. Switch to the Code window for the Calculate Investment form and navigate to the procedure for the Click event of the Calculate button. Then, click in the margin indicator bar to the left of the If statement to set a breakpoint at this statement.

11. Run the project. Then, click on the Calculate button without entering any values in the text boxes. When you do, Visual Basic should enter break mode at the breakpoint that you set in the previous step.

12. If the Debug toolbar isn't already displayed, right-click on the toolbar area and select Debug from the shortcut menu.

13. Click on the Step Into button repeatedly until you execute the MsgBox function, then click on the OK button to close the message box. When you do that, Visual Basic should switch back to the Code window and return to break mode. Then, click on the Step Into button until you execute the End Sub statement, which exits from break mode so you can enter more values into the Calculate Investment form.

Step through the future value calculation with valid data

14. Use the taskbar to switch to the Financial Calculations window. Then, enter some valid data for the future value calculation, and click on the Calculate command button. When you do, you should enter break mode at the breakpoint you set in step 10.

15. Click on the Step Into button repeatedly to move through the statements that perform the future value calculation until you've gone through the For...Next loop in the FutureValue function one time. Then, place the insertion point over the iIndex, Months, and FutureValue variables to check their values. Click on the Step Into button a few more times and check these variables again. This should clearly illustrate how this For...Next loop works. When you're done experimenting with the loop, click on the Step Out button to finish the loop and return to the form module, then click on the Step Into button a few more times until you execute the End Sub statement and exit from break mode.

16. Use the taskbar to switch to the Financial Calculations window, and note that the future value calculation is displayed in the Future Value text box. Then, click on the Close button in the Financial Calculations window to close it and return to the Visual Basic window.

17. Select the Clear All Breakpoints command from the Debug menu to remove the breakpoint that you set earlier in this exercise set.

18. If you're going to continue with this chapter, keep the project open. Otherwise, close the project without saving it.

How to use the debugging windows

Now that you know how to work with break mode, you're ready to learn how to use the primary debugging windows (the Immediate window, the Locals window, and the Watch window) as well as the Call Stack dialog box. Although Visual Basic also provides a Quick Watch feature, you can do what it offers more easily by using data tips. As a result, the Quick Watch feature is described but not illustrated.

How to use the Immediate window to work with values

You can use the Immediate window to display the values of variables and properties as shown in figure 4-5. Although you can also use the Auto Data Tips feature to display the values for variables and properties that appear in the Code window, you can use the Immediate window when the variable or property you want to display doesn't appear in the Code window. By default, the Immediate window is displayed when an application enters break mode. If it isn't, you can open it by clicking on the Immediate Window button in the Debug toolbar.

You can also use the Immediate window to execute code. For example, you can enter an assignment statement to change the value of a variable or property. Similarly, you can use the Immediate window to execute a Sub procedure or function or to display the value returned by the execution of a function. This can be useful for testing the result of a procedure with different arguments. When you do this, you can execute built-in functions as well as user-defined functions.

When you enter statements in the Immediate window, you should know that they're executed in the same context (or scope) as the application that's running. That means that you can't display the value of a variable that's out of scope and you can't execute a private procedure that's in a module that isn't currently executing. If you try to do that, Visual Basic displays a blank line or an error message. You can, however, display the value of a property of another form in the project or a property of one of its controls. To do that, just include the name of the form in the reference. Then, if you refer to a form that isn't currently loaded, it will be loaded. In this figure, for example, the statements in the Immediate window include the name of the Calculate Investment form since the standard module is currently executing.

You should also know that the statements you enter into the Immediate window remain there until you exit from the Visual Basic application or explicitly delete them. That way, you can use standard Windows techniques to edit and re-use the same statements from one execution of an application to another without having to re-enter them. To execute a statement that you've already entered in the Immediate window, just place the insertion point at the end of the statement and press the Enter key.

The Immediate window

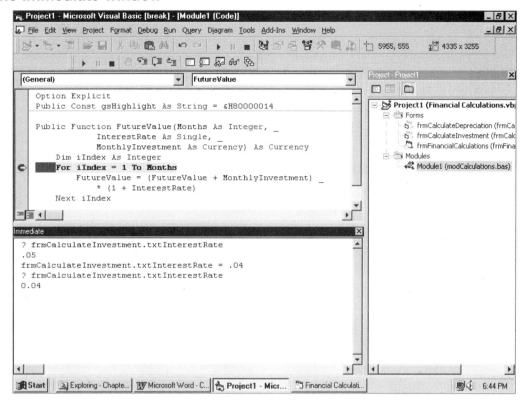

Description

- You can use the Immediate window to display and assign values. To display the Immediate window, press Ctrl+G, click on the Immediate Window button in the Debug toolbar, or select the Immediate Window command from the View menu.

- To display a value in the Immediate window, enter a question mark followed by the expression whose value you want to display. Then, press the Enter key.

- To assign a different value to a variable, property, or object, enter an assignment statement in the Immediate window. Then, press the Enter key.

- To execute functions and Sub procedures from the Immediate window, enter the name of the function or procedure followed by any arguments it requires. Then, press the Enter key. If you want to display the result of a function, precede the function call with a question mark.

- You can use the Print method in your application code to display values in the Immediate window as the application executes. When used in application code, the Print method must be preceded by the Debug object like this:

```
Debug.Print "iIndex = " & iIndex
```

Figure 4-5   How to use the Immediate window to work with values

How to use the Locals window
to monitor variables

The Locals window displays the values of all the variables that are in scope when an application enters break mode. At the top of this window, the name of the procedure that's currently executing is displayed. In figure 4-6, for example, the Locals window displays the values of all three variables in the CalculateFutureValue procedure of the frmCalculateInvestment module.

You can use the Locals window when you need to see the values of several variables that are used within the same procedure. Then, you can set a breakpoint at that procedure and display the Locals window to see those values. This is usually easier than using the Immediate window or using data tips to view the value of each variable.

In the Locals window in this figure, you'll notice that only the variables that are declared within the current procedure are displayed. In other words, the Locals window only displays local variables. If any variables are declared at the module level, the values of those variables are displayed under a special module variable that's included at the top of the Locals window. For a form module, this variable is the system variable Me. For a standard module, this variable is the name of the module. In either case, if you click on the plus sign to the left of this variable, you can see the module-level variables defined in the module along with the properties of the module and its controls.

Besides displaying the values of variables and properties, you can use the Locals window to change the values of those variables and properties. To do that, you simply highlight the value you want to change and enter a new value. Then, you can continue with the execution of the application.

The Locals window with three variables displayed

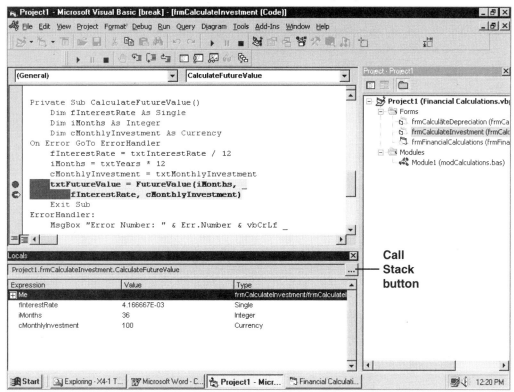

Description

- You can use the Locals window to display information about the variables within the scope of the procedure that's current when an application enters break mode. To display the Locals window, click on the Locals Window button in the Debug toolbar or select the Locals Window command from the View menu.

- To display properties and module-level variables, click on the plus sign (+) at the top of the window. For a form module, this will display the properties of the form and any controls it contains as well as any module-level variables. For a standard module, this will display any module-level variables.

- To change the value of a property or variable, click on the line that contains the property or variable, click on its value to highlight it, type a new value, and press the Enter key. If the value you enter isn't appropriate for the data type, an error message is displayed and the value isn't changed.

- To display the Call Stack dialog box shown in the next figure, click on the Call Stack button.

Figure 4-6   How to use the Locals window to monitor variables

How to use the Call Stack to monitor called procedures

Figure 4-7 shows how to use the Call Stack dialog box to monitor the execution of called procedures. When you display this dialog box, it lists all of the procedures that are currently active. In other words, the Call Stack dialog box displays a stack of called procedures, or a *call stack*.

The procedures listed in the Call Stack dialog box appear in reverse order from the order that they were called. So in this example, the procedure for the Click event of the Calculate button called the CalculateFutureValue procedure, which called the FutureValue function. To locate the statement in one procedure that called the next procedure, you can highlight the calling procedure in the Call Stack and click on the Show button. Then, Visual Basic switches to the Code window for the calling procedure and displays a triangle to the left of the calling statement.

The Call Stack dialog box

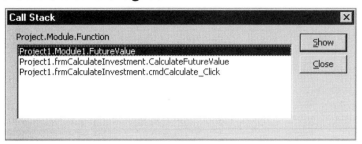

Description

- The Call Stack dialog box lists all of the procedures that are active when an application enters break mode. To display this dialog box, you can click on the Call Stack button in the Locals window. You can also press Ctrl+L, click on the Call Stack toolbar button in the Debug toolbar, or select the Call Stack command from the View menu.

- If the Call Stack dialog box lists more than one procedure, the current procedure is shown at the top of the dialog box and the procedures that called it are shown below it.

- You can use the Show button in the Call Stack dialog box to display the statement that passed control from the procedure that's highlighted to the next procedure. If, for example, you highlight the CalculateFutureValue procedure in the dialog box above and click on the Show button, Visual Basic displays the statement that called the FutureValue function in the Code window with a triangle to its left.

Figure 4-7   How to use the Call Stack to monitor called procedures

How to use the Watch window
to monitor expressions

Although you can display the values of expressions in the Immediate window, those values aren't updated automatically when they change. In contrast, the Watch window automatically updates the *watch expressions* that you enter into it. In addition, you can use the Watch window to enter break mode when the value of a watch expression becomes true or changes. Figure 4-8 shows how to use the Watch window.

To add a watch expression, you use the Add Watch dialog box shown in this figure. A watch expression can be any valid Visual Basic expression, and it doesn't have to exist in the application. For instance, the first expression in the Watch window in this figure checks to see if the FutureValue variable is greater than 1000 and returns a true or false value.

If you select an expression in the Code window before you display the Add Watch dialog box, that expression is displayed in the Expression text box and Visual Basic chooses the context that's appropriate for the expression. If, for example, you select a variable that's declared at the procedure level, the context is the current procedure in the current module. Although you can use the Context options in the Add Watch dialog box to change this context, you usually want to keep this context as specific as possible.

By default, the Watch Expression option is selected when you display the Add Watch dialog box. This option lets you use the Watch window to watch the expression whenever the application enters break mode. If you want the application to enter break mode when the watch expression becomes true or changes, you can select one of the other two Watch Type options. In this figure, for example, the watch expression uses the Break When Value Is True option. As a result, the application will enter break mode if the FutureValue variable becomes greater than 1000.

You can tell which Watch Type option is used for an expression by the icon that's displayed to the left of the expression in the Watch window. In this figure, for example, the first expression uses the Break When Value Is True option, the second and third use the Watch Expression option, and the fourth uses the Break When Value Changes option.

If the expression you add to the Watch window is an object, the Watch window will display a plus sign to the right of the Watch Type icon. Then, if you click on the plus sign, the properties of the object are displayed.

When and how to use the Quick Watch feature

You can use the Quick Watch feature to display the value of an expression that exists in your application code. To do that, you just highlight the expression and choose Quick Watch from the Debug menu or toolbar. Remember, though, that you can also display the value of an expression by displaying a data tip, so you really don't need this feature. Its one benefit is that it lets you add its expression to the Watch window by clicking on its Add button.

The Add Watch dialog box

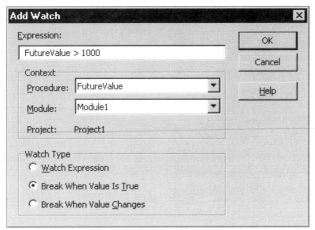

The Watch window

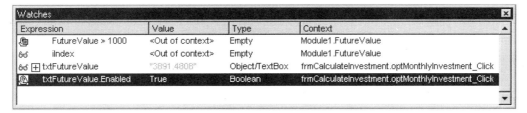

Description

- The Watch window lets you view the values of *watch expressions* while an application is in break mode. Once you add a watch expression, Visual Basic automatically displays the Watch window. You can also display the Watch window by clicking on the Watch Window button in the Debug toolbar or by selecting the Watch Window command from the View menu.

- To add a watch expression to the Watch window, select the Add Watch command from the Debug menu to display the Add Watch dialog box shown above. Then, enter a valid expression in the Expression text box, set the Context options, and select a Watch Type option.

- The Context options determine the scope of a watch expression. If an expression is out of scope, the Watch window will display a message instead of a value.

- The first Watch Type option lets you enter a watch expression that's displayed when the application enters break mode. The next two Watch Type options cause your application to enter break mode when the value of the watch expression becomes true or changes. The icon to the left of a watch expression in the Watch window indicates the watch type.

- To edit or delete a watch expression, right-click on the expression in the Watch window and select the Edit Watch or Delete Watch command from the shortcut menu.

Figure 4-8   How to use the Watch window to monitor expressions

Exercise set 4-2: Use the debugging windows

In this exercise set, you'll get a chance to experiment with the Immediate window, the Locals window, the Watch window, and the Call Stack.

Open the project

1. If it's not already open, open the Financial Calculations project you worked on in the last exercise set.

Use the Immediate window to display values and run a procedure

2. Open the Code window for the Calculate Investment form and navigate to the CalculateFutureValue procedure. Then, use the Debug toolbar to set a breakpoint on the assignment statement for the Future Value text box.

3. Run the project. Then, enter some valid data for the future value calculation and click on the Calculate command button. When you do, you should enter break mode at the breakpoint you set in the previous step.

4. If the Immediate window isn't already displayed, display it by clicking on the Immediate Window button in the Debug toolbar. If necessary, drag the title bar of the Immediate window to dock it as shown in figure 4-5.

5. Display the caption for the current form by typing this code into the Immediate window:

```
? Me.Caption
```

When you press the Enter key at the end of the line, Visual Basic should display the Caption property for the form.

6. Change the value that's in the Monthly Investment text box by typing this code into the Immediate window:

```
Me.txtMonthlyInvestment = 150
```

When you press the Enter key at the end of the line, Visual Basic should put the number 150 in the text box. To check this, use the taskbar to switch to the Financial Calculations window and look at the text box. Then, use the taskbar to switch back to the Visual Basic window.

7. Click on the Close button for the Immediate window to close it.

Use the Locals window to monitor variables and change properties

8. Use the Debug toolbar to display the Locals window. If necessary, drag the title bar of the Locals window to dock it as shown in figure 4-6. Then, note how the Locals window displays the values for the variables that are defined in the current procedure.

9. Click on the plus sign (+) to the left of the Me keyword to display a list of properties for the current form and its controls, and scroll the list to see how many properties you recognize. Next, click on the plus sign (+) to the left of one of the controls on the form, and note that you can also check the

properties for each control on the form. Then, scroll to the top of the Locals window and click on the minus sign (-) to the left of the Me keyword to collapse all properties and restore the Locals window to its original state.

10. Open the Code window for the standard module, set a breakpoint on the For…Next statement in the FutureValue function, and press F5 to continue running the procedure. This should execute all code up to the breakpoint that you just set, and you should see the five variables that are defined by the FutureValue function in the Locals window. Then, click on the Step Into button a few times to step through the For…Next loop, and notice how the iIndex and FutureValue variables change with each repetition of the loop. When you're satisfied that you understand how this loop works, click on the Call Stack button and experiment with the Call Stack dialog box. Last, remove the breakpoint from the For…Next statement and press F5 to continue.

11. Use the taskbar to switch to the Financial Calculations window, and click on the Calculate command button. When you do, you should enter break mode at the breakpoint in the CalculateFutureValue procedure. Next, change the value for the iMonths variable to zero by selecting the current value for this variable, typing a zero, and pressing Enter. Then, press F5 to finish running the procedure. To see the results of this calculation, use the taskbar to switch to the Financial Calculations window where the Future Value text box should contain zero.

12. Click on the Calculate command button to enter break mode. Then, close the Locals window by clicking on its Close button.

Use the Watch window as you step through code

13. Click on "iMonths" and select the Add Watch command from the Debug menu. In the Add Watch dialog box, edit the expression in the Expression box so it says "iMonths > 48", select the Break When Value Is True option, and click on the OK button. This should open the Watch window. Next, click on txtInterestRate and select Add Watch from the Debug menu again. This time, just click on the OK button to add the item to the Watch window.

14. Remove all breakpoints by selecting the Clear All Breakpoints command from the Debug menu, press F5 to continue executing the application, and use the taskbar to switch to the Financial Calculations window. Enter 3 as the Number of Years, click on the Calculate button, and notice that the application runs normally (no breakpoint). Then, enter 5 as the Number of Years and click on the Calculate button. This time, the application enters break mode and the two expressions are displayed in the Watch window.

15. Click on the Close button for the Watch window to close this window, and click on the End button to end the application.

16. Close the project, even if you're going to continue with this chapter. That will remove the items from the Watch window.

Other debugging techniques

In addition to the debugging commands and features presented so far in this chapter, you should know about the three other techniques for debugging Visual Basic applications that follow.

How to create a routine that handles specific types of trappable errors

Once you've identified the specific types of errors that your application is likely to encounter, you can use the Select Case statement with the Err object to create an error-handling routine like the one in figure 4-9. As you can see, this routine displays specific messages for two types of errors, and it displays a generic message for all other types of errors. Of course, you can handle the errors in any way that is appropriate with this same coding structure; you don't have to display error messages.

When you code an error-handling routine, you should realize that it also traps errors that occur in called procedures that don't have their own On Error statements. If, for example, the two procedures that are called by the procedure in this figure don't include On Error statements, the routine in this figure will handle any trappable errors that occur in those procedures. Otherwise, the errors that occur in those procedures will be handled by their own error-handling routines.

A routine that displays specific messages for two types of errors

```
Private Sub cmdCalculate_Click()
On Error GoTo ErrorHandler
    If optFutureValue Then
        CalculateFutureValue
    Else
        CalculateMonthlyInvestment
    End If
    Exit Sub
ErrorHandler:
    Select Case Err.Number
        Case 13
            MsgBox "You must enter numbers in the text boxes."
        Case 6
            MsgBox "The numbers you entered are too large. " & vbCrLf _
                & "Make sure to enter the interest rate as a decimal."
        Case Else
            MsgBox "Error Number: " & Err.Number & vbCrLf _
                & "Source: " & Err.Source & vbCrLf _
                & "Error Description: " & Err.Description
    End Select
End Sub
```

Description

- The procedure above shows how you can use the Select Case statement and the Err object to handle specific types of errors. In this case, specific messages are displayed for error number 13 and error number 6, while a general message is displayed for all other errors.

- When you code an On Error statement in one procedure, the error-handling routine also provides for trappable errors in any called procedure that doesn't include its own On Error statement.

- If you have any problem understanding this code, please refer back to figure 2-13 for information about the Select Case statement and to figure 2-16 for information about the On Error statement and the Err object.

Figure 4-9   How to create a routine that handles specific types of trappable errors

How to test an error-handling routine

To test a routine like the one shown in the previous figure, you can set up the conditions that force an error. For some types of errors, though, it can be time-consuming or impractical to set up the conditions that force an error. For those types of errors, you can use the Raise method of the Err object as shown in figure 4-10.

In this figure, the Raise method causes error number 7 to occur and Visual Basic sets the other properties of the Err object based on that error number. In particular, Visual Basic sets the Source property to the project name (Project1), and it sets the Description property to "Out of Memory."

When you're done debugging, you need to make sure to remove all statements that raise errors. To make it easy to find and remove debugging statements like this, you can code them at the left margin of the Code window as shown in this figure. Since you indent the other statements of a procedure, this makes the debugging statements easy to spot. You can also use the Find dialog box to find all statements like this. To access that dialog box, press Ctrl+F or select the Find command from the Edit menu.

The syntax of the Raise method

```
Err.Raise number[, source][, description]
              [, helpfile][, helpcontext]
```

A procedure that use the Raise method to test an error-handling routine

```
Private Sub cmdCalculate_Click()
On Error GoTo ErrorHandler
Err.Raise 7
    .
    .
    Exit Sub
ErrorHandler:
    MsgBox "Error Number: " & Err.Number & vbCrLf _
        & "Source: " & Err.Source & vbCrLf _
        & "Error Description: " & Err.Description
End Sub
```

The message box that's displayed when the code above is executed

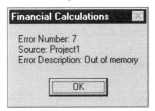

Description

- You can use the Raise method of the Err object to generate a run-time error during the execution of an application. This is useful when you want to test an error-handling routine.

- The only required argument of the Raise method is the number argument.

- The other arguments of the Raise method correspond to other properties of the Err object. If you don't specify these arguments, Visual Basic uses the values associated with the error number you specify. Or, if the number you specify isn't a valid error number, Visual Basic uses default values for these arguments.

- To get a list of valid error numbers, see the "Trappable errors" topic in Visual Basic online help.

Figure 4-10   How to test an error-handling routine

How to use compiler directives with debugging statements

If you use debugging statements like Err.Raise in a program, you'll want to be sure that these statements aren't included when you compile the program for distribution to its users. One way to do that is to delete these statements from the program. Another way is to use compiler directives as described in figure 4-11.

When you use *compiler directives*, you use the #If...Then...#Else directive to tell Visual Basic what statements to include in the compiled program. Although the syntax of this statement is similar to the syntax of the normal If statement, the conditions you specify must be based on one or more *conditional compiler constants*. In other words, you can't use regular program constants or variables in the conditions.

To declare a conditional compiler constant, you use the #Const directive. However, the expression that you assign to a constant like this can consist only of a literal value or another conditional compiler constant. In addition, you can't specify a data type for a compiler constant. Instead, Visual Basic uses the data type that's most appropriate for the value that's assigned to the constant.

In the example in this figure, you can see a typical use of compiler directives. Here, the compiler constant is assigned a value of True so the Err.Raise method is executed during debugging. Then, when the program is ready for production, you can assign a value of False to this constant so the debugging statement will be excluded and the normal statements will be included in the compiled program. Although you can omit the Else portion of the directive in a simple case like this one, you sometimes need to code both the If and the Else portions of the directive.

When you use compiler directives, you normally declare the compiler constants in the Declarations section of a module. However, even if they're coded in a procedure, they're treated as module-level constants so they're available to all the procedures in the module.

If you use the same compiler constants throughout the modules in a project, you can also define them as public constants. To do that, you specify the constants and their values in the Make tab of the Project Properties dialog box. To define the constant shown in this figure as public, for example, you enter

```
bDebug = +1
```

in the Conditional Compilation Argument text box. To define more than one constant, you separate them with colons.

When you use only a few debugging statements in an application, of course, you don't benefit much from the use of compiler directives. As your applications get more complex, though, you may find that you need to add a series of statements that help you debug it. Then, it's nice to be able to include them when you need them and exclude them when you don't, just by changing a constant.

The syntax of the #If..Then..#Else conditional directive

```
#If condition Then
    statements
[#Elseif condition-n Then
    statements] ...
[#Else
    statements]
#End If
```

The syntax of the #Const directive

```
#Const constantname = expression
```

A procedure that uses compiler directives

```
Option Explicit
#Const bDebug = True
    .
    .
Private Sub cmdCalculate_Click()
On Error GoTo ErrorHandler
#If bDebug Then
    Err.Raise 7
#Else
    If optFutureValue Then
        CalculateFutureValue
    Else
        CalculateMonthlyInvestment
    End If
#End If
ErrorHandler:
    MsgBox "Error Number: " & Err.Number & vbCrLf _
        & "Source: " & Err.Source & vbCrLf _
        & "Error Description: " & Err.Description
End Sub
```

Description

- A *compiler directive* tells Visual Basic whether or not to compile blocks of code. Compiler directives can be used to omit debugging statements from a compiled application without removing them from the source code.

- The #If...Then...#Else directive tells the compiler what statements to include based on the specified conditions. The conditions in this statement can include one or more *conditional compiler constants*, literals, and operators. To declare a conditional compiler constant, you use the #Const directive.

- Conditional compiler constants are always private to the module in which they're declared and are always evaluated as module-level variables even if they're declared within a procedure. However, you can also define public conditional compiler constants by specifying them in the Make tab of the Project Properties dialog box.

Figure 4-11   How to use compiler directives with debugging statements

Exercise set 4-3: Code and test an error-handling routine

In this exercise set, you'll first code a specialized error-handling routine and test it by deliberately entering invalid data. Then, you'll use the Err.Raise method to test your routine.

Open the project

1. Open the Financial Calculations project you worked on in the last exercise set.

Create a specialized error-handling routine

2. Open the Code window for the Calculate Investment form and navigate to the CalculateFutureValue procedure. Then, modify the error-handling routine in this procedure so it uses code like that shown in figure 4-9.

3. Press F5 to run the project. Next, enter 100 for the first three text boxes and click on the Calculate button. When you do, you should see a message box that says the numbers you entered are too large. Then, click on the OK button, change the value for the Interest Rate text box to .04, and click on the Calculate button. This time, the future value calculation should work correctly.

4. Change the value in the Years text box to "x" and click on the Calculate button. When you do, you should see a message box that says that you must enter numbers in the text boxes. Then, click on the OK button, change the value for the Years text box to 5, and click on the Calculate command button. This time, the future value calculation should work correctly.

5. Click on the Close button for the Financial Calculations window to close it and return to the Visual Basic window.

Use the Raise method to simulate an error

6. Press F1 to access the Help window, and use the Index tab to display the help topic for Trappable Errors. Note that error number 7 is the error that occurs when you run out of memory. Then, click on the Close button for the Help window to close it and return to the Visual Basic window.

7. Enter this code after the On Error statement at the top of the CalculateFutureValue procedure:

```
Err.Raise 7
```

8. Start the project, enter valid data into the first three text boxes, and click on the Calculate command button. When you do, you should see a message box that says you encountered error number 7. Then, click on the OK button to close the message box, and click on the Close button for the Financial Calculations window to close it and return to the Visual Basic window.

9. Move the Err.Raise statement you entered in step 7 to the top of the FutureValue function in the standard module, right after the Dim statement.

10. Start the project, enter valid data into the first three text boxes, and click on the Calculate command button. When you do, you should see a message box that says you encountered error number 7. This shows that the error-handling routine for the Click event of the Calculate button will handle trappable errors in the procedures and functions that it calls. Now, click on the OK button to close the message box, and click on the Close button for the Financial Calculations window to close it and return to the Visual Basic window.

Use a compiler directive

11. Enter the If portion of a compiler directive before and after the Err.Raise method in the FutureValue function so it looks like this:

```
#If bDebug Then
    Err.Raise 7
#End If
```

12. Choose the Properties command from the Project menu, click on the Make tab, and enter this code in the Conditional Compiler Argument text box:

```
bDebug = -1
```

13. Test the program to see that error 7 is raised by the compiled code. Next, use the Properties command in the Project menu to change the value of bDebug to 0 (false). Then, test the program again to see that error 7 isn't raised by the compiled code.

Clean up and save the project

14. Use the Properties command in the Project menu to reset the Startup Object to the Financial Calculations form. Then, test the application to make sure that it still works the way it's supposed to.

15. Click on the Save Project button to save the project and its forms. Then, exit from Visual Basic.

Perspective

If you have much debugging experience in other programming environments, you should now realize that Visual Basic provides a powerful set of debugging tools. By using them, you can set breakpoints at the start of critical portions of code. Then, you can step through the statements that follow each breakpoint, and you can review the values of the related variables and properties after each step. If necessary, you can also change values and alter the execution sequence of the statements. With tools like these, an inherently difficult job becomes more manageable.

Now, if you've completed the four chapters in this section of this book, you have all the programming skills you need to develop Visual Basic applications that don't retrieve and store data. You know how to use forms and controls to develop an effective user interface. You know how to use the syntax, statements, and functions of Visual Basic. And no matter what features you use, you know how to use the features that help you find and correct any bugs. With that as background, you're ready to move on to the next section. There, you'll learn how to develop applications that retrieve and update the data in a database.

Terms you should know

compile error
run-time error
break mode
data tip
breakpoint
margin indicator bar
Immediate window
Locals window
call stack
Watch window
watch expression
compiler directive
conditional compiler constant

Section 2

The essentials of database programming

In section 1, you learned how to use Visual Basic for developing applications that don't require the use of data that's stored in a database. In the real world, though, 90 percent or more of the Visual Basic applications do store and retrieve data. That's why this section is devoted to the essentials of database programming. When you complete it, you should be able to develop professional database applications that use the latest features of Visual Basic 6 including ADO, the Data Environment Designer, and the Data Report Designer.

In the first chapter in this section (chapter 5), you'll learn the concepts and terms that you need to know for database programming. In particular, you'll learn what the database management system (DBMS) is doing on the server while the Visual Basic interface that you develop for the clients is running. Then, in chapter 6, you'll learn how to develop a significant database application of your own using ADO, which is the preferred data access method of Visual Basic 6. As in section 1, exercise sets will guide you through the development of this application so you'll learn faster and better.

In the last five chapters in this section, you'll learn the skills that you need for developing database applications at a professional level. In chapters 7 and 8, you'll learn how to use ADO for more advanced applications. In chapter 9, you'll learn how to use the Data Environment Designer to build forms quickly and easily. In chapter 10, you'll learn how to use the Data Report Designer to develop the reports for an application. And in chapter 11, you'll learn how to use the Data View window to manage the database for an application. When you're done with the chapters in this section, you will have the skills of an entry-level database programmer in industry.

5

Introduction to database applications

Today, most Visual Basic applications are for multi-user systems that process the data stored in a database. Before you can develop an application like that, you need to be familiar with the concepts and terms that apply to database applications. In particular, you need to understand what the database management system is doing while your Visual Basic application is running.

To illustrate the database concepts, this chapter uses examples from Microsoft SQL Server 7.0. If you're using a different database management system, the concepts will be the same, although the implementation details may vary. As you will see, Visual Basic 6 is designed to work with any database that's supported by an OLE DB provider. And Visual Basic provides the providers for SQL Server, Oracle, and Access databases.

Introduction to multi-user database applications 172
The hardware components of a multi-user system 172
The software components of a typical multi-user database application 174

How a relational database is organized 176
How a table is organized 176
How the tables in a database are related 178
How the fields in a table are defined 180

How to use SQL to work with the data
in a relational database 182
How to query a single table 182
How to join data from two or more tables 184
How to modify the data in a table 186
How to use views, stored procedures, and triggers 188

How a DBMS provides for referential integrity,
security, and locking 190
How referential integrity works 190
How data security works 192
How locking works 194

Data access options and implementations 196
Common data access options 196
Common data access implementations 198

Client/Server implementations 200
Multi-tier systems and ActiveX components 200
Enterprise systems 202
Internet and intranet applications 204

Perspective 206

Introduction to multi-user database applications

In case you aren't familiar with multi-user systems, this first topic introduces you to the essential hardware and software components of a multi-user system. Then, the rest of this chapter presents additional information on these components and how you use them in database applications.

The hardware components of a multi-user system

Figure 5-1 presents the three hardware components of a multi-user system: the clients, the network, and the server. The *clients* are usually the PCs that are already available on the desktops throughout a company. And the *network* is the cabling, communication lines, network interface cards, hubs, routers, and other components that connect the clients and the server.

The *server* is a computer that has enough processor speed, internal memory (RAM), and disk storage to serve the clients of the system. This computer is usually a high-powered PC or a RISC system, but it can also be a mid-range system or a mainframe system. To back up the files of a system, a server usually has a tape drive or some other form of off-line storage. It may also have one or more printers or specialized devices that can be shared by the users of the system.

In a simple multi-user system, the clients and the server are part of a *local area network* (or *LAN*). However, two or more LANs can be connected as part of a *wide area network* (or *WAN*). Then, the clients that are on the LANs that are connected by the WAN can share data and communicate via services like e-mail.

The components of a multi-user system

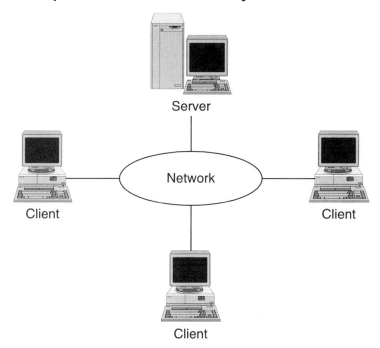

The three hardware components of a multi-user system

- The *clients* are the PCs, Macintoshes, or workstations of the system.
- The *server* is a computer that stores the files and databases of the system and provides services to the clients.
- The *network* consists of the cabling, communication lines, and other components that connect the clients and the servers of the system.

Figure 5-1   The hardware components of a multi-user system

The software components of a typical multi-user database application

Figure 5-2 presents the software components of a typical multi-user database application. In addition to a *network operating system* that manages the functions of the network, the server requires a *database management system (DBMS)* like Oracle or Microsoft SQL Server. This DBMS manages the databases that are stored on the server.

In contrast to a server, each client requires *application software* to perform useful work. This can be a purchased software package like a financial accounting package, or it can be custom software that's developed for a specific application. This book, of course, shows you how to develop custom software for database applications. This software runs with the operating system and the network software that must also be installed on the client.

Although the application software is run on the client, it uses data that's stored on the server. To make this communication between the client and the *data source* possible, the client requires an *ODBC (Open Database Connectivity) driver* or an *OLE DB provider*. If, for example, a SQL Server database is the data source, you can use either the ODBC driver or OLE DB provider for SQL Server. And if an Oracle database is the data source, you can use either the ODBC driver or OLE DB provider for Oracle. Whether you use an ODBC driver or an OLE DB provider depends on the technique you use to access the data. You'll learn about several of those techniques later in this chapter.

Once the software for both client and server is installed, the client communicates with the server via *SQL queries* (or just *queries*) that are passed to the DBMS through the ODBC driver or OLE DB provider. SQL, which stands for *Structured Query Language*, is an industry standard that makes communication between any application and any DBMS possible. After the client sends a query to the DBMS, the DBMS interprets the query and sends the results back to the client. (In conversation, SQL is pronounced as either S-Q-L or sequel.)

When the processing for an application is divided between the client and the server as illustrated in this figure, the system can be referred to as a *client/ server system*. Theoretically, at least, client/server systems let you balance the workload between the clients and the server so the system works more efficiently. Later in this chapter, you'll learn about some of the work that can be done by the DBMS on the server to lighten the work being done by the clients. Because multi-user systems are almost always client/server systems, we use those terms interchangeably in this book.

Client software, server software, and the SQL interface

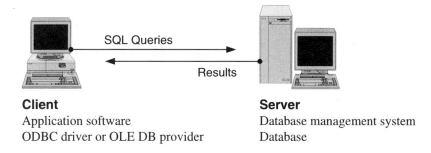

Client
Application software
ODBC driver or OLE DB provider

Server
Database management system
Database

Client software

- The *application software* does the work that the user wants to do. This type of software can be purchased or developed.
- The *ODBC driver* or *OLE DB provider* for the database lets the client application communicate with the *data source*.

Server software

- To store the databases of the client/server system, the server requires a *database management system* (*DBMS*) like Microsoft SQL Server, Sybase SQL Server, Oracle, or DB2.

The SQL interface

- The application software communicates with the database management system by sending *SQL queries* through the ODBC driver or OLE DB provider. When the DBMS receives a query, it provides a service like returning the requested data (*results*) to the client.

Figure 5-2   The software components of a typical multi-user database application

How a relational database is organized

In 1970, Dr. E. F. Codd developed a model for a new type of database called a relational database. This type of database eliminated some of the problems that were associated with earlier types of databases like hierarchical databases. By using the relational model, you can reduce data redundancy, which saves disk storage and leads to efficient data retrieval. You can also view and manipulate data in a way that is both intuitive and efficient. Today, relational databases are the de facto standard for client/server applications.

How a table is organized

The model for a *relational database* states that data is stored in one or more *tables*. It also states that each table can be viewed as a two-dimensional matrix consisting of *rows* and *columns*. The relational table in figure 5-3 illustrates this. Each row contains information about a single vendor.

In practice, the rows and columns of a relational database table are often referred to by the traditional terms, *records* and *fields*. In fact, some software packages use one set of terms, some use the other, and some use a combination. Throughout this book, these terms are used interchangeably.

If a table contains one or more columns that uniquely identify each row in the table, you can define these columns as the *primary key* of the table. For instance, the primary key of the Vendors table in this figure is the VendorID column. In this example, this column contains a number that is generated automatically by the DBMS, which SQL Server refers to as an *identity column*. Note, however, that a primary key doesn't have to be an identity column.

In addition to primary keys, some database management systems let you define keys that uniquely identify each row in a table. If, for example, there shouldn't be duplicates in the VendorName column, it can be defined as a *non-primary key*. In SQL Server, this is called a *unique constraint* or a *unique key*. The only difference between a unique key and a primary key is that a unique key can contain a null value and a primary key can't.

Indexes provide an efficient way to access the rows in a table based on the values in one or more columns. Because applications typically access table rows by referring to their key values, an index is automatically created for each key you define. However, you can define indexes for other columns as well. If, for example, you frequently need to sort the Vendor records by zip code, you can set up an index for that column. Like a key, an index can include one or more columns.

Although indexes can improve the efficiency of retrieval operations, they reduce the efficiency of insert, update, and delete operations. That's because the index has to be updated whenever a record is added or deleted or when the data in an index field is changed.

The Vendors table in the Accounts Payable database

Primary key   Columns

VendorID	VendorName	VendorAddress1	VendorAddress2
1	US Postal Service	Attn: Supt. Window Services	PO Box 7005
2	National Information Data Ctr	PO Box 96621	
3	Register of Copyrights	Library Of Congress	
4	Jobtrak	1990 Westwood Blvd Ste 260	
5	Newbrige Book Clubs	3000 Cindel Drive	
6	California Chamber Of Commerce	3255 Ramos Cir	
7	Towne Advertiser's Mailing Svcs	Kevin Windmer	3441 W Macarthur Blvd
8	BFI Industries	PO Box 9369	
9	Pacific Gas & Electric	Box 52001	
10	Robbins Mobile Lock And Key	4669 N Fresno	
11	Bill Marvin Electric Inc	4583 E Home	
12	City Of Fresno	PO Box 2069	

Rows

Concepts

- A *relational database* uses *tables* to store and manipulate data. Each table consists of one or more *records*, or *rows*, that contain the data for a single entry. Each row contains one or more *fields*, or *columns*, with each column representing a single item of data.

- Most tables contain a *primary key* that uniquely identifies each row in the table. The primary key often consists of a single field, but it can also consist of two or more fields.

- In addition to primary keys, some database management systems let you define one or more *non-primary keys*. In SQL Server, these keys are called *unique constraints* or *unique keys*. Like a primary key, a non-primary key uniquely identifies each row in the table.

- A table can also be defined with one or more *indexes*. An index provides an efficient way of accessing the data in a table. An index is automatically created for a table's primary and non-primary keys.

Figure 5-3   How a table is organized

How the tables in a database are related

The tables in a relational database can be related to other tables by values in specific columns. This is where the term *relational* comes from. The two tables shown in figure 5-4 illustrate this concept. Here, each row in the Vendors table is related to one or more rows in the Invoices table. This is called a *one-to-many relationship*.

Typically, relationships exist between the primary key in one table and the *foreign key* in another table. The foreign key is simply one or more columns in a table that refer to a primary key in another table. In SQL Server, relationships can also exist between a unique key in one table and a foreign key in another table.

Although one-to-many relationships are the most common, two tables can also have a one-to-one or many-to-many relationship. If a table has a *one-to-one relationship* with another table, the data in the two tables could be stored in a single table. Because of that, one-to-one relationships are used infrequently.

In contrast, a *many-to-many relationship* is usually implemented by using an intermediate table that has a one-to-many relationship with the two tables in the many-to-many relationship. In other words, a many-to-many relationship can usually be broken down into two one-to-many relationships.

The relationship between the Vendors and Invoices tables

Figure 5-4   How the tables in a database are related

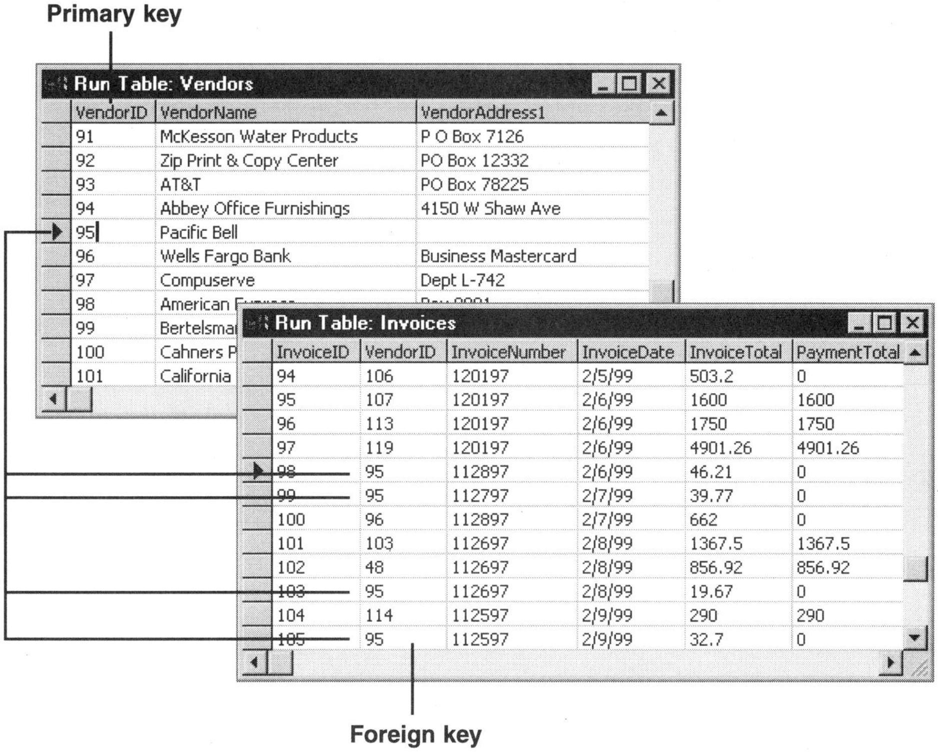

Concepts

- The tables in a relational database are related to each other through their key fields. For example, the VendorID field is used to relate the Vendors and Invoices tables above. The VendorID field in the Invoices table is called a *foreign key* because it identifies a related row in the Vendors table.

- Three types of relationships can exist between tables. The most common type is *a one-to-many relationship* as illustrated above. A table can also have a *one-to-one relationship* or a *many-to-many relationship* with another table.

How the fields in a table are defined

When you define a field in a table, you assign properties to it as indicated by the design of the Invoices table in figure 5-5. The most critical property for a field is its Datatype property, which determines the type of information that can be stored in the field. With SQL Server 7.0, you can choose from the *system data types* in this figure. You can also create your own *user-defined data types* that are based on the system data types. Because each data type has a specific format, you must be sure to assign the correct data type to each field.

The data types that you assign can also affect system performance. For example, a field with the *varchar* data type uses only as many bytes of storage as it needs. But a field with the *char* data type requires a fixed number of bytes no matter how many characters are actually stored in the field. So if a table has a large number of char fields and contains thousands of records, it will usually require more disk space than a table that uses varchar fields. This also affects the amount of data that is passed between the server and the client, which affects the performance of the client/server application. In general, then, you should use the *char* data type only when the data is a fixed size.

In addition to a data type, you can use defaults, check constraints, and rules to help maintain the validity of the data. A *default* provides a default value for a field when the user or the program doesn't enter anything into the field. If a default isn't specified and Null values aren't allowed for a field, the DBMS won't accept a record without a value in that field.

A *rule* or *check constraint* defines the acceptable values for a field. For example, you could define a check constraint for the Invoices table shown in this figure to make sure that the value in the InvoiceDueDate field is always greater than the value in the InvoiceDate field. Because a constraint is specified at the table level, not the field level, it can refer to two or more fields in the table. You can specify any number of constraints for a table.

When you use rules, you define them at the database level and then *bind* them to the appropriate fields in the database. For example, you can define a rule that requires the value in a field to be greater than zero. Then, you can bind that rule to every numeric field in the database that you want to contain a positive value. Note, however, that you can only bind a single rule to each field in the database. For that reason, check constraints are used more commonly than rules.

After you define the constraints and rules for a database, they're managed by the DBMS. If, for example, a user tries to add a record with data that violates a rule or constraint, the DBMS sends an appropriate error code back to the client without adding the record to the database. The client software can then respond to the error code.

The design of the Invoices table in SQL Server 7.0

Column Name	Datatype	Length	Precision	Scale	Allow Nulls	Default Value	Identity
InvoiceID	int	4	10	0			✓
VendorID	int	4	10	0			
InvoiceNumber	varchar	10	0	0			
InvoiceDate	datetime	8	0	0			
InvoiceTotal	money	8	19	4		(0)	
PaymentTotal	money	8	19	4		(0)	
CreditTotal	money	8	19	4		(0)	
TermsID	int	4	10	0		(1)	
InvoiceDueDate	datetime	8	0	0			

Common SQL Server data types

Type	Description
bit	A value of 1 or 0 that represents a True or False value.
char, varchar, text	Any combination of letters, symbols, and numbers.
datetime, smalldatetime	Alphanumeric data that represents a date and time. Various formats are acceptable.
decimal, numeric	Numeric data that is accurate to the least significant digit. The data can contain an integer and a fractional portion.
float, real	Floating-point values that contain an approximation of a decimal value.
int, smallint, tinyint	Numeric data that contains only an integer portion.
money, smallmoney	Monetary values that are accurate to four decimal places.
binary, varbinary, image	Binary strings.
cursor, timestamp, uniqueidentifier	A value that is always unique within a database.

Description

- The *data type* that's assigned to a field determines the type of information that can be stored in the field. Depending on the data type, you can also specify the length, precision, and scale for the field.

- A *default* is used for the value of a field if no value is specified for the field. You can specify a default at the field level as shown above or at the database level as a separate object. A default object can be bound to any number of fields in the database.

- You can also define check constraints and rules to restrict the values that can be entered into a field. *Check constraints* are defined at the table level and can refer to one or more fields in the table. *Rules* are defined at the database level as separate objects and can be *bound* to any number of fields in the database. You can also use a rule or check constraint to restrict the format of a field.

Figure 5-5   How the fields in a table are defined

How to use SQL to work with the data in a relational database

In this topic, you'll learn about the four SQL statements that you can use to manipulate the data in a database: the SELECT, INSERT, UPDATE, and DELETE statements. Although you can use other SQL statements to define the data in a database, the Visual Basic programmer usually doesn't use them. As a result, they aren't presented in this book.

Although SQL is a standard language, each DBMS is likely to have its own *dialect*, which includes extensions to the standard language. So when you use SQL, you need to make sure that you're using the dialect that's supported by your DBMS. In this chapter and throughout this book, all of the SQL examples are for Microsoft SQL Server's dialect, which is called *Transact-SQL*.

How to query a single table

Figure 5-6 illustrates how to use a SELECT statement to query a single table in a database. The syntax summary at the top of this figure uses conventions that you're probably familiar with if you've worked with other languages. Here, the capitalized words are SQL words and the lowercase words represent the items that you must supply. The brackets [ ] indicate that an item is optional; the bar (|) indicates a choice between the options on either side; and the elipsis (…) indicates that you can code a series of like items. To separate the items in a statement, you can use one or more spaces, and you can use indentation whenever it helps you improve the readability of a statement.

If you study the SELECT statement below the syntax summary, you can see how the two are related. Here, the SELECT statement retrieves fields from a table named Invoices. It selects a record from the Invoices table only if it has a balance due that's greater than zero. And it sorts the returned records by invoice date.

Please note in this SELECT statement that the last field in the query, BalanceDue, is calculated by subtracting PaymentTotal and CreditTotal from InvoiceTotal. In other words, a field by the name of BalanceDue doesn't actually exist in the database. This type of field is called a *calculated field*, and it exists only in the results of the query.

This figure also shows the *result set* that is returned by the SELECT statement. A result set is a logical table that's created temporarily within the database. The current record in the result set is identified by the *current row pointer*, or *current record pointer*. When you make a change to a result set, the change is reflected in the table that the result set was created from.

As you might guess, queries can have a significant effect on the performance of a client/server application. The more fields and records that are returned by a query, the more traffic the network has to bear. When you design a query, then, you should try to keep the number of fields and records to a minimum.

Simplified syntax for the SELECT statement

```
SELECT field-1 [, field-2]...
FROM table-1
[WHERE selection-criteria]
[ORDER BY field-1 [ASC|DESC] [,field-2 [ASC|DESC]...]
```

A SELECT statement that retrieves and sorts selected fields and records from the Invoices table

```
SELECT InvoiceNumber, InvoiceDate, InvoiceTotal,
    PaymentTotal, CreditTotal,
    InvoiceTotal - PaymentTotal - CreditTotal AS BalanceDue
FROM Invoices
WHERE InvoiceTotal - PaymentTotal - CreditTotal > 0
ORDER BY InvoiceDate
```

The result set defined by the SELECT statement

	InvoiceNumber	InvoiceDate	InvoiceTotal	PaymentTotal	CreditTotal	BalanceDue
Current row pointer ▶	P-0608	12/14/98	20551.18	0	0	20551.18
	989319-497	12/20/98	2312.2	0	0	2312.2
	989319-487	12/21/98	1927.54	0	0	1927.54
	97/553B	12/29/98	313.55	0	0	313.55
	97/553	12/30/98	651.29	0	0	651.29
	97/522	1/2/99	1962.13	0	0	1962.13
	203339-13	1/4/99	17.5	0	0	17.5
	0-2436	1/9/99	10976.06	0	0	10976.06
	963253272	1/11/99	61.5	0	0	61.5
	963253271	1/11/99	158	0	0	158
	963253269	1/11/99	26.75	0	0	26.75
	963253267	1/11/99	23.5	0	0	23.5
	2147483647	1/11/99	9.95	0	0	9.95
	963253264	1/12/99	52.25	0	0	52.25
	963253263	1/12/99	109.5	0	0	109.5
	43966316	1/19/99	10	0	0	10

Concepts

- The result of a SELECT query is a *result set* like the one shown above. A result set is a logical set of records that consists of all of the fields and records requested by the SELECT statement.

- The *current row pointer* identifies the current record in a result set. You can use this pointer to identify a record you want to update or delete from the result set. Any change to the result set is reflected in the table that the result set is based on.

- To select all of the fields in a table, you can code an asterisk (*) in place of the field names. For example, this statement will select all of the fields from the Invoices table:

```
SELECT * FROM Invoices
```

Figure 5-6   How to query a single table

How to join data from two or more tables

Figure 5-7 presents the syntax of the SELECT statement for retrieving data from two tables. This type of operation is called a *join* because the data from the two tables is joined together into a single result set. For example, the SELECT statement in this figure joins data from the Invoices and Vendors tables into a single result set.

An *inner join* is the most common type of join. When you use an inner join, records from the two tables in the join are included in the result set only if their related fields match. These matching fields are specified in the SELECT statement. In the SELECT statement in this figure, for example, records from the Invoices and Vendors tables are included only if the value of the VendorID field in the Vendors table matches the value of the VendorID field in one or more records in the Invoices table. If there aren't any invoices for a particular vendor, that vendor won't be included in the result set.

The second type of join is an *outer join*. With this type of join, all of the records in one of the tables are included in the result set whether or not there are matching records in the other table. In a *left outer join*, all of the records in the first table (the one on the left) are included in the result set. In a *right outer join*, all of the records in the second table are included. To illustrate, suppose that I had used a left outer join in the example in this figure. In that case, all of the records in the Vendors table would have been included in the result set even if no matching records were found in the Invoices table.

Although this figure shows only how to join data from two tables, you should know that you can extend this syntax to join data from additional tables. If, for example, you want to include line item data from a table named InvoiceLineItems in the results shown in this figure, you could code the FROM clause of the SELECT statement like this:

```
FROM Vendors
    INNER JOIN Invoices
        ON Vendors.VendorID = Invoices.VendorID
    INNER JOIN InvoiceLineItems
        ON Invoices.InvoiceID = InvoiceLineItems.InvoiceID
```

Then, you could include any of the fields in the InvoiceLineItems table in the field list of the SELECT statement.

SELECT statement syntax for joining two tables

```
SELECT field-list
FROM table-1
    {INNER | LEFT OUTER | RIGHT OUTER} JOIN table-2
    ON table-1.field-1 {=|<|>|<=|>=|<>} table-2.field-2
[WHERE selection-criteria]
[ORDER BY field-list]
```

A SELECT statement that joins data from the Vendors and Invoices tables

```
SELECT VendorName, InvoiceNumber, InvoiceDate, InvoiceTotal
FROM Vendors INNER JOIN Invoices
    ON Vendors.VendorID = Invoices.VendorID
WHERE InvoiceTotal >= 500
ORDER BY VendorName, InvoiceTotal DESC
```

The result set defined by the SELECT statement

VendorName	InvoiceNumber	InvoiceDate	InvoiceTotal
Bertelsmann Industry Svcs. Inc	509786	2/2/99	6940.25
Cahners Publishing Company	587056	2/2/99	2184.5
Computerworld	367447	2/2/99	2433
Data Reproductions Corp	40318	3/22/99	21842
Dean Witter Reynolds	112697	2/8/99	1367.5
Digital Dreamworks	120197	2/5/99	5000
Federal Express Corporation	963253230	1/17/99	739.2
Ford Motor Credit Company	120197	2/5/99	503.2
Franchise Tax Board	120197	2/6/99	1600
Fresno County Tax Collector	112697	2/8/99	856.92
IBM	Q545443	11/16/98	1083.58
Ingram	31359783	1/25/99	1575
Ingram	31361833	1/25/99	579.42
Malloy Lithographing Inc	0-2058	1/10/99	37966.19
Malloy Lithographing Inc	P-0259	12/19/98	26881.4

Concepts

- A *join* lets you combine data from two or more tables into a single result set. The type of join you choose determines how the data is combined.

- An *inner join*, also called an *equi-join*, returns records from both tables only if their related fields match. *An outer join* returns records from one table in the join (the LEFT or RIGHT table) even if the other table doesn't contain a matching record.

- Some database management systems support additional types of joins. For example, SQL Server supports *cross joins* and *full outer joins*.

Figure 5-7   How to join data from two or more tables

How to modify the data in a table

Figure 5-8 presents the basic syntax of the SQL INSERT, UPDATE, and DELETE statements. You use the INSERT statement to insert one or more records into a table. As you can see, the syntax of this statement is different depending on whether you're adding a single record or selected records.

To add a single record to a table, you specify the name of the table you want to add the record to, the names of the fields you're supplying data for, and the values for those fields. The example in this figure adds a record to a table named Terms, which contains three fields: TermsID, TermsDescription, and TermsDueDays. Because the value of the TermsID field is generated automatically, though, it's not included in the INSERT statement. If you're going to supply values for all the fields in a table, you can omit the field names, but then you must be sure to specify the values in the same order as the fields in the table.

To add selected records to a table, you include a SELECT statement within the INSERT statement. Then, the SELECT statement retrieves fields from one or more tables based on the conditions you specify, and the INSERT statement adds those records to another table. In the example in this figure, the SELECT statement selects all the fields from the records in the Invoices table that have been paid in full and inserts them into a table named InvoiceArchive.

To change the values of one or more fields in a table, you use the UPDATE statement. On this statement, you specify the name of the table you want to update, expressions that indicate the fields you want to change and how you want to change them, and a condition that indicates the record or records you want to change. In the example in this figure, the UPDATE statement changes the TermsID value to 4 for each record in the Invoices table that has a TermsID value of 1.

To delete records from a table, you use the DELETE statement. On this statement, you specify the table and a condition that indicates the records you want to delete. The DELETE statement in this figure deletes all the records from the Invoices table that have been paid in full.

INSERT INTO statement syntax for adding a single record

```
INSERT INTO table-name [(field-list)]
    VALUES (value-list)
```

A statement that adds a single record to a table

```
INSERT INTO Terms (TermsDescription, TermsDueDays)
    VALUES ("Net due 90 days", 90)
```

INSERT INTO statement syntax for adding selected records

```
INSERT INTO table-name (field-list)
    SELECT-statement
```

A statement that adds selected records from one table to another table

```
INSERT INTO InvoiceArchive
    SELECT * FROM Invoices
    WHERE InvoiceTotal - PaymentTotal - CreditTotal = 0
```

UPDATE statement syntax

```
UPDATE table-name
    SET expression-1 [,expression-2]…
    WHERE selection-criteria
```

A statement that changes the terms ID for selected records

```
UPDATE Invoices
    SET TermsID = 4
    WHERE TermsID = 1
```

DELETE statement syntax

```
DELETE FROM table-name
    WHERE selection-criteria
```

A statement that deletes all paid invoices

```
DELETE FROM Invoices
    WHERE InvoiceTotal - PaymentTotal - CreditTotal = 0
```

Figure 5-8   How to modify the data in a table

How to use views, stored procedures, and triggers

A *view* is a predefined query that's stored in a database. To create a view, you use the CREATE VIEW statement as shown in figure 5-9 to store the SELECT statement for the view with the database. To access the view, the client issues a SELECT statement that refers to the view. This causes a virtual table to be created from the SELECT statement in the view (a virtual table is just a temporary table that's created on the server). Then, the SELECT statement that referred to the view is executed on this virtual table to create the result set.

Although views can be quite useful, they require some additional overhead. That's because every time an application refers to a view, the view has to be created from scratch. If that's a problem, you can also restrict access to a database by using stored procedures.

A *stored procedure* is a set of one or more SQL statements that are stored together in a database. To create a stored procedure, you use the CREATE PROCEDURE statement as shown in this figure. To use the stored procedure, the client must send a request for it to be executed. Because that can be done in several different ways, the example in this figure uses *pseudocode* that gives the intent of the request but not the actual code for the request.

When the server receives the request, it executes the stored procedure. If the stored procedure contains a SELECT statement like the one in this figure, the result set is sent to the client. If the stored procedure contains INSERT, UPDATE, or DELETE statements, the appropriate processing is performed. Note that when you need to perform an operation that affects several records, using a stored procedure can be considerably more efficient than updating one record at a time.

One advantage of using a stored procedure instead of a view is that you can include *parameters* in a stored procedure as shown in this figure. Then, when you execute the procedure, you specify the value that you want to use for that parameter. In addition, stored procedures can contain *control-of-flow language*. For example, you can use If...Else language to determine the processing to be done based on specific conditions.

A *trigger* is a special type of stored procedure that is executed automatically when an insert, update, or delete operation is executed on a table. Triggers are used most often to maintain referential integrity as you'll see in the next figure. However, you can also use triggers to check the validity of data in a record that's being added to or changed in a table. Triggers give you more flexibility than rules and constraints because they can refer to any column in any table; they can contain conditional processing and error handling; and they can compare the state of a table before and after the operation that fired the trigger is executed.

A CREATE VIEW statement for a view named VendorsMin

```
CREATE VIEW VendorsMin As
    SELECT VendorName, VendorState, VendorPhone
    FROM Vendors
```

A SELECT statement from a client that uses the VendorsMin view

```
SELECT * FROM VendorsMin
    WHERE VendorState = "CA"
    ORDER BY VendorName
```

A CREATE PROCEDURE statement for a stored procedure named VendorsByState

```
CREATE PROCEDURE VendorsByState @State Char As
    SELECT VendorName, VendorState, VendorPhone
        FROM Vendors
        WHERE VendorState = @State
        ORDER BY VendorName
```

Pseudocode for executing the VendorsByState stored procedure from the client

```
Execute VendorsByState for State = "CA"
```

Concepts

- A *view* consists of a SELECT statement that's stored with the database. When an application refers to a view, a virtual table is created on the server that represents the view. Then, the result set is extracted from this view.

- Views can be used to restrict the data that a user is allowed to access or to present data in a form that's familiar to the user. In some databases, users may be allowed to access data only through views.

- A *stored procedure* is one or more SQL statements that have been compiled and stored with the database. A stored procedure can be started by application code on the client as indicated by the pseudocode above.

- Stored procedures can improve database performance because the SQL statements in each procedure are only compiled and optimized the first time they're executed. In contrast, SQL statements that are sent from a client to the server have to be compiled and optimized every time they're executed.

- A *trigger* is a special type of stored procedure that's executed, or *fired*, when records are inserted, updated, or deleted from a table. Triggers can be used to enforce referential integrity as described in figure 5-10. Triggers can also be used to check the validity of the data in a record that's being updated or added to a table.

- Because views, stored procedures, and triggers are stored as part of the database, they can be managed independently of the user interface for an application.

Figure 5-9   How to use views, stored procedures, and triggers

How a DBMS provides for referential integrity, security, and locking

When a Visual Basic application accesses the data in a database, the DBMS does what it can to keep the data accurate and protected. In particular, a DBMS automatically provides for referential integrity, data security, and locking based on the relationships and rules that have been defined for the database. As a result, you have little or no control over these functions as you develop a Visual Basic application. Nevertheless, you do need to understand these functions because they affect some of your coding and property settings.

How referential integrity works

Referential integrity means that records with foreign keys always have records with matching primary keys in another table. That means you can't add a record with a foreign key value if a primary key record with that value doesn't already exist. It also means you can't change a primary key value without changing the foreign key values in related records. And it means you can't delete a primary key record without deleting related foreign key records.

One way to enforce referential integrity is to define the primary key and foreign key relationships within the database. In SQL Server, these relationships are defined by *foreign key constraints* as shown in figure 5-10. When you define foreign key constraints, you are using what SQL Server calls *declarative referential integrity*, or *DRI*. This simply means that referential integrity is enforced automatically by the DBMS.

When you use DRI, you should be aware that you can't change a primary key value or delete a primary key record if related records exist. That's because SQL Server doesn't provide for *cascading* changes and deletes to related tables (although some database management systems do). If you want to be able to cascade changes and deletes with SQL Server, you can use triggers to enforce referential integrity instead of foreign key constraints.

A trigger can be executed when an insert, update, or delete operation is performed on a table. With SQL Server 6.5 and 7.0, you can create as many triggers as you need for each table, and each trigger can be fired for any combination of these operations. With earlier versions of SQL Server, though, only one trigger was allowed for each of these operations for each table.

The pseudocode in this figure illustrates how triggers work. In this case, the trigger is fired whenever a record in the Vendors table is updated. The trigger begins by checking to see if the primary key value in the Vendor record has changed. If it has, the trigger updates all the records in the Invoices table that have matching foreign keys so the relationship between the two tables is maintained. Note, however, that the trigger shown here is just a summary of what the trigger does, not the actual code, which would be far more complicated. Also note that the trigger isn't fired unless the update operation is successful.

The SQL Server dialog box for defining foreign keys

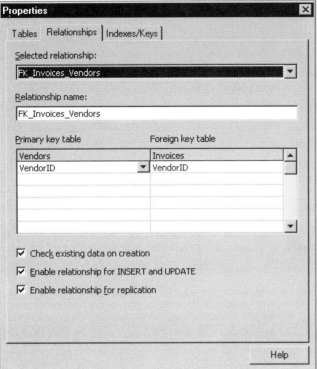

Pseudocode for a trigger that fires when a record in the Vendors table is updated

```
If the primary key value has changed Then
    Change all records in the Invoices table
    with matching foreign keys
```

Concepts

- *Referential integrity* means that the relationships between the tables are maintained correctly. That means that a table with a foreign key can't have records with foreign key values that don't have matching primary key values in the related table.

- In SQL Server, you can enforce referential integrity by defining *foreign key constraints* as shown above. When foreign keys are defined, you can't change a primary key value or delete a primary key record if related records exist.

- You can also enforce referential integrity using *triggers*. Triggers let you *cascade* changes from the primary keys in one table to the foreign keys in a related table. They also let you cascade deletes from the primary key table to the foreign key table.

Figure 5-10   How referential integrity works

How data security works

Data security determines who can access the tables and fields in a database. When you use Windows NT Server as the network operating system and SQL Server for database management, you actually have two layers of data security. NT Server controls who can log in to the network. And SQL Server controls who can access the objects and data in a database and what operations they can perform. This is summarized in figure 5-11.

To provide for network security, a network administrator sets up an account name and password for each user of the network. The administrator also determines what servers, files, and printers each user has access to. Then, when a user tries to connect to the network, NT Server asks for a valid name and password. If a user can't supply them, he or she isn't given access to the network and therefore can't access SQL Server data.

To provide for database security, a database administrator sets up a login ID and password for each user of a database. To do this with SQL Server 7.0, the administrator uses the SQL Server Login Properties dialog box. From this dialog box, the administrator can also grant access rights to individual databases.

After giving a user access to a database, the database administrator can use the Database User Properties dialog box shown in this figure to give the user specific capabilities and access rights. For instance, the database administrator can give the user permission to perform select, insert, update, and delete operations on the tables and views in the database and to execute stored procedures or to add foreign key constraints (DRI) to a table.

The dialog boxes for defining a user and setting user permissions

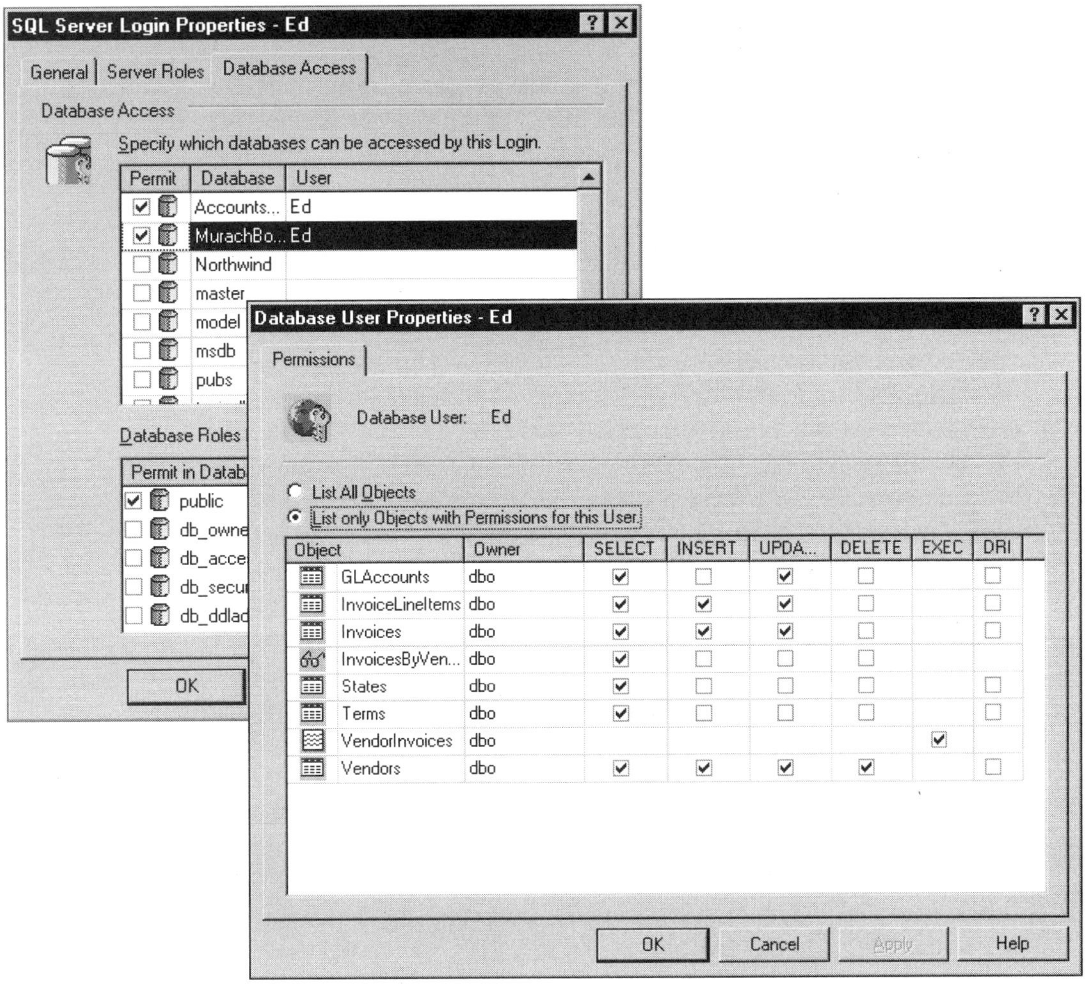

Concepts

- The *database security* provided by SQL Server determines who can log in to SQL Server, what databases and database objects (tables, views, etc.) each user has access to, and what operations each user can perform on the database and its objects.

- Before you can access a SQL Server database, you must log in to the network server. The server provides additional *network security* that determines what servers, files, and printers each user has access to.

- With Windows NT Security, user accounts on the server can be mapped to SQL Server login IDs so a user can connect to the network and log in to SQL Server at the same time.

Figure 5-11   How data security works

How locking works

Locking prevents two or more programs from changing the same data at the same time. To illustrate the need for locking, suppose program A accesses a record in the Vendors table to update the vendor's address. At the same time, program B accesses the same record to change the payment terms for the vendor. When program A finishes changing the address, the change is saved to the table. But when program B saves the same record with the updated payment terms, it replaces the record that program A just updated so the address returns to the old address. With a large database, of course, this type of problem should be rare, but it is nonetheless a problem that a business application must provide for.

SQL Server prevents this type of problem by automatically locking records. It does that by using the three lock types illustrated in figure 5-12. In the first diagram in this figure, program 2 and program 3 are retrieving data at the same time. Because these programs aren't updating the data, they have *shared locks* on the data, which means that other programs can still access the same data. Program 1, however, is attempting to update the data, so it has an *update lock* on the data. But it must wait until programs 2 and 3 are finished before it can actually update the data.

In the second diagram, programs 2 and 3 have finished and their shared locks have been released. When that happens, SQL Server upgrades program 1's update lock to an *exclusive lock* so it can update the shared data. At this point, no other programs can read or update this data. When program 1 finishes updating the data, however, the exclusive lock is released so other programs can access the data.

When SQL Server locks data, it must also determine the size of the lock to use. It does that dynamically based on the resources that are required to perform the requested operation. In general, SQL Server locks data by rows for single record transactions and by pages for batch transactions that include multiple rows. If many rows or pages in the same table are locked at the same time, though, SQL Server will automatically increase the lock size to the entire table using a process called *lock escalation*.

SQL Server lock types

Lock type	Description
Shared	Lets other programs acquire shared or update access to the same data.
Update	Lets other programs acquire shared access to the same data.
Exclusive	Prevents other programs from accessing the same data.

An update lock waiting for shared locks to be released

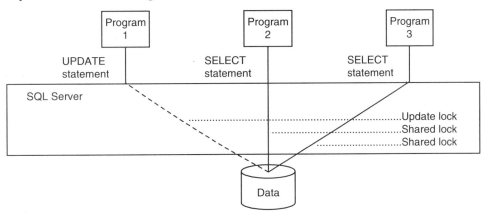

An update lock that's been updated to an exclusive lock

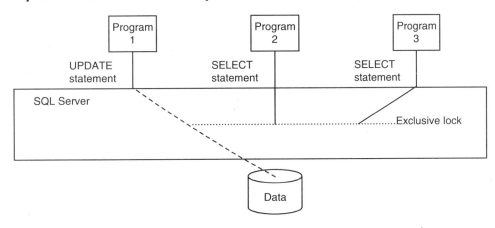

Concepts

- *Locking* prevents one user from accessing data that is being modified by another user. Locking is implemented automatically by SQL Server.

- SQL Server uses three types of locks as described above. *Shared locks* are used for statements like SELECT that don't change data. *Update locks* are used to lock data that SQL Server intends to modify. Update locks are upgraded to *exclusive locks* when the data is actually updated.

- Data can be locked by rows, pages, or tables. SQL Server determines the lock size dynamically.

Figure 5-12   How locking works

Data access options and implementations

Visual Basic 6 provides several different options for working with a database. In this topic, I'll describe the most commonly-used options and point out the advantages and disadvantages of each. Then, I'll compare two of the most common implementations so you can see for yourself how they differ.

Common data access options

Figure 5-13 presents some of the most common options for accessing data from a Visual Basic application. *DAO*, or *Data Access Objects*, is an option that's been used frequently in the past. When you use DAO, your data requests are processed by the *Jet database engine* before they're passed on to the ODBC driver. (If the request is for data in a Jet database, ODBC can be bypassed as indicated in this figure.) Because Jet was originally designed to be used with databases created in Access, though, it doesn't support some of the features of the more powerful client/server databases like SQL Server and *Oracle*. And even with recent improvements that have been made to Jet, its use can still reduce program efficiency.

With Visual Basic 5, Microsoft introduced a new data access option called *RDO*, or *Remote Data Objects*. Unlike DAO, RDO requests are passed directly to ODBC so they can be processed more efficiently. In addition, it can take advantage of many of the advanced features provided by client/server databases, like asynchronous queries, server-side cursors, and multiple result sets. Unfortunately, the features of RDO were limited, which made it difficult to use.

Microsoft's solution was a new data access option, called *ADO*, or *ActiveX Data Objects*. Like RDO, ADO requests aren't processed by Jet, so it can take advantage of the features of many client/server databases. In addition, it has features and flexibility that RDO doesn't have. Because of that, it is the preferred method for accessing data with Visual Basic 6; it is the method that we recommend for developing new applications; and it is the method that you'll learn how to use in the next six chapters.

As you will see in the next chapter, ADO is based on an *object model* that lets you refer to data using the same syntax that you use for referring to objects like forms and controls. Although RDO and DAO are also based on object models, the ADO model is both simplified and improved.

In contrast, *ODBC API (application programming interface)* isn't based on an object model. Instead, it provides a low-level interface to the ODBC driver, which means that you have more control over its functions. Although this can lead to efficient access of ODBC databases, the programming for it can be cumbersome. As a result, you should only use this approach when the other access methods don't provide the capabilities you need.

Common options for accessing data from Visual Basic

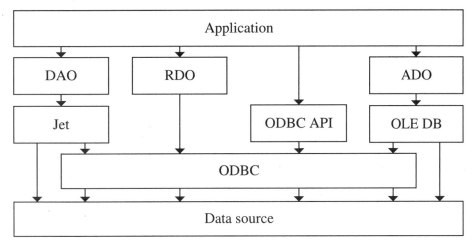

Description

- The recommended data access method for Visual Basic 6 is *ADO*, or *ActiveX Data Objects*. To communicate with a data source, ADO uses an OLE DB provider. If a provider isn't available for the specific data source you want to access, you can use one of the generic OLE DB providers.

- Before Visual Basic 6, *DAO*, or *Data Access Objects*, was the most common access method. When you use DAO, your data requests are processed by the Jet database engine and then by an ODBC (Open Database Connectivity) driver.

- *Remote Data Objects* (*RDO*) is similar to DAO, but it bypasses Jet and communicates directly with ODBC. Although RDO also provides a variety of features that aren't available when you use DAO, it lacks the ease of use and flexibility of ADO.

- ODBC API provides a low-level interface to ODBC data. Although ODBC API can be the most efficient technique for accessing data, it is also the most cumbersome to use.

- If you don't have an OLE DB provider for a database but you do have an ODBC driver for it, you can use the OLE DB provider for ODBC drivers that comes with Visual Basic 6. Then, you can use ADO, the provider, and the driver to access the data in the database, although this isn't as efficient as going directly from the OLE DB provider to the database.

- OLE DB providers can access data that ODBC drivers can't access. With OLE DB, for example, you can access data in the form of e-mail, spreadsheets, and word processing documents.

Figure 5-13   Common data access options

Common data access implementations

Figure 5-14 illustrates how an application accesses a SQL Server database when using DAO or ADO. As you can see, the most significant difference is that DAO requests are processed by the Jet database engine and an ODBC driver before they're passed on to SQL Server. In contrast, ADO requests are handled by an OLE DB provider.

One of the advantages of using Jet is that it provides features that aren't available with some client/server databases. These features include complex crosstab queries, TOP queries, multiple levels of grouping or totals, DAO functions, user-defined functions, and heterogeneous joins. However, the disadvantage of using these features with an ODBC database like SQL Server is that they can't be processed on the server. So if a query uses any of these features, all of the records that satisfy the other conditions of the query have to be returned to the client so Jet can apply the requested feature. That means that more data is passed from the server to the client, which makes the application less efficient. Because of that, you'll want to avoid using these features when accessing ODBC databases. But if you're not going to use the features of Jet, then it really doesn't make sense to use Jet, or DAO, at all.

In addition to bypassing Jet, ADO also handles resources more efficiently. In particular, it has a smaller footprint than DAO so it uses less memory on the client. It also lets you use the same connection for processing multiple requests for data, while DAO requires a separate connection for each data request. Finally, ADO uses a simpler object model than DAO, which makes it more flexible and easier to use.

In the next six chapters, you're going to learn how to use ADO for working with a SQL Server database so you may want to take one last look at this figure to remember how this works. When you do the exercise sets in those chapters, though, you may not have access to a SQL Server database running on a server. In that case, you can download an Access version of the practice database from our web site to your PC. With just a few differences, ADO works the same with an Access database as it does with a SQL Server database, and the exercise sets guide you through those differences.

How an application accesses a SQL Server database using DAO

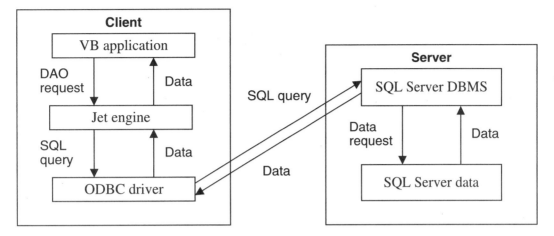

How an application accesses a SQL Server database using ADO

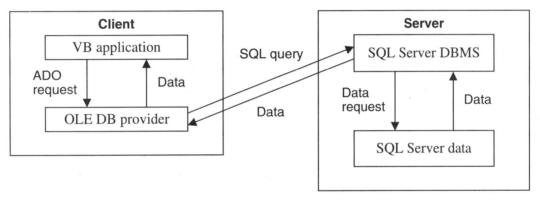

Description

- When a VB application issues a DAO request, the request is passed to the Jet database engine where it is converted to a SQL query. Then, the query is passed to the ODBC driver for the database to be accessed where it is converted to the SQL *dialect* of the database. Finally, the query is passed to the DBMS for the database, which processes the query.

- If a query includes features provided by Jet that aren't supported by the DBMS, some or all of the query may have to be processed by Jet. Then, all the data that Jet needs for processing the query must be sent from the server to the client. Because of that, using DAO and Jet isn't as efficient as using ADO.

- When an application issues an ADO request, the request is passed directly to the OLE DB provider for the database. The OLE DB provider converts the request to a SQL query that can be processed by the DBMS and then passes it to the DBMS.

- ADO is more efficient than DAO not only because it bypasses Jet, but because it handles resources more efficiently. In addition, it has a simplified object model.

Figure 5-14   Common data access implementations

Client/Server implementations

If you refer back to figure 5-1, you can see the architecture of a simple client/server system: one server, two or more clients, and a local area network. In the real world, though, client/server systems are more complicated than that.

Multi-tier systems and ActiveX components

Today, most client/server systems are *two-tier systems*. The first tier is the client, which does the *front-end processing*. The second tier is the server, which does the *back-end processing*. And all of the processing is done by either the client or the server.

In contrast, figure 5-15 presents a three-tier client/server system. Here, the clients are the first tier; the *component server* is the second tier; and the *database server* is the third tier. In a *multi-tier* (or *n-tier*) *system*, you add more servers to this physical configuration.

In the *three-tier system* shown in this figure, the component server is used to store and execute *ActiveX components*. When you implement functions as ActiveX components, the components can be re-used by any applications that need those functions, including applications developed in Visual Basic. With Visual Basic 6, these components may reside anywhere on the local network or they may be accessed through the Internet. The use of ActiveX components and component servers can also simplify the maintenance of an application later on. In chapter 13, you'll learn how to use Visual Basic to create and use ActiveX components.

Although components can be stored on a single component server as shown in this figure, they can also be stored on the clients, on database servers, on additional component servers, and on Internet servers. How they're deployed, of course, can have a significant effect on the performance of the system.

A three-tier physical implementation of a client/server application

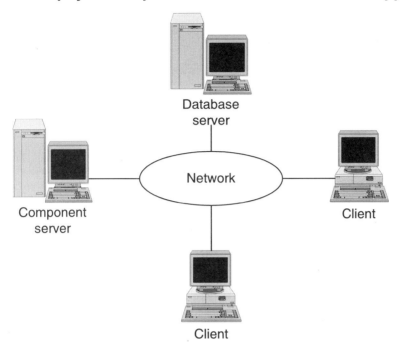

Concepts

- You can use Visual Basic to create *ActiveX components* that perform functions that can be used by more than one application on the network.

- One way to implement these components is to store them on a *component server* that's separate from the *database server*. The system then has three physical tiers so it can be called a *three-tier system*.

- The component objects do not have to be deployed as a third physical tier, however. They can be deployed on the clients, on the database server (still a two-tier system), on two or more component servers (an *n-tier,* or *multi-tier*, *system*), or on an Internet server.

- The primary benefits of using ActiveX components are (1) the components can be used by any applications that need their functions, and (2) the components are easier to maintain when they're on a separate server.

- To help manage the client requests for ActiveX components, the component server can use a service called Microsoft Transaction Server (MTS).

Figure 5-15   Multi-tier systems and ActiveX components

Enterprise systems

The term *enterprise system* refers to all of the computers of a large, often multi-national, company. Today, an enterprise system is likely to consist of at least one mainframe, a number of mid-range systems like DEC or AS/400 systems, a number of client/server systems, and some file server systems. (A *file server* is a machine that stores the files and databases used by the clients but doesn't do any of the processing associated with those files.) The problem, of course, is to connect these mixed platforms so all the people in the enterprise have access to the data they need. To complicate the problem, mid-range and mainframe systems weren't originally designed to communicate with PCs or PC networks.

To help standardize the communication between PCs, mid-range computers, and mainframes, IBM established a protocol called *System Network Architecture* (*SNA*). Today, that architecture can lead to communications between systems like those shown in figure 5-16. Here, the clients of a client/ server system can get data from the mainframe of the enterprise as well as from the AS/400 for the branch. To make this possible, a second server on the system called an *SNA server* provides a *gateway* to the AS/400 and mainframe.

The purpose of this figure is just to show one way that client/server systems and the other computers in an enterprise can communicate. This enhances the value of client/server systems because it lets each client get the data it needs from whatever computer has that data. The real-world complexities of implementing this type of connectivity, though, are far beyond the scope of this book.

A client/server system for an enterprise

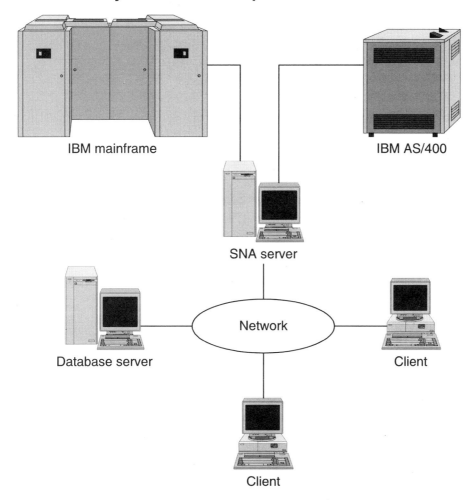

IBM mainframe

IBM AS/400

SNA server

Network

Database server

Client

Client

Concepts

- *Enterprise system* is a general term for the computer system of a large company with many geographic locations.

- Today, an enterprise system is likely to consist of file server systems, client/server systems running on more than one platform, mid-range systems like AS/400s, and a mainframe system.

- One of the major challenges of an enterprise system is providing the data that users need when they need it. This data may come from a database server on a local network, but it may also come from a database at a distant location on another network, a mid-range system, or a mainframe.

- IBM's *System Network Architecture* (*SNA*) makes it possible for the clients on a client/server system to communicate with AS/400s and mainframes. This communication is done through *gateways*. When you use Microsoft's SNA Server, the server becomes the gateway.

Figure 5-16   Enterprise systems

Internet and intranet applications

Today, more and more applications are being deployed on the Internet. The main reason for that is that an Internet application can be accessed from any computer that has access to the Internet. So, for example, if a company has offices in several locations, a single copy of the application can be placed on an *Internet server* rather than installing a copy of the application at each location. Similarly, if a company has a wide area network in place, an application can be placed on an *intranet server* on that network so that it can be accessed from any computer that has access to the wide area network.

Both Internet and intranet applications are *web-based applications*. That means that they reside on a web site, and they can be accessed using a *web browser*. They are also written in a platform-independent language like HTML so they can be accessed by any type of client.

As you can imagine, security is critical for applications that are placed on an Internet or intranet server. At the least, each application should require a user to enter a valid user ID and password. In addition, security can be implemented for the entire web site where an application resides.

Why is this of interest to the Visual Basic programmer? Because Visual Basic 6 is the first version that provides tools for developing Internet applications. And in chapter 14, you'll see how you can use these tools to develop a simple application. There, you'll see that you use many of the skills that you've learned in the other chapters of this book as you develop these applications.

A client/server system that's deployed on the Internet

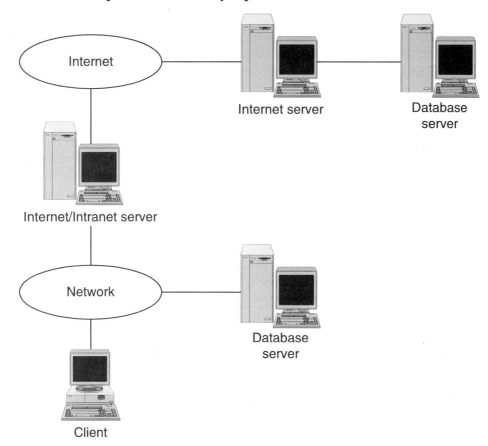

Concepts

- A client accesses an Internet application by using a *browser* like Microsoft Internet Explorer or Netscape Navigator. The browser connects to the Internet application by specifying a *Uniform Resource Locator*, or *URL*, like www.murach.com.

- Typically, browser requests go through an *Internet server* on the local network, which provides security for both incoming and outgoing requests. The server then sends the request to the Internet via a modem or a direct line.

- When the Internet application is located, the main or default *HTML page* is sent back to the local network where it is made available to the client.

- The data for an Internet application is typically stored on a database server that's connected to the Internet server. However, it can also be stored on the Internet server or on another server on the Internet.

- Internet applications, also referred to as *web-based applications*, can also be stored on an *intranet server* on the local network. Then, the clients can use browsers to access them just as if they were on the Internet.

Figure 5-17   Internet and intranet applications

Perspective

This chapter has introduced you to the hardware and software components of a multi-user system and described what takes place on the server side of a database application. With that as background, you are now ready to develop the client software for a database application. In the next chapter, then, you'll learn how to develop an application that maintains the data in a single table.

Because the effective use of a database is so critical to the success of business applications, the rest of the chapters in this section also focus on database programming. In chapters 7 and 8, for example, you'll learn how to use ADO for building forms that require data from two or more tables. And in chapters 9, 10, and 11, you'll learn how to use three of the new tools that come with Visual Basic 6 to build forms, develop reports, and work with databases.

Terms you should know

client	inner join
network	outer join
server	view
local area network (LAN)	stored procedure
wide area network (WAN)	trigger
database management system (DBMS)	referential integrity
data source	foreign key constraint
ODBC driver	declarative referential integrity (DRI)
OLE DB provider	cascading changes or deletes
SQL query (or just query)	data security
Structured Query Language (SQL)	locking
client/server system	shared lock
relational database	update lock
table	exclusive lock
row (or record)	lock escalation
column (or field)	DAO (Data Access Objects)
primary key	Jet database engine
identity column	RDO (Remote Data Objects)
non-primary key	ADO (ActiveX Data Objects)
unique constraint (or unique key)	object model
index	ODBC API
one-to-many relationship	two-tier system
foreign key	front-end processing
one-to-one relationship	back-end processing
many-to-many relationship	component server
data type	database server
default	multi-tier (or n-tier) system
rule	three-tier system
check constraint	ActiveX component
SQL dialect	enterprise system
calculated field	Internet server
result set	intranet server
current row (or record) pointer	web-based application
join	web browser

6

Introduction to database programming

Now that you know the concepts and terms that you need for database programming, this chapter shows you how to develop database applications of your own. First, you'll learn how to use a special control called an ADO data control to build bound forms. Then, you'll learn how to build forms without using a data control, called unbound forms. When you complete this chapter, you should be able to develop simple database applications of your own.

Basic skills for building bound forms 208
How to use an ADO data control to process data 208
ADO data control and bound control properties 210
Cursor options 212
Locking options 214
How to build the connection string for an ADO data control 216
Property settings for the bound Vendors form 218
Code for the bound Vendors form 218
Exercise set 6-1: Build a bound form 220

How to work with ActiveX data objects 222
The ActiveX Data Object model 222
Common ADO properties and methods 224
Techniques for working with ADO objects through code 226
Exercise set 6-2: Enhance the bound form 228

Basic skills for building unbound forms 230
How the unbound version of the Vendors form works 230
How to process data without using a data control 232
How to open a connection to a database 234
How to open a recordset 236
How to use a control array 238
Code for the unbound Vendors form 240
Exercise set 6-3: Build an unbound form 250

Perspective 252

Basic skills for building bound forms

The fastest and easiest way to develop a form that accesses data is to add an ADO data control to the form. As you'll see, you can use a data control to define the data that's available to a form and to perform some of the most common data processing functions. Because you work with the data by binding other controls to the data control, forms that use data controls are commonly referred to as *bound forms*.

How to use an ADO data control to process data

Figure 6-1 presents the form that you'll learn how to build in this chapter. As you can see, it uses an *ADO data control* to access the data in vendor records. This data control provides built-in functions for navigating through the records in the recordset defined by the data control and for displaying, adding, and updating the records in the recordset. That makes it easy to create a form that lets the user maintain records.

Recordset is a term that ADO uses to refer to a result set and its associated cursor. The result set contains the data returned by a query, and the *cursor* provides the mechanism that lets you identify specific records in the result set so you can display, update, and delete those records. You'll learn more about recordsets and cursors throughout this chapter.

To display the individual fields in the recordset that's defined by a data control, you use *bound controls*. As the name implies, a bound control is bound to a specific field in the recordset. Each of the text boxes on the Vendors form in this figure, for example, is bound to a field in the recordset defined by the data control shown at the bottom of the form. Then, when you use the data control to move to a different record in the recordset, the fields in the record are automatically displayed in the controls that are bound to those fields. And when you change the data in a bound control, the data is automatically saved to the recordset when you move to another record.

By default, a data control doesn't let the user add records to the recordset. To do that, you have to change the EOFAction property of the data control to adDoAddNew. Then, if the user clicks on the navigation button to move to the next record and the last record is already displayed, a new blank record is added to the recordset and displayed on the form. When the user enters the data for the new record and moves to another record, the new record is saved to the recordset.

Although the data control provides for adding and updating records, it doesn't provide for deleting records. So if you want the user to be able to delete records, you have to provide for that function through code. You'll see how to do that later in this chapter.

A form that uses an ADO data control to maintain vendor records

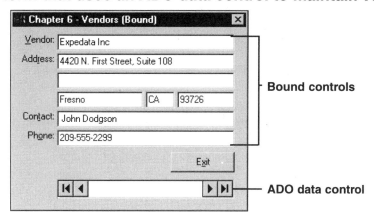

Description

- An *ADO data control* defines the *recordset* for a form and provides functions for navigating, displaying, adding, and updating records. Because these functions are built into the data control, it isn't necessary to add code for these functions to the application.

- You can use *bound controls* to work with the fields in the current record of the recordset that's defined by a data control. Then, the field values are displayed automatically in the bound controls.

- A data control contains the four navigation buttons shown above. From left to right, these buttons let you move to the first, previous, next, and last records in the underlying recordset.

- You can also use the data control to add records to the recordset. To do that, just set the EOFAction property of the data control to adDoAddNew (see figure 6-2). Then, when the user clicks on the navigation button to move to the next record and the last record is already displayed, a new blank record is added.

- When the user clicks on one of the navigation buttons to move to another record, the current record is automatically updated if the data in any of the bound controls has been changed. If the user closes the form before moving to another record, though, the changes are lost.

- Some functions, like deleting records, aren't built into the data control. To provide for these functions, you use Visual Basic code.

Figure 6-1   How to use an ADO data control to process data

ADO data control and bound control properties

Figure 6-2 presents some of the properties of an ADO data control and bound controls. Before you start learning about the properties, though, please note that the ADO data control is *not* the data control that's included in the standard Toolbox. Before you can use the ADO data control, you need to add it to the Toolbox by using the Components command in the Project menu.

You use the ConnectionString property of the data control to tell ADO how to connect to the data source. This property provides information like the OLE DB provider that you want to use, the name of the server where the data resides, and the name of the database that you want to access.

You can also include a user name and password as part of the connection string. An alternative, though, is to enter this information in the UserName and Password properties of the data control. Note, however, that this information must be included in one place or the other before the connection can be established. If it isn't, the connection will fail.

The RecordSource property identifies the data in the data source that you want to access. If you want to access all of the fields and records in a table, the RecordSource property can simply be the name of the table. More likely, though, the RecordSource property will be a SQL SELECT statement that specifies the tables, fields, and records that you want to access.

The CommandType property identifies the type of information that's included in the RecordSource property. If the RecordSource property contains the name of a table, for example, you set the CommandType property to adCmdTable. And if the RecordSource property contains a SELECT statement, you set the CommandType property to adCmdText. To be sure that these properties are synchronized, you can use the dialog box that's displayed when you click on the Build button for the RecordSource property. Note, however, that the CommandType property is used for efficiency only. If you leave it at its default of adCmdUnknown, ADO will determine what type of information the RecordSource property contains.

The CursorLocation and CursorType properties define the cursor to be used. You'll learn more about these properties in figure 6-3. And in figure 6-4, you'll learn about the LockType property, which controls the type of locking that's used for the records in the recordset.

The last two data control properties in this figure, BOFAction and EOFAction, control what happens when the user tries to move to the previous record when the first record is already displayed, or tries to move to the next record when the last record is already displayed. By default, the first or last record remains the current record, which is usually what you want. If you want to be able to use the data control to add records to the recordset, though, you can change the EOFAction property to adDoAddNew.

After you set the data properties of the data control, you can create the bound controls for the form. For each control, you use the DataSource and DataField properties to identify the data control and the field in the recordset that you want to bind to the control. You can also use the DataFormat property to set the format that will be used to display the data.

Some of the data properties of the ADO data control

Property	Description
ConnectionString	A string that contains all the information necessary to connect to a data source.
RecordSource	The name of a table or a SQL statement that identifies the fields and records to be retrieved from the data source.
CommandType	Identifies the type of information specified in the RecordSource property. The options are adCmdText (for a SQL statement), adCmdTable, adCmdStoredProc, and adCmdUnknown (default).
CursorLocation	The location of the cursor engine. See figure 6-3 for details.
CursorType	The type of cursor to be used. See figure 6-3 for details.
LockType	The type of lock to be used. See figure 6-4 for details.
MaxRecords	The maximum number of records that can be returned to the recordset. The default is zero, which means that all records that satisfy the query are returned.
UserName	The user name to use when logging in to a data source. If a user name isn't included in the ConnectionString property, it must be specified for this property.
Password	The password to use when logging in to a data source. If a password isn't included in the ConnectionString property, it must be specified for this property.
EOFAction	Determines what happens when the user tries to move past the last record in the recordset. The options are adDoMoveLast (default), adStayEOF, and adDoAddNew.
BOFAction	Determines what happens when the user tries to move past the first record in the recordset. The options are adDoMoveFirst (default) and adStayBOF.

Some of the data properties of a bound control

Property	Description
DataSource	Identifies the data control that defines the recordset you want the control bound to.
DataField	Identifies the field in the recordset that you want the control bound to.
DataFormat	The format that will be used to display the data.

Notes

- The ADO data control isn't included in the Toolbox by default. To add it to the Toolbox, use the Components command in the Project menu as described in chapter 3.
- If the CommandType property doesn't match the information in the RecordSource property, an error occurs.

Figure 6-2   ADO data control and bound control properties

Cursor options

To work with the individual records in a result set, you use *cursors*. Because the type of cursor you choose and the location of that cursor can have a dramatic effect on the efficiency of an application, you'll want to carefully consider your options. You set these options using the CursorLocation and CursorType properties of the data control as described in figure 6-3.

The CursorLocation property determines whether the cursor, along with the associated result set, will be stored on the client or on the server. By default, a data control is set to use *client-side cursors*. In that case, all of the data in the cursor and the associated result set is sent to the client when the form is loaded. Although this improves response time once the application is in use, it takes longer to load the form. Also, if you add or delete records in the recordset, you may have to refresh the recordset by using the Requery method, which you'll learn about later in this chapter.

The alternative is to use *server-side cursors*. With these cursors, the cursor and the result set are stored on the server, and data is sent to the client only when it's requested. There are two drawbacks, though. First, server-side cursors require additional server resources. Second, they may not provide all of the functionality of client-side cursors. You'll learn more about that in chapters 7 and 8.

Of course, to use server-side cursors, you need to use a DBMS like SQL Server that supports them. If you set the CursorLocation property to adUseServer and the DBMS doesn't support server-side cursors, the OLE DB provider will change this property back to client-side cursors without notifying you.

Once you decide where the cursor will be stored, you can set the CursorType property to indicate the type of cursor you want to use. If you choose to use server-side cursors, you can use any of the four cursor types as long as they're supported by the DBMS. If you want to be able to see the changes, additions, and deletions made to the underlying table by other users, for example, you can use a *dynamic cursor*. Keep in mind, though, that dynamic cursors require more overhead, so you'll want to use them only when necessary.

An alternative to a dynamic cursor is a *keyset cursor*. With a keyset cursor, you can see the changes made by other users and you aren't able to access records that have been deleted by other users. However, you can't see records that are added by other users like you can with a dynamic cursor. Because keyset cursors require less overhead than dynamic cursors, though, they're more practical for most applications.

If you don't need to see changes, additions, or deletions made by other users, you can use a *static cursor*. Typically, you use static cursors when you need to retrieve but not make changes to the records in a result set. For example, you can use a static cursor to create a report. Although you can add, update, and delete records when using a static cursor, that's usually not as efficient as using a keyset cursor. Note, however, that a static cursor is the only

CursorLocation options

Option	Description
adUseClient	The cursor and its associated result set reside on the client. Client-side cursors improve response time, but increase network traffic since all of the data must be sent to the client when the cursor is created.
adUseServer	The cursor and its associated result set reside on the server. Server-side cursors minimize network traffic and reduce the load on the client, but require additional resources on the server and may not provide the functionality of client-side cursors.

CursorType options

Option	Description
adOpenDynamic	Opens a dynamic cursor, which includes changes, additions, and deletions made to the database by other users. Uses keys to identify individual records. Cannot be used to create sorted result sets from SQL Server data.
adOpenKeyset	Opens a keyset cursor, which includes changes made to the database by other users. Additions made by other users aren't visible, but records deleted by other users are no longer accessible. Uses keys to identify individual records.
adOpenStatic	Opens a static cursor, which doesn't include changes, additions, and deletions made to the database by other users. This is the only type of cursor that can be created on the client with ADO.
adOpenForwardOnly	Opens a forward-only cursor. This cursor is like a static cursor, but you can only scroll forward through the records. This type of cursor isn't available when you define a recordset using a data control.

Notes

* The changes, additions, and deletions that are made available by a cursor are automatically included in any recordset that contains that data. No additional processing is required to view these changes.
* If you use client-side cursors (adUseClient), Visual Basic automatically sets the cursor type to adOpenStatic without notifying you, no matter what you set the CursorType property to.

Figure 6-3   Cursor options

type of cursor that's supported by ADO on the client. If you select one of the other types of cursors when the CursorLocation property is set to adUseClient, the OLE DB provider changes the CursorType property to adOpenStatic without notifying you.

The last cursor type is a *forward-only cursor*. This is similar to a static cursor except that you can only use it to move forward through the records in the result set. Although this type of cursor isn't available when you define a recordset using a data control, you can use it when you define a recordset through code as you'll see later in this chapter.

Locking options

Figure 6-4 presents the locking options that are available when you work with recordsets using ADO. How these options actually affect the locks that are applied to the data in the result set depend on the locking scheme that's defined by the DBMS. In this figure, for example, I've indicated how each locking option affects the locks that are placed on SQL Server data. The locking scheme for another DBMS may be different.

By default, ADO uses *optimistic locking*. With this type of locking, the assumption is that two people are unlikely to be editing the same record at the same time. So the record isn't locked until it's actually updated. Then, if by some chance the record has changed since it was retrieved, a trappable error occurs and the record isn't updated. If you're updating each record as it's changed, you'll use the adLockOptimistic option to implement optimistic locking. If you're updating records in a batch, you'll use the adLockBatchOptimistic option.

If you want to be sure that no other users can change a record after you retrieve it, you can use *pessimistic locking*. With this type of locking, the record is locked when it's retrieved so no other users can change it. Because this requires additional overhead, however, you shouldn't use it unless it's critical that other users not be able to change the same records. To implement pessimistic locking, use the adLockPessimistic option for the LockType property.

If you're only going to retrieve data but not update it, you may want to use the adLockReadOnly option. With this option, no locking is required since the data can't be changed.

LockType options

Option	Description
adLockReadOnly	Data can be viewed, but not modified. When used with SQL Server data, this causes a shared lock to be placed on the records so other users can access and change the data at the same time.
adLockPessimistic	Causes the records to be locked immediately so other users can't change them. When used with SQL Server data, this causes an update lock to be placed on the records when they're retrieved. The update lock is up-graded to an exclusive lock when the records are actually updated.
adLockOptimistic	Causes the records to be locked when they're updated. When used with SQL Server data, this causes a shared lock to be placed on the records when they're retrieved. Then, when the Update method is issued, the shared lock is upgraded to an update lock. And when the records are actually updated, the update lock is upgraded to an exclusive lock.
adLockBatchOptimistic	Used for updating records in batches instead of one at a time.

Note

- See figure 5-12 in chapter 5 for a more detailed explanation of how locking works with SQL Server.

Figure 6-4   Locking options

How to build the connection string
for an ADO data control

The easiest way to create a connection string is to build it as illustrated in figure 6-5. From the Property Pages dialog box, you choose the Use Connection String option, which is the default. When you first display this dialog box, the Use Connection String text box is empty. In this figure, though, the dialog box shows the beginning of the connection string for the Vendors form.

To build the connection string, you click on the Build button to display the Data Link Properties dialog box. The first tab of this dialog box lets you choose the OLE DB provider you want to use. As you can see, this list includes providers for Access (Jet 3.51), Oracle, and SQL Server databases. In addition, it includes a provider for ODBC drivers. If you need to access an ODBC database for which an OLE DB provider isn't available, you can use this provider to connect to the ODBC driver for that database. Then, the ODBC driver can connect to the database.

After you select a provider, you can click on the Next button to display the Connection tab of this dialog box. In this tab, you enter the name of the server that contains the database you want to access, the information that's required to log on to the server, and the name of the database you want to access. When you're done, you can click on the Test Connection button to be sure that the information you've entered is correct and you can connect to the database.

Before you can test a connection, you have to enter a valid user name and password. The exception is if you're using Windows NT integrated security. With integrated security, the name that the user enters to log on to the network is mapped to a SQL Server login ID, so a separate user name and password aren't required.

By default, the user name you enter is saved in the connection string but the password isn't. If you want to include the password in the connection string, check the Allow Saving of Password box. And if you want to omit the user name and password from the connection string, you can delete these entries before you click on the OK button to create the connection string. You can also enter a blank password into the connection string by selecting the Blank Password option. If the user name or password isn't included in the connection string, though, you need to supply them in the UserName and Password properties of the ADO data control.

The Advanced tab of the Data Link Properties dialog box provides advanced options, and the All tab lists all of the options for the selected provider, including some that aren't available from the other tabs. In general, though, you won't need to change any of these options.

The dialog boxes for building a connection string

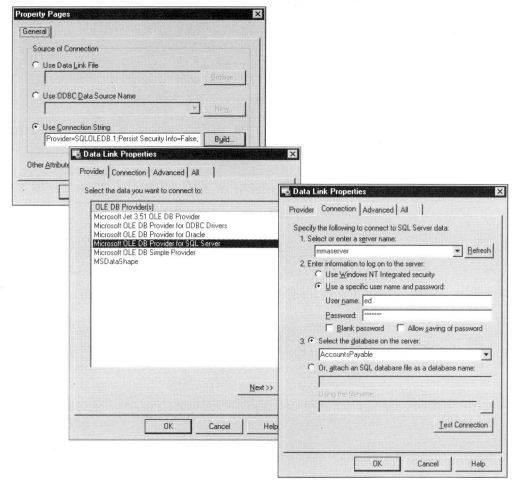

Description

- To display the General tab of the Property Pages dialog box for an ADO data control, click on the Build (...) button to the right of the ConnectionString property in the Properties window. To display all of the tabs of the Property Pages dialog box, right-click on the control and select the ADODC Properties command from the shortcut menu.

- To build a connection string, select the Use Connection String option and click on the Build button. Select the OLE DB provider you want to use from the Provider tab of the Data Link Properties dialog box, then click on the Next button and complete the Connection tab.

- You can also connect to a data source using a data link file or an ODBC data source, but those options aren't presented in this book.

Figure 6-5   How to build the connection string for an ADO data control

Property settings for the bound Vendors form

Figure 6-6 presents the critical property settings for the bound version of the Vendors form in figure 6-1. Here, the ConnectionString property of the data control indicates that the SQLOLEDB provider (the one for Microsoft SQL Server) will be used to access a database named AccountsPayable on a server named mmaserver. Notice that the user name and password aren't included in this string. Instead, they're included in the UserName and Password properties of the data control.

Because the recordset that's defined by the RecordSource property of the data control may return a significant amount of data, the CursorType property is set to adUseServer so the cursor and its associated result set are stored on the server. That way, only the records that are requested by the user will be sent to the client. To process those records efficiently, the CursorType property is set so a keyset cursor will be used.

The other property setting that you should notice is the setting for the EOFAction property. Because it's adDoAddNew, the user will be able to add new records by moving to the end of the recordset and then clicking on the navigation button that moves to the next record.

Once you've defined the data properties for a data control, you can set the Name property of the control to an appropriate name starting with the prefix *ado* like adoVendors. Then, you can bind all of the text boxes on the Vendors form to the fields in the recordset that's defined by the data control.

To bind a text box control, for example, you set its DataSource property to the name of the data control, adoVendors. Then, you drop down the list for the DataField property and select the name of the field that the control should be bound to. The text box that contains the vendor name, for example, should be bound to the field named VendorName, and the text box that contains the name of the contact person should be bound to the field named VendorContact.

Another text box property you may want to set is the MaxLength property. This property restricts the number of characters that can be entered into a text box. If the VendorName field is defined so that it can contain a maximum of 50 characters, for example, you may want to set the MaxLength property of the text box that's bound to that field to 50. By default, the MaxLength property is set to 0, which means that the user can enter any number of characters. If you don't change this default and the user enters more characters than are allowed by the field, an error may occur when the database is updated or the data may be truncated.

Code for the bound Vendors form

Figure 6-6 also shows the code that's required for the Vendors form. As you can see, this code is for the Click event procedure of the Exit command button. When the user clicks on this button, the form will be unloaded and the program will end. Because all of the other program functions are built into the data control, no other code is required.

The data properties for the ADO data control on the Vendors form

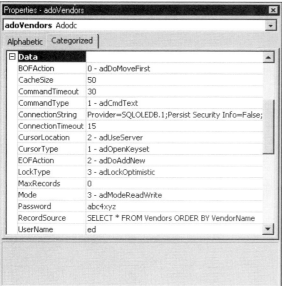

The property settings for a SQL Server database (shown above)

- The ConnectionString property specifies a SQL Server database named AccountsPayable on a server named mmaserver:

      Provider=SQLOLEDB.1;Persist Security Info=False;
          Data Source=mmaserver;Initial Catalog=AccountsPayable

- The RecordSource property specifies that the source of data for the data control is all of the fields in the Vendors table sorted by vendor name. The CommandType property is set to adCmdText to indicate that the RecordSource property contains a SQL statement.

- The CursorLocation property is set to adUseServer so the cursor is stored on the server. Then, the CursorType property is set to adOpenKeyset so the updating can be done as efficiently as possible.

- The BOFAction property is set to adDoMoveFirst, which means that the current record pointer will stay on the first record if the user tries to move past the beginning of the recordset. The EOFAction property is set to adDoAddNew, which means that a new record will be added if the user tries to move past the end of the recordset.

- All of the text boxes on the Vendors form are bound to the data control shown above through the DataSource property of the control. Then, each control is bound to a different field in the data source through the DataField property.

The code for the bound version of the Vendors form

```
Private Sub cmdExit_Click()
    Unload frmVendors
End Sub
```

Figure 6-6   Property settings and code for the bound version of the Vendors form

Exercise set 6-1: Build a bound form

In this exercise set and in all of the other exercise sets in this section, will use an Accounts Payable database. How do you get access to it? First, if you're in a training or classroom environment, a SQL Server version of this database may be available on a server that you can access. Then, you just need to find out what the connection details are like data source name, initial catalog, user name, and password. In appendix B, you can find the specifications for this database.

More likely, though, you'll be learning on your own so you'll use a Jet (Access) version of this database. In that case, you can download the database from our web site to your PC as described in appendix A. Or, if your PC doesn't have Internet access, you can use the Visual Data Manager that comes with Visual Basic to create a Jet database. You can also learn how to do that in appendix A.

In general, the exercise sets work the same whether you're using a SQL Server or a Jet database. The only differences are in the way that you connect to the database. As a result, all of the exercise sets in this section guide you through both types of connections. But please make sure that you're doing the steps under the headings that apply to the type of database you're using.

Start a new project and prepare it for use with ADO

1. Start Visual Basic and begin a Standard EXE project. Next, change the Name property of the form to frmVendors, the Caption property to Vendors (C6 Bound), the BorderStyle property to Fixed Single, and the StartUpPosition property to CenterScreen. Then, use the Properties command in the Project menu to change the ProjectName property to C6Bound.

2. Click on the Save Project toolbar button, click on the Create New Folder button in its dialog box, and create a new folder named Chapter 6 Bound. Then, save the form and project in that folder as frmVendors and C6Bound.

3. Use the Components command in the Project menu to add the Microsoft ADO Data Control 6.0 to the Toolbox. Then, add an ADO data control to the bottom of the form, change its Name property to adoVendors, and delete the text from the Caption property.

Connect the data control to a SQL Server database

4. *If you're using a SQL Server database*, set the Data properties for the data control as shown in figure 6-6. Next, click on the button for the ConnectionString property to display the Property Pages dialog box. Then, with the Use Connection String option selected, click on the Build button to display the Data Link Properties dialog box, and complete the Provider and Connection tabs as shown in figure 6-5, but with the server, user, password, and database entries that are required at your site. Last, click on the Test Connection button to test the connection. If it works, return to the Form window. Otherwise, fix the entries so the connection works.

Connect the data control to a Jet database

5. *If you're using a Jet database*, set the RecordSource, CommandType, and EOFAction properties for the data control as in figure 6-6, but leave the Cursor-Location property as adUseClient because Jet doesn't support server-side cursors, leave the CursorType property as adOpenStatic, and leave the Password and UserName properties blank because security isn't implemented for the Jet database.

6. Click on the button for the ConnectionString property to display the Property Pages dialog box. Next, with the Use Connection String option selected, click on the Build button to display the Data Link Properties dialog box. Then, select the Microsoft Jet 3.51 OLE DB Provider in the Provider tab, and select the database that's on your PC in the Connection tab (that's the only entry you need to make). Last, click on the Test Connection button to test the connection. If it works, return to the Form window. Otherwise, fix the entries so the connection works.

Add the labels and bound text boxes to the form

7. Add the label and text box controls to the form so it looks like the one in figure 6-1. To bind each text box control to the data control, set its DataSource property to adoVendors, and select the field you want to display in the control from the list for the DataField property. Set the Name property of the VendorName text box to txtName so you can refer to it from the code you'll add in the next exercise set.

8. Press F5 to start the application and display the form and its data. Use the navigation buttons on the data control to move from one record to another. Change the data in the name field of a record, then move to another record and back to the record you changed to see that the change was saved.

9. Click on the Last navigation button to move to the last record, then click on the Next button to display a blank record. (If a blank record isn't displayed, you need to change the EOFAction property of the data control to adDoAddNew.) Now, enter the data for a new record, click on the Previous button, and click on the Next button to see that the new record has been added. Then, click on the Close button in the upper right corner of the form to close the form.

Add the Exit command button and test some error conditions

10. Add an Exit command button to the form as shown in figure 6-1, change its Name property to cmdExit, change its Caption property to E&xit, and add the procedure shown at the bottom of figure 6-6 in the Code window.

11. Start the application again, click on the Last navigation button to move to the last record in the recordset, and click on the Next button to display a blank record. Next, click on the Previous button without entering any data so ADO displays an error message indicating that you can't insert an empty row into a table. Then, click on the OK button to return to the blank form.

12. Enter a name in the Vendor text box of the blank form, then click on the Previous button so ADO displays a message indicating that you must enter a city. That's because the definition for this field indicates that it can't be null. You also need to supply values for the State and ZipCode fields because they can't be null either. Now, click on the Exit button to end the application.

13. Save the project, and leave it open if you're going to continue.

How to work with ActiveX data objects

When you use ADO, you work with the properties, methods, and events of the data objects defined by the ActiveX Data Object model. Even when you use an ADO data control to process data, you're still using the ADO object model, although most of the operations are done for you behind the scenes.

The ActiveX Data Object model

Figure 6-7 presents the basic structure of the ActiveX Data Object model. This object model defines a hierarchy of data objects that you can use to interact with the data in a data source. When you connect to a data source, for example, a Connection object is created. And when you retrieve records from the data source, a Recordset object is created within the specified Connection object. In this chapter, you'll learn the basics of working with Connection and Recordset objects, and you'll learn more about these objects and the other ADO objects in later chapters.

The shaded objects in the ADO model in this figure represent *collections* of two or more of the same type of object. For instance, there can be a collection of Field objects within a Recordset object, and there can be a collection of Parameter objects within a Command object. As you'll soon see, you can use the coding techniques you learned in chapter 2 to work with the objects in these collections.

Like the form and control objects that you're already familiar with, data objects have properties, methods, and events that you can use for working with them. That means that you can use the same object syntax that you use for working with forms and controls to work with data objects like recordsets and fields. In the next figure, you'll be introduced to the properties and methods you'll use most often, and you'll be introduced to some of the common events in chapter 7.

Before you can use the ADO model for a project, you have to include a reference to it in your project. Although that's done automatically when you add an ADO data control to a form, you need to include a reference to this model when you do all of the ADO operations through code. You'll learn more about that later in this chapter.

If you've used DAO for database programming in the past, you might want to compare that model with the ADO model. If you do, you'll notice that the ADO model has fewer objects than the DAO object model, which makes ADO easier to use. In addition, ADO is more flexible than DAO. In terms of function, the ADO Connection object is similar to the DAO Database object, and the ADO Command object is similar to the DAO QueryDef object.

The ActiveX Data Object (ADO) model

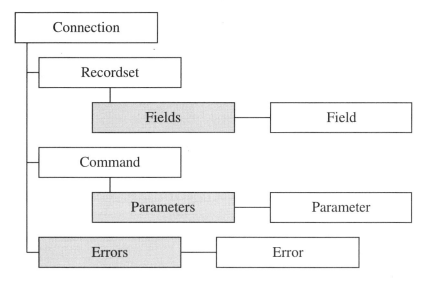

Concepts

- The ActiveX Data Object (ADO) model consists of a variety of *collections* and objects. A collection is simply a set of objects of the same type. The most common objects and collections are shown above (the collections are shaded).

- The Connection object represents a connection to a data source. You can use this object when you open recordsets and execute commands using the Recordset and Command objects.

- A Recordset object represents a set of records returned from a query. You can use the Fields collection of this object to refer to specific fields in the recordset.

- A Command object contains the definition of a command, such as a SQL statement, the name of a table, or the name of a stored procedure. You can use the Parameters collection of this object to create parameter queries or to specify arguments for a stored procedure.

- The Errors collection contains one or more Error objects that contain information about the most recent errors that occurred in response to an ADO operation. You can use these objects to get more information than the Visual Basic Err object provides.

- Although you can define two or more recordsets or commands using the same Connection object, they aren't stored in collections as are the Field, Parameter, and Error objects.

- The ADO model lets you access a data source using an object-oriented interface. That means you can use the same syntax to access data objects that you use to access objects like forms and controls. The ADO model also provides a variety of properties, methods, and events for working with the ActiveX data objects.

Figure 6-7   The ActiveX Data Object model

Common ADO properties and methods

Figure 6-8 presents the ADO properties and methods that you're most likely to use in an application. As you can see, all of these properties and methods are for Connection or Recordset objects, and some can be used with both. For instance, you can use the Open method with a Connection object to create a connection to a data source or with a Recordset object to create a recordset from the data source.

Four of the properties shown in this figure—ConnectionString, CursorLocation, CursorType, and LockType—correspond to properties of the ADO data control. Similarly, two other properties correspond to arguments that can be included in the ConnectionString property: the Provider property and the DefaultDatabase property (which corresponds to the Initial Catalog argument). As a result, you shouldn't have any trouble using these properties if you understand how to use the data control properties and connection string arguments.

The two Recordset properties that don't correspond to data control properties or connection string arguments are BOF and EOF. These properties indicate whether you have reached the beginning or end of the recordset. When you use these properties, you should realize that they're not set to True until you try to move past the beginning or end of the recordset. If, for example, the current record pointer is on the last record in the recordset and you try to move to the next record, the EOF property is set to True. Once the BOF or EOF property is changed to True, however, the current record is undefined. Before you can continue processing the recordset, then, you have to move the current record pointer to a valid record.

Another property that you haven't seen before is the RecordCount property of a Recordset object. This property indicates the number of records in the recordset. It is available as soon as the recordset is opened.

If you've used DAO in the past, you should notice that this property in a DAO recordset object indicates the number of records in the recordset that have been accessed, not the total number of records in the recordset. Because of that, you have to *populate* a DAO recordset by moving to the last record in the recordset before you get the count of all the records. With ADO, though, you don't have to do that.

Something else you don't have to do with ADO that you have to do with DAO is use the Edit method to move a record to the *copy buffer* for editing. That's because the changes you make to a record when using ADO are made directly to the recordset rather than to a copy of the data in the copy buffer. Then, when you execute the Update method, the changes you made to the recordset are saved to the underlying data source. Likewise, when you add a record using ADO, a blank record is added to the recordset instead of to the copy buffer as in DAO. And the Update method saves the new record to the underlying data source.

Common ADO properties

Property	Object	Description
ConnectionString	Connection	A string that contains all the information necessary to connect to a data source.
Provider	Connection	The name of the OLE DB provider for the connection.
DefaultDatabase	Connection	The database that's accessed when you open a recordset or execute a command using the Connection object.
CursorLocation	Connection Recordset	The location of the cursor engine. Server-side cursors are the default.
BOF EOF	Recordset	A true or false value that indicates whether or not the beginning or end of a recordset has been reached.
CursorType	Recordset	The type of cursor to be used.
LockType	Recordset	The type of lock to be used.
RecordCount	Recordset	The number of records in a recordset.

Common ADO methods

Method	Object	Description
Open	Connection Recordset	Opens a connection to a data source or opens a recordset from a data source.
AddNew	Recordset	Adds a new record to a recordset.
Update	Recordset	Saves the current record in a recordset.
Delete	Recordset	Deletes the current record from a recordset.
MoveFirst MoveLast MovePrevious MoveNext	Recordset	Moves to the first, last, previous, or next record in a recordset.
Requery	Recordset	Re-executes the query to refresh the recordset.
Close	Connection Recordset	Closes the object. If you don't close an object explicitly, it's closed automatically when the module that creates it is closed.

Figure 6-8   Common ADO properties and methods

Techniques for working with ADO objects through code

In the next topic of this chapter, you'll learn how to use ADO properties and methods in an actual application. Before you do that, though, I want to present some basic techniques that you can use for working with ADO objects through code. These techniques are illustrated in figure 6-9.

Before you can use an ADO object, you have to declare a variable that will contain a reference to the object. To do that, you use the Dim statement just as you do for other variables. Then, to create an *instance* of the object and store a reference to that object in the variable, you use the Set statement with the New keyword as shown in this figure. The first Set statement, for example, creates an instance of the ADO Connection object and assigns it to a variable named cnAP. The second Set statement creates an instance of the ADO Recordset object and assigns it to a variable named rsVendors.

The third Set statement in this figure assigns a value of Nothing to the rsVendors object variable. This releases the system resources that were being used by the object. After you assign a value of Nothing to an object variable, though, you can no longer use that variable to refer to the object.

The next group of statements in this figure shows how to work with ADO variables. The first statement, for example, uses the Open method of a Recordset object to create a recordset from the Vendors table. Then, the second statement assigns the value of the VendorName field in that recordset to a text box named txtName. Here, the field is referred to by the recordset name, the *bang operator* (!), and the field name. However, you can also refer to a field by coding the recordset name, collection name, and field name like this:

```
rsVendors.Fields!VendorName
```

Since the Fields collection is the default, though, it's usually omitted when you're referring to a field.

Because an ADO data control doesn't provide for all of the functions you may need to perform on a recordset, ADO provides a way to refer to that recordset through the data control. To do that, you use the Recordset property of the data control as shown in the procedure in this figure. This procedure deletes the current record from the recordset defined by the adoVendors data control. After this record is deleted and the MoveNext method is executed, the procedure checks to see if the EOF condition is true. If it is, that indicates that the last record in the recordset was deleted. In that case, the Requery method refreshes the recordset and the MoveLast method moves to the last record in the recordset.

If you wonder why the Requery method is necessary in this procedure, it's due to a limitation of ADO when server-side cursors are used. If you omit this method, an error will occur when the MoveLast method is executed indicating that the row that you're trying to move to has been deleted. In other words, ADO doesn't let you move to the new last row in a recordset after you've deleted the last row of the original recordset. Although this only occurs when you're using server-side cursors, this is the type of complexity that you have to deal with when you're developing database applications.

Typical declarations for ADO variables

```
Dim cnAP As Connection
Dim rsVendors As Recordset
```

Typical assignment statements for ADO variables

```
Set cnAP = New Connection
Set rsVendors = New Recordset
Set rsVendors = Nothing
```

Typical statements for working with ADO variables

```
rsVendors.Open "Vendors",cnAP,adOpenKeyset,adLockOptimistic,adCmdTable
txtName = rsVendors!VendorName
If rsVendors.EOF Then rsVendors.MoveLast
rsVendors.Close
```

A procedure that deletes a record from the data source associated with a data control

```
Private Sub cmdDelete_Click()
    If MsgBox("Are you sure you want to delete this record?", _
              vbYesNo + vbDefaultButton2 + vbQuestion) = vbYes Then
        adoVendors.Recordset.Delete
        adoVendors.Recordset.MoveNext
        If adoVendors.Recordset.EOF Then
            adoVendors.Recordset.Requery
            adoVendors.Recordset.MoveLast
        End If
    End If
End Sub
```

Description

- Use the Dim statement (Private or Public) to declare an object variable for an ADO object.

- After you declare an object variable for an ADO object, you use the Set statement to create an *instance* of the object and assign a reference to the object to the variable. To do that, you use the New keyword and the name of the ADO object.

- To disassociate a variable from the object it refers to, assign a value of Nothing to the variable. Then, the system resources associated with the object are released.

- After you create an instance of an object, you can refer to its properties, methods, and events in code.

- You can also refer to the properties and methods of a Recordset object defined by an ADO data control. To do that, you use the Recordset property of the data control as shown above.

- To refer to a field in a recordset, code the recordset name, the *bang operator* (!), and the field name as in rsVendors!VendorName.

Figure 6-9   Techniques for working with ADO objects through code

Exercise set 6-2: Enhance the bound form

In this exercise set, you'll start by adding a delete function to the Vendors form you created in exercise set 6-1. Then, you'll change the function of the data control so it doesn't provide for adding records, and you'll provide this function through code. When you're done, the Vendors form should look like this:

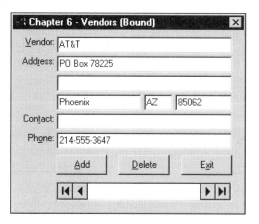

Add a delete function to the form

1. If necessary, open the application you created for exercise set 6-1 and display the Vendors form. Then, add a command button to this form to the left of the Exit button, change the name of this button to cmdDelete, and change its caption to &Delete.

2. Double-click on the Delete button to start its Click event procedure in the Code window. Then, add this code to the procedure:

```
If MsgBox("Are you sure you want to delete this record?", _
    vbYesNo + vbDefaultButton2 + vbQuestion) = vbYes Then
        adoVendors.Recordset.Delete
        adoVendors.Recordset.MoveNext
        If adoVendors.Recordset.EOF Then
            adoVendors.Recordset.Requery
            adoVendors.Recordset.MoveLast
        End If
End If
txtName.SetFocus
```

If you're using a Jet database, though, you can omit the Requery method from this code since it's not required when you're using client-side cursors.

3. Before you run the application, make sure the name of the text box that contains the vendor name and the name used in the last line of code are the same. Then, run the application, display a vendor you want to delete, and click on the Delete button. When the confirmation message is displayed, click on the No button to see that the record isn't deleted. Then, click on the Delete button again and delete the record. (If the vendor has related invoices and cascading deletes aren't in effect, you won't be able to delete the vendor record.)

4. Add a new record to the form, then try to delete it. *If you're using a SQL Server database with server-side cursors*, this should work correctly. But *if you're using a Jet database and client-side cursors*, the following error message will be displayed:

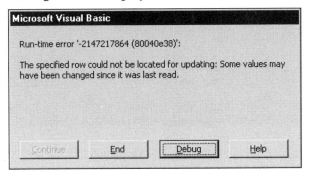

Then, click on the Debug button to see that the error occurred on the Delete method, and click on the End button in the toolbar to end the application. Because of the way client-side cursors work, you can't delete a new record without requerying the recordset first. And because that function isn't easy to implement in a bound form, the best solutions are (1) to avoid including add and delete functions on the same form or (2) develop an unbound form that works the way you want it to (you'll learn how to do that in the next section).

Use code to implement the add function

5. Change the EOFAction property of the data control to adDoMoveLast so the data control can't be used to add records. Then, add a command button to the left of the Delete button on the form with the name cmdAdd and the caption &Add.

6. Double-click on the Add button to display its Click event procedure in the Code window. Then, add the following code to the procedure:

```
adoVendors.Recordset.AddNew
txtName.SetFocus
```

7. Start the form, and click on the Last navigation button to move to the last record in the recordset. Then, click on the Next button to see that a new record isn't added.

8. Click on the Add button to add a new record, enter the information for the new record, and note the vendor name. Then, click on the Previous button to save the record, and click on the Next button to redisplay the new record.

9. Try to add another record with the same vendor name that you used in step 8. If the database has a unique constraint on the vendor name field, a message will be displayed that says you can't do that. Then, close the form.

10. Save the project and keep Visual Basic open if you're going to continue. Or, exit from Visual Basic if you want to take an extended break, because the rest of this chapter, which shows you how to develop unbound forms, can be taxing.

Basic skills for building unbound forms

The trouble with a data control is that its built-in functions limit the way the user interface works. To get around these limitations, though, you can build a form without using a data control, called an *unbound form*. Then, you can code all the functions of the user interface so it works just the way you want it to. When you complete this topic, you should be able to create simple unbound forms of your own.

How the unbound version of the Vendors form works

Figure 6-10 shows you what the unbound version of the Vendors form looks like and describes how it works. As you review this figure, you'll notice that the form provides some functions that weren't provided by the bound form. For example, the unbound form lets the user cancel out of an add or modify operation. It also displays an error message if the update of a new or existing record can't be done for some reason. Although you could probably figure out a way to implement these functions in a bound form, it wouldn't be easy.

To provide for navigation from one record to another, four command buttons at the bottom of this unbound form replace the data control of the bound form. Note, however, that they don't provide for the add and update functions that are built into a data control. Instead, these functions are implemented as separate command buttons on the form. That makes the form more intuitive for the user, and it simplifies the logic of the program.

To further improve the interface, the Add, Update, Delete, and navigation command buttons are enabled only when it makes sense. For example, the Update button isn't enabled in the form shown in this figure because none of the data in the form has been changed. As soon as the user changes any of this data, however, this button becomes available. By enabling and disabling these command buttons as the user works with the form, you limit what the user can do and maintain better control over the use of the form.

A form that uses code to maintain vendor records

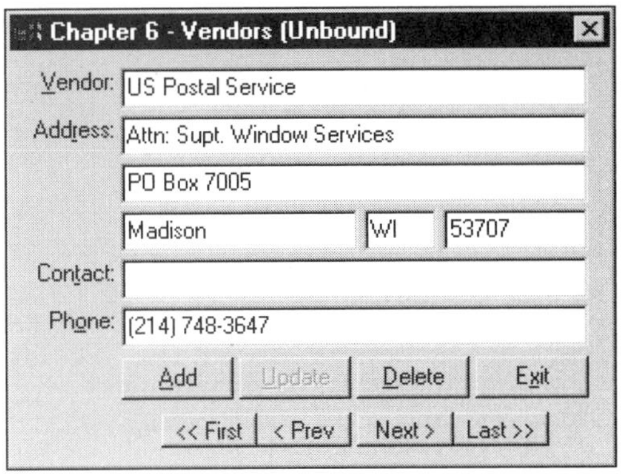

Description

- Unlike the bound version of the Vendors form, the navigation buttons in the unbound version shown above provide only for navigating through the recordset. They do not control the addition of new records or the updating of existing records.

- When an existing record is first displayed, the Update button is disabled as shown above. As soon as the user makes a change to the data in the form, however, the Update button is enabled and the Add, Delete, and navigation buttons are disabled. To save the changes, the user must click on the Update button or press the Enter key to activate the Update button (it's set as the default). To cancel the changes, the user can press the Escape (Esc) key.

- When the user clicks on the Add button, the controls are cleared, the Update button is enabled, and the Add, Delete, and navigation buttons are disabled. After the data for the new record is entered into the form, the user can save the record by clicking on the Update button or pressing the Enter key. To cancel the addition, the user can press the Esc key.

- If the user clicks on the Update button to add a new record or modify an existing record and a required field hasn't been entered, a message box is displayed identifying the field. If any other type of error occurs, a message box is displayed indicating that the record couldn't be saved. After acknowledging the error, the user can correct the entry and click on the Update button again or press the Esc key to cancel the operation.

- When the user clicks on the Delete button, a dialog box is displayed to confirm the delete operation. If the user confirms the operation, the record is deleted and the next record in the recordset is displayed.

Figure 6-10   How the unbound version of the Vendors form works

How to process data without using a data control

When you create an unbound form, you use Visual Basic code to provide the functions that are built into the data control. Figure 6-11 lists these functions and indicates what methods and statements you use to implement them and when each of them needs to be performed. Later in this chapter, when you see the code for the Vendors form, you'll see how these functions are actually implemented.

The key to developing an unbound form is knowing what events you need to respond to and what processing needs to be done in response to those events. Although the events aren't listed for the functions in this figure, you shouldn't have much trouble figuring out what the appropriate events are from the information in the last column in the table. For example, you'll want to open the connection and recordset for the form on the Load event of the form, which occurs when the form is first opened. And you'll want to save a new record or changes to an existing record when the user clicks on the Update button. Notice that because the controls on the form aren't bound to a data control, you have to provide the code for moving the data from the current record to the controls and from the controls to the current record.

You should also notice in this figure that a new record isn't added to the recordset until the user accepts the data for the new record by clicking on the Update button. Although you could add a record when the user clicks on the Add button, that's not necessary since the controls on the form aren't bound to the underlying recordset. This will make more sense when you see the complete code for this form.

Although this figure lists all of the functions that are needed to replace the functions of the data control, it doesn't list other functions that may be required by the Vendors form. When the user changes the data in one of the controls on the form, for example, the program must enable and disable the command and navigation buttons accordingly. Similarly, when the user presses the Escape key, the program must cancel the add or modify operation that was being performed.

Data control functions that must be provided through code

Function	Method or statement	When it should be executed
Open connection	Open method (Connection object)	When the form is loaded
Open recordset	Open method (Recordset object)	When the form is loaded
Recordset navigation	MoveFirst, MovePrevious, MoveNext, and MoveLast methods	When the user clicks on a navigation button or when other events require this movement
Move values from fields to controls	Assignment statements	When the recordset is opened, when the user clicks on a navigation button, when a record is deleted, and when changes to a record are canceled
Clear control values	Assignment statements	When the user indicates that he or she wants to add a record to the recordset
Add a new record to the recordset	AddNew method	When the user indicates that the recordset should be updated with the data for a new record
Move values from controls to current record, and update the recordset	Assignment statements, Update method	When the user indicates that the recordset should be updated with the data for a new record or the changes to an existing record
Close the connection and the recordset	Close method	When the users indicates that the connection or recordset is no longer needed

Description

- When you use code to process data, you must provide for the same functions that are provided by the data control. That includes opening the connection and recordset, navigating through and displaying the records in the recordset, adding new records to the recordset, and updating existing records.

- In addition to the data functions shown above, additional functions may be required when certain events occur. When the user changes the data in a control, for example, the Update button is enabled. Then, the user must click on the Update button to save the changes.

Note

- Before you can use ADO in an unbound form, you must include a reference to the ADO library. To do that, choose the References command from the Project menu and then select the Microsoft ActiveX Data Objects 2.0 Library option.

Figure 6-11   How to process data without using a data control

How to open a connection to a database

To open a connection to a database, you use the Open method of the Connection object as illustrated in figure 6-12. As you can see in the syntax for this method, you can code three arguments. The ConnectionString argument contains the information needed to connect to the data source and is stored in the Connection object's ConnectionString property. However, if you set the ConnectionString property before you open the connection, you can omit this argument. Also, if you include user ID and password information in the connection string, you can omit the UserID and Password arguments.

This figure also shows the arguments that you can code in the connection string. If you compare these arguments with the information that you include in the ConnectionString property of a data control, you'll see that it's nearly identical. Note, however, that most of the arguments can be coded with two different keywords. For example, you can use either Server or Data Source to specify the name of the server where the database resides, and you can use either Database or Initial Catalog to specify the name of the database. In contrast, when you build a connection string for a data control, ADO uses the Data Source and Initial Catalog keywords.

The example in this figure also shows how you can use the CursorLocation property of a Connection object to specify the location of the cursor. In this case, the cursor will be stored on the client, although the default is to store the cursor on the server. Notice that you must set the CursorLocation property before you open the connection because this property has no effect on an open connection.

If you look back to figure 6-8, you'll see two additional properties you can use with a Connection object. You can use the Provider property to set the OLE DB provider for a connection before you open it. And you can use the DefaultDatabase property to set or change the database that's specified in the connection string. You may want to do that, for example, if you want to let the user select from a list of databases that are available. Then, you can omit the Database argument from the connection string when you open the connection, present a list of available databases that the user can select from, and set the DefaultDatabase property depending on the user's selection. In most cases, though, you'll just include the Database argument in the connection string.

The syntax of the Open method for a Connection object

```
connection.Open [ConnectionString][, UserID][, Password]
```

Argument	Description
ConnectionString	A string that contains connection information (see the table below)
UserID	The user name to use when opening a connection to the data source
Password	The password to use when opening a connection to the data source

ConnectionString arguments for a SQL Server database

Argument	Description
Provider	The name of the OLE DB provider (SQLOLEDB)
Server/Data Source	The name of the server where the database resides
Database/ Initial Catalog	The name of the database
UID/UserID	The user name to use when connecting to the data source
PWD/Password	The password to use when connecting to the data source

Statements that open a connection to a SQL Server database

```
Dim cnAP As Connection
Set cnAP = New Connection
cnAP.CursorLocation = adUseClient
cnAP.Open "Provider=SQLOLEDB;Server=mmaserver;" _
        & "Database=AccountsPayable", "ed", "abc4xyz"
```

Notes

- The OLE DB provider name for SQL Server is SQLOLEDB. You can specify the provider for a Connection object in the ConnectionString argument as shown above, or you can set the Connection object's Provider property before you open the connection.

- You must supply a user ID and password in either the ConnectionString argument or in the UserID and Password arguments. If you don't, the connection will fail. If you specify a user ID and password in the UserID and Password arguments, they override any user ID and password specified in the ConnectionString argument.

- If you omit the Database/Initial Catalog argument from the connection string, you can identify the database after you open the connection by setting the Connection object's DefaultDatabase property.

Figure 6-12   How to open a connection to a database

How to open a recordset

Figure 6-13 shows you how to open a recordset using the Open method of the Recordset object. You shouldn't have any trouble figuring out how to use the various arguments of this method since they're similar to the properties that you use to define the recordset for a data control. In fact, the only argument that doesn't correspond directly to a data control property is the ActiveConnection argument.

In most cases, you'll use the ActiveConnection argument to identify the Connection object you want to use to open the recordset as illustrated by the first example in this figure. Here, an existing Connection object named cnAP is used to open a recordset object named rsVendors. Because a string containing a SELECT statement is used for the Source argument, the Options argument is set to adCmdText. The other arguments indicate that a keyset cursor will be created and optimistic locking will be used.

The second example in this figure shows how you can open a recordset without using a Connection object. Here, the ActiveConnection argument refers to a string that contains the connection information. When this Open method is executed, ADO actually creates a Connection object based on the information you supply. Unfortunately, you can't refer directly to this object through code like you can when you create a Connection object explicitly. And that means that you can't use the same connection for two or more recordsets. As a result, you'll want to use this technique only with applications that use a single recordset.

The syntax of the Open method for a Recordset object

```
recordset.Open [Source][, ActiveConnection][, CursorType]
               [, LockType][, Options]
```

Argument	Description
Source	A SQL statement, the name of a table, the name of a stored procedure, or a Command object (presented in chapter 8).
ActiveConnection	A valid Connection object or a string that contains all the necessary connection information.
CursorType	The type of cursor to be used for the recordset. The options are adOpenForwardOnly (default), adOpenKeyset, adOpenDynamic, and adOpenStatic.
LockType	The type of locking to be used for the recordset. The options are adLockReadOnly (default), adLockPessimistic, adLockOptimistic, and adLockBatchOptimistic.
Options	The type of information specified in the Source argument if it's not a Command object. The options are adCmdText (for a SQL statement), adCmdTable, adCmdStoredProc, and adCmdUnknown (default).

Statements that open a recordset with a SELECT statement and a Connection object

```
Dim rsVendors As Recordset, strSQL As String
Set rsVendors = New Recordset
strSQL = "SELECT * FROM Vendors ORDER BY VendorName"
rsVendors.Open strSQL, cnAP, adOpenKeyset, adLockOptimistic, adCmdText
```

Statements that open the same recordset using a connection string and no Connection object

```
Dim strConnection As String
strConnection = "Provider=SQLOLEDB;Server=mmaserver;" _
                & "UID=ed;PWD=abc4xyz;Database=AccountsPayable"
rsVendors.Open strSQL, strConnection, adOpenKeyset, _
               adLockOptimistic, adCmdText
```

Notes

- The Options argument helps ADO determine the type of information that's specified in the Source argument. If you omit this argument, ADO must make additional calls to the OLE DB provider to determine the type of data source, which can degrade performance. If the Options argument doesn't match the information in the Source argument, an error will occur.

- You can open a recordset without first creating a Connection object as shown in the second example above. If you need to open two or more recordsets on the same database, however, you can improve performance by creating a Connection object that can be used by all the recordsets.

Figure 6-13   How to open a recordset

How to use a control array

If two or more controls on a form perform similar functions, you may want to implement them as a *control array*. For instance, the command buttons that provide for navigation on the unbound Vendors form can be implemented as a control array. As you'll soon see, using a control array can simplify your code.

Figure 6-14 shows how to create and use a control array. To create an array, you just give two or more controls the same name. When you change the name of the second control to match the first one, Visual Basic warns you that the form already contains a control with that name. Then, if you continue with the name change, Visual Basic assumes that you want to create an array and gives each control a different index number starting with zero. In this example, you can see that both command buttons are named cmdNavigate, but their Index properties have different values.

Although the controls in an array appear as individual controls on the form, they're treated as a group. That means that when you click on a control in an array, an event occurs on the array, not on the individual control. However, the index value of the control that the event actually occurred on is passed to the event procedure. That way, you can use the index value within the procedure to determine what processing takes place.

The procedure in this figure illustrates how this works. Here, the control array consists of the four navigation buttons on the unbound Vendors form that let the user move to the first, previous, next, and last records in a recordset named rsVendors. When the user clicks on one of these buttons, this procedure is executed and the index value of the button that was clicked is stored in the variable named Index. Then, the procedure uses a Select Case statement to test the index value and determine which button was clicked.

If the index value is zero, for example, that means that the user clicked on the First button so the MoveFirst method is executed. And if the index value is one, that means that the user clicked on the Prev button so the MovePrevious method is executed. Notice that after the MovePrevious method is executed, the procedure checks to be sure that the current record pointer hasn't moved past the beginning of the file. If it has, the MoveFirst method is executed to move the pointer back to the first record. Similar processing is done if the user clicks on the Next button.

The properties for two controls in an array

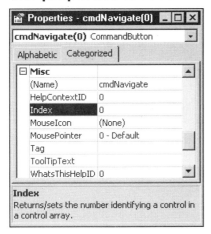
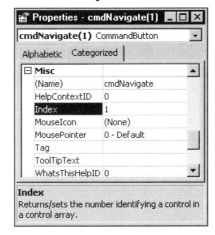

Code for working with the control array

```
Private Sub cmdNavigate_Click(Index As Integer)
    Select Case Index
        Case 0
            rsVendors.MoveFirst
        Case 1
            rsVendors.MovePrevious
            If rsVendors.BOF Then rsVendors.MoveFirst
        Case 2
            rsVendors.MoveNext
            If rsVendors.EOF Then rsVendors.MoveLast
        Case 3
            rsVendors.MoveLast
    End Select
End Sub
```

Description

- To create a control array, you add two or more controls of the same type to the form. Then, you change the names of the controls so they're all the same and Visual Basic sets the Index property of each control so it's unique.

- To refer to a control in an array, you use the control name followed by its index number in parentheses, starting with zero for the first control in the array as in this example:

    ```
    cmdNavigate(0)
    ```

- When you create a control array, the controls in the array are treated as a group. That means that you code a single event procedure for the entire array rather than coding an event procedure for each control in the array.

- When an event occurs on a control in an array, Visual Basic passes an argument to the event procedure that contains the index of the control that the event occurred on. Then, you can use that index to determine the processing that's done as shown above.

Figure 6-14   How to use a control array

Code for the unbound Vendors form

Figure 6-15 presents the complete code for the unbound Vendors form. Although this code is five pages long, it's worth taking the time to understand every procedure in it.

The Declarations section of the form module (1) contains the definitions of three variables and one constant that are used throughout the form. The first two variables are used to refer to the connection to the Accounts Payable database and the Vendors recordset. The third variable is used to indicate whether a new record is being added to the recordset. And the constant is used in the title bar of any dialog box that's displayed. Notice that the prefixes in these names start with an *m* to indicate that their scope is module-level.

In the event procedure for the Load event of the form (2), an instance of the Connection and Recordset objects are created and the connection and recordset are opened. Note that since the CursorLocation property of the connection isn't specified, server-side cursors will be used. In addition, the Open method of the recordset creates a keyset cursor, which is appropriate since the Vendors form lets users add, update, and delete records.

After opening the connection and recordset, the Load procedure calls three general procedures. The first procedure, LoadControls (3), moves the values from the fields in the current record in the recordset to the associated controls on the form. Notice that this procedure uses a With statement so the reference to the Vendors recordset doesn't have to be included on each assignment statement. Otherwise, a reference to a field would look like this:

```
mrsVendors!VendorName
```

If you look closely at the assignment statements in this LoadControls procedure, you'll see that four of them assign a field that's concatenated with a zero-length string (& ""). These concatenations are required because the database definition for each of these fields allows it to be null, but Visual Basic doesn't allow a null to be displayed in a text box. With the concatenation, though, a null field becomes a zero-length string, which is not the same as a null, and the error is avoided.

The second procedure that's called from the Load procedure is SetCommandButtons (4). This procedure enables or disables the Add, Delete, and Update command buttons and sets the Default property of the Update button based on the Boolean value that's passed to it. Since this value is True the first time this procedure is called, the Add and Delete buttons are enabled, the Update button is disabled, and the Default property of the Update button is set to False. By coding this procedure with a Boolean argument, you can also use this procedure to reverse these property settings as you'll see later in this program.

The third general procedure that's called from the Load procedure, SetNavigationButtons (5), works like the SetCommandButtons procedure. It receives a Boolean value of True or False and then uses that value to enable or disable the four navigation buttons on the form. Notice that because these command buttons are part of a control array, this procedure uses an index to refer to each control.

Visual Basic code for the unbound Vendors form

```
Option Explicit                                                      1
Dim mcnAP As Connection
Dim mrsVendors As Recordset
Dim mbAddNew As Boolean
Const msDialogTitle = "Chapter 6 - Vendors (Unbound)"


Private Sub Form_Load()                                              2
    Set mcnAP = New Connection
    Set mrsVendors = New Recordset
    mcnAP.Open "Provider=SQLOLEDB;Server=mmaserver;" _
            & "Database=AccountsPayable", "ed", "abc4xyz"
    mrsVendors.Open "SELECT * FROM Vendors ORDER BY VendorName", _
                    mcnAP, adOpenKeyset, adLockOptimistic, adCmdText
    LoadControls
    SetCommandButtons True
    SetNavigationButtons True
End Sub


Private Sub LoadControls()                                          3
    With mrsVendors
        txtName = !VendorName
        txtAddress1 = !VendorAddress1 & ""
        txtAddress2 = !VendorAddress2 & ""
        txtCity = !VendorCity
        txtState = !VendorState
        txtZipCode = !VendorZipCode
        txtContact = !VendorContact & ""
        txtPhone = !VendorPhone & ""
    End With
End Sub


Private Sub SetCommandButtons(bVal As Boolean)                     4
    cmdAdd.Enabled = bVal
    cmdUpdate.Enabled = Not bVal
    cmdUpdate.Default = Not bVal
    cmdDelete.Enabled = bVal
End Sub


Private Sub SetNavigationButtons(bVal As Boolean)                  5
    Dim i As Integer
    For i = 0 To 3
        cmdNavigate(i).Enabled = bVal
    Next
End Sub
```

Figure 6-15   Code for the unbound version of the Vendors form (part 1 of 5)

When the user clicks on a navigation button, the Click event procedure for the Navigate control array (6) is executed. This procedure uses a Select Case statement to determine which button was clicked and then executes the appropriate Move method on the recordset. In this statement, each case provides for one index value for the array of navigation buttons. When the index value is zero, for example, it means that the user clicked on the First button so the MoveFirst method is executed. And when the index value is one, it means that the user clicked on the Prev button so the MovePrevious method is executed. But if that method moves the current record pointer past the beginning of the file (the BOF property is true), the MoveFirst method is executed to move the pointer back to the first record. In this way, the Select Case statement provides for all four buttons in the array.

After the Select Case statement repositions the current record pointer, the LoadControls procedure (3) is called to display the current record. Then, the SetCommandButtons (4) and SetNavigationButtons (5) procedures are called to reset the state of the command and navigation buttons, and the focus is moved to the control named txtName, which is the first editable control on the form.

When the user clicks on the Add button, the Click event procedure for this control (7) is executed. This procedure starts by setting the mbAddNew variable to true to indicate that a record is going to be added to the recordset. Next, the ClearControls procedure (8) is called, which moves empty strings ("") to the controls on the form so the user can enter the data for the new record into them. Then, the SetCommandButtons procedure (4) is called, but this time the value that's passed to this procedure is False. That causes the Add and Delete command buttons to be disabled and the Update button to be enabled and set as the default command button. Finally, the last statement in this procedure moves the focus to the txtName control.

Please note that the recordset isn't affected by any of the statements in the cmdAdd_Click procedure. Instead, the controls are cleared so the user can enter the data for a new record into the controls. Then, if the user clicks on the Update button, the cmdUpdate_Click event procedure adds a new blank record to the recordset, moves the data from the controls to that record, and updates that record.

Visual Basic code for the unbound Vendors form

```
Private Sub cmdNavigate_Click(Index As Integer)                    6
    With mrsVendors
        Select Case Index
            Case 0
                .MoveFirst
            Case 1
                .MovePrevious
                If .BOF Then .MoveFirst
            Case 2
                .MoveNext
                If .EOF Then .MoveLast
            Case 3
                .MoveLast
        End Select
    End With
    LoadControls
    SetCommandButtons True
    SetNavigationButtons True
    txtName.SetFocus
End Sub
```

```
Private Sub cmdAdd_Click()                                         7
    mbAddNew = True
    ClearControls
    SetCommandButtons False
    txtName.SetFocus
End Sub
```

```
Private Sub ClearControls()                                        8
    txtName = ""
    txtAddress1 = ""
    txtAddress2 = ""
    txtCity = ""
    txtState = ""
    txtZipCode = ""
    txtContact = ""
    txtPhone = ""
End Sub
```

Figure 6-15   Code for the unbound version of the Vendors form (part 2 of 5)

When the user clicks on the Update button, the Click event procedure (9) for that button is executed. This procedure starts by using an On Error statement to enable an error-handling routine that's coded at the end of the procedure. After the On Error statement, the update procedure calls a function named ValidData (10) from within an If statement. This function checks that a value has been entered into each required field. To do that, it starts by declaring a string variable that is used to display a message to the user if a required field isn't entered. Then, it uses an If statement to check each required field for an empty string. If a field does contain an empty string, the focus is moved to that field and the message variable is assigned an appropriate value. If none of the required fields contain an empty string, the value of the function is set to True. Note, however, that it isn't necessary to set the value of this function to False if a field is invalid because that's the default value of a Boolean variable. Finally, if any of the fields are invalid, the ValidData procedure uses a MsgBox function to display an error message.

If the data is valid, the update procedure (9) checks the mbAddNew variable to determine if a record is being added. If this variable is true, the AddNew method is executed to add a new blank record to the recordset. Next, a procedure named LoadRecord (11) is called to move the values from the form controls to the current record. After that, the Update method is used to save the record to the Vendors table. This works whether the data for a new record or an updated record is being saved. Then, the mbAddNew variable is set to False, the SetCommandButtons (4) and SetNavigationButtons (5) procedures are called, and the focus is moved to the txtName control. Finally, the Exit Sub statement ends the procedure and prevents the error-handling routine that follows from being executed.

However, this error-handling routine is executed if an error occurs at any time during the execution of the update procedure (9). For instance, since the database has a unique constraint that prohibits duplicate vendor names, an error will occur when the Update method tries to save a record with a duplicate name to the Vendors table. Then, the first statement in the error-handling routine calls a procedure named DisplayErrorMessage (16), which uses the MsgBox function to display the Number, Description, and Source properties of the Err object.

This is followed by a statement that uses the CancelUpdate method to cancel the update if the EditMode property of the Vendors recordset indicates that a new blank record has been added to the recordset (adEditAdd). In this procedure, this condition will only exist if the AddNew method was successful but the Update method wasn't. In that case, the blank record needs to be removed from the recordset, which is done by the CancelUpdate method.

Visual Basic code for the unbound Vendors form

```
Private Sub cmdUpdate_Click()                                            9
On Error GoTo ErrorHandler
    If ValidData Then
        If mbAddNew Then mrsVendors.AddNew
        LoadRecord
        mrsVendors.Update
        mbAddNew = False
        SetCommandButtons True
        SetNavigationButtons True
        txtName.SetFocus
    End If
    Exit Sub
ErrorHandler:
    DisplayErrorMessage
    If mrsVendors.EditMode = adEditAdd Then mrsVendors.CancelUpdate
End Sub
```

```
Private Function ValidData() As Boolean                                 10
    Dim strMessage As String
    If txtName = "" Then
        txtName.SetFocus
        strMessage = "You must enter a vendor name."
    ElseIf txtCity = "" Then
        txtCity.SetFocus
        strMessage = "You must enter a city."
    ElseIf txtState = "" Then
        txtState.SetFocus
        strMessage = "You must enter a state code."
    ElseIf txtZipCode = "" Then
        txtZipCode.SetFocus
        strMessage = "You must enter a zip code."
    Else
        ValidData = True
    End If
    If Not ValidData Then
        MsgBox strMessage, vbOKOnly, msDialogTitle
    End If
End Function
```

```
Private Sub LoadRecord()                                                11
    With mrsVendors
        !VendorName = txtName
        !VendorAddress1 = txtAddress1
        !VendorAddress2 = txtAddress2
        !VendorCity = txtCity
        !VendorState = txtState
        !VendorZipCode = txtZipCode
        !VendorContact = txtContact
        !VendorPhone = txtPhone
    End With
End Sub
```

Figure 6-15   Code for the unbound version of the Vendors form (part 3 of 5)

When the user clicks on the Delete command button, the Click event procedure for the control (12) is executed. This procedure is similar to the event procedure you saw in figure 6-9. It uses the MsgBox function to confirm the delete operation and executes the Delete method if it's confirmed. Then, it moves to the next record and checks the EOF property. If this property is true, it requeries the recordset and moves to the last record. Finally, this procedure loads the form controls, sets the command and navigation buttons, and moves the focus to the txtName control.

Before I go on, you should know that the Delete method in this procedure may not work if the vendor record that's being deleted has related invoice records and referential integrity is in effect. In that case, the vendor record can be deleted only if the related invoice records are also deleted. In other words, cascading deletes must be in effect for the relationship between the Vendors and Invoices tables. If cascading deletes aren't in effect, you'll probably want to add code that checks for related invoices or that traps the appropriate error. You'll have a better idea how to do that after you read the next two chapters.

When the user changes any of the data in the text boxes on the form, the Change event procedure for the changed control is executed. Although only three of these procedures are shown in this figure (13), the complete code must include one change procedure for each text box. Each of these procedures must call the SetNavigationButtons procedure to disable the navigation buttons, and call the SetCommandButtons procedure to disable the Add and Delete buttons and enable the Update button.

Visual Basic code for the unbound Vendors form

```
Private Sub cmdDelete_Click()                                    12
On Error GoTo ErrorHandler
    If MsgBox("Are you sure you want to delete this record?", _
            vbYesNo + vbDefaultButton2 + vbQuestion, msDialogTitle) _
        = vbYes Then
        With mrsVendors
            .Delete
            .MoveNext
            If .EOF Then
                .Requery
                .MoveLast
            End If
            LoadControls
        End With
    End If
    SetCommandButtons True
    SetNavigationButtons True
    txtName.SetFocus
    Exit Sub
ErrorHandler:
    DisplayErrorMessage
End Sub
```

```
Private Sub txtName_Change()                                     13
    SetNavigationButtons False
    SetCommandButtons False
End Sub

Private Sub txtAddress1_Change()
    SetNavigationButtons False
    SetCommandButtons False
End Sub
    .
    .
    .

Private Sub txtPhone_Change()
    SetNavigationButtons False
    SetCommandButtons False
End Sub
```

Figure 6-15   Code for the unbound version of the Vendors form (part 4 of 5)

Anytime the user presses a key, the KeyDown event occurs. If the KeyPreview property of the form is set to True, this event occurs on the form. Otherwise, it occurs on the control that has the focus. For the purposes of this application, the KeyPreview property of the form has been set to True so a single KeyDown procedure (14) can be used.

The KeyDown procedure begins by checking whether the Esc key was pressed, which indicates that the user wants to cancel the current operation. If it was pressed, the LoadControls procedure is called to move the field values from the current record in the recordset to the controls on the form. If the user pressed the Esc key while adding a record, that causes the last record that was displayed to be redisplayed. If the user was modifying a record, that causes the record to be redisplayed with its original values.

To understand how that works, you have to remember that the recordset isn't updated until the user clicks on the Update button. Until then, only the values of the controls are changed. So if the user is adding a record, the current record is the record that was displayed before the user clicked on the Add button. And if the user is modifying a record, the current record contains the field values before they were modified. After the current record is redisplayed in the form, the SetCommandButtons and SetNavigationButtons procedures are called to reset the state of these buttons. In addition, if a record was being added when the Esc key was pressed, the mbAddNew variable is reset to False.

The last event procedure (15) occurs when the user clicks on the Exit button. This procedure closes the Connection and Recordset objects and releases the resources used by these objects by setting the object variables that refer to them to Nothing. Then, the procedure unloads the form to end the application.

Now that you've browsed through all the procedures in the program, you may want to review them to see how they work together. If you do, you'll find seven general procedures: LoadControls, LoadRecord, ClearControls, SetCommandButtons, SetNavigationButtons, ValidData, and DisplayErrorMessage. The name of each procedure is designed to give a clear indication of what each procedure does, and you need similar procedures whenever you develop a maintenance application.

The event procedures, of course, call the general procedures whenever they are needed. So once you code the general procedures, it's relatively easy to code most of the event procedures. The only difficult ones are those that use the ADO methods: the one for the Load event of the form, the one for the Click event of the cmdNavigate array; the one for the Click event of the cmdUpdate button; and the one for the Click event of the cmdDelete button.

When you start developing a program, of course, you may not know what general procedures you're going to need. As you code the event procedures, though, you'll discover functions that are needed by more than one event procedure. Then, you can move the code for those functions from the event procedures into general procedures.

Visual Basic code for the unbound Vendors form

```
Private Sub Form_KeyDown(KeyCode As Integer, Shift As Integer)          14
    If KeyCode = vbKeyEscape Then
        LoadControls
        SetCommandButtons True
        SetNavigationButtons True
        If mbAddNew Then mbAddNew = False
    End If
End Sub
```

```
Private Sub cmdExit_Click()                                              15
    mrsVendors.Close
    mcnAP.Close
    Set mrsVendors = Nothing
    Set mcnAP = Nothing
    Unload frmVendors
End Sub
```

```
Private Sub DisplayErrorMessage()                                       16
    MsgBox "Error Code: " & Err.Number & vbCrLf & _
        "Description: " & Err.Description & vbCrLf & _
        "Source: " & Err.Source, vbOKOnly + vbCritical, msDialogTitle
End Sub
```

Figure 6-15   Code for the unbound version of the Vendors form (part 5 of 5)

Exercise set 6-3: Build an unbound form

In this exercise set, you will create an unbound form like the one in figure 6-10. To do that, you will implement all of the database functions through code.

Start a new project and prepare it for coding

1. Start a new Standard EXE project. Then, change the Name property of the form to frmVendors, the Caption property to Vendors (C6 Unbound), the KeyPreview property to True, the BorderStyle property to Fixed Single, and the StartUpPosition property to CenterScreen.

2. Use the Properties command in the Project menu to change the ProjectName property to C6Unbound, and use the References command to add a reference to the Microsoft ActiveX Data Objects 2.0 Library. Next, click on the Save Project button to display the Save File As dialog box, and use the Create New Folder button to create a new folder named Chapter 6 Unbound. Then, save the form and project in this folder with the names frmVendors and C6Unbound.

3. Add the label and text box controls to the form and change the Caption and Alignment properties of the label controls so they look like those in figure 6-10. Then, enter these names for the Name properties of the text boxes: txtName, txtAddress1, txtAddress2, txtCity, txtState, txtZipCode, txtContact, and txtPhone.

4. Add the four command buttons for the navigation functions at the bottom of the form. Change the Caption properties of these buttons so they appear as in figure 6-10. Then, change the name of each button to cmdNavigate starting with the left button and moving to the right. When you change the name of the second button, a message will be displayed that asks whether you want to create a control array. Click on Yes, then change the names of the remaining buttons and notice that the Index properties of these buttons range from 0 through 3.

Start the coding

5. Open the Code window, and enter the following statements in the Declarations section:

```
Dim mcnAP As Connection
Dim mrsVendors As Recordset
```

6. Enter the procedure for the Load event of the form shown in part 1 of figure 6-15, excluding the call to the SetCommandButtons procedure since those buttons haven't been added to the form yet. As you enter the arguments for the Open methods of the Connection and Recordset objects, be sure they're appropriate for the database you're using.

    If you're using a SQL Server database, you may have to change the Provider, Server, UserID, and Password arguments for the Open method of the Connection object so they are appropriate for your system.

If you're using a Jet database, you need to change the arguments for the Open method for the Connection object so it uses the Jet OLE DB driver and the right path to the database :

```
mcnAP.Open "Provider=Microsoft.Jet.OLEDB.3.51;" & _
    "Data Source=C:\Murach\VB6\Databases\AccountsPayable.mdb"
```

You also need to change the CursorType argument in the Open method for the Recordset object to adOpenStatic. (Since Jet doesn't support server-side cursors, it will automatically use client-side cursors.)

7. Enter the LoadControls and SetNavigationButtons procedures shown in part 1 of figure 6-15. Then, enter the procedure for the Click event of the cmdNavigate control array as shown in part 2 of this figure, excluding the call to the SetCommandButtons procedure.

8. Start the application to test the form. Next, use the navigation buttons to display the records in the recordset. Enter a change for a record, move to another record, and back to the changed record to see that the change wasn't saved since that code hasn't been entered yet. If necessary, fix any bugs and test again. Then, click on the Close button and return to the Code window.

Add the add, update, and delete functions to the form

9. Add the Add, Update, Delete, and Exit command buttons shown in the form in figure 6-10. Change the Caption properties for these buttons so they appear as shown in this figure, and change the Name properties to cmdAdd, cmdUpdate, cmdDelete, and cmdExit.

10. Open the Code window and add statements to the Declarations section to declare a Boolean variable named mbAddNew and a constant named msDialogTitle as shown in part 1 of figure 6-15. Then, add the general procedure named SetCommandButtons, and add calls to this procedure from the Load event procedure for the form and the Click event procedure for the control array as shown in this figure. You will now have entered all of the code in figure 6-15 through the navigation procedure.

11. Add the remaining code in figure 6-15. Try to do this by entering, testing, and debugging a few procedures at a time.

12. When you've got all the procedures entered, test all of the functions of the application. To start, modify an existing record to see how that works. Next, add a record to see how that works. Then, delete the record you just added. If necessary, fix any bugs and test again.

13. Click on the Exit button to close the form. Then, save the form and project.

Perspective

This goal of chapter has been to introduce you to database programming and the range of what it can entail. Although you can develop bound forms that display data with relative ease, developing bound forms that update, add, and delete records can get somewhat complicated. Beyond that, though, you'll often want to develop unbound forms that are more intuitive for the user and that work just the way you want them to...but that gets even more complicated.

If you've taken the time to do the exercise sets in this chapter, you should now have a good understanding of what database programming is and what you need to know to become proficient at it. But there's much more to learn about database programming than what's in this chapter. So in the next two chapters of this section, you'll learn some additional skills for building bound and unbound forms. And in the last three chapters, you'll learn how to use some of the new Visual Basic 6 tools for building forms, developing reports, and working with databases.

Terms you should know

bound form
ADO data control
recordset
cursor
bound control
client-side cursor
server-side cursor
dynamic cursor
keyset cursor
static cursor
forward-only cursor
optimistic locking
pessimistic locking
collection
populate
copy buffer
instance
bang operator
unbound form
control array

7

How to build bound forms with ADO

In chapter 6, you learned the basic skills for building both bound and unbound forms that access and maintain data with ADO. Now, you'll learn some additional skills for building bound forms with ADO. In particular, you'll learn how to use some of the special Visual Basic controls for working with data. You'll also learn the coding techniques that you need for building bound forms.

When you finish this chapter, you should be able to develop bound forms at a professional level for a wide variety of database applications. Then, in chapter 8, you can learn how to build unbound forms with ADO. You'll need those skills when you build applications that require the extra control that you can only get through unbound forms.

How to work with bound controls **254**
Two forms that use bound controls 254
How to work with the DataList and DataCombo controls 256
How to work with the DataGrid control 258
How to set the properties for a DataGrid control 260
Property settings for the controls on the Vendors form 262
Why this application uses client-side cursors 264
Exercise 7-1: Build the Vendors form 266

Coding techniques for bound forms **268**
How to use some common events for an ADO data control 268
How to use the MoveComplete event of an ADO data control 270
How to use the Error event of an ADO data control 272
The code for the standard module of the Vendors application 274
The code for the Vendors form 274
Bugs that occur when using a Jet database 276
Exercise set 7-2: Write the code for the Vendors form 278

The property settings and code
for the New Vendor form **280**
The property settings for the New Vendor form 280
The code for the New Vendor form 282
More about bugs that occur when using a Jet database 284
Exercise set 7-3: Build the New Vendor form 286

Perspective **288**

How to work with bound controls

In chapter 6, you learned how to build a bound Vendors form that used text boxes for all of the bound data. Now, you'll learn how to use some of the new Visual Basic 6 controls for bound data as you build an enhanced version of the bound Vendors form plus a New Vendor form.

Two forms that use bound controls

Figure 7-1 presents the enhanced version of the bound Vendors form along with a New Vendor form. When the user selects a vendor from the DataCombo control at the top of the Vendors form, the application displays the information for that vendor in the other controls on the form. Here, a DataList control is used to list the unpaid invoices for the vendor, and a DataGrid control is used to display the detail for each of the unpaid invoices.

The DataCombo, DataList, and DataGrid controls are special controls called *data-bound controls*. They became available with Visual Basic 6, and they are designed to work with OLE DB providers and ADO. In fact, if you want to use ADO, you can't use the standard DBCombo, DBList, and DBGrid controls because they're designed to work with ODBC drivers and DAO.

To add a vendor to the database, the user can click on the New button on the Vendors form. This displays the New Vendor form. Then, the user can enter new vendor data into the seven text boxes and two DataCombo controls.

As you learn how to build these forms, you'll discover that each of the data-bound controls uses an ADO data control as its data source. The DataCombo control that displays the vendor names, for example, gets its data from an ADO data control that uses the Vendors table as its source of data. Similarly, the DataList and DataGrid controls get their data from an ADO data control that uses the Invoices table as its source of data.

Although the controls on these forms get their data from ADO data controls, you don't see the data controls when the application is running because their Visible properties are set to False. The data controls are hidden because the functions that are provided by the visible interface of the data control—navigating through existing records and adding new records—are implemented using other techniques. For example, navigation on the Vendors form is provided by the Vendor Name DataCombo control, and the addition of new records is provided by the New command button. That makes the form more intuitive to the user, but still takes advantage of the data control for moving data between the recordset it defines and the bound controls on the form.

When you use two or more data controls on the same form, you have to make sure that they're *synchronized*. When you use the DataCombo control to select a different vendor, for example, you want to be sure that the correct invoice information is displayed in the DataList and DataGrid controls. Later in this chapter, you'll learn that you can use the events and methods of the data controls and the data-bound controls to synchronize this data.

The Vendors and New Vendor forms

Vendors (C7 Bound)

Vendor Selection
Vendor Name:
| Malloy Lithographing Inc | ▼ | New | Delete |

→ **DataCombo control**

Vendor Information:
5411 Jackson Road
PO Box 1124
Ann Arbor, MI 48106
(313) 555-6113

Unpaid Invoices:
P-0608
0-2436

YTD Purchases:
$213,039.65

→ **DataList control**

Last Transaction Date:
March 28, 1999

→ **Multi-line textbox**

Unpaid Invoice Detail

Invoice No.	Invoice Date	Invoice
▶ P-0608	12/14/98	$20,
0-2436	1/9/99	$10,

Vendor Record: 66 of 122

DataGrid control

New Vendor

New Vendor Information

Name: American Office Supply
Address: 2134 W. Main St.
          Suite 936
City: San Luis Obispo
State: CA ▼   94472
Contact: Ed Koop
Phone: 805-555-7498
Terms: Net due 30 days ▼

OK   Cancel

Description

- The primary purpose of the Vendors form is to display the vendor and invoice information for a specific vendor.
- The DataCombo control on the Vendors form lets the user choose the name of a vendor from a drop-down list. Then, the data for that vendor is displayed.
- If the user clicks on the New button on the Vendors form, the New Vendor form is displayed so the user can enter the data for a new vendor. Then, the user can click on the OK button to add the record to the database, or click on the Cancel button to cancel the operation and close the form.
- If the user clicks on the Delete button on the Vendors form, the current record is deleted. However, this button is disabled if the vendor has any unpaid invoices.
- The DataList control on the Vendors form displays the invoice numbers for all of the selected vendor's unpaid invoices.
- The DataGrid control on the Vendors form displays detail information for all of the selected vendor's unpaid invoices.
- The *multi-line text box* is just a text box with its MultiLine property set to True. In this application, it is used to display some of the fields in the vendor record.

Figure 7-1   Two forms that use bound controls

How to work with the DataList and DataCombo controls

Figure 7-2 presents the properties of the DataList and DataCombo controls that you're most likely to use. The DataSource and DataField properties work just like they do for any other bound control. They identify a data source and a field in the recordset associated with that data source. When you use an ADO data control as the data source, this binds the control to the data source. In the New Vendor form in the previous figure, for example, the Terms DataCombo control is bound to the TermsID field in the recordset associated with the Vendors data control.

In contrast, the RowSource property identifies the data source that defines the recordset used to populate the control, and the ListField property identifies the field in that recordset that should be displayed. For the Terms DataCombo control in the New Vendor form in the previous figure, the RowSource property identifies the data control for the Terms table and the ListField property identifies the TermsDescription field in that table. As a result, the terms description for the current vendor is displayed in the DataCombo control.

For now, you can assume that data controls are going to be used as the data sources for both the DataSource and RowSource properties. In chapter 9, though, you'll learn how to create a DataEnvironment object that you can use instead of a data control as the data source or row source. Then, you use the DataMember or RowMember property to identify the Command object within the DataEnvironment object that delivers the recordset that you want.

Another property that you may need to set for a DataCombo or DataList control is the BoundColumn property. This property identifies the field in the recordset defined by the RowSource property that is passed to the field identified by the DataField property. For example, the BoundColumn property for the Terms DataCombo control in the New Vendor form specifies the TermsID field, which is the field that's common to both the Vendors and Terms tables.

Later, when you write the code for a form, you can use the BoundText property when you need to get the current value of the column that's bound by the BoundColumn property. You can also use the Text property when you need to refer to the text in the control. You'll see this illustrated in the code for the Vendors form.

Note, however, that you may not need to set all of the properties in figure 7-2 for each DataCombo or DataList control that you use. For instance, the DataCombo and DataList controls on the Vendors form in the previous figure are not bound to a data control by the DataSource field. Instead, this is handled by code. You'll understand why this is necessary after you review the property settings and code for this application, and you'll understand this even better after you do the exercise sets for this chapter.

Some of the properties of the DataList and DataCombo controls

Property	Description
DataSource	The name of the data source that the control is bound to. This is usually a data control or a DataEnvironment object.
DataMember	If you select a DataEnvironment object for the DataSource property, use this property to select the Command object that you want to use.
DataField	The name of the field that the control is bound to.
RowSource	The name of the data source that provides the data to be displayed. This is usually a data control or a DataEnvironment object.
RowMember	If you select a DataEnvironment object for the RowSource property, use this property to select the Command object that you want to use.
ListField	The name of the field in the data source defined by the RowSource and RowMember properties that's displayed by the control.
BoundColumn	The field defined by the RowSource property that is used to pass data to the field defined by the DataSource and DataField properties. This can be the same field that's used in the ListField property.
BoundText	This property returns or sets the value of the current field specified by the BoundColumn property.
DataFormat	Determines the format in which the bound data is displayed.
MatchEntry	Determines how the data in a control is searched as text is entered. 0 – dblBasicMatching (the default) only matches the first character entered with the items in the list, while 1 – dblExtendedMatching matches all the characters entered with the items in the list.
Style	(DataCombo only) Determines whether the list portion of a combo box drops down or is fixed. It also determines whether text can be entered into the text portion of the combo box.

Description

- When you use a DataCombo or DataList control, you can bind the control to a field that's defined by one ADO data control but display data from a field that's defined by another ADO data control. The field that's specified in the BoundColumn property is the field that's common to both of the recordsets that are defined by the data controls.

- To bind a DataList or DataCombo control to a field, use the DataSource and DataField properties. To display data in a DataList or DataCombo control, use the RowSource and ListField properties.

- If you create a DataEnvironment object as shown in chapter 9, you can use it for a DataSource or RowSource property. In that case, you use the DataMember or RowMember property to specify the command that you want to use within the DataEnvironment object.

Note

- Before you can use the DataList and DataCombo controls, you need to add the Microsoft DataList Controls 6.0 (OLEDB) to your Toolbox.

Figure 7-2   How to work with the DataList and DataCombo controls

How to work with the DataGrid control

If you want to display more than one record from a recordset at the same time, you can use a DataGrid control like the one shown in the form in figure 7-1. In this example, this control is bound to a recordset defined by an ADO data control. This recordset contains all of the unpaid invoices for the current vendor, and each column in the grid is bound to a different field in the recordset.

Like the DataList and DataCombo controls, you can also bind a DataGrid control to a DataEnvironment object. Then, you use the DataMember property of the control to identify the Command object that defines the recordset for the control. You'll learn more about using using DataEnvironment and Command objects in chapter 9.

Figure 7-3 shows how to work with this type of grid control. After you add a DataGrid control to a form, you set its DataSource property to identify the ADO data control that it's bound to. Once you've done that, you can use the Retrieve Fields command in the shortcut menu for the grid control to retrieve all the fields from the recordset that's defined by the data control. When you do that, each of the fields appears as a column in the grid as shown in this figure.

To edit the columns in the grid, you use the Edit command in its shortcut menu. When you select this command, the grid enters *UI-active mode*. From this mode, you can use the commands in the shortcut menu (which is somewhat different from the one shown) to add, copy, delete, and move columns. You can also change column widths or the row heights while you're in this mode by dragging the column and row dividers.

The shortcut menu for a DataGrid control

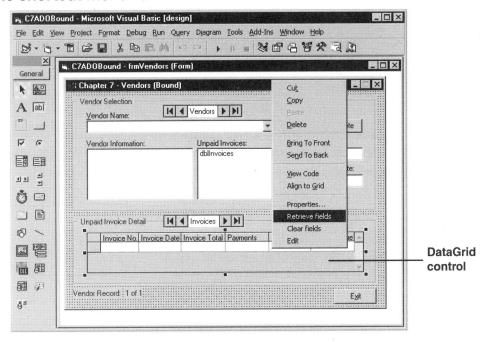

DataGrid control

Description

- You use the DataSource property of the DataGrid control to establish its source of data. This property provides the name of the ADO data control that the grid is bound to.

- Once you bind a DataGrid control to an ADO data control, you can use the Retrieve Fields command in the DataGrid's shortcut menu to add fields to the grid. When you do that, each field in the recordset defined by the data control becomes a column in the DataGrid.

- If you choose the Edit command from its shortcut menu, the DataGrid enters into *UI-active mode*. In this mode, you can use the commands in the UI-active shortcut menu to change the layout of the columns and rows in the DataGrid control.

- The Cut, Copy, Paste, Delete, Insert, and Append commands in the UI-active shortcut menu let you manipulate the columns in a DataGrid control. To select the column you wish to work with, click on the column header. To select two or more columns, drag over the column headers.

- You can also change individual column widths while in UI-active mode by dragging the column dividers. And you can change the height of all the rows by dragging a row divider.

- To exit from UI-active mode, click anywhere outside the DataGrid control.

Note

- Before you can use the DataGrid control, you need to add the Microsoft DataGrid Control 6.0 (OLEDB) to your Toolbox.

Figure 7-3   How to work with the DataGrid control

How to set the properties for a DataGrid control

Figure 7-4 presents some of the properties of the DataGrid control. These properties are displayed on the tabs of the Property Pages dialog box that you can display by selecting the Properties command from the shortcut menu for the control. Some of these properties are also available from the Properties window.

In addition to the four tabs referred to in this figure, four other tabs are available in the Property Pages dialog box. These tabs let you set properties that affect how the Tab and arrow keys work, what colors and fonts are used, and how splits work if the grid is split into two or more panes.

The AllowAddNew, AllowDelete, and AllowUpdate properties in the General tab determine what you can do with the data in the grid. By default, you can update records but you can't add or delete records.

In contrast, the Columns tab provides properties for each column in the grid. Although the initial values of these properties are set when you retrieve the fields from the ADO data control, some of these values change when you change the grid in UI-active mode. For each column, the Caption property contains the text that's displayed at the top of the column, which by default is the field name.

The Layout tab also provides properties for each column. Three of the properties in this tab that you might want to change are Locked, AllowSizing, and Alignment. If you change the Locked property to True, the user won't be able to change the data in the column even if updating is allowed.

The Format tab lets you set the FormatType property, which determines the format in which fields are displayed. As a result, you will frequently want to change the default format settings.

The Property Pages dialog box for a DataGrid control

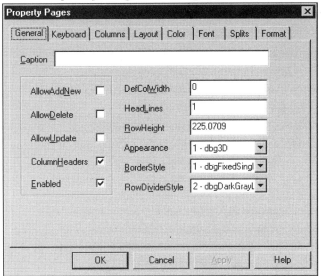

Common DataGrid properties

Tab	Property	Description
General	AllowAddNew	Determines whether records can be added to the grid. By default, records can't be added.
General	AllowDelete	Determines whether records can be deleted from the grid. By default, records can't be deleted.
General	AllowUpdate	Determines whether records in the grid can be modified. By default, records can be modified.
Columns	Caption	The text that's displayed in the column header for the selected field. The default caption is the name of the field.
Columns	DataField	The field that the selected column is bound to.
Layout	Locked	Determines whether data in the selected column can be edited. By default, the columns aren't locked.
Layout	AllowSizing	Determines whether the selected column can be sized by the user. By default, columns can be sized.
Layout	Alignment	The position of the data in the selected column. The default is left aligned.
Format	FormatType	The format that's used to display the data in the selected column.

Operation

- To access the Properties Pages dialog box, choose the Properties command from the shortcut menu for the DataGrid control.
- To set the properties for a field in the Columns, Layout, or Format tab, you select the field you want to format before you set its properties.

Figure 7-4   How to set the properties for a DataGrid control

Property settings for the controls on the Vendors form

Figure 7-5 shows the property settings for the data-bound controls on the Vendors form in figure 7-1. To make this form work the way you want it to, you need to add two hidden ADO data controls to the form along with the text box, DataCombo, DataList, and DataGrid controls.

If you study the properties for the ADO data controls, you can see that the RecordSource property for each control is a SELECT statement. For instance, the SELECT statement for the Vendors data control gets all of the records in the Vendors table sorted in VendorName sequence. This data is automatically retrieved when the application starts and the Vendors form is loaded.

In contrast, the SELECT statement for the Invoices control gets selected fields from the Invoices table, but only when the VendorID field has a value of -1. Since no vendor has an ID of -1, though, no records are returned. This SELECT statement is coded this way because you only want to retrieve invoice information *after* a vendor has been selected. As you will see later, code is used to provide a different SELECT statement for the RecordSource property whenever a vendor is selected. You still need to provide a starting SQL statement for the RecordSource property, though, or an error will occur when the form that uses the ADO data control is loaded.

If you look at the LockType and Mode properties for the two data controls, you can see that they vary based on what the application needs to do with the records that are retrieved. Since records can be deleted from the Vendors table, the properties for the Vendors data control are set so the records can be read or written and so the locking is optimistic. On the other hand, since the records in the Invoices table can't be changed or deleted, the properties for the Invoices data control are set so the records can only be read.

Once the properties are set for the data controls, you can set the properties for the YTD Purchases and Last Transaction Date text boxes as shown in this figure. Here, you can see that they are bound to the Vendors data control via the DataSource and DataField properties just as the text boxes were bound in chapter 6. You can also see that the Locked properties are set to True so users can't change the data in these fields, and the DataFormat properties are set so the data is easier to read.

In contrast, the multi-line text box isn't bound to a data source. This means that the application must provide code that populates this text box. Note, however, that its MultiLine property is set to True so the data can fill two or more lines within the box.

Basic property settings for the two ADO data controls

Property	Value
CommandType	1 – adCmdText
ConnectionString	Provider=SQLOLEDB;Server=<server name>;Database=AccountsPayable
CursorLocation	3 – adUseClient
CursorType	3 – adOpenStatic
Password	Your password
UserName	Your user name
Visible	False

Other property settings for the two ADO data controls

Property	Vendors control	Invoices control
Name	adoVendors	adoInvoices
Caption	Vendors	Invoices
LockType	3 – adLockOptimistic	1 – adLockReadOnly
Mode	3 – adModeReadWrite	1 – adModeRead

RecordSource	SELECT *
	 FROM Vendors
	 ORDER BY VendorName
		SELECT InvoiceNumber, InvoiceDate, InvoiceTotal,
		    PaymentTotal, CreditTotal,
		    InvoiceTotal - PaymentTotal - CreditTotal
		    AS BalanceDue
		 FROM Invoices
		 WHERE VendorID = -1

Property settings for the text boxes

Property	YTD Purchases	Last Transaction Date	Vendor Information
Name	txtYTDPurchases	txtLastTranDate	txtVendorInfo
DataSource	adoVendors	adoVendors	
DataField	YTDPurchases	LastTranDate	
DataFormat	Currency	Date (MMMM d, yyyy)	
Locked	True	True	True
MultiLine	False	False	True

Figure 7-5   Property settings for the controls on the Vendors form (part 1 of 2)

If you look at the property settings for the DataCombo and DataList controls, you may be surprised to see that they aren't bound to a data source via the DataSource property. However, their RowSource and ListField properties are set so these controls display data that's retrieved through the Vendors and Invoices data controls. In contrast, the DataGrid control is bound to the Invoices data control through its DataSource property.

After you set the data source for the DataGrid control, you can retrieve the fields for the grid. Since the SELECT statement for the Invoices data control lists six fields (five from the Invoices table plus one calculated field named BalanceDue), that's the number of columns that the grid will include. Then, you can use the Property Pages dialog box to set the properties shown in this figure for the General, Splits, Columns, Layout, and Format tab. These properties just format the grid the way you want it.

Why this application uses client-side cursors

Perhaps you've noticed that both data controls used by this Vendors form use client-side cursors. In addition, as you will soon see, the three data controls that are used by the New Vendor form use client-side cursors. That may lead you to wonder why client-side cursors are used if it's true that server-side cursors work more efficiently for some applications.

The short answer is that you can't get this application to work with server-side cursors. To start, you can't use an ORDER BY clause in a SQL statement that's used as the RecordSource property for a data control with server-side cursors, and there are other problems too. In fact, when I contacted the Microsoft help staff, they recommended using client-side cursors. Perhaps that explains why the Visual Basic default is client-side cursors. In our experience, the more you try to work with server-side cursors, the more you realize that they have some serious limitations.

Basic property settings for the DataCombo, DataGrid, and DataList controls

Property	DataCombo control	DataList control	DataGrid control
Name	dbcVendors	dblInvoices	dbgInvoices
RowSource	adoVendors	adoInvoices	
ListField	VendorName	InvoiceNumber	
BoundColumn	VendorID		
DataSource			adoInvoices
Style	2 – dbcDropdownList		

General and Splits tab settings for the DataGrid control

Tab	Property	Setting
General	AllowUpdate	Not checked
Splits	Scrollbars	2 - dbgVertical

Columns, Layout, and Format tab settings for the columns of the DataGrid control

Column	Caption (Columns tab)	DataField (Columns tab)	Alignment (Layout tab)	FormatType (Format tab)
Column 0 (InvoiceNumber)	Invoice No.	InvoiceNumber	0 – dbgLeft	General
Column 1 (InvoiceDate)	Invoice Date	InvoiceDate	2 – dbgCenter	Date
Column 2 (InvoiceTotal)	Invoice Total	InvoiceTotal	1 – dbgRight	Currency
Column 3 (PaymentTotal)	Payments	PaymentTotal	1 – dbgRight	Currency
Column 4 (CreditTotal)	Credits	CreditTotal	1 – dbgRight	Currency
Column 5 (BalanceDue)	Balance Due	BalanceDue	1 – dbgRight	Currency

Notes

- Before you can use the DataList and DataCombo controls, you need to add the Microsoft DataList Controls 6.0 (OLEDB) to your Toolbox.
- Before you can use the DataGrid control, you need to add the Microsoft DataGrid Control 6.0 (OLEDB) to your Toolbox.

Figure 7-5   Property settings for the controls on the Vendors form (part 2 of 2)

Exercise 7-1: Build the Vendors form

Starting with this exercise set, the instructions will be less explicit than they have been in the earlier chapters based on the assumption that you now know how to do most of the basic development functions. In this first exercise set, you'll build a Vendors form like the one in figure 7-1. In exercise set 7-2, you'll add the code that makes this form work the way you want it to. And in exercise set 7-3, you'll add the New Vendor form and its code.

Start a new project and prepare it for use with ADO

1. Start Visual Basic and begin a Standard EXE project. Then, change the Name property of the form to frmVendors, the Caption property to Vendors (C7 Bound), and the StartUpPosition property to CenterScreen. Last, use the Properties command in the Project menu to change the ProjectName property to C7Bound.

2. Click on the Save Project toolbar button to display the Save File As dialog box, and use the Create New Folder button to create a new folder named Chapter 7 Bound. Then, save the form and project in this folder with the names frmVendors and C7Bound.

3. Use the Components command in the Project menu to add these components to the Toolbox: Microsoft ADO Data Control 6.0 (OLEDB), Microsoft DataGrid Control 6.0 (OLEDB), and Microsoft DataList Controls 6.0 (OLEDB).

Add the controls to the new form

4. Use the Toolbox to add the required controls to the new form so it looks something like this:

5. Set the properties for the two ADO data controls as summarized in figure 7-5 (part 1). Make sure that the ConnectionString, Password, and UserName properties are appropriate for the type of database you're using, just as you did for the exercises in chapter 6.

6. Set the properties for the labels, frames, and command buttons on your own using figure 7-1 as a guide. For the label at the bottom of the form, enter "Vendor Record: " as its Caption property. When this form is running, though, this property will be changed by code. Also, set the Name property of this label to lblRecordNum, and set the Name properties of the command buttons to cmdNew, cmdDelete, and cmdExit.

7. Then, set the properties for the text boxes, DataCombo, DataList, and DataGrid controls as summarized in figure 7-5 (part 2), but not including the properties for the DataGrid tabs.

8. Select the Retrieve Fields command from the shortcut menu for the DataGrid control. If you've set the other properties right, that should create DataGrid columns for the six fields specified in the SELECT statement for the Invoices data control.

9. Select the Properties command from the shortcut menu for the DataGrid control, and set the tab properties that are summarized in figure 7-5.

10. To make the final adjustments to the DataGrid control, select the Edit command from its shortcut menu so you enter UI-active mode. Then, drag the column dividers so all six columns fit in the grid.

Test and save the form

11. Start the project. If you've done everything right, the form should look something like the one in figure 7-1. Then, you should also be able to select a vendor from the drop-down DataCombo list by using the mouse or the up and down arrow keys on the keyboard, and you should be able to see data in the YTD Purchases and Last Transaction Date boxes. Note, however, that this data doesn't change when you select a new vendor. Note also that there isn't any data in the other controls. To get this form to work right, you need to code the required procedures, which you'll do in the next exercise set.

12. Save the project and form in their current states. Next, change the Visible property for each data control in the Vendors form to True, and delete the WHERE clause from the SELECT statement in the RecordSource property of the Invoices data control. Then, test the project again. This time you should see data in the DataList and DataGrid controls, and you should be able to move from one invoice to another by using the scroll bars on these controls. You should also be able to change the data in the two text boxes by using the Vendors data control, and you should be able to change the data in the DataGrid control by using the Invoices data control. Note, however, that the Vendors data and the Invoices data isn't synchronized because that has to be done with code.

13. Close the project *without saving it* so the project reverts back to the way it was in step 11.

Coding techniques for bound forms

Now that you know how to use some of the special controls for working with bound forms, you'll learn some coding techniques for working with these forms. In particular, you'll learn how to code procedures for some common events that occur as an ADO control is used.

How to use some common events for an ADO data control

Figure 7-6 summarizes some of the common events that occur as you use an ADO data control. For instance, the EndOfRecordset event occurs when the application tries to move past the end of a recordset, and the Error event occurs when an error occurs during an operation performed by the data control. You can then use these events to trigger procedures that perform the processing that needs to be done.

Some of the most useful events are those that start with the word *Will* and those that end with the word *Complete*. For instance, the WillMove event occurs before the current position in the recordset associated with the data control changes, and the MoveComplete event occurs after the current position changes. Similarly, the WillChangeRecord event occurs before a record in the recordset is changed, and the ChangeRecordComplete event occurs after it is changed.

In this figure, you can see how the WillChangeRecord event can be used to trigger a procedure that checks the validity of a zip code field before the current record is actually updated. Here, the procedure calls a function named ValidZipCode to do the validity checking. Then, if the zip code isn't valid, the MsgBox function is used to display an error message. In addition, the adStatus parameter is set to a constant value (adStatusCancel) that cancels the change that's in progress.

If you study the Sub statement for the procedure in this figure, you can see that four arguments (or *parameters*) are used with this event procedure. To enter these parameters into your code, you can select the data control from the Object list at the top of the Code window and the event from the Event list. Then, the Sub and End Sub statements are generated automatically along with the parameter list.

Incidentally, when you try to look up information about these events, you'll find them listed as methods, not events. But don't let that confuse you. If, for example, you type in EndOfRecordset in the MSDN Help system, you'll see an entry for the EndOfRecordset method. Nevertheless, that entry will give you the information you need.

Some common events for an ADO data control

Event	Occurs ...
EndOfRecordset	When the application tries to move past the end of the recordset.
Error	After a data access error occurs during an operation performed by the data control.
WillMove MoveComplete	Before and after the current position in the recordset changes.
WillChangeField FieldChangeComplete	Before and after the changes are made to a specific field in the recordset.
WillChangeRecord RecordChangeComplete	Before and after changes are made to one or more records in the recordset.
WillChangeRecordset RecordsetChangeComplete	Before and after changes are made to the recordset object itself.

The parameters for a WillChangeRecord event procedure

Parameter	Description
adReason	The reason this event has occurred.
cRecords	The number of records that will be affected.
adStatus	A status value that you can set to cancel the operation that caused this event.
pRecordset	The name of the recordset associated with this event.

A WillChangeRecord event procedure that validates an entry

```
Private Sub adoVendors_WillChangeRecord(ByVal adReason _
        As ADODB.EventReasonEnum, _
    ByVal cRecords As Long, _
    adStatus As ADODB.EventStatusEnum, _
    ByVal pRecordset As ADODB.Recordset)
  If Not ValidZipCode Then
    MsgBox "Invalid zip code. Please re-enter.", _
        vbInformation + vbOKOnly, "Invalid data entry"
    adStatus = adStatusCancel
    txtZipCode.SetFocus
  End If
End Sub
```

Differences between the event declarations for ADO 2.0 and ADO 2.1

- When you upgrade from ADO 2.0 to ADO 2.1, the pRecordset parameter that is automatically declared as ADODB.Recordset must be manually changed to ADODB.Recordset20. This is a documented problem that you can read about by downloading knowledge base article Q222145 from the http://support.microsoft.com web site.

- This affects the pRecordset parameters for all of the ADO data control events listed above, except the Error event.

Figure 7-6   How to use some common events for an ADO data control

How to use the MoveComplete event of an ADO data control

When another record in the recordset associated with a data control becomes the current record, the MoveComplete event occurs on the data control. Then, you can use this event to perform operations like synchronizing the data in related recordsets with the current record.

In figure 7-7, for example, you can see how this event can be used in two different procedures. The first procedure displays the value of the AbsolutePosition property of the recordset in the Caption property of the data control. This causes the record number for the current record to be displayed in the middle of the data control.

In the second procedure in this figure, you can see how this event can be used to synchronize the data in one data control with the current record in another data control. Here, a data control named adoVendors defines a recordset that contains all of the records in a table of vendors, and a second data control named adoInvoices defines a recordset that contains all of the records in a table of invoices that are related to the current vendor. Then, when the current vendor changes, the MoveComplete event is used to update the recordset associated with the adoInvoices data control so it displays the invoices for the new current vendor.

To do that, the event procedure first constructs a SELECT statement in a string variable. This SELECT statement selects only those invoices that have a vendor ID equal to the value in the VendorID field in the Vendors recordset. Then, the procedure sets the RecordSource property of the Invoices data control equal to the value of the SELECT statement in the string variable. Last, after the RecordSource property is changed, the Refresh method of the Invoices data control is executed to rebuild the recordset based on the new RecordSource property.

If you're using ADO 2.1 instead of ADO 2.0, please remember that the pRecordset parameter in the two procedures in this figure must be changed to

```
pRecordset As ADODB.Recordset20
```

This is summarized at the bottom of the previous figure.

The parameters for a MoveComplete event procedure

Parameter	Description
adReason	The reason this event has occurred.
pError	If an error occurred during this event, this parameter will contain the error number. Otherwise, it's not set.
adStatus	A status value that you can set to cancel the operation that caused this event.
pRecordset	The name of the recordset associated with this event.

A MoveComplete event procedure that displays the current record number in the data control

```
Private Sub adoVendors_MoveComplete(ByVal adReason _
        As ADODB.EventReasonENum, _
    ByVal pError As ADODB.Error, adStatus As ADODB.EventStatusEnum, _
    ByVal pRecordset As ADODB.Recordset)
    adoVendors.Caption = "Record " & adoVendors.Recordset.AbsolutePosition
End Sub
```

A MoveComplete event procedure that synchronizes the data in one data control with the current record in another data control

```
Private Sub adoVendors_MoveComplete(ByVal adReason _
        As ADODB.EventReasonENum, _
    ByVal pError As ADODB.Error, adStatus As ADODB.EventStatusEnum, _
    ByVal pRecordset As ADODB.Recordset)
    Dim strSQL as String
    strSQL = "SELECT InvoiceNumber, InvoiceDate, InvoiceTotal, " & _
                "PaymentTotal, CreditTotal, " & _
                "InvoiceTotal - PaymentTotal - CreditTotal " & _
                    "AS BalanceDue " & _
            "FROM Invoices " & _
            "WHERE InvoiceTotal - PaymentTotal - CreditTotal > 0 " & _
                "AND VendorID = " & adoVendors.Recordset!VendorID
    adoInvoices.RecordSource = strSQL
    adoInvoices.Refresh
End Sub
```

Description

- The MoveComplete event occurs after the current record pointer is moved to a new record. This event is typically used to synchronize the data defined by the data control's recordset with the data in another recordset.

- The AbsolutePosition property returns the absolute position of the current record in the recordset. To use this property, you must be using a client-side cursor.

- The Refresh method rebuilds the data control's recordset. You can use this method to update a recordset after you change the RecordSource property of the data control.

Figure 7-7   How to use the MoveComplete event of an ADO data control

How to use the Error event
of an ADO data control

When you use an ADO data control to work with data, the data control automatically handles ADO errors for you. It does that by displaying a dialog box like the one shown at the top of figure 7-8. As you can see, the message is just a brief description of the error that occurred.

If you want to replace this default error-handling with custom processing or if you want to provide additional processing when an error occurs, you can code a procedure for the Error event of the data control. Note, however, that this event only occurs when you perform an operation by clicking on one of the navigation buttons on the data control. It does not occur when you execute a method on the recordset object that's associated with the data control.

In this figure, you can see a simple procedure for the Error event of an ADO data control. This procedure displays the values in four of the parameters that are passed to it when the event occurs: ErrorNumber, Description, Scode, and Source. As a result, this message is more complete than the default message.

After the message is displayed, the procedure in this figure sets the fCancelDisplay parameter to True. As a result, the default processing for the error is cancelled and only the custom message is displayed. If this parameter weren't changed, both the default and the custom message would be displayed.

A default message for an ADO data control error

The parameters for an Error event procedure

Parameter	Type	Description
ErrorNumber	Long	The error number associated with the error that occurred.
Description	String	A brief description of the error that occurred.
Scode	Long	The error code that's returned from the server.
Source	String	The name of the source that caused the error.
HelpFile	String	The full path to a help file that contains more information about the error.
HelpContext	Long	The help context number used to find help information about the error.
fCancelDisplay	Boolean	A boolean value that you can set to display or cancel the default error message. If you set this to True, the default message isn't displayed.

An Error event procedure that displays an error message

```
Private Sub adoVendors_Error(ByVal ErrorNumber As Long, _
        Description as String, ByVal Scode As Long, _
        ByVal Source As String, ByVal HelpFile As String, _
        ByVal HelpContext As Long, fCancelDisplay As Boolean)
    Dim strMessage As String
    strMessage = "Error number: " & ErrorNumber & vbCrLf & _
                 "Description: " & Description & vbCrLf & _
                 "Code: " & Scode & vbCrLf & "Source: " & Source
    MsgBox strMessage, vbOKOnly + vbCritical, "Data control error"
    fCancelDisplay = True
End Sub
```

Description

- The Error event is triggered when a data access error occurs during an operation that's performed by a data control, not when you issue a method on a recordset that's associated with a data control.

- When a data access error occurs during an operation that's done by a data control, the data control automatically displays a dialog box that describes the error. Although this message is usually adequate, you can code an Error event procedure that provides custom information.

Figure 7-8   How to use the Error event of an ADO data control

The code for the standard module of the Vendors application

Now that you've learned how to use some of the events for an ADO data control, you should understand the code for the Vendors application. To start, figure 7-9 presents the code for its standard module. The global constant can be used as the title for any message boxes that are displayed by the procedures in any of the other modules. The public procedure can be called by the error-handling routine in any procedure in any module of this application.

The code for the Vendors form

Figure 7-9 also presents the code for the procedures in the Vendors form module. Here, the Form_Load procedure (1) sets the Text property of the dbcVendors DataCombo control to the first vendor name in the Vendors recordset. That causes the Change event of the control to fire. As you'll see in a minute, that procedure synchronizes the other data on the form with the current vendor.

Right after the Load event for a form occurs, the Activate event occurs. Unlike the Load event, which occurs only when the form is loaded, the Activate event occurs each time the form becomes the active form. In this figure, the Form_Activate procedure (2) is used to set the focus on the DataCombo control so the user can use it to select a vendor.

When a user selects a different vendor from the DataCombo control or when the Text property of the control is changed through code, the dbcVendors_Change procedure (3) is executed. It consists of one statement that uses the Find method of the recordset defined by the Vendors data control to set the current record to the one that has its VendorID field equal to the value in the BoundText property of the DataCombo control. The fourth argument for this Find method (adBookmarkFirst) is a constant that indicates that the search should start with the first record in the recordset.

After the current record in the Vendors recordset is changed, the Change procedure calls the FormatVendorInfo procedure (4), which populates the multi-line text box (txtVendorInfo) with vendor information. To do that, it uses a series of Immediate If functions (IIfs) that check to see whether the next field in the Vendors recordset is null or blank. If it is, nothing is added to the multi-line text box; otherwise, the field is added to the previous contents of the text box. This coding ensures that blank lines won't be displayed in the text box.

When the FormatVendorInfo procedure finishes, control returns to the Change procedure (3). This procedure then sets the RecordSource property of the Invoices data control to a new SQL statement and issues the Refresh command. That synchronizes the Vendors recordset with the Invoices recordset so only the invoices for the current vendor are displayed in the DataGrid control and in the DataList control.

After the data controls are synchronized, the next statement uses an IIf function to set the Enabled property of the Delete button. If the value of the

Code for the standard module

```
Option Explicit
Public Const gsDialogTitle = "Chapter 7 - Vendors (bound)"
```

```
Public Sub DisplayErrorMessage()
    MsgBox "Error code: " & Err.Number & vbCrLf & "Error description: " & _
            Err.Description & vbCrLf & "Error source: " & Err.Source, _
            vbOKOnly + vbCritical, gsDialogTitle
End Sub
```

Code for the Vendors form

```
Option Explicit
```

```
Private Sub Form_Load()                                                    1
    dbcVendors.Text = adoVendors.Recordset!VendorName
End Sub
```

```
Private Sub Form_Activate()                                                2
    dbcVendors.SetFocus
End Sub
```

```
Private Sub dbcVendors_Change()                                            3
    Dim strSQL As String
    adoVendors.Recordset.Find "VendorID = " & dbcVendors.BoundText, , , _
                            adBookmarkFirst
    FormatVendorInfo
    strSQL = "SELECT InvoiceNumber, InvoiceDate, InvoiceTotal, " & _
            "PaymentTotal, CreditTotal, " & _
            "InvoiceTotal - PaymentTotal - CreditTotal AS BalanceDue " & _
            "FROM Invoices " & _
            "WHERE InvoiceTotal - PaymentTotal - CreditTotal > 0 AND " & _
            "VendorID = " & adoVendors.Recordset!VendorID
    adoInvoices.RecordSource = strSQL
    adoInvoices.Refresh
    cmdDelete.Enabled = IIf(adoInvoices.Recordset.RecordCount > 0, _
                            False, True)
    lblRecordNum = "Vendor Record: " & adoVendors.Recordset.AbsolutePosition _
                & " of " & adoVendors.Recordset.RecordCount
End Sub
```

Notes

- When I first coded the procedures for this form, I divided the code in the Change procedure (3) between two event procedures. Then, the dbcVendors_Change procedure contained only the statement that uses the Find method, while an adoVendors_MoveComplete procedure contained all of the other code. That worked because the MoveComplete event occurs whenever the position in the recordset changes.

- The trouble with using the MoveComplete event, though, is that it occurs whenever the current record changes. As a result, the MoveComplete procedure is executed unnecessarily when the MoveNext method is executed in the Delete procedure and later when the New Vendor form is used to add a record to the recordset. That's why it's better to put all the code in the Change procedure.

Figure 7-9   The code for the standard module and the Vendors form (part 1 of 2)

RecordCount property of the Invoices recordset is greater than zero, which means there are unpaid invoices for the vendor, the Delete button is disabled. Otherwise, it's enabled. Then, the last statement sets the Caption property of the label control at the bottom of the Vendors form so it displays both the absolute position and the total number of records in the Vendors recordset.

When the user clicks on the Delete button in the Vendors form, the cmdDelete_Click procedure (5) is executed. This event procedure first displays a message box to confirm the deletion. Then, if the user clicks on the Yes button, the vendor is deleted, the record position is adjusted, the recordset is refreshed, the Text property of the DataCombo control is set to the vendor name in the current record, and the focus is moved to that control. But if an error occurs during this process, the error-handling routine calls the DisplayErrorMessage procedure in the standard module.

When the user clicks on the New button in the Vendors form, the cmdNew_Click procedure (6) displays the New Vendor form. The 1 after the Show method for the New Vendor form indicates that the form is *modal*. That means that it remains the active form until the user either adds a record or cancels the operation. In other words, the user can't switch to another form until the modal form is closed.

Bugs that occur when using a Jet database

The primary goal of this book is to teach you how to develop database applications that use the database management systems that Visual Basic is especially designed for: SQL Server and Oracle. When you're learning, though, you're likely to use an Access (or Jet) database running on your own PC for testing the applications you develop. Unfortunately, that may lead to bugs that you won't encounter when you're using a SQL Server database.

If, for example, you're using the Learning Edition of Visual Basic with an Access database, the Find method in the Change procedure (3) will blow up the first time it's executed. That's a problem with the Jet OLE DB provider. To work around that problem, you need to code a procedure that replaces the use of the Find method, as shown in appendix C.

But even if you're using the Professional or Enterprise Edition of Visual Basic, the Jet OLE DB provider won't work right for this application. After the cmdDelete_Click procedure (5) deletes a record, for example, the vendor name of the deleted record still appears in the Vendors combo box. This is due to a timing problem within Visual Basic that lets the Vendors data control get refreshed before the record in the recordset has had time to be deleted.

A quick and dirty solution is to add a loop after the Delete method with the To value adjusted to the speed of your PC (large enough to slow the refresh function down, but not so large that the processing delay is noticeable):

```
Dim lngLoop As Long
For lngLoop = 1 To 1000000
Next lngLoop
```

The right solution, though, is for Microsoft to fix the bugs in the Jet provider.

Code for the Vendors form (continued)

```
Private Sub FormatVendorInfo()                                           4
    With adoVendors.Recordset
        txtVendorInfo = ""
        txtVendorInfo = IIf(!VendorAddress1 = " " Or _
            IsNull(!VendorAddress1),  txtVendorInfo, !VendorAddress1 & vbCrLf)
        txtVendorInfo = IIf(!VendorAddress2 = " " Or  _
            IsNull(!VendorAddress2), txtVendorInfo, _
            txtVendorInfo & !VendorAddress2 & vbCrLf)
        txtVendorInfo = txtVendorInfo & !VendorCity & ", " & _
            !VendorState & " " & !VendorZipCode & vbCrLf
        txtVendorInfo = IIf(!VendorContact = " " Or _
            IsNull(!VendorContact), txtVendorInfo, _
            txtVendorInfo & !VendorContact & vbCrLf)
        txtVendorInfo = IIf(!VendorPhone = " ", txtVendorInfo, _
            txtVendorInfo & !VendorPhone)
    End With
End Sub
```

```
Private Sub cmdDelete_Click()                                           5
On Error GoTo ErrorHandler
    If MsgBox("Delete this vendor?", _
            vbYesNo + vbDefaultButton2 + vbQuestion, _
            gsDialogTitle) = vbYes Then
        With adoVendors.Recordset
            .Delete
            .MoveNext
            If .EOF Then .MoveLast
            adoVendors.Refresh
            dbcVendors.Text = !VendorName
        End With
        dbcVendors.SetFocus
    End If
    Exit Sub
ErrorHandler:
    DisplayErrorMessage
End Sub
```

```
Private Sub cmdNew_Click()                                             6
    frmNewVendor.Show 1
End Sub
```

```
Private Sub cmdExit_Click()                                            7
    Unload Me
End Sub
```

Figure 7-9   The code for the standard module and the Vendors form (part 2 of 2)

Exercise set 7-2: Write the code for the Vendors form

In this exercise set, you'll write the code that makes the Vendors form that you created in exercise set 7-1 work the way you want it to. You'll also add a standard module that includes one general procedure that can be called from a procedure in the Vendors module or later from a procedure in the New Vendor module.

Start the project and add a standard module

1. Open the C7Bound project that you created in exercise set 7-1.

2. Add a standard module to the project by selecting Add Module from the Project menu. Next, set the Name property to modStandard. Then, save the module by right clicking on it in the Project Explorer and selecting Save modStandard.

3. Add the global constant and Sub procedure shown in figure 7-9 to the standard module.

Add the code for the Vendors form that makes it display the right data

4. Add the Form_Load and Form_Activate procedures shown in figure 7-9 to the Vendors module. Then, test the project to see that a vendor name now appears in the DataCombo box when the application starts.

5. Add the dbcVendors_Change procedure shown in figure 7-9 to the Vendors module, omitting the call to the FormatVendorInfo procedure. Then, test the project to see that the data in the YTD Purchases and Last Transaction Date boxes changes when you select a new vendor in the DataCombo box. *If you're using the Learning Edition of Visual Basic and the program blows up on the Find method*, make the programming changes that are presented in appendix C.

6. Add the call to the FormatVendorInfo procedure, then enter that procedure. *If you're using a Jet database*, though, use an empty text string ("") in the If conditions instead of a text string that contains one space. This is due to the differences in the way SQL Server and Access handle empty strings.

7. Test the project. At this point, all of the data for each vendor should be displayed properly as you move from one vendor to another. If not, you need to debug the project.

Add the Delete and Exit procedures

8. Add the cmdDelete_Click procedure shown in figure 7-9 to the Vendors module. Next, add this statement right after the On Error statement:

    ```
    Err.Raise 76
    ```

    Then, test the project to make sure that the DisplayErrorMessage procedure in the standard module works properly. Last, end the application, return to the Code window, and delete the Err.Raise statement. (You won't test the delete function itself until the next exercise set.)

9. Add the cmdExit_Click procedure shown in figure 7-9. Then, test the project to makes sure that it works right.

Save the project

10. At this point, you haven't added the code for the cmdNew_Click procedure because you haven't yet created the New Vendor form. You'll do that in the next exercise set. For now, save the project, and leave it open if you're going to continue.

The property settings and code for the New Vendor form

Now that you know how the Vendors form works, you should have no trouble understanding how the New Vendor form works. After you study its property settings and code, you can build this form in the last exercise set for this chapter.

The property settings for the New Vendor form

Figure 7-10 presents the property settings for the three data controls and the two DataCombo controls that are used by the New Vendor form shown in figure 7-1. The other controls on this form are just a frame, labels, text boxes, and command buttons so you should already know how to set their properties.

Since new records will be added to the recordset defined by the adoVendors data control, the Mode property for this control is set to adModeReadWrite. The LockType property for this control is set to adLockOptimistic. In contrast, since the recordset defined by the States and Terms data controls will only be read, their Mode and LockType properties are set to adModeRead and adLockReadOnly.

Note also that the initial RecordSource property for the Vendors data control is set to a SELECT statement that doesn't return any records. That's because this form is only used to add new vendors to the database. In contrast, the RecordSource properties for the other data controls are set to SELECT statements that retrieve all of the records in the States and Terms tables.

After you set the properties for the data controls, you can set the properties for the State and Terms DataCombo controls. For the Terms control, the DataSource and DataField properties bind it to the TermsID field in the recordset defined by the Vendors data control. Then, the RowSource and ListField properties are set so this box displays the values in the TermsDescription field in the recordset defined by the Terms data control. Last, the BoundColumn property is required so the value in the TermsID field in the current Terms record (not the terms description in the DataCombo control) is passed to the TermsID field in the Vendors record when the new record is updated.

The property settings for the States DataCombo control are similar to those for the Terms control. The main difference is that the field displayed in the control (StateCode) is the same as the field that the control is bound to (VendorState). As a result, the BoundColumn property doesn't need to be set because you want the value in the DataCombo control to be passed to the data source field (VendorState) when the new record is updated.

For both DataCombo controls, dbcDropDownList is used as the Style property. This prevents a user from entering text into the text portion of the control. That way, the user can't enter invalid data.

Basic property settings for the three ADO data controls

Property	Value
CommandType	1 – adCmdText
ConnectionString	Provider=SQLOLEDB;Server=<server name>;Database=AccountsPayable
CursorLocation	3 – adUseClient
CursorType	3 – adOpenStatic
Password	Your password
UserName	Your user name
Visible	False

Other property settings for the ADO data controls

Property	Vendors control	States control	Terms control
Name	adoVendors	adoStates	adoTerms
Caption	Vendors	States	Terms
Mode	3 – adModeReadWrite	1 – adModeRead	1 – adModeRead
LockType	3 – adLockOptimistic	1 – adLockReadOnly	1 – LockReadOnly
RecordSource	SELECT * FROM Vendors WHERE VendorID = -1	SELECT * FROM States ORDER BY StateCode	SELECT * FROM Terms ORDER BY TermsID

Property settings for the DataCombo controls

Property	State combo box	Terms combo box
Name	dbcStates	dbcTerms
RowSource	adoStates	adoTerms
ListField	StateCode	TermsDescription
DataSource	adoVendors	adoVendors
DataField	VendorState	TermsID
BoundColumn		TermsID
Text	<blank>	<blank>
MatchEntry	1 – dblExtendedMatching	1 – dblExtendedMatching
Style	2 – dbcDropDownList	2 – dbcDropDownList

Note

* The DropDownList style for a DataCombo control prevents the user from entering a value in the text portion of the control that isn't in the list.

Figure 7-10   The Property settings for the New Vendor form

The code for the New Vendor form

Figure 7-11 presents all the code for the New Vendor form, which is displayed when the user clicks on the New button on the Vendors form. Once the New Vendor form becomes the active window, its Activate event occurs so its Form_Activate event procedure (1) is executed. Within this procedure, the AddNew method creates a new record in the Vendors recordset, which clears the data-bound controls on the form. Then, the SetFocus method is used to set the focus in the first text box on the form.

After the form is displayed with cleared controls, the user can enter data for a new vendor record. Then, if the user clicks on the OK button to add the vendor to the database, the cmdOK_Click procedure (2) issues the Update method to update the new record with the data that the user has entered. After that, this procedure issues these statements:

```
frmVendors.adoVendors.Refresh
frmVendors.dbcVendors.Text = adoVendors.Recordset!VendorName
```

The first one refreshes the data control on the Vendors form so it is aware of the new record. The second one sets the Text property of the DataCombo control on the Vendors form to the name of the new vendor. When that happens, the Change event of that control is fired. If you look back to figure 7-9, you'll see that this procedure uses the Find method to locate the new vendor record so it's displayed on the form. Then, control returns to the cmdOK_Click procedure. This procedure ends by hiding the New Vendor form, which makes the Vendors form the active window.

If the user decides to cancel the record addition by clicking on the Cancel button on the New Vendor form, the cmdCancel_Click procedure (3) is executed. This procedure uses the CancelUpdate method to discard the record that was added by the Form_Activate procedure. Then, it issues the Hide method for the New Vendor form so the Vendors form becomes the active window.

The next procedure (4) is activated when the Validate event occurs for the zip code text box. This event, as you may remember from chapter 3, occurs after the focus leaves a control and moves to a control that has its CausesValidation property set to True. As a result, you can use it to trigger a procedure that checks the validity of the data that the user has entered into the control. In this case, the procedure calls a function named ValidZipCode (5), which checks the zip code for validity and returns a value of True if it's valid or False if it's invalid. Then, if the value is False, the procedure displays an error message and sets the Cancel argument to True so the focus stays on the zip code text box.

If you study the ValidZipCode function (5), you can see that it first checks to make sure that entries have been made in both the state and zip code controls. If they haven't, this procedure doesn't do anything. But if they have, the procedure finds the record in the States table that has a state code equal to the one in the text portion of the State DataCombo control. Then, it checks to see if the first five characters in the zip code text box are less than the value in the

Code for the New Vendor form

```
Option Explicit
```

```
Private Sub Form_Activate()                                                1
On Error GoTo ErrorHandler
    adoVendors.Recordset.AddNew
    txtName.SetFocus
    Exit Sub
ErrorHandler:
    DisplayErrorMessage
End Sub
```

```
Private Sub cmdOK_Click()                                                  2
On Error GoTo ErrorHandler
    adoVendors.Recordset.Update
    frmVendors.adoVendors.Refresh
    frmVendors.dbcVendors.Text = adoVendors.Recordset!VendorName
    frmNewVendor.Hide
    Exit Sub
ErrorHandler:
    DisplayErrorMessage
    txtName.SetFocus
End Sub
```

```
Private Sub cmdCancel_Click()                                              3
    adoVendors.Recordset.CancelUpdate
    frmNewVendor.Hide
End Sub
```

```
Private Sub txtZipCode_Validate(Cancel As Boolean)                        4
    If Not ValidZipCode Then
        MsgBox "Invalid zip code", vbOKOnly + vbInformation, gsDialogTitle
        txtZipCode = ""
        Cancel = True
    End If
End Sub
```

```
Private Function ValidZipCode() As Boolean                                 5
    ValidZipCode = True
    If txtZipCode <> "" And dbcStates.BoundText <> "" Then
        With adoStates.Recordset
            .Find "StateCode = '" & dbcStates.Text & "'", , , adBookmarkFirst
            If  Val(Left(txtZipCode, 5)) < !FirstZipCode Or _
                Val(Left(txtZipCode, 5)) > !LastZipCode Then
                ValidZipCode = False
            End If
        End With
    End If
End Function
```

Figure 7-11   The code for the New Vendor form (part 1 of 2)

FirstZipCode field in the States table or greater than the value in the LastZipCode field. If they are, the zip code is invalid so ValidZipCode is set to False and the procedure ends.

The last procedures for the New Vendor form are designed to highlight (or select) the text in any text box that the focus moves to. Since none of these text boxes contain text when the form is first displayed, this has no value at first. But if the user wants to return to a field that has already been entered, this makes it easier to modify the entry by typing over it.

As you can see in this figure, the first seven procedures (6) are for the GotFocus events of the seven text boxes on the form. Each of these calls a procedure named HilightText that requires the name of the control to be highlighted as its only argument.

In the HilightText procedure (7), you can see that the SelStart property of the control that's passed to the procedure is set to 0 and the SelLength property is set to the length of the Text property for the control. These properties determine the portion of the text that is highlighted when the focus moves to a control.

Although these highlighting procedures are of limited value on a New Vendor form like this, I wanted you to see this technique so you can use it when you build a form for updating existing data. If, for example, you want to enhance this application so it provides for changing an existing record, you can add a Change button to the Vendors form that displays a Change Vendor form. Then, you can move the HilightText procedure to the standard module and make it a Public procedure so it can be called by either the New Vendor or Change Vendor form.

More about bugs that occur when using a Jet database

When you use the Jet OLE DB provider to add a record to the recordset in the cmdOK_Click procedure (2) for the New Vendor form, another bug becomes apparent. This time the application blows up when it tries to execute the Find method in the dbcVendors_Change procedure for the Vendors form. The problem is that the BoundText property, which should be the Vendor ID of the new record, is null so the data for the new record can't be found.

If you step through the procedures using the F8 key, though, the Find method works. So here again, the bug is apparently due to a timing problem within Visual Basic. Specifically, the Find method is executed before the Update is complete so the VendorID isn't available in the BoundText property.

Another quick and dirty solution is to add a delaying loop after the Update method in the cmdOK_Click procedure (2), something like this:

```
Dim lngLoop As Long
For lngLoop = 1 to 10000000
Next lngLoop
```

But here again, this isn't an acceptable solution. A better solution is to develop the application using unbound forms. And the right solution is for Microsoft to get the Jet provider working right so you can use it with confidence.

Code for the New Vendor form (continued)

```
Private Sub txtName_GotFocus()                                    6
    HilightText txtName
End Sub

Private Sub txtAddress1_GotFocus()
    HilightText txtAddress1
End Sub

Private Sub txtAddress2_GotFocus()
    HilightText txtAddress2
End Sub

Private Sub txtCity_GotFocus()
    HilightText txtCity
End Sub

Private Sub txtZipCode_GotFocus()
    HilightText txtZipCode
End Sub

Private Sub txtContact_GotFocus()
    HilightText txtContact
End Sub

Private Sub txtPhone_GotFocus()
    HilightText txtPhone
End Sub
```

```
Private Sub HilightText(ctl As Control)                          7
    ctl.SelStart = 0
    ctl.SelLength = Len(ctl)
End Sub
```

Figure 7-11   The code for the New Vendor form (part 2 of 2)

Exercise set 7-3: Build the New Vendor form

In this exercise set, you'll build the New Vendor form shown in figure 7-1, add the code for it, and complete the Vendors application.

Start the project and add a new form to the project

1. Open the C7Bound project you created in exercise set 7-1 and enhanced in exercise set 7-2.

2. Add a new form to the project, change the Name property of the form to frmNewVendor, change the Caption property to New Vendor, and change the BorderStyle property to Fixed Single. Then, save the new form as frmNewVendor in the same folder as the other project files.

Add the controls to the New Vendor form

3. Add the required controls to the new form so it looks something like this:

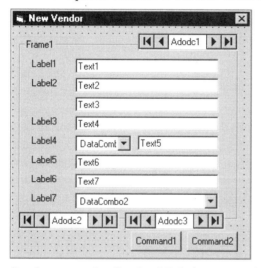

4. Set the properties for the ADO data controls and the DataCombo controls as summarized in figure 7-10. *If you're using an Access database*, though, use the Microsoft Jet 3.51 OLE DB Provider.

5. Set the AutoSize property for all Label controls to True. Then, set the Caption properties for the frame, label, and command button controls so the form looks something like the one in figure 7-1.

6. Set the Cancel property of the Cancel command button to True so it will be activated when you press the Esc key.

7. Set the DataSource and DataField properties for all the text boxes so they are bound to the proper fields in the recordset that's specified by the Vendors data control. Then, set the TabIndex properties for the text boxes and command buttons from 0 through 11 starting with the nine text box and DataCombo controls and ending with the OK and Cancel buttons. Also, set the Name properties for these controls as appropriate.

Add the code for the New Vendor form

8. Add the cmdNew_Click procedure shown in figure 7-9 to the Vendors module. Then, run the project, click on the New button to display the New Vendor form, and experiment with this form to see what works without any coding. In particular, notice how you can use the DataCombo controls to select the data for a field.

9. Add the code for the first three procedures shown in figure 7-11 to the New Vendor module. Then, run the project, click on the New button, enter a new record with valid data in the New Vendor form, and click on the OK button to add the record to the database and return to the Vendors form.

10. If necessary, fix any bugs and continue. *If you're using an Access database* and the program blows up on the Find method, you need to add a loop delaying the processing after the Update method in the cmdOK_Click procedure of the New Vendor form as shown on page 284.

11. With the project running, select the vendor record that you added in step 9, and delete it by clicking on the Delete button. *If you're using an Access database* and the deleted record still appears in the combo box of the Vendors form, you need to add a delaying loop after the Delete method in the cmdDelete_Click procedure as shown on page 276.

12. Add the code for the fourth and fifth procedures shown in figure 7-11 to the New Vendor module. *If you're using the Learning Edition*, though, replace the Find method with the code in appendix C. Then, run the project, and try to add a new record with an invalid zip code. You shouldn't be able to.

13. Add the code for the txtCity_GotFocus and HilightText procedures shown in figure 7-11 to the New Vendor module. Then, run the program, enter a city in the City box, move the focus to another text box, and move the focus back to the City box. The city that you entered should now be selected so you can replace it just by typing a new name. If you want to, you can now return to the Code window and enter the GotFocus procedures for the other text boxes, but that isn't necessary.

Add a Change Vendor form to the application (optional)

14. Want to test yourself? Add a Change command button to the Vendors form, add a Change Vendor form to the application, and add the code that makes this new form work. The Change Vendor form should look and work like the New Vendor form, but its Caption should be Change Vendor and it should let the user change the information for the current vendor.

The quickest way to develop this new form is to make a copy of the New Vendor form. To do that, first change its name to frmChangeVendor and save it as frmChangeVendor.frm. Then, you can use the Add Form command in the Project menu to add the existing form named frmNewVendor back into the project.

Save the project and exit from Visual Basic

15. Save the project and exit from Visual Basic. Then, congratulate yourself because you've created an application that has many of the marks of a professional application.

Perspective

The primary goal of this chapter has been to show you how to use the controls and coding techniques that you need for developing complete business applications using bound forms with ADO. Now, by using the controls and techniques that have been presented, you should be able to start developing business applications of your own.

A second goal of this chapter has been to help you understand the advantages and disadvantages of bound forms. Although the use of bound forms is often tempting because of the minimal coding requirements, the built-in functions of the ADO data controls and other data-bound controls limit the way the user interface can work. In addition, the relationships between the property settings and the code can be difficult to establish and maintain. And that can lead to serious debugging problems.

That's why the next chapter shows you how to create the same application using unbound controls. When you finish it, you'll be better able to decide when to use a bound form for an application and when to use an unbound form. You'll also have a better understanding of what it takes to develop a solid database application using either bound or unbound forms.

Terms you should know

data-bound control
synchronized controls
multi-line text box
UI-active mode
parameter
modal form

8

How to build unbound forms with ADO

In chapter 6, you learned the basic skills for building unbound forms that access and maintain data with ADO. Now, you'll learn some additional skills for building unbound forms with ADO. In particular, you'll learn how to use the standard ListBox and ComboBox controls to work with data, and you'll learn how to use the MSFlexGrid control. You'll also learn the coding techniques that you need for building unbound forms. When you finish this chapter, you should be able to develop unbound forms at a professional level for a wide variety of database applications.

How to work with unbound controls **290**
Three forms that use unbound controls 290
How to work with the ListBox and ComboBox controls 292
How to work with the MSFlexGrid control 294
Property settings for the controls on the Vendors form 296
Exercise set 8-1: Build the Vendors form 298

Coding techniques for unbound forms **300**
How to work with Command objects 300
How to work with stored procedures that contain parameters 302
How to check for ADO and OLE DB provider errors 304
How to work with Connection and Recordset events 306
How to use transaction processing 308
How to create a connection string using a login form 310
The code for the standard module of the Vendors application 312
The code for the Vendors form 312
Exercise set 8-2: Write the code for the standard module
and Vendors form 320

**The property settings and code for the Login
and New Vendor forms** **322**
The property settings for the Login and New Vendor forms 322
The code for the Login form 324
The code for the New Vendor form 326
Exercise set 8-3: Build the New Vendor and Login forms 332

Perspective **334**

How to work with unbound controls

When you build an unbound form, you don't use the special DataList and DataCombo controls that you use with bound forms. Instead, you use the ListBox and ComboBox controls that are available from the standard Toolbox. Similarly, instead of a DataGrid control, you use the Microsoft FlexGrid (MSFlexGrid) control. In the topics that follow, you'll learn how to use all three of these controls to work with the data in an unbound form.

Three forms that use unbound controls

Figure 8-1 presents an unbound version of the Vendors application that you studied in chapter 7. The unbound Vendors and New Vendor form perform the same basic functions as the bound versions in the previous chapter, while the Login form performs a function that can't be done with a bound form.

Like the bound Vendors form, the unbound form uses a combo box that lets the user select a vendor. It also uses a list box to display unpaid invoices, and it uses a grid to display the detail information for unpaid invoices. Unlike the bound form, though, this form uses standard combo box and list box controls instead of data-bound controls, and it uses an MSFlexGrid control instead of a data-bound grid control. Similarly, the State and Terms combo boxes on the New Vendor form are implemented with standard combo box controls.

Because the controls on these forms are all unbound, you have to use Visual Basic code to populate them with the appropriate data. You also have to use code to synchronize the invoice data on the Vendors form with the current vendor record and to display the information for a new vendor on the Vendors form after you add it by using the New Vendor form.

The Login form in this figure is used to accept connection information from the user. Then, that information is used to build a connection string that's used to open a connection to the database. This form wasn't used in the bound Vendors application in chapter 7 because there's no way to pass the information from a login form to the data control in a bound form without loading the form first. But since the connection properties of the data control must be set before the form is loaded, this technique can only be used with unbound forms.

The three forms of the enhanced unbound Vendors application

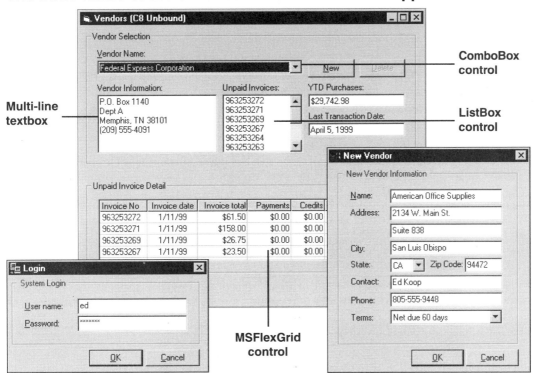

Description

- This unbound version of the Vendors application performs the same functions as the bound version presented in chapter 7. To display the information for a vendor, you select the vendor name from the combo box at the top of the Vendors form. And to add or delete a vendor, you click on the New or Delete button on the Vendors form.

- The unbound Vendors application starts by displaying a login dialog box that lets the user enter a user name and password. The information in this form is used to create the connection string that's used to open a connection to the database.

- Because no bound controls are used on the Vendors and New Vendor forms, each control on these forms is populated and synchronized through code. Standard ComboBox controls are used for the Vendor Name data on the Vendors form and for the State and Terms data on the New Vendor form. A standard ListBox control is used to display the unpaid invoices on the Vendors form. And an MSFlexGrid control is used to display detail information for the unpaid invoices.

- Like the bound version of the Vendors form, the unbound Vendors form uses a multi-line text box to display the general information about a vendor including address, contact person, and phone number.

Figure 8-1   Three forms that use unbound controls

How to work with the ListBox and ComboBox controls

Figure 8-2 shows how to work with the standard ListBox and ComboBox controls. Although you were introduced to these controls in chapter 3, this figure presents some of the properties and methods that you need for working with the data in a recordset.

When you create a standard list box or combo box, its list is empty. To populate the control, you have to provide the list items in the List property. To do that as you design the form, you can enter the items into the box that drops down from the List property. In most cases, though, you'll want to populate the control as the program executes. To do that, you use the AddItem method.

The LoadVendors procedure in this figure illustrates the use of the AddItem method. This procedure reads through the records in a recordset named mrsVendors and loads the value of the VendorName field for each record into the list. It also loads the value of the VendorID field for each record into the ItemData property of the new list item (the item identified by the NewIndex property). This property can contain a number that's associated with the list item. It is particularly useful when you need to associate the items in the list with other data in the form by a field (like VendorID) that's different than the field that's displayed in the list (like VendorName).

Once you populate a list box or combo box, you can refer to a specific item in the list by using its index value. For example, the following statement assigns the value of the first item in a combo box named cboTerms to a string variable named strTerms:

```
strTerms = cboTerms.List(0)
```

To get the value of the item that's currently selected in a list box or combo box, you can use the Text property of the control like this:

```
strTerms = cboTerms.Text
```

And to work with the currently selected item, you can use the ListIndex property of the control like this:

```
cboTerms.RemoveItem cboTerms.ListIndex
```

You'll see how statements like these are used in the Vendors application later in this chapter.

Some of the properties of the ListBox and ComboBox controls

Property	Description
ItemData	An array of numbers with each number corresponding to an item in the list or combo box.
List	An array of text strings that define the items in the list or combo box.
ListCount	The number of items in the list or combo box.
ListIndex	The index of the item that's currently selected in the list or combo box.
NewIndex	The index of the last item that was added to the list or combo box.
Sorted	Determines whether or not the items in the list or combo box are sorted alphabetically.
Style	For a list box, determines if a checkbox is displayed next to each entry in the list. For a combo box, determines if the list portion drops down or is fixed and if text can be entered in the text box portion of the control.
Text	The value of the item that's currently selected in the list or combo box.

Some of the methods of the ListBox and ComboBox controls

Method	Description
AddItem	Adds an item to the list or combo box. If the list is sorted, the item is added in the appropriate position in the list. Otherwise, it's added at the end of the list.
Clear	Clears the list or combo box.
RemoveItem	Removes the item with the specified index from the list or combo box.

A procedure that populates a ComboBox control from a recordset

```
Private Sub LoadVendors()
    With mrsVendors
        Do Until .EOF
            cboVendors.AddItem !VendorName
            cboVendors.ItemData(cboVendors.NewIndex) = !VendorID
            .MoveNext
        Loop
    End With
End Sub
```

Description

- If the items displayed in the ListBox or ComboBox control are fixed, you can use the List property to enter items as you design the form. Otherwise, you can use the AddItem method to add items to the list as the program executes as shown in the procedure above.

- You can use the ItemData property to associate a numeric key field with each item that you add to a ListBox or ComboBox list. This is useful if you need to synchronize the item that's displayed in the ListBox or ComboBox control with other controls on the form using the key field.

Figure 8-2   How to work with the ListBox and ComboBox controls

How to work with the MSFlexGrid control

The MSFlexGrid control lets you display data in a row and column format like the one for a DataGrid control. Unlike the DataGrid control, though, you have to use code to populate the MSFlexGrid control. Within the code, you use the properties shown in figure 8-3.

When you first create a MSFlexGrid control, it contains two rows and two columns, and those values are stored in the Rows and Cols properties. If you will be populating the grid with data from a variable number of records as in the Vendors application, it isn't necessary to change the value in the Rows property until the form is run. Then, you can set this property based on the number of records in the recordset that's used to populate the control. In contrast, the number of columns is usually fixed so you can set the Cols property when you define the control.

When you set the Rows or Cols property, be sure to include any column or row headers displayed in the grid. The Unpaid Invoice Detail grid in the Vendors form, for example, includes one row that contains the column headings as shown at the top of this figure. As a result, the total number of rows will be one more than the number of rows in the recordset. As you can see in figure 8-3, the number of columns and rows used for the headings are specified by the FixedCol and FixedRows properties, which are typically set when the control is defined.

The FormatString property contains a string that determines the appearance of the rows and columns in the grid. You can use this property to specify the width and alignment of each column and the text that's displayed at the top of each column. You can also use it to specify the text that's displayed to the left of each row. This figure shows the FormatString property for the Unpaid Invoice Detail grid.

To refer to the value of a specific cell in a grid, you first have to make that cell the *active cell*. To do that, you set the Col property to the number of the column that the cell is in, and you set the Row property to the number of the row that the cell is in. Note, however, that the columns and rows in a grid are numbered from zero. After you set these properties, you can use the Text property to refer to the value of the cell that they refer to. To refer to the value of the cell in the second row (row number 1) of the first column (column number 0), for example, you can use code like this:

```
Dim sActiveCell As String
msgInvoices.Col = 0
msgInvoices.Row = 1
sActiveCell = msgInvoices.Text
```

You'll see a complete example of how to populate a MSFlexGrid control in the code for the unbound Vendors form.

The MSFlexGrid control used in the unbound Vendors form

Invoice No	Invoice date	Invoice total	Payments	Credits	Balance due ▲
963253272	12/24/98	$61.50	$0.00	$0.00	$61.50
963253271	12/24/98	$158.00	$0.00	$0.00	$158.00
963253269	12/24/98	$26.75	$0.00	$0.00	$26.75 ▼

Common MSFlexGrid properties

Property	Description
Rows	The number of rows in the grid, including the header row.
Cols	The number of columns in the grid, including the header column.
FixedRows	The number of rows used for column headings. These rows don't move as you scroll vertically.
FixedCols	The number of columns used for row headings. These columns don't move as you scroll horizontally.
FormatString	Defines the widths of the columns in the grid, the alignment of the data in each column, and the text in the column and row headers.
Col	The number of the column that contains the active cell. Columns are numbered beginning with zero.
Row	The number of the row that contains the active cell. Rows are numbered beginning with zero.
Text	The value of the cell that's defined by the current column and row.

The FormatString property for the grid shown above

<Invoice No |^Invoice date |> Invoice total|>   Payments|>   Credits|> Balance due

Description

- By default, the Rows and Cols properties provide for two columns and two rows in the MSFlexGrid control. The first column and first row are fixed and can be used for headings as indicated by the FixedCols and FixedRows properties.

- To specify the alignment of the data in each column in the grid, you use the characters > (right-align), < (left-align), and ^ (center) in the FormatString property as shown above. You can also specify the text to be displayed in the column header for each column. And you can specify the width of the column by including spaces in the header text. To divide the column definitions, you use the pipe character: |.

- If the grid includes row headers, you can also define the text to be displayed in each row of the header. To do that, follow the column definitions with a semicolon and then the text for each row separated by pipe characters. The length of the longest heading is used as the width of the column.

- You can identify a specific cell in the grid by setting the Col and Row properties. Then, you can use the Text property to refer to the contents of that cell.

Figure 8-3   How to work with the MSFlexGrid control

Property settings for the controls on the Vendors form

Figure 8-4 presents the property settings for the controls on the Vendors form. As you study these settings, notice that none of them refer to the data that they will display. Because these controls are unbound, they will have to be populated through code.

Three of the properties for the MSFlexGrid control in this figure weren't presented in figure 8-3 and have been changed from their defaults. The Highlight property is set so selected cells aren't highlighted unless the grid has the focus, in contrast to the default which is to always highlight selected cells. The ScrollBars property is set so only a vertical scroll bar is displayed, in contrast to the default which is to display both vertical and horizontal scroll bars. And the SelectionMode property is set so selections are made by row, instead of the default which is to allow individual cells to be selected. Note that these properties only affect the appearance of the grid and not the way it functions.

Basic property settings for the Vendors ComboBox control

Property	Value
Name	cboVendors
Sorted	True
Style	2 – Dropdown list

Basic property settings for the Unpaid Invoices ListBox control

Property	Value
Name	lstInvoices
TabStop	False

Property settings for the MSFlexGrid control

Property	Value
Name	msgInvoices
Rows	2
Cols	6
FixedRows	1
FixedCols	0
FormatString	<Invoice No I^Invoice date I> Invoice totalI> PaymentsI> CreditsI> Balance due
Highlight	2 – flexHighlightWithFocus
ScrollBars	2 – flexScrollBarVertical
SelectionMode	1 – flexSelectionByRow
TabStop	False

Property settings for the text boxes

Property	Vendor Information	YTD Purchases	Last Transaction Date
Name	txtVendorInfo	txtYTDPurchases	txtLastTranDate
Locked	True	True	True
MultiLine	True	False	False
TabStop	False	False	False
Text	<blank>	<blank>	<blank>

Note

- The property names and options for the MSFlexGrid control are listed above as they appear in the Properties window. If you use the Property Pages dialog box to set these properties, though, some of them appear differently. For example, the FormatString property appears as just Format, and the ScrollBars options are None, Horizontal, Vertical, and Both.

Figure 8-4   Property settings for the controls on the Vendors form

Exercise set 8-1: Build the Vendors form

In this exercise set, you'll build an unbound Vendors form like the one in figure
8-1. Then, in exercise set 8-2, you'll add the code for this form, and you'll
create a standard module for this application. Finally, in exercise set 8-3, you'll
add the Login and New Vendor forms and their code to the application.

Start a new project and prepare it for use with ADO

1. Start Visual Basic and begin a Standard EXE project. Then, change the Name
    property of the form to frmVendors, the Caption property to Vendors (C8
    Unbound), and the StartUpPosition property to CenterScreen. Last, use the
    Properties command in the Project menu to change the ProjectName property
    to C8Unbound.

2. Save the form and project with the names frmVendors and C8Unbound in a
    new folder named Chapter 8 Unbound.

3. Use the References command in the Project menu to add the Microsoft
    ActiveX Data Objects 2.0 Library to the project. Then, use the Components
    command in the Project menu to add the Microsoft FlexGrid Control 6.0 to
    the Toolbox.

Add controls to the new form

4. Use the toolbox to add the required controls to the new form so it looks
    something like this:

5. Set the Caption properties for the labels, frames, and command buttons on your own using the form in figure 8-1 as a guide. For the label at the bottom of the form, enter "Vendor Record:" as its Caption property. When this form is run, this property will be changed by code. Next, set the Name property of this label to lblRecordNumber, and set the Name property of the command buttons, to cmdNew, cmdDelete, and cmdExit.

6. Set the properties for the ComboBox, ListBox, MSFlexGrid, and TextBox controls as shown in figure 8-4. Adjust the spacing in the FormatString property of the MSFlexGrid control as necessary to create the appropriate column widths.

Test and save the form

7. Start the project. If you've done everything right, the form should look something like the one in figure 8-1. Because you haven't entered any code for this form, though, no data is displayed on the form and none of the functions are operational.

8. Close the form by clicking on the Close button in the title bar. Then, save the project, and leave it open if you're going to continue.

Coding techniques for unbound forms

Now that you know how to use some of the controls for working with unbound forms, you'll learn some coding techniques for working with them.

How to work with Command objects

The Vendors form in the Vendors application shown in figure 8-1 uses a Command object to populate the Invoices grid for the current vendor. A Command object contains the definition of a query and is particularly useful for creating *parameter queries*. This type of query contains parameters that you can use to change the *criteria* for the query. For instance, the criteria for the Invoices grid is that the VendorID field in an Invoice record must be equal to the VendorID field in the current vendor record.

Figure 8-5 shows how to work with Command objects. To start, you use the Dim and Set statements to create the Command object. Then, you set the three properties shown in this figure to define the command. In particular, you set the CommandText property to the SQL statement you want to execute. You can also set this property to the name of a stored procedure or table.

To implement a parameter query with a Command object, you code a question mark wherever you want to use a parameter in the SQL statement. For each question mark, a Parameter object is automatically added to the Parameters collection of the Command object. Then, to set the value of a parameter, you use the Value property of its Parameter object as shown in this figure (Value is the default property). You can set other properties of a Parameter object to define other characteristics such as its data type and whether it's used for input or output, but the defaults are usually what you want.

Once you create a Command object and assign values to any parameters it will use, you use the Execute method to execute the command. If you're executing a command that returns rows, you assign the result to a Recordset object as illustrated by the first example in this figure. This opens the recordset based on the query in the Command object. Then, as the program executes, you can change the values of the parameters and use the Execute method to re-execute the query with the new parameter values.

If you use a Command object to create a recordset, you should know that the recordset is always opened read-only with a static cursor (client-side) or a forward-only cursor (server-side). That means you can't make changes to the data using ADO methods like Update and Delete. However, you can execute other commands that contain SQL statements that change the data.

You can also use a Command object to execute a query that doesn't return records. This is illustrated by the second coding example in this figure. In this example, the command will delete paid invoices from the Invoices table. Notice that one argument is included for the Execute method in this example. After the command is executed, the variable that's specified for this argument will contain the number of records that were affected by the command. In this example, that variable is used to display a count of the records that were

Common properties of the Command object

Property	Description
ActiveConnection	The Connection object that will be used to connect to the database.
CommandText	The text of the command to be executed. This can be the name of a stored procedure, a SQL statement, or the name of a table.
CommandType	Indicates how the CommandText property should be evaluated. Typical options are adCmdText (for a SQL statement), adCmdTable, adCmdStoredProc, adCmdUnknown, and adExecuteNoRecords (for a query that doesn't return any rows).

Code that creates and executes a Command object that returns rows

```
Dim mrsInvoices As Recordset, mcmdInvoices As Command
Set mcmdInvoices = New Command
mcmdInvoices.ActiveConnection = mcnAP
mcmdInvoices.CommandText = "SELECT * FROM Invoices WHERE VendorID = ?"
mcmdInvoices.CommandType = adCmdText
mcmdInvoices.Parameters(0) = mrsVendors!VendorID
Set mrsInvoices = mcmdInvoices.Execute
```

Code that creates and executes a Command object that deletes records

```
Dim mcmdInvoices As Command, lRecordCount As Long
Set mcmdInvoices = New Command
mcmdInvoices.ActiveConnection = mcnAP
mcmdInvoices.CommandText = "DELETE FROM Invoices " & _
    "WHERE InvoiceTotal - PaymentTotal - CreditTotal = 0"
mcmdInvoices.CommandType = adExecuteNoRecords
mcmdInvoices.Execute lRecordCount
MsgBox lRecordCount & " records deleted"
```

Description

- A Command object contains the definition of a query. To create a Command object, you use the Dim and Set statements as shown above. Then, you set the properties of the Command object to define the query that will be executed.

- To use parameters in the SQL statement for a Command object, code a question mark (?) for each parameter. For each question mark, one Parameter object is added to the Parameters collection of the Command object. Then, you can set the Value property of each Parameter object to the value you want for that parameter.

- To execute the query defined by a Command object, you use the Execute method of the Command object. If the query returns rows, you assign the result set to an object variable. Otherwise, you simply execute the Command object.

- The first argument for the Execute method returns a Long variable that represents the number of records affected by the command.

Figure 8-5   How to work with Command objects

deleted by the command. Although you can code other arguments for the Execute method, this is the one you're most likely to use.

Although you typically use Command objects to execute queries, you can also execute a query using the Execute method of a Connection object. This works just as it does for a Command object, except that you include the text of the query you want to execute as the first argument of the Execute method, and you can't use parameters. To execute the Delete query shown in figure 8-5 with a Connection object, for example, you use code like this:

```
mcnAP.Execute "DELETE FROM Invoices " & _
    "WHERE InvoiceTotal - PaymentTotal - CreditTotal = 0", _
    lRecordCount, adExecuteNoRecords
```

This technique is useful when you only need to execute a query once during the execution of a program. If you need to execute a query more than once, you'll want to create a Command object for the query.

How to work with stored procedures that contain parameters

If you code parameters in the SQL statement for a Command object as shown in figure 8-5, ADO creates the Parameter objects for you. If the parameters are included in a stored procedure, though, ADO has no way of knowing what the definitions of those parameters are. In that case, you have to create the Parameter objects explicitly as shown in figure 8-6.

The example in this figure shows you how to execute a stored procedure that contains a single parameter. Here, the CreateParameter method is used to define the Parameter object and assign it to a variable. The arguments of this method indicate that the parameter is named ID, it will hold an integer that will be used as input, it can be up to four characters in length, and it's initial value is the value of the VendorID field in the current vendor record.

Before you can use a Parameter object, you have to add it to the Parameters collection of the Command object. To do that, you use the Append method of the Parameters collection as illustrated in this example. Note, however, that if the stored procedure contains two or more parameters, they must be appended to the Command object in the same order that they're defined in the stored procedure.

After you create the Parameter objects and append them to the Parameters collection, you're ready to execute the procedure. To do that, you use the Execute method just as you would for any other command. Then, to change the values of the parameters used by the stored procedure, you set the Value properties of the Parameter objects and re-execute the command as illustrated in the second coding example in this figure.

Incidentally, you also have to create and append Parameter objects when you use parameter queries with an Access (Jet) database. This is due to the way the Jet OLE DB provider works. So if you use an Access database as you do the exercise sets for this chapter, you'll become more familiar with these methods.

The syntax of the CreateParameter method

```
Set Parameter = Command.CreateParameter([Name][, Type][, Direction]
                                            [, Size][, Value])
```

Arguments of the CreateParameter method

Argument	Description
Name	A string that specifies the name of the Parameter object.
Type	The data type of the Parameter object.
Direction	A constant that indicates whether the parameter is used for input, output, or both input and output, or whether it will contain the return value from a stored procedure.
Size	The maximum number of characters that a parameter value will contain.
Value	A default value for the Parameter object.

A stored procedure that contains one parameter

```
Create Procedure spVendorInvoices @ID int As
    SELECT VendorID, InvoiceNumber, InvoiceDate, InvoiceTotal
    FROM Invoices WHERE VendorID = @ID
```

Code that executes the stored procedure

```
Dim mrsInvoices As Recordset
Dim mcmdInvoices As Command, mprmInvoices As Parameter
Set mcmdInvoices = New Command
mcmdInvoices.CommandText = "spVendorInvoices"
mcmdInvoices.CommandType = adCmdStoredProc
Set mprmInvoices = mcmdInvoices.CreateParameter("ID", adInteger, _
    adParamInput, 4, grsVendors!VendorID)
mcmdInvoices.Parameters.Append mprmInvoices
Set mrsInvoices = mcmdInvoices.Execute
```

Code that changes the parameter value and re-executes the stored procedure

```
mprmInvoices.Value = grsVendors!VendorID
Set mrsInvoices = mcmdInvoices.Execute
```

Description

- Before you can run a stored procedure that contains parameters, you have to define the parameters in your application. To do that, you use the CreateParameter method of the Command object to create each Parameter object.

- After you create a Parameter object, you add it to the Parameters collection of the Command object using the Append method of that collection. Then, when you execute the command, the parameters are passed to the stored procedure.

- You can change the value of a parameter using the Value property of a Parameter object. Then, you can use the Execute method of the Command object to re-execute the stored procedure with the new parameter value.

Figure 8-6   How to work with stored procedures that contain parameters

How to check for ADO and OLE DB provider errors

When an error occurs in response to an ADO operation, the Visual Basic Err object is updated with information about that error. Then, you can trap the error by coding an On Error statement, and you can respond to the error by coding an error-handling routine like the first one in figure 8-7. Notice that this routine checks for specific errors using constants that are associated with the error numbers, and some of the most common ADO error numbers and codes are listed at the top of this figure. For a complete list of ADO errors, you can look up the *ADO Error Codes* topic in online help.

In addition to ADO errors, an ADO operation can cause OLE DB provider errors. In that case, the Err object doesn't always contain detailed information about what actually caused the operation to fail. To get the additional information you need about a provider error, though, you can use the Error objects in the ADO Errors collection. This collection is accessed through the ADO Connection object.

The bottom portion of figure 8-7 describes some of the properties of the Error object and presents a routine for handling these types of errors. Note that each time an error occurs, the Errors collection can contain one or more Error objects. To refer to a specific object in the collection, you use its index number. For example, you can refer to the first object in the Errors collection like this:

```
Errors(0)
```

In most cases, the first object in the Errors collection contains the most detailed information about the error, so you'll want to use this object to display information about the error to the user. If other objects are available, they typically contain higher-level information. These objects can sometimes be useful when you're debugging a program.

If you look at the second error routine in this figure, you'll see that it starts by checking the Count property of the Errors collection. If the value of this property is greater than zero, it means that a provider error has occurred. In that case, the first object in the Errors collection is used to display an error message to the user. If the value of this property is zero, it means that a Visual Basic or ADO error occurred. In that case, the Err object is used to display error information.

If a provider error occurs, you'll want to be sure to clear the Errors collection when you're done displaying its error information. To do that, you use the Clear method of the Errors collection as shown in this figure. That resets the Count property of this collection to zero so the next time an error occurs, the error-handling routine executes the appropriate code.

Common ADO error codes

Number	Constant	Description
3001	adErrInvalidArgument	The program is using the wrong type of arguments, the arguments are out of range, or the arguments conflict.
3021	adErrNoCurrentRecord	Either the current record has been deleted, or the BOF or EOF property is True.
3265	adErrItemNotFound	The requested object couldn't be found in the collection referenced by the application.
3421	adErrDataConversion	The program is trying to perform an operation using the wrong type of data.

An error routine that checks for specific errors

```
Dim sMessage As String
If Err.Number = adErrNoCurrentRecord Then
    If mrsVendors.BOF and mrsVendors.EOF Then
        sMessage = "No data in recordset."
    Else
        sMessage = "Record has been deleted."
    End If
Else
    sMessage = "Error number: " & Err.Number & vbCrLf & Err.Description
End If
MsgBox sMessage, vbOKOnly + vbCritical, "Error"
```

Some of the properties of the Error object

Property	Description
Number	The number associated with the error
Description	Text that describes the error
Source	The object that caused the error

An error routine that checks for provider errors

```
If gcnAP.Errors.Count > 0 Then
    MsgBox "Error code: " & gcnAP.Errors(0).Number _
        & vbCrLf & " Description: " & gcnAP.Errors(0).Description _
        & vbCrLf & "Source: " & gcnAP.Errors(0).Source, _
        vbOKOnly + vbCritical, gsDialogTitle
    gcnAP.Errors.Clear
Else
    MsgBox "Error code: " & Err.Number & vbCrLf & "Description: " _
        & Err.Description, vbOKOnly + vbCritical, gsDialogTitle
End If
```

Description

- The Error objects in the ADO Errors collection contain information about the most recent OLE DB provider errors that occurred in response to an ADO operation.
- The first object in the Errors collection usually contains the most detailed information about the error. You typically use this object to display information to the user.

Figure 8-7   How to check for ADO and OLE DB provider errors

How to work with Connection and Recordset events

In chapter 7, you learned how to use some of the events that occur on a data control when you work with bound forms. When you work with unbound forms, similar events are available for the Connection and Recordset objects. These events are summarized in figure 8-8.

The events you'll use most often are the ones that fire when you change the current position in a recordset (WillMove and MoveComplete), when you change a field in a record (WillChangeField and ChangeFieldComplete), when you change a record in a recordset (WillChangeRecord and ChangeRecordComplete), or when you change the recordset (WillChangeRecordset and ChangeRecordsetComplete). For example, you can use the WillChangeField event to validate the value that's entered for a field before the change is applied to the current record. You can use the WillChangeRecord event to validate one or more fields in a record before the record is saved. And you can use the ChangeRecordsetComplete or MoveComplete events to synchronize the data on one or more forms after the recordset is requeried or the current position changes.

You can use some of the other events in this figure when you perform an *asynchronous operation*. If, for example, you know that a query that's executed by a Command object may take more than a few seconds to complete, you may want to execute the command asynchronously. That means that while the command is executing, the application can perform other operations. Then, when the command finishes, the FetchComplete event fires so the application can react accordingly. To run an asynchronous operation, you set the Option argument for the Execute method of a Command object or the Open method of a Recordset or Connection object to an appropriate value like adExecuteAsynch for a Command object.

One event that's particularly useful for asynchronous operations is FetchProgress. This event fires periodically as records are retrieved asynchronously into a Recordset object. When this event fires, several arguments are passed to it as shown by the example in this figure. The first two arguments indicate the number of records that have been returned and the total number of records to be returned. You can use the values of these arguments to display the progress of the operation to the user.

Before you can use any of the Connection and Recordset events, you have to declare the object using the WithEvents keyword as shown in this figure. When you do that, the objects and their events will appear in the drop-down lists in the Code window so you can create event procedures for them. Note, however, that the WithEvents keyword can only be used with a Connection or Recordset object that's declared in a form or class module (see chapter 13). It can't be used in a standard module.

Connection object events

Event	When it fires
BeginTransComplete, CommitTransComplete, RollbackTransComplete	After the BeginTrans, CommitTrans, or RollbackTrans methods complete
WillConnect, ConnectComplete	Before and after you open a connection to a data source
Disconnect	After you close a connection to a data source
WillExecute, ExecuteComplete	Before and after you execute a query by executing a Connection or Command object or opening a Recordset object.
InfoMessage	When additional information is returned from the provider about the current connection operation

Recordset object events

Event	When it fires
EndOfRecordset	When you try to move to a record that's past the end of the recordset
FetchProgress	Periodically during an asynchronous retrieval operation
FetchComplete	After all the records have been retrieved by an asynchronous operation
WillMove, MoveComplete	Before and after the current position in the recordset changes
WillChangeField, ChangeFieldComplete	Before and after changes are made to a specific field in the record
WillChangeRecord, ChangeRecordComplete	Before and after changes are made to one or more records in the recordset
WillChangeRecordset, ChangeRecordsetComplete	Before and after changes are made to the recordset

How to use the FetchProgress event procedure

```
Private Sub mrsInvoices_FetchProgress(ByVal Progress As Long, _
        ByVal MaxProgress As Long, adStatus As ADODB.EventStatusEnum, _
        ByVal pRecordset As ADODB.Recordset)
    lblFetchProgress.Caption = Progress & " out of " & MaxProgress & _
        " records returned."
End Sub
```

Description

- To use events with Connection and Recordset objects, you need to declare the objects using the WithEvents keyword like this:

```
Dim WithEvents mcnAP As Connection
Dim WithEvents mrsInvoices As Recordset
```

- Some of these events are used with *asynchronous operations*. With this type of operation, program execution can continue while the operation completes.

Figure 8-8   How to work with Connection and Recordset events

How to use transaction processing

When you process a group of closely related transactions, you sometimes need to treat them as a single transaction. Then, if one of the transactions in the group fails, you can *rollback* the changes made to all of the transactions in the group. Otherwise, if all transactions are successful, you can *commit* all the changes. This type of processing can be referred to as *transaction processing*.

To illustrate, suppose you want to save all the paid invoices from an Invoices table to an archive table and then delete all the paid invoices from the Invoices table. However, you don't want to archive an invoice unless the related delete operation is successful. To do that, you can treat all the archive and delete operations as a single transaction that can be rolled back if any part of it isn't successful.

Figure 8-9 shows how to use transaction processing with ADO. As you can see, the methods that you use to implement transaction processing operate on a Connection object. Before you begin transaction processing, then, you must create the Connection object you want to use.

To start a transaction, you use the BeginTrans method. Then, if all of the operations in the transaction are performed successfully, you can use the CommitTrans method to commit the changes to the data source. If any of the operations fail, however, you can use the RollbackTrans method to reverse the changes that were made to the data source. Note that only the operations that change the data source are included in the transaction. So, for example, the statement in this figure that opens the connection is not reversed if the transaction is rolled back.

When you use transactions, you should be aware that a transaction is never committed unless you execute the CommitTrans method. So, if the application ends or the Connection object falls out of scope while a transaction is in progress, all of the changes that have been made to any recordsets on that connection are automatically rolled back. And if a Connection object is closed explicitly with the Close method while a transaction is in progress, an error occurs.

A procedure that uses transaction processing

```
Private Sub ArchiveInvoices()
    Dim strSQL as String
    Dim mcnAP as Connection
    Dim mcmdInvoices as Command
On Error GoTo ErrorHandler
    Set mcnAP = New Connection
    Set mcmdInvoices = New Command
    mcnAP.CursorLocation = adUseClient
    mcnAP.BeginTrans
    mcnAP.Open "Provider=SQLOLEDB;Server=mmaserver;" & _
               "Database=AccountsPayable;User ID=ed;Password=abc4xyz"
    mcmdInvoices.ActiveConnection = mcnAP
    mcmdInvoices.CommandType = adCmdText
    strSQL = "INSERT INTO InvoiceArchive SELECT * FROM Invoices " & _
             "WHERE InvoiceTotal - PaymentTotal - CreditTotal = 0"
    mcmdInvoices.CommandText = strSQL
    mcmdInvoices.Execute
    strSQL = "DELETE FROM Invoices WHERE " & _
             "InvoiceTotal - PaymentTotal - CreditTotal = 0"
    mcmdInvoices.Execute
    mcnAP.CommitTrans
    Exit Sub
ErrorHandler:
    DisplayErrorMessage
    mcnAP.RollbackTrans
End Sub
```

Description

- By default, each SQL statement and each ADO method that changes the data source is treated by the OLE DB provider as a separate *transaction*. However, you can use the BeginsTrans, CommitTrans, and RollbackTrans methods of a Connection object to treat a sequence of statements or methods as a single transaction. This is often referred to as *transaction processing*.

- The BeginTrans method starts the transaction. Then, if the operations in the transaction complete successfully, you can use the CommitTrans method to save the changes to the data source. But if an error occurs during any part of the transaction, you can use the RollbackTrans method to discard any changes made to the data source.

- The data that's affected by a transaction is typically locked for the duration of the transaction. Because of that, you should avoid lengthy transactions and transactions that are interrupted for user input.

- You can also implement transactions using the SQL BEGIN TRAN, COMMIT TRAN, and ROLLBACK TRAN statements. These statements are similar to the ADO methods used for transaction processing, but provide some additional flexibility.

Figure 8-9   How to use transaction processing

How to create a connection string using a login form

Figure 8-10 shows how you can create a login form that accepts connection information from the user. You can use a form like this to provide security for an application. Then, only those users with a valid user name and password can access the application.

The code for implementing the login form is straightforward. When the user clicks on the OK button in this form, the Click event procedure begins by checking that a user name and password have been entered. If not, an appropriate error message is displayed. Otherwise, a connection string is generated using the values that were entered into the form.

After the connection string is generated, the login form opens a connection using the connection string. If the connection is successful, the login form is unloaded and the Vendors form is displayed. If the connection fails, however, the error-handling routine at the end of this procedure is executed. This routine assumes that the error is caused by an invalid user name or password and displays an appropriate message. Keep in mind, however, that other errors could occur and you'd probably want to provide for them as well. After the user responds to the error message that's displayed, he or she can correct the user name and password and try to log on again.

A form that accepts login information

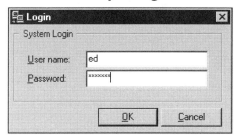

Code that creates a connection string and opens the connection

```
Private Sub cmdOK_Click()
On Error GoTo ErrorHandler
    Dim strConnect As String
    If txtUserName = "" Or txtPassword = "" Then
        MsgBox "You must enter a user name and password.", _
            vbOKOnly + vbInformation, gsDialogTitle
        txtUserName.SetFocus
    Else
        strConnect = "Provider=SQLOLEDB;Server=mmaserver;" & _
            "Database=AccountsPayable;User ID=" & txtUserName & _
            ";Password=" & txtPassword
        gcnAP.Open strConnect
        Unload Me
        frmVendors.Show
    End If
    Exit Sub
ErrorHandler:
    MsgBox "The user name and password you entered are invalid.", _
        vbOKOnly + vbCritical, gsDialogTitle
    txtUserName.SetFocus
End Sub
```

Notes

- You can hide the characters that are entered for a password by setting the PasswordChar property of the text box to a *placeholder character* (usually, an asterisk). Then, the placeholder character is displayed instead of the actual characters that are entered.

- You can create a login form similar to the one shown above by selecting the Login Dialog option from the Add Form dialog box. However, the code that's generated for the form isn't very useful, so you're probably better off creating your own form.

Figure 8-10   How to create a connection string using a login form

The code for the standard module of the Vendors application

Now that you've learned some of the coding techniques for working with unbound forms, you should understand the code for the Vendors application. To start, figure 8-11 presents the code for its standard module. This procedure consists of two Public variables, a Public constant, and two Public procedures. Because these variables, constant, and procedures are defined in a standard module, they can be accessed by all the other modules in the application. For example, the DisplayErrorMessage procedure in this module is called by both the Vendors and New Vendor forms. Notice that this procedure checks for both provider errors and for Visual Basic or ADO errors.

The second procedure in this module is called from all three of the forms in this application. It's used to highlight the text in a text box when the focus is moved to that text box. You'll see the code that calls this procedure in a minute. When the procedure is called, the control that receives the focus is passed to it as an argument. Then, the SelStart property of this control is set to 0 so that the highlight will start at the beginning of the text in the control, and the SelLength property is set to the numbers of characters that have been entered into the control. As you can see, the number of characters is retrieved using the Len function. The result is that all of the characters in the text box are highlighted.

The code for the Vendors form

Figure 8-11 also presents the code for the Vendors form module. To start, the Declarations section of this module (1) declares two variables. The first variable is for the Invoices recordset that will be used to display the invoices for a vendor. And the second variable is for the Command object that will be used to retrieve the invoices.

The first event procedure in the Vendors form module is for the Intialize event of the form (2). This event occurs when an instance of the form is created, which happens automatically the first time the form is referred to from the application. This event occurs before the Load event of the form, and is typically used to initialize the data for the form before it's displayed.

The Initialize procedure in the Vendors form begins by creating instances of the Vendors and Invoices recordset and the Invoices Command object. Then, it opens the Vendors recordset, and sets the appropriate properties of the Invoices command. Notice that although the SELECT statement in the Invoices command contains a parameter, this procedure doesn't set the value of that parameter or open a recordset based on the command. That's taken care of when the Text property of the Vendors combo box is set to the current vendor in the Load procedure of the form. You'll see how that works in a minute. If an error occurs during the Initialize procedure, the error routine calls the DisplayErrorMessage procedure defined in the standard module and then ends the application by executing an End statement.

Code for the standard module

```
Option Explicit                                                              1

Public gcnAP As Connection
Public grsVendors As Recordset
Public Const gsDialogTitle = "Chapter 8 - Vendors (unbound)"
```

```
Public Sub DisplayErrorMessage()                                             2
    If gcnAP.Errors.Count > 0 Then
        MsgBox "Error code: " & gcnAP.Errors(0).Number _
            & vbCrLf & " Description: " & gcnAP.Errors(0).Description _
            & vbCrLf & "Source: " & gcnAP.Errors(0).Source, _
            vbOKOnly + vbCritical, gsDialogTitle
        gcnAP.Errors.Clear
    Else
        MsgBox "Error code: " & Err.Number & vbCrLf & "Description: " _
            & Err.Description & vbCrLf & "Source: " & Err.Source, _
            vbOKOnly + vbCritical, gsDialogTitle
    End If
End Sub
```

```
Public Sub HilightText(ctl As Control)                                       3
    ctl.SelStart = 0
    ctl.SelLength = Len(ctl)
End Sub
```

Code for the Vendors form

```
Option Explicit                                                              1

Dim mrsInvoices As Recordset
Dim mcmdInvoices As Command
```

```
Private Sub Form_Initialize()                                                2
On Error GoTo ErrorHandler
    Set grsVendors = New Recordset
    Set mrsInvoices = New Recordset
    Set mcmdInvoices = New Command
    grsVendors.Open "SELECT * FROM Vendors ORDER BY VendorName", _
        gcnAP, adOpenStatic, adLockOptimistic, adCmdText
    mcmdInvoices.ActiveConnection = gcnAP
    mcmdInvoices.CommandText = "SELECT InvoiceNumber, InvoiceDate, " _
        & "InvoiceTotal, PaymentTotal, CreditTotal," _
        & "InvoiceTotal-PaymentTotal-CreditTotal AS BalanceDue " _
        & "FROM Invoices WHERE VendorID = ? " _
        & "AND InvoiceTotal-PaymentTotal-CreditTotal > 0"
    mcmdInvoices.CommandType = adCmdText
    Exit Sub
ErrorHandler:
    DisplayErrorMessage
    End
End Sub
```

Figure 8-11   The code for the standard module and the Vendors form (part 1 of 4)

As you review the code in the Initialize procedure, you'll notice that it doesn't create or open the Connection object that's used by the Recordset and Command objects. As you'll see later, that's done in the Login form module. This code is in the Login module so the connection can be tested to be sure that a valid user name and password are entered before the Login form is closed.

If the Initialize procedure completes successfully, the procedure for the Load event of the form is executed (3). This procedure loads the Vendors combo box with the names of all the vendors in the Vendors recordset. Then, it uses the MoveFirst method to move the current record pointer to the first record in the Vendors recordset, and it sets the Text property of the combo box to the name of that vendor. Because that statement changes the value of the combo box, it causes the Click event procedure (4) for the combo box to be executed. This procedure is also executed any time the user selects a vendor from the combo box.

The first statement in the Click event procedure for the Vendors combo box finds the selected vendor in the Vendors recordset. That's necessary because selecting a vendor from the combo box simply changes the Text property of the combo box. It doesn't affect the Vendors recordset in any way. To locate the selected vendor, the procedure uses a Find method that contains the VendorID associated with that vendor. Since this value was stored in the ItemData property when the combo box was loaded, the value in this property is used to locate the appropriate vendor.

After the record is located, the label in the lower left corner of the form is changed to reflect the position of the current vendor record in the recordset. Then, the FormatVendorInfo procedure (5) is called to format the data that's displayed in the text boxes on the form, and the list box that will display a list of the unpaid invoices for the vendor is cleared. Next, the value of the first parameter for the Invoices command is changed so it contains the VendorID of the current vendor, and the Invoices recordset is filled by executing the Invoices command. If that recordset contains any invoices, the FillInvoiceControls procedure (6) is called to load the Invoices list box and grid, and the Delete command button is disabled so the vendor record can't be deleted. If no invoices are found for the vendor, the Rows property of the invoice grid is set to 1 so only the header row is displayed, and the Delete command button is enabled so the vendor can be deleted.

Code for the Vendors form (continued)

```
Private Sub Form_Load()                                                    3
   With grsVendors
       Do Until .EOF
           cboVendors.AddItem !VendorName
           cboVendors.ItemData(cboVendors.NewIndex) = !VendorID
           .MoveNext
       Loop
       .MoveFirst
       cboVendors.Text = !VendorName
   End With
End Sub
```

```
Private Sub cboVendors_Click()                                             4
    grsVendors.Find "VendorID = " & cboVendors.ItemData(cboVendors.ListIndex), _
        , , adBookmarkFirst
    lblRecordNumber = "Vendor Record: " & grsVendors.AbsolutePosition & " of " _
        & grsVendors.RecordCount
    FormatVendorInfo
    lstInvoices.Clear
    mcmdInvoices.Parameters(0) = grsVendors!VendorID
    Set mrsInvoices = mcmdInvoices.Execute
    If mrsInvoices.RecordCount > 0 Then
        FillInvoiceControls
        cmdDelete.Enabled = False
    Else
        msgInvoices.Rows = 1
        cmdDelete.Enabled = True
    End If
End Sub
```

```
Private Sub FormatVendorInfo()                                             5
    With grsVendors
        txtVendorInfo = ""
        txtVendorInfo = IIf(!VendorAddress1 = " " Or _
            IsNull(!VendorAddress1), txtVendorInfo, !VendorAddress1 & vbCrLf)
        txtVendorInfo = IIf(!VendorAddress2 = " " Or _
            IsNull(!VendorAddress2), txtVendorInfo, _
            txtVendorInfo & !VendorAddress2 & vbCrLf)
        txtVendorInfo = txtVendorInfo & !VendorCity & ", " & _
            !VendorState & " " & !VendorZipCode & vbCrLf
        txtVendorInfo = IIf(!VendorContact = " " Or _
            IsNull(!VendorContact), txtVendorInfo, _
            txtVendorInfo & !VendorContact & vbCrLf)
        txtVendorInfo = IIf(!VendorPhone = " ", txtVendorInfo, _
            txtVendorInfo & !VendorPhone)
        txtYTDPurchases = Format(!YTDPurchases, "Currency")
        txtLastTranDate = Format(!LastTranDate, "MMMM d, yyyy")
    End With
End Sub
```

Figure 8-11   The code for the standard module and the Vendors form (part 2 of 4)

The FillInvoiceControls procedure (6) starts by setting the Rows property of the Invoices grid to one more than the number of records in the Invoices recordset. An additional row is needed to display the information in the column headers. Then, a For...Next statement is used with the MoveNext method to load the data from each record in the Invoices recordset into a row in the grid. Since the first row of the grid contains the column headings, the counter that's used by the For...Next statements starts at a value of 1 (the second row) and is incremented by 1 until it reaches the value of the RecordCount property. Then, the first statement within the For...Next loop sets the Row property of the grid to the value of the counter.

Because some of the columns in the grid need to be formatted, each column is loaded by a separate statement. To do that, the Col property is initially set to zero to indicate that the active cell is in the first column. Next, the value of the InvoiceNumber field is loaded into the cell in the current row of that column. Then, the Col property is set to one, the next field is loaded, and so on. Note that if the fields didn't need to be formatted or if all the fields were formatted the same way, you could code another For...Next statement that processes each column within the For...Next loop that processes each row. In that case, you would use a column counter variable to refer to each field in the current record by its index number rather than referring to the fields by name. After the fields in each record are loaded into the appropriate columns in the grid, the last statement before the MoveNext method adds the InvoiceNumber of the current record to the Invoices list box.

If the user clicks on the Delete button to delete a vendor record, the Click event procedure for that button (7) is executed. This procedure begins by displaying a message to confirm the delete operation. If the user confirms the operation, the vendor name is removed from the combo box list and the record is deleted. Then, the current record pointer is repositioned and the name of the current vendor is displayed in the combo box. As before, this change to the Text property causes the Click event of the combo box to fire, which causes the information for the current vendor to be displayed on the form.

Code for the Vendors form (continued)

```
Private Sub FillInvoiceControls()                                           6
    Dim intRecordCounter As Integer
    With msgInvoices
        .Rows = mrsInvoices.RecordCount + 1
        For intRecordCounter = 1 To mrsInvoices.RecordCount
            .Row = intRecordCounter
            .Col = 0
            .Text = mrsInvoices!InvoiceNumber
            .Col = 1
            .Text = mrsInvoices!InvoiceDate
            .Col = 2
            .Text = Format(mrsInvoices!InvoiceTotal, "Currency")
            .Col = 3
            .Text = Format(mrsInvoices!PaymentTotal, "Currency")
            .Col = 4
            .Text = Format(mrsInvoices!CreditTotal, "Currency")
            .Col = 5
            .Text = Format(mrsInvoices!BalanceDue, "Currency")
            lstInvoices.AddItem mrsInvoices!InvoiceNumber
            mrsInvoices.MoveNext
        Next intRecordCounter
    End With
End Sub
```

```
Private Sub cmdDelete_Click()                                              7
On Error GoTo ErrorHandler
    Dim intIndex As Integer
    If MsgBox("Delete this vendor?", vbYesNo + vbDefaultButton2 + vbQuestion, _
            gsDialogTitle) = vbYes Then
        cboVendors.RemoveItem cboVendors.ListIndex
        With grsVendors
            .Delete
            .MoveNext
            If .EOF Then .MoveLast
            cboVendors.Text = !VendorName
        End With
    End If
    Exit Sub
ErrorHandler:
    DisplayErrorMessage
End Sub
```

Figure 8-11 The code for the standard module and the Vendors form (part 3 of 4)

If the user clicks on the New button to add a new vendor, the Click event procedure for that button (8) is executed. This procedure simply displays the New Vendor form as a modal form.

The user can also display the detail information for an invoice in the Invoices grid by clicking on the invoice number for that invoice in the Invoices list box. Then, the Click event procedure of the list box (9) is executed. This procedure starts by setting the Row property of the grid to 1 (the first row that contains invoice data) and the Col property of the grid to 0 (the column that contains the invoice number). Then, it uses a Do loop to locate the row that contains the invoice number that the user clicked on in the Invoices list box. When it finds that row, it sets the TopRow property of the grid to that row number, which causes that row to be displayed at the top of the grid.

The last event procedure in this module (10) is fired when the user clicks on the Exit button. This procedure unloads the main form to end the application.

Code for the Vendors form (continued)

```
Private Sub cmdNew_Click()                                              8
    frmNewVendor.Show 1
End Sub
```

```
Private Sub lstInvoices_Click()                                        9
    With msgInvoices
        .Row = 1
        .Col = 0
        Do Until .Text = lstInvoices.Text
            .Row = .Row + 1
        Loop
        .TopRow = .Row
    End With
End Sub
```

```
Private Sub cmdExit_Click()                                           10
    Unload Me
End Sub
```

Figure 8-11   The code for the standard module and the Vendors form (part 4 of 4)

Exercise set 8-2: Write the code for the standard module and Vendors form

In this exercise set, you will add code to the Vendors form that you created in exercise set 8-1 so this form works the way you want it to. You'll also create the standard module that's used by the Vendors application.

Start the project and add a standard module

1. Open the C8Unbound project that you created in exercise set 8-1.

2. Add a standard module to the project, set its Name property to modStandard, and save the module in the folder for this project.

3. Add the two global variables, the global constant, and the two global procedures shown in part 1 of figure 8-11 to the standard module.

Add the code for the Vendors form that makes it display the right data

4. Add the two Dim statements shown in part 1 of figure 8-11 to the Declarations section of the Vendors form. *If you're using a Jet database,* you'll also need to code a Dim statement for a Parameter object named mprmInvoices.

5. Enter the Form_Initialize procedure for this form. *If you're using a Jet database*, though, you'll need to add these statements following the statement that sets the CommandType property of the command:

```
Set mprmInvoices = mcmdInvoices.CreateParameter("ID", _
    adInteger, adParamInput, 4)
mcmdInvoices.Parameters.Append mprmInvoices
```

This creates and sets the value for the Parameter object that a Jet database requires.

6. Because the Connection object that's used by this application is created and opened in the Login form and you haven't created the Login form yet, you'll need to add some code to the Form_Initialize procedure so it'll work correctly. First, add these two statements following the three Set statements at the beginning of the procedure:

```
Set gcnAP = New Connection
gcnAP.CursorLocation = adUseClient
```

Next, enter a statement to open the connection. The format of this statement will depend on whether you're accessing a Jet or SQL Server database.

If you're using a SQL Server database, the statement will look something like this:

```
gcnAP.Open "Provider=SQLOLEDB;Server=mmaserver;" & _
           "Database=AccountsPayable;User ID=ed;" & _
           "Password=abc4xyz"
```

But be sure to change the Provider, Server, User ID and Password parameters so they're appropriate for the database you're accessing.

If you're using a Jet database, the statement will look something like this:

```
gcnAP.Open "Provider=Microsoft.Jet.OLEDB.3.51;" & _
      "Data Source=C:\Murach\VB6\Databases\AccountsPayable.mdb"
```

7. Enter the code for the Form_Load procedure shown in figure 8-11 (part 2). Next, run the project to see that the combo box is loaded with the names of all the vendors in the Vendors recordset, but the information for that vendor isn't displayed in the other controls on the form. Select a different vendor from the Vendors combo box to see that the name of the vendor you selected is now displayed in the text box portion of the combo box. Then, click on the Close button to close the form.

8. Enter the code for the cboVendors_Click procedure in figure 8-11 (part 2). ***If you're using a Jet database***, though, you'll need to replace the shaded statement with this statement:

```
mprmInvoices.Value = grsVendors!VendorID
```

    Also, ***if you're using the Learning Edition of Visual Basic***, you need to know that the Find method isn't implemented by the OLE DB Provider that comes with it. To fix this problem, please see the notes in appendix C for chapter 8.

9. Enter the code for the FormatVendorInfo and FillInvoiceControls procedures shown in figure 8-11 (parts 2 and 3). ***If you're using a Jet database***, be sure to replace the text strings in the If conditions that contain a single space with empty strings (""). Then, run the project. Now, the information for the first vendor should be displayed in the form when the form first opens, and you should be able to display the information for other vendors by selecting the vendor from the Vendors combo box. If your application doesn't work this way, you'll need to debug it.

Add the remaining code to the Vendors form

10. Enter the code for the cmdDelete_Click and cmdNew_Click procedures as shown in figure 8-11 (parts 3 and 4) and test the project. Because you haven't created the New Vendor form yet, you'll get an error when you click on the New button. However, you should be able to delete a vendor by clicking on the Delete button.

11. Close the form, then enter the code for the lstInvoices_Click and cmdExit_Click procedures shown in figure 8-11 (part 4). Then, run the project one more time. Locate a vendor that has several invoices like Federal Express, then click on the fourth or fifth invoice in the Invoices list box to see that the details for that invoice are now displayed at the top of the Invoices grid. When you're done, click on the Exit button to close the form and end the application.

12. If everything worked right, save the project and leave it open if you're going to continue.

The property settings and code for the Login and New Vendor forms

Now that you know how the Vendors form works, you should have no trouble understanding how the Login and New Vendor forms work. After you study the property settings and code for these forms, you can build them in the last exercise set for this chapter.

The property settings for the Login and New Vendor forms

Figure 8-12 presents the property settings for the text boxes, combo boxes, and command buttons on the Login and New Vendor forms. Except for the PasswordChar property for the Password text box on the Login form, you should already be familiar with these properties. As described in figure 8-10, the PasswordChar property lets you display a placeholder character in place of the characters entered by the user. In this case, an asterisk is displayed for every character entered into the Password text box so the password isn't visible.

The New Vendor form includes two combo boxes that let the user select a state and payment terms for the vendor. As you can see by the Style property for these controls, the combo boxes are implemented as drop-down lists. That means that the user must select an item from the list. No other values are allowed.

Also notice that the Cancel property of the Cancel buttons on the Login and New Vendor forms is set to True. That way, the user can cancel out of these forms simply by pressing the Esc key. Also notice that the Default property of the OK buttons is set to True, which means that their Click event procedures are executed by default when the user presses the Enter key.

Property settings for the text boxes on the Login form

Property	User name	Password
Name	txtUserName	txtPassword
PasswordChar		*

Property settings for the text boxes on the New Vendor form

Property	Name	Address(1)	Address(2)	City
Name	txtName	txtAddress1	txtAddress2	txtCity

Property	Zip code	Contact	Phone
Name	txtZipCode	txtContact	txtPhone

Property settings for the combo boxes on the New Vendor form

Property	State	Terms
Name	cboStates	cboTerms
Sorted	True	False
Style	2 – Dropdown List	2 – Dropdown List

Property settings for the command buttons on the Login and New Vendor forms

Property	OK button	Cancel button
Name	cmdOK	cmdCancel
Cancel	False	True
Default	True	False

Note

- Be sure to clear the Text property for all text boxes on both forms so they're blank when they're first displayed.

Figure 8-12   The property settings for the Login and New Vendor forms

The code for the Login form

Figure 8-13 presents the code for the Login form. This form is set as the startup object for the project, so it's the first form that's displayed when the project starts. Before the application continues, the user must enter a valid user name and password into this form so a connection to the data source can be established.

When this form is first loaded, the Load event of the form (1) creates a new instance of the Connection object that was declared in the standard module of the application as a Public variable (see part 1 of figure 8-11). Then, it sets the CursorLocation property of the connection so client-side cursors are used.

If the user clicks on the Cancel button on this form or presses the Esc key, the Click event procedure for this button (2) is executed. This procedure displays a message box that verifies that the user wants to end the application. If the user clicks on the Yes button in this box, the form is unloaded and the application ends. If the user clicks on the No button, the focus is moved to the User Name text box on the Login form so the user can enter a name and password.

When the user clicks on the OK button to accept a user name and password, the Click event procedure of that button (3) is executed. This procedure begins by checking that a user name and password have been entered. The assumption here is that a password is always required, which may not be the case. If a password isn't required on your system, you can omit the code that checks for an entry in this control.

If both a user name and password have been entered, the procedure builds a connection string in the strConnect variable using the information that was entered on the form. Notice that the Provider, Server, and Database specifications are hardcoded into this string. Although you could let the user enter this information on the Login form, that usually isn't necessary.

After building the connection string, it's used to open a connection to the data source. If the connection is successful, the Login form is unloaded and the Vendors form is displayed. If the connection isn't successful, the error-handling routine is called.

The error-handling routine starts by checking the Count property of the Errors object to see if a provider error occurred. If so, the routine checks the Number property of the first Error object to see if the error was due to a failed login, indicating that the user name or password is invalid. If so, an appropriate error message is displayed and the user can then re-enter the user name and password. If any other type of error occurs—either a provider error, a Visual Basic error, or an ADO error—an error message is displayed, the form is unloaded, and the application ends. (Incidentally, you can find out what the error number is for a missing password by letting it happen and trapping the error. Then, you can use that error number in your code.)

The last two procedures in this module (4) occur when the focus moves to one of the text boxes on the Login form. Both of these procedures call the HilightText procedure in the application's standard module. As you may recall, this procedure highlights the text in the text box to make it easier for the user to change.

Code for the Login form

```
Private Sub Form_Load()                                                  1
    Set gcnAP = New Connection
    gcnAP.CursorLocation = adUseClient
End Sub
```

```
Private Sub cmdCancel_Click()                                            2
    If MsgBox("Exit application?", vbYesNo + vbQuestion, _
            gsDialogTitle) = vbYes Then
        Unload Me
    Else
        txtUserName.SetFocus
    End If
End Sub
```

```
Private Sub cmdOK_Click()                                                3
On Error GoTo ErrorHandler
    Dim strConnect As String
    If txtUserName = "" Or txtPassword = "" Then
        MsgBox "You must enter a user name and password.", _
            vbOKOnly + vbInformation, gsDialogTitle
        txtUserName.SetFocus
    Else
        strConnect = "Provider=SQLOLEDB;Server=mmaserver;" & _
            "Database=AccountsPayable;User ID=" & txtUserName & _
            ";Password=" & txtPassword
        gcnAP.Open strConnect
        Unload Me
        frmVendors.Show
    End If
    Exit Sub
ErrorHandler:
    If gcnAP.Errors.Count > 0 Then
        If gcnAP.Errors(0).Number = -2147217843 Then
            MsgBox "The user name and password you entered are invalid.", _
                vbOKOnly + vbInformation, gsDialogTitle
            txtUserName.SetFocus
        Else
            MsgBox "Unable to connect to the data source.", _
                vbOKOnly + vbCritical, gsDialogTitle
            Unload Me
            End
        End If
        gcnAP.Errors.Clear
    Else
        MsgBox "Error code: " & Err.Number & vbCrLf & "Description: " & _
            Err.Description, vbOKOnly + vbCritical, gsDialogTitle
        Unload Me
        End
    End If
End Sub
```

```
Private Sub txtUserName_GotFocus()                                       4
    HilightText txtUserName
End Sub

Private Sub txtPassword_GotFocus()
    HilightText txtPassword
End Sub
```

Figure 8-13   The code for the Login form

The code for the New Vendor form

Figure 8-14 presents the code for the New Vendor form, which is displayed when the user clicks on the New button on the Vendors form. In the Declarations section of this form (1), you can see that a single variable is declared for the States recordset. Since this recordset is used to load the States combo box and to validate the zip code entered by the user, it must be declared at the module level. In contrast, the Terms recordset is declared as a local variable within the procedure that loads the Terms combo box because it's not used outside of that procedure.

When the New Vendor form is first loaded, the Load event procedure (2) begins by creating an instance of the States Recordset object. Then, it opens this recordset and calls the LoadStates and LoadTerms procedures to load the States and Terms combo boxes.

The LoadStates procedure (3) loops through the records in the States recordset and adds an item to the States combo box list for each record. When the loop ends, the recordset is at the end of the file (EOF), so the MoveFirst method is used to move the record pointer to the first record. If the recordset remains at EOF, the ValidZipCode procedure (8) that uses the States table won't work with some versions of the OLE DB providers.

The LoadTerms procedure (4) works similarly, except that it first declares the Terms recordset, then creates an instance of the recordset and opens the recordset. It also sets the ItemData property of each item that's added to the list to the TermsID field of the terms record. This is the field that will be saved in the new vendor record. At the end of this procedure, the object variable that's used to refer to the Terms recordset is set to Nothing since this recordset isn't needed after the combo box is loaded.

Each time the New Vendor form is displayed, the Activate event procedure (5) is executed. When the form is first loaded and displayed, this event occurs after the Initialize and Load events of the form. This event is typically used to modify the menus and toolbar on a form. In this case, however, it's used to clear the controls on the form so the user can enter a new record. Notice that the States and Terms combo boxes are cleared by setting their ListIndex properties to -1, which indicates that no selection has been made. The last statement in this procedure moves the focus to the first text box on the form so the user can begin entering data.

Code for the New Vendor form

```
Dim mrsStates As Recordset                                                1
```

```
Private Sub Form_Load()                                                   2
    Set mrsStates = New Recordset
    mrsStates.Open "States", gcnAP, adOpenStatic, adLockOptimistic, _
        adCmdTable
    LoadStates
    LoadTerms
End Sub
```

```
Private Sub LoadStates()                                                  3
    With mrsStates
        Do Until .EOF
            cboStates.AddItem !StateCode
            .MoveNext
        Loop
        .MoveFirst
    End With
End Sub
```

```
Private Sub LoadTerms()                                                   4
    Dim rsTerms As Recordset
    Set rsTerms = New Recordset
    With rsTerms
        .Open "Terms", gcnAP, adOpenStatic, adLockOptimistic, adCmdTable
        Do Until .EOF
            cboTerms.AddItem !TermsDescription
            cboTerms.ItemData(cboTerms.NewIndex) = !TermsID
            .MoveNext
        Loop
    End With
    Set rsTerms = Nothing
End Sub
```

```
Private Sub Form_Activate()                                               5
    txtName = ""
    txtAddress1 = ""
    txtAddress2 = ""
    txtCity = ""
    cboStates.ListIndex = -1
    txtZipCode = ""
    txtContact = ""
    txtPhone = ""
    cboTerms.ListIndex = -1
    txtName.SetFocus
End Sub
```

Figure 8-14   The code for the New Vendor form (part 1 of 3)

When the user clicks on the OK button to accept a vendor record, the Click event procedure for that button (6) is executed. This procedure starts by calling the ValidData function (7) to be sure that the user entered a value in all of the required fields. The ValidData function also calls the ValidZipCode procedure (8) to be sure that the zip code is valid for the state code. This procedure is similar to the one you saw in the bound New Vendor form in chapter 7. If any of the required fields are omitted or if the zip code is invalid, an error message is displayed and the new record isn't added. To understand how this works, you need to remember that the initial value of a Boolean variable, in this case, ValidData, is False. So the If statement that tests ValidData in the Click event procedure is False unless the value of ValidData is set to True.

If all of the data is valid, ValidData is set to True and the Click event procedure continues by adding a new record to the Vendors recordset. Then, it calls the LoadRecord procedure (9), which moves the data from the controls on the New Vendor form to the fields in the new vendor record. Before the recordset is updated, though, the name of the new vendor is saved in a local variable. I'll explain this statement and why it's necessary in just a moment. After that statement, the Update method is used to save the new record and the Vendors recordset is requeried. The requery is necessary to synchronize the recordset with the data on the server. If you didn't requery the recordset, you would run into problems if you tried to delete the new record.

After the recordset is requeried, a Find method is used to locate the record for the new vendor. Here, you can see that the record is located by using the vendor name that was saved in the local variable. In this case, the VendorID field can't be used because it's generated automatically when the new record is saved, so there's no way of knowing what it will be.

Unfortunately, though, searching for a vendor by name causes two potential problems. First, if the VendorName field isn't defined as a unique field, the find operation may locate a record other than the one you just added. Because of that, this field and any other fields that you will use to locate records in a table should be defined as unique in the database (with a unique constraint).

Second, the Find method won't work if the vendor name contains one or more single quotes (apostrophes). That's because the entire name must be enclosed in single quotes within the text string that's passed to the Find method so it will be interpreted properly by the OLE DB provider. But if the name contains a single quote (as in Ed's Computers), the provider will interpret it as the end of the name and the remaining text won't be evaluated properly. To avoid this problem, a Replace function is used to replace any single quotes within the vendor name with two single quotes when its value is assigned to the local variable. Then, the string will be evaluated properly. (This is a SQL convention that's supported by all SQL interpreters that conform to the ANSI rules.)

After the new vendor record is located, the vendor name is added to the Vendors combo box on the Vendors form. Because this combo box is sorted, the new vendor will automatically appear in alphabetical sequence. Next, the Text property of the combo box is set to the new vendor name so that vendor is

Code for the New Vendor form (continued)

```
Private Sub cmdOK_Click()                                                    6
On Error GoTo ErrorHandler
    Dim strVendorName As String
    If ValidData Then
        grsVendors.AddNew
        LoadRecord
        strVendorName = Replace(grsVendors!VendorName, "'", "''")
        grsVendors.Update
        grsVendors.Requery
        grsVendors.Find "VendorName = '" & strVendorName & "'"
        With frmVendors
            .cboVendors.AddItem grsVendors!VendorName
            .cboVendors.ItemData(.cboVendors.NewIndex) = grsVendors!VendorID
            .cboVendors.Text = grsVendors!VendorName
        End With
        frmNewVendor.Hide
    End If
    Exit Sub
ErrorHandler:
    DisplayErrorMessage
    If grsVendors.EditMode = adEditAdd Then grsVendors.CancelUpdate
    txtName.SetFocus
End Sub
```

```
Private Function ValidData() As Boolean                                      7
    Dim strMessage As String
    If txtName = "" Then
        txtName.SetFocus
        strMessage = "You must enter a vendor name."
    ElseIf txtCity = "" Then
        txtCity.SetFocus
        strMessage = "You must enter a city."
    ElseIf cboStates.ListIndex = -1 Then
        cboStates.SetFocus
        strMessage = "You must select a state."
    ElseIf txtZipCode = "" Then
        txtZipCode.SetFocus
        strMessage = "You must enter a zip code."
    ElseIf cboTerms.ListIndex = -1 Then
        cboTerms.SetFocus
        strMessage = "You must select the terms."
    Else
        If ValidZipCode Then
            ValidData = True
        Else
            txtZipCode.SetFocus
            strMessage = "The zip code is invalid."
        End If
    End If
    If Not ValidData Then
        MsgBox strMessage, vbOKOnly + vbInformation, gsDialogTitle
    End If
End Function
```

Figure 8-14   The code for the New Vendor form (part 2 of 3)

selected. That, in turn, causes the Click event of the combo box to fire. If you look back at the procedure for this event in part 2 of figure 8-11, you'll see that it formats and displays the information for the vendor.

If the processing in the Click event procedure completes without any errors, the New Vendor form is hidden and the Vendors form appears with the information for the new vendor displayed. If an error occurs, however, the error-handling routine calls the DisplayErrorMessage procedure in the standard module. Then, the routine checks the EditMode property of the Vendors recordset to determine if the error occurred during the update of that record. If it did, this property will have a value of adEditAdd since a new record has been added but hasn't been saved. If, for example, the user tries to add a record with a duplicate vendor name and the database has a unique constraint on that field, an error will occur and the EditMode property will have that value. In that case, the CancelUpdate method is issued so the new record is discarded. Then, the user can make the appropriate changes to the data in the New Vendor form and try to add the record again.

The ValidZipCode function (8) works by locating the record for the state code that was entered by the user. Then, it checks to be sure that the zip code that was entered falls within the range of zip codes for that state.

The LoadRecord procedure (9) moves the values in the text boxes and combo boxes on the form to the appropriate fields in the new record. Here, you should notice the difference in the assignment statements for the VendorState and TermsID fields. Although both of these statements load a field with data from a combo box, the VendorState field is loaded with the Text value of the selected item and the TermsID field is loaded with the ItemData value. That's because the TermsDescription field is displayed in the combo box, but the TermsID field is saved in the vendor record.

Curiously, if you're using this code with the Jet 4.0 OLE DB provider (the one you get with Access 2000), you can't omit the default Text property as shown in this figure. If you do, a null value is assigned to the field in the recordset. In other words, for this procedure to work right, the first assignment statement has to be coded as

```
!VendorName = txtName.Text
```

and the seven assignment statements that follow also have to explicitly name the Text property. This of course shouldn't be required, and it's particularly vexing since this worked right with the Jet 3.51 OLE DB provider.

The next seven procedures (10) call the HilightText procedure in the standard module whenever the focus moves to one of the text boxes on the form. The last procedure (11) hides the New Vendor form when the user clicks on the Cancel button on that form or presses the Esc key while that form is active.

Code for the New Vendor form (continued)

```
Private Function ValidZipCode() As Boolean                                    8
    ValidZipCode = True
    With mrsStates
        .Find "StateCode = '" & cboStates.Text & "'", , , adBookmarkFirst
        If Val(Left(txtZipCode, 5)) < !FirstZipCode Or _
            Val(Left(txtZipCode, 5)) > !LastZipCode Then
            ValidZipCode = False
        End If
    End With
End Function
```

```
Private Sub LoadRecord()                                                      9
    With grsVendors
        !VendorName = txtName
        !VendorAddress1 = txtAddress1
        !VendorAddress2 = txtAddress2
        !VendorCity = txtCity
        !VendorState = cboStates
        !VendorZipCode = txtZipCode
        !VendorContact = txtContact
        !VendorPhone = txtPhone
        !TermsID = cboTerms.ItemData(cboTerms.ListIndex)
    End With
End Sub
```

```
Private Sub txtName_GotFocus()                                               10
    HilightText txtName
End Sub

Private Sub txtAddress1_GotFocus()
    HilightText txtAddress1
End Sub

Private Sub txtAddress2_GotFocus()
    HilightText txtAddress2
End Sub

Private Sub txtCity_GotFocus()
    HilightText txtCity
End Sub

Private Sub txtZipCode_GotFocus()
    HilightText txtZipCode
End Sub

Private Sub txtContact_GotFocus()
    HilightText txtContact
End Sub

Private Sub txtPhone_GotFocus()
    HilightText txtPhone
End Sub
```

```
Private Sub cmdCancel_Click()                                                11
    frmNewVendor.Hide
End Sub
```

Figure 8-14   The code for the New Vendor form (part 3 of 3)

Exercise set 8-3: Build the New Vendor and Login forms

In this exercise set, you'll build the New Vendor form shown in figure 8-1 and add the code for it. Then, you'll have the option of building the Login form for this application and adding the code to create and test a connection based on the user name and password that you enter into this form. You may want to do that if you're accessing data in a SQL Server database or in a Jet database that's password protected. If you're accessing data in a Jet database that isn't password protected, though, the Login form isn't necessary.

Start the project and add a new form

1. Open the C8Unbound project you created in exercise set 8-1 and enhanced in exercise set 8-2.

2. Add a new form to the project, change its Name property to frmNewVendor, change its Caption property to New Vendor, and change its BorderStyle property to Fixed Single. Then, save the form with the name frmNewVendor in the same folder as the other project files.

Build and test the New Vendor form

3. Add the frame, labels, text boxes, standard combo boxes, and command buttons to the form so it looks like the one in figure 8-1. Then, set the Caption properties of the frame and labels so they look like those in that figure, and set the properties for the text boxes, combo boxes, and command buttons as shown in figure 8-12.

4. Add the code in part 1 of figure 8-14 to the form. Then, start the project and click on the New button in the Vendors form to display the New Vendor form. Drop down the lists for the States and Terms combo boxes and select a different value from each. At this point, that's all you can do with this form other than to enter data into the text boxes. So close the form and end the application.

5. Add the code for the cmdOK_Click procedure in part 2 of figure 8-14. *If you're using the Learning Edition of Visual Basic*, though, you need to know that the Find method in the middle of this procedure isn't implemented by the OLE DB Provider that comes with it. To fix this problem, please see the notes in appendix C for chapter 8.

6. Add the remaining code in parts 2 and 3 of figure 8-14. Then, run the application. Display the New Vendor form and click on its OK button without entering any data. What error message is displayed?

7. With the form still running, enter the data for all the required fields in a vendor record, but enter an invalid zip code. Then, click on the OK button. Is an error message displayed? If not, you'll need to fix the code that validates the zip code.

8. Enter a correct zip code, then press the OK button to add the record to the Vendors recordset. Now, the information for that vendor should be displayed in the Vendors form.

9. Click on the New button to display the New Vendor form again. Enter a name for the new vendor, then press the Esc key to cancel out of the form. Select the vendor record that you added in step 8, and delete it by clicking on the Delete button. Then, end the application.

Build and test the Login form (optional)

10. Add another new form to the project. Then, change the Name property of the form to frmLogin, change the Caption property to Login, change the BorderStyle property to Fixed Dialog, and change the StartUpPosition property to CenterScreen. Save the new form with the name frmLogin.

11. Add the frame, labels, text boxes, and command buttons to the Login form so it looks like the form in figure 8-1. Set the Caption properties of the frame and labels so they appear as shown in that figure, then set the properties for the text boxes and command buttons as shown in figure 8-12.

12. Add the code shown in figure 8-13 to the Login form. Be sure to change the connection string arguments depending on the type and location of the database you want to access.

13. Because the Login form includes code that creates and opens the Connection object that's used by the other forms in the application, you'll need to remove the code you added to the Vendors form to perform those functions. In particular, you need to remove the Set statement that creates an instance of the connection, the assignment statement that sets the value of the CursorLocation property, and the statement that opens the connection. These statements can be found in the procedure for the Initialize event of the Vendors form.

14. Change the StartupObject property of the project to the Login form. Then, run the application. When the Login form is displayed, press the Enter key without entering a user name or password to see what happens. Then, enter an invalid user name or password to see what happens. Finally, enter a valid user name and password. When you click on the OK button, the Vendors form should be displayed. If not, you'll need to debug the project.

Save the project and exit from Visual Basic

15. Save the project and exit from Visual Basic. If you were able to create this application successfully and if you understand all the code, you're well on your way to having the skills of a professional programmer.

Perspective

If you completed the exercise sets for this chapter, you should now have a good idea of what it takes to develop professional applications using unbound forms. Although this chapter only presents the most common controls for working with unbound forms, you should be able to use other controls using similar techniques. The same goes for the coding techniques presented in this chapter. If you understood the techniques presented here, you should be able to develop techniques of your own for performing other operations.

This chapter should also give you an idea of what the advantages of using unbound forms are. In particular, because you work directly with ADO objects rather than through the data control, you have more control over the operations that are performed. Also, because you code each operation explicitly, you don't have to guess what's going on behind the scenes through a bound control. Although unbound forms may take longer to develop initially, they're often easier to test, maintain, and debug.

Terms you should know

active cell
parameter query
criteria
asynchronous operation
transaction processing
commit
rollback
placeholder character

9

How to use the Data Environment Designer to build forms

The Data Environment Designer is a new feature of Visual Basic 6 that lets you create ADO Connection and Command objects with relative ease. Once you've created these objects, you can use them to build forms. You can also use these objects with the Data Report Designer that's presented in the next chapter to create the reports for an application. In short, the Data Environment Designer is a powerful new development tool that every Visual Basic 6 developer should be familiar with. Although this tool isn't available with the Learning Edition of Visual Basic, you can get a good appreciation for what it can do and how you use it just by reading this chapter.

Basic skills for working with the Data Environment Designer **336**
How to work with the Data Environment Designer 336
How to edit or create a Connection object 338
How to create a Command object 340
How to build a bound form from a Command object 342
How to change the mapping defaults 344
How to use Data Environment objects in code 346
Exercise set 9-1: Develop a bound form 348

Other skills for working with Command objects **350**
How to use the Query Designer to create a query 350
How to use the Advanced tab to set Command properties 352
How to use the Relation tab to define a parent-child relationship 354
How to use the Grouping tab to define record groups 356
How to use the Aggregates tab to define aggregate fields 358
How to use the Parameters tab for queries that use parameters 360
Exercise set 9-2: Create the Command objects for a new project 362

An enhanced Vendors application **364**
The enhanced Vendors form 364
The properties for the data-bound controls 366
The code for the Vendors application 368
Exercise set 9-3: Build an enhanced Vendors form 370

Perspective **372**

Basic skills for working with the Data Environment Designer

To get you started right with the Data Environment Designer, you'll first learn how to create Designer, Connection, and Command objects. Then, you'll learn how to use a Command object to quickly build a bound form, and you'll learn how to refer to the Data Environment objects in code so you can add the code to the form that makes it work the way you want it to. After that introduction, exercise set 9-1 will guide you through the development of a simple bound form that will illustrate some of the power of this feature.

How to work with the Data Environment Designer

Figure 9-1 shows the Data Environment Designer window that you can open from Visual Basic 6. Within this window, you can see four *Data Environment objects* that have been created for this project. At the top of the window, you can see a *DataEnvironment object* (deAP) that has one *Connection object* (conAP) followed by two *Command objects* that use its connection: the Vendors object and the VendorInvoices object. After each Command object, you can see the fields that are returned by the command. All of the objects that you create in this window use ADO for accessing the data.

Before you can use a DataEnvironment object, you need to create at least one Connection object and one Command object for it. Then, you can use the Command object to create a bound form. You can refer to the Connection object and Command object through code as you create an unbound form. Or, you can use a combination of the two techniques to build forms.

Although you can create more than one DataEnvironment object for a single project, you'll normally use just one for each project. Similarly, although you can create more than one Connection object for a DataEnvironment object, you'll normally create just one. Then, you'll use that connection for all of the commands that are required by your project.

The Data Environment Designer window

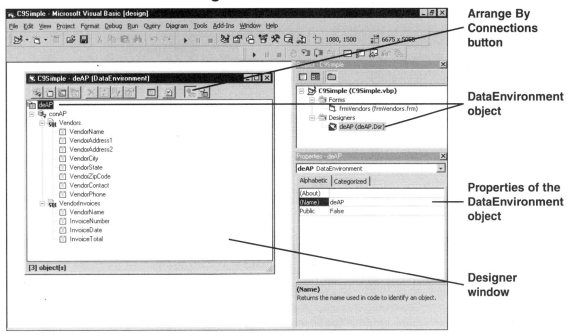

Arrange By
Connections
button

DataEnvironment
object

Properties of the
DataEnvironment
object

Designer
window

Description

- The Data Environment Designer is a new feature with Visual Basic 6. It lets you create Connection and Command objects that you can use for building forms and developing reports with ADO.

- To open the Designer window, you can select More ActiveX Designers from the Project menu and then select Data Environment. Or, you can right-click in the Project Explorer window, then select Add, More ActiveX Designers, and Data Environment from the subsequent menus.

- When the Designer window is opened for the first time for a project, one DataEnvironment object and one Connection object are shown. To change the name of the DataEnvironment object, select it in either the Designer or Project Explorer window, then change the name in the Properties window.

- To change the way the objects are arranged in the Data Environment Designer window, click on the Arrange By Connections or the Arrange By Objects toolbar buttons. (The Arrange By Connections view is shown above.)

- To remove a DataEnvironment object from a project, select the object in the Project Explorer window and chose the Remove command from either the Project menu or the shortcut menu.

Figure 9-1   How to work with the Data Environment Designer

How to edit or create a Connection object

Figure 9-2 shows how to create a Connection object with the Data Environment Designer. In this case, the resulting object is like a Connection object that you create through code as shown in chapter 8. In fact, as you will soon see, the Connection object has the same ADO methods, properties, and events that you were introduced to in chapter 8.

To edit or create a Connection object, you can use the techniques that are presented in this figure. To start, you'll want to edit the Connection object that is automatically created when you open the Designer window for the first time. Once the Data Link Properties dialog box is displayed, you can complete the Provider and Connection tabs just as you did for the exercise sets in chapters 6 and 7.

When you create a new Connection object, it is added to the Designer window. In addition, if you open the Data View window that's presented in chapter 11, you'll see all of the Connection objects for the Designer. Note, however, that you can only use the Data View window to manage database objects like stored procedures, tables, and views. You can't use that window to edit Data Environment objects. To do that, you have to use the Designer window.

The Provider and Connection tabs of the Data Link Properties dialog box

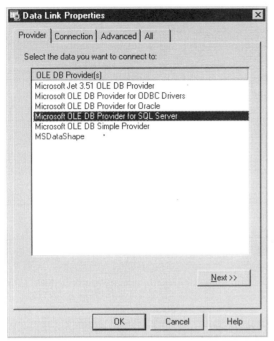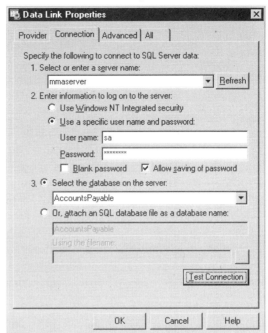

Description

- To edit a Connection object, select that object in the Designer window and click on the Properties button in the Designer toolbar. Or, right-click on the Connection object and select Properties from its shortcut menu.

- To create a new Connection object, click on the Add Connection button in the Designer toolbar. Or, click on the Arrange By Objects toolbar button to display the Connections folder, then right-click on that folder and select Add Connection from its shortcut menu.

- When the Data Link Properties dialog box is displayed, you must complete the Properties and Connection tabs as you did in chapters 6 and 7 (see figure 6-5 for more detail).

- When you add a Connection object to the Designer window, it's also added to the Data View window that's presented in chapter 11. However, you have to use the Designer window, not the Data View window, to edit the properties of the Connection object or to see its Command objects.

Figure 9-2   How to edit or create a Connection object

How to create a Command object

Figure 9-3 shows how to create a Command object. After the General tab of the Properties dialog box is displayed, you need to give the object a command name and select one of the Connection objects that you've created. Then, to establish the data source, you either (1) choose a stored procedure, table, or view, or (2) enter an SQL statement that does the query that you want.

After you complete the General tab, you can use the five other tabs to enhance the query or modify the default settings. You'll learn how to use these tabs after you do the first exercise set for this chapter. You'll also learn how to use the Query Designer that you access by clicking on the SQL Builder button. It lets you build an SQL query by using a graphical interface instead of entering the query from scratch. But first, I want you to see how easy it is to build a bound form from a Command object.

The General tab of the Properties dialog box for a Command object

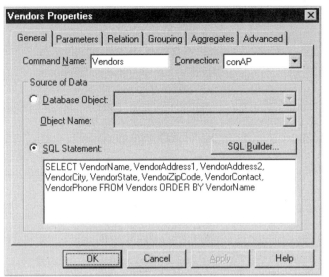

Description

- To create a new Command object, click on the Add Command button on the Designer toolbar, or right-click on the Command folder and select Add Command from its shortcut menu. This displays the General tab of the Properties dialog box for the Command object.

- From the General tab, you enter a name for the command, and you choose one of the Connection objects that has been created for the DataEnvironment object. Then, if you click on the Database Object button, you can select Stored Procedure, Table, or View from the first drop-down list and the stored procedure, table, or view that you want to use as the data source from the Object Name list. Or, if you click on the SQL Statement button, you can enter an SQL statement as the data source.

- To build an SQL statement for a command using a graphical interface, you can click on the SQL Builder button. You can learn how to use this interface in figure 9-7.

- In figures 9-8 through 9-12, you can learn how to use the other five tabs of the Properties dialog box. As you will see, the Relation, Grouping, and Aggregates tabs let you create more complicated queries; the Advanced tab lets you change the default ADO settings like those for CursorType and LockType; and the Parameters tab lets you adjust the properties of the Parameter objects that are used with queries that use parameters.

- To edit a Command object, click on the Properties button in the Designer toolbar, or right-click on the object and select Properties from its shortcut menu.

Figure 9-3   How to create a Command object

How to build a bound form from a Command object

Figure 9-4 shows how to create a bound form by dragging and dropping a Command object or individual fields of that object onto a form. To do that, of course, both the Designer window and the Form window have to be visible as shown in this figure. By default, bound text box controls are added to the form for all fields that don't have the Boolean data type, and one label is added before each field to identify it. As you will see in the next figure, though, you can change these defaults.

To bind each text box control to its related field, the DataSource, DataMember, and DataField properties are set automatically. If you check these properties for a control, you'll see that the DataSource property is set to the name of the DataEnvironment object, and the DataMember property is set to the name of the Command object.

After you've added the controls to the form, you can move and edit them as usual. In practice, you'll probably want to reposition some of the controls since they're added to the form in columns. You may also want to edit the labels so they provide more descriptive names.

Once you've got those controls set up the way you want them, you need to add navigation controls to the form so the user can move from one record to another. You also need to add the code to the form that makes it work the way you want it to. For the simple form in this figure, for example, you could add First, Previous, Next, and Last command buttons for navigation and an Exit button to exit from the application. Then, you could add the code that makes these buttons work.

A bound form that was created from a Command object

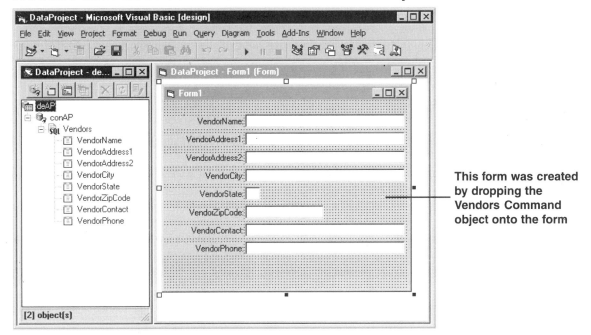

This form was created by dropping the Vendors Command object onto the form

Description

- To create a bound form from a Command object, drag the object and drop in onto the form. Then, one bound control is added to the form for each field that's defined by the command, and all of the data properties for each control are set automatically. By default, a label that identifies each bound control is also added to the form.

- To add individual fields to a form, expand the Command object in the Designer window so it shows all the fields defined by the object. Then, drag-and-drop one field name at a time onto the form.

- By default, text boxes are used as the bound controls for all fields except for Boolean fields, which default to check box controls. However, you can change these defaults as shown in the next figure.

- If you look at the Data properties for a bound control that has been added to the form in this way, you will see that the DataSource property is set to the designer name (deAP), the DataMember property is set to the command name (Vendors), and the DataField property is set to the field name.

- After you add the controls to the form, you can move or edit them in the usual ways.

- To complete a form, you need to add navigation controls that let the user move from one record to another. For a simple application like the one above, you can add command buttons that use the MoveFirst, MoveLast, MoveNext, and MovePrevious methods.

Figure 9-4   How to build a bound form from a Command object

How to change the mapping defaults

Figure 9-5 shows how to change the *mapping* defaults for a category of data types, a specific data type, or a specific field. If, for example, you want all of the fields that have the Currency data type mapped to masked edit controls instead of text boxes, you can use the Options dialog box as shown in this figure. You can also use that dialog box to stop identifying labels from being added to a form when you drag fields onto it.

Similarly, if you want to change the mapping for a single field in a command, you can use the Field Properties dialog box for that field. You can also use that dialog box to change the Caption property of the field that is used to identify it.

In either dialog box, you use the Control list to select the control that you want the category, data type, or field mapped to. This list contains all of the controls that are registered on your machine including ActiveX controls. Note, however, that any changes you make to the defaults apply only to the project you're working on. If you start a new project, the original defaults are reinstated.

The Options and Field Properties dialog boxes

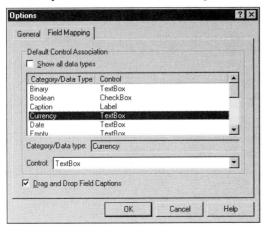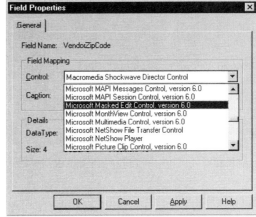

Description

- When you drop a Command object or fields on a form, the fields are *mapped* to specific types of controls based on the defaults that have been set. By default, one identifying label is also added to the form for each field. However, you can use the Options dialog box to change these general defaults. And you can use the Field Properties dialog box to change the mapping default or caption for a single field.

How to use the Options dialog box to change the general defaults

- To display the Options dialog box, click on the Options button in the Designer toolbar.
- To change the default mapping for a category of data types, choose the category in the Category/Data Type column, then choose the control from the Control list.
- To change the default mapping for a specific data type, check the Show All Data Types box. Then, choose the data type in the Category/Data Type column, and choose the control from the Control list.
- To stop identifying labels from being added to a form, uncheck the Drag And Drop Field Captions box.

How to use the Field Properties dialog box to change the defaults for specific fields

- To display the Field Properties dialog box, right-click on the field name in the Designer window and select Properties from its shortcut menu.
- To change the default control that will be used for the field, choose the control from the Control list.
- To change the label caption for a field from its default value (the name of the field), change the Caption entry.

Figure 9-5   How to change the mapping defaults

How to use Data Environment objects in code

Figure 9-6 shows how you can refer to Data Environment objects in code. These objects include one Recordset object that is automatically created for each Command object that returns a recordset. The names of these Recordset objects are the related command names preceded by the letters *rs*.

After you enter the name of a DataEnvironment object in the Code window followed by a dot, the completion list shows the names of the Connection and Recordset objects that you can enter next. Then, after you enter the name of one of those objects followed by a dot, the completion list shows the names of the properties and methods that you can use.

The properties and methods that are available are the same ones that you can use with a Connection or Recordset object that you create through code. This includes the BeginTrans, CommitTrans, and RollbackTrans methods for a Connection object. Since these methods aren't available when you use an ADO data control as a data source, this means that you can do transaction processing with a Designer that you can't do with a data control.

You can also enter procedures for the events that occur as the Data Environment objects are used. To do that, you first need to open the Code window for the *Designer module*. Then, you can select the DataEnvironment object, the Connection object, or the Recordset object that you want from the Object list and the event that you want from the Event list. That will automatically generate the Sub and End Sub statements that you need for the procedure.

Although the DataEnvironment object has only Initialize and Terminate events, the Connection and Recordset objects have the events that were presented in chapter 8. For instance, you can use the WillChangeRecord event to trigger a procedure that validates the data that is going to be used to update a record before it is actually updated.

A completion list for a DataEnvironment object

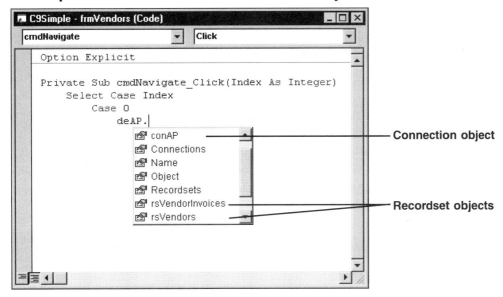

Connection object

Recordset objects

Statements that refer to properties and methods

```
deAP.rsVendors.RecordCount
deAP.rsVendorInvoices.EOF
deAP.rsVendorInvoices.Find
deAP.conAP.CursorLocation
```

Description

- When you create a Connection object, it is automatically added to the completion list for a DataEnvironment object as shown above. In addition, one Recordset object is created for each Command object, and it too is added to the completion list. The name of each recordset consists of the prefix *rs* followed by the name of the command.

- For each Connection, Command, and Recordset object that you create with the Data Environment Designer, you can use the properties and methods that you used with the Connection, Command, and Recordset objects that you created through code in chapter 8.

- You can also use code to respond to Designer, Connection, and Recordset events. To do that, select the Designer in the Project Explorer window and click the View Code button in its toolbar to display the Code window for the Designer module. Then, to create a procedure for an event, select the Designer (DataEnvironment), Connection, or Recordset object from the Object list at the top of the Code window, and select the event from the Event list.

- A DataEnvironment object has only two events: Activate and Terminate. In contrast, Connection, Command, and Recordset objects have the same events that you were introduced to in chapter 8.

Figure 9-6   How to use Data Environment objects in code

Exercise set 9-1: Develop a bound form

In this exercise set, you'll create a simple bound form using a Data
Environment Designer. That will give you a quick idea of how useful this new
feature can be.

Start a new project

1. Start Visual Basic and begin a Standard EXE project.

2. Set the Name property of the form to frmVendors, its Caption property to
    Vendors (C9 Simple), and its StartUpPosition property to CenterScreen.
    Then, close the Form window for the form.

3. Change the project name to C9Simple. Then, save the project and form with
    the names C9Simple and frmVendors in a new folder named Chapter 9
    Simple.

Add a Data Environment Designer to the project

4. Add a Data Environment Designer to the project by selecting More ActiveX
    Designers from the Project menu and clicking on Data Environment. Then,
    change the name of the designer to deAP, and save the designer with that
    name.

Edit the Connection object

5. From the Data Environment Designer window, open the Properties dialog box
    for the Connection object that's shown. Then, set the properties so you
    connect to the AccountsPayable database that you've been using for the
    exercise sets in chapters 6 through 8.

6. With the Properties window still open, test the connection. Then, return to the
    Designer window, and rename the Connection object as conAP.

Add a Command object

7. Add a Command object to the Designer window by clicking on the Add
    Command button on the Data Environment Designer toolbar.

8. Open the Properties dialog box for this Command object, change its name to
    Vendors, and set its connection to conAP. Then, click on the SQL statement
    button, and enter this SQL statement:

```
SELECT VendorName, VendorAddress1, VendorAddress2,
       VendorCity, VendorState, VendorZipCode,
       VendorContact, VendorPhone
    FROM Vendors ORDER BY VendorName
```

Build a bound Vendors form

9. Open the Form window for the Vendors form so you can see both the Data Environment Designer window and the Form window. Then, drag the Vendors Command object from the Designer window and drop it in the upper left corner of the form. This should add text boxes and labels for all the fields of the command to the form. If necessary, you can drag all of the controls at once to position them properly on the form.

10. Add five command buttons to the bottom of the form: four for navigation and one to exit from the form. Then, reposition the controls, delete unnecessary labels, and change the other labels so the form looks like something like this:

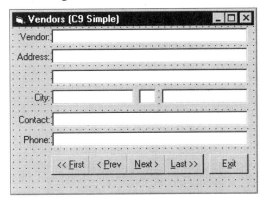

11. Test the project to see how this form works without any code. Although the data for the first record in the recordset should be displayed, none of the command buttons will work. So click on the Close button for the form to exit.

Add the code for the command buttons

12. Add the code for the navigation buttons using the MoveFirst, MovePrevious, MoveNext, and MoveLast methods and the EOF and BOF properties of the recordset named rsVendors. You can either set these navigation buttons up as an array as shown on pages 238 and 239 in chapter 6, or code one Click event procedure for each button.

13. Add the code to exit from the application when the Exit button is clicked.

Test and save the project

14. Test the project to make sure that it works correctly. When the form appears, you should see the data for the first vendor in the recordset. Then, click on the different navigation buttons to move through the list of vendors. And click on the Exit button to end the application.

15. Save the project. Then, use the Remove Project command in the File menu to remove it so you can start a new project in the next exercise set.

Other skills for working with Command objects

Now that you've seen how you can use the Data Environment Designer to create Command objects and build forms, this chapter presents the full range of techniques for creating Command objects. In particular, you'll learn how to use the Query Designer to create the SQL queries for a Command object, and you'll learn how to use the other five tabs of the Properties dialog box for a Command object.

How to use the Query Designer to create a query

Figure 9-7 shows the Query Designer window that opens when you click on the SQL Builder button on the General tab of the Properties dialog box for a Command object. You can then use this graphical interface to create a SQL query without even knowing the proper syntax for it. When you get the query the way you want it and close the Query Designer window, the query can be saved as the SQL statement for the Command object. This is usually easier and more accurate than entering the code for the statement directly into the General tab.

When the Query Designer window opens, no tables are shown in the *diagram pane*. However, the Data View window that's described in chapter 11 is also opened. Then, after you position the two windows so both are visible, you can drag the tables that you want to include in the query from the Data View window to the Query Designer window. In this figure, you can see that two tables have been added to the diagram pane, and a join line shows that the tables are related.

In the *grid pane*, you can see the fields that are going to be included in the query. To add fields to this pane, you just check the boxes before the field names that are shown in the diagram pane. You can also enter an expression in the Column column to create a calculated field, and you can enter a name in the Alias column to give the calculated field a name. Here, a calculated field is given the name BalanceDue (because the expression is too wide for the Column column, only part of it is visible).

Once the fields have been added to the grid pane, you can use the Sort Type column to identify any fields that the returned rows should be sorted by and the Sort Order column to give the order of precedence for the sort if more than one field is identified. Here, for example, the rows should be sorted in ascending sequence by just the VendorName field. Similarly, you can use the Criteria and Or columns to establish any criteria that should be used for selecting the rows that will be included in the query. Here, only those rows that have a BalanceDue value that's greater than zero should be included.

As you create the query, the *SQL pane* shows the current version of the resulting SQL statement. You can also run this query at any time to display the selected records in the *results pane*. That way you can be sure that the query works the way you want it to.

The Query Designer window for a query that retrieves data from two tables

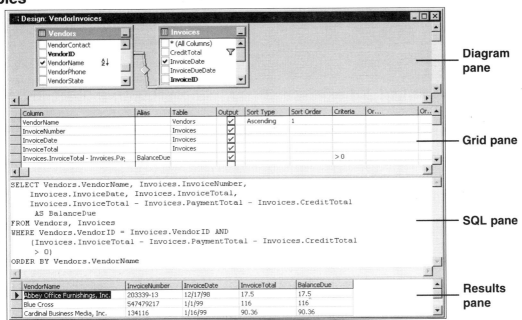

Diagram pane

Grid pane

SQL pane

Results pane

Description

- When you're creating or editing a Command object, you can use the Query Designer to generate the SQL query that you need. To do that, click the SQL Builder button on the General tab of the Properties dialog box for a Command object (see figure 9-3).

- When the Query Designer starts, the Data View window that's described in chapter 11 is also opened. Then, to add tables to the query, you drag them from the Data View window and drop them in the *diagram pane* of the Query Designer.

- To include a field in the query and add it to the *grid pane*, check its box in the diagram pane. To include all the fields in a table, check the All Columns box. To include a calculated field, enter an expression in the Column column.

- To sort the records based on one or more fields, choose Ascending or Descending from the drop-down list in the Sort Type column.

- To select the records to be included in the results, enter criteria in the Criteria and Or columns of the grid pane. If you want to use a field to select records but you don't want to include it in the results, remove the check mark from the Output column for the field.

- To execute the SQL statement that's shown in the *SQL pane*, select the Run command from the Query menu or the shortcut menu. If the query returns a recordset, the data is displayed in the *results pane*. Otherwise, you'll see a message indicating how many records were affected by the query.

- To save the SQL statement in the Command object, close the Query Designer window and click Yes in the resulting dialog box.

- To resize a pane, drag its top or bottom boundary. To hide or show a pane, use the Hide Pane command in the shortcut menu or the Show Panes submenu of the View menu.

Figure 9-7   How to use the Query Designer to create a query

In chapter 11, you can learn how to use the Query Designer for creating other types of queries like Insert and Update queries. When you use the Data Environment for building forms, though, you just use Select queries to get the data that you need.

How to use the Advanced tab
to set Command properties

Figure 9-8 shows the Advanced tab of the Properties dialog box for a Command object. Here, you can set some of the properties for the recordset that a Command object returns like cursor location, cursor type, and lock type. These are the same properties that you normally set when you develop a bound or unbound application.

When you create a new Command object, it has the default settings shown in the figure. In most cases, these are the settings you need if you're using the command for building a form. However, if the command you're creating adds, updates, or deletes records, you need to change the lock type property. Otherwise, you'll get an error message when your application runs.

The Advanced tab of the Properties dialog box

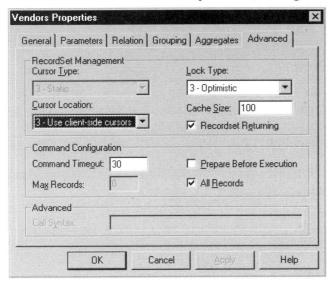

The default settings

Cursor Type:	3 – Static
Cursor Location:	3 – Use client-side cursors
Lock Type:	1 – Read Only
Recordset Returning:	Checked

Description

- The Advanced tab of the Properties dialog box for a Command object lets you change the default settings for the recordset that it returns.
- If you select server-side cursors for a Command object, you can select Forward Only, Keyset, Dynamic, or Static as the cursor type. If you select client-side cursors, you can only use a Static cursor type.
- If you're going to delete, update, or add records in the recordset for the Command object, you need to change the lock type from its Read Only default to Pessimistic, Optimistic, or Batch Optimistic.
- By default, the All Records option is checked, which causes all records in the recordset to be sent to the client if you're using client-side cursors. To limit the number of records returned, though, you can uncheck the All Records box and enter the maximum number of records that you want returned in the Max Records box.
- If you want the Command object to be compiled before it's executed, check the Prepare Before Exection box. If you select this option, the application will take longer to start up, but will run faster thereafter.

Figure 9-8   How to use the Advanced tab to set Command properties

How to use the Relation tab to define a parent-child relationship

Figure 9-9 shows how to use the Relation tab of the Properties dialog box. From this tab, you can set up a *parent-child relationship* between two Command objects based on one field that is common to the recordsets for both commands. If, for example, you want to set up a relationship between a Vendors and an Invoices recordset, you can base the relationship on the VendorID field that's in both recordsets. Often, when you choose the common field for a relationship like this, you use the primary key in the parent recordset and a foreign key in the child recordset.

Once you set up a parent-child relationship, the child recordset is changed whenever the value in the parent field changes. As a result, any controls that are bound to the child command will be updated with the new data. This makes it relatively easy to set up an MSFlexGrid or a DataGrid for the recordset. You'll see this illustrated when you do the last exercise set in this chapter.

If you look in the Designer window in this figure, you can see that the child command (Invoices) is subordinate to the parent command (Vendors). If necessary, you can then add other levels of subordination like an InvoiceLineItems command that's subordinate to the Invoices command. When you set up relationships like that, you're creating *hierarchical recordsets*, or a *command hierarchy*.

To view this hierarchy, you can select the parent command in the Designer window and choose the Hierarchy Info option from its shortcut menu. Then, from the Hierarchy Information dialog box, you can either view the SQL Shape command that created the parent-child relationship or the ADO hierarchy.

Before you continue, you should know that the recordset for a child command is not available in the completion list as you enter code. However, you can refer to a child recordset using any one of these forms:

```
deAP.rsVendors!Invoices
deAP.rsVendors.Fields!Invoices
deAP.rsVendors.Fields("Invoices")
```

In this case, no matter which form you use, you're referring to the Invoices recordset in the Fields collection of the Vendors recordset. Then, the Value property contains all of the records in the recordset. You'll see how this works when you do exercise set 9-3.

The Relation tab of the Properties dialog box

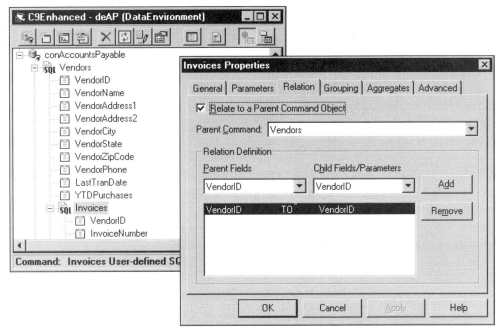

Description

- The Relation tab of the Properties dialog box for a Command object lets you define a *parent-child relationship* between two recordsets based on a common field in the two recordsets. Then, whenever the value in that field in the parent recordset changes, the child recordset is automatically updated so it contains the child records that relate to the parent.

- The easiest way to create a Command object for a child is to right-click on the Command object for the parent and select the Add Child Command from the shortcut menu or Designer toolbar. Then, some of the required entries are made automatically in the General and Relation tabs. Otherwise, you can create a parent command and convert it to a child command by setting up a parent-child relationship in the Relation tab.

- In the Relation tab, be sure that the Relate to a Parent Command Object box is checked. Next, select the Command object that you want to use as the parent from the Parent Command list. Then, in the Relation Definition section, select the parent and child fields that establish the relationship and click on the Add button to add them to the relationship list. If the relationship is based on more than one set of fields, you can repeat this process as you add other sets of fields to the list.

- If you try to exit from the Relation tab with the Relate to a Parent Command Object box unchecked, you'll receive an error message that says the relationship hasn't been properly defined.

Figure 9-9   How to use the Relation tab to define a parent-child relationship

How to use the Grouping tab
to define record groups

Figure 9-10 shows how to use the Grouping tab in the Properties dialog box. Here, another child command has been created that's subordinate to the Vendors command. Since this child command is designed to get the invoice totals for each vendor, it is named InvoiceTotals.

When the Grouping tab for a command is first displayed, the Fields in Command list shows all the fields in the recordset for the command. Then, you can move one or more fields from this list to the Fields Used for Grouping list. In this example, the VendorID is the only field used for grouping so the invoice records will be grouped by vendor. Later, you can use the Aggregates tab to define aggregate fields that perform functions based on this grouping.

When you use grouping, you should know that the records in the Command object are sorted based on the fields in the group. The records in the Command object shown in this figure, for example, will be sorted by VendorID. That makes sense since the records can't be grouped by VendorID unless they're sorted by VendorID. In addition, if the records are grouped by more than one field, they're sorted in the order they appear in the Fields Used for Grouping list. Note that the sort order that's specified by a group overrides any sort order that's specified in the SQL statement for the Command object. Normally, then, you won't include an ORDER BY clause in the SELECT statement for a Command object that uses grouping.

After you establish a grouping, two folders are added to the Designer window. The Summary fields folder contains all of the fields used for the grouping. The Detail fields folder contains all of the fields defined by the command including the fields used for grouping.

When you use child commands with grouping for building forms, you may be surprised by some of the results. Later in this chapter, for example, you'll see a Vendors form that displays the data from a child Invoices command in a DataGrid as well as the data for two aggregate fields that are based on the grouping shown in this figure. To start, I thought that I could include the grouping and aggregate fields in the same command that I used for populating the DataGrid. But when I defined the grouping and ran the application, the DataGrid didn't work. The solution was to remove the grouping from the Invoices child command and to create a second child command named InvoiceTotals that defined only the fields and grouping needed for the aggregate fields.

The Grouping tab of the Properties dialog box

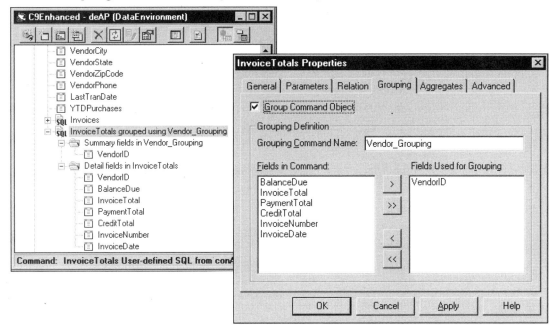

Description

- The Grouping tab of the Properties dialog box for a Command object lets you define groups of records based on the values in one or more fields. You can then use the Aggregates tab to define fields that receive the results of functions that are performed on the records in each group. You can also use the Data Report Designer to establish report breaks for each group.

- To define a group, check the Group Command Object box on the Grouping tab. This displays all of the fields retrieved by the command in the Fields in Command list. Then, to add a field to the Fields Used for Grouping list, select its field name and click on the > button. Or, to remove a field from the Fields Used for Grouping list, select its field name and click on the < button.

- You can define groups for both parent and child commands.

- In the Designer window, one folder is created for the Summary fields and another for the Detail fields that are defined for a Command object. If you expand these folders, you can see the field names for these fields.

Figure 9-10   How to use the Grouping tab to define record groups

How to use the Aggregates tab
to define aggregate fields

Figure 9-11 shows how to use the Aggregates tab of the Properties dialog box to define *aggregate fields*. Each aggregate field receives the value of a function that's performed on one of the fields in all of the records of a group, a child recordset, or a parent recordset. In this example, the Sum function will be performed on the BalanceDue field for all of the records in each vendor grouping and the result will be placed in the aggregate field named BalanceDueSum. Similarly, the Count function can be performed on the VendorID field (or the InvoiceTotal or BalanceDue field) to get the number of invoices for each vendor and the result will be placed in the aggregate field named InvoiceCount.

If the Command object is a parent, you can also define an aggregate field that performs a function on one of the fields in all of the records in the recordset. Although the result is referred to as a *grand total*, that total can actually be the result of any one of the functions listed in this figure.

After you define one or more aggregate fields, they are added to the folder for summary fields as shown in this figure. To distinguish them from grouping fields, though, the aggregate fields are preceded by an icon that includes a plus and minus sign. Also, if you create one or more grand total fields for a parent command, a grand total folder that contains these fields is added to the Designer window. Later, as you build a form, you can drag and drop any of these fields onto the form.

When you define an aggregate field, you should realize that you're actually adding a SQL function to the SQL statement that creates the recordset for the Command object. This is a part of the standard SQL language. As a result, the database management system performs the function, and you don't have to perform the function in the Visual Basic application that runs on the client.

The Aggregates tab of the Properties dialog box

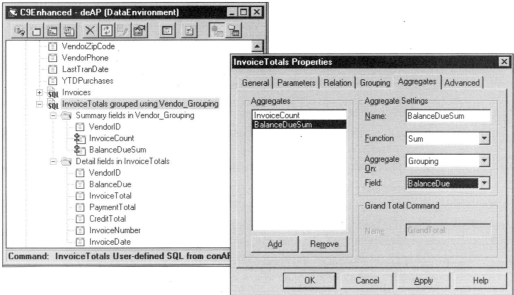

Aggregate functions

Any, Average, Count, Maximum, Minimum, Standard Deviation, Sum

Description

- The Aggregates tab of the Properties dialog box for a Command object lets you define aggregate fields that receive the values derived by functions. These functions can be performed on the records in a group, the records in a child recordset, or all of the records in a recordset.

- To create an aggregate field, click on the Add button. Then, enter a name in the Name box, choose a function from the Function list, choose what the aggregate should be based on from the Aggregate On list, and choose the field that the aggregate performs the function on from the Field list.

- If you create a grand total aggregate field, you also need to enter a name in the Name box within the Grand Total Command frame. Note, however, that you can only create a grand total for a parent command.

- Before you can define an aggregate field based on a child command, you need to define the group in the Grouping tab.

- In the Designer window, an aggregate field is displayed with a plus and minus sign next to its name in the Summary fields folder. If you define one or more grand total fields, a GrandTotal folder is also created.

Figure 9-11   How to use the Aggregates tab to define aggregate fields

How to use the Parameters tab for queries that use parameters

Figure 9-12 shows the Parameters tab of the Properties dialog box for a Command object. This tab applies only to the Parameter objects that are used by Command objects that are based on SQL statements or stored procedures that use parameters, not on the Command or Recordset objects themselves. As a result, you probably won't need to change any of the parameter properties that are available through this tab. And you probably shouldn't change any of these properties because that may lead to errors.

One property that you may want to set, though, is the Value property. This can be useful during the development and testing of an application, because it sets an initial value for the selected parameter. When you're done with the testing, of course, you delete this property value.

A stored procedure and the Parameters tab of the Properties dialog box

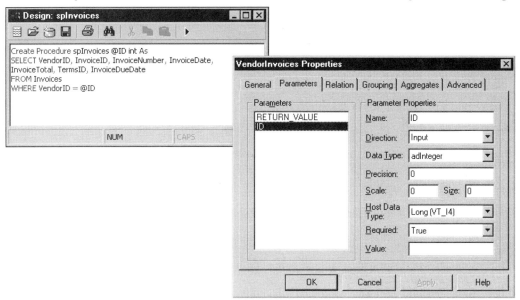

Description

- The Parameters tab of the Properties dialog box for a Command object applies only to SQL queries or stored procedures that use parameters. Then, you can use this tab to adjust the properties for the related Parameter objects.

- The Parameters list includes each Parameter object used by a query. This includes the RETURN_VALUE parameter for a stored procedure.

- To change the properties for a specific Parameter object, click on the parameter name in the Parameters list, then change any of the properties.

- In general, you shouldn't need to change any of the properties for a parameter, and you may cause debugging problems if you do. The only exception is the Value property, which can be used to set the initial value for a Parameter object.

- To use parameters in a SELECT statement, you code a ? for each parameter just as you do for Command objects that you create through code (see pages 300 and 301). Then, a parameter is created for each ?, and you can modify its properties from the Parameters tab.

Figure 9-12   How to use the Parameters tab for queries that use parameters

Exercise set 9-2: Create the Command objects for a new project

In this exercise set, you'll create some Command objects for an enhanced Vendors application. Then, in exercise set 9-3, you build a bound form that uses these commands.

Create a new project

1. Start a new Standard EXE project. Then, set the Name property of the form to frmVendors, its Caption property to Vendors (C9 Enhanced), and its StartUpPosition property to CenterScreen.

2. Change the project name to C9Enhanced. Then, save the project and form with the names C9Enhanced and frmVendors in a new folder named Chapter 9 Enhanced.

3. Add the Designer file you created in exercise set 9-1 to this project. To do that, right-click in the Project Explorer window, select Add from its shortcut menu, and select Add File from its submenu. Then, open the Chapter 9 Simple folder that you created in the last exercise set, and double-click on the file named deAP. Since you're not going to save this file with a new name, the Command objects that you create in this exercise set will be added to the original file.

Modify the Vendors command

4. Double-click on the DataEnvironment object in the Project Explorer window to open the Designer window. Next, right-click on the Vendors command that you created in the last exercise set, select Properties to open up its dialog box, and open the Query Designer for the command. Then, add the VendorID, LastTranDate, and YTDPurchases fields to the SQL query, and remove the VendorContact field by clicking on the appropriate fields in the Diagram pane. When you're done, close the Query Designer window and save the query.

5. Re-open the Properties dialog box for the Vendors command, and click on the Advanced tab. Then, set the Lock Type property to Optimistic since you'll be updating the fields in the recordset that this command returns.

Add the Invoices child command

6. Select the Vendors Command object in the Designer window, and click on the Add Child Command button in the toolbar. As you can see, this adds a child command that's subordinate to the Vendors command. Then, open the Properties window for the child command, change its name to Invoices, click on the SQL statement option, and click on the SQL Builder button to open both the Query Designer and the Data View windows.

7. Size and position the Query Designer and Data View windows so you can see both at the same time. In the Data View window, expand the Data Environment Connections folder, the Connection object, and the Tables folder

so you can see all of the tables in the database. Then, drag the Invoices table to the diagram pane in the Query Designer window.

8. Maximize the Query Designer window so you have room to work, and add these fields to the query: VendorID, InvoiceNumber, InvoiceDate, InvoiceTotal, PaymentTotal, and CreditTotal. Next, enter this expression for the next field in the grid pane

```
InvoiceTotal - PaymentTotal - CreditTotal
```

and enter BalanceDue in its Alias column. Then, enter > 0 in its Critera column. When you're done, select the Run command from the Query menu to make sure that the query gets the right fields and records. When you're satisfied that it does, close the Query Designer window and save the query.

9. Open the Properties dialog box for the Invoices command. In the General tab, you should see the query you just designed. Next, click on the Relation tab and finish setting up the parent-child relationship by clicking on the Add button. Then, click on the OK button to close the Properties dialog box.

Add the InvoiceTotals child command

10. Select the Connection object in the Designer window, and add a Command object. At this point, the new command is a parent command.

11. Open the new command's Properties dialog box, and name the command InvoiceTotals. Then, open the Query Designer window, add the Invoices table to its diagram pane, and create this SQL statement for the command:

```
SELECT VendorID,
    InvoiceTotal - PaymentTotal - CreditTotal AS BalanceDue
    FROM Invoices
    WHERE (InvoiceTotal - PaymentTotal - CreditTotal > 0)
```

12. After you've saved the SQL query, re-open the Properties dialog box, and use the Relation tab to set up a parent-child relationship with the Vendors command based on just the VendorID field. Then, use the Grouping tab to create a grouping based on the VendorID field.

13. With the Properties dialog box still open, use the Aggregates tab to create a field named InvoiceCount that uses the Count function to count the entries in either the VendorID or BalanceDue field (the results should be the same either way). Then, create a field named BalanceDueSum that uses the Sum function to add the values in the BalanceDue field. After you close this dialog box, note that the command is now a child of the Vendors command.

Add the States Command object

14. Add one more Command object to the Designer window. It should be named States, and it should get all the fields from the States table.

Save and run the project

15. Save the project and then test it. If you see a blank form, it means that the underlying Connection and Command objects are working. Then, you can close the form. But leave the project open if you're going to continue.

An enhanced Vendors application

At this point, you should know how to create the Command objects that you need for building forms and developing reports. So the rest of this chapter will show you how you can use some of these commands as you build a form.

The enhanced Vendors form

Figure 9-13 shows an enhanced Vendors form that gets data from four different command objects. The basic vendors information comes from the fields in a Vendors command. The invoice data in the grid comes from a child Invoices command that's subordinate to the Vendors command. The two fields to the right of the address information get their data from aggregate fields that are defined in an InvoiceTotals command. And the State combo box gets its data from a States command that gets all the records from a States table.

When you use this Vendors form, you can modify the data in the address and phone fields. Then, the update takes place when you move to another vendor. In addition, you can delete a vendor record by clicking on the Delete button, but only if the vendor doesn't have any unpaid invoices. That's why the Delete button is disabled in this figure.

Once you've defined the Command objects, you can build most of this form just by dragging and dropping fields from the Designer window onto the form. However, since the default control for a child command is the MSFlexGrid, you may want to replace it with the improved DataGrid control. You'll see how this works when you do the last exercise set for this chapter.

The enhanced Vendors form

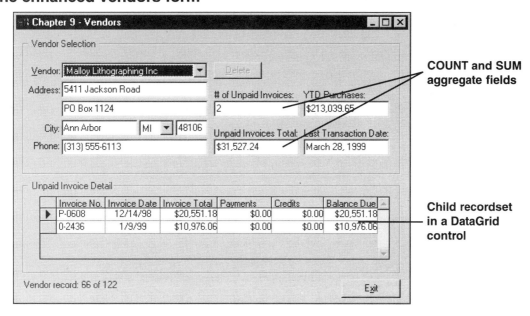

COUNT and SUM aggregate fields

Child recordset in a DataGrid control

Description

- In this Vendors form, the user can select a vendor from the DataCombo control, update the data for a vendor in the address and phone text boxes, and delete the current vendor by clicking on the Delete button (but only if the vendor doesn't have any unpaid invoices).

- The Vendors form uses one Connection and four Command objects: a parent Vendors command, a parent States command (for the States DataCombo control), a child Invoices command for the data in the grid, and a child InvoiceTotals command that defines the aggregate fields.

- You can build this form by dragging and dropping the appropriate commands and fields onto the form. By default, though, the Invoices child data is displayed in an MSFlexGrid control. Then, to improve the way the data is displayed, you can replace it with a DataGrid control.

Figure 9-13   The enhanced Vendors form

The properties for the data-bound controls

Figure 9-14 presents the properties for the bound controls on the Vendors form shown in the previous figure. For all of these controls, the DataSource property identifies the DataEnvironment object. Then, the DataMember and DataField properties for each text box identify the Command object and field for each text box. And the DataMember property identifies the Command object that will supply all of the fields that are displayed in the DataGrid control.

In contrast, if you look at the properties for the two DataCombo controls, you can see that the RowMember and ListField properties identify the Command object and field that's in the list for each control. In addition, the DataMember and DataField properties for the States control identify the Command object and field that should receive the current state value when a record is updated.

When you drag and drop a field onto a form, the binding properties are set automatically. However, you usually need to change some of the other properties of the controls. For instance, since the text boxes for address and phone in this example can be changed by the user, you should set their TabIndex properties so the user can tab from one box to the next in sequence. You should also set the TabStop properties for the other text boxes to False and their Locked properties to True so their values can't be changed. And if you're going to use code to refer to any of the controls that you dropped on the form, you may want to modify their names so they're more descriptive.

The DataSource property for all of these controls

*   deAP

The Data properties for the text boxes

Name	DataMember	DataField	DataFormat
txtAddress1	Vendors	VendorAddress1	General
txtAddress2	Vendors	VendorAddress2	General
txtZipCode	Vendors	VendorZipCode	General
txtPhone	Vendors	VendorPhone	General
txtYTDPurchases	Vendors	YTDPurchases	Currency
txtLastTranDate	Vendors	LastTranDate	Date
txtInvoiceCount	InvoiceTotals_Grouping	InvoiceCount	General
txtInvoiceSum	InvoiceTotals_Grouping	BalanceDueSum	Currency

The Data properties for the DataGrid control

Name	DataMember
dbgInvoices	Invoices

The Data properties for the DataCombo controls

Name	DataMember	DataField	RowSource	RowMember	ListField
dbcVendors			deAP	Vendors	VendorName
dbcStates	Vendors	VendorState	deAP	States	StateCode

Other properties that need to be set for the Vendors DataCombo control

*   Set the BoundColumn property to VendorID.
*   Set the Style property to dbcDropDownList.

Notes

*   The DataSource, DataMember, and DataField properties for text boxes are set automatically when you drag a field from the Designer window and drop it on a form. Similarly, some of the Data properties for other types of controls are set automatically when you drop commands or fields on a form.
*   The DataFormat property for a control is not set automatically, although the default setting is General.

Figure 9-14   The properties for the data-bound controls on the Vendors form

The code for the Vendors application

Figure 9-15 shows the minimum code that's required for the Vendors form in figure 9-13. It provides for displaying the data for a vendor when the user selects a vendor, and it provides for deleting a vendor when the user clicks on the Delete button. This figure omits the other types of code that you would normally include in an application like this so the focus is clearly on the use of the Data Environment objects.

When the application starts, the DataEnvironment object is created along with the Connection and Command objects you defined for it. This all happens behind the scenes before the first form is displayed. Then, the Form_Load procedure (1) sets the Text property of the DataComboBox so that the name of the first vendor in the rsVendors recordset is displayed.

Whenever the vendor name in the DataCombo box changes, the dbcVendors_Change procedure (2) runs. Here, the Find method for the recordset created by the Vendors command is used to get the data for the selected vendor. Then, this statement is used to get the data for the child recordset for that vendor:

```
Set rsInvoices = deAP.rsVendors!Invoices.Value
```

This sets the Recordset object that this procedure defines to the value of the recordset returned by the Invoices child command, which is accessed through the Fields collection of the Vendors recordset. After that statement, the Enabled property of the Delete button is set based on the RecordCount property for the Invoices recordset. Then, the rsInvoices variable is set to Nothing because that recordset is no longer needed.

If the user clicks on the Delete button, the cmdDelete_Click procedure (3) is executed. Its code is just like the code for the comparable procedure in the chapter 7 application except the ReFill method is used to re-populate the DataCombo control after the vendor record has been removed from the underlying recordset. That's necessary because the list of vendors in the control isn't updated automatically when a vendor is deleted from the recordset. In contrast, the chapter 7 application uses the Refresh method of the data control that supplies the list of vendors, which causes the list to be updated automatically. This is just one difference between using a data control and a Command object in a data environment.

When the user clicks on the Exit button, the last procedure in the form module (4) is executed. It first checks to see if the address information for the current vendor has been edited, but not updated. If so, the current record is updated before the form is closed and the application ends.

The last procedure in this figure is designed to illustrate the use of the designer module. It is executed whenever the application moves to a new record in the Vendors record set, and it updates the record number in the label control at the bottom of the form. This shows that event procedures for Data Environment objects must be coded in the Designer module, not the Form module. In practice, though, you would probably code the statement in this procedure right before the last statement in the dbcVendors_Change procedure so you wouldn't need to use the Designer module.

Code for the Form module

```
Option Explicit
```

```
Private Sub Form_Load()                                                    1
    dbcVendors.Text = deAP.rsVendors!VendorName
End Sub
```

```
Private Sub dbcVendors_Change()                                            2
    Dim rsInvoices As Recordset
    deAP.rsVendors.Find "VendorID = '" & dbcVendors.BoundText _
        & "'", , , adBookmarkFirst
    Set rsInvoices = deAP.rsVendors!Invoices.Value
    cmdDelete.Enabled = IIf(rsInvoices.RecordCount = 0, True, False)
    Set rsInvoices = Nothing
End Sub
```

```
Private Sub cmdDelete_Click()                                              3
On Error GoTo ErrorHandler
    If MsgBox("Delete this vendor?", vbYesNo + vbDefaultButton2 + _
               vbQuestion, "Delete OK") = vbYes Then
        With deAP.rsVendors
            .Delete
            .MoveNext
            If .EOF Then .MoveLast
            dbcVendors.ReFill
            dbcVendors.Text = !VendorName
        End With
    End If
    dbcVendors.SetFocus
    Exit Sub
ErrorHandler:
    MsgBox "Error code: " & Err.Number & vbCrLf & _
            "Description: " & Err.Description & vbCrLf & _
            "Source: " & Err.Source, _
            vbOKOnly + vbCritical, "Delete Error"
End Sub
```

```
Private Sub cmdExit_Click()                                                4
    If deAP.rsVendors.EditMode = adEditInProgress Then deAP.rsVendors.Update
    Unload Me
End Sub
```

Code for the Designer module

```
Private Sub rsVendors_MoveComplete(ByVal adReason As ADODB.EventReasonEnum, _
            ByVal pError As ADODB.Error, adStatus As ADODB.EventStatusEnum, _
            ByVal pRecordset As ADODB.Recordset)
    frmVendors.lblVendorRecord = "Vendor record: " _
        & deAP.rsVendors.AbsolutePosition & " of " & deAP.rsVendors.RecordCount
End Sub
```

Figure 9-15   The code for the Vendors application

Exercise set 9-3: Build an enhanced Vendors form

In this exercise set, you'll use the Command objects that you created in the last exercise set to build an enhanced version of the Vendors form that looks something like this:

Build the form

1. If necessary, open the C9 Enhanced project you created in exercise set 9-2. Then, open, size, and position the Designer and Form windows so you can drag objects from the Designer window and drop them on the form.

2. Select the VendorName field in the Designer window, and select Properties from its shortcut menu. In the resulting dialog box, change its field mapping so it uses a Microsoft DataCombo control. Then, do the same for the VendorState field.

3. Drag and drop the Vendors Command object onto the form. When you do, you should see a control and label created for each field defined by the query. In addition, you should see two MSFlexGrid controls at the bottom of the form, one for each child command. Since you don't need the second grid control, delete it.

4. Delete the labels for the VendorID, VendorAddress2, VendorState, and VendorZipCode fields, and delete the text box for the VendorID field. Then, modify the label captions and rearrange the controls so they have the layout shown above.

5. In the Designer window, open the folders for the InvoiceTotals command, and drag the InvoiceCount and InvoiceSum fields to the form. Then, modify the label captions and position the controls as shown above.

6. Change the properties for the Vendors and States DataCombo controls as shown in figure 9-14, and be sure to set the BoundColumn and Style

properties for the Vendors control too. Also, set the DataFormat properties for the three text boxes that don't use the General format. Then, set the TabStop, TabIndex, and Locked properties for the controls.

7. Right-click on the MSFlexGrid control, and select the Retrieve Structure command from its shortcut menu so the fields in the child command are added to the control. Then, run the project. At this point, the data for the first record should be displayed in the controls, you should be able to select an item from the DataCombo lists for Vendors and States, you should be able to tab through the updateable fields, and the other fields should be locked.

8. Because the DataGrid control works better than the MSFlexGrid control, delete the FlexGrid control and add the DataGrid control in its place. To do that, you'll have to use the Components command in the Project menu to add the control to the Toolbox. Once it's sized and positioned properly, set its data properties as shown in figure 9-14, and use the Retrieve Fields command in its shortcut menu to add the fields to the grid. Then, use the Edit and Properties commands in its shortcut menu to adjust the column widths, change the column headings, and change the formatting. If necessary, refer back to figure 7-5 for the specifics on how to do that. When you're done, run the project to make sure this grid works right.

9. Add the two command buttons and the label at the bottom of the form that complete the user interface. Then, set the properties for these controls.

Add the code

10. Code and test the procedures in the form module shown in figure 9-15 one procedure at a time. After you've added the first two procedures, you should be able to display and modify the data for any vendor that you select in the Vendors DataCombo control. After you add the third procedure, you be able to delete any vendor record that doesn't have any unpaid invoices. (Be sure that the Lock Type property for the Vendors command is set to Optimistic if you encounter any problems with its methods.)

11. Switch to the Code window for the Designer module, and add the code for the last procedure in figure 9-15. If you're using ADO 2.1, the pRecordset parameter must be manually coded as ADODB.Recordset20 (see page 269). Then, run the program one last time to make sure that the record number displays properly in the label at the bottom of the form.

Save the application

12. Save the application and exit from Visual Basic.

Perspective

If you've done the exercise sets for this chapter, you should now appreciate the benefits that you get from using the Data Environment Designer for building forms. First, you can quickly create the Command objects that you need, even if they require elaborate SQL statements. Second, you can quickly build a bound form by dragging commands and fields from the Designer window and dropping them on a form.

On the other hand, the Data Environment Designer also brings with it some of the shortcomings that are related to bound forms. In particular, like a data control, the Designer provides for some built-in functions that you have no control over through code and that you may not fully understand. For industrial-strength applications, that can lead to serious debugging problems. And to compound the problem, because the Designer is a new feature, its documentation is weak. If you doubt these difficulties, try to add a New Vendor form like the one in chapter 9 to the application that you created in exercise sets 9-2 and 9-3.

With that as background, it's probably best to use the Designer for developing bound forms that display data but don't update it. In addition, though, you'll use the Designer for creating the Command objects that you use for developing reports as shown in the next chapter. For that purpose, the Designer has all strengths and no weaknesses.

Terms you should know

Data Environment Designer
Data Environment objects
DataEnvironment object
Connection object
Command object
mapping
designer module
Query Designer
diagram pane
grid pane
SQL pane
results pane
parent-child relationship
hierarchical recordsets
command hierarchy
aggregate field
grand total

10

How to use the Data Report Designer to develop reports

With previous versions of Visual Basic, Microsoft included a third-party product for developing reports called Crystal Reports. Although this product is still available with Visual Basic 6, the preferred tool for developing reports with Visual Basic 6 is its new Data Report Designer.

When you use the Data Report Designer, you usually get the data for reports through commands that have been created with the Data Environment Designer that's presented in chapter 9. As a result, you need to read chapter 9 before you read this chapter. Like the Data Environment Designer, the Data Report Designer isn't available with the Learning Edition of Visual Basic, but this chapter will nevertheless give you a solid appreciation for how you use it.

Basic skills for developing a data report **374**
How to create a data report from a DataEnvironment object 374
How to work in the Data Report window 376
How to add predefined fields to a report 378
How to format, preview, and print a report 380
Exercise set 10-1: Create a simple data report 382

How to add grouping and totals to a data report **384**
How to create groups based on any field in a report 384
How to create groups based on hierarchical relationships 386
How to add functions to a report 388
Exercise set 10-2: Create a report with grouping and totals 390

How to use code to work with a data report **392**
How to preview or print a data report 392
How to create a form that opens reports 394
How to modify a report at run-time 396
How to create a data report without a DataEnvironment object 398
Exercise set 10-3: Create a form for printing reports 400
Exercise set 10-4: Modify a report at run-time 401

Perspective **402**

Basic skills for developing a data report

The first topics in this chapter present the basic skills you need to develop reports using a DataEnvironment object. After you open a new report and associate it with a Command object in the data environment, you add controls to the report much as you do when you create a form. You can also add pre-defined fields to a report that contain information like the date and page number. Then, you can format and preview the report to make sure it looks the way you want it to before you print it. After you learn these skills, the first exercise set in this chapter will guide you through the development of a simple report.

How to create a data report from a DataEnvironment object

Figure 10-1 shows you how to use the Data Report Designer to create a report and associate it with a Command object in a data environment. When you start a new report, it contains the five default sections shown in this figure. When you associate the report with a Command object, though, these sections will change to match the command definition. The name of the Detail section will change, for example, depending on the name of the Command object. In addition, if the Command contains a grouping or child commands, Group Header and Group Footer sections will be added to the report.

To associate a report with a DataEnvironment object, you set the DataSource property of the report to the name of that object. Then, you set the DataMember property to the name of the Command object you want to base the report on. Finally, you apply the structure of the Command object to the report using the Retrieve Structure command that's available from the shortcut menu of the Data Report window. Note that when you retrieve the command structure, any changes you've made to the report are lost. So you'll want to use the Retrieve Structure command before you add any controls to the report.

When you add a data report to a Visual Basic project, it appears under the Designers folder in the Project Explorer with a default name like DataReport1. Before you save the report, then, you'll want to change its Name property to something descriptive. We also suggest that you include the prefix *dr* on the name to identify it as a data report.

By the way, you can also add existing data reports to a project. To do that, you use the Add File command in the Project menu or the shortcut menu for the Project Explorer.

A new data report that's based on a DataEnvironment object

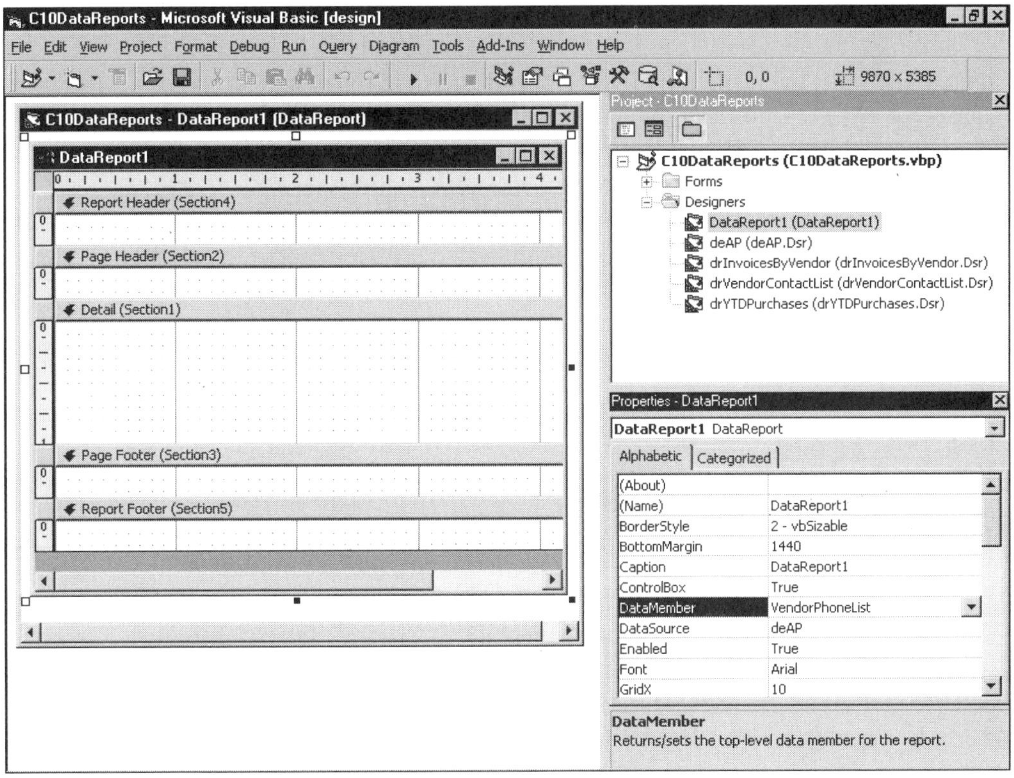

Description

- Before you create a data report, create a DataEnvironment object and define a Connection object to connect to the database that contains the data for the report. Then, create a Command object that defines the data for the report. See chapter 9 for details.

- To create a data report, select Add Data Report from the Project menu, use the list for the Add toolbar button to select Data Report, or use the shortcut menu for the Project Explorer window. This opens the Data Report window with a report that contains five default sections: Report Header, Page Header, Detail, Page Footer, and Report Footer.

- To associate the data report with the Command object you created, set the DataSource property of the report to the name of the DataEnvironment object that contains the Command object, and set the DataMember property to the name of the Command object.

- To format the sections of the report based on the structure of the Command object, select the Retrieve Structure command from the shortcut menu of the Data Report window. This creates custom names for the sections of the report and, if the Command object is defined with a grouping or with a child command, adds the appropriate group headers and footers to the report. See figures 10-5 and 10-6 for details on grouping.

Figure 10-1   How to create a data report from a DataEnvironment object

How to work in the Data Report window

Figure 10-2 shows you how to work in the Data Report window. In this example, the report is associated with a Command object named VendorPhoneList. Notice that the name of the Detail section of this report has been changed to reflect the name of this object.

To add a field from the Command object to the report, you simply drag it from the Data Environment Designer window to the section of the report where you want it to print. In most cases, you'll add the fields to the detail section of the report. If you use grouping as described later in this chapter, though, you can also add the grouped fields to the Group Header or Group Footer section of the report. As you work, if you try to add a field or any other control to a section where it's not appropriate, the mouse pointer will be displayed as a circle with a line through it indicating that the control can't be added to that section.

When you add a control by dragging a field from the Designer window, the DataMember and DataField properties of the text box that's created are set automatically so the control is associated with the appropriate field. In addition, a label that identifies the field is added to the report with its default Caption property set to the field name. You can change this property using standard techniques. Because the label is added to the Detail section of the report along with the control for the field, you may want to move it to another section. In the report in this figure, for example, the labels have been moved to the Page Header section so they'll print at the top of each page as column headings.

You can also add controls to a report by using the tools in the DataReport section of the Toolbox. These tools are available whenever the Data Report window has the focus. You can use these tools to add additional labels to the report that contain information like the report name. You can add labels that contain predefined fields as described in the next figure. You can add Function controls that contain summary information as described in figure 10-7. And you can add graphic images, lines, and shapes that improve the appearance of the report.

As you add controls to a report, you may need to change the size of one or more sections to accommodate the controls. In particular, you'll want to change the size of the Detail section so it provides just enough space for one record as illustrated in this figure. If you include additional space at the top or bottom of this section, that space will be included above or below each record in the report when it's printed.

After you add a control to a report, you can work with it much as you do the controls on a form. If you display the shortcut menu for a control, for example, it includes a variety of options for working with controls. One option that's particularly useful is the one that lets you center a control in a section. You'll use that option often to center the report and page headings for your reports.

The design of a report that prints a list of vendor phone numbers

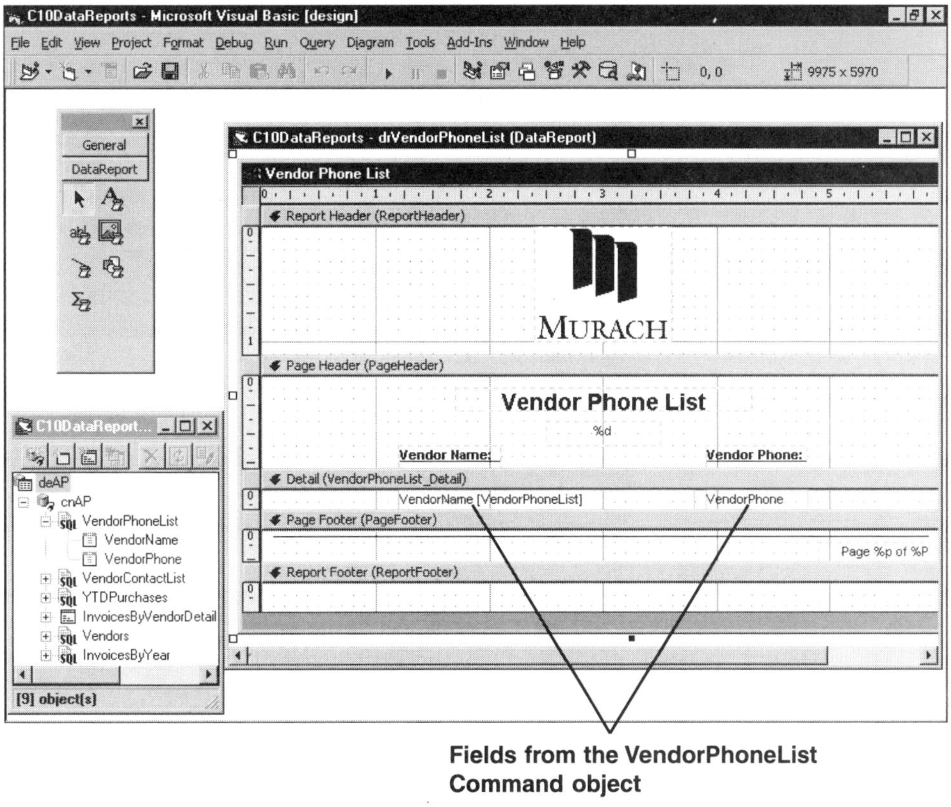

Fields from the VendorPhoneList
Command object

Description

- To add a field to a report, drag it from the list of fields for the Command object in the Data Environment Designer window to the appropriate section of the report. This adds a text box to the report for that field along with a label that identifies the field.

- When you add a field to a report, the DataMember and DataField properties of the text box that's created are set automatically so they refer to the appropriate field. You can also create a control that displays a field by adding a text box to the report and then setting its DataMember and DataField properties manually.

- To add other controls to a report, select the control from the DataReport section of the Toolbox and then drag in the report to place and size the control. The DataReport controls let you create labels, text boxes, images, lines, shapes, and functions.

- After you add a control to a report, you can move, size, and modify it by using many of the same techniques you use with form controls. You can also use the shortcut menu for a control to perform a variety of operations, including aligning and centering.

- To change the height of a section, drag the bottom border of the section. To change the width of all the sections in the report, drag the right border of the report.

Figure 10-2   How to work in the Data Report window

How to add predefined fields to a report

Most reports include a date to indicate when they were printed. In addition, if a report will print on two or more pages, page numbers are usually included. To make it easy to add this type of information to a report, the Data Report Designer includes the predefined fields shown in figure 10-3.

To add a predefined field to a report, you can use the shortcut menu for the section where you want to add it as shown in this figure. When you do, a label is added to the report that contains the code for the field in its Caption property. Then, if you need to, you can change this property to include additional information. The label in the lower right corner of the Page Footer section of the report in this figure, for example, includes the codes for two predefined fields along with some text. You can also create a field like this by adding a label to the report and then entering the text and code directly into its Caption property.

The shortcut menu for inserting a predefined field

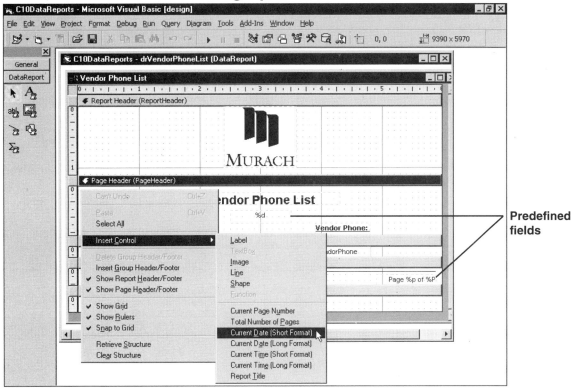

Codes for predefined fields

Code	Description
%p	The current page number
%P	The total number of pages
%d	The current date (short format)
%D	The current date (long format)
%t	The current time (short format)
%T	The current time (long format)
%i	The report title (from the Title property of the DataReport object)

Description

- To add a predefined field to a report, display the shortcut menu for the section where you want to add the field and then select the field you want to add from the Insert Control submenu.

- You can also include a predefined field by adding a label control and then including the code for the field in the control's Caption property.

Figure 10-3   How to add predefined fields to a report

How to format, preview, and print a report

Once you're done adding the controls to a report, you're ready to preview it to make sure it's formatted the way you want. The easiest way to do that is to change the Startup Object property of the project to the name of the report. Then, when you run the project, the report will be displayed in print preview as shown in figure 10-4. From this view, you can scroll through the pages of the report and zoom in and out of the report.

If a report isn't formatted the way you want it, you can exit from print preview and make any necessary changes to the report layout. To change the margins for the page, you can use the four report properties shown in this figure. And to change where page breaks occur, you can use the two section properties.

The vendor phone list report in print preview

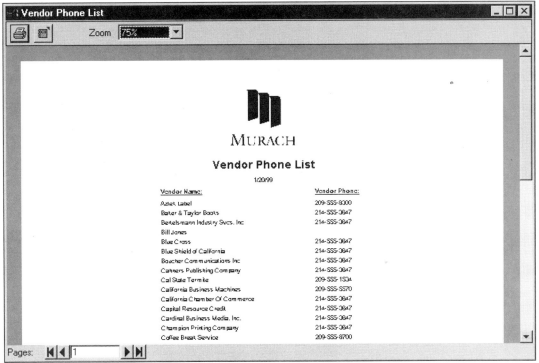

The properties for formatting a report for printing

Object	Property	Description
Report	TopMargin BottomMargin LeftMargin RightMargin	The margins of the report in twips. By default, the margins are set to 1440, or approximately one inch.
Section	ForcePageBreak	Forces a page break before or after the section. The available settings are rptPageBreakNone, rptPageBreakBefore, rptPageBreakAfter, and rptPageBreakBeforeAndAfter.
	KeepTogether	Causes the section to begin printing on the following page if the whole section won't fit on the current page. The available settings are True and False.

Description

- To preview a report, set the Startup Object property of the project to the name of the data report. Then, run the project.

- You can use the controls in the Print Preview window to zoom in and out of the report and to scroll through the pages of the report. To print the report, click on the Print toolbar button.

- To change the margins of a report or to control where page breaks occur, use the Report and Section properties shown above.

Figure 10-4   How to format, preview, and print a report

Exercise set 10-1: Create a simple data report

In this exercise set, you'll create a report that lists the names and phone numbers of the vendors in the Vendors table. To do that, you'll start by using the techniques you learned in chapter 9 to create a DataEnvironment object, a Connection object that accesses the AccountsPayable database, and a Command object that defines the fields used by the report. Then, you'll use the skills you've just learned to create the report.

Start a new project and create a DataEnvironment, Connection, and Command object

1. Start Visual Basic and begin a Standard EXE project. Then, remove the default form from the project without saving it.

2. Create a new DataEnvironment object. Then, change the Name property of that object to deAP, and change the Name property of the default Connection object to cnAP.

3. Display the Data Link Properties dialog box for the Connection object, and enter the appropriate options to connect to the AccountsPayable database.

4. Add a Command object to the connection, and display its Properties dialog box. Next, set the Command Name property to VendorPhoneList, and be sure that the Connection property is set to cnAP. Then, click on the SQL Statement option, enter the statement that follows, and click on the OK button to save these properties:

```
SELECT VendorName, VendorPhone FROM Vendors
    ORDER BY VendorName
```

5. Change the Project Name property for the project to C10DataReports. Then, save the DataEnvironment object with the name deAP in a new folder named Chapter 10 Data Reports, and save the project with the name C10DataReports in the same folder.

Create the Data Report

6. Select Add Data Report from the Project menu to add a report to the project. Next, set the Name property of the report to drVendorPhoneList, and set the Caption property to Vendor Phone List. Then, select deAP for the DataSource property and VendorPhoneList for the DataMember property.

7. Right-click on the report, and select Retrieve Structure. Then, click on the Yes button in the dialog box that's displayed to replace the existing report layout.

8. Open the Data Environment Designer window, expand the cnAP connection so you can see the VendorPhoneList command, and expand that command so you can see the fields it contains. Then, drag the VendorName and VendorPhone fields from the Designer window to the Detail section of the report.

9. Drag the labels for the vendor name and phone fields to the Page Header section. Then, change the Font properties of the labels so they're bold and underlined, and change their Caption properties to add a space after the word Vendor.

10. Align the labels and fields so they look like the ones in figure 10-2. Then, drag the bottom border of the Detail section so it's as small as possible, and drag the right border of the report so there's as much space to the right of the vendor phone as there is to the left of the vendor name.

11. Change the Startup Object property of the project to the name of the data report, and run the application. This should display the list of vendor names and phone numbers in print preview. Enlarge the preview window so you can see both columns and several rows of the report. Then, drop down the Zoom list and select 75% so you can see more of the report, and use the buttons at the bottom of the window to display each page of the report. When you're through experimenting, close the preview window.

12. Increase the size of the Page Header section so you can add the information shown in figure 10-2. Then, drag the Vendor Name and Vendor Phone labels back to the bottom of that section, and add a label at the top of the section. Set the Caption property of this label as shown, set its Font property to Bold 18 point, and set its Alignment property to rptJustifyCenter. Last, right-click on the label, choose the Center in Section option in the shortcut menu, and select Horizontally from the submenu to center the label in the section.

13. Right-click in the Report Header section below the label you just added, highlight the Insert Control option, and select Current Date (Short Format). This adds a label with the code %d to the form. Set the Alignment property of this control to rptJustifyCenter, and center the control in the section.

14. Increase the size of the Report Header section. Then, add a label, set its Caption property to Mike Murach & Associates, set its Alignment property to rptJustifyCenter, and change its Font property to Italic 14 point. If necessary, increase the size of the label to display its caption, then center the label in the section. Also, if necessary, adjust the size of the section.

15. Add a line control to the top of the Page Footer section as shown in figure 10-2. Then, add a label below this line and position it at the right end of the line. Set the Caption property of this control so it displays as shown in that figure, and set its Alignment property to rptJustifyRight.

16. Run the project to display the report in print preview. Notice the date in the page header, and notice the page number in the page footer. Move to the second page of the report and notice that the report header isn't included on that page. Close the preview window and make any adjustments so the report prints the way you want it to. In particular, adjust the LeftMargin property of the report so the report is centered on the page.

Save the project and report

17. Save the project, and save the report in the Chapter 10 folder with the name drVendorPhoneList. But leave the project open if you're going to continue.

How to add grouping and totals to a data report

Many of the reports you create will be grouped by one or more fields in the data source. For example, if a report prints a list of invoices, you might want to group the invoices by vendor. Then, you can print subtotals for each vendor, and you can print totals for the entire report. The following topics will present the basic skills for adding grouping and totals to a report.

How to create groups based on any field in a report

In chapter 9, you learned how to add grouping to a Command object. Figure 10-5 reviews the procedure for doing that. In addition, it shows you how the grouping in a Command object is applied to a report that prints the invoices for each vendor.

The Command object in this figure is grouped by the VendorID and VendorName fields. Note that because both of these fields are unique in the Vendors table, only one of them is actually required to create the grouping for the report. As you'll see in a minute, though, you need to specify both of these fields to format the report as shown in this figure.

When you set the DataMember property for the report, you'll notice that selections are available for both the summary fields and the detail fields defined by the Command object. For the Command object in this figure, for example, you'll see items named Vendor_Grouping and InvoicesByVendorDetail. To include groups in the report, you need to select the Grouping item.

When you retrieve the structure of a grouping into a report, a Group Header and a Group Footer section are added to the report for the group. Then, you can add any fields in the group to those sections. Remember from chapter 9 that when you create a group, the fields in the group appear in a Summary fields folder in the Data Environment Designer window, and all the fields appear in the Detail fields folder. You can add a summary field only to the Group Header, Group Footer, or Detail section, and you can add a detail field only to the Detail section.

In the report in this figure, both the VendorID and VendorName fields have been added to the Group Header section. That way, these fields will only print once for each vendor. That's why both of these fields were included in the group. If the group had been defined using only the VendorID field, the VendorName could have been added only to the Detail section. But that would mean that it would print for each invoice, which probably isn't what you want.

A report that groups invoices by vendor

Description

- You can use the Grouping tab in the Properties dialog box for a Command object to group the records retrieved by the command. To display this dialog box, right-click on the Command object and select Properties from the shortcut menu.

- To create a group, check the Group Command Object box, enter the name you want to use for the group, and select the fields you want to include in the group. The fields you include in the group should be the fields you want to add to the Group Header or Group Footer section of the report.

- After you create a group, it will appear in the Data Environment Designer window with two subordinate folders. The first folder contains the summary fields for the group (the fields you selected in the Grouping tab), and the second folder contains the detail fields (the fields in the original Command object).

- If you base a report on a Command object that includes grouping, the appropriate Group Header and Group Footer sections are added to the report when you retrieve the structure of the Command object. Then, you can add the summary fields in the group to one of those sections, and you can add the detail fields to the Detail section.

Figure 10-5   How to create groups based on any field in a report

How to create groups based on hierarchical relationships

If you use the Data Environment Designer to design a Command object that establishes parent-child relationships, the Command object can be used to generate the groups for a report as shown in figure 10-6. Here, the Command object defines a recordset that includes data from three tables. The records in the Vendors table are related to the records in the Invoices table through the VendorID field. And the records in the Invoices table are related to the records in the InvoiceLineItems table through the InvoiceID field. This can be referred to as a *command hierarchy*.

When this Command object is used with a report, a structure like the one shown in this figure is generated. As you can see, this report includes Group Header and Footer sections for the vendors that will contain vendor information and Group Header and Footer sections for the invoices that will contain invoice information. Then, the Detail section will contain information about the line items for each invoice.

Because groups are usually easier to define than command hierarchies, you'll probably use groups for most of the reports you create. If you need to create a report with two or more levels of grouping, though, you need to use a command hierarchy because you can create only a single level of grouping with the grouping feature.

A report with two levels of groupings and the Command objects used to create its structure

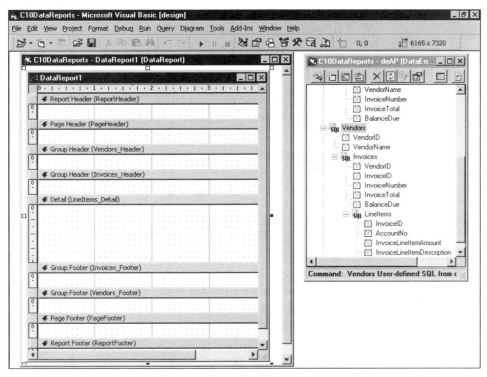

Description

- You can use the techniques presented in chapter 9 to create a *command hierarchy* that consists of two or more levels of parent-child relationships. In this example, the Vendors command includes an Invoices child command that includes a LineItems child command.

- When you retrieve the structure of a command hierarchy into a data report, Group Header and Group Footer sections are added to the report for each parent command in the hierarchy. Then, you can add the fields in the parent commands to the appropriate group sections, and you can add the fields in the child command to the Detail section.

Figure 10-6   How to create groups based on hierarchical relationships

How to add functions to a report

If a report contains groups, you'll usually want to add subtotals for each group. In addition, you'll want to add totals for the entire report. To do that, you can use the Function control as described in figure 10-7.

When you first add a Function control to a report, it's not bound to any field in the report. Then, to bind the control to a field, you set its DataMember property to the name of the Command object for the report, and you set the DataField property to the name of the field you want to summarize. After that, the name of that field appears in the control as shown in this figure.

By default, a Sum function is performed on the selected field. However, you can perform other functions by changing the FunctionType property of the control to one of the settings shown in this figure. If you want to include a count of the records for each vendor, for example, you can change the FunctionType property to rptFuncRCnt.

If you want a function to operate only on the records in each group of a report, you can add it to the Group Footer section for that group. In this figure, for example, two functions have been added to this section that will calculate the invoice total and balance due for the invoices for each vendor. To operate on all the records in a report, you add the function to the Report Footer section of the report. These are the only two sections where you can add functions.

Another way to add a function to a report is to add an aggregate field to the Command object, which you learned how to do in chapter 9. Then, you can drag that field onto the report. The advantage of this is that you can add an aggregate field to a Group Header or Group Footer section or to the Detail section. You might want to do that, for example, to include a count of invoice records in the group header for a vendor. The drawback is that aggregate fields can't be included in the Report Footer section. In addition, aggregate fields require more database overhead. Because of that, you normally use aggregates only when you need to include summary information in the Group Header or Detail section.

The functions in the Invoices By Vendor Detail report

Settings for the FunctionType property

Setting	Description
rptFuncSum	Calculates the sum of the values in the field.
rptFuncAve	Calculates the average of the values in the field.
rptFuncMin	Returns the minimum value in the field.
rptFuncMax	Returns the maximum value in the field.
rptFuncRCnt	Counts the number of rows in the section.
rptFuncVCnt	Counts the number of non-null values in the field.
rptFuncDEV	Calculates the standard deviation.
rptFuncERR	Calculates the standard error.

Description

- To add a function to a report, add a Function control. Then, set the FunctionType property of the control to one of the functions shown above, set the DataMember property to the Command object that the report is based on, and set the DataField property to the field you want to perform the function on.

- You can place a function in either a Group Footer section or in the Report Footer section. If you place it in a Group Footer section, the calculation will be performed for each group of records. If you place it in the Report Footer section, the calculation will be performed on all the records for the report.

- You can also create a function by adding an aggregate field to the Command object for the report and then adding that field to the report. Unlike a function control, you can place an aggregate field in the Detail section or a Group Header section. However, you can't place it in the Report Footer section.

Figure 10-7   How to add functions to a report

Exercise set 10-2: Create a report with grouping and totals

In this exercise set, you'll create a data report like the one in figure 10-7 that prints all the invoices in the Invoices table grouped by vendor. To do that, you'll define a Command object that uses grouping. When you're done, the report should look something like this:

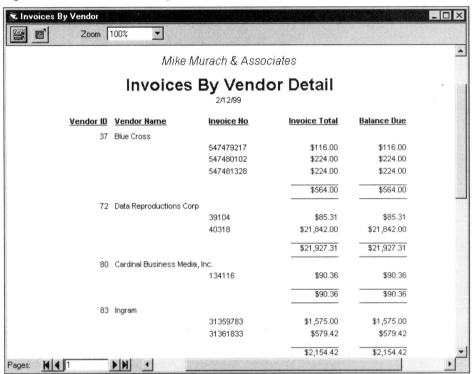

Open the project and create a Command object with grouping

1. Open the C10DataReports project you created in exercise set 10-1. Then, open the Data Environment Designer window for the deAP object, and add a new Command object to the cnAP connection.

2. Display the Properties dialog box for the new command, change the Command Name property to InvoicesByVendor, and make sure that the Connection property is set to cnAP.

3. Click on the SQL Statement option, and click on the SQL Builder button to display the Query Designer. Then, use the designer to create a query that includes the VendorID and VendorName fields from the Vendors table and the InvoiceNumber and InvoiceTotal fields from the Invoices table. Also, include a calculated field named BalanceDue that's derived by subtracting the PaymentTotal and CreditTotal fields in the Invoices table from the InvoiceTotal field. Set the criteria for this field so only records with a balance due greater than zero are included. When you're done, close the Query window and save the query.

4. Display the Properties dialog box for the command again, and click on the Grouping tab. Then, check the Group Command Object box, change the Grouping Command Name to Vendor_Grouping, add the VendorID and VendorName fields to the group, and click on the OK button.

5. Expand the folder for the Command object so you can see the Summary fields and Details fields folders that were created. Then, expand these folders to see the fields in each one.

Create a data report that uses grouping

6. Start a new data report, set its Name property to drInvoicesByVendorDetail, set its Caption property to Invoices By Vendor Detail, set its DataSource property to deAP, and set its DataMember property to Vendor_Grouping. Then, use the Retrieve Structure command to format the report.

7. Drag the VendorID and VendorName fields in the Summary fields folder of the InvoicesByVendor Command object to the Group Header section of the report. Then, drag the labels for these fields to the Page Header section.

8. Drag the fields in the Detail fields folder to the Detail section of the report, and drag the labels for these fields to the Page Header section. Then, format and align the labels and fields so they look like the controls in figure 10-7. Be sure to change the DataFormat properties of the InvoiceTotal and BalanceDue fields to Currency.

9. Add two Function controls to the Group Footer section as shown in figure 10-7. Set the DataMember property of these controls to InvoicesByVendor, and set the DataField properties to InvoiceTotal and BalanceDue. Then, add the same functions with the same properties to the report footer.

10. Add the remaining labels and lines shown in figure 10-7 to the report, and add a label to the Report Header with the caption Mike Murach & Associates. Then, align and format these controls, and set the margin properties of the report so it's centered on the page.

11. Change the Startup Object property of the project to the name of the report, and run the project. Then, review the report layout in print preview, and make any necessary changes so it looks the way you want it to. Last, change the KeepTogether property of the Detail section to True, and run the report again. How does this affect the page breaks?

12. If you have a printer available to you, print the report by clicking on the Print button. Then, close the preview window.

Save the project and the report

13. Save the project, and save the new report with the name drInvoicesByVendorDetail in the Chapter 10 folder. But leave the project open if you're going to continue.

How to use code to work with a data report

Now that you know how to create a data report, you're ready to learn how to work with a data report using Visual Basic code. In particular, you'll learn the methods that you can use to preview or print a report. You'll learn how to create a form that makes reports available to the user. You'll learn how to refer to the sections and controls on a report so you can modify it at run-time. And just to complete the picture, you'll learn how to create a report without using a DataEnvironment object.

How to preview or print a data report

Figure 10-8 presents the two methods of the DataReport object you can use to preview or print a report. To preview a report, you use the Show method. To print a report, you use the PrintReport method.

When you use the PrintReport method, you can include several arguments. The ShowDialog argument determines whether the Print dialog box is displayed before the report is printed. If you display this dialog box, the user can select the printer where the report will be printed as well as the pages and the number of copies to be printed. The other arguments let you specify whether all the pages of the report or a specific range of pages are printed. If you omit these arguments, all the pages are printed.

The syntax of the Show method

```
datareport.Show
```

The syntax of the PrintReport method

```
datareport.PrintReport [ShowDialog][, Range][, PageFrom][, PageTo]
```

Argument	Description
ShowDialog	Determines if the Print dialog box is displayed before the report is printed. This argument is set to False by default.
Range	Determines what pages of the report are printed. The available settings are rptRangeAllPages (the default) and rptRangeFromTo. If you specify rptRangeFromTo, you must also specify the PageFrom and/or PageTo option.
PageFrom PageTo	The numbers of the first and last pages to be printed. If you omit PageFrom, the report is printed from page 1. If you omit PageTo, the report is printed through the last page.

A statement that displays a report in Print Preview

```
drVendorPhoneList.Show
```

A statement that displays the Print dialog box for a report

```
drYTDPurchases.PrintReport True
```

A statement that prints the first five pages of a report

```
drInvoicesByVendorDetail.PrintReport , rptRangeFromTo, , 5
```

Description

- You can issue the Show or PrintReport method from a form or standard module. See figure 10-9 for more information on creating a form that opens reports.
- You can also export the text in a report to a file using the ExportReport method. For more information, see online help.

Figure 10-8   How to preview or print a data report

How to create a form that opens reports

Figure 10-9 presents a form that you can use to make reports available to the user. Here, the form includes an array of option buttons where each button represents a specific report. To print a report, the user selects an option and clicks on the Print button. Although there are other ways to give users access to reports, this example gives you a general idea of how to include reports in an application.

This figure also presents the code for the Click event of the Print button. This procedure uses a Select Case statement to determine which option is selected. Then, it uses a Show method to display the appropriate report in print preview. Of course, you could also use the PrintReport method to print the report directly to the printer or to display the Print dialog box so the user can select the printer and the pages and copies to be printed.

A form for opening reports

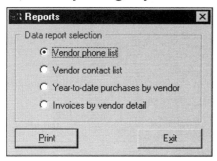

The code for the Click event of the Print command button

```
Private Sub cmdPrint_Click()
    Screen.MousePointer = vbHourglass
    Select Case True
        Case optReport(0)
            drVendorPhoneList.Show
        Case optReport(1)
            drVendorContactList.Show
        Case optReport(2)
            drYTDPurchases.Show
        Case optReport(3)
            drInvoicesByVendorDetail.Show
    End Select
    Screen.MousePointer = vbDefault
End Sub
```

Description

- The code above uses a Select Case statement to determine which option on the form is selected. Then, it uses the Show method to preview a report based on the selection.

- The MousePointer property of the Screen object is set to vbHourglass at the beginning of the Click event procedure so an hourglass is displayed as the report is being generated. The pointer is changed back to its default at the end of the procedure.

Figure 10-9   How to create a form that opens reports

How to modify a report at run-time

If you need to generate two reports that use the same data and have similar layouts, you can do that by modifying a single report at run-time. With just a couple modifications, for example, you could use the Invoices By Vendor Detail report shown in figure 10-7 to print an Invoices By Vendor Summary report like the one in figure 10-10. As you can see, this report includes the invoice totals for each vendor but doesn't include the invoice details.

You can use Visual Basic code to modify a report by changing the properties of the sections and controls in the report. To refer to the sections of a report, you use the Sections collection of the DataReport object. As with other collections, you can refer to a member of the collection by name or by index number. Because the names of report sections tend to be long, you're usually better off using index numbers as shown in the code in this figure. The first section in the report, which is usually the Report Header section, has index number 1. The second section, which is usually the Page Header section, has index number 2. And so on.

To refer to a control on a report, you use the Controls collection of the section that contains the control. Although you can use index numbers or names to refer to controls, you usually use names so they're easier to identify in the code. In that case, you'll want to change the names of the controls to be modified to reflect their contents.

The layout for the report that's used to create the detail or summary report is also presented in this figure. If you compare this layout with the layout for the detail report shown in figure 10-7, you'll notice two differences. First, the label in the Page Header section that identifies the report has been changed to just Invoices By Vendor. Then, the code that prints the report will add the word "Detail" or "Summary" to the end of this label depending on which report is to be printed.

Second, the VendorID and VendorName fields have been added to the Group Footer section. That way, this information is printed along with the summary information for each vendor when the summary report is printed.

The code that prints these reports is included in a form that lets the user select the form to be printed. This code assumes that the form is implemented like the one in figure 10-9, and one option is available for each report. Although you might think that you could include this code in the report itself, you can't. That's because the DataReport object doesn't include a Load event that you can use to set these properties.

If the user chooses to print a summary report, the code begins by adding the word "Summary" to the end of the label that contains the report title. Then, it hides the Group Header and the Detail sections of the report so they won't print. It also hides the invoice number label in the Page Header section of the report since the invoice numbers aren't included on the summary report. And it hides the lines above and below the summary totals in the Group Footer section so they won't print. In contrast, if the user chooses to print a detail report, the code adds the word "Detail" to the end of the report title, and it hides the controls for the VendorID and VendorName fields in the group footer.

The summary report and the data report used to create it

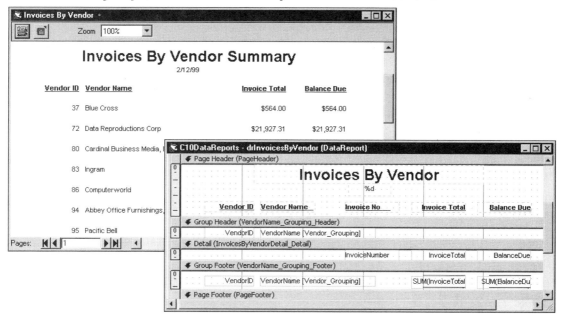

The code for printing the Invoices by Vendor report

```
If optReport(0) Then
    With drInvoicesByVendor
        .Sections(2).Controls("lblReportTitle").Caption _
            = .Sections(2).Controls("lblReportTitle").Caption & " Summary"
        .Sections(3).Visible = False
        .Sections(4).Visible = False
        .Sections(2).Controls("lblInvoiceNumber").Visible = False
        .Sections(5).Controls("lneSum1").Visible = False
        .Sections(5).Controls("lneSum2").Visible = False
        .Sections(5).Controls("lneSum3").Visible = False
        .Sections(5).Controls("lneSum4").Visible = False
        .Show
    End With
Else
    With drInvoicesByVendor
        .Sections(2).Controls("lblReportTitle").Caption _
            = .Sections(2).Controls("lblReportTitle").Caption & " Detail"
        .Sections(5).Controls("txtSumVendorID").Visible = False
        .Sections(5).Controls("txtSumVendorName").Visible = False
        .Show
    End With
End If
```

Description

- You can refer to the sections of a report and the controls in each section by using their index numbers or names. The sections of a report are numbered in the order that they appear in the report, starting with index number 1 for the report header. The controls in each section are numbered in the order you add them to the section.

Figure 10-10   How to modify a report at run-time

Although you can use the technique shown in this figure to modify a report at run-time, it usually makes more sense to create a separate report for each layout. After you create and save the first report, you can modify it to create the second report and then use the Save As command to save it with a different name. Note, however, that there are a couple of advantages to modifying a report at run-time. First, report maintenance can be easier since you only have to modify one report layout for two or more related reports. Second, a single report takes up less disk space. The drawback to this, of course, is that it takes time to write the code that modifies the report.

How to create a data report without a DataEnvironment object

Although you'll usually create a data report based on a Command object that's defined within a DataEnvironment object, you can also create a data report through code. To do that, you use code like that presented in figure 10-11. As you review this code, you'll see that it's similar to the code you use to define the data source for an unbound form. Like the code in figure 10-10, this code is included in the form that's used to print the report and not in the report itself.

When this form is loaded, the Load event procedure creates an instance of the Connection object and opens the connection. Then, when the user selects which report to print, the Execute method of the Connection object is used to execute the SELECT statement that defines the data source for the report, and the result of this statement is stored in a recordset variable. After that, the DataSource property of the report is set to the value of that variable. As a result, when the report is run, it will use the recordset referenced by that variable as its source of data.

For this to work, you have to specify the field that a control will refer to when you design the report. To do that, you add a text box to the report and set its DataField property to the name of the field you want it to display. Because the data source isn't specified until the report is run, though, it's not available as you're designing the report. That means you have to manually enter the names of the fields for each control. Because of that difficulty, you will probably avoid using this method for creating reports.

Code for a form that displays unbound reports

```
Option Explicit
Dim cn As Connection
Dim rs As Recordset

Private Sub Form_Load()
    Set cn = New Connection
    cn.Open "Provider = SQLOLEDB;Server=mmaserver;" _
        & "Database=AccountsPayable", "ed", "abc4xyz"
End Sub

Private Sub cmdPrint_Click()
    Screen.MousePointer = vbHourglass
    Select Case True
        Case optReport(0)
            Set rs = cn.Execute("SELECT VendorName, VendorPhone " _
                & "FROM Vendors ORDER BY VendorName")
            Set drVendorList.DataSource = rs
            drVendorList.Show
        Case optReport(1)
            Set rs = cn.Execute("SELECT VendorName, VendorContact " _
                & "FROM Vendors ORDER BY VendorName")
            Set drVendorContactList.DataSource = rs
            drVendorContactList.Show
        Case optReport(2)
            .
            .
            .
    End Select
    Screen.MousePointer = vbDefault
End Sub
```

Description

- To create a data report without using a DataEnvironment object, you open a Connection object and create a Recordset object on that connection using the Execute method. Then, you set the DataSource property of the data report to the Recordset object.

- Because the DataReport object doesn't have a Load event, you have to set its data source from a form or standard module.

- When you design a data report that's not associated with a DataEnviroment object, you include a field from the data source by adding a text box to the report and then setting its DataField property to the name of the field.

Figure 10-11   How to create a data report without a DataEnvironment object

Exercise set 10-3: Create a form for printing reports

In this exercise set, you'll create a form like the one in figure 10-9 for printing reports. Then, you'll use this form to preview the two reports you created in exercise sets 10-1 and 10-2.

Open the project and add a form

1. Open the project you created in exercise set 10-1 and modified in exercise set 10-2. Then, add a form to this project, set its Name property to frmReports, set its Caption property to Reports, set its BorderStyle property to FixedSingle, and set its StartUpPosition property to CenterScreen.

2. Save the form with the name frmReports in the Chapter 10 folder.

Add controls to the form

3. Add a frame to the form and change its Caption property so it appears as in figure 10-9. Then, add two option buttons within this frame, change the name of both buttons to optReport to create a control array, change the Caption property of the first button to Vendor phone list, and change the Caption property of the second button to Invoices by vendor detail.

4. Add the Print and Exit buttons shown in figure 10-9 and set their Name properties to cmdPrint and cmdExit. Also, set the Default property of the Print button to True. Then, size and position the controls on the form so it looks the way you want it to.

Add code to the form

5. Add code like that shown in figure 10-9 to the Click event procedure of the Print button. Since your form contains only two options, the Select Case statement should contain only two cases.

6. Add the Click event procedure for the Exit button.

7. Change the Startup Object property of the project to this form and run the application. When the form is displayed, click on the Print button to display the Vendor Phone List in print preview. Then, close the preview window, select the other report, and preview it. When you're done, close the preview window and close the form.

8. Change the Show method for the Vendor Phone List to PrintReport, and specify True for the ShowDialog argument so the Print dialog box will be displayed. Then, run the application again, and click on the Print button. This should display the Print dialog box. If you have access to a printer, select the Pages option, enter 1 in the From and To boxes, and click on the OK button. Otherwise, click on the Cancel button to close this dialog box.

Save the project

9. Close the form and save the project. But leave the project open if you're going to continue.

Exercise set 10-4: Modify a report at run-time

In this exercise set, you'll create a report like the one in figure 10-10 that can be modified at run-time to generate a summary or a detail report. Then, you'll modify the form you created in the last exercise set to print these two reports.

Open the project and create a new report

1. Open the project you created and modified for this chapter. Then, use the Save As command to save the drInvoicesByVendorDetail report with the name drInvoicesByVendor in the Chapter 10 folder.

Modify the report

2. Open the Data Report window for this report, change the Name property of the report to drInvoicesByVendor, and change its Caption property to Invoices By Vendor.

3. Change the Caption property for the label that contains the report title to Invoices By Vendor. Next, open the Data Environment Designer window for the deAP object, and drag the VendorID and VendorName fields from the Summary fields folder of the InvoicesByVendor command to the Group Footer section of the report. Then, delete the labels for these fields, and size and position their text boxes as shown in figure 10-10. Be sure to set the Alignment property of the VendorID text box to rptJustifyRight.

4. Change the Name properties of the controls that you will refer to from code. In particular, change the name of the report title label to lblReportTitle; the Invoice No label to lblInvoiceNumber; the lines above and below the summary totals in the Group Footer section to lneSum1, 2, 3, and 4; the text box for VendorID in the Group Footer section to txtSumVendorID; and the text box for the VendorName in the Group Footer section to txtSumVendorName.

Modify the form

5. Open the Form window for the frmReports form and add a third option button. Set this button's Name property to optReport so it's included in the control array, and set its Caption property to Invoices by vendor summary.

6. Open the Code window for the form, and enter code like that shown in figure 10-10 to format and preview the summary and detail reports.

7. Run the application. When the Reports form is displayed, select the detail report and click on the Print button. This report should look just like the one you created in exercise set 10-2. If not, make the necessary changes.

8. Close the preview window, select the summary report from the Reports form, and click on the Print button. The report should look like the one in figure 10-10. If not, make the necessary changes.

Save the project and exit from Visual Basic

9. Save the project and exit from Visual Basic.

Perspective

If you did the exercise sets for this chapter, you should now have a good idea of how you can use the Data Report Designer to develop reports. To become proficient with this tool, though, you may want to take the time to do some additional experimentation. In particular, you may want to try using a command hierarchy to create a report that contains two or more levels of grouping. You may want to try using the various summary functions. And you may want to try using aggregates to include summary information in the Group Header or Detail section of a report. If you can do those tasks, you should be able to develop the reports you need for business applications.

Terms you should know

command hierarchy

11

How to use the Data View window to work with databases

From the Data View window, you can work with the components of the database used by an application. That makes it easy to perform tasks like creating tables, views, and stored procedures without having to leave the Visual Basic environment. The alternative is to leave Visual Basic and use the tools that come with the DBMS for the database.

Before you use the Data View window, you should realize that it isn't available with the Learning Edition of Visual Basic 6. You should also realize that this window is designed for working with SQL Server and Oracle databases, not Access databases. As a result, the only operations you can perform on an Access database from this window are adding, modifying, and deleting records from existing tables and views. If you want to do more than that with an Access database, you can work with it directly from Access or by using the Visual Data Manager that's available from the Visual Basic Add-Ins menu (you'll find an introduction to this tool in appendix B).

Introduction to the Data View window 404
Basic skills for working in the Data View window 404
How to create a data link 406
Exercise set 11-1: Create a data link and view database objects 408

How to work with tables 410
How to create or modify a table 410
How to work with constraints, relationships, indexes, and keys 412
How to add or change table data 414
Exercise set 11-2: Modify the data and design of a table 416

How to work with other database objects 418
How to create or modify a database diagram 418
How to create or modify a view 420
How to create a query 422
How to create or modify a stored procedure 424
How to create or modify a trigger 426
Exercise set 11-3: Create a database diagram and other database objects . 428

Perspective 432

Introduction to the Data View window

Figure 11-1 illustrates the Data View window that you can access from within Visual Basic. When you open this window for the first time, it includes two empty folders: one for *data links* and one for *Data Environment connections*. Then, before you can work with the objects in a database, you have to create either a data link or connection to it. Since chapter 9 shows you how to create and use a Data Environment connection, this chapter shows you how to create and use a data link.

When you work with a database in the Data View window, you should realize that you're actually using a program called Microsoft Visual Database Tools. With Visual Basic 5, this program was available only with the Enterprise Edition, and it was accessed through Microsoft Visual Studio. With Visual Basic 6, however, this program is available with both the Professional and Enterprise Editions and it is accessed through the Data View window.

Basic skills for working in the Data View window

If you expand the folder for a data link or Data Environment connection as shown in figure 11-1, you'll see folders that contain the database objects for that data link. These include database diagrams, tables, views, and stored procedures. Then, to start a function, you right-click on an object to display its shortcut menu and choose the function you want. The shortcut menu in this figure, for example, shows the functions that are available for a table, and similar functions are available for the other objects in a database.

At this point, you may be wondering when you would use a data link to work with a database and when you would use a Data Environment connection. The answer is that you should use a Data Environment connection only when you also need to use it to build forms and reports as described in chapters 9 and 10. Otherwise, you're better off using a data link.

One advantage of using a data link is that it is persistent across projects. So once you create a data link, you can use it from any Visual Basic project. In fact, you can create and use data links without even opening a project. That's possible because the data link information is stored in the Windows Registry. In contrast, when you create a Data Environment connection, it's stored with the project and is available only from that project. Also, because the connection is stored with the project, that project requires additional resources.

The Data View window with a shortcut menu displayed

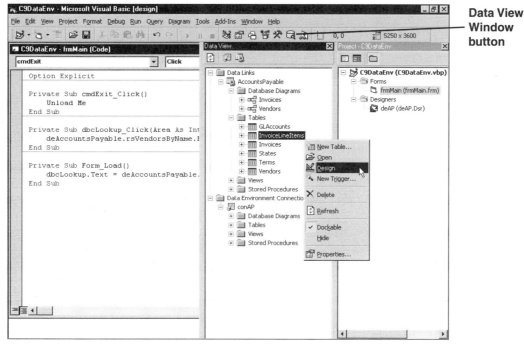

Data View
Window
button

Description

- The Data View window displays the objects in the data links and Data Environment connections you create. To display this window, click on the Data View Window button in the toolbar or choose the Data View Window command from the View menu.

- To start database functions from the Data View window, expand the data link or Data Environment connection folder and subfolders so you can see the object you want to work with. Then, right-click on the object and select the function you want from the shortcut menu that appears.

Notes

- Before you can see the objects in a database, you must create a data link or a Data Environment connection for that database.

- You can perform the same database functions using a data link and a Data Environment connection. You only need to create a Data Environment connection, though, if you want to use it to build forms or reports as shown in chapters 9 and 10.

Figure 11-1   Basic skills for working in the Data View window

How to create a data link

Figure 11-2 shows the dialog box that you use to create a data link. Notice that this is the same dialog box that you can use to build a connection string for an ADO data control. If you've read chapter 6, then, you already know how to complete this dialog box. The only difference is that when you click on the OK button to accept the information for the data link, the link is added to the Data View window where you can enter a name for it.

The Connection tab in this figure is for a SQL Server database. Here, you enter the name of the server where the database resides and any information that's required to log on to that server. Then, you can use the drop-down list to select the database that you want to access.

If you use a specific user name and password to log on to the server, you'll probably want to save that information with the data link. That way, you won't have to enter it each time you use the data link. Although the user name is saved automatically, the password isn't saved unless you select the Allow Saving of Password option.

The Provider and Connection tabs of the Data Link Properties dialog box

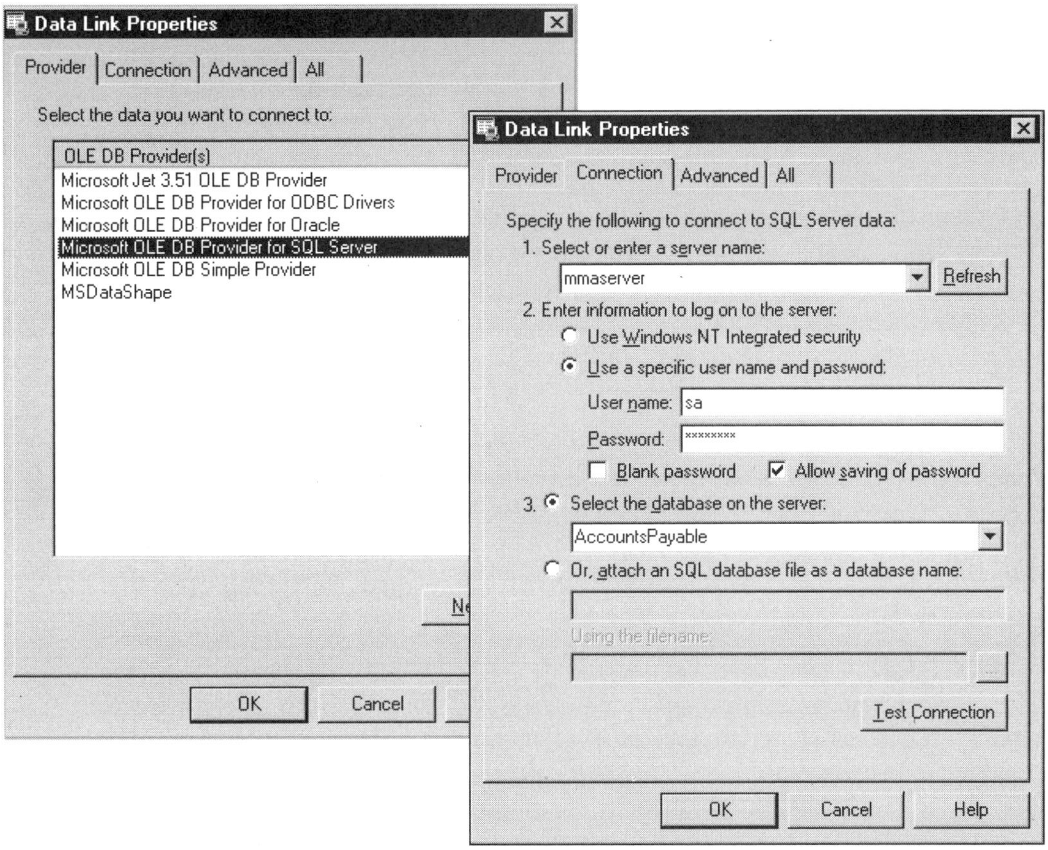

Operation

- To display the Data Link Properties dialog box, click on the Add a New Data Link button in the Data View window toolbar. Or, right-click on the Data Links folder and select Add a Data Link from the shortcut menu.

- On the Provider tab, select the OLE DB provider that you want to use, click on the Next button to display the Connection tab, and complete the entries for that tab. Then, click on the OK button to complete the data link.

Notes

- See figure 6-5 in chapter 6 for more information on completing the Data Link Properties dialog box.

- If you omit the user name and password from the Connection tab, you will be asked to enter them when you try to expand the data link in the Data View window.

- To change the properties for an existing data link, select Modify from the shortcut menu for the data link.

Figure 11-2   How to create a data link

Exercise set 11-1: Create a data link and view database objects

In this exercise set, you'll use the Data View window to create a data link and view the database objects that this links you to. If you're using the Learning Edition of Visual Basic 6, though, this window isn't available to you.

Start Visual Basic and open the Data View window

1. Start Visual Basic. When the New Project dialog box is displayed, click on the Cancel button so no project is opened. Then, click on the Data View Window button in the toolbar to open the Data View window. If no one else has used your system to create data links, this window should contain one folder for data links and one folder for Data Environment connections, but those folders should be empty.

Create a data link for a SQL Server database

2. Right-click on the Data Links folder and select Add a Data Link to display the Provider tab of the Data Link Properties dialog box. Then, select the Microsoft OLE DB Provider for SQL Server option, and click on the Next button to display the Properties tab.

3. In the Properties tab, enter the name of the server where your database resides, and enter the information required to log on to the server. If you enter a user name and password, be sure to select the Allow Saving of Password option so the password is saved with the data link. Then, select the database that you want to connect to from the drop-down list. If a blank list is displayed, that means that you have provided invalid log on information so correct the information you've entered and try to select the database again. Last, click on the OK button to create the data link.

Create a data link for an Access database

4. Right-click on the Data Links folder and select Add a Data Link to display the Provider tab of the Data Link Properties dialog box. Then, select the Microsoft Jet 3.51 OLE DB Provider option, click on the Next button to display the Connection tab, and select the database that you're going to use. You don't have to enter any logon information. Last, click on the OK button to create the data link.

Name the data link and view the data in the database

5. At this point, the Data View window will look like this:

While the data link name is still selected, enter "AccountsPayable" and press the Enter key.

6. Right-click on the data link you just created to see the options that are available from the shortcut menu. Then, press the Esc key to close the menu. Now, double-click on the data link or click on the plus sign to the left of the link to expand its folder. *If the data link is for a SQL Server database*, you should see folders named Database Diagrams, Tables, Views, and Stored Procedures. *If the data link is for an Access database*, though, you should see only the Tables and Views folders. Right-click on each of these folders to see the options that are available.

7. Expand the Tables folders to see the tables that the database contains. Then, right-click on any table to see the options that are available.

8. Click on the plus sign to the left of any table to see what fields it contains. Then, double-click on a field to display its properties. When you're done reviewing its properties, close the dialog box that's displayed.

9. If you created a project for chapter 9, open that project. Notice that the Data Environment connection you created for that chapter is now displayed in the Data View window along with the data link you created. Expand the folder for that connection, and then expand the subfolders to see that you have access to the same objects that you have access to through the data link. Right-click on each object to see that you also have access to the same functions.

10. If you didn't create a project for chapter 9, open any other project or open a new project to see that the data link you created is available from that project.

Clean up the environment

11. Use the Remove Project command in the File menu to close the current project, but keep Visual Basic running with the Data View window open if you're going to continue with this chapter. Otherwise, close the Data View window and exit from Visual Basic.

How to work with tables

If you need to create a new table in a database, you can do that using the Data View window. You can also modify the definition of an existing table, including its check constraints, relationships, indexes, and keys. And you can add, modify, and delete records.

How to create or modify a table

Figure 11-3 shows the window you use to design a table. In this case, the design of an existing table is being modified, but the window that's displayed when you create a new table is identical except for its title.

Each row in the design window for a table represents a field in the table and each column represents a property of that field. To define a new field for a table, then, you simply enter its properties in an empty row in the window.

If you need to insert a new row between two existing rows, you can do that using the shortcut menu shown in this figure. Just select the row below where you want to insert the new row by clicking on its row selector, and then select the Insert Column command from the shortcut menu for that row. This inserts a new row into this window, which represents a column (field) in the table, so don't let the command name confuse you. If you need to insert two or more fields into the table, select the number of rows you want to insert before you select the Insert Column command, and that number of rows is inserted above the first row you highlighted.

If you try to select two or more adjacent rows, you'll notice that you can't do it by dragging across their row selectors as you can in other applications. Instead, you have to select the first row and then hold down the Shift key as you select the last row. If you need to select nonadjacent rows, you can do that by holding down the Ctrl key as you click on the row selector for each row.

You can also use the shortcut menu to delete one or more columns or to set the primary key for the table. When you set the primary key, a key icon appears in the row selector for the fields in the key. The primary key of the Invoices table in this figure, for example, is the InvoiceID field.

When you modify the design of an existing table, you should keep in mind that you can't make a change that will affect the integrity of the table. For example, you can't change the data type of a field if existing records contain data that can't be stored with that data type. And you can't delete a field that's defined as a foreign key to another table. If you try to do that, Visual Basic will display an error message when you try to save the table and the change won't be saved.

The design of the Invoices table in the Accounts Payable database

Column Name	Datatype	Length	Precision	Scale	Allow Nulls	Default Value	Identity	Identity Seed	Identity Increment
InvoiceID	int	4	10	0			✓	1	1
VendorID	int	4	10	0					
InvoiceNumber	varchar	10	0	0					
InvoiceDate	datetime	8	0	0					
InvoiceTotal	money	8	19	4		(0)			
PaymentTotal	money	8	19	4		(0)			
CreditTotal	money	8	19	4		(0)			
TermsID	int	4	10	0		(1)			
InvoiceDueDate	datetime	8	0	0					

Shortcut menu:
- 🔑 Set Primary Key
- Insert Column
- Delete Column
- 🖼 Properties

Operation

- To add a new table to a database, right-click on the Tables folder in the Data View window and select New Table from the shortcut menu that's displayed. A dialog box will ask you to enter a name for the table. Then, the New Table window is displayed.

- To modify an existing table, right-click on the table in the Data View window and select Design from the shortcut menu. Then, the Design Table window shown above is displayed.

- To define a new field for the table, enter the properties for the field in an empty row in the design window. See figure 5-5 in chapter 5 for a description of the properties you can specify for a field.

- To set the primary key for the table, click on the row selector to the left of the key field to highlight it and then select Set Primary Key from the shortcut menu for the selection. To select two or more fields, hold down the Ctrl key as you select them.

- To insert a field above an existing field, highlight the existing field and select Insert Column from the shortcut menu for the field. To delete a field, highlight its row and select Delete Column from its shortcut menu.

- To display the properties for the table, select Properties from its shortcut menu. The Properties dialog box lets you work with constraints, relationships, indexes, and keys as shown in figure 11-4.

- To save the changes to a table's design, select the Save *tablename* command from the File menu. If you close the design window without saving the table, you will be asked if you want to save the changes.

Note

- If an error occurs when you save a table, a message is displayed that describes the error. Then, you can click on the OK button to return to the design window and correct the error.

Figure 11-3   How to create or modify a table

How to work with constraints, relationships, indexes, and keys

Figure 11-4 shows two tabs of the dialog box that's displayed when you select Properties from the shortcut menu for a table. This dialog box lets you define check constraints, indexes, and keys for the table. It also lets you modify, but not create, the relationships between the table and other tables in the database. Later in this chapter, you'll learn how to create these relationships using a database diagram.

Check constraints are used to limit the data or the format of the data that can be entered into a field. The check constraint in this figure, for example, limits the InvoiceDueDate fields to dates that are greater than the InvoiceDate field. Although you can refer to as many fields as you need to in a single constraint, you can refer only to fields in that table. For more information on the expressions you can code for a check constraint, see the help topic "Defining a Check Constraint Expression."

If you create or modify a check constraint for a table that contains data, the default is to check the existing data to be sure that it meets the constraint. If that's not what you want, you can remove the check mark from the Check Existing Data on Creation box at the bottom of the dialog box. Then, the data is checked only when new records are added to the table.

You can also disable a constraint so you can add, modify, and delete records that destroy the referential integrity of the database. You may need to do that, for example, when you're testing a new application. To allow these types of changes, you remove the check mark from the Enable Constraint for INSERT and UPDATE box. You can also disable a constraint when you replicate a database by removing the check mark from the Enable Constraint for Replication box.

The Indexes/Keys tab of the Properties dialog box lets you change the columns that are included in the primary key. It also lets you create other indexes or nonprimary keys (called *unique constraints*) on the table. By default, Visual Basic creates a non-unique index (duplicate values are allowed) when you click on the New button. To create a unique index (duplicate values aren't allowed), though, you can select the Create UNIQUE option and then select the Index option. And to create a unique constraint, you can select the Create UNIQUE and Constraint options.

You can also create a *clustered index* by selecting the Create as CLUSTERED option. When you create a clustered index, the records in the table are sorted in sequence by index value. Because of that, a table can include only one clustered index.

The Tables and Indexes/Keys tabs of the Properties dialog box

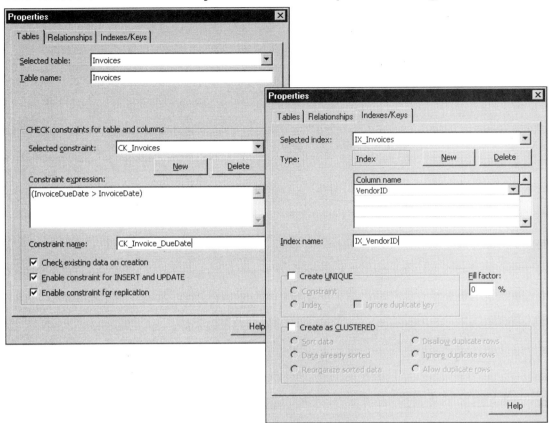

Description

- To display the Properties dialog box shown above, right-click on the table in design view to display the shortcut menu shown in figure 11-3 and select Properties.

- To create a check constraint, click on the New button in the Tables tab of the Properties dialog box. Then, enter the constraint and the name you want to use for the constraint, and select the appropriate options.

- To create an index or nonprimary key, click on the New button in the Indexes/Keys tab of the Properties dialog box. Then, select the columns you want to include in the index or key, enter a name for the index or key, and select the remaining options as appropriate. You can also use this tab to modify, but not create, the primary key for the table.

- To modify an existing constraint, index, or key, select it from the drop-down list and then make the necessary changes.

- You can use the Relationships tab to modify the relationship between two tables. To create a relationship, you work in the Database Diagram window as shown in figure 11-6.

Figure 11-4   How to work with constraints, relationships, indexes, and keys

How to add or change table data

Figure 11-5 shows how to work with the data in a table. From the Run Table window shown in this figure, you can add records to the end of the table or modify or delete existing records. Note, however, that if an operation will cause data integrity rules to be broken, an error message is displayed and the operation won't be performed. So, for example, you can't enter data with the wrong data type into a field, and you can't delete a record if it has related records in another table and cascading deletes aren't implemented.

When you display the data in a table, you're actually working with a tool called the Query Designer, which you'll learn more about later in this chapter. For now, though, you should realize that when you open a table, a SELECT statement is executed that retrieves all of the fields and records from the table. That data is then displayed in the results pane of the Query Designer, which is the pane you see in this figure.

The data in the Invoices table

InvoiceID	VendorID	InvoiceNumber	InvoiceDate	InvoiceTotal	PaymentTotal	CreditTotal	TermsID	InvoiceDueDate
89	99	509786	2/11/99	6940.25	6940.25	0	2	2/27/99
90	108	121897	2/12/99	450	450	0	2	3/2/99
91	80	134116	2/12/99	90.36	0	0	3	3/15/99
92	80	133560	2/12/99	175	175	0	2	3/3/99
93	104	120197	2/14/99	5000	5000	▶ Run		3/1/99
94	106	120197	2/14/99	503.2	0	Clear Results		3/1/99
95	107	120197	2/15/99	1600	1600			3/1/99
96	113	120197	2/15/99	1750	1750	⤒ First		3/1/99
97	119	120197	2/15/99	4901.26	4901.26	⤓ Last		3/1/99
98	95	112897	2/15/99	46.21	0	▼ Next		3/12/99
99	95	112797	2/16/99	39.77	0	▲ Previous		3/11/99
100	96	112897	2/16/99	662	0	Row...		3/7/99
101	103	112697	2/17/99	1367.5	1367.5	▶✳ New		2/24/99
102	48	112697	2/17/99	856.92	856.92			2/24/99
103	95	112697	2/17/99	19.67	0			3/10/99
104	114	112597	2/18/99	290	290	✂ Cut		2/23/99
105	95	112597	2/18/99	32.7	0	Copy		3/9/99
106	95	112497	2/19/99	16.33	0	Paste		3/8/99
107	95	112397	2/19/99	16.33	0			3/7/99
108	117	111897	2/22/99	16.62	16.62			2/25/99
109	102	109596	2/25/99	41.8	0	Hide Pane		3/24/99
110	72	39104	3/3/99	85.31	0			4/2/99
						Properties		

Operation

- To display the data in a table, double-click on the table in the Data View window or right-click on the table and select Open from the shortcut menu. The data is then displayed in the Run Table window shown above.

- To change the data in a field, move the cursor to that field and enter the changes. The changes are saved as soon as you move to another record.

- To add a new record, enter the data for the record into the blank row at the bottom of the table. You can move to that row using the scroll bar or by selecting New from the shortcut menu. The new record is saved as soon as you move to another record.

- To cancel the changes to a field, press the Esc key while the cursor is in that field. If the data in the field hasn't changed, the changes in the entire record are canceled.

- To delete a record, select it by clicking on its row selector and then press the Delete key. You will be asked to confirm the delete operation.

- To change the width of a column in the window, drag the vertical line on the right side of the column heading for that column to the desired width. To change the height of all the rows in the window, drag the horizontal line at the bottom of any row to the desired height.

Note

- If you don't change the data in the Run Table window within a specified time limit, a message is displayed asking if the data can be cleared. If you clear the data, you can display it again by selecting Run from the shortcut menu.

Figure 11-5   How to add or change table data

Exercise Set 11-2: Modify the data and design of a table

In this exercise set, you will modify the data in the GLAccounts table. Then, you'll modify the design of the table by adding a check constraint to it. If you're using an Access database, please remember that the Data View window will only let you modify the data in the table so you can only do steps 1 through 4 in this exercise set.

Modify the data in a table (for Access and SQL Server users)

1. If necessary, start Visual Basic without opening a project and open the Data View window. Then, expand the folders in that window so you can see the tables in the database.

2. Double-click on the GLAccounts table in the Data View window to display the table data. Next, drag the vertical bar to the right of the AccountDescription heading until you can see all of the data in that column. Then, click in that column for the record with account number 181 and add the word "Costs" to the end of the description. Notice the pencil in the row selector for that record, which indicates that the record has changed. Press the Tab key to move to the next record and save the changes. Last, return to the field you just changed and change it back the way it was.

3. Right-click on the table and select New from the shortcut menu to move to the bottom of the table. Next, enter a new record with an account number of 1000 and an account description of Investment Funds into the blank row at the bottom of the table. Then, press the Tab key to save the new record. Last, delete the new record by clicking on the row selector for the record and pressing the Delete key.

4. If you're using an Access database, close the Data View Window and close Visual Basic. Otherwise, continue with the next steps.

Modify the design of the GLAccounts table (for SQL Server users)

5. Right-click on the GLAccounts table and select Design from the shortcut menu so the Design Table window is displayed.

6. Change the data type for the AccountDescription field to Numeric. Next, select the Save GLAccounts command from the File menu so the dialog box to the right is displayed. Notice that the Vendors and InvoiceLineItems tables will also be saved since they are related to the GLAccounts table.

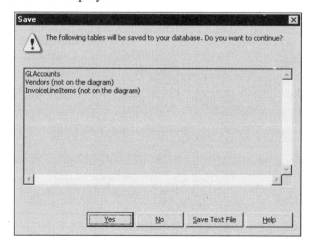

7. Click on the Yes button to save the changes. When you do, a dialog box with an error message is displayed because existing data in the table conflicts with the new data type. Then, click on the OK button. And if the Save Change Script dialog box is displayed to ask whether you want to save the VBScript file for this change, click on the No button. When you're back in the Design Table window, change the data type back to varchar.

8. Enter a new field at the bottom of the table so it looks like this:

Column Name	Datatype	Length	Precision	Scale	Allow Nulls	Default Value	Identity	Identity Seed	Identity Increment
AccountNo	int	4	10	0					
AccountDescription	varchar	50	0	0					
AccountBalance	numeric	9	18	0		(0)			

    Right-click anywhere in the Design Table window and select Properties from the shortcut menu to display the Properties dialog box. Next, click on the New button in the Tables tab and enter this for the constraint expression:

    `(AccountNo > 0 and AccountNo < 1000)`

    Then, enter CK_GLAccounts_AccountNo for the constraint name and close the dialog box to save the constraint. Last, close the Design Table window to save the changes. If Visual Basic displays a dialog box that asks whether you want to save a VBScript file for this change, click on the No button.

Change the data in the GLAccounts table (for SQL Server users)

9. Double-click on the GLAccounts table to display the table data, and notice that the value in the AccountBalance column for each record is zero since that was the default you entered for that field.

10. Right-click on the table and select New from the shortcut menu to move to the bottom of the table. Next, enter 1000 as the account number and Investment Fund as the account description. Then, press the Tab key twice to save the new record. At this point, a dialog box will display a message that indicates that the account number you just entered conflicts with the check constraint you created. So click on the OK button, and press the Esc key to cancel the new record.

11. Close the Run Table window, and open the GLAccounts table in design view again. Next, delete the new AccountBalance field you added by right-clicking on the row that defines it and selecting Delete Column from the shortcut menu. Then, display the Properties dialog box for the table and click on the Delete button in the Tables tab to delete the constraint you added. When you're done, close the Properties dialog box and close the Design Table window to save the changes. If Visual Basic displays a dialog box that asks whether you want to save a VBScript file for this change, click on the No button.

12. If you're going to continue, keep Visual Basic running with the Data View window open. Otherwise, close this window and exit from Visual Basic.

How to work with other database objects

In the pages that follow, you'll learn how you can use the Data View window to work with database diagrams, views, queries, stored procedures, and triggers. As you read these pages, though, please keep in mind that they present just an introduction to what you can do. For more detailed information, see the help topics for the Data View window.

How to create or modify a database diagram

Figure 11-6 shows the Database Diagram window that you use for defining a relationship between two tables. In this example, the diagram includes four tables. Here, a relationship has already been defined between the Vendors and Invoices tables, the Vendors and Terms tables, and the Invoices and Terms tables, and a relationship is being defined between the Vendors and GLAccounts tables.

The easiest way to create a relationship between two tables is to drag the row selector for the foreign key of one table to the title bar of the table that has the primary key. When you do that, the Create Relationship dialog box is displayed. Then, you can use this dialog box to verify that the correct fields and options have been selected for the relationship. If necessary, after you create a relationship, you can use the Relationships tab of the Properties dialog box shown in figure 11-4 to modify it.

When you add a table to a database diagram, all of the field names are displayed by default. This is illustrated by the Vendors, Terms, and GLAccounts tables in this figure. However, you can also display a table in several other views by selecting a new view from the shortcut menu for the table. For the Invoices table in this diagram, I selected Keys from the shortcut menu so only the key fields are displayed. Notice that the foreign keys as well as the primary keys are included in this view.

You can also display all of the properties for the fields in a table by selecting Column Properties from the shortcut menu. When you do, the table will be displayed as shown in figure 11-3. Then, you can use the techniques shown in that figure to work with the table. In fact, when you display the design of a table in that view, you're actually displaying a database diagram for a single table.

Although you can create a single database diagram that includes all of the tables in a database, you're more likely to create several diagrams that represent different segments of the database. To start, for example, you can create a Vendors diagram like the one in this figure that includes only the tables directly related to the Vendors table. Then, you can create another diagram to show only the tables that are related to another table like the Invoices table. As you create these diagrams, you can include one table in as many different diagrams as you need.

A database diagram that includes the Vendors table and all related tables

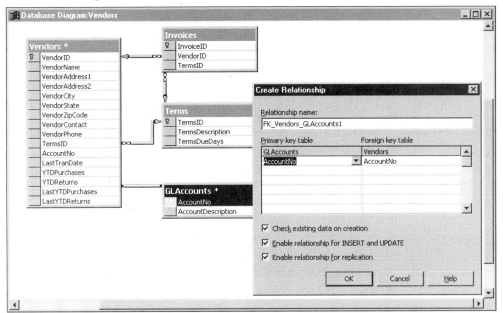

Operation

- To create a new database diagram, right-click on the Database Diagrams folder and select New Diagram from the shortcut menu. To modify an existing diagram, right-click on the diagram and select Open. The Database Diagram window is then displayed.

- To add tables to a diagram, drag them from the Tables folder in the Data View window to the Database Diagram window. By default, the names of all the fields in the table will be displayed as shown in the Vendors table above.

- To display a table in a different view, select another option from the top of the shortcut menu for the table. The options are to display just the key fields, just the table name, or the properties for each field, or to create your own custom view.

- To create a relationship between two tables, drag the row selector for the foreign key in one table to the title bar of the primary key table. Then, select the appropriate options in the Create Relationship dialog box that's displayed. A foreign key constraint will be defined on the primary key table and a relationship line will be added to the diagram.

- If a relationship has already been defined between two tables, a relationship line will appear when they're added to the diagram. A key at the end of a line represents the one side of a relationship, and an infinity sign represents the many side of a relationship.

Figure 11-6   How to create or modify a database diagram

How to create or modify a view

Figure 11-7 shows how you can create and modify a view. A view, as you may remember from chapter 5, is simply a SELECT statement that's stored as a separate object in the database. The View Designer shown in this figure lets you create that SELECT statement using a graphical interface.

As you can see in this figure, the View window consists of four panes. The *diagram pane* shows the tables and fields that are used by the view. To add a table to this pane, just drag it from the Data View window to the pane. You can also drag an existing view to this pane if you want to base the new view on the existing view.

If a relationship exists between two tables that you add to the diagram pane, a join line appears automatically as shown in this figure. By default, an inner join is created, which means that records from the two tables are included in the results of the view only if their related fields match. If you want to create an outer join, though, you can do that by right-clicking on the join line and selecting the appropriate option from the shortcut menu that's displayed. You can also create a join between two tables for which a relationship hasn't been defined. Note, however, that doing that does not create a relationship between the tables.

To include a field in the view, you simply check its box in the diagram pane. That field is then added to the *grid pane*. You can also select a field directly from the drop-down Column list in the grid pane.

To select the records that you want to include in the view, you enter criteria in the Criteria and Or columns of the grid pane. The view shown in this figure, for example, will include only invoices with a balance greater than zero. To accomplish that, a calculated field is included in the view that uses the InvoiceTotal, PaymentTotal, and CreditTotal fields to determine the balance of each invoice. If you want to use a calculated field for specifying criteria but you don't want to include that field in the view results, you can remove the check mark from the Output column for that field.

As you create a view, a SELECT statement is generated and displayed in the *SQL pane*. You can also type directly into this pane, but you usually won't need to do that.

Once you have the view defined the way you want it, you can execute it to be sure that it returns the data you want. When you do that, the results are displayed in the *results pane* at the bottom of the window. You can also display just the results pane for an existing view by selecting Open from the shortcut menu for the view in the Data View window.

A view that retrieves data from two tables

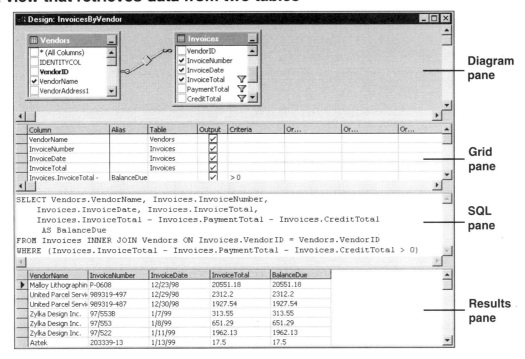

Diagram pane

Grid pane

SQL pane

Results pane

Operation

- To create a new view, right-click on the Views folder in the Data View window and select New View from the shortcut menu. To modify an existing view, right-click on the view and select Design from the shortcut menu. A View window like the one above is then displayed.

- To add tables to a view, drag them from the Data View window to the *diagram pane* of the View window. If a relationship exists between two tables, a join line appears.

- To change how two tables are joined, right-click on the join line and select the appropriate option from the shortcut menu that appears. To create a join between two tables, drag the key field in one table to the key field in the other table.

- To include a field in the view and add it to the *grid pane*, check its box in the diagram pane. To include all the fields in a table, check the All Columns box.

- To select the records to be included in the results, enter criteria in the Criteria and Or columns of the grid pane. If you want to use a field to select records but you don't want to include it in the results, remove the check mark from the Output column for the field.

- As you work in the diagram and grid panes, a SQL statement is generated in the *SQL pane*. To execute this statement, select the Run command from the shortcut menu or the Query menu. The results of the view are displayed in the *results pane*.

- To save the view, select Save View from the File menu and enter a name for the view.

Figure 11-7   How to create or modify a view

How to create a query

Although you can't save a query as a separate object in a SQL Server database, you can use the Data View window to create SQL statements that you can then copy and paste into an application. You can also run the SQL statements that you create in the Data View window.

To create a query, you use a tool called the Query Designer. Although the Query Designer isn't available directly from the Data View window, you can get to it by opening a table or view as described in figure 11-8. Then, you can use the techniques described in this figure to create and run the query.

You use the Query Designer in much the same way that you use the View Designer. The biggest difference is that the Query Designer lets you create queries other than Select queries. The query in this figure, for example, is an Insert query that inserts selected records from the Invoices table into a table named InvoiceArchive. In this case, only the invoices that have a zero balance are selected.

To create the query in this figure, I started by opening the Invoices table to display all of the fields and records in that table in the results pane. Then, I used the Show Panes command in the View menu to display the other panes in the window. When I did that, the following statement was displayed in the SQL pane:

```
SELECT * FROM Invoices
```

Next, I added a field to the query that calculates the balance due for an invoice, and I entered criteria for that field so only records with a balance due equal to zero are selected. Then, I ran the query to be sure that the correct records were selected.

After that, I selected Insert from the Change Type submenu of the Query menu to change the Select query to an Insert query. When I did that, I was asked to enter the name of the table that the records were to be appended to. The resulting SQL statement is shown in this figure. Notice that the results pane in this figure is dimmed to show that the SQL statement was changed after the results were generated. Then, you can run the new SQL statement to perform the database operation that it specifies.

Although the procedure for creating each type of query differs, you shouldn't have any trouble creating other types of queries as long as you understand how they work. To create an Update query, for example, you have to specify the fields you want to update and how you want them updated. And to create a Make-table query, you have to specify the name of the table you want to create.

Once you create a query using the Query Designer, you can copy the statement in the SQL pane to the clipboard. Then, you can paste it into the appropriate location in the Code window for the application. Without the Query Designer, you have to enter a query manually and hope that it works the way you want it to.

A query that inserts invoice records into the InvoiceArchive table

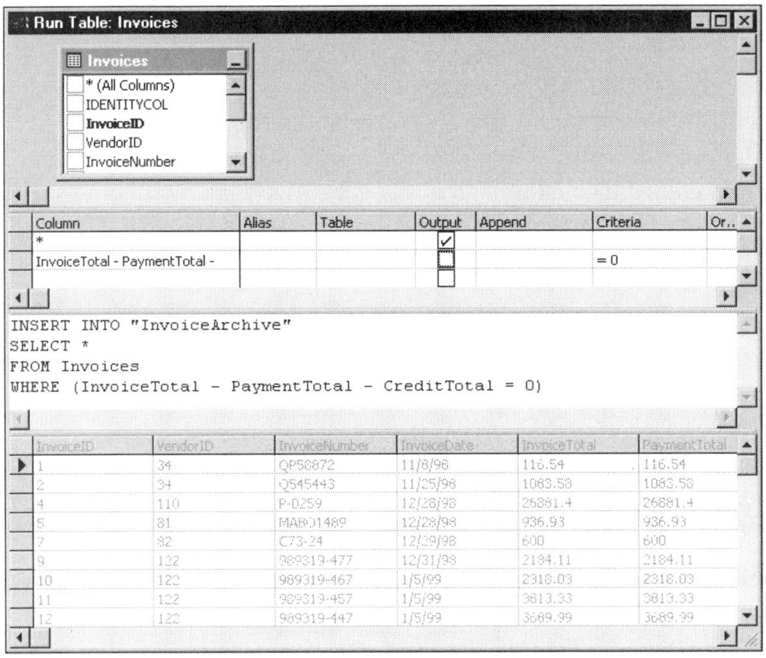

Operation

- To create a query, open a table or view that you want to use in the query. This displays the results pane for that table or view. Then, use the Show Panes command in the View menu to display the diagram, grid, and SQL panes for the query.

- To create a Select query, use the information in figure 11-7 for creating a view. You will also be able to sort the query on one or more fields using the Sort Type and Sort Order columns that are displayed in the grid pane or the Sort Ascending and Sort Descending commands in the Query menu.

- To create an Insert, Update, Delete or Make-table query, select that option from the Change Type submenu of the Query menu. Then, complete the grid pane as necessary to define the query.

- After you create a query, you can copy the statement in the SQL pane to the clipboard and paste it into your application. Or, you can run the query. However, you can't save a query as an object in the database.

- To run the query, select the Run command from the shortcut menu or the Query menu. If the query returns records, they will be displayed in the results pane. Otherwise, a message indicating the number of records that were affected is displayed.

- Before you create a query that changes the data in a database, you may want to create and execute a Select query that retrieves the records that will be affected. Then, when you change it to another type of query, the criteria you specified for the Select query are maintained.

Figure 11-8   How to create a query

How to create or modify a stored procedure

Figure 11-9 shows how you can create or modify a stored procedure. To do that, you work in the Source Code Editor window. When you create a new stored procedure in this window, a template is displayed that you can use as a guide for creating the procedure. This template contains a default procedure name that you can replace with a custom name; the general syntax for two parameter definitions that you can replace with your own definitions if the procedure will use parameters; and sample statements that you can replace with the text of the stored procedure.

The stored procedure shown in this figure consists of a single SELECT statement that includes a parameter. This is the stored procedure that is used in the application in chapter 8 to retrieve the invoices for a vendor. As you can see, the parameter is defined in the first line of the procedure after the name of the procedure. Then, when the application executes this procedure, it passes the value of the VendorID field to the procedure, which is used as the value of this parameter.

Although the stored procedure in this figure is simple, you can create stored procedures that are extremely complex. For example, you can create stored procedures that maintain the referential integrity of the tables in a database instead of using foreign keys or triggers. As an application programmer, though, you're not likely to do that. Instead, you'll probably use stored procedures for relatively straightforward operations like Select, Insert, Update, and Delete queries.

The template for a new stored procedure

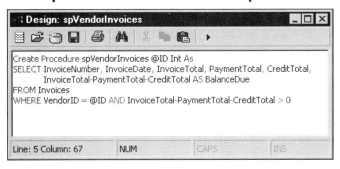

A stored procedure that includes a parameter

```
Create Procedure spVendorInvoices @ID Int As
SELECT InvoiceNumber, InvoiceDate, InvoiceTotal, PaymentTotal, CreditTotal,
       InvoiceTotal-PaymentTotal-CreditTotal AS BalanceDue
FROM Invoices
WHERE VendorID = @ID AND InvoiceTotal-PaymentTotal-CreditTotal > 0
```

Operation

- To create a new stored procedure, right-click on the Store Procedures folder in the Data View window and select New Stored Procedure from the shortcut menu. The Source Code Editor window is then displayed with a template that you can use as a guide for creating the procedure.

- To use the stored procedure template, replace the default name (StoredProcedure*n*) with the name you want to use. If the stored procedure will include parameters, replace the comment that shows the parameter syntax with the parameter definitions. Otherwise, delete this comment. Then, replace the comment after the As keyword with the text of the stored procedure.

- To modify an existing stored procedure, right-click on the procedure in the Data View window and select Design from the shortcut menu.

- To save a stored procedure, click on the Save To Database toolbar button in the Source Code Editor window, or select Save from the File menu.

Figure 11-9   How to create or modify a stored procedure

How to create or modify a trigger

In chapter 5, you learned that a trigger is a special type of stored procedure that's executed when records are inserted, updated, or deleted from a table. Because a trigger is associated with a specific table, it doesn't appear in a separate folder in the Data View window like stored procedures do. Instead, you have to expand a table in the Data View window to see the triggers for that table.

To work with triggers, you use the Source Code Editor window just as you do when you work with stored procedures. When you create a new trigger though, a different template is provided as shown in figure 11-10. As you can see from this template, you can use a trigger for an insert, update, or delete operation or any combination of those operations.

The trigger shown in this figure is used to maintain referential integrity between the Invoices and InvoiceLineItems tables when a record is deleted from the Invoices table. To do that, it deletes any records in the InvoiceLineItems table that have the same value in the InvoiceID field as the invoice record that was deleted. If you take a minute to review this trigger, you should get a pretty good idea of how it works.

Like stored procedures, you can create triggers that are quite complex. Because triggers are typically used to maintain referential integrity and implement business rules, though, they're more likely to be implemented by database administrators than by application programmers.

The template for a new trigger on the Invoices table

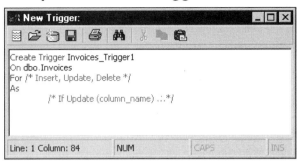

A trigger that deletes invoice line items related to a deleted invoice

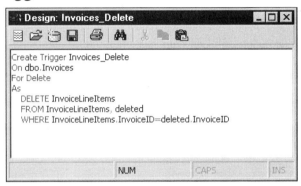

Operation

- To create a new trigger for a table, right-click on the table in the Data View window and select New Trigger from the shortcut menu. The Source Code Editor window is then displayed with a template that you can use as a guide for creating the trigger.

- To use the trigger template, replace the default name (*tablename*_Trigger1) with the name you want to use. Change the For clause so it indicates the operations for which you want the trigger to fire (Insert, Update, and/or Delete). Then, replace the comment after the As keyword with the text of the trigger.

- To save a trigger, click on the Save To Database toolbar button in the Source Code Editor window, or select Save from the File menu. When you expand the table that contains the trigger in the Data View window, the trigger will appear along with the list of fields in the table.

- To modify an existing trigger, right-click on the trigger in the Data View window and select Design from the shortcut menu.

Figure 11-10   How to create or modify a trigger

Exercise set 11-3: Create a database diagram and other database objects

In this exercise set, you will create a database diagram, view, query, stored procedure, and trigger. To do these exercises, you need to use a SQL Server database since these functions aren't available for an Access database.

Create a database diagram

1. If necessary, start Visual Basic and open the Data View window. Then, expand the Data Links folder and the AccountsPayable folder so you can see the subordinate folders.

2. Right-click on the Database Diagrams folder and select New Diagram to open the Database Diagram window. Then, expand the Tables folder in the Data View window, and drag the Vendors, Invoices, Terms, and GLAccounts tables to the Database Diagram window. Assuming that the relationships between these tables have already been defined, the diagram should look something like the one in figure 11-6.

3. Right-click on the relationship line between the Vendors and GLAccounts tables, select Delete Relationship From Database from the shortcut menu to delete the relationship, and click on the Yes button when the confirmation dialog box is displayed.

4. Drag the row selector for the AccountNo field in the GLAccounts table to the Vendors table to display the Create Relationship dialog box. Make sure that the settings appear as shown in figure 11-6, and click on the OK button to create the relationship.

5. Right-click on each of the tables in the diagram and select Keys from the shortcut menu so only the key fields are displayed. The diagram should now look something like this:

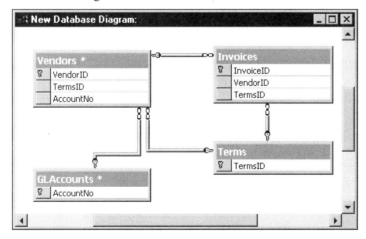

6. Close the Database Diagram window and click on the No button in the dialog box that's displayed so this diagram isn't saved.

Create a view

7. Right-click on the Views folder in the Data View window and select New View from the shortcut menu to open the New View window. Then, drag the Vendors and Invoices tables from the Data View window to the diagram pane of the New View window. When you do that, a join line should appear between the two tables. If it doesn't, drag the VendorID field in the Vendors table to the VendorID field in the Invoices table to create the join.

8. Click on the check box for the VendorName field in the Vendors table and the InvoiceNumber, InvoiceDate, and InvoiceTotal fields in the Invoices table. Next, notice the SELECT statement that's created in the SQL pane. Then, select the Run command from the Query menu, and scroll through the results pane to view the results of this statement.

9. Click in the Criteria column for the InvoiceTotal field in the Grid pane and enter the expression "> 500". Next, press the Enter key and notice that the results pane is dimmed. Also notice that a funnel appears to the right of the InvoiceTotal field in the Diagram pane to indicate that the view is filtered by that field. Then, run the query again with the new criteria. The window should now look something like this:

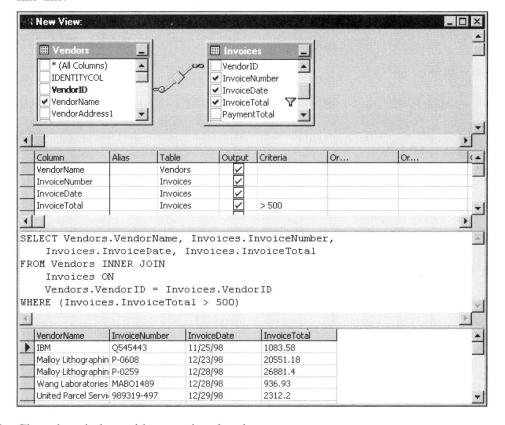

10. Close the window without saving the view.

Create a query

11. Double-click on the Invoices table in the Data View window to display the data in that table. Then, use the Show Panes command in the View menu to display the diagram, grid, and SQL panes.

12. Enter this expression in the second row of the grid pane as shown in figure 11-8:

```
InvoiceTotal - PaymentTotal - CreditTotal
```

Then, enter BalanceDue in the Alias column of that row and enter the expression "= 0" in the Criteria column.

13. Select the Run command from the Query menu to display the results of the query. Then, scroll to the last column in the results pane to display the BalanceDue column and notice that the value in each record is zero.

14. Select the Make Table option from the Change Type submenu of the Query menu to change the query from a Select query to a Make-table query. When prompted, enter InvoiceArchive as the name of the table to be created. Then, notice that the SELECT statement in the SQL pane has been changed to a SELECT INTO statement. Now, remove the check mark from the Output column of the BalanceDue field so it's not included in the query results. At this point, the query should look like this:

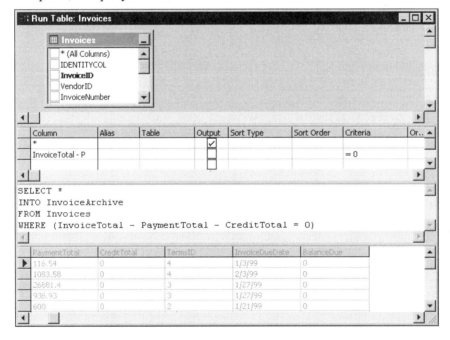

15. Run the query. Visual Basic then displays a dialog box that shows the number of records that were affected by the query. Click on the OK button in this dialog box, and close the window.

16. Click on the Refresh Data View button in the Data View window, then expand the AccountsPayable folder and the Tables folder so you can see the InvoiceArchive table you just created. Next, double-click on the table to see the records that were added to this table. Then, close this window, right-click on the InvoiceArchive table in the Data View window, select Delete from the shortcut menu, and delete the table.

Create a stored procedure

17. Right-click on the Stored Procedures folder in the Data View window and select New Stored Procedure to display the Source Code Editor. Visual Basic then displays a template in this window like the one in figure 11-9.

18. Highlight the default name for the stored procedure and replace it with the name spVendorInvoices. Next, highlight the next few lines of code that begin with /* and end with */ and replace them with the parameter definition "@ID Int". Then, highlight the comment and the Return statement following the As keyword and replace them with the SELECT statement shown in the stored procedure in figure 11-9.

19. Click on the Save To Database button in the Source Code Editor window to save the stored procedure with the name you entered in the Create Procedure statement. Then, close the Source Code Editor window.

20. Refresh the Data View window, and expand the AccountsPayable and Stored Procedures folder to see the procedure you just created. Then, delete the stored procedure using the Delete command in its shortcut menu.

Create a trigger

21. Right-click on the Invoices table in the Data View window and select New Trigger from the shortcut menu to display the Source Code Editor window. Visual Basic then displays a template like the one in figure 11-10.

22. Change the name of the trigger to Invoices_Delete, replace the comment on the For clause with the word "Delete," and replace the comment following the As clause with the DELETE statement shown in the trigger in figure 11-10.

23. Click on the Save to Database button in the Source Code Editor window to save the trigger. Then, close this window.

24. Refresh the Data View window, and expand the AccountsPayable and Tables folders. Next, expand the Invoices table to see the trigger you just created. Then, delete the trigger using the Delete command in its shortcut menu.

Exit from Visual Basic

25. Close the Data View window, and exit from Visual Basic.

Perspective

Although the database for a business application is typically designed and implemented by a database administrator, an application programmer may need to develop some of the tables, views, stored procedures, and triggers that are required for testing an application. In addition, the application programmer may need to review the objects of a database to see which ones are available and how they are defined. In either case, the Data View window makes that relatively easy without ever leaving Visual Basic. As a result, this is an important new feature of Visual Basic 6.

At this point, if you've read all of the chapters in this section, you have all the skills you need for developing database applications. With those skills, you should be able to develop bound forms quickly and easily whenever they're appropriate. You should also be able to develop unbound forms whenever an application requires the careful treatment that can be only be done through coding. And with either type of form, you can use the skills presented in this chapter to review and manage the database objects that your application uses.

Terms you should know

data link
Data Environment connection
check constraint
unique constraint
clustered index
diagram pane
grid pane
SQL pane
results pane

Section 3

Other development skills

This four chapters in this section present other development skills that every Visual Basic programmer should at least be aware of. To make these chapters as easy to use as possible, they are designed as independent modules. That means you can read them in whatever order you prefer; you don't have to read them in sequence.

In chapter 12, you can learn how to enhance a user interface by adding menus, toolbars, a status bar, and help information to it. You normally do this enhancement after you've got the rest of the application working the way you want it to.

In chapter 13, you can learn more about object-oriented programming. In particular, you'll learn how to create class modules that define your own objects with their own properties and methods. You'll also learn how to use those class modules by including them in a standard project or by deploying them as ActiveX components.

In chapter 14, you can learn how to use Visual Basic for developing Internet applications. There, you'll learn how to create dynamic web pages by using DHTML. You'll also learn how to create IIS applications by using Web Classes.

Last, chapter 15 shows you how to distribute a completed application on the clients of a system. There, you'll learn how to create a setup program that delivers all the files that are needed by the clients. Then, you can run the setup program on each client to install the application.

12

How to enhance the user interface

Once you have the forms of an application working right, you can enhance the user interface by adding a startup form, menus, toolbars, a status bar, and help information. You may also want to add a splash form to the application or change from a single-document interface to a multiple-document interface. By making these additions and changes, you improve the appearance of the application at the same time that you make it easier to use.

An introduction to user interfaces 436
Single-document and multiple-document interfaces 436
Splash forms and startup forms 438
How to start an application with a splash form 440
Two quick ways to add help information 442
Exercise set 12-1: Start an MDI interface 444

How to add menus, toolbars, and status bars 446
How to create menus 446
How to create a toolbar using a PictureBox control
and command buttons 448
How to create a toolbar using Toolbar and ImageList controls 450
How to create a status bar 452
How to use code to work with menus, toolbars, and status bars 454
Exercise set 12-2: Enhance the interface 456

How to use the Microsoft Help Workshop 458
An overview of the Microsoft Help Workshop 458
How to create a topic file 460
How to create a contents file 462
How to map a help topic to a numeric value 464
How to compile and test the help project 466
How to use a help file in a Visual Basic application 468
Exercise set 12-3: Add help information 470

Perspective 474

An introduction to user interfaces

When you develop business applications with Visual Basic, you normally use either a single-document or a multiple-document interface. How you use other features of the user interface, such as menus, toolbars, and startup forms, depends on which type of interface you choose. So this chapter starts by presenting two typical interfaces. Then, the remaining topics in this chapter show you how to implement specific features of the user interface.

Single-document and multiple-document interfaces

Figure 12-1 shows two versions of the Accounts Payable application. The first version uses a *single-document interface (SDI)*. Notice that each form in this version has its own menu. Although toolbars weren't required for this particular application, each form in an SDI interface can also have its own toolbar.

The second version uses a *multiple-document interface (MDI)*. Here, the parent form contains a menu and toolbar that are available to all of the child forms. As you'll see later in this chapter, you can use code to modify the menu and toolbar depending on what form is active and what operations are available.

The parent form in the MDI application in this figure also includes a status bar. A bar like this can be set up to display a number of information items. Although you can add a status bar to any form in either an SDI or MDI interface, it makes most sense to use one on a parent form.

Single-document interface (SDI)

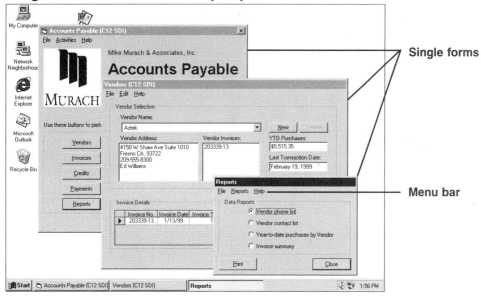

Multiple-document interface (MDI)

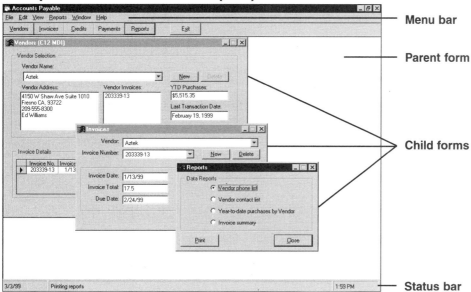

Description

- The forms in an SDI application typically contain their own menus and toolbars.
- The parent form in an MDI application typically contains menus and a toolbar that are used by all the child forms. A parent form can also contain a status bar.

Figure 12-1   Single-document and multiple-document interfaces

Splash forms and startup forms

When your application consists of more than one form, you usually need to provide a *startup form* that directs the user to the other forms of the application. This is illustrated by the second form in figure 12-2, which is the first form in an SDI application. In an MDI application, the parent form can be used as the startup form, but often a special child form is used within the parent form to provide information about the application.

When you start an application, you may want to load all of the forms of the application, but show only the startup form. Then, you can show the other forms as they are required by the user. Although this takes the application longer to start up, the forms appear quickly once the startup procedure has been completed. One alternative is to load each form as it is required by the user. Another alternative is to load the primary forms when the application starts and the other forms as they are needed.

If there is a significant delay before the first screen is displayed by an application, you may want to start the application by displaying a *splash form* (or *splash screen*) like the one at the top of this figure. This type of screen shows the user that the startup procedure is in progress. Then, to show the user that progress is being made, you can change the caption of a label on the splash form as you move through the startup procedure, or you can change the Value property of a progress bar like the one shown in this figure.

Incidentally, a ProgressBar control is one of eight controls that are included in the Microsoft Windows Common Controls 6.0. To add these controls to the Toolbox, you use the Components command in the Project menu. Three of the other controls in this group that are useful when you're enhancing the user interface are the Toolbar, ImageList, and StatusBar controls.

A splash form for the Accounts Payable application

Descriptive label
ProgressBar control

A startup form for the SDI version of the Accounts Payable application

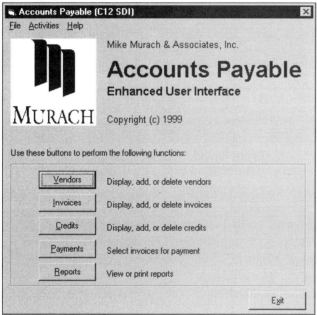

Notes

- You can use the Splash Screen option in the Add Form dialog box to create a splash form. The splash form that's created contains a template for the information commonly included on a splash form.
- You can use a label control on a splash form that changes as the startup procedure executes to tell the user what tasks the application is performing.
- You can use a ProgressBar control on the splash form to show what portion of the startup procedure has been completed.
- You can set the Screen.MousePointer property to vbHourglass for a splash form so the mouse pointer appears as an hourglass when it's positioned over the form. To return to the default arrow, set the MousePointer property to vbDefault.

Figure 12-2   Splash forms and startup forms

How to start an application with a splash form

After you add a startup form or splash form to an application, you need to change the properties of the application so it starts by loading the right form. To do that, you access the Project Properties dialog box that's shown in figure 12-3. In this example, the startup object is a form named frmSplash, which is the splash form for the application.

The code in this figure shows how you can use the Load event procedure for the splash form to load the primary forms of the application and to show the progress of this startup procedure. The first statement in this procedure displays the splash form. This is necessary because by default, the form isn't displayed until the Load procedure finishes. But because the purpose of this form is to show the progress of the Load procedure, you have to issue the Show method explicitly to display the form at the start of this procedure.

The Show method in this procedure is followed by a DoEvents function. This function passes control to the Windows operating system so it does the events that are already in its queue. Otherwise, Windows decides what the priorities of the events in its queue are and executes them based on those priorities. But that may mean that the form isn't displayed at the beginning of this procedure, even though the Show method is the first statement. The DoEvents function is useful whenever you want to make sure that all the commands in the queue are executed before the procedure continues.

The next two statements assign a value of 10 to the Value property of the ProgressBar control and a message that indicates what form is being loaded to the Caption property of the Label control. In later statements, the procedure displays four more progress messages in the Label control and five updated values in the ProgressBar control to show the user how the startup procedure is progressing.

The last two statements in this procedure show the startup form and unload the splash form. The Show method for the startup form is required because loading a form doesn't also display it.

When you load the forms at the beginning of an application, you'll want to make sure that the forms aren't unloaded when the user closes them. Instead, they should be unloaded only when the user ends the application. To close a form without unloading it, you use the Hide method of the form. You may also want to remove the built-in Close button in the title bar of the form so the user can't click on it to unload the form. The easiest way to do that is to change the ControlBox property of the form to False. Note that this also removes the Maximize and Minimize buttons from the title bar.

You can also use a splash form to load a parent form and the child forms for an MDI application. If you do that, you'll want to change the AutoShowChildren property of the MDI form to False. Otherwise, the child forms will be displayed as they're loaded.

The Project Properties dialog box that sets the startup form

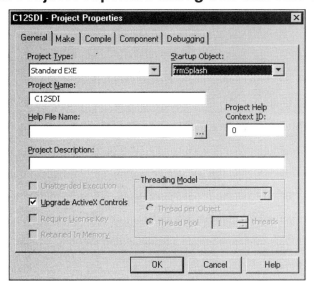

Code for the Load event procedure of the splash form

```
Private Sub Form_Load()
    frmSplash.Show
    DoEvents
    prgFormLoad.Value = 10
    lblLoadStatus = "Now loading 'Startup' form..."
    Load frmMain
    prgFormLoad.Value = 30
    lblLoadStatus = "Now loading 'Vendors' form..."
    Load frmVendors
    prgFormLoad.Value = 40
    lblLoadStatus = "Now loading 'New Vendor' form..."
    Load frmNewVendor
    prgFormLoad.Value = 60
    lblLoadStatus = "Now loading 'Invoices' form..."
    Load frmInvoices
    prgFormLoad.Value = 80
    lblLoadStatus = "Now loading 'Reports' form..."
    Load frmReports
    prgFormLoad.Value = 100
    frmMain.Show
    Unload frmSplash
End Sub
```

Notes

- To hide, but not unload a form, use the Hide method of the form.
- To prevent a user from unloading a form by clicking on the built-in Close button in the title bar, you can remove this button by changing the ControlBox property of the form to False.
- If you use a splash form to load the child forms, change the AutoShowChildren property of the parent form to False so the child forms aren't displayed when they're loaded.

Figure 12-3   How to start an application with a splash form

Two quick ways to add help information

Because Visual Basic applications use the standard Windows interface, users who are already familiar with other Windows applications should quickly adapt to Visual Basic applications. In addition, you should try to design and develop each application so it is as easy to use as is practical. Nevertheless, almost all applications can benefit from the addition of at least a minimum amount of help information.

In figure 12-4, you can see two quick ways to add help information to an application. To provide a ToolTip for a control, for example, you just add the tip to the ToolTipText property of the control. And to provide help information that's available from the Help menu, you can develop a simple form that displays the information.

One form that's usually made available from the Help menu is an About form like the one shown in this figure. An About form typically includes information about the application such as its version number and copyright date. The About form in this figure also contains a command button that displays information about the system that's in use. To create a form like this, you can choose the About Dialog option from the Add Form dialog box. Then, the System Info button and the code that's necessary to display the system information when this button is clicked is included in the form automatically.

Beyond that, you can build a complete help system for an application that's comparable to one for a commercial application. To do that, you can use a Help editor or compiler. Later in this chapter, you'll learn the basics of using the Help compiler that comes with Visual Basic 6, called the Microsoft Help Workshop. As you'll see, this tool makes it easy to develop more sophisticated help systems when the techniques shown in figure 12-4 aren't enough.

A ToolTip for a toolbar button

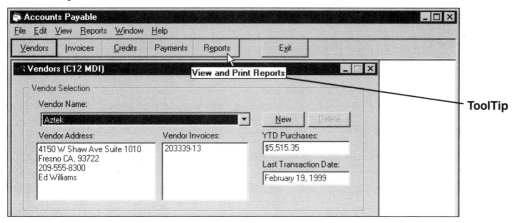

Description

- To provide a ToolTip for any control on a form, enter the tip into its ToolTipText property. This tip is automatically displayed when you position the mouse pointer over the control.

A form used to display help information

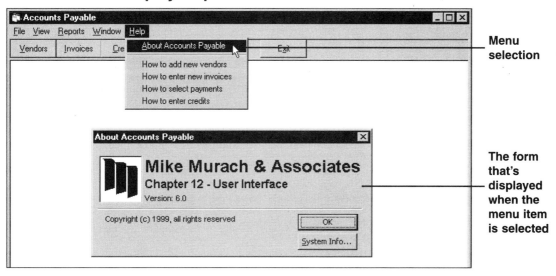

Description

- To display help information for a menu selection, you can develop a form that provides the information.

- To create an About form like the one shown above, you can use the About Dialog option in the Add Form dialog box. The form that's generated includes the System Info button and the code needed to display the system information.

Figure 12-4   Two quick ways to add help information to a form

Exercise set 12-1: Start an MDI interface

In this exercise set, you'll create a simple MDI application with a single child form. You'll also create a splash form that will be used to start the application, and you'll add some basic help information.

Start a new project

1. Start Visual Basic and begin a Standard EXE project. Next, right-click on the default form (Form1) in the Project Explorer and use the Remove command to remove it from the project.

2. Select the Add MDI Form command in the Project menu to add an MDI form to the project. Enlarge the form so that it covers most of the screen, change its Name property to frmMain, change its Caption property to Accounts Payable, and change its WindowState property to Maximized.

3. Use the Add Form and Add Module commands in the Project menu to add the forms and module you created for the exercise sets in chapter 7 to this project.

4. Change the ProjectName property for the project to C12MDI and the Startup Object property to frmMain. Then, use the References command in the Project menu to add Microsoft ActiveX Data Objects 2.0 Library.

5. Save the project with the name C12MDI in a new folder named Chapter 12 MDI, and save the MDI form with the name frmMain. Then, right-click on the Vendors form in the Project Explorer and use the Save As command to save the form in the Chapter 12 folder. Do the same for the New Vendors form and the standard module.

Add menus to the MDI form and create a child form

6. Use the Menu Editor as described in chapter 3 to add File, View, and Help menus to the form. (Be sure to include an ampersand at the beginning of the caption for each menu so you can use the keyboard to access them.) The File menu should contain an Exit command named mnuExit, the View menu should contain a Vendors command named mnuVendors, and the Help menu should contain an About Accounts Payable command named mnuAbout. When you're done, click on the OK button to exit from the Menu Editor and then click on each menu to see the commands that are displayed.

7. Add code to the Click event procedure of each menu command to implement its function. The Exit command should unload the form, the Vendors command should display the form named frmVendors, and the About Accounts Payable command should display a modal form named frmAbout (Show 1), which you'll create in step 16.

8. Display the frmVendors form, change its Caption property to Vendors (C12), its MDIChild property to True, and change its BorderStyle property to Fixed Single. Next, change the name of the Exit button to cmdClose and its Caption property to &Close. Then, change the name of the cmdExit_Click procedure to cmdClose_Click.

9. Start the application, pull down the View menu, select the Vendors command to display the Vendors form, and click on the Close button in that form to close the form. Then, pull down the File menu and select the Exit command to end the application. If everything worked the way it should, save the project. Otherwise, make the necessary changes before saving it.

Create a splash form

10. Select the Add Form command from the Project menu and select the Splash Screen option from the Add Form dialog box that's displayed. Then, change the Caption property of the CompanyProduct label to your name, and delete the remaining labels except for Product and Version.

11. Add a label near the bottom of this form, and change its Caption property to "Loading Accounts Payable forms…". Then, open the Code window for the form and delete the Form_KeyPress and Frame1_Click event procedures.

12. Notice that the Form_Load procedure sets the Caption properties for the Product and Version labels. After these statements, add this code:

```
frmSplash.Show
DoEvents
Load frmMain
Load frmVendors
frmMain.Show
Unload frmSplash
```

13. Change the code for the Click event of the Close button on the Vendors form so it hides the form instead of unloading it, and change the ControlBox property of the form to False to remove the Close button from the title bar.

14. Change the AutoShowChildren property of the parent form to False so the Vendors form isn't displayed when the parent form is loaded.

15. Change the Startup Object property of the project to frmSplash, and test the application to see that it works (the splash form may be displayed for only a moment in this simple application). Then, close the application, save the project, and save the splash form with the name frmSplash.

Add help information

16. Use the About Dialog option in the Add Form dialog box to add an About form to the project. Then, delete the App Description and Warning labels and add your own entries for the Application Title and Version labels.

17. Enter "Select a vendor from the list" into the ToolTipText property of the Vendor combo box on the Vendors form.

18. Run the application, and move the pointer over the combo box to see the ToolTip. Next, select the About Accounts Payable command in the Help menu to display the About form, and click on the System Info button to see the information that's displayed. When you're done, close the dialog boxes and end the application.

19. Save the project, and save the About form with the name frmAbout.

How to add menus, toolbars, and status bars

Menus and toolbars let the user access the functions of an application in familiar ways, while status bars can display general information about the system or application. In the topics that follow, you'll learn how to add menus, toolbars, and status bars to an application. Then, in the last topic, you'll learn how to use code to work with menus, toolbars, and status bars.

How to create menus

Figure 12-5 reviews and expands on the information presented in chapter 3 on how to use the Menu Editor dialog box to create the menus for a form. If you need to refresh your basic skills for creating menus, you can refer back to figure 3-13.

The menus in figure 12-5 are the ones for the parent form of the MDI application shown in figure 12-1. Notice in that figure, though, that the Edit menu shown in figure 12-5 isn't displayed. That's because the Visible property of this menu has been set to False since it doesn't apply to the form that's currently displayed. You'll learn how to make these types of changes to a menu through code in figure 12-9.

When you create the menus for a parent form, you'll usually include a Window menu. Then, if you check the WindowList property for that menu, it will automatically display all of the open child forms and you can use it to switch between those forms.

You may also want to include other commands in the Window menu that let you arrange the open child forms. Then, you can use the Arrange method of the parent form to implement those functions. If, for example, you include a Tile command on this menu, you can execute this statement when that command is selected:

```
Me.Arrange vbTileHorizontal
```

For a list of all the arguments you can code on the Arrange method, see the Help topic for this method.

You can also use the Menu Editor to create *popup menus* that are activated when the user clicks the right mouse button on a form or control. If these menus are different than the drop-down menus, you need to turn their Visible properties off so they aren't displayed with the drop-down menus. However, you can also use the menus in the menu bar as popup menus. In figure 12-9, you'll see the coding requirements for a popup menu.

The Menu Editor dialog box

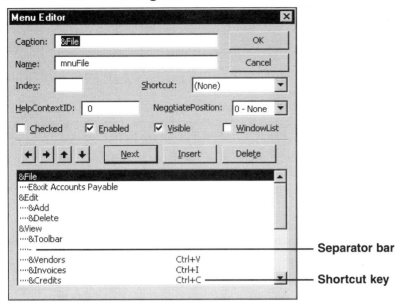

Separator bar

Shortcut key

Drop-down menus

- To access the Menu Editor dialog box, display the form and click on the Menu Editor icon in the toolbar or choose Menu Editor from the Tools menu.

- The Caption and Name properties are required for all menu objects, and the prefix *mnu* is commonly used in the name of a menu object.

- You can use the ellipsis (…) at the end of the Caption property to identify menu commands that lead to dialog boxes. And you can use a single hyphen (-) in the Caption property to display a separator bar between menu commands.

- To create a Window menu that lists all of the open child forms in a parent form, select the WindowList property. Then, you can use this menu to switch between the open forms.

Popup menus

- To create a *popup* (or *shortcut*) *menu* that's different from the other menus, remove the check mark from the Visible property. Then, you can use code to test whether the right mouse button has been clicked and, if so, to display the popup menu (see figure 12-9).

- Some controls provide built-in popup menus. If, for example, you right-click on any masked text box control, a popup menu is displayed with these standard Windows commands: Undo, Cut, Copy, Paste, Delete, and Select All.

Figure 12-5   How to create menus

How to create a toolbar using a PictureBox control and command buttons

Figure 12-6 shows how to create a simple toolbar by placing command buttons on a PictureBox control. The only trick here is to set the Align property of the picture box to Align Top. Once you do that, the picture box automatically extends from the left side of the form to the right side. Then, you can adjust the Height property of the picture box so it's just slightly larger than the height of the command buttons you add to it.

Since toolbar buttons often duplicate functions that are already available from other controls on the form or from the menu system, you'll often code a toolbar button so it calls an existing procedure. You'll see how to do that in figure 12-9.

If you want to create toolbar buttons that have icons on them, you can add graphic images to the command buttons. To do that, set the Picture property of the command button to the graphic you want to display, and set the Style property to Graphical. Note that when the properties are set this way, the text in the Caption property is still displayed on the command button. If you want to display just a graphic, delete the text in the Caption property.

If you want to use graphic images on toolbar buttons, you'll probably need to get or create some images. The preferred format for this purpose is the icon format, which is designed for small graphic files. All icon files have a small number of pixels (usually 32 by 32 or 16 by 16) and have ico as the extension. Although the Standard and Professional editions of Visual Basic include many common icons, they don't include icons for specialized functions like the ones you're likely to need for business applications. Then, if you can't buy the icons you need from another source, you can use the Image Editor that comes with both editions of Visual Basic to design your own icons. You can find the Image Editor in the \Common\Tools\Vb\Imagedit folder on Disk 1 of the Visual Basic CDs.

From a practical point of view, though, it's usually best to avoid the use of icons when you're developing business applications. After all, it's easier to understand the words on a command button than it is to guess what an icon represents. And if you avoid the use of icons, you also eliminate the need to provide ToolTips for the icons. On the other hand, it's relatively easy to create toolbar buttons with ToolTips, as long as you're satisfied with the icons that are already available on your PC.

A toolbar created using a picture box and command buttons

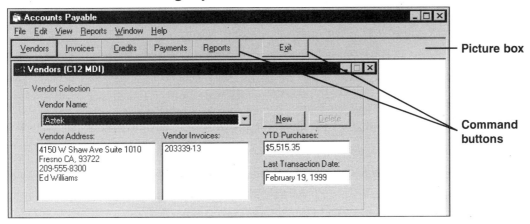

Description

- Add a PictureBox control to the form to create a toolbar area as shown above. If you set the Align property for this control to Align Top, it automatically reaches across the width of the form.

- Add a command button within the toolbar area for each button on the toolbar. Then, write the code for the click event of each command button.

- To place a graphic image on a command button, change the Style property for the command button to Graphical and use the Picture property to select a graphic file, preferably one with the ico (icon) extension.

- To create a ToolTip for the button, use its ToolTipText property.

Figure 12-6   How to create a toolbar using a PictureBox control and command buttons

How to create a toolbar using Toolbar and ImageList controls

Another way to create a toolbar is to use the Toolbar control as described in figure 12-7. This control is part of the Microsoft Windows Common Controls 6.0, which you can add to the Toolbox using the Components command in the Project menu. This also adds the ImageList control to the Toolbox. You can use this control in conjunction with the Toolbar control as you'll learn in a moment.

When you add a Toolbar control to a form, it appears at the top of the form below any menus or other toolbars that you've added to the form. Then, you can use the Buttons tab of the Property Pages dialog box shown in this figure to add buttons to the toolbar. As you add buttons, they're assigned index numbers beginning with 1. You can use those index numbers to refer to the individual buttons in code. Alternatively, you can set the Key or Tag property for each button to a unique value that you can refer to in code.

The buttons on a Toolbar control can display text, a graphic image, or both. To display text, just set the Caption property for that button. To display a graphic image, you first need to create an image list by adding an ImageList control to the form. Note that the ImageList control is invisible when the form is run, so it doesn't matter where you place it on the form.

After you add an ImageList control to the form, you add the images you want to use on the toolbar buttons to the image list using the Images tab in its Property Pages dialog box. Each image you add is assigned an index number that you can then use to refer to the image from the Toolbar control. To do that, you set the Image property of the toolbar button to the index number of the image. But first, you have to set the ImageList property of the Toolbar control (on the General tab) to the name of the ImageList control that contains the images.

You can also add space between two buttons on a toolbar by adding a button between them and changing the Style property of that button to tbrSeparator. This adds a fixed amount of space between the controls. To add more space, change the Style property to tbrPlaceholder and set the Width property to the width of the space. The other Style options let you add a check box, a group of buttons, or a drop-down list to the toolbar.

As you can see, using the Toolbar control is much more complicated than using a PictureBox control and command buttons, particularly if you want to include graphic images on the buttons in the toolbar. However, the Toolbar control lets you create more sophisticated toolbars and gives you more control over their appearance. Unless your application requires this, though, you're better off using just a PictureBox control and command buttons because they're easier to work with and they're standard Toolbox controls.

A toolbar created using a Toolbar and ImageList control

The properties for a toolbar button

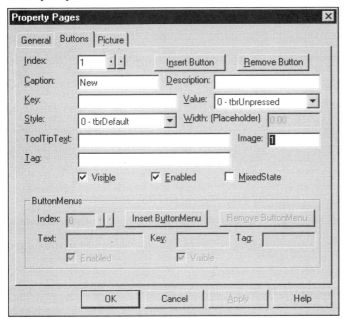

Description

- When you add a Toolbar control to a form, it is automatically placed at the top of the form below the menus and reaches across the width of the form.

- To add buttons to the toolbar, click on the Insert Button button in the Buttons tab of its Property Pages dialog box. The buttons are assigned index values beginning with 1. You can use the Index property or the values you enter in the Key or Tag properties to refer to the buttons through code.

- To include text on a button, enter the text in the Caption property. To include a graphic image on a toolbar button, set the ImageList property on the General tab to the name of the ImageList control that includes the image. Then, set the Image value to the Index number for the image that you want from the image list.

- To create an image list, add an ImageList control to the form. Then, use the Images tab of its Property Pages dialog box to add the images that you want to use on the toolbar buttons. As you add each image, an Index number is assigned to it.

- To respond to the user clicking on a button in the toolbar, write code for the ButtonClick event of the Toolbar control as described in figure 12-9.

Figure 12-7   How to create a toolbar using the Toolbar and ImageList controls

How to create a status bar

Figure 12-8 shows you how to create a *status bar*. Like the Toolbar and ImageList controls, the StatusBar control is part of the Microsoft Windows Common Controls 6.0. You can use this control to display system information or the text or graphics that you specify. The status bar shown in this figure, for example, consists of three *panels* that display the system date and time along with an indication of the operation that's being performed.

When you first add a status bar to a form, it consists of a single panel. To add panels to the status bar, you use the Panels tab of its Property Pages dialog box as shown in this figure. As you add panels, they're assigned index numbers that uniquely identify each panel. In addition, you can specify unique values for the Key and Tag properties of each panel.

By default, the Style property of a panel is set to sbrText. This setting lets you display any text you specify as illustrated by the second panel in the status bar shown in this figure. You can specify the text to be displayed by setting the Text property in the Panels tab or by setting this property through code as shown in the next figure.

You can also set the Style property to display selected system information in a panel. The Style property for the panel shown in this figure, for example, is set to sbrDate. This causes the system date to be displayed as illustrated by the first panel in the status bar. To see what other settings are available, you can drop down the list for this property.

Another property you're likely to change is the MinimumWidth property. By default, this property is set to 1440, which is the width of the first panel in the status bar shown in this figure. If you're using a panel to display messages to the user, you'll want to increase this value.

If you want to use a status bar only to display messages, an easy way to do that is to change the Style property of the status bar to sbrSimple. Then, the status bar will consist of a single panel that spans the width of the status bar. To specify the text that's displayed in the panel, you set the SimpleText property of the status bar.

A status bar that displays the date, time, and current operation

The properties for the first panel in the status bar

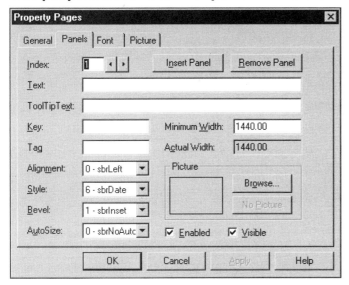

Description

- When you add a StatusBar control to a form, it is automatically placed at the bottom of the form and reaches across the width of the form.

- By default, a status bar contains a single *panel*. To change the properties for this panel or to insert or remove panels, use the Panels tab of the Property Pages dialog box for the status bar.

- Each panel in a status bar is assigned an Index number. You can use this number to refer to the panel through code. You can also use the Key and Tag properties to uniquely identify the panels in the status bar and refer to them in code.

- The Style property determines the information that's displayed in the panel. The default value for this property is sbrText, which displays the text you specify in the Text property. The other options display specific information, such as the date or time or an indication of whether Caps Lock or Num Lock are on.

- To change the width of a panel, set the MinimumWidth property. This width won't change unless you resize the status bar and the AutoSize property for the panel is set to something other than its default of sbrNoAuto.

- You can display a picture in a status bar panel by setting the Picture property, and you can display a ToolTip for a panel by setting the ToolTipText property.

- To create a status bar that contains a single panel for displaying text only, set the Style property of the status bar (in the General tab) to sbrSimple. Then, set the SimpleText property to the text you want to display.

Figure 12-8   How to create a status bar

How to use code to work with menus, toolbars, and status bars

Figure 12-9 shows some typical procedures for working with menu commands, toolbar buttons, and status bar panels. The first procedure is for the Click event of the Delete command in the Edit menu. However, since the delete function has already been provided for by the Click event procedure for the Delete command button, the menu command procedure simply calls the command button procedure: cmdDelete_Click.

Similarly, the second procedure in this figure is for the Click event of a toolbar button that displays the Vendors form. But since that function is already provided for by the Vendors command in the View menu, the procedure just calls the procedure for that menu command.

The third procedure in this figure is for the ButtonClick event of a Toolbar control (there is no Click event for a Toolbar control). For the ButtonClick event, Visual Basic passes a Button object to the procedure. Then, the code can refer to the Index, Key, or Tag property that was set when the button was defined to determine which button was clicked. In this example, the Key property is used, and the code for each button calls an existing procedure.

The fourth procedure shows or hides a toolbar when the Toolbar command on the View menu is clicked. This code uses the Checked property to display a check mark on the menu command when the toolbar is shown and to remove the check property when the toolbar is hidden. It also uses the Visible property to show and hide the toolbar. Another way to code this function is like this:

```
mnuViewToolbar.Checked = Not mnuViewToolbar.Checked
pbxToolbar.Visible = Not pbxToolbar.Visible
```

Here, the Not operator is used to reverse the values of the Checked and Visible properties.

The fifth procedure is for the MouseUp event of a form, but similar code can be used for a control (and the MouseDown event can be used instead of the MouseUp event). When the MouseUp event occurs, four arguments are passed to the procedure. This procedure uses the Button argument in an If statement to determine whether the right mouse button (2) has been clicked. If it has, the code uses the PopupMenu method of the form to display the View menu.

The sixth procedure shows how to modify the menus on a parent form at run time so they're appropriate for the active child form. It changes the Visible property of the Edit menu to True (it's hidden by default), then changes the Add and Delete commands in that menu to indicate what will be added or deleted.

An alternative to modifying the menus is to include a separate menu system for the parent form and each child form that requires different menus. Then, if the active child form has menus, the menus for that form replace the menus of the parent form. But if the active child form doesn't have menus or if no child form is active, the menus of the parent form are displayed.

The last procedure in this figure shows how to change the text in a status bar panel. Here, the panel is referred to by its index, and the Text property of the panel is set to a text string.

Code for the Click event of a menu object

```
Private Sub mnuEditDelete_Click()
    cmdDelete_Click
End Sub
```

Code for the Click event of a toolbar command button

```
Private Sub cmdVendors_Click()
    mnuViewVendors_Click
End Sub
```

Code for the ButtonClick event of a Toolbar control

```
Private Sub Toolbar1_ButtonClick(ByVal Button As MSComctlLib.Button)
    If Button.Key = "New" Then
        frmNewVendor.Show 1
    ElseIf Button.Key = "Delete" Then
        DeleteVendor
    End If
End Sub
```

Code that shows or hides a toolbar

```
Private Sub mnuViewToolbar_Click()
    If mnuViewToolbar.Checked Then
        mnuViewToolbar.Checked = False
        pbxToolbar.Visible = False
    Else
        mnuViewToolbar.Checked = True
        pbxToolbar.Visible = True
    End If
End Sub
```

Code for a popup menu

```
Private Sub Form_MouseUp(Button As Integer, _
        Shift As Integer, X As Single, Y As Single)
    If Button = 2 Then
        PopupMenu mnuView
    End If
End Sub
```

Code that modifies a menu on a parent form when a child form becomes active

```
Private Sub Form_Activate()
    With frmAP
        .mnuEdit.Visible = True
        .mnuEditAdd.Caption = "&Add Vendor"
        .mnuEditDelete.Caption = "&Delete Vendor"
    End With
End Sub
```

Code for changing the text in a status bar panel

```
Private Sub Form_Activate()
    frmAP.sbAPStatus.Panels(2).Text = "Displaying form"
End Sub
```

Figure 12-9   How use code to work with menus, toolbars, and status bars

Exercise set 12-2: Enhance the interface

In this exercise set, you'll enhance the menus in the MDI application you created in exercise set 12-1 by adding a different menu to the Vendors form. Then, you'll add a toolbar with two buttons that let you display the Vendors form and exit from the application. Finally, you'll add a status bar to the parent form.

Add menus to the Vendors form

1. Open the project you created in exercise set 12-1, display the Vendors form, and start the Menu Editor. Then, add File, Edit, and Help menus to this form with the same File and Help commands as in the parent form and with New and Delete commands named mnuNew and mnuDelete in the Edit menu.

2. Open the Code window for the Vendors form, and enter this code at the end of the dbcVendors_Change procedure:

```
mnuDelete.Enabled = cmdDelete.Enabled
```

This will disable the Delete menu command if the Delete command button is disabled.

3. Enter the code for the Click events of the New and Delete menu commands so they perform the functions of the New and Delete command buttons as illustrated in the first example in figure 12-9. Then, enter the code for the Click event of the Exit command in the File menu so it unloads the parent form (frmMain), and enter the code for the Click event of the About command in the Help menu so it displays the About form.

4. Run the application, and notice that only the menus that are defined in the parent form are displayed. Then, open the Vendors form using the View menu and notice that only the menus defined in that form are displayed.

5. With the application still running, drop down the Edit menu and notice that the Delete command in this menu is disabled if the Delete command button in the Vendors form is disabled. Then, select the New command from the Edit menu to display the New Vendor form, click on the Cancel button in this form to close it, and select the Exit command in the File menu to end the application.

Add a toolbar to the parent form

6. Use the Components command in the Project menu to add the Microsoft Windows Common Controls 6.0 to the Toolbox. Then, display the parent form and add a Toolbar control to it.

7. Right-click on the Toolbar control and select Properties from its shortcut menu to display the Property Pages dialog box. Then, click on the Buttons tab, click on the Insert Button command button to add a toolbar button, and set both its Caption and Key properties to Vendors.

8. Insert another button, set its Style property to PlaceHolder, and set its Width property to 5000. Then, insert one last button, set its Caption property to E&xit and its Key property to Exit, and close the Property Pages dialog box.

9. Open the Code window for the parent form and enter this code for the ButtonClick event of the Toolbar:

```
Private Sub Toolbar1_ButtonClick(ByVal Button As MSComctlLib.Button)
    If Button.Key = "Vendors" Then
        frmVendors.Show
    ElseIf Button.Key = "Exit" Then
        mnuExit_Click
    End If
End Sub
```

10. Start the application and click on the Vendors toolbar button to display the Vendors form. Then, click on the Exit toolbar button to end the application.

11. Add an ImageList control anywhere on the parent form, display its Property Pages dialog box, click on the Insert Picture button in the Images tab, and insert any picture you like. (You can find a variety of images in the Common\Graphics folder of Disk 1 of the Visual Basic CDs or in the C:\Program Files\Microsoft Office\Clipart folders if you use Microsoft Office.) Notice that an index value of 1 is assigned to this image. Then, add a second image with an index value of 2, and close the dialog box.

12. Display the Property Pages dialog box for the toolbar you created earlier, and set the ImageList property in the General tab to the ImageList control you just created. Next, click on the Buttons tab and set the Image property of the first button to 1 and of the third button to 2. Last, close the dialog box and notice that the images have been added to the toolbar buttons.

Add a status bar to the parent form

13. Add a StatusBar control to the bottom of the parent form, change its Height property to 375, display its Property Pages dialog box, and click on the Panels tab. Then, change the Alignment property for the default panel to sbrCenter, change the Style property to sbrDate, and click on the Apply button to apply these settings to the status bar.

14. Click on the Insert Panel button to insert another panel, and display the properties for the new panel by changing the Index number to 2. Then, change the MinimumWidth property to 8640, change the Bevel property to sbrNoBevel, and click on the OK button to apply the settings and close the dialog box.

15. Open the Code window for the Vendors form, and enter this statement in the procedure for the Activate event of the form:

```
frmMain.StatusBar1.Panels(2).Text = "Displaying Vendors"
```

16. Test the application to see how this looks. Then, close the application and save the project.

How to use the Microsoft Help Workshop

Visual Basic 6 provides a Help compiler called the Microsoft Help Workshop that lets you create custom help for your applications. In the following topics, you'll learn the basics of using this program. Keep in mind, however, that there's more you can do with the Help Workshop than what's presented here. For more information, see the Help Authoring Guide that's installed as part of the Microsoft Help Workshop.

An overview of the Microsoft Help Workshop

Figure 12-10 presents an overview of the Microsoft Help Workshop. Here, you can see the Project window for a *help project* (file extension hpj) that was created for the Accounts Payable application. When this project is compiled, it's saved in a *help file* (file extension hlp) that you can refer to from your application. If you include a Help menu in your application, for example, you can include a command on that menu that will display a Help Topics dialog box. This dialog box can contain Contents, Index, and Find tabs like those in other Microsoft applications.

If you review the settings for this project, you'll see that it refers to two files: C12Help.rtf and C12Help.cnt. C12Help.rtf is the *topic file* for the project. This file contains the text for each topic that you want to display from your help system. It also defines the entries that will be included in the Index tab of the Help Topics window and the topic titles that will be used in the Find tab. You create this file using a word processing program like Microsoft Word as you'll see in the next figure.

C12Help.cnt is the *contents file* for the project. This file defines the headings and topics that will be displayed in the Contents tab of the Help Topics dialog box. By organizing the topics in a logical sequence, you can help a user become familiar with your application quickly and easily. If you omit the contents file, the Contents tab doesn't appear in the Help Topics dialog box.

In addition to providing a Help Topics dialog box, you can use the Help Workshop to provide *context-sensitive help*. Before you can do that, though, you have to map context-sensitive topics to numeric values. Then, you can use the numeric values to refer to those topics from your application.

The best way to create a new help system is to start by creating a topic file with a few help topics. Then, you can include that file in a help project and test the help project to be sure that it works the way you want it to. Next, you can enter the remaining help topics and test the project again. After you've entered and tested all of the topics, you can create and test the contents file. Just as you did with the topic file, you may want to start by creating just a portion of the contents file to be sure that it works the way you want it to. Finally, if you want to use any of the topics to display context-sensitive help, you can map them to numeric values and then test the project again.

The Project window for a Microsoft Help Workshop project

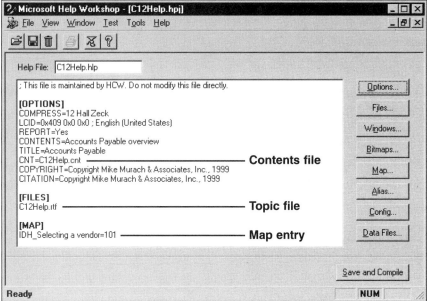

Description

- To install the Microsoft Help Workshop, run the Setup.exe file in the Common/Tools/Vb/Hcw folder on Disk 1 of the Visual Basic CDs.

- To create a *help project*, start the Help Workshop and select the New command from the File menu. Then, select Help Project from the dialog box that's displayed.

- To develop the topics that you want the help system to display, use a word processing program like Microsoft Word that lets you save the file in Rich Text format. Then, to include the *topic file* in a help project, click on the Files button and add the file to the dialog box that's displayed.

- To create a *contents file* that specifies how the help topics will appear in the Contents tab of the Help Topics dialog box, select the New command from the File menu. Then, select Help Contents from the dialog box that's displayed. To include the contents file in a help project, identify it in the Files tab of the Options dialog box that's displayed when you click on the Options button.

- To provide *context-sensitive help* from your application, use the Map button to create *map entries* that map the topic IDs in the topic file to numeric values that you can use in your application.

- After you set all the appropriate options for the project, save and compile the project to create a *help file* that you can use from your application.

Figure 12-10   An overview of the Microsoft Help Workshop

How to create a topic file

Figure 12-11 shows you how to create a topic file using Microsoft Word. Here, you can see that each topic is entered on a separate page of the document. Each topic is also formatted the way it will appear when it's displayed in the Help window.

To identify each topic, you associate it with a topic ID. To do that, you insert a footnote at the beginning of the topic using a number sign (#) as the custom footnote mark. In Microsoft Word, you insert a footnote by selecting the Footnote command from the Insert menu. Then, you enter the footnote mark into the Custom Mark text box in the dialog box that's displayed. When you click on the OK button in this dialog box, Word adds a footnote at the bottom of the page and lets you enter the text for the footnote. In this case, the text is the ID for the topic you're entering. (If you're using another word processor to create your topic file, refer to its help information to find out how to enter footnotes.) In general, we recommend that you use topic IDs that are descriptive like the ones shown in this figure so they're easy to remember.

If a topic will be used to display context-sensitive help, you should use the prefix IDH_ for the topic ID as shown in the fifth footnote in this figure. Then, the Help Workshop recognizes it as a context-sensitive topic and, when you compile the project, warns you if you haven't mapped the topic to a numeric value.

In addition to the footnote that defines the topic ID for each topic, you can enter a footnote that identifies index entries for the topic. The third footnote shown in this figure, for example, includes two indexes entries for a single topic. Notice that this footnote uses the letter K as the footnote mark. Also notice that the two index entries in the footnote are separated by a semicolon. You can include as many index entries as you want for each topic. Then, when the user selects any of the entries from the Index tab of the Help Topics dialog box, the associated topic is displayed.

You can also include a footnote that specifies the title to be used for the topic. To do that, you use a dollar sign ($) as the footnote mark. The text you specify in this footnote is used as the title for the topic in the Find tab of the Help Topics dialog box. Because of that, a topic isn't included in the Find tab unless you include a $ footnote for it. This title is also used in other locations in Help, such as in the History window. So although this footnote isn't required, you'll want to include it for most help topics.

If you want to be able to jump to a topic from within another topic, you can create a *hotspot* in the topic as shown in this figure. To do that, you format the hotspot with a double-underline. (In Word, you do that with the Font command in the Format menu.) Then, you enter the name of the topic that you want to jump to right after the hotspot text with no space between the hotspot and the topic ID. Because you don't want the topic ID to appear in the help topic when it's displayed, you also need to format the ID so it's hidden. When you display a topic that contains a hotspot, the hotspot appears as green text with a single underline.

A topic file created in Microsoft Word

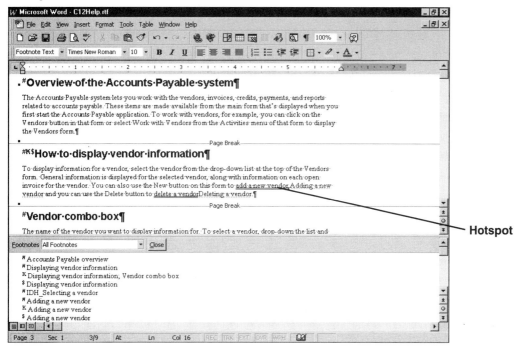

Hotspot

Common footnote marks you can use with help topics

Mark	Description
#	Required. Defines the topic ID for the topic.
K	Identifies entries to be included in the help index.
$	Specifies the title for the topic.

Description

- To create a topic file, enter the text for each topic as you want it to appear in help. Then, separate each topic with a page break.
- To define the topic ID, add a footnote at the beginning of the topic using the # footnote mark. If the topic will be used to provide context-sensitive help, use the prefix IDH_ for the topic ID.
- To include a topic in the help index, add another footnote using the K footnote mark. Separate multiple index entries with semicolons.
- If you want to display a topic in the Find tab of the Help Topics dialog box, add a footnote at the beginning of the topic using the $ footnote mark.
- To create a *hotspot* that jumps from one topic to another, format the hotspot text with a single or double underline, enter the ID of the topic you want to jump to right after the hotspot, and format that topic ID as hidden text.
- When you're done entering the topics, save the document in Rich Text format.

Figure 12-11   How to create a topic file

You can also create a hotspot that displays a topic in a pop-up box rather than in the Help window. To do that, you format the hotspot with a single underline. Then, the hotspot appears as green text with a dashed underline. In this case, only the first paragraph of the topic is displayed in the pop-up box. If you want to display more than one paragraph, you need to separate the paragraphs with line breaks instead of paragraph marks.

When you're done entering the topics and footnotes for a help file, you save the file in Rich Text format. Then, you can add it to a help project.

How to create a contents file

Figure 12-12 shows how to create a contents file for a help project. To start, you select the New command from the File menu and then select Help Contents from the dialog box that's displayed. Then, a Contents window like the one shown in this figure is displayed.

To add an entry to the contents file, click on the Add Above or Add Below button. When you do, the Edit Contents Tab Entry dialog box shown in this figure is displayed. By default, the Topic option is selected in this dialog box. To add a topic to the contents file, enter the title you want to appear in the Contents tab and the topic ID for the topic. When you click on the OK button, the topic is added to the list box in the Contents window.

If you look at the Edit Contents dialog box in this figure, you'll see that you can also specify a help file and a window type for each topic in the contents file. If a contents file refers to topics in more than one help file, you can use the Help File text box to tell the Help Workshop which help file contains each topic. By default, the Help Workshop will look for the topic in the help file you specify in the Default Filename text box in the Contents window. If all of the topics included in the contents file are in a single help file, then, this is the only entry that's required.

You can also define custom windows for displaying your help topics using the Windows button in the Project window (see figure 12-10). If you want to use one of these windows for a topic, enter the name of the window in the Window Type text box. To find out how to create custom windows, see the *Customizing Help Windows* topics in the Help Authoring Guide.

To add a heading to the contents file, click on one of the Add buttons and select the Heading option from the Edit Contents Tab Entry dialog box. When you do, all of the text boxes except for Title will be disabled. Then, enter the heading you want to add and click on the OK button to add it to the contents list.

After you add a heading or topic, you can use the Edit button to modify it or the Remove button to delete it. You can also use the Move Right and Move Left buttons to create a contents list with more than one level of headings. After you create a new heading, for example, you can click on the Move Right button to make that heading subordinate to the one above it.

A contents file for a help project

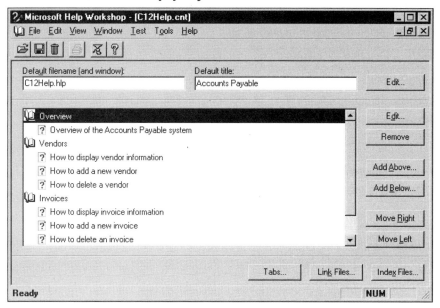

The dialog box for adding a topic to the contents file

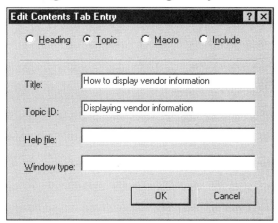

Description

- To start a contents file, select the New command from the File menu in the Help Workshop window, then select Help Contents from the dialog box that's displayed.

- Enter the name of the help file that contains the help topics as the Default file name, and enter the title you want to display in the Help Topics dialog box as the Default title.

- Use the list box and the buttons to its right to design the contents file. When you click on one of the Add buttons, the Edit Contents Tab Entry dialog box is displayed so you can enter the information for the heading or topic.

Figure 12-12   How to create a contents file

How to map a help topic to a numeric value

Figure 12-13 shows you how to map a help topic to a numeric value. You'll need to do that if you want to use the topic to display context-sensitive help. Then, you can use the numeric value to refer to the topic from your Visual Basic application.

To map a topic to a numeric value, or *context ID*, you click on the Map button in the Project window for the help project. When you do that, the Map dialog box shown in this figure is displayed. In this case, the dialog box contains a single map entry that maps the topic ID *IDH_Selecting a vendor* to the number 101. This is the entry that you saw in the [MAP] section of the project shown in figure 12-10.

To map a topic to a numeric value, you click on the Add button in the Map dialog box to display the Add Map Entry dialog box shown in this figure. This dialog box lets you enter a topic ID and the number you want to map it to. You can also enter a comment that's saved with the map entry and displayed in the Project window.

By default, the Help Workshop recognizes topic IDs with the prefix IDH as topics that will be used to display context-sensitive help. Then, when you compile the project, the topics are checked to be sure that each topic with this prefix has been mapped to a numeric value so you can refer to it directly from your Visual Basic application. If you use prefixes other than IDH, you can enter the prefixes at the bottom of the Map dialog box. Then, the Help Workshop will check for those prefixes when you compile the project.

The dialog boxes for mapping topic IDs

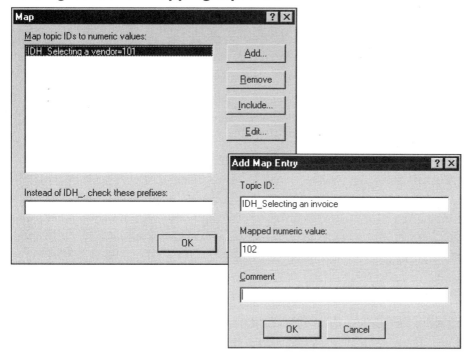

Description

- To map a help topic to a numeric value, click on the Map button in the Project window to display the Map dialog box. Then, click on the Add button and enter a topic ID and the numeric value you want to map it to in the Add Map Entry dialog box.

- To remove a previously mapped topic ID, highlight it in the Map dialog box and click on the Remove button. To edit a previously mapped topic ID, highlight the topic and click on the Edit button.

- The numeric value that a topic is mapped to is often referred to as a *context ID* because it's used to provide context-sensitive help from a Visual Basic application.

- If you use prefixes other than IDH_ to identify context-sensitive topics, you can enter those prefixes at the bottom of the Map dialog box. Then, when you compile the project, the Help Workshop will check all topics with those prefixes to be sure that they are mapped to numeric values.

- Topics that are mapped to numeric values appear in the [MAP] section of the project file as shown in figure 12-10.

Figure 12-13   How to map a help topic to a numeric value

How to compile and test the help project

Before you compile and save a help project, you need to set some project options. In particular, you need to be sure that you've included the appropriate topic and contents files. To do that, you use the Options dialog box shown in figure 12-14.

To identify the topic and contents files, you use the Files tab of the Options dialog box. If a project includes more than one topic file, you can add or delete files by clicking on the Change button to display the Topic Files dialog box. You can also display this dialog box by clicking on the Files button in the Project window.

By default, a help file is saved in the same folder as the project file with the same name as the project file but with the extension hlp. Although you can change the name or location of this file by entering the file specification in the Help File text box in the Files tab, you'll usually use the default.

If a help project includes a contents file, the text you specify for the default title in that file is displayed in the title bar of the Help Topics dialog box. If your project doesn't include a contents file, though, or if the contents file doesn't specify a default title, you'll want to specify a default title in the General tab of the Options dialog box. If a title isn't specified in the contents or project file, the name of the help file is displayed in the title bar.

When you compile a project file to create a help file, you may want to compress the help file so it takes up less space. This is particularly true if you're going to distribute the file by diskette. To compress a file, you use the options on the Compression tab of the Options dialog box. In most cases, though, you'll select the Maximum option to compress the file as much as possible.

You can also create a *full-text search index* using the options on the FTS tab. Then, the user can use the Find tab of the Help Topics dialog box to search for any word in any help topic. In most cases, though, this isn't necessary because the Find Setup Wizard that's displayed the first time you access the Find tab lets you create this file.

After you set the project options, you can compile and save the project file by clicking on the Save and Compile button in the Project window. When the Help Workshop is done compiling the project, a window is displayed that contains some statistics related to the compilation and indicates any errors that occurred.

If the project compiles cleanly, you're ready to test it. To do that, click on the Run WinHelp button in the toolbar to display the View Help File dialog box. Then, if you click on the View Help button, the Help Topics dialog box for your help file is displayed and you can navigate through it to see how it works. You can also use the View Help File dialog box to display individual topics for mapped topic IDs.

The General and File options for a help project

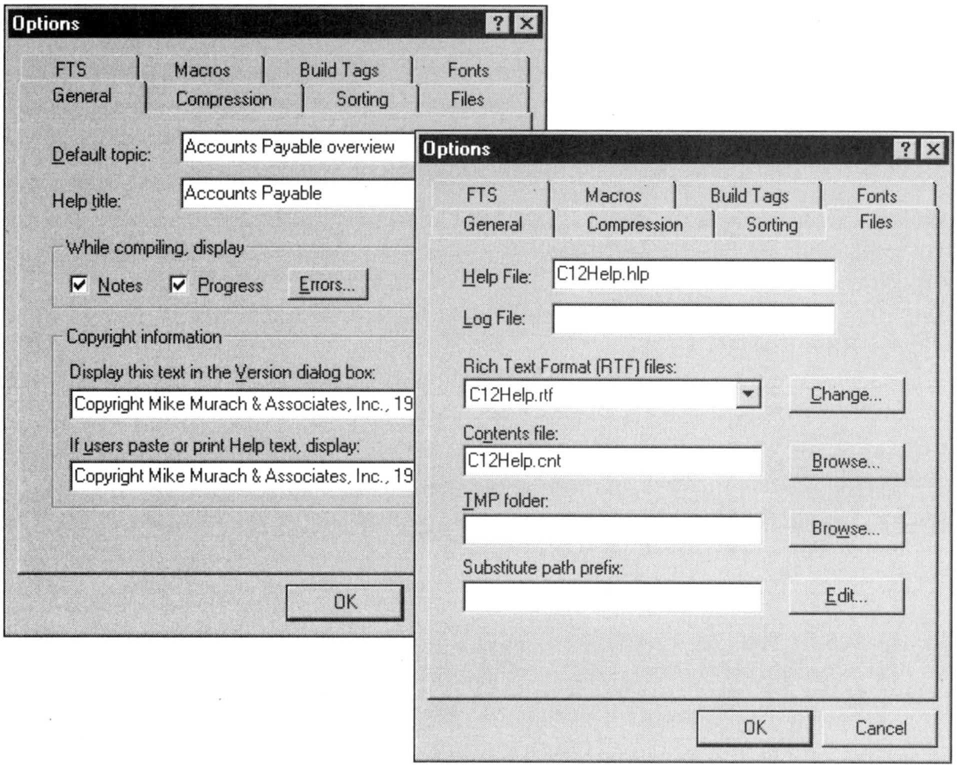

Description

- To display the Options dialog box, click on the Options button in the Project window.

- The General tab of the Options dialog box lets you specify the default topic that's displayed when the user selects a topic that's not available. It also lets you specify the title that's displayed in the title bar of the Help Topics dialog box.

- The Compression tab lets you compress the help file so that it takes up less space. The default is to not compress this file.

- The Files tab lets you specify the names and locations of the help file for the project, the rich text file that contains the topics for the help system, and the contents file.

- The FTS tab lets you create a *full-text search* index that includes every word in the help topics. This index is used to implement the Find tab of the Help Topics dialog box.

- To compile a help project and save it to a help file, click on the Save and Compile button in the Project window.

- To test a help file, click on the Run WinHelp toolbar button in the Project window. The dialog box that's displayed lets you display the Help Topics dialog box for the help file or the Help window for a mapped topic ID.

Figure 12-14   How to compile and test the help project

How to use a help file in a Visual Basic application

Once you're sure that a help file works the way you want it to, you're ready to use it from your Visual Basic application. Figure 12-15 shows you how to use a help file to display a Help Topics dialog box or to display context-sensitive help.

The quickest way to provide help information for a project is to set its HelpFile property to the name of the help file you want to use. Then, the Help Topics dialog box for that file is displayed any time the user presses F1 while the application is running.

To display context-sensitive help when the user presses the F1 key, you have to set the right properties for a project, form, or control. For instance, to display context-sensitive help for a project, you set its ProjectHelpContextID property to the context ID of the topic you want to display. (Remember that the context ID is the numeric value that a topic is mapped to when using the Help Workshop.) And to display context-sensitive help for a form or control, you set its HelpContextID property to the appropriate context ID.

Another common way to implement help is to display the Help Topics dialog box when the user selects a command like Contents or Index from the Help menu. To do that, you add a CommonDialog control to the form and set the properties in the Help tab of its Property Pages dialog box as shown in this figure. Here, the HelpFile property is set to the name of the help file, and the HelpCommand property is set so the Help Topics dialog box will be displayed. To find out what values are available for the HelpCommand property, you can use the Object Browser to display the HelpConstants for the CommonDialog control. Note, however, that this information tells you to use a value of 3 to display the Help Topics dialog box. If you're using version 4.0x of the Help Workshop, though, this will display the default topic instead of the Help Topics dialog box. To display the Help Topics dialog box, you have to use a value of 11 as shown in this figure.

After you set the properties for the CommonDialog control, you use its ShowHelp method to display help as shown in the procedure in this figure. In this case, the procedure is executed when the user selects the menu command named mnuContents. You can use a similar procedure to display help when the user performs other actions like clicking on a toolbar button or command button.

You can also use the CommonDialog control to display a specific help topic when the user selects a command like "How to add new vendors." To do that, you set its HelpContext property to the context ID of the topic you want to display, and you set the HelpCommand property to 1. If necessary, you can change the HelpContext and HelpCommand properties of the CommonDialog control through code depending on which command the user selects.

The Help tab for a CommonDialog control

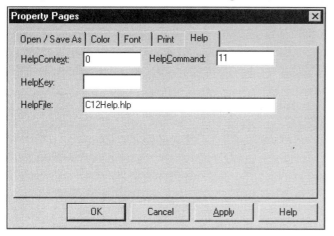

Code that displays the help file from a menu

```
Private Sub mnuContents_Click()
    cdlHelp.ShowHelp
End Sub
```

How to display a help file using a CommonDialog control

- Set the HelpFile property to identify the help file you want to use. If the help file is stored in the same folder as the application, you can omit the path as shown above. Otherwise, you'll need to include the path in the file specification.

- Set the HelpCommand property to identify the type of help you want to display. To display the Contents tab of the Help dialog box, for example, set this property to 11. To find out what the other settings are for this property, use the Object Browser to display the HelpConstants for the CommonDialog control.

- If you want to display a specific help topic, you can set the HelpCommand property to 1 and the HelpContext property to the context ID of the help topic.

How to display help information when the user presses the F1 key

- To display the Contents tab of the Help window when the user presses F1, enter the path and file name of the help file in the Help File Name box on the General tab of the Project Properties dialog box (see figure 12-3).

- To display context-sensitive help when the focus is on a form or control, set the HelpContextID property of the form or control to the context ID of the help topic.

Figure 12-15   How to use a help file in a Visual Basic application

Exercise set 12-3: Add help information

In this exercise set, you'll use the Microsoft Help Workshop to create a simple help file, and use it in the project you created in exercise sets 12-1 and 12-2. As simple as this help file is, though, this is a time-consuming exercise set that you may want to skip until you have an imminent need for these skills.

Install the Microsoft Help Workshop

1. If you haven't already installed the Microsoft Help Workshop on your system, insert Disk 1 of the Visual Basic 6.0 CDs into your CD-ROM drive. Then, use the Explorer to locate the Setup.exe file in the Common/Tools/Vb/Hcw folder, and double-click on this file to install the Workshop.

Create a topic file

2. For this exercise set, you need to use a file in Rich Text Format like the one below. If you're taking a course and can get the file from your instructor, you just need to save the file in the Chapter 12 MDI folder with the name C12Help.rtf. Otherwise, you have to create the document by using a word processing program like Microsoft Word. Then, you have to add footnotes to it and save it as summarized in the next three steps.

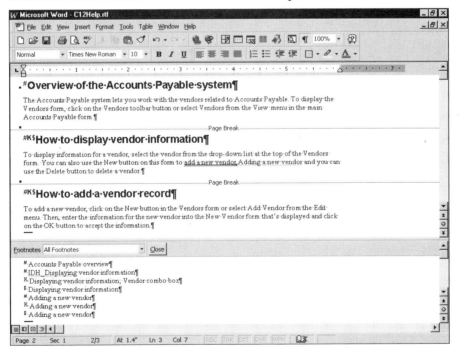

3. After you've entered the three topics on three separate pages, place the insertion point at the beginning of the first topic and use the Footnote feature to insert the first footnote shown above to define the topic ID (with Word, you use the Footnote command in the Insert menu). Do the same for the second topic, making sure to prefix the topic ID with IDH_ so you can use it as a

context-sensitive topic. Then, insert two more footnotes for the second topic to identify index entries and specify a title for the topic. Last, place the insertion point at the beginning of the third topic and insert the last three footnotes.

4. Select the text "add a new vendor" in the second topic, and format it with a double underline (with Word, use the Fonts command in the Format menu). Then, enter the topic ID for the third topic right after this underlined text, and format it so it's hidden (with Word, use the Fonts command again).

5. Save the document in Rich Text Format with the name C12Help in the Chapter 12 MDI folder. Then, close the file and Microsoft Word.

Create a help project

6. Click on the Start button in the Windows Task bar, locate the Help Workshop in the Programs menu, and click on it to start this program. If a tip is displayed, click outside its dialog box to close it.

7. Select New from the File menu, select Help Project from the New dialog box that's displayed, and click on the OK button to display the Project File Name dialog box. Then, navigate to the Chapter 12 MDI folder, enter C12Help as the file name, and save the project file in that folder.

8. Click on the Files button in the Project window to display the Topic Files dialog box, click on the Add button, and add the topic file you created earlier in this exercise set. Then, click on the OK button to close the Topic Files dialog box.

9. Click on the Options button in the Project window, enter "Accounts Payable overview" for the Default topic, and enter "Accounts Payable" for the Help title. Then, click on the OK button to accept these settings, and click on the Save and Compile button to save the project and create a help file. At this point, review the information that's displayed for the compilation to be sure that no errors occurred. If any errors did occur, correct them and compile the project again. Then, close the compilation window by clicking on its Close button or choosing the Close command in the File menu.

Display the help file from your Visual Basic application

10. With the Help Workshop still open, open the Visual Basic application you created for this chapter. Next, select the Properties command from the Project menu and use the Build button for the Help File Name box to enter the path and file name for the help file you just created (C12Help).

11. Start the application and press F1. That should display the Index tab of the Help Topics dialog box with three topics shown. If it doesn't, open the Vendors form and press F1 again. If that still doesn't work, open the New Vendor form and press F1. In our tests, that has always worked. If the help information isn't displayed all three times, though, it indicates that there's a bug in Visual Basic, not in your application or the Workshop. (We hope, of course, that Microsoft fixes this bug soon and that this exercise set still gives you a feel for how you develop help information for an application.)

12. With the Help window still open, double-click on the *Displaying vendor information* topic to display that topic in the Help window. Next, click on the hotspot for adding a new vendor to display that topic. Then, click on the Contents button. The *Overview of the Accounts Payable system* topic should be displayed because the help file doesn't contain a contents file and you specified this topic as the default.

13. Click on the Index button to return to the Index tab of the Help Topics dialog box, and click on the Find tab. Since this is the first time you've used this tab, the Find Setup Wizard dialog box will be displayed. Select the Maximize search capabilities option, click on the Next button, and click on the Finish button in the next dialog box to create the find list. Next, select the *Adding a new vendor* topic and click on the Display button to display that topic. Then, close the Help window and end the application.

Create a contents file

14. Switch to the Help Workshop and create a contents file by selecting the New command from the File menu and Help Contents from the dialog box that's displayed. Then, enter C12Help.hlp for the Default file name and Accounts Payable for the Default title.

15. Click on the Add Above button, select the Heading option from the dialog box that's displayed, and enter "Overview" for the Title. Then, click on the OK button to add that heading to the Contents window.

16. With the Overview heading highlighted, click on the Add Below button, enter "Overview of the Accounts Payable system" for the Title, enter "Accounts Payable overview" for the Topic ID, and click on the OK button to add this topic below the Overview heading. Then, add another heading named "Vendors," and add the topics for displaying vendor information and for adding a new vendor below that heading (remember that the footnotes with the # signs in the Rich Text document are the ones that identify the topic IDs).

17. Click on the Save toolbar button and save the file in the Chapter 12 folder with the name C12Help. The file extension *cnt* will be added automatically.

18. Switch back to the Project window and click on the Options button. Next, click on the Files tab, enter the name of the contents file that you just created into the Contents file text box, and click on the OK button. Then, save and compile the project.

19. Click on the Run WinHelp toolbar button, and click on the View Help button in the View Help File dialog box that's displayed. This should display the Contents tab of the Help Topics dialog box. Now, double-click on the Overview folder to see the topic in that folder, and double-click on the *Overview of the Accounts Payable system* topic to display that topic in the Help window. Then, close the Help window and close the View Help File dialog box.

Create and use a context-sensitive help topic

20. Switch back to the Project window, and click on the Map button. Next, click on the Add button in the Map dialog box that's displayed, enter "IDH_Displaying vendor information" for the Topic ID, enter 1 for the Mapped numeric value, and click on the OK button to add this map entry to the Map dialog box. Then, click on the OK button to return to the Project window where you should now see a [Map] section with the entry you just created. If you do, compile and save the project.

21. Switch back to Visual Basic, display the Vendors form, and change its HelpContextID property to 1. Next, run the application and press F1 with only the parent form displayed to see whether the Help Topics dialog box is displayed. Close that dialog box, display the Vendors form, and press F1 again. This time, the help topic on displaying vendor information should be displayed since the context ID you entered for this form is mapped to that topic. If either test fails, the problem is probably a bug in Visual Basic, not something that you've done wrong. To make sure, though, open the New Vendor form and press F1 to see whether that still works. Now, close the Help window and end the application.

Display help information from a menu command

22. Open the parent form and display the Menu Editor. Add a menu command to the Help menu with the Caption "Contents and Index" and the name mnuContents. Then, click on the OK button to close this dialog box.

23. Use the Components command in the Project menu to add the Microsoft Common Dialog Control 6.0 to the Toolbox, and add this control to the parent form. Next, display the Property Pages dialog box for this control, click on the Help tab, enter 11 for the HelpCommand property, and enter C12Help.hlp for the HelpFile property. Then, click on the OK button to accept these settings.

24. Display the Code window for the parent form, and enter this statement for the Click event of the menu command named mnuContents:

```
CommonDialog1.ShowHelp
```

Then, run the application and select the Contents and Index command from the Help menu to see that the Help Topics dialog box is displayed. After you experiment with this way of accessing the help information, close this dialog box and end the application.

25. Close and save the Visual Basic project and the Help Workshop project.

Perspective

If you take some time to experiment with the features presented in this chapter, you'll see that they're all relatively easy to use. Nevertheless, they can significantly improve the impression that an application makes on its users. And they can help the users of the application work more efficiently.

Terms you should know

single-document interface (SDI)
multiple-document interface (MDI)
startup form
splash form
popup menu
status bar
panel
help project
help file
topic file
contents file
context-sensitive help
map entry
hotspot
context ID
full text-search index

13

How to create and use class modules and ActiveX components

Class modules are the basis of *object-oriented programming (OOP)*. They define the objects that you can use to build an application. Although many objects are available to you when you develop applications in Visual Basic, you can also define new objects by creating your own class modules. In this chapter, you'll learn how to create and use class modules. Then, you'll learn the concepts and techniques for implementing class modules as ActiveX components.

How to create and use class modules 476
An overview of class modules 476
How to use the properties and methods of a class object 478
How to create a class module 480
How to define class properties 482
How to define class methods 484
How to define and use class events 486
The code for the Book Order class module 488
The code for the Book Order form module 490
Exercise set 13-1: Create the Book Order application 492

An enhanced version of the Book Order application 494
How the enhanced application works 494
The code for the enhanced class module 496
The code for the enhanced form module 500
Exercise set 13-2: Enhance the Book Order application 502

How to create and use ActiveX components 504
An overview of ActiveX components 504
How an application communicates with ActiveX components 506
A general procedure for creating and testing an ActiveX component 508
How to create an ActiveX project 510
How to set the properties for an ActiveX project 512
How to use ActiveX components 514

The benefits of using class modules 516
Exercise set 13-3: Create and use an ActiveX component 517

Perspective 518

How to create and use class modules

In the following topics, you'll learn the basic concepts and techniques for creating and using class modules. In particular, you'll learn how to define the properties, methods, and events you want the class module to provide. And you'll learn how to use those properties, methods, and events from other modules.

An overview of class modules

Figure 13-1 shows the structure of a project that contains a *class module*, which by definition defines an *object class*. Here, you can see that a class module can contain private code that can't be accessed by other modules as well as public code that can be accessed by other modules in the project. This public code defines the properties and methods that the other modules can use.

For the most part, the code you use to create class modules is the same as the code you use within form and standard modules. To define a method within a class module, for example, you code public Sub procedures and functions. And to define a property within a class module, you can declare a public variable. You already know how to do both of those tasks.

Another way to define properties is to use code that provides access to private variables in the class module. In addition, you can define events within a class module that your application can respond to. You'll learn how to define and use property procedures and events later in this chapter.

After you create a class module, you use it in the other modules of the project by creating an *instance* of it, called a *class object*, that's assigned to an object variable. Then, you can use that object variable to access the properties, methods, and events of the object. You can also create more than one instance of a class module within an application. In that case, each instance is a separate object that contains its own data.

One of the benefits of using class modules is that they let you create objects that can be used by more than one application. An object that provides methods for calculating freight charges, for example, can be used by both accounts payable and order processing applications. Because a class module is stored in a separate file just like a form or standard module, you can include it in any application that can use its functions. The trick to designing class modules, though, is making them generic enough to be used in two or more applications without making them so simple that they aren't much use. You'll understand that difficulty much better by the time you complete this chapter.

How you use a class module in a standard project

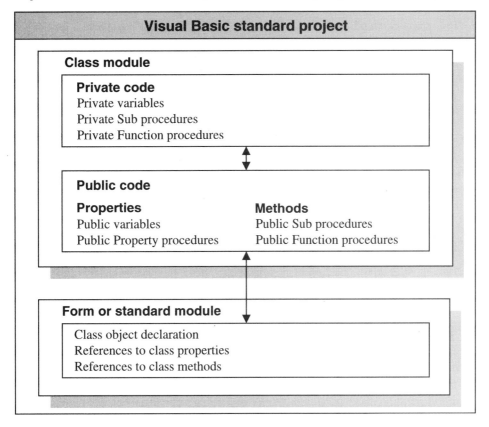

Visual Basic standard project

Class module

Private code
Private variables
Private Sub procedures
Private Function procedures

Public code

Properties
Public variables
Public Property procedures

Methods
Public Sub procedures
Public Function procedures

Form or standard module
Class object declaration
References to class properties
References to class methods

Concepts

- A *class module* defines an *object class*. To define the methods for an object class, you code public procedures and functions. To define the *properties* for an object class, you code public variables or *property procedures* that provide access to private variables.

- To use a class module from another module, you create an instance of the object class and assign it to an object variable. Then, you can use the object variable to access the properties and methods of the *class object*.

- You can also define events within a class module. Then, when an event occurs in a class object, you can respond to it from the module that created the instance of the object.

- A class module that's created within a standard project can be accessed only from the modules in that project. To use the same class module in another project, you have to copy it into that project.

Figure 13-1   An overview of class modules

How to use the properties and methods of a class object

Figure 13-2 presents a simple Book Order application that uses a class module. This application lets the user select a book from a combo box and enter a quantity for that book. Then, the application gets the price of the selected book and calculates the amount of the order.

This figure also presents a summary of the properties and methods in the Book Order class module and shows how most of them are used by the application. After the user selects a book and enters a quantity, those values are stored in properties of the class object. Next, the CalcBookTotal method is used to get the price of the selected book and calculate the total amount of the order. Because that method saves the price and amount as properties of the class object, they can then be retrieved by the form module and displayed in the form.

As you review the code in this figure, you can see that you create an instance of an object class the same way you create an instance of other objects like forms or connections. In this example, the instance is created at the same time the object variable is declared by coding the New keyword in the variable declaration. However, you can also code two separate statements to perform these functions like this:

```
Private mclsBookOrder As BookOrder
Set mclsBookOrder As New BookOrder
```

This figure also shows that the syntax you use to refer to the properties and methods of a class object is identical to the syntax you use to refer to the properties and methods of other objects. In general, you code the name of the object, followed by the dot operator, followed by the name of the property or method and any arguments it requires. (Although the properties and methods in this example don't use arguments, you'll see some later in this chapter that do.) If the Auto List Members feature is on, you'll see a list of the properties and methods that are available for the object when you enter the object name followed by a dot operator in the Code window. And you'll see the definitions of any arguments that are required by the property or method when you enter the its name followed by a space. That makes class objects as easy to work with as any other objects.

Please note that to use the properties and methods of a class object, you don't need to know how they're implemented. You just need to know what their names are, what they're for or what they do, and what arguments (if any) each method requires. As you'll see later in this chapter, that's important when you use class modules that are implemented as ActiveX components because you may not have access to the code in the class modules.

A form that uses the BookOrder class module

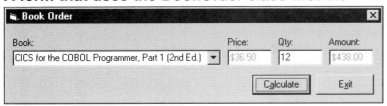

The properties of the BookOrder class module

Property	Description
BookDesc	The description of the book selected by the user that's passed to the class module.
BookQty	The quantity of books entered by the user that's passed to the class module.
BookPrice	The price of the ordered book that's used to populate the Price text box.
BookAmount	The sales amount of the ordered book that's used to populate the Amount text box.

The methods of the BookOrder class module

Method	Description
BookDescriptions	Returns a recordset that contains the descriptions of all the books in the BookPrices table. It's used to populate the Book combo box.
CalcBookAmount	Gets the price of a book and multiplies the price by the quantity to get the sales amount of the ordered book.

Code that declares an object variable and creates an instance of the object class

```
Private mclsBookOrder As New BookOrder
```

Code that sets the values of two properties, executes a method, and retrieves the values of two properties

```
Private Sub cmdCalculate_Click()
    If cboBook.ListIndex <> -1 And mskQty <> "" Then
        mclsBookOrder.BookDesc = cboBook
        mclsBookOrder.BookQty = mskQty
        mclsBookOrder.CalcBookAmount
        mskPrice = mclsBookOrder.BookPrice
        mskAmount = mclsBookOrder.BookAmount
    Else
        MsgBox "You must select a book and enter a quantity."
    End If
End Sub
```

Code that frees the resources used by an object variable

```
Private Sub Form_Unload
    Set mclsBookOrder = Nothing
End Sub
```

Figure 13-2   How to use the properties and methods of a class object

How to create a class module

Figure 13-3 shows how to create a class module. One way to do that is to choose the Class Module option from the Add Class Module dialog box. Then, you use your normal coding techniques to add code to the module. Another way to create a class module is to choose the VB Class Builder option from this dialog box. Then, some of the code in the class module is generated for you.

When you choose the VB Class Builder option, a simple graphical interface is displayed that lets you define the properties, methods, and events for a class. Then, Visual Basic creates a coding framework for the properties, methods, and events that you define, but you still have to add the specific code that implements these elements. Although you may want to use this tool the first few times you create a class module because it may help you understand the coding that's required, it's just as easy to enter the code yourself once you become familiar with it.

In addition to creating new class modules, you can add existing class modules to a project. In other words, you can reuse class modules that were written for other projects. To do that, use the Existing tab of the Add Class Module dialog box to locate a module and add it to your project. However, if you make changes to the class module after you add it to your project, be sure to save it as a new class module so the original class module remains unchanged.

In addition to the definitions of properties, methods, and events that you code in a class module, you can code two event procedures. These are for the Initialize and Terminate events of the module. Since the Initialize event occurs whenever you create an instance of the class module, you typically use its event procedure to initialize any data used by the object as shown by the class module in this figure. Since the Terminate event occurs when the last reference to a class object created from the class module is removed or when the object goes out of scope, you typically use its event procedure to perform housekeeping tasks like releasing the resources used by any objects defined in the module.

Before you save a class module, you should change its Name property to something that clearly identifies it because that's the name that you use to refer to the class module from other modules in the project. You should also save the module with this name. In this figure, the name is BookOrder to indicate that it provides the properties, methods, and events that you need for creating an order for books. However, you can also add a prefix like *c* to the name to identify it as a class module.

The dialog box for adding a class module

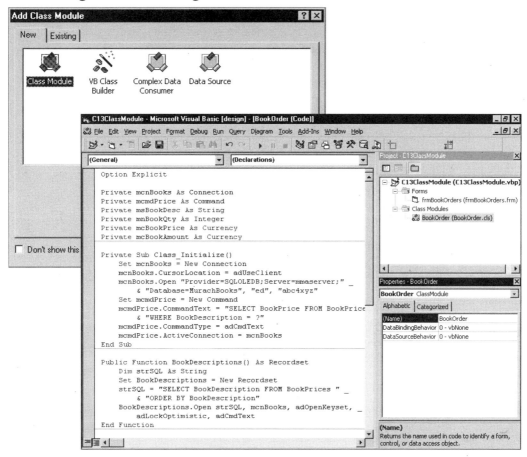

Description

- You can use the Add Class Module dialog box shown above to create a new class module or to add an existing class module. To display this dialog box, choose the Add Class Module command from the Project menu.

- To create a new class module from scratch, select the Class Module option from the New tab. Then, you can use the Code window and the Add Procedure command in the Tools menu to add the code for the class module just as you do for form and standard modules.

- To use the VB Class Builder to create a new class module, select the VB Class Builder option from the New tab. The VB Class Builder helps you create the code framework for the properties, methods, and events to be included in the class module. Then, you can use the Code window to add the specific code for these elements.

- To add an existing class module to a project, select the module from the Existing tab.

Figure 13-3   How to create a class module

How to define class properties

You can define a class property using one of two techniques. First, you can declare a variable as Public as shown in the first example in figure 13-4. Then, the variable can be accessed, and changed, from any other module in the project. If you want to restrict the access to a property, though, or if you want to perform some additional processing when a property is accessed, you can implement it using a *property procedure* as illustrated by the second, third, and fourth examples in this figure. In all three of these examples, a variable that defines a property is declared as Private. Then, a property procedure provides the code that sets or retrieves the value of that variable.

The property procedures in the second example define a read/write property. In this case, the Property Get procedure retrieves the value of the private variable, and the Property Let procedure sets the value of this variable. Notice that these two procedures accomplish the same thing as declaring the variable as public. The difference, though, is that you can easily add code to the property procedures if you need to. So this is the recommended technique for defining properties.

The third example shows the definition for a write-only property. Here, a Property Let procedure is used to set the value of a private variable. Because a Property Get procedure isn't included, though, the value of the property can't be retrieved. Notice that this procedure also includes code that checks the value of the property before it's assigned to the variable.

The fourth example shows the definition for a read-only property. Here, a Property Get procedure is used to retrieve the value of a private variable. In this case, the variable is a field in a recordset that's defined within the procedure. Like the Property Let procedure in the third example, this Property Get procedure performs some additional processing. Specifically, it defines a recordset based on a Command object that uses a parameter.

You'll notice in the two Property Let procedures in this figure that the argument that contains the value that's assigned to the private variable is defined using the ByVal keyword. That way, if the value of the argument is changed within the procedure, it won't affect the value of the variable in the calling module. That's one way to insure that the class module and the calling module are independent of one another.

A read/write property that's implemented as a public variable

```
Public mnBookQty As Integer
```

A read/write property that's implemented using property procedures

```
Private mnBookQty As Integer

Public Property Let BookQty(ByVal BookQty As Integer)
    mnBookQty = BookQty
End Property

Public Property Get BookQty() As Integer
    BookQty = mnBookQty
End Property
```

A write-only property that's implemented using a Property Let procedure

```
Private mnBookQty As Integer

Public Property Let BookQty(ByVal BookQty As Integer)
    If BookQty > 0 And BookQty < 1000 Then
        mnBookQty = BookQty
    Else
        MsgBox "You must enter a quantity between 1 and 999."
    End If
End Property
```

A read-only property that's implemented using a Property Get procedure

```
Public Property Get BookPrice() As Currency
    Dim rsPrice As Recordset
    mcmdPrice.Parameters(0) = BookDesc
    Set rsPrice = mcmdPrice.Execute
    BookPrice = rsPrice!BookPrice
End Property
```

Description

- A public variable declared within a class module is treated as a property and can be accessed directly by any other module in the project.

- To protect a variable from direct access or to perform some additional processing when a variable is accessed, you can declare the variable as private and use property procedures to provide access to it.

- A Property Get procedure gets the value of a private variable. Within the procedure, you assign the value of that variable to the procedure name just as you do for a Function procedure. Then, that value is passed back to the calling procedure.

- A Property Let procedure assigns a value to a private variable. This procedure must accept at least one argument that contains the value to be assigned. Similarly, a Property Set procedure assigns a value to a private object variable (not illustrated).

Figure 13-4   How to define class properties

How to define class methods

Figure 13-5 shows you how to define the methods for a class module. In general, you just code Public Sub procedures and functions. Because you do that using the same techniques you use to code procedures in form and standard modules, you shouldn't have any trouble defining methods.

If a method requires one or more values to perform its function, those values can be made available by using one of two techniques. First, before the method is called from another module, that module can pass the values as properties. This is illustrated by the first example in this figure. Here, the book description that's used as the parameter of a Command object is saved in a private variable named msBookDesc. And the book quantity that's used to calculate the amount is saved in a private variable named mnBookQty.

A second technique is to pass the values directly to the method as arguments. This is illustrated by the second and third examples in this figure. In the second example, the method is implemented as a Sub procedure that gets the book price, calculates the amount, and saves the price and amount in private variables. Then, the calling module can retrieve these values using properties of the class module.

The third example implements the method as a function. Here, the book price is retrieved and saved in a private variable that can later be accessed by using a property of the class module. Then, the amount is calculated and returned directly to the calling procedure.

One criterion you can use to decide whether to pass values as properties or as arguments is whether the values will be used by other procedures in the class module. If so, you'll want to pass the values as properties so they can be accessed from any procedure in the module. Otherwise, you can just pass the values as arguments to the procedure that uses them.

When you define a method that requires arguments, you may want to include one or more arguments that are optional. To do that, you use the Optional keyword on the argument definition like this:

```
Optional ByVal Discount As Currency
```

When you include optional arguments, though, they must be coded after any required arguments.

If you look back at figure 13-4, you'll see that you can also code arguments on property procedures. In fact, you always include an argument on a Property Let procedure to accept the value to be assigned to the property. In contrast, it's less common to include an argument on a Property Get procedure. For instance, the Property Get procedure in the fourth example in figure 13-4 could just as easily have been coded as a function. In fact, if you compare this procedure to the Function procedure in figure 13-5, you'll see that they're nearly identical. The main difference is that the Property Get procedure returns the book price to the calling procedure, and the Function procedure returns the amount. As you can see, then, you have a variety of options to choose from when creating a class module.

A method that performs a calculation using private variables

```
Public Sub CalcBookAmount()
    Dim rsPrice As Recordset
    mcmdPrice.Parameters(0) = msBookDesc
    Set rsPrice = mcmdPrice.Execute
    mcBookPrice = rsPrice!BookPrice
    mcBookAmount = mcBookPrice * mnBookQty
End Sub
```

A method implemented as a Sub procedure with arguments

```
Public Sub CalcBookAmount(ByVal BookDesc As String, _
        ByVal BookQty As Integer)
    Dim rsPrice As Recordset
    mcmdPrice.Parameters(0) = BookDesc
    Set rsPrice = mcmdPrice.Execute
    mcBookPrice = rsPrice!BookPrice
    mcBookAmount = mcBookPrice * BookQty
End Sub
```

A method implemented as a function with arguments

```
Public Function BookAmount(ByVal BookDesc As String, _
        ByVal BookQty As Integer) As Currency
    Dim rsPrice As Recordset
    mcmdPrice.Parameters(0) = BookDesc
    Set rsPrice = mcmdPrice.Execute
    mcBookPrice = rsPrice!BookPrice
    BookAmount = mcBookPrice * BookQty
End Sub
```

Description

- You define a class method by coding a public Sub or Function procedure within a class module.

- If a method requires one or more values from the calling procedure to perform its function, those values can be passed to the class module as properties before the method is executed. Then, those values can be used by any procedures in the class modules.

- Values can also be passed directly to a method as arguments. Then, those values can be used only within the procedure that defines the method.

Figure 13-5   How to define class methods

How to define and use class events

Figure 13-6 shows the code that's required to define and use a class event. The code shown in this example creates a CalculateComplete event for the Book Order class object. This event occurs at the end of the CalcBookAmount method. When it occurs, the event procedure in the form module retrieves the values of two properties of the class object. Although this example is simplistic, it does illustrate the concepts and techniques for defining and using class events.

In the class module, you use the Event statement to declare the event at the module level. On this statement, you include the name of the event and any arguments that will be passed to the event when it occurs. Then, you code the RaiseEvent statement anywhere within the module to cause the event to occur. If the event requires arguments, this statement must pass those arguments to the event.

To respond to an event from a form module, you have to do two things. First, you have to declare the class module that contains the event with the WithEvents keyword. Since you can't use this keyword and the New keyword together, you have to code a separate Set statement to create an instance of the object class. In most cases, you'll code that statement in the Load event procedure of the form.

Second, you have to code an event procedure for the event just as you code an event procedure for any other event. After you declare the class object with the WithEvents keyword, the object appears in the first drop-down list at the top of the Code window, and the event appears in the second drop-down list. So you can use those lists to create the appropriate Sub and End Sub statements for the procedure.

When the RaiseEvent statement in the class module is executed, it causes the event procedure in the form module to be executed. After the statements in this procedure are executed, control returns to the statement following the RaiseEvent statement in the class module. Then, program execution continues as usual.

The syntax of the Event statement

```
[Public] Event eventname [(argumentlist)]
```

The syntax of the RaiseEvent statement

```
RaiseEvent eventname[(argumentlist)]
```

Code for a class module that defines an event

```
Option Explicit
Public Event CalculateComplete()

Public Sub CalcBookAmount(ByVal BookDesc As String, ByVal BookQty As Integer)
    .
    .
    RaiseEvent CalculateComplete
End Sub
```

Code for a form module that uses the event

```
Option Explicit
Private WithEvents mclsBookOrder As BookOrder

Private Sub Form_Load()
    Set mclsBookOrder = New BookOrder
    .
    .
End Sub

Private Sub cmdCalculate_Click()
    If cboBook.ListIndex <> -1 And mskQty <> "" Then
        mclsBookOrder.CalcBookAmount cboBook, mskQty
    Else
        MsgBox "You must select a book and enter a quantity."
    End If
End Sub

Private Sub mclsBookOrder_CalculateComplete()
    mskPrice = mclsBookOrder.BookPrice
    mskAmount = mclsBookOrder.BookAmount
End Sub
```

Description

- To declare an event within a class module, you code an Event statement at the module level. Then, you can code a RaiseEvent statement within any procedure in that module to cause the event to occur.

- To respond to an event within a form module, you must declare the class object using the WithEvents keyword. Then, the object and event will appear in the lists in the Code window, and you can use standard procedures to add an event procedure for that event.

- When an event occurs, control is passed to the event procedure for that event. If the event is defined with arguments, the arguments are passed also. When the event procedure completes, control is returned to the statement after the RaiseEvent statement that caused the event to occur.

Figure 13-6   How to define and use class events

The code for the Book Order class module

Figure 13-7 presents the complete code for the Book Order class module. The Declarations section of this module (1) declares six private variables that are used within the module. The first two variables define the Connection object that will be used to connect to the MurachBooks database and the Command object that will be used to retrieve the price of a book. Because no property procedures are coded for these variables, they can't be accessed from outside the class module. In contrast, a Property Let or a Property Get procedure has been coded for each of the other four variables, which means that they can be accessed as properties of the class module.

When an instance of the object class is created, the Initialize event procedure (2) of the class object is executed. This procedure opens a connection to the MurachBooks database and defines the Command object that will be used to get the price of a book.

The BookDescriptions function (3) is coded as a public procedure, which makes it available as a method from the form module. This function retrieves all of the book descriptions from the BookPrices table in the MurachBooks database. Then, it returns the recordset that contains those descriptions to the calling procedure in the form module.

The two Property Let procedures in the class module (4) simply set the values of two private variables to values passed from the form module. These values are for the book description selected by the user and the quantity entered by the user in the form module. Then, the CalcBookAmount procedure (5) uses these variables to get the price of the selected book and to calculate the amount for the book. Here, the price and amount are saved in private variables, which can be retrieved through the two Property Get procedures (6).

The last procedure in this class module is for the Terminate event of the module. This procedure sets the object variables that are used to refer to the Connection and Command objects to Nothing so the resources used by these objects are released.

Code for the Book Order class module

```
Option Explicit                                                              1
Private mcnBooks As Connection
Private mcmdPrice As Command
Private msBookDesc As String
Private mnBookQty As Integer
Private mcBookPrice As Currency
Private mcBookAmount As Currency


Private Sub Class_Initialize()                                               2
    Set mcnBooks = New Connection
    mcnBooks.CursorLocation = adUseClient
    mcnBooks.Open "Provider=SQLOLEDB;Server=mmaserver;" _
        & "Database=MurachBooks", "ed", "abc4xyz"
    Set mcmdPrice = New Command
    mcmdPrice.CommandText = "SELECT BookPrice FROM BookPrices " _
        & "WHERE BookDescription = ?"
    mcmdPrice.CommandType = adCmdText
    mcmdPrice.ActiveConnection = mcnBooks
End Sub


Public Function BookDescriptions() As Recordset                             3
    Dim strSQL As String
    Set BookDescriptions = New Recordset
    strSQL = "SELECT BookDescription FROM BookPrices " _
        & "ORDER BY BookDescription"
    BookDescriptions.Open strSQL, mcnBooks, adOpenStatic, _
        adLockOptimistic, adCmdText
End Function


Public Property Let BookDesc(ByVal BookDesc As String)                      4
    msBookDesc = BookDesc
End Property

Public Property Let BookQty(ByVal BookQty As Integer)
    mnBookQty = BookQty
End Property


Public Sub CalcBookAmount()                                                 5
    Dim rsPrice As Recordset
    mcmdPrice.Parameters(0) = msBookDesc
    Set rsPrice = mcmdPrice.Execute
    mcBookPrice = rsPrice!BookPrice
    mcBookAmount = mcBookPrice * mnBookQty
End Sub


Public Property Get BookPrice() As Currency                                 6
    BookPrice = mcBookPrice
End Property

Public Property Get BookAmount() As Currency
    BookAmount = mcBookAmount
End Property


Private Sub Class_Terminate()                                               7
    Set mcnBooks = Nothing
    Set mcmdPrice = Nothing
End Sub
```

Figure 13-7   The code for the Book Order class module

The code for the Book Order form module

Figure 13-8 presents the code for the Book Order form module. To start, this module declares the variable that will be used to refer to the Book Order class object (1). Because this declaration contains the New keyword, it also creates an instance of the object class.

When the form is first loaded, the Load event procedure (2) is executed. This procedure declares a recordset variable, and calls the BookDescriptions method of the BookOrder class object to retrieve the records for this recordset. Then, it uses a Do loop to retrieve each record in the recordset and load the book description in each record into the Book combo box on the form.

When the user clicks on the Calculate button on the form, the Click event procedure for that button (3) is executed. This procedure starts by checking to be sure that the user has selected a book and entered a valid quantity. If not, an error message is displayed. Otherwise, the procedure sets the BookDesc property of the class object to the selected book, and it sets the BookQty property to the entered quantity. Then, it calls the CalcBookTotal method to get the price of the book and calculate the amount. Because the price and amount are stored in properties of the class object, the next two statements retrieve the values of those properties.

The last two procedures (4) are executed when the user clicks on the Exit button. The Click event procedure for that button unloads the form, which causes the Unload event of the form to occur. Then, the Unload event procedure sets the variable that refers to the Book Order object to Nothing so its resources are released. This statement is coded in the Unload event procedure rather than in the Click event procedure for the Exit button so it also occurs when the user closes the form by clicking on the built-in Close button for the form.

This illustrates how the use of a class module can simplify the code in a form module. For instance, the form module gets data from one of the tables in the MurachBooks database without any of the complexities normally associated with doing that. Similarly, the form module gets the amount (unit price times quantity) without even coding an expression. This simplicity in the form module, of course, is made possible by the complexity in the class module. So the trick is to design class modules that improve programmer productivity overall.

Code for the Book Order form module

```
Option Explicit                                                          1
Private mclsBookOrder As New BookOrder


Private Sub Form_Load()                                                  2
    Dim rsBooks As Recordset
    Set rsBooks = mclsBookOrder.BookDescriptions
    Do Until rsBooks.EOF
        cboBook.AddItem rsBooks!BookDescription
        rsBooks.MoveNext
    Loop
End Sub


Private Sub cmdCalculate_Click()                                         3
    If cboBook.ListIndex <> -1 And Val(mskQty) > 0 Then
        mclsBookOrder.BookDesc = cboBook
        mclsBookOrder.BookQty = mskQty
        mclsBookOrder.CalcBookAmount
        mskPrice = mclsBookOrder.BookPrice
        mskAmount = mclsBookOrder.BookAmount
    Else
        MsgBox "You must select a book and enter a valid quantity."
    End If
End Sub


Private Sub cmdExit_Click()                                              4
    Unload Me
End Sub

Private Sub Form_Unload(Cancel As Integer)
    Set mclsBookOrder = Nothing
End Sub
```

Figure 13-8   The code for the Book Order form module

Exercise set 13-1: Create the Book Order application

In this exercise set, you'll create the Book Order application that you've just studied. To run that application, though, you need access to the MurachBooks database that contains the BookPrices table. If you're taking a course, a SQL Server version of this database may be available to you. Otherwise, you can download a Jet version of this database from our web site or create your own version of this Jet database as described in Appendix A.

If you're using the Learning Edition of Visual Basic 6, you should remember that masked edit boxes aren't available with this edition. As a result, you'll have to use text boxes in their place in step 3, and you'll have to adjust the properties and code for these boxes accordingly.

Start a new project and prepare it for use with ADO

1. Start Visual Basic and begin a Standard EXE project. Then, change the Name property of the form to frmBookOrders, the Caption property to Book Order, the BorderStyle property to Fixed Single, and the StartUpPosition property to CenterScreen. Last, change the ProjectName property to C13ClassModule.

2. Use the References command in the Project menu to add a reference to the Microsoft ActiveX Data Objects 2.0 Library. Then, save the form and project with the names frmBookOrders and C13ClassModule in a new folder named Chapter 13 Class Module.

Add controls to the Book Orders form

3. Use the Components command in the Project menu to add the Microsoft Masked Edit Control 6.0 to the Toolbox. Then, use the Toolbox to add the labels, combo box, masked edit boxes, and command buttons to the form so it looks like the one in figure 13-2. Be sure to set the Disabled properties of the Price and Amount boxes to False so data can't be entered into them. You'll also need to set the Height property of the masked edit controls so that they have the same height as the combo box.

4. Set the Name property of the combo box to cboBook, and set its Style property to Dropdown List. Set the Name properties of the masked edit boxes to mskPrice, mskQty, and mskAmount, and set their Format properties so their values will display the way you want them to. Also, set the TabStop properties of the Price and Amount boxes to False since no data can be entered into them. Finally, set the Name properties of the command buttons to cmdCalculate and cmdExit, and set the Default property of the Calculate button to True.

Enter the code for the class module and form module

5. Select the Add Class Module command from the Project menu, then select the Class Module option to add a new class module. Set the Name property of the class module to BookOrder, then save the class module with the same name in the Chapter 13 Class Module folder.

6. Enter the code for the Declarations section and the Class_Initialize and BookDescriptions procedures shown in figure 13-7. Be sure to change the connection string so you can access the appropriate database. *If you're accessing a Jet database*, you'll also need to add this command to the Declarations section:

    ```
    Dim mprmPrice As Parameter
    ```

    And you'll need to add these commands to the end of the Initialize procedure:

    ```
    Set mprmPrice = mcmdPrice.CreateParameter("BookDesc", _
        adVarChar, adParamInput, 50)
    mcmdPrice.Parameters.Append mprmPrice
    ```

7. Switch to the Code window for the form module, and enter the statement in the Declarations section in figure 13-8. Then, enter the Form_Load procedure shown in that figure. As you enter the Set statement in that procedure, notice that the properties and methods of the class module are listed for you when you enter the name of the class object followed by a dot operator. If this list isn't displayed, display the Options dialog box and select the Auto List Members option in the Editor tab.

8. Run the application. Drop down the combo box to see that it's been loaded with the names of the available books. Then, click on the Close button to close the form.

9. Enter the remaining code in figure 13-7 into the class module. *If you're accessing a Jet database*, you'll need to replace the statement in the CalcBookAmount procedure that assigns a value to the parameter of the Command object with this statement:

    ```
    mprmPrice.Value = msBookDesc
    ```

10. Enter the remaining code in figure 13-8 into the form module. Then, run the application. Select a book, enter a quantity, and click on the Calculate button. When you do, the price and amount should be displayed on the form. If not, you'll need to debug the application before you move on.

Save the project

11. Save the project and leave it open if you're going to continue.

An enhanced version of the Book Order application

Although the application you've just seen illustrates the basic concepts and techniques for creating and using class modules, it lacks the functionality of a real world application. So now you'll be introduced to an enhanced version of the Book Order application that gives you a better idea of what a class module can do.

How the enhanced application works

Figure 13-9 presents the enhanced version of the Book Order form along with the properties for the main controls on the form. As you can see, this form lets the user select up to three books. For each book that's selected, the user must enter a quantity. Then, when the user clicks on the Calculate button, the application retrieves the price of each book, calculates the amount for each book, and calculates the sales total for all the books. This application also applies a discount based on the total number of books that are ordered and subtracts this discount from the sales total to get the final total.

This form implements the Book, Price, Qty, and Amount controls as control arrays. As a result, the Name property is the same for the controls in each array, and the Index property uniquely identifies each control. Because these controls are implemented as arrays, this form can easily be extended to provide for as many book selections as necessary.

The enhanced Book Order form also includes a New button. When the user clicks on this button, all of the controls on the form are cleared so the user can enter a new order.

An enhanced Book Order form

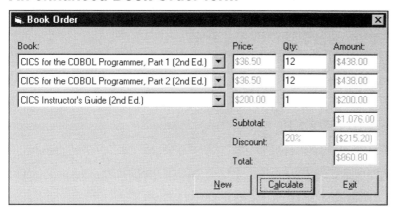

Property settings for the Book combo box and masked edit control arrays

Property	Book	Price	Qty	Amount
Name	cboBook	mskPrice	mskQty	mskAmount
Enabled	True	False	True	False
Format	n/a	$#,##0.00;($#,##0.00)	#,##0	$#,##0.00;($#,##0.00)
Style	2 – Dropdown List	n/a	n/a	n/a
TabStop	True	False	True	False
Index	0, 1, and 2	0, 1, and 2	0, 1, and 2	0, 1, and 2

Property settings for the other masked edit controls

Property	Subtotal	Discount Pct	Discount	Total
Name	mskSubtotal	mskDiscountPct	mskDiscount	mskTotal
Enabled	False	False	False	False
Format	$#,##0.00;($#,##0.00)	0%	$#,##0.00;($#,##0.00)	$#,##0.00;($#,##0.00)
TabStop	False	False	False	False

Property settings for the command buttons

Property	New	Calculate	Exit
Name	cmdNew	cmdCalculate	cmdExit
Default	False	True	False

Description

- To calculate an order, the user selects one or more books, enters a quantity for each book, and clicks on the Calculate button. Then, the application gets the price for each book, calculates the sales amount for each book, and calculates the subtotal, discount, and total for the entire order.

- To start a new order, the user clicks on the New button. Then, all the combo boxes and masked edit boxes are cleared.

Figure 13-9   The form and the control properties for the enhanced application

The code for the enhanced class module

Figure 13-10 presents the code for the class module of the enhanced Book Order application. This code starts by declaring the five variables that will be used within this module (1). Notice that all of these variables are declared as Private so they can't be accessed directly by the form module. Because the values of the last three variables need to be retrieved by the form module, though, Property Get procedures are used to expose them as read-only properties.

The Initialize procedure for the module (2) establishes a connection to the MurachBooks database and defines the Command object that will be used to retrieve the prices for the books. The code in this module is identical to the code in the simple Book Order class module presented earlier in this chapter.

The BookDescriptions function (3) is also identical to the function in the simple class module. It opens a recordset that contains the descriptions of all the books in the BookPrices table. Then, that recordset is passed back to the calling procedure in the form module where it's used to populate the Book combo boxes. Because this procedure is defined as Public, it can be referred to from the form module as a method of the class module.

The BookPrice function (4) is similar to the CalcBookAmount procedure in the original class module. Instead of retrieving the book price and saving it in a private variable, however, it returns the price directly to the form module. Then, the form module can calculate the amount using that price and the quantity entered by the user. Because of that, it's not necessary to pass the quantity to the class module.

Because the book description is needed to get the price for a book, this value must be passed from the form module to the class module. In the original class module, this value was passed as a property and stored in a module-level variable. In the enhanced class module, however, this value is passed as an argument of the BookPrice function. Because this value isn't used by any other procedures in the class module, you don't have to save it in a module-level variable.

Code for the enhanced class module

```
Option Explicit                                                          1
Private mcnBooks As Connection
Private mcmdPrice As Command
Private mfDiscountPct As Single
Private mcDiscount As Currency
Private mcTotal As Currency


Private Sub Class_Initialize()                                           2
    Set mcnBooks = New Connection
    mcnBooks.CursorLocation = adUseClient
    mcnBooks.Open "Provider=SQLOLEDB;Server=mmaserver;" _
            & "Database=MurachBooks", "sa", "password"
    Set mcmdPrice = New Command
    mcmdPrice.CommandText = "SELECT BookPrice FROM BookPrices " _
        & "WHERE BookDescription = ?"
    mcmdPrice.CommandType = adCmdText
    mcmdPrice.ActiveConnection = mcnBooks
End Sub


Public Function BookDescriptions() As Recordset                         3
    Dim strSQL As String
    Set BookDescriptions = New Recordset
    strSQL = "SELECT BookDescription FROM BookPrices " _
        & "ORDER BY BookDescription"
    BookDescriptions.Open strSQL, mcnBooks, adOpenStatic, _
        adLockOptimistic, adCmdText
End Function


Public Function BookPrice(ByVal BookDesc As String) As Currency         4
    Dim rsPrice As Recordset
    mcmdPrice.Parameters(0) = BookDesc
    Set rsPrice = mcmdPrice.Execute
    BookPrice = rsPrice!BookPrice
End Function
```

Figure 13-10   The code for the enhanced BookOrder class module (part 1 of 2)

The CalculateTotals procedure (5) calculates the discount to be applied to an order and calculates the total order amount. To do that, the procedure needs the total quantity of books that were ordered and the total of the amounts (the order subtotal). Because these values are calculated in the form module, they are passed as arguments to the CalculateTotals procedure. Then, this procedure uses a Select Case statement to determine the discount percent based on the quantity, after which it calculates the discount amount based on the subtotal amount. Finally, it calculates the order total.

The CalculateTotals procedure stores the discount percent, discount amount, and order total as private variables. Then, three Property Get procedures (6) are used to return these values to the form module. The last procedure in this module (7) sets the two object variables used by the module to Nothing so the resources used by these objects are released.

Code for the enhanced class module (continued)

```
Public Sub CalculateTotals(ByVal Qty As Integer, _                          5
                           ByVal Subtotal As Currency)
    Select Case Qty
        Case 0 To 9
            mfDiscountPct = 0
        Case 10 To 24
            mfDiscountPct = 0.1
        Case 25 To 99
            mfDiscountPct = 0.2
        Case 100 To 249
            mfDiscountPct = 0.25
        Case 250 To 999
            mfDiscountPct = 0.3
        Case Else
            MsgBox "The total number of books must be less than 1000."
    End Select
    mcDiscount = Subtotal * mfDiscountPct * -1
    mcTotal = Subtotal + mcDiscount
End Sub
```

```
Public Property Get DiscountPct() As Single                                 6
    DiscountPct = mfDiscountPct
End Property

Public Property Get Discount() As Currency
    Discount = mcDiscount
End Property

Public Property Get Total() As Currency
    Total = mcTotal
End Property
```

```
Private Sub Class_Terminate()                                               7
    Set mcnBooks = Nothing
    Set mcmdPrice = Nothing
End Sub
```

Figure 13-10   The code for the enhanced BookOrder class module (part 2 of 2)

The code for the enhanced form module

Figure 13-11 shows the code for the enhanced form module. This code starts by declaring a private variable (1) that will be used to refer to the BookOrder object. Because this statement includes the New keyword, it also creates an instance of the object class.

The procedure for the Load event of the form (2) populates the three combo boxes used on the form. This procedure is the same as the Load procedure in the simple Book Order form module except that it loads the book descriptions into three combo boxes instead of one. To get the book descriptions, it uses the BookDescriptions method of the class module to get a recordset that contains one record for each book. Then, it uses a Do loop to read through the records and load the book descriptions into each combo box.

Notice that this procedure refers to each combo box explicitly by its index number. If more than three combo boxes were included on the form, though, you could use a For...Next loop within the Do loop to load the book descriptions. Then, the For...Next loop could vary the index numbers of the combo boxes so the book descriptions are added to each one.

When the user clicks on the Calculate button, the event procedure (3) must do several things. First, it must get the price of each book that the user selected and entered a valid quantity for. To do that, it uses a For...Next loop to process each item. The code in this loop starts by checking to be sure that a book was selected and a quantity greater than zero was entered. If so, the BookPrice method of the class module is used to get the price of the book. Because this method uses the book description to get the book price, the value in the Book combo box is passed to the method. And because the method is implemented as a function that returns the price, the method is included in an assignment statement that assigns the price to the appropriate Price control.

After the price of a book is retrieved, the procedure uses it to calculate the amount, which is assigned to the appropriate Amount control. Then, the quantity and subtotal are accumulated in local variables named nQty and cSubtotal. These variables are used later in this procedure.

After all the line items are processed, the nQty variable is checked to be sure that at least one book was ordered. If not, an error message is displayed. Otherwise, the cSubtotal variable is assigned to the Subtotal masked edit control. Then, the nQty and cSubtotal variables are passed to the CalculateTotals method of the class module. After this method calculates the discount percent, discount amount, and order total, these values are retrieved from the class module using the DiscountPct, Discount, and Total properties, and these values are assigned to the appropriate controls on the form.

If the user clicks on the New button in the form, the Click event procedure for that button (4) is executed. This procedure clears all of the controls on the form so the user can enter a new order.

The last two procedures in the form module (5) unload the form and release the resources used by the class object.

Code for the enhanced form module

```
Option Explicit                                                              1
Private mclsBookOrder As New BookOrder


Private Sub Form_Load()                                                      2
    Dim rsBooks As Recordset
    Set rsBooks = mclsBookOrder.BookDescriptions
    Do Until rsBooks.EOF
        cboBook(0).AddItem rsBooks!BookDescription
        cboBook(1).AddItem rsBooks!BookDescription
        cboBook(2).AddItem rsBooks!BookDescription
        rsBooks.MoveNext
    Loop
End Sub


Private Sub cmdCalculate_Click()                                             3
    Dim nIndex As Integer
    Dim cSubtotal As Currency
    Dim nQty As Integer
    For nIndex = 0 To 2
        If cboBook(nIndex).ListIndex <> -1 And Val(mskQty(nIndex)) > 0 Then
            mskPrice(nIndex) = mclsBookOrder.BookPrice(cboBook(nIndex))
            mskAmount(nIndex) = mskPrice(nIndex) * mskQty(nIndex)
            nQty = nQty + mskQty(nIndex)
            cSubtotal = cSubtotal + mskAmount(nIndex)
        End If
    Next
    If nQty > 0 Then
        mskSubtotal = cSubtotal
        mclsBookOrder.CalculateTotals nQty, cSubtotal
        mskDiscountPct = mclsBookOrder.DiscountPct
        mskDiscount = mclsBookOrder.Discount
        mskTotal = mclsBookOrder.Total
    Else
        MsgBox "Please select one or more books and enter valid quantities."
    End If
End Sub


Private Sub cmdNew_Click()                                                   4
    Dim nIndex As Integer
    For nIndex = 0 To 2
        cboBook(nIndex).ListIndex = -1
        mskQty(nIndex) = ""
        mskPrice(nIndex) = ""
        mskAmount(nIndex) = ""
    Next nIndex
    mskSubtotal = ""
    mskDiscountPct = ""
    mskDiscount = ""
    mskTotal = ""
End Sub


Private Sub cmdExit_Click()                                                  5
    Unload Me
End Sub

Private Sub Form_Unload(Cancel As Integer)
    Set mclsBookOrder = Nothing
End Sub
```

Figure 13-11   The code for the enhanced BookOrder form module

Exercise set 13-2: Enhance the Book Order application

In this exercise set, you'll enhance the Book Order application you created in the last exercise set so it lets the user select up to three books and applies a discount based on the total number of books ordered. Here again, *if you're using the Learning Edition of Visual Basic 6*, you'll have to use text boxes instead of the masked edit boxes and adjust the properties and code accordingly.

Open the project

1. If it's not already open, open the project named C13ClassModule that you created in exercise set 13-1.

Add controls to the Book Order form

2. Add the combo box and masked edit controls for two additional line items as shown in figure 13-9. The easiest way to do that is to copy each existing control and then paste it back onto the form. When you do that, a dialog box will be displayed that asks if you want to create a control array, and you should click on the Yes button in this dialog box. When you're done adding these controls, make sure that their properties are set as in figure 13-9.

3. Add the remaining masked edit controls and their associated labels to the form, and set their properties as in figure 13-9. Then, add the New button, set its Name property to cmdNew, and set its Caption property so it appears as shown in that figure.

4. Set the TabIndex properties of the controls with tab stops so the focus will move from left to right and top to bottom when the user presses the Tab key.

Add the code for the class module and the form module

5. Switch to the Code window for the class module. In the Declarations section, delete all of the variable declarations except the ones for the Connection and Command objects.

6. Delete the two Property Let and the two Property Get procedures. Next, add a public function named BookPrice including an argument and an As clause as shown in the procedure in figure 13-10 (part 1). Then, copy the first four lines in the CalcBookAmount procedure to the BookPrice procedure, and change the name of the msBookDesc variable used in the second statement to just BookDesc so this statement uses the BookDesc argument that's passed to the procedure. Also, change the name of the mcBookPrice variable in the last statement in this procedure to just BookPrice so the price is assigned to the function. Finally, delete the CalcBookAmount procedure.

7. Switch to the Code window for the form module, and enhance the code for the Load event procedure so it looks like the procedure in figure 13-11.

8. Delete the code from the cmdCalculate_Click event procedure. Then, add the three Dim statements and the For…Next loop to this procedure as shown in figure 13-11.

9. Run the application. Then, select one or more books, enter a quantity for each, and click on the Calculate button. The price and amount for each book should be displayed, but the other controls should be empty.

10. End the application, and return to the Code window for the class module. Enter the declarations for the three additional module-level variables shown in figure 13-10. Then, enter the code for the CalculateTotals and Property Get procedures shown in part 2 of figure 13-10.

11. Switch to the Code window for the form module. Enter the rest of the code for the cmdCalculate_Click procedure shown in figure 13-11. Then, enter the code for the cmdNew_Click procedure shown in that figure.

12. Run the application. Click on the Calculate button without selecting any books to see the message that's displayed, and click on the OK button in this dialog box to close it. Then, select one or more books, enter quantities for those books so the total quantity is greater than nine, and click on the Calculate button. This should display the subtotal, discount percent, discount amount, and order total. If they're not displayed or if the correct amounts aren't displayed, you'll need to debug the application. Otherwise, click on the New button to clear the form, and experiment with it on your own. When you're done, end the application.

13. Save the project.

Add an event to the class module

14. Switch to the Code window for the class module, and enter an Event statement in the Declarations section as shown in figure 13-6. Then, add a RaiseEvent statement like the one shown in that figure to the end of the CalculateTotals procedure.

15. Switch to the Code window for the form module. Change the declaration for the mclsBookOrder object variable in the Declarations section so it contains the WithEvents keyword as shown in figure 13-6. You'll need to remove the New keyword from this statement since it can't be used with WithEvents.

16. Add a Set statement at the beginning of the Load event procedure to create an instance of the BookOrder object class as shown in figure 13-6. Next, select the mclsBookOrder object from the first drop-down list in the Code Window so Visual Basic generates the Sub and End Sub statements for the CalculateComplete event of this object. Then, move the three assignment statements at the end of the CalculateTotals procedure to the CalculateComplete event procedure.

17. Run the application. Select one or more books, enter quantities so the total quantity is greater than nine, and click on the Calculate button. The application should work just as it did before.

18. Close the project without saving the changes.

How to create and use ActiveX components

Once you know how to create class modules, you're just one step away from creating ActiveX components. After you learn what these components are and what benefits they offer, you'll learn how to create and use them.

An overview of ActiveX components

An *ActiveX component* is an *executable (EXE)* or *dynamic link library (DLL)* that contains one or more class modules. Like a class module in a standard project, a class module in an ActiveX project can contain properties, methods, and events. However, the properties, methods, and events defined in a class module in an ActiveX project are exposed at the global level. That means that they are available to any project that has access to the component rather than only to the other modules in the project.

Figure 13-12 illustrates the difference between using class modules created in a standard project and class modules created in an ActiveX project. As you can see, a class module created in a standard project must be included in every project that uses it. In contrast, a class module in an ActiveX project exists separately from any project that uses it. One of the benefits of using ActiveX components, then, is that the size of each project that uses them is reduced.

Another benefit of using ActiveX components is that they simplify maintenance. If, for example, an ActiveX component resides on a network server, you can change that component without changing any of the client applications that use the component. When you're done, the modified component is immediately available to the projects that use it.

A third benefit of using ActiveX components is that they don't have to reside on the clients that use them. Although they can reside on the local machine, they can also reside on another user's machine on the same network or on a network server called a *component server*. When components are stored on a component server, the processing for the applications that use them can be balanced more evenly between the client and the server.

Although this chapter focuses on ActiveX components, you should know that you can also create two other types of ActiveX objects with Visual Basic: *ActiveX controls* and *ActiveX documents*. An ActiveX control is a customized control that you can use in any project, and many of the controls that come with Visual Basic are ActiveX controls. There's usually no point in making your own controls, however, since just about every component you'll need either comes with Visual Basic or can be purchased from a third-party vendor.

In contrast, an ActiveX document is an application object that you can add to an ActiveX document container. For instance, Word, Excel, and Access can be used as ActiveX documents, and the Microsoft Internet Explorer can be used as an ActiveX document container.

Two projects that use the same class modules

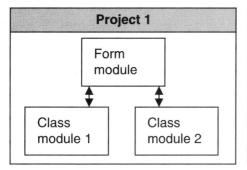
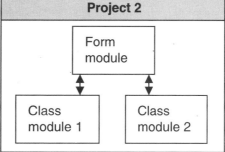

Two projects that use the same ActiveX component

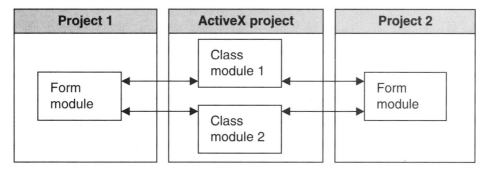

Description

- *ActiveX components* are stand-alone units of executable code that can be used by any application that supports ActiveX technology. An ActiveX component can contain one or more class modules.

- ActiveX components let you access the same code from more than one application. You don't have to include the code in each application like you do with class modules.

- When you modify an ActiveX component, the changes are immediately available to all the applications that use it.

Figure 13-12   An overview of ActiveX components

How an application communicates with ActiveX components

Microsoft developed ActiveX technology based on its *Component Object Model*, or *COM*. This model specifies the low-level functionality and interface needed for objects and programs that support ActiveX to communicate with each other. As shown in figure 13-13, a program interacts with ActiveX components through the COM interface. With COM, an application can communicate only with ActiveX components that reside on the same machine as the application, and these components can be referred to as *local components*.

If an application needs to communicate with components on other machines, called *remote components*, it uses another interface called the *Distributed Component Object Model*, or *DCOM*. Notice in this figure, though, that an application doesn't communicate directly with DCOM. Instead, all requests for ActiveX components go through COM. Then, if COM determines that the component is on a remote machine, it passes the request on to DCOM.

COM keeps track of ActiveX components through the use of a unique ID that's given to each component when it's created. This unique ID is commonly referred to as the *Class Identifier*, or *CLSID*. However, it can also be referred to as the *Globally Unique Identifier* (*GUID*) or the *Universally Unique Identifier* (*UUID*). No matter what you call it, though, no two components anywhere will have the same ID. That way, COM always knows which component to use and where to find it.

Before you can use an ActiveX component from an application, you must *register* it on the machine that will run the application. When you register a component, information about the component, including its unique ID, is placed in the system registry. You'll learn how to register a component on your machine later in this chapter.

ActiveX technology

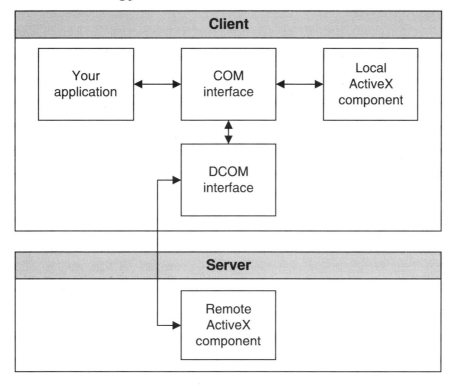

Description

- ActiveX components can reside on the same machine as the applications that use them, or they can reside on another machine on the network. A machine that hosts ActiveX components is typically called a *component server*.

- If an ActiveX component resides on the same machine as the application that uses it, the application communicates with the component using the *Component Object Model*, or *COM*. This model keeps track of ActiveX components using the unique ID that's assigned to each component when it's registered.

- If an ActiveX component resides on a machine other than the one where the application that uses it resides, COM passes the request on to the *Distributed Component Object Model*, or *DCOM*. With DCOM, you can access components that reside on a local network, an intranet, or the Internet.

- The COM and DCOM interfaces are transparent to your Visual Basic applications. As a result, if the component is properly installed and *registered*, you can use standard techniques to work with its class modules.

Note

- Although Windows 98 supports DCOM by default, Windows 95 doesn't. To use DCOM with Windows 95, you can download the file named DCOM98.EXE from the Microsoft web site.

Figure 13-13   How an application communicates with ActiveX components

A general procedure for creating and testing an ActiveX component

Figure 13-14 presents a general procedure you can use to create and test ActiveX components. In general, you create the server project that contains the component (steps 1-3), you create the client project (step 4), and you test the two together on your local machine (step 5). Then, if the component will reside on a local machine, you're done. Otherwise, you can install the component on the remote server where it will reside (step 6), install the client application on a local machine (step 7), and test the two together (step 8).

Although you can start by creating a separate project for an ActiveX component as indicated by this figure, you may want to start by creating a class module within the project that contains the code for the client application. In fact, we recommend that you do that if you haven't worked with class modules before. Then, when you get the class module working the way you want it, you can start an ActiveX project, add the class module to it, and remove the class module from the client project.

This figure also describes the four types of files that you can create for an ActiveX component. The name of each file that's created is the name of the project, and the extension is the file type shown in this figure. All of these files can be created when you build the project in step 3 of the procedure.

The main file that's created for a component, and the only one that's required for all components, is the EXE or DLL file. This file contains the executable code for the component. In the next figure, you'll learn about the difference between these two types of files and when to use them.

If a component will reside on a remote machine, you also need to create TLB and VBR files for the component. These files provide information that client applications use to communicate and work with the remote component. As you'll see in chapter 15, these files must be installed on the client machine along with the client application that uses the component.

How to create and test an ActiveX component

1. Create the ActiveX project and enter the code for the project (see figure 13-15).

2. Set the properties for the ActiveX project and save the project (see figure 13-16).

3. Use the Make command on the File menu to build the project. This compiles the project and creates the DLL or EXE and the TLB and VBR files for the component.

4. Create the client project and select the component from the References dialog box (see figure 13-17). Enter the required code, set the project properties, and save the project.

5. Run the client project and test the component. If you make changes to the component, use the Make command again to recreate the VBR, TLB, and DLL or EXE files for the component.

6. If the component will reside on a remote server, use the Package and Deployment Wizard to create a setup program for the component as described in chapter 15. Then, run the setup program to install the component on the server.

7. Use the Package and Deployment Wizard to create a setup program for the client project as described in chapter 15. Be sure to include a reference to the VBR file for the remote component. Then, run the setup program to install the client on your machine.

8. Run the client application and test the component.

Types of files that are created for a component

File type	Description
EXE or DLL	Contains the executable code for the component. Also contains information about the component's properties, methods, and events that's used by the Object Browser and client applications when the component resides on the local machine.
TLB	Contains information about the component's properties, methods, and events. This file is used by the Object Browser and client applications when the component resides on a remote server.
VBR	Contains information that's used by client applications to locate the component when it resides on a remote server.

Figure 13-14   A general procedure for creating and testing an ActiveX component

How to create an ActiveX project

Figure 13-15 shows you how to create an ActiveX project. To start, you need to decide whether to create an EXE or DLL project. In general, you create a DLL if the component will reside on the same machine as the client application because a DLL runs *in-process*, or in the same address space, as the client application. If the component will run on remote server, though, you create an EXE, which runs *out-of-process*, or in its own address space.

After you select the type of project you want to create, Visual Basic creates the project with a single class module. Then, you can create the code for that class module just as you would for any other class module. You can also add existing class modules to the project or create additional class modules.

You can also include standard modules and form modules in an ActiveX project. These modules, of course, can be referred to only from the other modules in the project. They can't be referred to from outside the project like the class modules can.

Before you save and build an ActiveX project, you should make sure that the properties for each class module in the project are set correctly. In particular, you'll want to make sure that the Instancing property is set to MultiUse. When you create a class module in an ActiveX project, MultiUse is the default. When you create a class module in a standard project, however, the default for this property is Private. If you add a class module that was created in a standard project to an ActiveX project, then, you'll want to make sure you change this property. In addition, you'll want to be sure that the Name property is set the way you want it since this is the name you'll use to access the object class.

How to create an ActiveX project

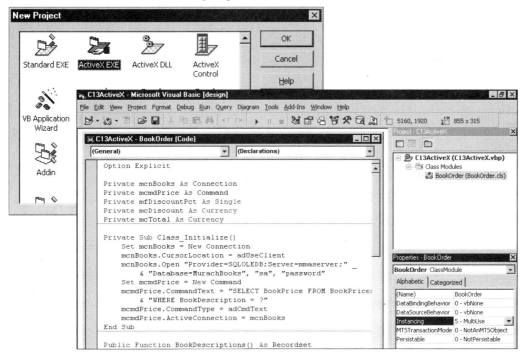

Description

- To create an ActiveX project, choose the ActiveX EXE or ActiveX DLL option from the New Project dialog box shown above. The type of ActiveX project you create depends mostly on where the component will reside.

- If the component will reside on the same machine as the application that uses it, you usually create it as a DLL (dynamic link library). Since a DLL runs *in-process*, which means that it runs in the same address space as the application that uses it, it's usually faster than an EXE.

- If the component will reside on a remote server, you usually create it as an EXE. This type of component is an executable program that runs *out-of-process*, which means that it runs in its own address space.

- When you start an ActiveX DLL or EXE project, a single class module is created by default. However, you can create other class modules for the project, and you can add standard or form modules to the project.

- By default, the Instancing property of a class module is set to MultiUse, which is the option you want for most DLL and EXE projects.

Figure 13-15   How to create an ActiveX project

How to set the properties for an ActiveX project

After you enter the code for an ActiveX project, but before you save or build the project, you need to set the project properties as described in figure 13-16. Three of these properties are available from the General tab of the Project Properties dialog box, and three others are available from the Component tab. To display the Project Properties dialog box, select the Properties command from the Project menu.

Although you've already seen the three properties in the General Tab, they're particularly important when used in an ActiveX project. As you can see, the Project Name and Project Description properties are used by the Object Browser. In addition, the Project Description property is used by the References dialog box shown in the next figure. As a result, if other programmers will be using the component, you should be sure to provide meaningful names for these properties.

The Startup Object property typically identifies the first module that's executed when an application starts. For an ActiveX component, though, you usually leave this property at its default setting of none. That way, no extra code is executed when the first instance of an object class in the component is created. If for some reason you do need to execute code when the first instance of an object class is created, though, you can code a Sub Main procedure and choose the Sub Main option for the Startup Object property.

The Start Mode, Remote Server Files, and Version Compatibility properties are specific to ActiveX projects. Except for the Remote Server Files property, these properties are usually set the way you want them by default. If you're creating a remote component, though, you'll want to turn on the Remote Server Files property, which isn't selected by default. This will create the VBR and TLB files that are needed for a client application to communicate and work with a remote component. These files aren't needed for a local component because the client has direct access to the EXE or DLL file for the component.

Once you have the properties for an ActiveX project set properly, you can save and build the project. Then, you can use it from any application on the same machine. If you want to deploy the component on a remote machine, though, you need to create a setup program as described in chapter 15.

If you display the Project Properties dialog box after you build a component with the Project Compatibility option selected, you'll see that Visual Basic displays the name of the executable file in the text box below the compatibility options as shown in this figure. Then, if you change the component and build it again, Windows will use the same unique ID number for the new version of the component that it used for the original version. That way, the change will not affect any applications that already refer to the component, which is usually what you want.

Project properties for an ActiveX component

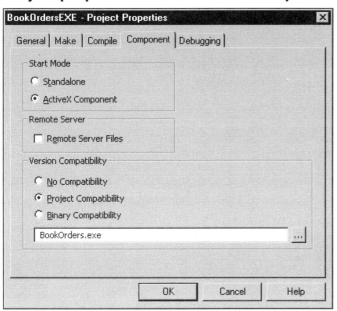

The General tab

Property	Description
Project Name	Specifies the name of the type library that's used to identify the component in the Object Browser.
Project Description	Specifies the text that's displayed for the component in the Details pane of the Object Browser and in the References dialog box.
Startup Object	Specifies the module that's executed when the component is first accessed. For an ActiveX component, this option is usually set to (none), which is the default.

The Component tab

Property	Description
Start Mode	Determines whether the application is started as a standalone application or as an ActiveX server (component) when it's run within Visual Basic. By default, the ActiveX Component option is on. (This property can't be changed for a DLL.)
Remote Server Files	Creates VBR and TLB files for the project when it's compiled. These files are used by client applications to access and use remote components, and this option isn't selected by default.
Version Compatibility	Determines the level of compatibility between different versions of a component. Project Compatibility is the default.

Figure 13-16   How to set the properties for an ActiveX project

How to use ActiveX components

Before you can use an ActiveX component from a client application, you have to register it on your machine as described in figure 13-17. If you created the component on your machine, it's already registered. Otherwise, you need to copy it to your machine and then register it by executing it if it's an EXE or using the REGSVR32 program if it's a DLL.

After you register the component, you can use it in an application by adding a *reference* to it. To do that, you use the References dialog box shown in this figure. If you try to create an instance of a class module in a component that's not referenced by the client application, Visual Basic will display a compile error stating that the user-defined type isn't defined.

The References dialog box includes all components that have been registered on the local machine. To use one of these components, just check its box. To use a component that has not been registered on the local machine, click on the Browse button to locate the component. After you locate and select the component you want, it's added to the Available References list. Then, you can refer to the component from the Code window, but you won't be able to execute the code until you register the component on your machine.

After you add a reference to an ActiveX component to a project, you can use any of the object classes it defines. To do that, just create an instance of the object class and refer to its properties and methods as described earlier in this chapter. If you don't know what properties and methods an object class defines, you can use the Object Browser or the Auto List Members feature to find out.

The dialog box for adding a reference for an ActiveX component

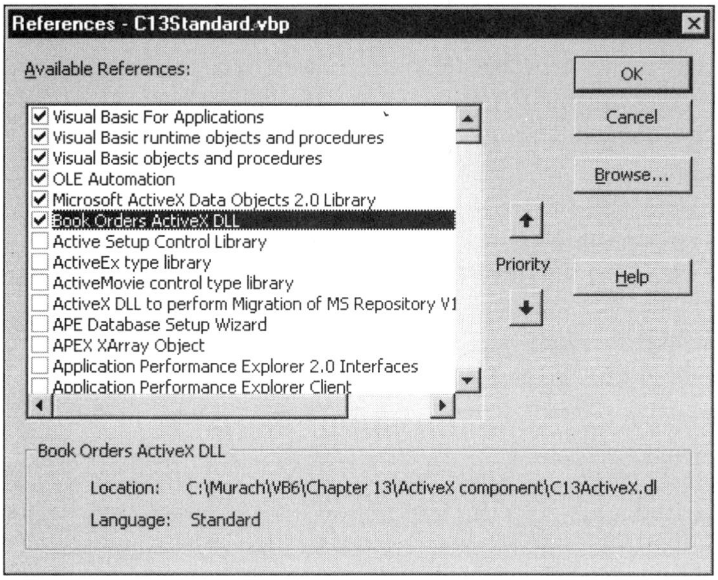

How to register an ActiveX component on your machine

- If you created the component on your machine, it's already registered. Otherwise, you need to begin by copying the component to the \Windows\System folder on your machine.

- If the component is implemented as an EXE, execute it to register it. If it's implemented as a DLL, use the REGSVR32.EXE program to register it.

- REGSVR32 is a DOS program that's installed in your \Windows\System folder by default. To use it, open a DOS window, change to the \Windows\System folder, and enter a command like this (where dllname is the name of the DLL you want to register):

```
regsvr32.exe dllname
```

- If you can't find REGSVR32 on your PC, you can find it on Disk 1 of the Visual Basic 6 disks in the Common\Tools\Vb\Regutils folder.

How to add a reference to an ActiveX component

- To use an ActiveX component in a client application, you select it from the References dialog box shown above. To access this dialog box, select the References command from the Project menu. The Available References list includes all the components that have been registered on your machine.

- If the component has not been registered on the local machine, you can click on the Browse button in the References dialog box to locate the component and add it to the Available References list. Then, you'll be able to refer to the component in code, but you won't be able to execute that code until you register the component on your machine.

Figure 13-17   How to use ActiveX components

The benefits of using class modules

Now that you've seen how to use class modules in standard and ActiveX projects, you can reflect on the benefits of using class modules in your projects. To start, let's assume that someone else has already developed the class modules that you need for an application. That certainly should make it easier for you to develop the application because all you have to do is use the properties and methods of the available objects.

A second benefit is improved maintenance of an application because all of the business processing, including the database processing, can be done in the class modules, while the user interface processing is done in the form modules. That should make it easier to find the code that needs to be changed. In addition, you can change the code in the class module without affecting the operation of the user interface.

If you can design objects that can be used by more than one application, a third benefit is reusability, which in turn can lead to improved programmer productivity. As you learned earlier in this chapter, though, the trick is designing objects that can be easily reused.

One last benefit that you get from using class modules is an improved way of thinking about application development. The more you think in terms of objects with clearly established properties and methods, the more you'll be able to take advantage of object-oriented technology. In the long run, learning to think in terms of objects will help you work faster at the same time that it helps you improve the maintainability and reliability of your applications.

The downside to the use of class modules is the complexity that it adds to the jobs of project managers and programmers. First, someone has to plan the class modules for the applications that they're going to be used by. Second, someone has to develop these modules, which some programming managers think is too difficult for the average programmer. Third, once the class modules have been developed, the programmers who are going to use them need to get full information about the objects, properties, methods, and events so they can use them effectively. In short, getting the potential benefits from the use of class modules presents some significant planning and management difficulties. To date, these difficulties have proven to be so substantial that they have clearly limited the use and value of class modules and ActiveX components in business applications.

Exercise set 13-3: Create and use an ActiveX component

In this exercise set, you'll create an ActiveX DLL project that contains the Book Order class module. Then, you'll use this ActiveX component in the Book Order project. *If you're using the Learning Edition of Visual Basic 6*, though, you won't be able to do this exercise set because your edition doesn't let you create ActiveX components.

Create an ActiveX DLL project and add the Book Order class module

1. Start a new project, and select the ActiveX DLL option from the New Project dialog box. This adds a class module to the new project by default. Then, right-click on the class module in the Project Explorer and use the Remove command to remove the module without saving it.

2. Select the Add Class Module command from the Project menu, and add the BookOrder class module you created in the last exercise set to the ActiveX project. Next, change the Instancing property of this module to MultiUse. Then, use the Save As command in the shortcut menu for the class module to save the module in a new folder named Chapter 13 ActiveX with the same name as the original class module.

3. Use the Properties command in the Project menu to set the Project Name property to C13ActiveX and the Project Description property to Book Orders ActiveX DLL. Next, use the References command in the Project menu to add a reference to the Microsoft ActiveX Data Objects 2.0 library to the project. Then, save the project with the name C13ActiveX in the Chapter 13 ActiveX folder.

4. Select the Make command from the File menu and save the files in the Chapter 13 ActiveX folder. Then, close the project.

Use the DLL file in the Book Order application

5. Open the Book Order project you created in the last exercise set. Next, right-click on the class module in the Project Explorer, and select the Remove command to remove the class module from the project. Then, right-click on the form module and use the Save As command to save the form in the Chapter 13 ActiveX folder.

6. Select the References command from the Project menu, and select the Book Orders ActiveX DLL reference from the dialog box that's displayed. Then, click on the OK button to save this reference and close the dialog box.

7. Use the Properties command in the Project menu to change the project name to C13Standard. Then, use the Save As command in the File menu to save the project with the name C13Standard in the Chapter 13 ActiveX folder.

8. Run the project and test it. It should work just as it did when it used the class module. If it doesn't, you'll need to debug it.

Close the project and exit from Visual Basic

9. Close the project and exit from Visual Basic.

Perspective

The goal of this chapter has been to introduce you to class modules and ActiveX components and to present the basic coding skills that are required to create and work with them. Beyond that, I hope that this chapter has helped you begin to see how you can use class modules and ActiveX components in your own development efforts. If you understand the class module that was presented in this chapter and can visualize it as an object, then this chapter has succeeded.

Terms you should know

object-oriented programming (OOP)
class module
object class
instance
class object
property procedure
ActiveX component
executable (EXE)
dynamic link library (DLL)
component server
ActiveX control
ActiveX document
Component Object Model (COM)
local component
remote component
Distributed Component Object Model (DCOM)
Class Identifier (CLSID)
Globally Unique Identifier (GUID)
Universally Unique Identifier (UUID)
registering a component
in-process execution
out-of-process execution

14

How to develop Internet applications

Visual Basic 6 includes two new features you can use to develop Internet applications from within the Visual Basic IDE. In this chapter, you will learn the basic skills for using these features. Note, however, that there's a lot more you need to know before you'll be able to develop full-fledged Internet applications. But this chapter should help get you started.

An introduction to building Internet applications **520**
An introduction to Internet applications 520
The two types of Internet applications you can build with Visual Basic ... 522
Features and requirements of DHTML and IIS applications 524

Basic skills for building a DHTML application **526**
An overview of DHTML applications 526
How to use the DHTML Page Designer 528
How to develop the code for a DHTML application 530
How to test and build a DHTML application 530

Basic skills for building an IIS application **532**
An overview of IIS applications 532
How to create an HTML page 534
How to use the Webclass Designer 536
How to develop the code for an IIS application 538
How to use webclass tags to display data on an HTML page 540
How to test and build an IIS application 540

Perspective **542**

An introduction to building Internet applications

Before you learn the techniques for building Internet applications in Visual Basic, you need to understand some basic concepts for working with Internet applications. In addition, you need to become familiar with the two different types of Internets applications that you can build with Visual Basic so you have a general idea of how they work. Then, you'll be better prepared to decide which type of application will work best for your specific situation.

An introduction to Internet applications

Figure 14-1 presents the interface for a simple Internet application. This application lets you select a vendor from a list of all the vendors in the Vendors table. Then, it displays some basic information for that vendor.

The code for an Internet application like the one shown in this figure is stored on a *web server* on the Internet or an intranet. To access the application from a client machine, you use a *browser*. The browser shown here is the Microsoft Internet Explorer, but others are available.

The *pages* of an Internet application make up its user interface much as the forms of a standard application make up its user interface. To develop the pages for an application, you use a language called the *HyperText Markup Language*, or *HTML*. This is a standard language that's used to develop documents for display on the World Wide Web.

To identify an Internet application from a browser, you enter its *Uniform Resource Locator*, or *URL*. The URL tells the browser the address of the application. The actual file that the URL points to depends on the type of application you're accessing. The URL in this figure, for example, points to an HTML page on the web site at www.murach.com. After you enter this URL, the browser locates the page and displays it on the client machine. Then, you can interact with that page to perform the functions of the application.

When you use Visual Basic to develop Internet applications, you use Visual Basic code to perform the processing of the application. As you'll see later in this chapter, you do that using many of the same coding techniques that you use with standard applications. When you develop Internet applications, though, you have access to additional object models.

Microsoft Internet Explorer with an Internet application displayed

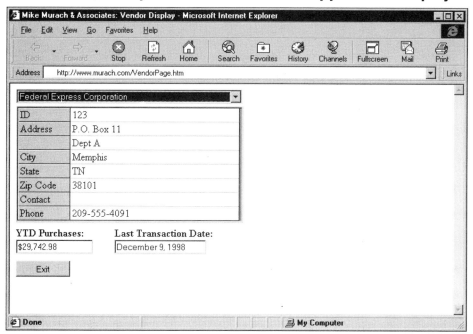

Concepts

- Internet applications reside on a *web server* on an intranet or the Internet. To access an Internet application from a client machine, you use a browser like Microsoft Internet Explorer or Netscape Navigator.

- To start an application from a browser, you enter its *Uniform Resource Locator*, or *URL*. The URL indicates the location of the application on the web server.

- The user interface for an Internet application consists of one or more *pages* written in the *Hypertext Markup Language*, or *HTML*. When you use Visual Basic to implement an Internet application, you can use Visual Basic code to interact with these pages.

Figure 14-1   An introduction to Internet applications

The two types of Internet applications you can build with Visual Basic

You can develop two types of Internet applications from within the Visual Basic environment: *DHTML* and *IIS*. Figure 14-2 presents a conceptual view of how these two types of applications work. Notice that to run a DHTML application, you enter the URL for the default page of the application. Then, that page points to the Visual Basic code for the application, which can point to other pages.

In contrast, the URL for an IIS application points to the ASP file for the *webclass* you want to execute. As you'll see later in this chapter, webclasses are the main components of IIS applications. They define the templates for the HTML pages that will be used by the file along with other custom webclass items.

The main job of the ASP file is to create an instance of the webclass that will be used by the client. Then, it starts the execution of the webclass, which causes the first page to be displayed by the browser. Notice that all requests for ASP files from the browser are processed by the Internet Information Server (IIS).

As you can see in this figure, DHTML and IIS applications have several similarities: They are both stored on a server, the Visual Basic code for both is stored in a DLL file, and they both work with HTML pages. You can also see that they're implemented somewhat differently, and you'll learn more about that later in this chapter. One of the biggest differences between these two type of applications, however, is where they're executed.

When you start a DHTML application, the DLL for the application is downloaded to the client where it's executed. Although that means it may take longer for the application to start, it also means that the application will respond more quickly to user input. In addition, the workload on the server is reduced, which can be a critical factor in the overall efficiency of the system.

In contrast, the DLL for an IIS application is executed on the server. Because a server is typically more powerful than the client machines that access it, that means the code can execute more efficiently. As you can imagine, though, a server can quickly become bogged down if it has to process a large number of applications at the same time. You'll want to keep that in mind when you decide whether to develop DHTML or IIS applications.

How a DHTML application works

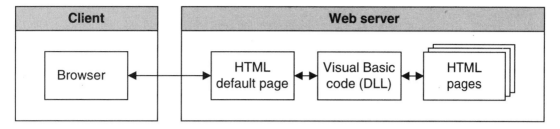

How an IIS application works

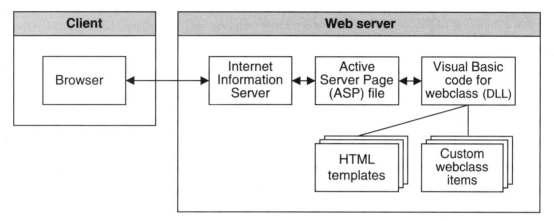

Description

- You can create two types of Internet applications using Visual Basic: DHTML, which stands for Dynamic Hypertext Markup Language, and IIS, which stands for Internet Information Server.

- A DHTML application consists of one or more *HTML pages* and the Visual Basic code that processes those pages. The URL for a DHTML application points to the default HTML page for the application. This page, in turn, points to the Visual Basic code for the application, which can display other pages.

- An IIS application consists of one or more webclasses. A *webclass* contains the templates for the HTML pages it uses along with the definitions of custom webclass items. A webclass also contains the Visual Basic code that processes the pages and web items.

- When you compile an IIS application, an *Active Server Page (ASP)* file is created for each webclass. The main purpose of an ASP file is to create an instance of a webclass and then execute it.

- The URL for an IIS application points to an ASP file. The URL is processed by the Internet Information Server, which manages the webclasses on the server.

Figure 14-2   The two types of Internet applications you can build with Visual Basic

Features and requirements of DHTML and IIS applications

Figure 14-3 outlines some of the features of DHTML and IIS applications. One difference between the two is the browsers that can be used to access them. Although you can use any browser to access an IIS application, you can use only Microsoft's Internet Explorer to access a DHTML application. Because of this restriction, DHTML is typically used to implement the applications for an intranet rather than the Internet. In contrast, IIS is typically used to implement applications for the Internet so that any browser can be used to access them. However, IIS can also be used to implement applications for an intranet if two or more browsers are used by the clients on the network.

Another difference between DHTML and IIS applications is the object model that's used to work with the pages of the application. DHTML uses its own object model that lets you refer to any element of a page and respond to its events. IIS uses the Active Server Pages object model to access and work with the information in an HTML page. In addition, you can use the properties, methods, and events of the webclasses and webitems in an IIS application to work with the HTML pages. You'll see how that works later in this chapter.

This figure also lists the system requirements for developing and running DHTML and IIS applications. Because you can access a DHTML application only using the Internet Explorer, you must have it installed on both the development system and any system that will use the application. Notice that the development system must have release 4.01 with Service Pack 1 or later, but release 4.0 or later is sufficient for a client system. Because the applications will run on the clients, they must also have the run-time version of Visual Basic along with any ActiveX components that are used by the application. If the clients don't have them, they are downloaded the first time a client requests the application.

To develop an IIS application, you need to have Windows NT Server or Workstation 4.0 or later or Windows 95 or 98. In most cases, you'll develop an IIS application using NT Workstation or Windows 95/98 and Peer Web Services or Personal Web Server with Active Server Pages. Then, you'll deploy it on an NT Server system that has Internet Information Server installed. Note that Internet Information Server, Peer Web Services, and Personal Web Server are all part of the NT 4.0 option pack and do not come with Visual Basic. To get the products you need, you can download them from Microsoft's web site at http://backoffice.microsoft.com/downtrial/optionpack.asp.

In addition to the requirements shown in this figure, you may want to install an HTML editor on the development system. Even if you're not responsible for developing the HTML for an application, you may want to be able to view it. In most cases, you can just use the NotePad program that comes with Windows to do that. If you'll be doing extensive development work, though, you'll probably want to install a more powerful program like Microsoft FrontPage.

Features of a DHTML application

- Designed to be run on an intranet
- Must be accessed using Microsoft's Internet Explorer 4.0 or later
- Uses the Dynamic HTML object model
- Processing is performed on the client machine
- Provides a graphical interface for creating HTML pages
- Provides faster response to events

System requirements for DHTML applications

Development system	Client system
Microsoft Internet Explorer 4.01 with Service Pack 1 or later	Visual Basic run-time version (downloaded the first time the application is run)
	ActiveX components (downloaded the first time the application is run)
	Internet Explorer 4.0 or later

Features of an IIS application

- Can be run on the Internet or on an intranet
- Can be accessed from any browser
- Uses the Active Server Pages object model
- Processing is performed on the web server
- Consists of a special type of object called a Webclass

System requirements for IIS applications

Development system	Client system
Windows NT Server 4.0 with Service Pack 3.0 or later and Internet Information Server 3.0 or later with Active Server Pages	Any browser such as Internet Explorer or Netscape Navigator
or	
Windows NT Workstation 4.0 with Service Pack 3.0 or later and Peer Web Services 3.0 or later with Active Server Pages	
or	
Windows 95/98 and Personal Web Server 3.0 or later with Active Server Pages	

Note

- The application code for both DHTML and IIS applications is stored separately from the HTML code.

Figure 14-3   Features and requirements of DHTML and IIS applications

Basic skills for building a DHTML application

You develop a DHTML application using techniques that are similar to the techniques you use to develop applications based on forms. Instead of developing forms using the Form Designer, however, you develop pages using the Page Designer. You'll learn the basic skills for working with the Page Designer in just a minute. But first, I want to present the interface and some code for a sample application.

An overview of DHTML applications

When you use the Page Designer to develop a DHTML page, the HTML code for the page is generated for you. That means that you don't need to know HTML to develop a DHTML application. And that's why you don't see any HTML code in the application shown in figure 14-4.

The application shown in this figure is the same one that was presented in figure 14-1. It displays information for the vendor that's selected from the list at the top of the page. If you look at the code for this application, you'll see that it looks similar to the code you've seen throughout this book. Notice in particular that you work with ADO objects the same way you do from any other application.

The biggest difference between a DHTML application and a standard forms-based application is that you use the DHTML object model to work with a page and the objects, or *elements*, it contains. The first two event procedures shown in this figure, for example, are for the Initialize and Load events of the page. These events are similar to the Initialize and Load events of a form. In fact, if you look at the code for these procedures, you'll see that it's almost identical to the code you'd expect to see in a form module. Instead of working with form objects, properties, and methods, however, it works with DHTML objects, properties, and methods.

For example, the Load procedure uses the createElement method of the Document object to create an Option element. Then, that element is used to load the vendor names into the selVendors element on the page (the element that contains the drop-down list of vendor names). Although the details of how this code works may not be obvious, you should be able to figure it out by using online help to learn about the objects and methods used in this example.

The last event procedure shown in this figure is for the onchange event of the selVendors element. This event is similar to the Change event for a combo box control on a form. You'll learn more about the events that are available for DHTML in figure 14-6.

The user interface and code for a DHTML application

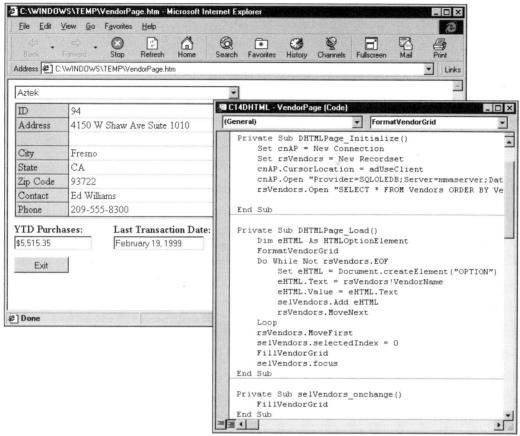

Description

- To create the user interface for a DHTML application, you use the DHTML Page Designer. This designer lets you create HTML pages using techniques similar to the techniques you use to create forms.

- When you use the DHTML Page Designer to create a page, the HTML code is generated for you. Because of that, you can create a DHTML application without knowing HTML.

- You use the DHTML object model to work with a page and its elements through code. You can use the object model to respond to events, set and retrieve properties, and call methods just as you do for other objects.

- You can use ADO objects in a DHTML application just as you do in any other application. You can work with ADO objects through code as shown above, or through a DataEnvironment object as described in chapter 9.

Figure 14-4   An overview of DHTML applications

How to use the DHTML Page Designer

Figure 14-5 presents the basic skills for working with the DHTML Page Designer. As you can see, the Page Designer window is divided into two panels. The treeview panel on the left lists the elements on the page in a tree view. The detail panel on the right shows the elements on the page. You use the detail panel to design the page using skills similar to those you use to design a form. You can use the treeview or detail panel to select an element on the page and to display the properties for that element. Notice that when you select an element in one panel, the element is automatically selected in the other panel.

You use the Toolbox to add most of the elements to a page. When the Page Designer window is open, an HTML tab will appear in the Toolbox as shown in this figure. Many of the elements on this tab are similar to controls that you add to forms. The TextField element, for example, is like a TextBox control, and the Select element is like a ComboBox control. A few of the elements, however, are specific to HTML. For example, the Submit element sends the data on the page to the specified URL when it's clicked, and the Hyperlink element jumps to the specified URL when it's clicked. In addition to the elements in the HTML tab of the Toolbox, you can add ActiveX controls from other tabs.

When you add an element to a page, you should know that you can position it using absolute positioning or relative positioning. The default is absolute positioning, which means that the element will appear exactly where you place it. With relative positioning, an element is placed in the next available position on the page. To switch to relative positioning, click on the Absolute Position Mode button on the toolbar to deselect it.

Unlike other elements, you don't use the Toolbox to add text to a page. Instead, you type it directly onto the page. To position the text vertically, you add or delete paragraph marks. To position it horizontally, you can use spaces or the alignment buttons in the toolbar. You can use other controls in the toolbar to format the text.

Since most Internet applications consist of more than one page, you'll probably need to add DHTML pages to the project. When you do that, VB will display a dialog box that asks if you want to save the HTML for the page as part of the project or in an external file. By default, the HTML is saved as part of the project. In that case, though, you can't view or edit the HTML code that's generated. If you need to do that, you'll want to save it in an external file. Then, you can use the Launch Editor button in the Page Designer toolbar to display the HTML file. By default, the file will be displayed in NotePad. To use a different editor, set the appropriate option in the Advanced tab of the Options dialog box. You can also save a page to an external file at a later time by clicking on the DHTML Page Designer Properties button in the Page Designer toolbar.

When you first open a new DHTML project, you'll notice that it includes a standard module in addition to the default page. This module contains two custom procedures. You can use one of the procedures to store information on the user's system in a file called a *cookie*. Then, the next time that user accesses the application, you can use the other procedure the retrieve the information.

The DHMTL Page Designer

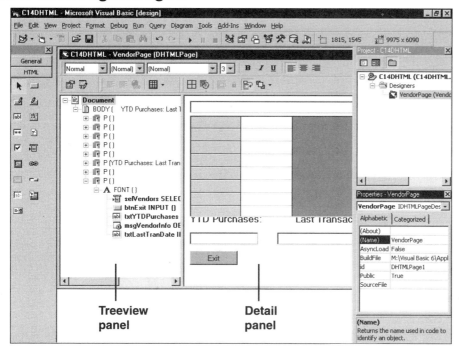

Treeview panel   **Detail panel**

Description

- To start a DHTML project, select the DHTML Application option from the New Project dialog box. By default, the DHTML project includes one standard module and one DHTML page.

- To open the Page Designer for the page, double-click on the page in the Project Explorer. To add a new page, select Add DHTML Page from the Project menu or the shortcut menu for the Project Explorer.

- The left panel of the Page Designer window (the treeview panel) lists all of the *elements* on the page in a tree view. The right panel of the Page Designer window (the detail panel) shows the elements as they will appear on the page.

- To add text to a page, type it on the page where you want it to appear. Then, use the controls in the toolbar at the top of the designer window to format the text.

- To add an element to a page, select it from the HTML tab of the Toolbox and then drag in the page where you want it to appear. You can also add ActiveX controls that appear in other tabs of the Toolbox to an HTML page.

- Many of the elements in the HTML tab of the Toolbox are similar to controls you use in forms. Others, like the Hyperlink element, are specific to web-based applications.

- To display the properties for an element, click on it in the left or right panel of the Page Designer window. To display the code for an element, double-click on it in either panel.

- To display the Code window for a page, double-click on any element on the page in either panel of the Page Designer window.

Figure 14-5   How to use the DHTML Page Designer

How to develop the code for a DHTML application

Like the code for other applications, the code for DHTML applications responds to events. You saw the code for three events in figure 14-4. Figure 14-6 presents some additional events you can use to work with the pages and elements in a DHTML application.

As you can see in this figure, the events you use to work with a DHTMLPage object are similar to the events you use to work with a form. In addition to these events, you can use other events like those listed in the figure to work with the elements on a page. Many of these events are similar to standard VB events. Note, however, that the event names are different from the VB names. Note also that not all of the possible events are listed in this figure. To find out what events are available for an element, use the drop-down lists in the Code window to select the element and display its events.

The first procedure in this figure is for the onchange event of the Select element that displays the available vendors. This event occurs whenever the user selects a different vendor, and its event procedure calls the FillVendorGrid procedure. That procedure uses the Find method of the vendors Recordset object to locate the selected vendor. Then, it loads the information from that record into the MSFlexGrid control on the form. If you've used this control before, you shouldn't have any trouble understanding how this code works. The thing to notice is that this code is the same as the code you'd use in a forms-based application except that the value of the VendorName field is retrieved from the Select element instead of a combo box.

How to test and build a DHTML application

To test a DHTML application, you run it just as you would any other application. When you run the application for the first time, Visual Basic displays the Debugging tab of the Project Properties dialog box. The options in this dialog box determine what happens when the application starts. By default, the first page that was created for the project is displayed when the application starts, which is usually what you want. If you want to display a different page, select that page from the drop-down list. Or, select one of the other options to execute another program, navigate to a URL, or do nothing until the appropriate component is created. Note that you can also execute a Sub Main procedure when the application starts just as you can for any other project.

When you're done testing and debugging the application, you can create the DLL for the project using the Make command in the File menu. In addition to creating the DLL, this command creates an HTML file for each page defined by the project. The pages are saved with the name and location you specify. If you previously saved a page to an external file, that file is used automatically. After you build the application, you can use the Package and Deployment Wizard as described in chapter 15 to deploy the application on a web server.

DHTMLPage events

Event	Description
Initialize	Occurs when an instance of the page is created. Typically used to initialize the data for the page.
Load	Occurs when the browser loads the page. Typically used to initialize the elements on the page.
Unload	Occurs when the user moves to another page or closes the application. Typically used to close objects and release resources used by object variables.
Terminate	Occurs when all object variables that refer to the page are set to Nothing or the object variables go out of scope.

Other common events and their Visual Basic equivalents

VB event	DHTML event	VB Event	DHTML event
Click	onclick	KeyPress	onkeypress
DoubleClick	ondblclick	KeyDown	onkeydown
MouseDown	onmousedown	KeyUp	onkeyup
MouseUp	onmouseup	GotFocus	onfocus
MouseMove	onmousemove	LostFocus	onblur
Change	onchange	Error	onerror

Code that loads the Vendor grid when a vendor is selected

```
Private Sub selVendors_onchange()
    FillVendorGrid
End Sub

Private Sub FillVendorGrid()
    Dim sVendorName As String
    sVendorName = Replace(selVendors.Value, "'", "''")
    rsVendors.Find "VendorName='" & sVendorName & "'", , , adBookmarkFirst
    With msgVendorInfo
        .Col = 1
        .Row = 0
        .Text = rsVendors!VendorID
        .Row = 1
        .Text = rsVendors!VendorAddress1 & ""
        .
        .
        .
    End With
    txtYTDPurchases.Value = Format(rsVendors!YTDPurchases, "Currency")
    txtLastTranDate.Value = Format(rsVendors!LastTranDate, "mmmm d, yyyy")
End Sub
```

Description

- The code for an HTML application responds to events on the DHTMLPage object and the elements on the page. Many of these events have Visual Basic counterparts.
- To refer to an element in code, you use its ID property, not its Name property.

Figure 14-6   How to develop the code for a DHTML application

Basic skills for building an IIS application

Unlike DHTML applications, you don't use a visual designer to build the pages of an IIS application. Instead, you have to use an HTML editor to create the pages using HTML code. You'll learn the basics for doing that in this section. In addition, you'll learn the basic skills for working with HTML pages within an IIS application.

An overview of IIS applications

Figure 14-7 presents an overview of an IIS application. Here, the first page of the application lists all of the vendors in the Vendors table. Although you may not be able to tell from this figure, the vendor name for each vendor is implemented as a *hyperlink*. When you click on the hyperlink for a vendor, a second page displays additional information for that vendor.

To create an IIS application, you define one or more *webclasses* using the Webclass Designer. The Webclass Designer lets you associate the HTML files for the application with templates in the webclass. You can also use the Webclass Designer to define custom *webitems*. Then, the code for the application can respond to events on the webclasses and the templates and custom webitems they contain.

The HTML code for the body of the page is also included in this figure. If you haven't worked with HTML code before, don't worry about how this code works. You'll learn more about it in the following topics. For now, just notice that the tags that are prefixed with WC@ are called *webclass tags*. Notice too that these tags are referred to in the code for the application. As you'll see, webclass tags are used to determine the data that will be displayed when the application is executed.

The Visual Basic code in this figure contains three event procedures. The first one is executed when the Start event of the webclass occurs. The second one is executed when the Respond event of the template named VendorList occurs. And the third one is executed when the ProcessTag event of the VendorList template occurs. You'll learn more about these objects and events later in this section.

The user interface, Visual Basic code, and HTML code for an IIS application

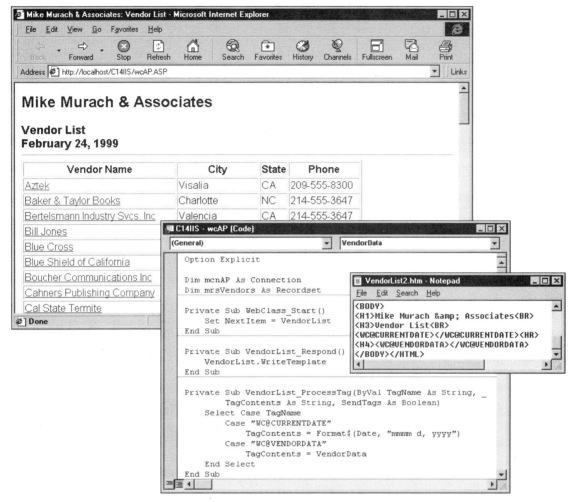

Description

- An IIS application consists of one or more webclasses. To create a webclass, you use the Webclass Designer.

- Each webclass can contain templates for the HTML files that define the user interface for the application. A webclass can also contain custom *webitems*.

- You can use special tags called *webclass tags* within an HTML file to identify text that will be replaced when the IIS application is run.

- The code for an IIS application responds to events on the webclass and the templates and custom webitems it contains.

Figure 14-7   An overview of IIS applications

How to create an HTML page

Figure 14-8 presents the HTML code for the page shown in figure 14-7 along with some common *HTML tags* that you can use to define a page. If you take a few minutes to study the information in this figure, you shouldn't have much trouble figuring out how the HTML code works.

In general, you code one tag at the beginning of a definition and one at the end of the definition. For example, you code the <HTML> and </HTML> tags at the beginning and end of a page, and you code the <BODY> and </BODY> tags at the beginning and end of the body of the page. The body of a page contains the information that's actually displayed on the page.

You can also create style sheets within an HTML page that can be used throughout the page. To do that, you use the <STYLE> and </STYLE> tags as shown in the figure to name and define the styles. Then, you refer to the styles by name whenever you want to use them. In this figure, for example, the style named H1 is used to format the company name that's displayed at the top of the page, the style named H2 is used to format the page title and date, and the style named DATA is use to format the data on the page. You can look back to figure 14-7 to see how these styles affect the appearance of the page. After you specify a style in the body of the page, that style is used for any text or data that follows until an end tag for that style or a start tag for another style is specified.

The alternative to using styles is to use the <FONT> and </FONT> tags to define the font for specific areas of the page. If you use the same font in more than one area, though, you're better off defining a style for it so you don't have to repeat the font characteristics. You can also use specific tags to boldface, italicize, underline, or center an area.

Another set of tags you're likely to use in an HTML file are <A HREF> and </A>. These tags identify a hyperlink that when clicked will display another HTML page. Hyperlinks are the main technique for navigating in a web-based application. You'll learn how to use hyperlinks in an IIS application later in this chapter.

You can also include input elements like buttons and text boxes on an HTML page using the <INPUT TYPE> tag. This tag lets you create a variety of elements based on the *type* you specify. For more information on using this tag or any of the other tags that are available, we recommend you check out the web site for the W3C World Wide Web Consortium at www.w3.org/MarkUp.

HTML code for the page shown in figure 14-7

```
VendorList2.htm - Notepad                          _ □ X
File  Edit  Search  Help
<HTML>
<HEAD>
<TITLE>Mike Murach & Associates: Vendor List</TITLE>
</HEAD>
<STYLE>
H1 {font-family: Arial;font-weight: bold;font-size: 24px;}
H2 {font-family: Arial;font-size: 18px;}
DATA {font-family: Arial;font-size: 14px;}
</STYLE>
<BODY>
<H1>Mike Murach &amp; Associates<BR>
<H2>Vendor List<BR>
<WC@CURRENTDATE></WC@CURRENTDATE><HR>
<DATA><WC@VENDORDATA></WC@VENDORDATA>
</BODY></HTML>
```

Common HTML tags

Tag	Description
<HTML> & </HTML>	A page
<HEAD> & </HEAD>	A page header
<TITLE> & </TITLE>	The title that's displayed in the browser's title bar
<STYLE> & </STYLE>	One or more style definitions
<FONT> & </FONT>	Font characteristics
<BODY> & </BODY>	The part of the page that's displayed in the browser
<B> & </B>; <I> & </I>; <U> & </U>; <CENTER> & </CENTER>	Boldfaced, italicized, underlined, or centered text
 ; <P>	A line or paragraph break
<HR>	A horizontal line
<A HREF=*url*> linktext </A>	A hyperlink
<INPUT TYPE=*type* value=*value* name=*name*>	An input element like a button or text box
<TABLE> & </TABLE>	A table
<TD> & </TD>; <TR> & </TR>	A table column or row
<IMG SRC=imagefile>	A JPEG or GIF image
<! & ->	A comment

Description

- You can use an application like NotePad or Microsoft FrontPage to create an HTML page. After you enter the code for the page, save it with the extension HTM.

- You define an HTML page using tags like those shown above. Most of the tags are coded in pairs around the text they affect. A few, however, are self-contained.

- You can also code special tags, called webclass tags, that identify the text that will be replaced when the application is run. See figure 14-11 for details.

Figure 14-8   How to create an HTML page

How to use the Webclass Designer

Figure 14-9 presents the basic techniques for creating the webclasses of an IIS application using the Webclass Designer. When you first start an IIS project, it consists of a single webclass. If you display that webclass in the Webclass Designer window shown in this figure, you'll see that it consists of two folders that are displayed in the treeview panel of the window. The HTML Template WebItems folder will contain the templates for the HTML pages used by the application, and the Custom WebItems folder will contain custom items that you create. The application in this figure, for example, contains two templates: one for the page shown in figure 14-7 and one for the page that's displayed when you click on one of the hyperlinks in the first page. Note, however, that this application doesn't use any custom webitems.

When you add a template to a webclass, you identify the HTML file that contains the code for the page. Then, VB creates a copy of that page and stores it in the same folder as the other files in the project. If the original file is in the same folder, VB adds a number suffix to the file name so you can distinguish it from the original file. (That's why the file shown in figure 14-8 is named VendorList2 and not VendorList.) In other words, the application doesn't use the original HTML file. That way, two or more programmers can use the same file and customize it any way they like without affecting the original file.

To display and modify the code associated with an HTML template, you highlight the template and click on the Edit HTML Template button in the Webclass Designer toolbar. Then, the file is displayed in the Windows NotePad program unless you specify a different editor. To specify a different editor, use the Advanced tab of the Options dialog box.

As you'll see in the next figure, only three events are available for working with the templates and custom webitems in a webclass. To add more functionality to an application, however, you can add custom events to the templates and custom webitems. If, for example, you want the user to be able to display additional information on the ViewVendor page, you can add a hyperlink to the page that, when clicked, fires a custom event that displays the additional information. To accomplish that, you use the URLFor method of the WebClass object to associate the hyperlink with the custom event. You'll learn the basics of using this method later in this chapter.

One more thing you should notice in this figure is the TagPrefix property for the ViewVendor webitem. This property indicates the prefix that's used for the webclass tags in the HTML file. In most cases, you'll use the default prefix of WC@. However, you can change this to any prefix you like, and you can use different prefixes for different webitems.

How to use the Webclass Designer

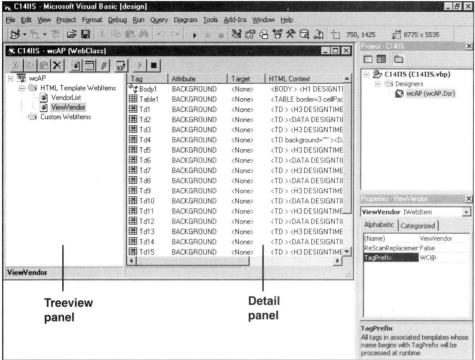

Description

- To start an IIS application, select the IIS Application option from the New Project dialog box. By default, the IIS project includes a single webclass.

- To open the Webclass Designer for a webclass, double-click on it in the Project Explorer. To add a new webclass, select Add Webclass from the Project menu or the shortcut menu for the Project Explorer.

- The left panel of the Webclass Designer window (the treeview panel) displays the templates and custom webitems defined for the webclass. The right panel (the detail panel) displays detail information for the selected webclass item.

- To add an HTML template to a webclass, click the Add HTML Template WebItem button in the Web Designer toolbar. Then, identify the HTML file in the dialog box that's displayed.

- To edit the HTML code for a template, highlight the template and click on the Edit HTML Template toolbar button. This displays the HTML file in your default HTML editor.

- To add a Custom WebItem, click on the Add Custom WebItem toolbar button.

- To add a custom event for a template or custom webitem, highlight the template or webitem and then click on the Add Custom Event toolbar button.

- The TagPrefix property for a template or custom webitem indicates the prefix that is used to identify webclass tags in the HTML code. The default prefix is WC@.

Figure 14-9   How to use the Webclass Designer

How to develop the code for an IIS application

Figure 14-10 presents the webclass and webitem events you can respond to in an IIS application. Then, the code in this figure illustrates how you might use three of these events. This code also uses a couple of the properties and methods that are available for WebClass and WebItem objects. To display the Code window for a webclass, you can double-click on the webclass or any webclass item in the treeview panel.

If you display the Code window when you first start an IIS project, you'll notice that the Start event of the webclass that's added to the project by default already includes some code. This code sends some information to the browser indicating that the start event was processed. To do that, it uses the Write method of the Response object, which is one of the objects in the ASP object model.

Normally, you'll replace the default code in the Start event with code like that shown in the first event procedure in this figure. In this case, the code sets the NextItem property of the webclass to the VendorList template. That causes the page associated with this template to be displayed when the user starts the webclass by entering the URL for its ASP file into a browser.

When the NextItem property is set to the name of a webitem, the Respond event for that webitem is fired. The second procedure in this figure shows the code for this event for the VendorList template. Here, the WriteTemplate method of the template is used to display the VendorList page in the browser that requested it.

The third procedure in this figure is for the ProcessTag event of the VendorList template. This event is fired when the WriteTemplate method is used to display a page in the browser and the page contains webclass tags. This event fires for each webclass tag in the file so the appropriate processing can be done for that tag. You'll learn the details of using webclass tags and the ProcessTag event in the next figure.

The only webitem event that's not illustrated in this figure is UserEvent. This event is fired for an event that's defined at run-time. In other words, it fires when an event occurs that's not defined by the webclass. In the next figure, for example, you'll see the procedure that's used to display the list of vendors on the VendorList page. Within this procedure, the URLFor method is used to define the hyperlinks that let the user display the ViewVendor page for each vendor. For now, just realize that for this to work, the Vendor ID of the selected vendor must be returned to the webclass. In this case, the Vendor ID is returned as the name of an event. Then, the UserEvent procedure can be used to display the information for the appropriate vendor.

Webclass events

Event	Description
Initialize	Occurs when an instance of the webclass is created.
BeginRequest	Occurs when the user issues a request from the browser to the webclass.
EndRequest	Occurs after the webclass processes a request and sends a response to the browser.
FatalErrorResponse	Occurs when the processing of a webclass is terminated due to an error.
Start	Occurs when the user starts the webclass from a browser by specifying the URL for the webclass' ASP file. Occurs after the BeginRequest event.
Terminate	Occurs when the web class goes out of scope.

Webitem events

Event	Description
Respond	Occurs when a webitem is activated by a user request if a custom event has not been defined for the item.
ProcessTag	Occurs when the WriteTemplate method is issued on a template. Used to replace the contents of webclass tags in the HTML page.
UserEvent	Occurs when an event defined at run-time is fired.

Code that responds to webclass and webitem events

```
Private Sub WebClass_Start()
    Set NextItem = VendorList
End Sub

Private Sub VendorList_Respond()
    VendorList.WriteTemplate
End Sub

Private Sub VendorList_ProcessTag(ByVal TagName As String, _
        TagContents As String, SendTags As Boolean)
    Select Case TagName
        Case "WC@CURRENTDATE"
            TagContents = Format$(Date, "mmmm d, yyyy")
        Case "WC@VENDORDATA"
            TagContents = VendorData
    End Select
End Sub
```

Description

- The code for an IIS application responds to events on the webclass and the webitems it contains.
- NextItem is a property of a webclass that indicates the next webitem to be processed.
- WriteTemplate is a method of a webclass that's used to send a template or custom webitem to the browser.

Figure 14-10   How to develop the code for an IIS application

How to use webclass tags to display data on an HTML page

Figure 14-11 shows how to use webclass tags in an IIS application. First, you include the tags in the HTML file as shown at the top of this figure. Note that the tags are included in the file in the location where the replacement text will appear at run-time. Also note that you can include default text between the starting and ending webclass tags. In fact, it's this text, or the *tag contents*, that are replaced when the page is displayed. In many cases, though, the tag contents are empty as in this example.

When the page is displayed, the ProcessTag event occurs for each webclass tag in the page. The arguments that are passed to this event include the tag name and the tag contents. Then, the tag name can be used to determine which tag is being processed, and the tag contents can be set to the appropriate value for that tag. The procedure in this figure, for example, sets the tag contents to the current date for the WC@CURRENTDATE tag. And it sets the tag contents to the value of the VendorData function for the WC@VENDORDATA tag. When the procedure finishes, the new tag contents are displayed on the page.

Now that you understand how to use webclass tags, you should take a minute to study the code in the VendorData function that creates the contents of the WC@VENDORDATA tag. As you can see, this function creates a string variable that contains HTML code. This code includes HTML tags that define a table that's used to display the vendor information. The vendor data that's included in the table is retrieved from a recordset that's created at the beginning of the function. (This code isn't shown in the figure, but it's the same as the code for any other ADO recordset.)

Because the name of each vendor is to be included on the page as a hyperlink, the <A HREF> tag is used to display the VendorName field. Within this tag, the URLFor method is used to identify the template that will be displayed when the hyperlink is clicked. This method also identifies the event that will fire when the hyperlink is clicked. In this case, the name of the event is the value of the VendorID field. Because that event isn't defined by the webclass, the UserEvent event will fire instead. Because the event name (VendorID) is passed to the UserEvent event, the procedure for that event can retrieve the vendor record for the VendorID and then use the WriteTemplate method to display the ViewVendor page.

How to test and build an IIS application

Before you run an application to test it, you'll want to be sure that the Start Component option in the Debugging tab of the Project Properties dialog box is set so the appropriate webclass is executed when the program starts. By default, the webclass that's included when you first start the project is set as the starting component, which is usually what you want.

HTML code that contains webclass tags

```
<WC@CURRENTDATE></WC@CURRENTDATE><HR>
<H4><WC@VENDORDATA></WC@VENDORDATA></H4></H3></H1>
```

Visual Basic code that replaces the contents of the webclass tags

```
Private Sub VendorList_ProcessTag(ByVal TagName As String, _
        TagContents As String, SendTags As Boolean)
    Select Case TagName
        Case "WC@CURRENTDATE"
            TagContents = Format$(Date, "mmmm d, yyyy")
        Case "WC@VENDORDATA"
            TagContents = VendorData
    End Select
End Sub

Private Function VendorData() As String
    Dim strHTML As String
        .
        .
    strHTML = "<TABLE CELLPADDING=1 BORDER=1>" & vbCr _
            & "<TR><TH><H4>Vendor Name</TH>" & vbCr _
            & "<TH>City</TH>" & vbCr & "<TH>State</TH>" & vbCr _
            & "<TH>Phone</TH>" & vbCr & "</TR>" & vbCr
    Do While Not mrsVendors.EOF
        strHTML = strHTML & "<TR>" & vbCr & "<TD><A HREF=""" _
                & URLFor(ViewVendor, CStr(mrsVendors("VendorID"))) _
                & """>" & mrsVendors!VendorName & "</A></TD>" & vbCr _
                & "<TD>" & mrsVendors!VendorCity & "</TD>" & vbCr _
                & "<TD>" & mrsVendors!VendorState & "</TD>" & vbCr _
                & "<TD>" & mrsVendors!VendorPhone & "</TD>" & vbCr _
                & "</TR>" & vbCr
        mrsVendors.MoveNext
    Loop
    strHTML = strHTML & "</TABLE>" & vbCr & "<HR><H3>"
    VendorData = strHTML
        .
        .
End Function
```

Description

- To display data on an HTML page, you use webclass tags. These are special tags that you use to identify the location of the data on the page.

- When you create a webclass tag, you prefix its name with the prefix specified in the TagPrefix property of the HTML template. Then, you code an end tag that's prefixed with a slash (/). You can also code default text (the tag contents) between the start and end tags.

- When a page that contains webclass tags is displayed at run-time, the ProcessTag event is fired. The procedure for this event receives the name of the current tag and the tag contents as arguments. You can use these arguments within the procedure to replace the tag contents with the appropriate data.

- The SendTags argument indicates whether the tags or only the tag contents are returned to the page. The default is to send only the tag contents.

Figure 14-11   How to use webclass tags to display data on an HTML page

The first time you run the application, Visual Basic displays a dialog box that lets you confirm the name of the *virtual directory* that will be created for the project. This virtual directory, also called a *virtual root*, is used during testing so the application can display its pages in the browser. When the application is deployed, it will be stored in a subdirectory of the home directory of the web server so it can be accessed by the browser.

When you're done testing and debugging an application, you use the Make command in the File menu to build it. This creates the DLL file for the application as well as the ASP file for each webclass. Then, you can use the Package and Deployment Wizard as described in chapter 15 to deploy the application on a web server.

Perspective

After reading this chapter, you should have a good idea of what's involved in developing Internet applications with Visual Basic. In addition, you should have a general feel for the strengths and weaknesses of DHTML and IIS applications. Because DHTML lets you develop the pages for an application using a graphic designer, for example, it's much easier to develop forms that contain a variety of elements that let you enter and update data. On the other hand, you can manipulate the HTML code for a page more easily with an IIS application.

Because this chapter presents only the basic concepts and skills you need for developing Internet applications, you'll want to learn more before you try to develop a sophisticated business application. The best way to do that is to review the material that's available with online help. This information is also included in printed format in the *Microsoft Visual Basic 6.0 Reference Library* that's available from Microsoft.

Terms you should know

web server	element
browser	cookie
page	hyperlink
Uniform Resource Locator (URL)	webclass
HyperText Markup Language (HTML)	webitem
HTML page	webclass tag
Dynamic HTML (DHTML)	HTML tag
Internet Information Server (IIS)	tag contents
Active Server Pages (ASP)	virtual directory (or virtual root)

15

How to distribute an application

After you complete a project, you need to install it on the machines that will run the application. To do that, you can use the Package and Deployment Wizard that comes with Visual Basic to create a setup program for it. Then, you can run that setup program to install the application and all of the files it requires on each of the client machines. Or, you can run the setup program to install the application on an intranet or Internet server so the clients can access the program from that server.

An introduction to the Package and Deployment Wizard 544
How the Package and Deployment Wizard works 544
How to install the Package and Deployment Wizard 546
How to start the Package and Deployment Wizard 546
How to work with the Package and Deployment Wizard 548

How to distribute an application 550
Step 1: Create the package 550
Step 2: Deploy the package 558
Step 3: Run the setup program to install the application 562
Exercise set 15-1: Install the Accounts Payable application 564

Other deployment issues 566
How to work with scripts 566
How to handle missing dependency information 568
How to create a dependency file for an ActiveX component or control 570
How to create an installation CD 570
A summary of the files in the Package and Support folders 572
How to deploy Internet applications 574
Exercise set 15-2: Install the Book Orders application 576

Perspective 578

An introduction to the Package and Deployment Wizard

The Package and Deployment Wizard is an add-in program that comes with Visual Basic. To help you understand this wizard, this chapter starts by describing how the wizard works. Then, it shows you how to install, start, and work with this wizard.

How the Package and Deployment Wizard works

Figure 15-1 shows how the Package and Deployment Wizard uses input files and creates output files. For the most part, the wizard automatically identifies all input files and automatically creates the required output files, including the setup program. However, the choices you make as you use the wizard can affect those input and output files.

To identify the input files, the Package and Deployment Wizard analyzes the project file. In particular, it checks the references that are specified in the References dialog box, and it checks the components that are specified in the Components dialog box. Then, the wizard creates the setup program, the setup list, and the compressed files that contain all of the other files that need to be installed if the application is to work right.

Each time you use the Package and Deployment Wizard, the wizard saves your choices in a *script*. Then, the next time you use the wizard, you can use or modify any of the previously saved scripts. As a result, a script is both an input and an output file.

If the application you're distributing includes any third party files or components, you should be sure to check their license agreements. That's because some manufacturers require that you pay a royalty fee each time the file or component is distributed to a new user. If you're not sure whether you can distribute a file or component without paying a royalty fee, be sure to contact the manufacturer. Note, however, that you can freely distribute the files in the Visual Basic Graphics, ODBC, Samples, and Icons folders.

Input and output files used by the Package and Deployment Wizard

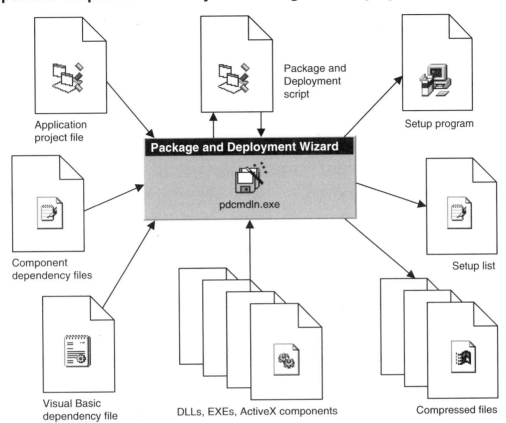

Description

- The Package and Deployment Wizard is a Visual Basic add-in that you can use to create a setup program named Setup.exe for a Visual Basic application. Then, you can use that setup program to *install* the application on one or more clients.

- The Package and Deployment Wizard stores information about all the required files in a file named Setup.lst. Then, when you run the setup program for the project, it uses the Setup.lst file to determine how each file is registered and installed.

- Besides creating the setup program and the Setup.lst file, the Package and Deployment Wizard compresses all the files required by the application and saves them to the location you specify. These files include the executable file for the project and all other files required by the application.

- When you use the Package and Deployment Wizard to package or deploy an application, it saves all of your choices in a *script*. Then, if you need to package or deploy the application again, you can use the script or you can modify the script.

Figure 15-1   How the Package and Deployment Wizard works

How to install the Package and Deployment Wizard

Figure 15-2 shows how to use the Add-In Manager dialog box to install the Package and Deployment Wizard as an *add-in program*. Once this wizard is installed, its command name appears on the Add-Ins menu for all Visual Basic applications.

How to start the Package and Deployment Wizard

After you install this wizard, you can start it by selecting the Package and Deployment Wizard command from the Add-Ins menu. Then, the wizard will run within the Visual Basic project and automatically select the current project as shown in the next figure. Since this is the most convenient and least error-prone way to start this wizard, this is the one that you'll use when you do the exercise sets for this chapter.

Note, however, that there are two other ways to run the Package and Deployment Wizard. First, you can run this wizard as a *stand-alone application* by selecting it from the Windows Start menu. Then, the Package and Deployment Wizard will run in its own window and you have to select the project you want to work with.

Second, you can run the Package and Deployment Wizard in *silent mode* by starting a DOS prompt and entering a command line with switches that identify the scripts to be used and other options. In this case, you don't see any dialog boxes except the one that notifies you that the operation is complete. Although this mode was designed to automate the distribution process, it's harder to use and it provides little advantage over using the wizard as an add-in program. For more information about using silent mode, though, you can look up "Silent mode, the Package and Deployment Wizard" in online help.

The Add-In Manager dialog box

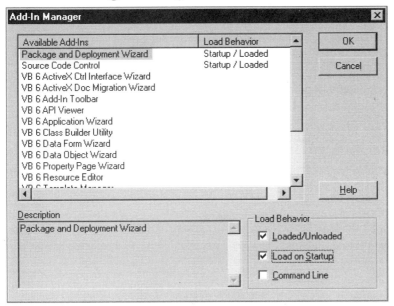

How to install the Package and Deployment Wizard as an add-in

1. Select the Add-In Manager command from the Add-Ins menu to display the dialog box shown above.

2. If necessary, select Package and Deployment Wizard from the Available Add-Ins list as shown above.

3. Check the Loaded/Unloaded and Load on Startup options as shown above.

4. Click on the OK button. After that, the Package and Deployment Wizard command will appear at the bottom of the Add-Ins menu.

Three ways to start the Package and Deployment Wizard

1. You normally start the wizard as an *add-in program* by selecting the Package and Deployment Wizard command from the Add-Ins menu. Then, it appears as a dialog box within Visual Basic, and it automatically selects the current project as shown in the next figure.

2. You can start the wizard as a *stand-alone application* by selecting it from the Windows Start menu. Then, it will run in its own window and you have to select the project you want to work with.

3. You can start the wizard in *silent mode* by issuing an appropriate command from a DOS prompt. When you use this method, the Package and Deployment Wizard dialog box isn't displayed.

Figure 15-2   How to install and start the Package and Deployment Wizard

How to work with the Package and Deployment Wizard

Before you start the Package and Deployment Wizard as an add-in program, you open the project you want to distribute. Then, you should use the References and Components dialog boxes to make sure that only required references and components are selected. However, since some of these references and components are added automatically, you shouldn't remove any unless you're certain that they aren't needed. Similarly, you should use the Project Properties dialog box to make sure that the Project Name and Project Description properties are set correctly. Last, you should use the Make command in the File menu to create an executable file for the project, and you should save the project.

Once you've done that housekeeping, you can start the Package and Deployment Wizard command from the Add-Ins menu. When the wizard starts, the dialog box in figure 15-3 is displayed. At the top of this screen, you can see the path and name for the project file.

In step 1 of the general procedure for distributing an application, you click on the Package button to *package* the project. Then, the wizard displays a series of dialog boxes that walk you through the packaging procedure. When you finish this procedure, the wizard creates the output files needed to install the project.

In step 2, you click on the Deploy button to *deploy* the project. After that, the wizard displays a series of dialog boxes that walk you through the deployment procedure. When you finish this procedure, the wizard copies the packaged files to the location that you have specified. Because the files are large, that usually means copying the package for the project to a shared network folder, a CD, or an intranet or Internet server, but the wizard can also copy the files to a series of diskettes.

In step 3, to complete the installation procedure, the setup program needs to be run from the client PCs. The most efficient way to do that is to run the setup program from a shared network folder or from an intranet or Internet server. But if the client PC doesn't have access to a server, you can run the setup program from a CD or diskettes.

The third button in the opening dialog box for the Package and Deployment Wizard lets you manage the scripts for the current project. If you click on this button, a dialog box is displayed that lets you rename, duplicate, and delete the *packaging scripts* that are created when you package a project or the *deployment scripts* that are created when you deploy a project. You'll learn more about the use of scripts as you proceed through this chapter.

The main screen for the Package and Deployment Wizard

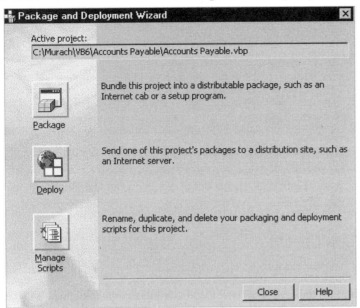

A general procedure for distributing an application

1. Click on the Package button to *package* the project. This package will include (1) the Setup.exe file, (2) the Setup.lst file, and (3) one or more compressed files that contain all files needed to install the project. In addition, this process will create a Support folder that contains the uncompressed versions of all files needed by the application.

2. Click on the Deploy button to *deploy* the package to a shared network folder, to diskettes, or to an intranet or Internet server. That way, the setup program will be available to other PCs.

3. Run the setup program from each end-user's PC to install all the files needed to run the application.

How to manage scripts

- To manage the scripts that the Package and Deployment Wizard uses, click on the Manage Scripts button. Then, you can use the Manage Scripts dialog box to rename, duplicate, and delete *packaging scripts* and *deployment scripts* (see figure 15-7).

Figure 15-3   How to work with the Package and Deployment Wizard

How to distribute an application

Now that you have a general idea of how the Package and Deployment Wizard works, you're ready for more details about each of the three major steps.

Step 1: Create the package

Figure 15-4 shows eight of the dialog boxes that you use to create a package for a project. These are the dialog boxes that are displayed when you click on the Package button in the first dialog box for the Package and Deployment Wizard. Although this may seem like a lot of dialog boxes, the defaults for most of them are set correctly when they're displayed so you usually don't need to change many of the options.

Before the first dialog box in this figure is displayed, other dialog boxes may be displayed that tell you that the project needs to be saved, compiled, or recompiled before you continue. In that case, you can usually click on the Yes button to save, compile, or recompile the project. Occasionally, though, that won't work right so you have to close the wizard and use the Save Project or Make commands from the File menu to save, compile, or recompile the project. Before you do that, you may also need to change some settings in the Project Properties dialog box.

Once that housekeeping is done, the Package Type dialog box in this figure is displayed, and you can select the type of package you want to create. For most projects, you will select the Standard Setup Package option. Later in this chapter, though, you'll learn when and how to use the Dependency File option to create a dependency file. In addition, you'll learn about using a third option, called the Internet Package option, that lets you create a package that can be deployed to the Internet.

In the Package Folder dialog box that's displayed next, you can select the folder that the package should be stored in once its created. By default, the wizard selects the folder that contains the project file, and the wizard suggests that a subfolder called Package be created for storing the package. If you accept this suggestion, the wizard displays a dialog box that tells you that it is about to create the Package folder. Then, you can click on the Yes button to create the folder. No matter what folder you select as the folder for the package, though, the wizard automatically creates a Support subfolder for it.

Later, when the wizard finishes its packaging procedure, the package is stored in both the Package and Support folders, but in two different formats. The Package folder usually contains the Setup.exe file, Setup.lst file, and a compressed file that contains all files that make up your application. The Support folder contains all the files that make up your application in an uncompressed form. This folder also includes a batch file that allows you to rebuild the compressed file if any of the existing project files are changed.

The Package Type dialog box

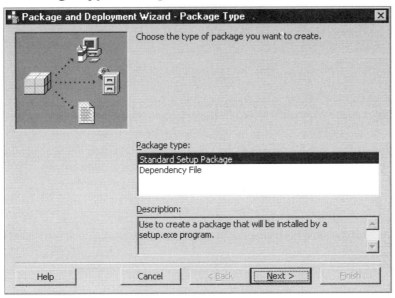

The Package Folder dialog box

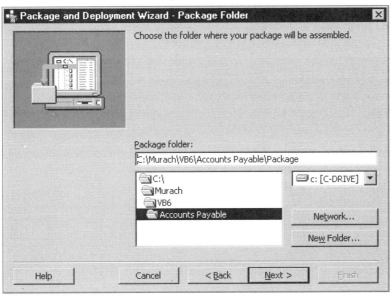

Figure 15-4   How to create a package (part 1 of 4)

The Included Files dialog box lists all files that the wizard intends to include in the setup program. This list includes files needed by your application as well as files used by the setup program itself. If you position the mouse pointer over the name for one of the files, the wizard will display a ToolTip that gives you some information about the file.

Since the wizard usually identifies the right files, you shouldn't need to make any changes to this dialog box. However, if you notice that a required file is missing, you can click on the Add button to add that file to the package. Similarly, if you're absolutely sure that an unnecessary file has been included, you can uncheck the box to the left of the file to remove the file from the package. When in doubt, though, it's better to include any questionable files.

The Cab Options dialog box lets you choose whether you want to create a single CAB file or multiple CAB files for the package. A *cabinet file*, or *CAB file*, is a type of compressed file that can contain one or more other files. It is similar to a ZIP file, but it was developed by Microsoft. By default, the wizard selects the Single Cab option so all of the setup files, with the exception of the Setup.exe and the Setup.lst file, are stored in a single CAB file. Since this is usually faster and easier than working with multiple files, you should use this option whenever you intend to deploy your application to a shared network folder, a CD, or to an intranet or Internet server.

The only time you don't want to use the Single Cab option is when you want to deploy your application to diskettes. In that case, you should select the Multiple Cabs option, and use the Cab Size combo box to select a cab size that corresponds to the diskette size that your PC uses. Then, when you deploy the application, the wizard will create CAB files that are small enough to fit on your diskettes. It will also copy the Setup.exe and Setup.lst files onto the first diskette.

The Included Files dialog box

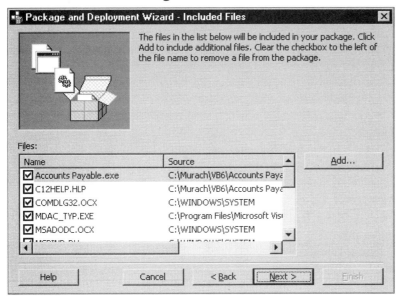

The Cab Options dialog box

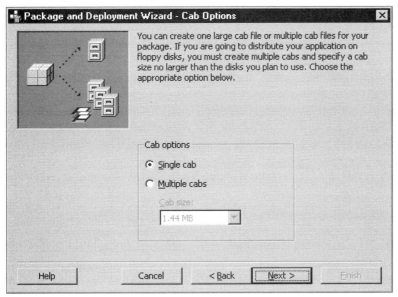

Figure 15-4   How to create a package (part 2 of 4)

After the Cab Options dialog box, the Installation Title dialog box is displayed. Although this dialog box isn't shown in this figure, it contains a single text box that you can use to set the title that will be used when the setup program is run. In addition, the title in this dialog box will be used as the default group and item name in the Start Menu Items dialog box that's shown next.

The Start Menu Items dialog box lets you choose where your application will appear in the Start menu. By default, the item for your application will appear in its own group directly below the Programs group. Since this is standard for most Windows applications, you can usually accept this setting.

If this isn't acceptable, though, you can use the four buttons on the right side of the dialog box to create new groups or items, to modify the properties of the selected groups or items, or to remove existing groups or items. For example, you can use the New Item button to add an item for the help file to the Accounts Payable group.

After that, the Install Locations dialog box shows the install locations for all of the files that will be installed by your setup program. Here, the wizard gives the install locations for the files as macros that may point to different paths depending on some system variables. Two of the most important macros are the $(WinSysPath) macro and the $(AppPath) macros.

The path specified by the $(WinSysPath) macro depends on the operating system. With Windows 95 and 98, the $(WinSysPath) macro refers to the Windows\System folder. With Windows NT, however, the same macro refers to the Windows\System32 folder. Either way, this folder contains the system files that are used by Windows and Windows applications, such as DLL, EXE, and OCX files.

The path specified by the $(AppPath) macro depends on the setup program. By default, most applications are installed in a subfolder of the Program Files folder on the C drive. For example, the Accounts Payable application is usually installed in the C:\Program Files\Accounts Payable folder. In that case, the $(AppPath) macro points to that folder. However, if the Accounts Payable application is installed in another folder, the $(AppPath) macro points to that folder. For information about the other install location macros, click on the Help button in this dialog box.

For most applications, the wizard sets the install locations appropriately. As a result, you usually don't need to change the install location for a file. If you want to change the default location for a file, though, you can click in the Install Location column and select a different macro from a drop-down list. In addition, you can specify a subfolder by typing a backslash and the folder name after the macro name as shown here:

```
$(AppPath)\Samples
```

Later, when you run the setup program, the setup program will create that subfolder.

The Start Menu Items dialog box

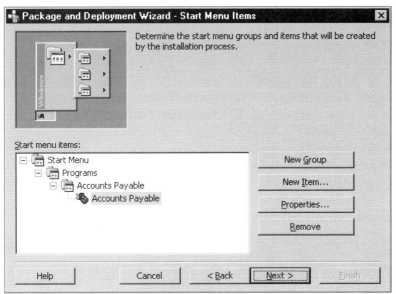

The Install Locations dialog box

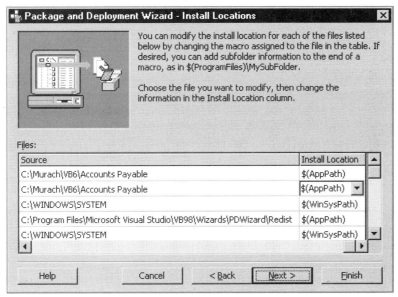

Figure 15-4   How to create a package (part 3 of 4)

The Shared Files dialog box lets you mark one or more files as shared. Then, if you uninstall your application, the shared files won't be removed until all other applications that use those files are uninstalled. Unless you develop several programs that share common files, though, you won't need to mark any files as shared.

Last, the Finished dialog box lets you enter a name for the packaging script. This script saves all the settings in the previous dialog boxes. Although you can accept the default script name of Standard Setup Package 1, you can also modify that default name as shown here. Similarly, if you've made changes to an existing script, you can save the current script under a new name.

When you click on the Finish button, the wizard displays a dialog box that contains a packaging report. This report usually tells you that the Package and Support folders have been created. After you read the report, you can save it by clicking on the Save button or you can close the dialog box by clicking on the Close button.

Note, however that this report may include a message that says, "You have included mdac_typ.exe in your installation package. If you will be installing this package on a Windows 95/98 system, it will require DCOM98 to install properly." All this means is that you may need to install DCOM98 on some systems before you run the applications that you install. If so, you can download information about installing DCOM98 and the files needed to install DCOM98 from Microsoft's web site.

The Shared Files dialog box

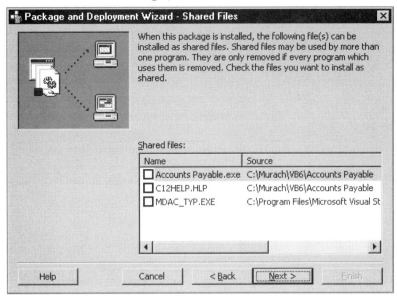

The Finished dialog box

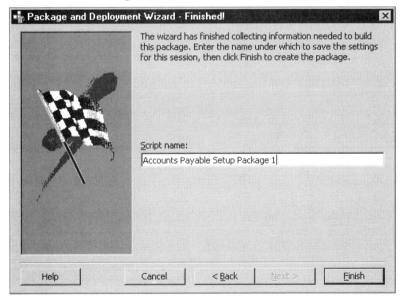

Figure 15-4   How to create a package (part 4 of 4)

Step 2: Deploy the package

Once you package an application, you can deploy it to a shared network folder as shown in figure 15-5. This figure shows four of the dialog boxes that are displayed when you click on the Deploy button in the main dialog box for the Package and Deployment Wizard. Although these dialog boxes show how to deploy an application to a network folder, you can also use them to deploy an application to diskettes or to an intranet or Internet server.

The Package to Deploy dialog box lets you select the package you want to deploy. To do that, you use the combo box to select the packaging script that you created when you created the package for the project.

Then, the Deployment Method dialog box lets you select the type of deployment. For most standard applications, you'll select the Folder option. But if you packaged the application into multiple CAB files, the Diskettes option will also be available. Similarly, if you want to deploy the application to an intranet or Internet server, you can select the Web Publishing option. You'll learn more about that later.

The Package to Deploy dialog box

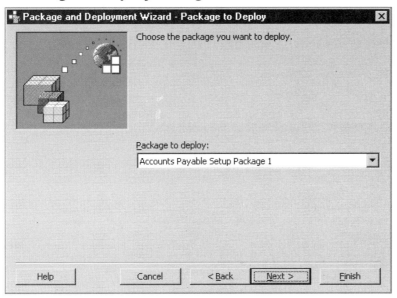

The Deployment Method dialog box

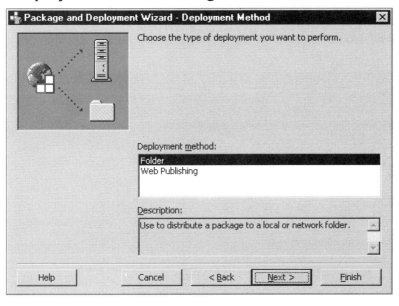

Figure 15-5   How to deploy a package (part 1 of 2)

The Folder dialog box lets you select the folder that will be used to store the setup program. If the network folder you want is mapped to a drive letter, you can select the drive from the drive combo box. Then, you can select the folder you want from the folder list box. Otherwise, you can click on the Network button to browse through all of the available folders on your network.

Most of the time, though, you'll want to create a subfolder that's subordinate to the one you select. To do that, you click on the New Folder button and enter the name of the subfolder. In this dialog box, for example, you can see that the name of the subfolder is Accounts Payable Setup, which is subordinate to the Visual Basic 6 folder. That way, anyone browsing the network can easily find the Setup.exe file that's used to install the Accounts Payable application.

In the Finished dialog box, you can accept the default name or enter a new name for the deployment script that has been created. This script contains all of the choices that you made in the deployment dialog boxes. In some cases, you will want to create one script for deploying a package to a folder, and then re-run the wizard to create another script for deploying the package to CD or diskettes.

When you click on the Finish button in this dialog box, you'll see a dialog box that gives you a deployment report. Usually, you can read this report and click on the Close button to close the report without saving it. But if you decide that there's a reason to save the report, you can click on the Save button to save it.

The Folder dialog box

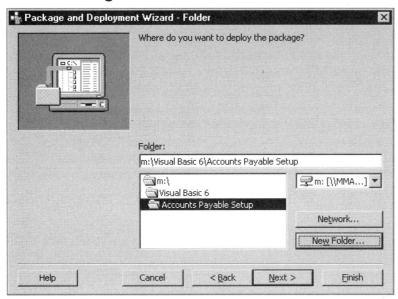

The Finished dialog box

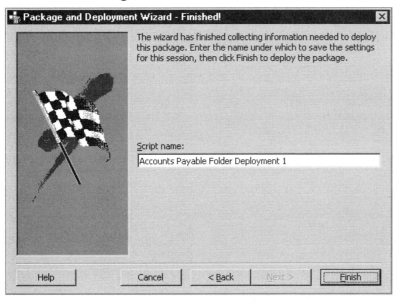

Figure 15-5   How to deploy a package (part 2 of 2)

Step 3: Run the setup program to install the application

After you deploy the application to a server, a CD, or diskettes, you need to install the application on each PC that is going to use it. To start this process, you find the folder that contains the setup program and double-click on its name as summarized in figure 15-6. There, you can see the dialog boxes that are displayed when you run a setup program that has been created by the Package and Deployment Wizard.

Like most setup programs, this setup program begins by welcoming you to the installation program and recommending that you close all applications that are running. Then, this setup program displays a dialog box that lets you confirm the folder that the application is going to be installed in. If the default folder is acceptable, you can click on the large icon on the left side of the dialog box to install the application. But if you want to change the installation folder, you can click on the Change Directory button.

If the setup program fails or the application doesn't install properly, you can use the Add/Remove Programs icon in the Control Panel to uninstall the application as summarized in this figure. Then, you can use the Package and Deployment Wizard to create a new setup package that corrects the problem.

The first setup dialog box

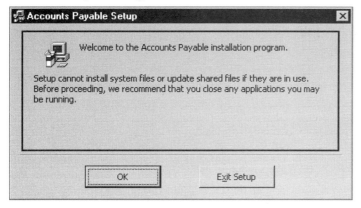

The second setup dialog box

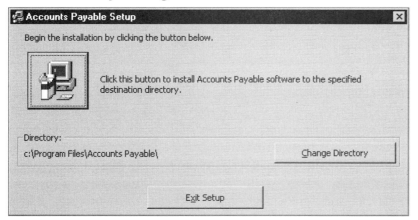

Description

- To install an application, start the Windows Explorer, navigate to the folder that contains the Setup.exe file for the application, and double-click on the file. When you do, the setup program displays dialog boxes like the ones shown above. To continue from the first dialog box, click on the OK button. To continue from the second dialog box, click on the large button that contains the computer icon.

- To cancel the setup procedure, you can click on the Exit Setup button in either dialog box. Then, the setup program will uninstall itself and any files that have been installed so far.

- To change the folder where the application will be installed, click on the Change Directory button in the second dialog box. Then, you can specify the folder you want used.

- To uninstall an application, open the Windows Control Panel, double-click on the Add/Remove Programs icon, select the application you want to remove, and click on the Add/Remove button.

Figure 15-6   How to use the setup program to install an application

Exercise set 15-1: Install the Accounts Payable application

In this exercise set, you'll create a setup program for the MDI version of the Accounts Payable application that you created in chapter 12. Then, you'll use this setup program to install this application, and you'll use the Control Panel to uninstall this application.

Use Visual Basic to open and test the application

1. Start Visual Basic and open the MDI version of the Accounts Payable project you created for chapter 12 (or one you created for chapter 6, 7, or 8).

2. Select the Project Properties command from the Project menu to display the Project Properties dialog box. Then, set the Project Name property to AccountsPayable, and save the project with the name Accounts Payable.

3. Test the project to make sure that it works correctly. If it doesn't, fix any problems before you continue.

4. Select the Add-In Manager command from the Add-Ins menu. This should display the Add-In Manager dialog box. Then, check the box for the Package and Deployment Wizard, check the Loaded/Unloaded option, check the Load on Startup option, and click on the OK button. When you do, Visual Basic should add the Package and Deployment Wizard command to the Add-Ins menu.

Use the Package and Deployment Wizard to create the package

5. Select the Package and Deployment Wizard from the Add-Ins menu. This should start the Package and Deployment Wizard with the current project selected. If you see a message that says you need to save the project before you can continue, click on the Yes button to save the project.

6. Click on the Package button. If you see a message that says the project must have an executable file, click on the Compile button to compile the project and create the executable file. If you see a message that says the source files are newer than the executable file, click on the Yes button to recompile the application.

7. Use the Next button to move through the nine dialog boxes of the wizard as shown in figure 15-4. In general, the default settings should be appropriate, but you should read all of the dialog boxes carefully to see what the wizard is doing. When you get to the last dialog box, enter Accounts Payable Setup Package 1 as the name of the script, but don't click on the Finish button.

8. With the last dialog box still open, use the Back button to review all settings. In particular, make sure that the Package subfolder has been created and selected. If you don't understand any of these dialog boxes, click on the Help button and review the help information. When you're satisfied with the wizard's settings, click on the Finish button, read the packaging report that's displayed, and click on the Close button.

Use the Package and Deployment wizard to deploy the package

9. Click on the Deploy button, select Accounts Payable Setup Package 1, and click on the Next button. Then, select the Folder option and click on the Next button.

10. Select or create the folder you want. If you have access to a network, select a network folder. Otherwise, create a new folder on your hard drive. When you're done, click on the Next button. Then, enter an appropriate deployment script name, and click on the Finish button.

11. Read the deployment report that's displayed. Then, click on the Close button to return to the main screen for the Package and Deployment Wizard.

12. Click on the Close button to close the Package and Deployment Wizard. Then, exit from Visual Basic.

Install the Accounts Payable application

13. If you deployed the application to a network folder, you can move to another PC running under Windows 95, NT, or 98 that has access to that folder. Otherwise, you can stay at your PC.

14. Close all open applications and start the Windows Explorer. Then, navigate to the deployment folder and double-click on the Setup.exe file. At the first setup dialog box, you can click on the OK button. At the second setup dialog box, the path for the application should be C:\Program Files\Accounts Payable. If so, continue to install the application. Otherwise, click on the Change Directory button to create and select the C:\Program Files\Accounts Payable folder, then continue the installation.

15. Use the Start menu to start the Accounts Payable application. To do that, select the Programs menu, the Accounts Payable submenu, and the Accounts Payable application. Then, test the application. When you're satisfied that the application works correctly, exit from it.

16. Use the Windows Explorer to navigate to the C:\Program Files\Accounts Payable folder. Notice how this folder contains the EXE file for the Accounts Payable application, the help file, and a text file that's used by the uninstall application.

Uninstall the Accounts Payable application

17. Open the Windows Control Panel and double-click on the Add/Remove Programs icon. Then, select Accounts Payable and click on the Add/Remove button. When Windows asks you if you're sure, click on the Yes button so the program is uninstalled.

18. Open the Start menu, select the Programs command, and notice that the Accounts Payable folder isn't available any more. Next, switch to the Windows Explorer and notice that the Program Files folder no longer contains the Accounts Payable folder. Then, exit from the Explorer.

Other deployment issues

Although this chapter has already presented the skills that you need for installing most applications, the rest of this chapter presents some other deployment issues that you should be aware of.

How to work with scripts

When you use the Package and Deployment Wizard to package and deploy a project, the wizard saves the packaging script and the deployment script. Later, if you need to package or deploy the project again, the wizard displays a list of the saved scripts as shown in figure 15-7 so you can choose the one you want to use. After you choose a script, you can click on the Finish button to run the entire script, or you can click on the Next button to move through the dialog boxes that let you modify the script.

Once a project contains several scripts, you may need to use the Manage Scripts dialog box to work with them as shown in this figure. You can use this dialog box to rename, duplicate, or delete any of the scripts for the project.

Although you often need just one packaging script and one deployment script for each project, there are reasons why you may want to have more than one packaging or deployment script for a project. If, for example, you want to deploy an application in a network folder as well as on a CD, you need two deployment scripts. Or, if the setup procedure doesn't work right, you can save the original package settings in one script while you experiment with new settings in other scripts.

The wizard dialog box that let's you select a script

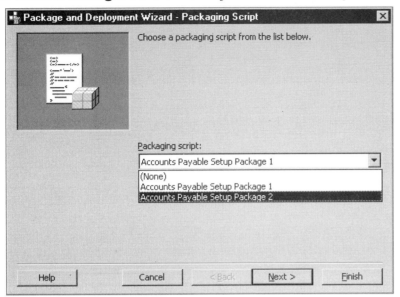

The Manage Scripts dialog box

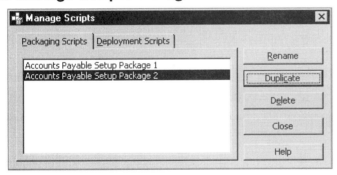

Desciption

- The first dialog box shown above is displayed when you begin packaging or deploying a project that already contains a script. From this dialog box, you can select the script you want. Then, you can click on the Finish button to execute the script or you can use the Next button to move though the script and modify it. You can also select the None option to start a new script that uses the default settings for the wizard.

- The second dialog box shown above can be used to rename, duplicate, or delete existing scripts. To access this dialog box, start the Package and Deployment Wizard and click on the Manage Scripts button.

Figure 15-7   How to work with scripts

How to handle missing dependency information

When you package a project, the Package and Deployment Wizard uses *dependency files* to determine what files need to be included for the project to run correctly when it's installed on another PC. First, it uses a file called Vb6dep.ini that indicates the files that are required by all Visual Basic 6 applications. Then, it checks the dependency files for each ActiveX component or control that the project uses. These files have the same name as the ActiveX DLL or EXE file, but they use a DEP extension. Later, if the Package and Deployment Wizard can't find the corresponding DEP file for an ActiveX component or control, it displays a dialog box like the one in figure 15-8.

When you encounter a dialog box like that one, you usually need to find or create the missing dependency information as summarized in this figure. If the file is a third-party ActiveX control or component, you may need to contact the vendor to obtain the DEP file. If, on the other hand, you used Visual Basic to create the ActiveX component or control, you can create the DEP file as shown in the next figure. When all DEP files are in the correct folders, you can restart the Package and Deployment Wizard and finish the packaging process.

Since some ActiveX components and controls don't need any files beyond the default Visual Basic files to run correctly, they aren't dependent on other files and don't need to include any dependency information. So if you think that the file listed in the Missing Dependency Information dialog box doesn't depend on other files, you can click on the OK button to continue the packaging process. Then, you can install the application and test it to see if it works correctly. If a needed file isn't included due to missing dependency information, though, the application won't install correctly and may crash when it's run.

If you're absolutely sure that a file doesn't depend on any other files, you can check the box to it's left in the Missing Dependency Information dialog box and click on the OK button. This will permanently mark the file as not having a DEP file. Then, the Missing Dependency Information dialog box won't be displayed for that file in the future.

If the file in the Missing Dependency Information dialog box is an EXE file that's deployed as a remote ActiveX component, you need to locate or create the TLB and VBR files for the component. When you create your own ActiveX EXE components, you can use Visual Basic to create those files. To do that, select the Properties command from the Project menu to display the Project Properties dialog box, click on the Component tab, and check the Remote Server Files option. Then, when you use the Make command from the File menu to build the EXE file for the project, the TLB and VBR files are also built.

The dialog box that's displayed when dependency information is missing

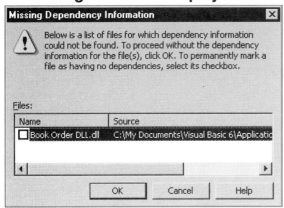

Two types of dependency files

File	Description
Vb6dep.ini	This is the master dependency file for Visual Basic 6. It identifies most of the DLL files that are needed by all Visual Basic applications.
*.dep	This is a file that contains a list of all files that are required by a component. Usually, this file is stored in the same folder as the component it describes.

Description

- To continue without dependency information, click on the OK button. If you do this, however, you can't be sure that the application will install correctly. If you want to permanently mark a file as not being dependent on any other files, you can check the box that precedes it before you click on the OK button.

- To get the dependency information for a file, note the file name and location, click on the Cancel button, and cancel out of the packaging process. Then, you can locate or create the appropriate DEP files and move them into the same folder as the corresponding DLL or EXE files. When all DEP files are accounted for, you can restart the wizard and finish the packaging process.

- For third-party ActiveX controls or components, you should find the DEP file and place it in the same folder as its DLL or EXE file. To do that, you may need to contact the vendor or download the DEP file from the an Internet site.

- For ActiveX controls or components that you created, you can use the Package and Deployment Wizard to create a DEP file as shown in the next figure.

Figure 15-8   How to handle missing dependency information

How to create a dependency file for an ActiveX component or control

If you used Visual Basic to create an ActiveX component (DLL or EXE) or control (OCX), you can use the Package and Deployment Wizard to create a dependency file for that component or control. Figure 15-9 shows how.

When you get to the Package Type dialog box, select the Dependency File option as shown in this figure. And when you get to the Package Folder dialog box, select the folder that contains the DLL, EXE, or OCX file for the component or control. These files are usually stored in the Windows\System or Windows\System32 folder.

How to create an installation CD

If you have access to a CD drive that can write on CDs, you can create an installation CD for your application. Although the procedure for creating a CD depends on the type of CD drive and creation software, the general idea is this. First, you use the Package and Deployment Wizard to deploy the application to a folder on your hard drive or on a network server. Then, you use your CD creation software to write the contents of that folder onto the CD. Usually, that means writing the files in the Package folder onto a CD.

The dialog box for creating a DEP file for an ActiveX component

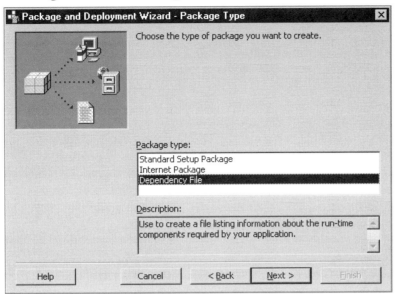

Package and Deployment Wizard - Package Type

Choose the type of package you want to create.

Package type:

Standard Setup Package
Internet Package
Dependency File

Description:

Use to create a file listing information about the run-time components required by your application.

| Help | Cancel | < Back | Next > | Finish |

Procedure

1. Use Visual Basic to open the project that was used to create the ActiveX component or control.

2. Select the Package and Deployment Wizard command from the Add-Ins menu.

3. Click on the Package button and use the wizard to create the DEP file. When you get to the Package Type dialog box shown above, click on the Dependency File option. When you get to the Package Folder dialog box, select the folder that contains the ActiveX component or control.

Notes

- ActiveX components are stored in DLL and EXE files.
- ActiveX controls are stored in OCX files.
- ActiveX components and controls are usually stored in the Windows\System or Windows\System32 folder.

Figure 15-9   How to create a dependency file for an ActiveX component or control

A summary of the files in the Package and Support folders

When you use the Package and Deployment Wizard to create a package, it creates the Package and Support folders shown in figure 15-10. This figure describes some of the most important files stored in these folders.

The Package folder contains all of the files that you need to deploy an application. In fact, when you use the Package and Deployment Wizard to deploy an application to a folder, it just copies the files in the Package folder to another folder. If you're curious about what type of information the Setup.lst file contains, you can use a text editor such as Notepad to open this file.

The Support folder contains a copy of the Setup.exe and Setup.lst files as well as the other files that are used by the Setup.exe file including Setup1.exe, Vb6stkit.dll, and St6unst.exe. In addition, it contains all DLL and OCX files that are needed by the application.

If you want to see what DLL and OCX files are included for your application, you can use the Explorer to review the contents of the Support folder. Before you'll be able to see the DLL files, though, you may need to change the view options so all system files are displayed. Although some DLL files like Msvbvm60.dll are required by all Visual Basic applications, other DLL files are required only when you use the References dialog box to add references to your project. Similarly, OCX files are required only when you use the Components dialog box to add components to your project. For example, the Msadodc.ocx file is required if you use the Microsoft ADO Data Control 6.0.

If your application uses a data access technology like ADO, a file named Mdac_type.exe will be included in the Support folder. At almost 8 megabytes, this file is often the largest file in the Support folder. However, it's an important file because it automatically installs the components you need for your data access technology.

The Package folder for the Accounts Payable application

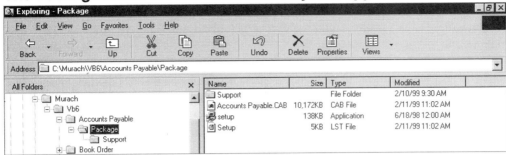

The Package folder

File	Description
Setup.exe	The file that starts the installation process.
Setup.lst	A text file that contains information about the installation including required files, installation locations, and changes to the Windows registry.
*.cab	Compressed files that contain the executable file for the application along with all other files that are included in the Support folder.

The Support folder

File	Description
Project.exe	The executable file for the project.
Stdole2.tlb	A run-time file that's needed by all Visual Basic applications.
Setup1.exe	The setup file that performs the main installation procedure for your application.
Vb6stkit.dll	The DLL that contains code that's used by Setup1.exe.
St6unst.exe	The utility that's used to uninstall an application when the setup procedure is terminated before it finishes.
*.dll	All DLL files that are used by the application. Some DLL files are needed by all Visual Basic applications. Other DLL files are specific to your application and are specified in the References dialog box.
*.ocx	All files for the ActiveX controls that are used by the application. These files are usually specified in the Components dialog box for the project.
MS-DOS Batch file	The batch file that automatically recreates the CAB files if you use the Package and Deployment Wizard to modify any settings.
Mdac_type.exe	A self-extracting executable that installs all of the necessary components needed for your data access technology. This file is only included when your application accesses data.

Figure 15-10   A summary of the files in the Package and Support folders

How to deploy Internet applications

You can use the Package and Deployment Wizard to deploy five types of applications to the Internet: (1) ActiveX controls, (2) ActiveX components, (3) ActiveX documents, (4) DHTML applications, and (5) IIS applications. For example, you could deploy the ActiveX component that you created in chapter 13 to a web site. Or, you could deploy either of the applications that are described in chapter 14 to a web site. Then, when a user accesses that web site with a web browser, the *Internet package* is downloaded to the user's PC.

To create an Internet package, start the Package and Deployment Wizard, click on the Package button, and select the Internet Package option from the Package Type dialog box. Then, the wizard will step you through the packaging process, although the specific details will depend on the type of application. When you finish this process, the wizard will create the primary CAB file that's used as the setup program by the web browser.

To deploy an Internet package, start the Package and Deployment Wizard and click on the Deploy button. Then, you can use the resulting dialog boxes to deploy the application to a web site. In figure 15-11, for example, you can see two of the screens for deploying the Book Orders EXE component to the Internet. Here, the Items to Deploy dialog box shows the two items that will be deployed to the Internet. The first file is the primary CAB file that contains the EXE file for the component and all of the other required files. The second file is a text file that contains the HTML that's automatically generated for the component.

When the Web Publishing Site dialog box asks for the URL (Uniform Resource Locator) for the web server as well as the web publishing protocol that you want to use, you should start by specifying the protocol. For simple file distribution like deploying an installation package, FTP (File Transfer Protocol) is often faster since it was designed for that. In contrast, although HTTP (HyperText Transfer Protocol) is the standard protocol of the Web, it is often slower for file transfers. Because it's graphical, though, it allows for such things as interactive setup programs that FTP cannot deliver.

Once you choose the transfer protocol and enter the appropriate URL, the wizard will attempt to contact the server. If successful, the wizard will display the Finished dialog box and deploy your package. If the wizard cannot contact the server, though, a message box reports the error. Then, you must correct all errors so that the wizard can connect to the server and continue on to the Finished dialog box.

The Items to Deploy dialog box

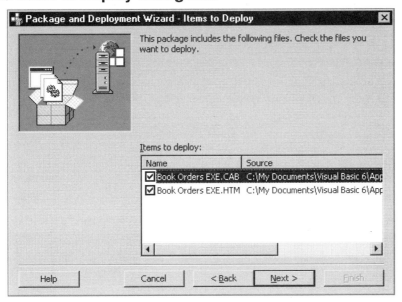

The Web Publishing Site dialog box

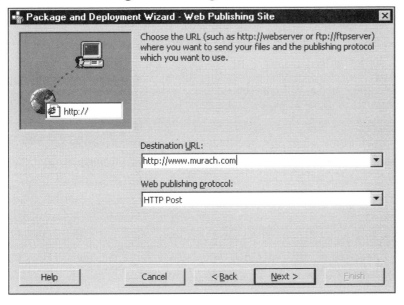

Figure 15-11   Two of the dialog boxes for deploying an Internet application

Exercise set 15-2: Install the Book Orders application

In this exercise set, you'll install and uninstall the Book Orders application that you created in chapter 13. Since this application uses the Book Order ActiveX component that you created in chapter 13, you'll need to create a DEP file for the ActiveX component. *If you're using the Learning Edition of Visual Basic 6*, though, you won't be able to do this exercise set because that edition doesn't let you create ActiveX components

Open and test the Book Orders application

1. Start Visual Basic and open the Book Orders project you created for chapter 13.

2. Select the References command from the Project menu so Visual Basic displays the References dialog box. Then, make a note of the references that are checked. If any of the references in this dialog box aren't used by the application, you can uncheck their boxes.

3. Select the Properties command from the Project menu so Visual Basic displays the Properties dialog box. On the General tab, set the Project Name property to BookOrders. On the Make tab, change the Version property to version 2.0.

4. Test the project to make sure it works correctly. If it doesn't, fix any problems before you continue.

Encounter missing dependency information for the Book Order component

5. Select the Package and Deployment Wizard from the Add-Ins menu, click on the Package button, and move through the wizard's dialog boxes. After you complete the Package Folder dialog box, you should see a dialog box like the one shown in figure 15-8. Then, click on the Cancel button for this dialog box, click on the Cancel button for the wizard, and close the main screen for the wizard.

6. Select the Remove Project command from the File menu to close the Book Orders project.

Create a DEP file for the Book Order component

7. Open the Book Order DLL project that you used to create the BookOrder component.

8. Select the Package and Deployment Wizard from the Add-Ins menu, click on the Package button, and move through the wizard's dialog boxes. In the Package Type dialog box, select the Dependency File option. In the Package Folder dialog box, select the same folder as the one that contains the DLL file. In the *Cab Information Screen dialog box*, accept the default options. (This dialog box lets you package the DEP file into a CAB file for

distribution on the web.) And in the Finished dialog box, accept the default name. When you're done, click on the Finish button to create the DEP file.

9. Close the Book Order DLL project by selecting the Remove Project command from the File menu.

Package and deploy the Book Orders application

10. Open the Book Orders project and select the Package and Deployment Wizard from the Add-Ins menu.

11. Click on the Package button and move through the dialog boxes that follow to create a package for the Book Orders application. This should be similar to the steps you used to package the Accounts Payable application in the previous exercise set.

12. Click on the Deploy button and use the dialog boxes that follow to deploy the Book Orders application to a folder called Book Orders Setup. This should be similar to the steps you used to deploy the Accounts Payable application in the previous exercise set.

13. Click on the Close button to close the Package and Deployment Wizard. Then, exit from Visual Basic.

Install and uninstall the Book Orders application

14. If you deployed the application to a network folder, you can move to another PC running under Windows 95, NT, or 98 that has access to that folder. Otherwise, you can stay at your own PC.

15. Close all open applications and start the Windows Explorer. Then, navigate to the Book Orders Setup folder and double-click on the setup.exe file. At the first setup dialog box, you can click on the OK button. At the second setup dialog box, you can continue the installation.

16. Use the Start menu to start the Book Orders application. Then, test the application to make sure it works correctly.

17. Open the Windows Control Panel and double-click on the Add/Remove Programs icon. Then, select the Book Orders option and click on the Add/Remove button. When Windows ask you if you're sure, click on the Yes button so the program is uninstalled.

18. Exit from the Windows Explorer.

If you have now completed all of the chapters in this book, you know a lot about all phases of application development. You should also be ready to start developing and distributing business applications of your own. Congratulations!

Perspective

Although the Package and Deployment Wizard makes it easy to package and deploy an application, there's still a lot of room for error. As a result, the process of packaging and deploying an application often ends up being a process of trial and error. Fortunately, though, the wizard saves all of your settings in scripts, which is a big help when you have to troubleshoot packaging or deployment problems.

* * *

If you have now completed this book, we hope you've enjoyed the journey. In section 1, we hope you began to appreciate the power of the Integrated Development Environment and the range of the Visual Basic language. In section 2, we hope you saw the potential of Visual Basic for developing database applications as well as the inherent difficulties of working with bound forms, Data Environment objects, and client/server technology. And in section 3, we hope you've seen the range of what's involved as you deliver professional applications to your users.

Of course, because Visual Basic is such a large subject, it takes several years on the job before you come close to mastering it. The good news is that you already know enough to start developing professional business applications on your own. Besides that, you should have the concepts, skills, and perspective that you need for learning whatever else you need to know as you develop those applications. If that's the case, this book has done its job. And we thank you for reading it.

Terms you should know

script
add-in program
install
standalone application
silent mode
package
deploy
packaging script
deployment script
cabinet file (CAB file)
dependency file
Internet package

Appendixes

The first two appendixes that follow give you the information that you need for doing the exercise sets for sections 2 and 3. If you're going to use Access databases for those applications, please read appendix A. If you're going to use SQL Server databases, please read appendix B.

In contrast, appendix C presents additional information for users of the Learning Edition of Visual Basic 6. In particular, it summarizes which exercise sets you can and cannot do, and shows you what changes you need to make to the applications for chapters 7 and 8 if you want them to work correctly.

How to download or create the Access databases

If you do the exercise sets in this book, you're going to need two Access (Jet) databases. For chapters 6 through 12, you need the Accounts Payable database. For chapter 13, you need the Murach Books database. The specifications for these databases are presented first in this appendix so you can see how they relate to the applications that use them.

The easiest way to get these databases on your PC is to download them from our web site. This is a simple procedure that takes just a few minutes. After you download them, you can update the dates in the Accounts Payable database by running a simple Visual Basic application that is downloaded with the databases.

If you don't have access to the Internet, you can use the Visual Data Manager that comes with Visual Basic 6 to create the Access databases, define their tables, and enter some test data into these tables. The procedures for doing that are also described in this appendix.

Last, this appendix shows you how to create an ODBC data source for an Access database. Then, you can connect to the Access database by using the OLE DB provider for ODBC drivers. Although you shouldn't need to do this, you should realize that this is another way to connect to an Access database.

The AccountsPayable database **582**
The Vendors table 582
The Invoices table 583
The Terms table 583
The States table 584
The GLAccounts table 584

The MurachBooks database **585**
The BookPrices table 585

How to download and update the Access databases **586**
How to download the databases 586
How to update the dates in the Accounts Payable database 586

How to create the databases **588**
How to define the tables of a database 588
How to add test data to a database 592

How to create an ODBC data source **594**

The AccountsPayable database

The applications that you develop in the exercise sets for chapters 6 through 12 use the AccountsPayable database. This database consists of five tables: Vendors, Invoices, Terms, States, and GLAccounts. The specifications for these tables are presented on the following pages.

For each table, the specifications include the names of the fields in the table, the type of data that each field contains, an indication of whether the fields are required or if they have a default value, and the indexes that are required. This is the information you'll need if you define the tables using the Visual Data Manager as described later in this appendix. This information can also help you understand the operation of the applications that use them. For example, because the VendorName field in the Vendors tables is defined with a unique index, you can't add two records with the same vendor name to the table. And, even though the TermsID and AccountNo fields are required, you don't have to enter values for them because they have default values.

The Vendors table

Table Structure

Field name	Type	Size	Other properties
VendorID	Long	4	AutoIncrField
VendorName	Text	50	Required
VendorAddress1	Text	50	
VendorAddress2	Text	50	
VendorCity	Text	50	Required
VendorState	Text	2	Required
VendorZipCode	Text	10	Required
VendorContact	Text	50	
VendorPhone	Text	50	
TermsID	Integer	2	Required; Default is 3
AccountNo	Integer	2	Required; Default is 570
LastTranDate	Date/Time	8	
YTDPurchases	Currency	8	Default is 0
YTDReturns	Currency	8	Default is 0
LastYTDPurchases	Currency	8	Default is 0
LastYTDReturns	Currency	8	Default is 0

Indexes

Name	Field	Other properties
VendorID	VendorID	Primary; Unique
VendorName	VendorName	Unique

The Invoices table

Table structure

Field name	Type	Size	Other properties
InvoiceID	Long	4	AutoIncrField
VendorID	Long	4	Required
InvoiceNumber	Text	20	Required
InvoiceDate	Date/Time	8	Required
InvoiceTotal	Currency	8	Required
PaymentTotal	Currency	8	Default is zero
CreditTotal	Currency	8	Default is zero
TermsID	Integer	2	Required; Default is 3
InvoiceDueDate	Date/Time	8	Required

Index

Name	Field	Other properties
InvoiceID	InvoiceID	Primary; Unique

The Terms table

Table structure

Field name	Type	Size	Other properties
TermsID	Integer	2	Required
TermsDescription	Text	50	Required
TermsDueDays	Integer	2	Required

Test data

TermsID	TermsDescription	TermsDueDays
1	Net due 10 days	10
2	Net due 20 days	20
3	Net due 30 days	30
4	Net due 60 days	60
5	Net due 90 days	90

The States table

Table structure

Field name	Type	Size	Other properties
StateCode	Text	2	Required
FirstZipCode	Text	10	Required
LastZipCode	Text	10	Required

Test data

StateCode	FirstZipCode	LastZipCode
CA	90000	96699
NY	09000	14999
TN	37000	38599

The GLAccounts table

Table structure

Field name	Type	Size	Other properties
AccountNo	Integer	2	Required
AccountDescription	Text	50	Required

Test data

AccountNo	AccountDescription
100	Cash
110	Accounts Receivable
120	Book Inventory
552	Postage
570	Office Supplies

The MurachBooks database

The applications that you develop in the exercise sets for chapter 13 use the MurachBooks database. This database consists of a single table called the BookPrices table, and that table contains only three fields.

The BookPrices table

Table structure

Field name	Type	Size	Other properties
BookID	Text	4	Required
BookDescription	Text	50	Required
BookPrice	Currency	8	Required

Test data

BookID	BookDescription	BookPrice
CC1R	CICS for the COBOL Programmer, Part 1 (2nd Ed.)	$36.50
CC2R	CICS for the COBOL Programmer, Part 2 (2nd Ed.)	$36.50
CIGR	CICS Instructor's Guide (2nd Ed.)	$200.00
DB21	DB2 for the COBOL Programmer, Part 1	$36.50
DB22	DB2 for the COBOL Programmer, Part 2	$36.50
VB6	Murach's Visual Basic 6	$45.00

How to download and update the Access databases

If you follow the procedures in this appendix, you can download the two databases that you'll need for the exercise sets in sections 2 and 3 in just a few minutes. Then, you can run an update program that is downloaded with the databases to update the dates in the AccountsPayable database.

How to download the databases

Figure A-1 shows how to download the Access databases from our web site. To do that, you can download a Zip file that contains the AccountsPayable database, the MurachBooks database, and a DateUpdate program. The Zip file is a compressed, executable file that expands into the uncompressed versions of all the folders and files that it represents. Once you've downloaded the Zip file, you can expand the file by double-clicking on it in the Explorer window. This creates the Murach, VB6, and Databases folders and stores the three files in the Databases folder.

How to update the dates in the Accounts Payable database

Figure A-1 also shows how to update the dates that are used in the Vendors and Invoices tables of the Accounts Payable database. In short, you just double-click on the DateUpdate.exe file. It compares the dates in the tables with the current date, then updates all of the dates in the tables so they correspond to the current date.

How the downloaded databases are stored on your PC

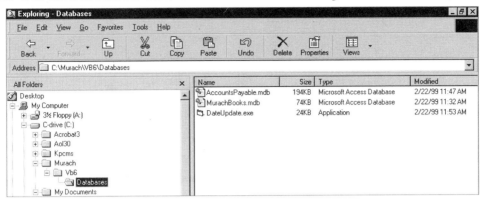

How to download and expand the databases

1. Start your Internet browser and go to *www.murach.com*. Then, find the Access database download for *Murach's Visual Basic 6* book. You can do that by finding the book first and then the downloads, or vice versa. But how you do that may vary from one version of our web site to another. When you find the database download, click on it. This downloads a single Zip file named VB6Databases.exe and saves it in the default folder on your PC.

2. Start the Windows Explorer and navigate to the folder on your PC that contains the Zip file. Then, double-click on the VB6Databases.exe file. This creates the folders and files for the AccountsPayable and MurachBooks databases and places them in the C:\Murach\VB6\Databases folder.

How to update the dates in the Accounts Payable database

- Double-click on the DateUpdate.exe file in the Databases folder. This updates all of the dates in the Vendors and Invoices tables relative to the current date.

Figure A-1   How to download and update the Access databases

How to create the databases

If you don't have access to the Internet, you can create your own AccountsPayable and MurachBooks databases. To do that, you can use either Access, which you probably have on your PC, or an add-in program called the Visual Data Manager that comes with Visual Basic 6. After you use one of these programs to define the tables for each database, you can use the program to add a few records to each table. That should be all that you need for testing the applications that you develop.

Of the two programs, Access is more powerful and easier to use. So if you have it on your PC and know how to use it, you'll probably want to use that program for creating the databases. In case you don't have Access, though, the pages that follow show you how to use the Visual Data Manager to define the tables of the databases and then add data to those tables.

If you use Access to create the tables in the AccountsPayable database, keep in mind that the settings that were presented in the table specifications earlier in this appendix are for defining the tables with the Visual Data Manager. If you use Access to create the tables, the settings will be somewhat different. Because the Access settings are similar, though, you shouldn't have much trouble figuring out what they should be. In addition to these settings, you may want to define the primary keys for the Terms, States, and GLAccounts tables. Then, you can define the relationships between all the tables in the database so referential integrity will be enforced. You can't do that using the Visual Data Manager.

How to define the tables of a database

The three parts of figure A-2 show how to use the Visual Data Manager to define the tables of a database. In short, you use the Add Field dialog box to add the fields to the table, you use the Add Index dialog box to add any indexes to the table, and you use the Table Structure dialog box to build the table.

How to start the Visual Data Manager

1. Start Visual Basic, but don't open a project. Then, select the Visual Data Manager command from the Add-Ins menu to display the VisData window.

How to create a new database

2. Select the New command from the File menu. Then, select Version 7.0 MDB from the Microsoft Access submenu to display this dialog box:

3. Use this dialog box to save the database as AccountsPayable or as MurachBooks. Then, click on the Save button to display the Database Window for the database.

How to create a new table

4. Right-click in the Database Window and select the New Table command. This will display the Table Structure dialog box.

5. Enter the name of the table in the Table Name text box.

How to add fields to a table

6. Click on the Add Field button to display the Add Field dialog box:

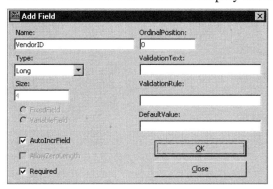

7. Use this dialog box to enter a name for the field and to set the properties for the field. Then, click on the OK button. Continue in this manner until you've added all the fields for the table. To determine the name and properties for each field, refer back to the table specifications at the start of this appendix. When you're done, click on the Close button.

Figure A-2   How to define the tables in a database (part 1 of 3)

How to add indexes to a table

8. Click on the Add Index button to display the Add Index dialog box:

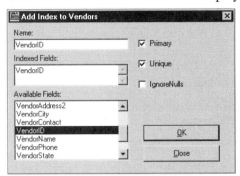

9. Use this dialog box to add the indexes that the table requires. To determine the name and properties for each index, refer back to the table specifications. When you're done, click on the Close button.

How to build the table

10. When you're done adding fields and indexes, the Table Structure dialog box should look something like this:

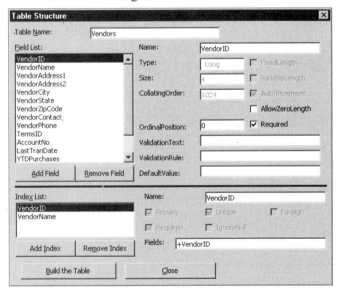

Figure A-2   How to define the tables in a database (part 2 of 3)

11. Click on the Build the Table button. The Visual Data Manager then builds the table and displays it in the Database Window like this:

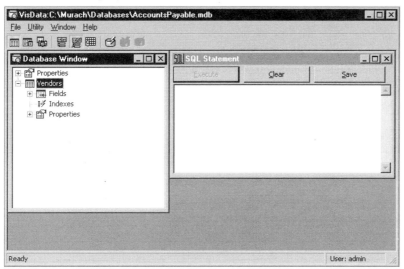

How to create other tables

12. To create the other tables that the database requires, repeat steps 4 through 11.

How to modify the definitions for a table

13. If you discover that you need to modify the definitions for a table, right-click on the table in the Database Window and select the Design command from the shortcut menu. This displays the Table Structure dialog box, which you can use to change the properties for fields and indexes. For some properties, though, you may need to remove the field or index and then add it again.

Figure A-2   How to define the tables in a database (part 3 of 3)

How to add test data to a database

After you define the tables for a database, you need to add test data to those tables. At first, though, you need to add just a few records to each table. That will be adequate for testing most Visual Basic applications. In fact, your first test runs are likely to be more efficient if you keep the number of records in each table to a minimum. Later, after you have a working version of an application, you can add other records that test specific procedures of your application.

Although figure A-3 shows how to use the Visual Data Manager to add test data to a table, you can also use the Data View window that's described in chapter 11 for that purpose. Or, if you used Access to create the database, you can use Access to add the test data. Later, after you develop working versions of the Visual Basic applications for chapters 6 through 8, you can use those applications to add more records to the Vendors table of the AccountsPayable database.

When you add data to the Vendors table, you can use whatever data you want for the names, addresses, and other required fields. When you add data to the Invoices table, though, you need to make sure that the value in the VendorID field corresponds to the value in one of the VendorID fields in the Vendors table. To do that, you can use the Visual Data Manager to open the Vendors table and find the VendorID for the vendor you want. Then, you can use the Visual Data Manager to open the Invoices table and enter the invoices for that vendor.

How to add test data to a table

1. Start Visual Basic, but don't open a project. Then, select the Visual Data Manager command from the Add-Ins menu to open the VisData window.

2. Select the Open Database command from the File menu. Then, select the Microsoft Access command from the submenu, and use the Open dialog box to open the database that you want to add data to.

3. Right-click on the table and select the Open command. Then, VisData displays a form that you can use for adding, editing, and deleting records:

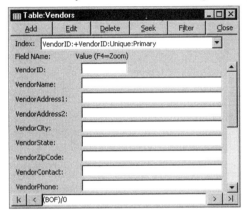

4. Click on the Add button to display a form that you can use to add a record:

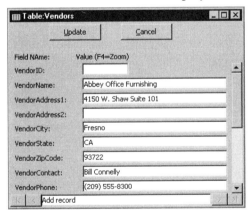

5. Enter the data for the record and click on the Update button to add it to the database table.

6. Repeat steps 4 and 5 until you've added all the test data for the table.

How to edit the data in a record

7. You can use the first form shown above to check the data that you've entered. Then, if you need to edit the data, click on the Edit button and use the second form shown above to modify the record.

Figure A-3   How to add test data to a table

How to create an ODBC data source

If you want to experiment with the use of ODBC drivers as another way to connect to a database, you can use the OLE DB provider for ODBC drivers in conjunction with the Access ODBC driver. To make that work, though, you also need to create an ODBC data source for the Access ODBC driver as shown in figure A-4.

How to create an ODBC data source

1. Open the Windows Control Panel and double-click on the ODBC (32-bit) icon. This displays the ODBC Data Source Administrator dialog box with the User DSN tab displayed.

2. Click on the Add button to display a dialog box that lists all of the available ODBC drivers.

3. Select the Microsoft Access Driver option, and click on the Finish button. This dialog box is then displayed:

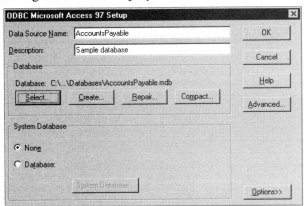

4. Enter a name and description for the data source.

5. Click on the Select button and find the Access database you want to use. When you're done, the path to the database should be displayed as shown above.

6. Click on the OK button. That displays the Data Source Administrator dialog box with the new data source shown in it:

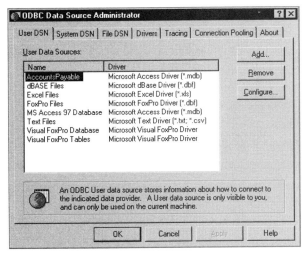

7. Click on the OK button.

Figure A-4   How to create an ODBC data source

B

The specifications for the SQL Server databases

If you're using this book in a classroom or training environment, your PC may be attached to a server that has the SQL Server databases. Then, you can use those databases instead of the Access databases as you do the exercise sets for sections 2 and 3. As you work, you can review the specifications that follow to see how the databases relate to the applications that use them.

If you're the instructor or administrator who's responsible for setting up these SQL Server databases, there are several ways that you can do that. Perhaps the best way, though, is this. First, use SQL Server to create the databases. Second, download the Access versions of these databases as described in Appendix A. Third, use Access to export the tables to SQL Server. After that, you can use the Data View window of Visual Basic 6 to adjust the table definitions to the specifications in this appendix.

Another alternative is to use the Access Upsizing Wizard to upsize the Access databases to SQL Server databases. This is described on pages 500 to 505 of our book called *Client/Server Programming: Access 97*. If you don't have Access on your system, though, you have to use SQL Server to create the databases. Then, you can use either SQL Server or the Data View window of Visual Basic 6 to define the tables in the databases and add data to them.

The AccountsPayable database **598**
The Vendors table 598
The Invoices table 599
The States table 599
The Terms table 600
The GLAccounts table 600
The MurachBooks database **601**
The BookPrices table 601

The AccountsPayable database

The applications that you develop in the exercise sets for chapters 6 through 12 use the AccountsPayable database. This database consists of five tables: Vendors, Invoices, Terms, States, and GLAccounts. The applications for chapter 6 use just the Vendors table. The applications for chapters 7 through 10 use all but the GLAccounts table. And chapter 11 has you experiment with only the GLAccounts table.

The specifications for these tables are presented on this page and the three pages that follow. When you develop a Visual Basic application that uses one of these tables, you should review the specifications for the table so you can see how they will affect the operation of the application. Note, for example, that the VendorName field in the Vendors table is defined with a unique constraint, so you can't add two records with the same vendor name to the table. Similarly, if a field is defined as No Nulls without a default, you can't add a new record to the table if that field doesn't contain data.

The Vendors table

Table Structure

Column name	Datatype	Length	Notes
VendorID	int	4	Key field; identity field
VendorName	varchar	50	No nulls
VendorAddress1	varchar	50	
VendorAddress2	varchar	50	
VendorCity	varchar	50	No nulls
VendorState	char	2	No nulls; foreign key of States table
VendorZipCode	varchar	10	No nulls
VendorContact	varchar	50	
VendorPhone	varchar	50	
TermsID	int	4	No nulls; foreign key of Terms table; default is 3
AccountNo	int	4	No nulls; foreign key of GLAccounts table; default is 570
LastTranDate	datetime	8	
YTDPurchases	money	8	No nulls; default is zero
YTDReturns	money	8	No nulls; default is zero
LastYTDPurchases	money	8	No nulls; default is zero
LastYTDReturns	money	8	No nulls; default is zero

Indexes

Name	Column	Other properties
PK_Vendors	VendorID	Primary; Unique
IX_VendorName	VendorName	Unique; Constraint

The Invoices table

Table structure

Column name	Datatype	Length	Notes
InvoiceID	int	4	Key field; identity field
VendorID	int	4	No nulls; foreign key of Vendors table; index with nonunique keys
InvoiceNumber	varchar	10	No nulls
InvoiceDate	datetime	8	No nulls
InvoiceTotal	money	8	No nulls; default is zero
PaymentTotal	money	8	No nulls; default is zero
CreditTotal	money	8	No nulls; default is zero
TermsID	int	4	No nulls; foreign key of Terms table
InvoiceDueDate	datetime	8	No nulls

The States table

Table structure

Column name	Datatype	Length	Notes
StateCode	char	2	Key field
FirstZipCode	int	4	No nulls
LastZipCode	int	4	No nulls

Sample data

StateCode	FirstZipCode	LastZipCode
CA	90000	96699
NY	09000	14999
TN	37000	38599

The Terms table

Table structure

Column name	Datatype	Length	Notes
TermsID	int	4	Key field; identity field
TermsDescription	varchar	50	No nulls
TermsDueDays	smallint	2	No nulls

Sample data

TermsID	TermsDescription	TermsDueDays
1	Net due 10 days	10
2	Net due 20 days	20
3	Net due 30 days	30
4	Net due 60 days	60
5	Net due 90 days	90

The GLAccounts table

Table structure

Column name	Datatype	Length	Notes
AccountNo	int	4	Key field
AccountDescription	varchar	50	No nulls

Sample data

AccountNo	AccountDescription
100	Cash
110	Accounts Receivable
120	Book Inventory
552	Postage
570	Office Supplies

The MurachBooks database

The applications that you develop in the exercise sets for chapter 13 use the MurachBooks database. This database consists of a single table named BookPrices table, and it contains only three fields.

The BookPrices table

Table structure

Column name	Datatype	Length	Notes
BookID	varchar	4	Key field
BookDescription	varchar	50	No nulls
BookPrice	smallmoney	4	No nulls

Sample data

BookID	BookDescription	BookPrice
CC1R	CICS for the COBOL Programmer, Part 1 (2nd Ed.)	$36.50
CC2R	CICS for the COBOL Programmer, Part 2 (2nd Ed.)	$36.50
CIGR	CICS Instructor's Guide (2nd Ed.)	$200.00
DB21	DB2 for the COBOL Programmer, Part 1	$36.50
DB22	DB2 for the COBOL Programmer, Part 2	$36.50
VB6	Murach's Visual Basic 6	$45.00

Special considerations for users of the Learning Edition

The Learning Edition of Visual Basic is an inexpensive edition that lets you get off to a good start with Visual Basic. Obviously, though, it doesn't include all of the features of the more expensive Professional or Enterprise editions. In addition, the Jet OLE DB provider doesn't work the same way that it does in the other editions. This appendix summarizes the limitations and differences that you should be aware of.

Differences by chapter **604**
Chapter 3 604
Chapters 5 and 6 604
Chapters 7 and 8 604
Chapters 9, 10, and 11 604
Chapter 13 604
Chapter 14 604
Chapter 15 604
Coding changes for the exercise sets **605**
Chapter 7 coding changes 605
Chapter 8 coding changes 606

Differences by chapter

The summary that follows presents the differences between what the chapters in the book present and what the Learning Edition provides.

Chapter 3

Since the Microsoft Masked Edit Control 6.0 isn't available with the Learning Edition, you need to use text boxes instead of masked edit controls in exercise set 3-2.

Chapters 5 and 6

Everything in the Learning Edition works the way it's presented in the text. However, the Learning Edition only provides the OLE DB provider for Jet databases and the OLE DB provider for ODBC databases. When you do the exercise sets for chapter 6, then, you should use the Jet OLE DB provider.

Chapters 7 and 8

For the exercise sets in chapters 7 and 8, you need to make the coding changes that follow this summary because the Find method isn't supported.

Chapters 9, 10, and 11

The Data Environment Designer, Data Report Designer, and Data View window aren't available with the Learning Edition.

Chapter 13

Although you can create class modules just as this chapter shows, the applications in exercise sets 13-1 and 13-2 use masked edit controls, which aren't included with the Learning Edition. As a result, you need to use text boxes for these controls. In addition, since the Learning Edition doesn't support the creation of ActiveX components, you can't do exercise set 13-3.

Chapter 14

The Learning Edition doesn't support the features presented in this chapter.

Chapter 15

Although the Learning Edition supports the wizard presented in this chapter, you can't do exercise set 15-2 because it installs an ActiveX component and the creation of those components isn't supported by this edition.

Coding changes for the exercise sets

Chapter 7 coding changes

1. Use the OLE DB provider for ODBC drivers for all of the ADO data controls that are used in the exercise sets for this chapter. To use that provider, though, you also need to create an ODBC data source, which you can learn how to do at the end of appendix A.

2. Because the Find method doesn't work with the Jet OLE DB provider that comes with the Learning Edition, comment out this statement in the dbcVendors_Change procedure in the Vendors form module:

```
adoVendors.Recordset.Find "VendorID = " & dbcVendors.BoundText, _
    , , , adBookMarkFirst
```

and replace it with this statement:

```
FindVendorByID
```

Then, code this procedure in the same form module:

```
Private Sub FindVendorByID()
    With adoVendors.Recordset
        .MoveFirst
        Do Until !VendorID = dbcVendors.BoundText
            .MoveNext
        Loop
    End With
End Sub
```

3. Comment out this statement in the ValidZipCode procedure:

```
.Find "StateCode = '" & dbcStates.BoundText & "'", , , _
    adBookMarkFirst
```

and replace it with this statement:

```
FindStateData
```

Then, code this procedure in the same form module:

```
Private Sub FindStateData()
    With adoStates.Recordset
        .MoveFirst
        Do Until !StateCode = dbcStates.BoundText
            .MoveNext
        Loop
    End With
End Sub
```

Chapter 8 coding changes

1. Because the Find method doesn't work with the Jet OLE DB provider that comes with the Learning Edition, comment out this statement in the cboVendors_Click procedure in the Vendors form module:

    ```
    grsVendors.Find "VendorID = " & _
        cboVendors.ItemData(cboVendors.ListIndex), , , adBookMarkFirst
    ```

    and replace it with this statement:

    ```
    FindVendorByID
    ```

    Then, code this procedure in the same form module:

    ```
    Private Sub FindVendorByID()
        With grsVendors
            .MoveFirst
            Do Until !VendorID = _
                    cboVendors.ItemData(cboVendors.ListIndex)
                .MoveNext
            Loop
        End With
    End Sub
    ```

2. Comment out this statement in the cmdOK_Click procedure in the New Vendor form module:

    ```
    grsVendors.Find "VendorName = '" & strVendorName & "'"
    ```

    and replace it with this statement:

    ```
    FindVendorByName(strVendorName)
    ```

    Then, code this procedure in the same form module:

    ```
    Private Sub FindVendorByName(Name As String)
        With grsVendors
            .MoveFirst
            Do Until !VendorName = Name
                .MoveNext
            Loop
        End With
    End Sub
    ```

Index

A

About form, 442

Access 97, 597

Access database, 581-595

download, 586

Active cell (MSFlexGrid), 294

Active Server Page, 523, 524

ActiveConnection property (Command object), 301

ActiveForm property (MDIForm object), 134

ActiveX component, 200, 504-517, 574

remote, 568

ActiveX control, 504, 574

ActiveX Data Objects, 196, 222

ActiveX document, 504, 574

Add Form dialog box, 104

Add Module command (Project menu), 52

Add Procedure command (Tools menu), 26

Add-in program, 546

AddItem method (ComboBox control), 293

AddNew method (ADO), 225

ADO, 196, 198

Errors collection, 304

properties and methods, 224

ADO data control

events, 268

processing data with, 208

properties, 210

Aggregate fields (Command object), 358

Alignment property, 15

DataGrid control, 261

AllowAddNew property (DataGrid control), 261

AllowDelete property (DataGrid control), 261

AllowSizing property (DataGrid control), 261

AllowUpdate property (DataGrid control), 261

Application

DHTML, 574

IIS, 574

Internet and intranet, 204

web-based, 204

Application software, 174

Argument

ByRef, 90

ByVal, 90, 482, 484

coding, 30

in functions, 92

in procedures, 90

optional, 484

Property procedure, 483-484

Arithmetic expressions, 66

Arrays

in code, 70

of controls, 238

AS/400, 202

ASP, 523, 524

Assignment statement, 62

Asynchronous operation, 306

Auto Data Tips option, 141

Auto List Members feature, 28

Auto Quick Info feature, 30

Auto Syntax Check option, 141

AutoShowChildren property (MDIForm object), 440

B

Back-end processing, 200

Background Compile option, 141

Bang operator, 226

BEGIN TRAN statement (SQL), 309

BeginTrans method (Connection object), 308

BeginTransComplete event (Connection object), 307

Binary data type (SQL Server), 181

Bit data type (SQL Server), 181

BOF property (ADO), 225

BOFAction property (ADO data control), 211

Bookmark, 50

Boolean data type (VB), 59

BorderStyle property (Form object), 15

Bound control, 208, 254-261

Bound form, 208-229, 253-288

building from Command object, 342

building with ADO, 208-229, 253-288

Bound New Vendors form (chapter 7)

code, 282-285

property settings, 280

Bound Vendors form (chapter 7)

code, 274-277

BoundColumn property (DataCombo control), 257

BoundText property (DataCombo control), 257

Break command, 147

Break in Class Module option, 141

Break mode, 142

Break on All Errors option, 141

Break on Unhandled Errors option, 141
Breakpoint, 144
Browser, 204, 520
Bugs
    when using a Jet database, 276, 284
    when using the Learning Edition, 276
Built-in functions
    example, 98
    summary, 94
ButtonClick event (Toolbar control), 450
ByRef keyword, 90
Byte data type (VB), 59
ByVal keyword, 90

C

CAB file, 552
Cabinet file, 552
Call Stack, 154
Call statement, 90
Cancel property (Form object), 15
Caption property, 15
    DataGrid control, 261
Cascading changes and deletes, 190
CD, 570
ChangeComplete events
    ADO data control, 269
    Recordset object, 307
Char data type (SQL Server), 181
Check box, 4, 116
Check constraint, 180
    working with, 412
CheckBox control, 115
Child form, 128, 436
    creating, 130
    writing code for, 134
Class event, 486
Class Identifier, 506
Class library, 124
Class module, 476-503
Class object, 476
Classes list in Object Browser, 124
Clear method (ComboBox control), 293
Click event, 22
Client, 172
Client/Server architecture, 200-205
Client/Server system, 174
Client-side cursor, 212
Close method (ADO), 225
CLSID, 506
Clustered index, 412

Code
    Calculate Investment form (chapter 1), 40
    Login form (chapter 8), 324
    New Vendors form (chapter 7), 282-285
    New Vendors form (chapter 8), 326-331
    Vendors form (chapter 6), 240-249
    Vendors form (chapter 7), 274-277
    Vendors form (chapter 8), 312-319
    Vendors form (chapter 9), 368
Coding guidelines, 54
Col property (MSFlexGrid control), 295
Collections (ADO), 222
Cols property (MSFlexGrid control), 295
Column, 176
Columns property (DataGrid control), 261
COM, 506
Combo boxes, working with, 118
ComboBox control, 115, 290
    working with, 118, 292
Command button, 4
    Picture property, 448
    Style property, 448
Command hierarchy, 354
Command object, 336
    ADO, 223
    advanced properties, 352
    building bound forms, 342
    changing mapping defaults, 344
    creating, 340
    defining aggregate fields, 358
    defining parent-child relationships, 354
    grouping fields, 356
    other skills, 350-361
    parameters, 360
    working with, 300
CommandButton control, 115
CommandText property (Command object), 301
CommandType property
    ADO data control, 211
    Command object, 301
Comment, 48
COMMIT TRAN statement (SQL), 309
CommitTrans method (Connection object), 308
CommitTransComplete event (Connection object), 307
Compile error, 34
Compile on Demand option, 141
Compiler directives for debugging, 164
Component
    ActiveX, 504-517, 574
    local, 506

registering, 506
remote, 506, 568
Component Object Model, 506
Component server, 200, 504
Components command (Project menu), 120
Components dialog box, 120
Concatenate, 62
Conditional compiler constants, 164
Conditional expressions, 68
ConnectComplete event (Connection object), 307
Connection events, 306
Connection object, 223, 234, 336, 338
Connection string
    building for ADO data control, 216
    creating with login form, 310
ConnectionString property, 211, 225, 216
Const keyword, 64
Constants, 58, 64-65, 97
Constraints, 176, 180, 412
Container control, 114
Contents file, 458, 462
Context ID (help file), 465
Context-sensitive help, 458, 469
Continuation character, 48
Continue command, 147
Control, 4
    adding to a form, 10
    adding to the Toolbox, 120
    aligning, 10
    bound, 254-261
    data-bound, 254-261
    in standard Toolbox, 114
    selecting, 10
    sizing, 10
    unbound, 290
Control array, 238
ControlBox property (Form object), 15
Controlling application execution, 146
Cookie, 528
Copy buffer, 224
CREATE PROCEDURE statement (SQL), 188
CREATE VIEW statement (SQL), 188
CreateParameter method (Command object), 302
Criteria, 300
Currency data type (VB), 59
Current record pointer, 182
Current row pointer, 182
Cursor, 208, 212
Cursor data type (SQL Server), 181
CursorLocation property (ADO data control), 211

CursorLocation property (ADO), 225
CursorType property (ADO), 211, 225

D

DAO, 196, 198
Data Access Objects, 196
Data access options, 196
Data-bound control, 254
Data control, 115, 208
    events, 268
Data Environment Designer, 336
Data Link Properties dialog box, 216, 339, 407
Data link, 404, 406
Data objects (ADO), 222
Data processing without a data control, 232
Data report
    adding fields to, 376
    adding predefined fields to, 378
    changing the margins, 380
    creating, 374, 398
    creating totals, 388
    form for displaying, 394
    grouping on fields, 384
    grouping on relationships, 386
    modifying at run-time, 396
    previewing and printing, 380
Data Report Designer, 374
Data security, 192
Data source, 174, 594
Data tip, 142
Data types
    for Visual Basic variables, 58-59
    for SQL Server fields, 181
Data View window, 404, 597
Database, 588
    Access, 581-595
    Jet, 581-595
    relational, 176
    security, 192
    SQL Server, 597-602
    test data, 592
Database diagram, 418
Database management system, 174
Database server, 200
DataCombo control, 254-257
DataEnvironment object, 336
    creating a report from, 374
    using in code, 346
DataField property
    bound control, 211

DataCombo control, 257
DataGrid control, 261
DataFormat property (DataCombo control), 257
DataGrid control, 254
    properties, 260
    working with, 258
DataList control, 254-257
DataMember property (DataCombo control), 257
DataReport object, 392
DataSource property
    bound control, 211
    DataCombo control, 257
Date data type (VB), 59
Date function, 95
Datetime data type (SQL Server), 181
DateValue function, 95
DblClick event, 22
DBMS, 174
DCOM, 506
DCOM98, 507, 556
Debug object, 151
Debug toolbar, 142
Debugging applications, 34, 140-165
Debugging commands, 146
Debugging windows, 150-157
Debugging with compiler directives, 164
Decimal data type (SQL Server), 181
Declarations section, 61
Declarative referential integrity, 190
Default property, 15, 29
Default values for fields, 180
DefaultDatabase property (ADO), 225
Delete method (ADO), 225
DELETE statement (SQL), 186
Dependency file, 568-571
Deploy an application, 548, 558-561, 574
Deployment issues, 566-577
Deployment script, 548
Description property
    Err object, 82
    Error object, 305
Designer module, 346
DHTML
    application, 522-525, 526-531, 574
    event, 530
Diagram pane, 350, 420
Dialect (SQL language), 182
Dim keyword, 61
DirListBox control, 115
Disconnect event (Connection object), 307
Distribute an application, 543-577

Distributed Component Object Model, 506
DLL, 504, 508, 510
Do...Loop statement, 80, 490, 500
Dot operator, 28
Double data type (VB), 59
Download databases, 586
DRI, 190
DriveListBox control, 115
Dynamic cursor, 212
Dynamic HTML, 522-525, 526-531
Dynamic link library, 504

E

Edit toolbar, 50
Element, 526
Enabled property, 15
End command, 147
End Function statement, 93
End Sub statement, 24, 90
EndOfRecordset event
    ADO data control, 269
    Recordset object, 307
Enterprise Edition, xvi
Enterprise system, 202
EOF property (ADO), 225
EOFAction property (ADO data control), 211
Err object, 82
Error event (ADO data control), 269, 272-273
Error handling, 82, 160, 162
Error object, 304
Error trapping, 82
Errors collection, 223
Event, 4
    ADO data control, 268
    Class object, 486
    Connection object, 306
    Control object, 22
    DHTMLPage object, 530
    Form object, 22
    Recordset object, 306
    Webclass, 538
    Webitem, 538
Event-driven programming, 22
Event procedure, 22, 24
Event statement, 486
Exclusive lock (SQL Server), 194
Executable file, 6, 42, 504
ExecuteComplete event (Connection object), 307
Exit Sub statement, 82
Explorer-style interface, 128

F

FetchComplete event (Recordset object), 307
FetchProgress event (Recordset object), 307
Field, 176
Fields collection (ADO), 223
File server, 202
File Transfer Protocol, 574
FileListBox control, 115
Fixed-length string, 59
FixedCols property (MSFlexGrid control), 295
FixedRows property (MSFlexGrid control), 295
Float data type (SQL Server), 181
For Each...Next statement, 78
For...Next statement, 78, 500
Foreign key, 178
Foreign key constraint, 190
Form, 4
　　bound, 208-229, 253-288
　　modal, 130
　　modeless, 130
　　splash, 438, 440
　　startup, 106, 438
　　unbound, 230-237, 300-311
Form Layout window, 110
Form module, 24
Form window, 8, 24
FormatNumber function, 40
FormatString property (MSFlexGrid control), 295
FormatType property (DataGrid control), 261
Forward-only cursor, 212
Frame control, 115
Front-end processing, 200
FTP, 574
Full-text search index (help file), 466
Function control, 388
Function statement, 93
Functions, 92
　　Visual Basic, 94
FV function, 30, 95

G

General procedure, 26
Global variable, 60
Globally Unique Identifier, 506
GotFocus event, 22
Grid pane (Query Designer window), 350
Grid pane (View window), 420
Grouping (Command object), 356
GUID, 506

H

Handling errors, 160
Hardware components of multi-user systems, 172
Help, 32
　　adding, 442
　　compiling and testing, 466
　　creating a contents file, 462
　　creating a help project, 458
　　creating a topic file, 460
　　footnote marks for help topics, 461
　　mapping topics to numeric values, 464
　　using in an application, 468
HelpCommand property, 469
HelpContextID property, 469
HelpFile property, 469
Hide method (Form object), 440
Hierarchical recordsets (Command object), 354
Hotspot (help), 460
HScrollBar control, 115
HTML, 520, 526
HTML page, 204, 522, 527, 532, 534
HTTP, 574
Hyperlink, 532
Hyperlink element, 528
HyperText Markup Language, 520
HyperText Transfer Protocol, 574

I

IDE, 8
Identity column, 176
If statement, 74
IIf function, 95
IIS application, 522-525, 532-541, 574
Image control, 115
Image data type (SQL Server), 181
Image Editor application, 448
ImageList control, 450
Immediate window, 150
Index, 176, 412
InfoMessage event (Connection object), 307
Initialize event, 480, 488, 496, 526
Inner join, 184
In-process, 510
Input mask, 122
InputBox function, 95, 98
INSERT statement (SQL), 186
Installing an application, 508, 562-563
Instance, 134, 226, 476-480, 522
InStr function, 95, 99

Int data type (SQL Server), 181
Int function, 95
Integer data type (VB), 59
Integrated Development Environment, 8
Internet application, 520-541, 574
    DHTML, 522-525, 526-531
    IIS, 522-525, 532-541
Internet Explorer, 521, 524
Internet Information Server, 522-525
Internet package, 574
Internet server, 204
ItemData property (ComboBox control), 293

J

Jet database, 581-595
    bugs, 276, 284
Jet database engine, 196
Join, 184

K

Key
    foreign, 178
    non-primary, 176
    primary, 176-178
    unique, 176
    working with, 412
Keyset cursor, 212

L

Label (VB), 82
Label control, 4, 115
LAN, 172
Learning Edition, xvi, 276, 603-606
Left function, 95, 99
Left outer join, 184
Len function, 95, 99
Line control, 115
List box control, 118
List property (ComboBox control), 293
ListBox control, 115, 290, 292, 293
ListCount property (ComboBox control), 293
ListField property (DataCombo control), 257
ListIndex property (ComboBox control), 293
Load event
    Form, 22
    Page, 526
Load statement, 440
Local area network, 172
Local component, 506
Local variable, 60

Locals window, 152
Lock escalation, 194
Lock type (SQL Server), 194
Locked property, 15
    DataGrid control, 261
Locking, 194
Locking options, 214
LockType property
    ADO, 225
    ADO data control, 211
Logical error, 34
Logical operators, 68
Login form, 290, 310, 324
Long data type, 59
LostFocus event, 22
LTrim function, 95, 99

M

Main procedure, 106
Mainframe, 202
Make command, 509, 530
Many-to-many relationship, 178
Map entry, 458, 464
Mapping defaults, 344
Masked edit box, 122
MatchEntry property (DataCombo control), 257
MaxButton property (Form object), 15
MaxRecords property (ADO data control), 211
MDI, 124, 436
MDI form, 130
MDIChild property (Form object), 130
Me keyword, 134
Members list, 124
Menu, 132, 446, 454
Menu Editor, 132, 446
Methods, 28
    ADO, 225
    Class object, 479, 484
    ComboBox object, 293
    Connection object, 234, 308
    DataReport object, 392
    Debug object, 151
    ListBox object, 293
    Recordset object, 236
Microsoft Developer Network, 32
Microsoft Help Workshop, 458
Microsoft Internet Explorer, 521, 524
Mid function, 95, 99
Mid-range computer, 202
MinButton property (Form object), 15
Modal form, 130

Modeless form, 130
Module
    class, 476-503
    form, 24
    standard, 24, 52
    designer, 346
Module-level variable, 60
Money data type (SQL Server), 181
MousePointer property (Screen object), 438
Move method (ADO), 225
MoveComplete event
    ADO data control, 268-271
    Recordset object, 307
MSDN browser, 32
MSFlexGrid control, 290, 294, 295
MsgBox function, 96, 98
Multi-line text box, 255, 291
Multiple-document interface, 124, 436
Multi-tier system, 200
Multi-user database, 174
Multi-user system, 172

N

Name property, 15
Naming recommendations, 54
Nested If statements, 74
Netscape Navigator, 521
Network, 172
    security, 192
Network operating system, 174
New command (File menu), 6
New keyword, 134, 226
NewIndex property (ComboBox control), 293
Non-primary key, 176
Now function, 95
N-tier system, 200
Number property
    Err object, 82
    Error object, 305
Numeric data type (SQL Server), 181
Numeric data types (VB), 59

O

Object, 4
    Command, 340-361
    Connection, 223, 234, 336, 338
    DataEnvirontment, 336, 346
    DataReport, 392
    Debug, 151
    Err, 82
    Error, 304
    Form, 4, 14
    Recordset, 223, 236
    Screen, 438
    WebClass, 538
    WebItem, 538
Object Browser, 124
Object class, 476
Object data type (VB), 59
Object Linking and Embedding, 114
Object model
    ADO, 222
    DHTML, 527
Object variable, 134
Object-oriented programming, 475
ODBC, 174
ODBC API, 196
ODBC data source, 594
ODBC driver, 196
OLE control, 115
OLE DB Provider, 174, 196, 304
On Error statement, 82
One-dimensional array, 70
One-to-many relationship, 178
One-to-one relationship, 178
OOP, 475
Open command (File menu), 6
Open Database Connectivity, 174
Open method
    ADO, 225
    Connection object, 234
    Recordset object, 236
Optimistic locking, 214
Option button, 4, 116
Option Explicit statement, 62
OptionButton control, 115
Options dialog box, 29, 31, 140
Oracle, 196
Order of precedence
    arithmetic expression, 66
    conditional expression, 68
Outer join, 184
Out-of-process, 510

P

Package, 548, 550-557
    Internet, 574
Package and Deployment Wizard, 544-549
Packaging script, 548
Page Designer (DHTML), 526, 528

Page event, 531
Page, see HTML page
Panel (status bar), 452
Parameter object, 302
Parameter query, 300
Parameters
    collection (ADO), 223
    Command object, 360
    stored procedure, 188, 302
Parent form, 128, 130, 436
Parent-child relationship, 354
Password property (ADO data control), 211
PasswordChar property (text box), 311
Peer Web Server, 524
Personal Web Server, 524
Pessimistic locking, 214
Picture property (Command button), 448
PictureBox control, 115, 448
Placeholder character, 311
Pmt function, 42
Populating
    ComboBox control, 293
    DAO recordset, 224
Popup menu, 446
Primary key, 176-178
Print method (Debug object), 151
Printing code, 42
PrintReport method (DataReport object), 392
Private keyword, 24, 61, 90
Private procedure, 24
Procedure
    calling, 90
    coding, 90
    Function, 92
    monitoring, 154
    property, 482
    Sub, 90
    Sub Main, 106
Procedure-level variable, 60
Professional Edition, xvi
ProgressBar control, 438
Project, 6, 18
Project Explorer, 8, 108
Project Properties command (Project menu), 52, 106, 512
Properties, 12, 15, 28
    ADO data control, 210
    Class object, 478, 482
    ComboBox control, 293
    DataCombo control, 257
    DataGrid control, 260
    DataList control, 257
    ListBox control, 293
    MSFlexGrid control, 295
    project, 512
Properties window, 8
Property Get procedure, 482, 488, 498
Property Let procedure, 482, 488
Property settings
    Calculate Investment form (chapter 1), 16, 38
    Login form (chapter 8), 322
    New Vendors form (chapter 7), 280
    New Vendors form (chapter 8), 322
    Vendors form (chapter 6), 218
    Vendors form (chapter 7), 262-265
    Vendors form (chapter 8), 296
    Vendors form (chapter 9), 366
Provider property (ADO), 225
Public keyword, 61, 90

Q

Query, 182, 422
    Delete, 187
    Insert, 187
    Parameter, 300
    Select, 182-185
    Update, 187
Query Designer, 350, 422
Quick Watch feature, 156

R

Raise method, 162
RaiseEvent statement, 486
RDO, 196
Real data type (SQL Server), 181
Record, 176
RecordCount property (ADO), 225
Recordset, 208
Recordset events, 306
Recordset object, 223, 236
RecordSource property (ADO data control), 211
Reference, 233, 514
Referential integrity, 190
Register, 506
REGSVR32, 514
Relational database, 176
Relational operators, 68
Relationships between tables, 412
Rem keyword, 49
Remote component, 506, 568
Remote Data Objects, 196

Remove method (ComboBox control), 293
Report
    adding fields to, 376
    adding predefined fields to, 378
    changing the margins, 380
    creating, 374, 398
    creating totals, 388
    form for displaying, 394
    grouping on fields, 384
    grouping on relationships, 386
    modifying at run-time, 396
    previewing and printing, 380
Requery method (ADO), 225
Restart command, 147
Result set, 182
Results pane (Query Designer window), 350
Results pane (Data View window), 420
Resume statements, 82
Right function, 95, 99
Right outer join, 184
Rnd function, 95
ROLLBACK TRAN statement (SQL), 309
RollbackTranComplete event (Connection object), 307
RollbackTrans method (Connection object), 308
Row, 176
Row property (MSFlexGrid control), 295
RowMember property (DataCombo control), 257
Rows property (MSFlexGrid control), 295
RowSource property (DataCombo control), 257
Rule, 180
Run to Cursor command, 147
Run-time errors, 34

S

Scope of variables, 60
Screen object, 438
Script, 544, 566
    deployment, 548
    packaging, 548
SDI, 124, 436
Select Case statement, 76, 498
SELECT statement (SQL), 182, 184
Server, 172
Set Next Statement command, 147
Set statement, 226
Setup CD, 570
Setup.exe file, 572
Setup program, 544
Server-side cursor, 212
Shape control, 115

Shared locks (SQL Server), 194
Show method (DataReport object), 392
Show method (Form object), 440
Show Next Statement command, 147
ShowInTaskbar property (Form object), 15
Silent mode, 546
Single data type (VB), 59
Single-document interface, 124, 436
SLN function, 95
Smalldatetime data type (SQL Server), 181
Smallint data type (SQL Server), 181
Smallmoney data type (SQL Server), 181
SNA server, 202
Sorted property (ComboBox control), 293
Source property (Error object), 305
Splash form, 438, 440
SQL, 174
SQL pane, 350, 420
SQL query, 174
SQL Server database, 597-602
SQL Server data types, 181
SQL Server lock types, 194
SQL statements, 184
Stand-alone application, 546
Standard EXE option, 6
Standard module, 24, 52
    code for Vendors application, 312-313
Start command, 147
Startup form, 106, 438
Startup Object, 53, 106
StartUpPosition property (Form object), 15
Statement
    assignment, 62
    Call, 90
    Do...Loop, 80, 490, 500
    End Function, 93
    End Sub, 24, 90
    Event, 486
    Exit Sub, 82
    For Each...Next, 78
    For...Next, 78, 500
    Function, 93
    If, 74
    Load, 440
    On Error, 82
    Option Explicit, 62
    RaiseEvent, 486
    Resume, 82
    Select Case, 76, 498
    Set, 226

Sub, 24, 90
summary, 86
With, 84
Static cursor, 212
Static keyword, 61
Status bar, 452, 454
StatusBar control, 452
Step Into command (debugging), 147
Step Out command (debugging), 147
Step Over command (debugging), 147
Stored procedure, 188, 302, 424
String data type (VB), 59
Structured Query Language, 174
Style property
ComboBox control, 293
CommandButton control, 448
DataCombo control, 257
Sub Main procedure, 106
Sub procedure, 90
Sub statement, 24, 90
Submit element, 528
SYD function, 95
Synchronizing controls, 254, 271
System data types, 180
System Network Architecture, 202

T

TabIndex property, 15
Table, 176
adding or changing data, 414
creating or modifying structure, 410
TabStop property, 15
Tag contents, 540
Terminate event, 480, 488, 499
Text box, 4
multi-line, 255, 291
Text data type (SQL Server), 181
Text property, 15
ComboBox control, 293
MSFlexGrid control, 295
TextBox control, 115
Three-tier system, 200
Time function, 95
Timer control, 115
Timestamp data type (SQL Server), 181
Tinyint data type (SQL Server), 181
TLB file, 508, 512, 568
Toolbar
code for working with, 454
creating with PictureBox control, 448
creating with Toolbar control, 450

Toolbar control, 450
Toolbox, 8
adding controls, 120
control summary, 114
ToolTip, 442
Topic file, 458, 460
Transaction processing, 308
Transact-SQL, 182
Trappable error, 82
Trapping specific errors, 160
Trigger, 188
creating and modifying, 426
Two-dimensional array, 70
Two-tier system, 200

U

UI active mode, 258
Unbound control, 290
Unbound form
basic building skills, 230-237
building with ADO, 290-334
coding techniques, 268-277
New Vendors form (chapter 8), 326-331
Vendors form (chapter 6), 240-249
Vendors form (chapter 8), 296, 312-319
Uniform Resource Locator, 204, 520, 574
Unique constraint, 176, 412
Unique key, 176
Uniqueidentifier data type (SQL Server), 181
Universally Unique Identifier, 506
Unload event, 22
Update lock (SQL Server), 194
Update method (ADO), 225
UPDATE statement (SQL), 186
URL, 204, 520, 574
User-defined constant, 64
User-defined data type, 180
UserName property (ADO data control), 211
UUID, 506

V

Val function, 40, 95
Validate event, 122
Varbinary data type (SQL Server), 181
Varchar data type (SQL Server), 181
Variable-length string, 59
Variables
assigning values, 62
controlling scope, 60
declaring, 58
monitoring, 152

Variant data type (VB), 59
VB Class Builder, 480
VBR file, 508, 512, 568
View, 188
   creating or modifying, 420
View window, 420
Visible property, 15
Visual Basic functions, 94, 98
Visual Basic statements, 86
Visual Data Manager, 588-595
VScrollBar control, 115

W

WAN, 172
Watch expression, 156
Watch window, 156
Web browser, 204
Web server, 520
Web-based application, 204
Webclass Designer (IIS), 536
Webclass, 522, 532, 536, 538
Webclass tag, 532, 535, 540
Webitem, 532, 538
Wide area network, 172
WillChange event
   ADO data control, 269
   Recordset object, 307
WillConnect event (Connection object), 307
WillExecute event (Connection object), 307
WillMove event (ADO data control), 269
WillMove event (Recordset object), 307
WindowList property (menus), 446
With statement, 84
WithEvents keyword, 486
Wizard, Package and Deployment, 544-549

#Const directive, 164
#If...Then...Else directive, 164

Client/Server Programming: Access 97

Anne Prince and Joel Murach

Access 97 is a powerful tool for developing client/server (database) applications, especially for departmental or small business systems. And yet, most Access books limit you to working within Access, rather than teaching you what you need to know to handle databases in enterprise systems.

That's where this book comes in. It carefully explains all the pieces that are involved in developing a database application, shows you how they work together, and fills in the gaps that might trip you up otherwise...all at a pace that's right for the professional programmer. In fact, at the end of the first 4 chapters (just 157 pages), you'll be writing your first true client/server application, using Access as the front-end and DAO as the data access method. The data itself can be in an Access database or in an ODBC database such as SQL Server whose tables are linked to Access tables.

Then, the remaining 10 chapters make you a more proficient programmer, as you learn how to: build sophisticated forms and do more complex database processing using DAO...improve an application's performance by accessing the data with ODBCDirect instead of DAO...enhance the user interface with a splash screen, menus, toolbars, and online help... develop reports using Access' built-in report generator ...use class modules and ActiveX components (you can't create these in Access, but your applications can use them)...and test, debug, and deploy an application on the clients.

Access 97, 14 chapters, 558 pages, **$40.00**
ISBN 1-890774-01-4

Client/Server Programming: Visual Basic 5

Anne Prince and Ed Koop

Although most new client/server projects today are developed using Visual Basic 6, some companies are still maintaining VB5 applications. So if you need to know VB5, here's the book for you. It teaches you about older technologies that aren't covered in our VB6 book so you'll know how to handle them when you come across them in earlier applications.

As you might guess, this book teaches many of the same skills that our VB6 book covers: how to develop a Visual Basic application, how to do database programming, how to test, debug, and distribute your applications, how to write and use ActiveX components, and so on. Since you already know VB6, you can skim a lot of this material. But you'll also learn about VB5 features that were dropped or pre-empted by new features in VB6:

* how to develop bound and unbound forms with DAO, the preferred access method in VB5

* how to use Crystal Reports, the standard add-in for creating reports

* how to use the Visual Data Manager to create simple databases that you can use for testing your programs

So you'll be glad you have this book close at hand whenever a VB5 question comes up because it gives the professional perspective and answers you can't find in other VB5 books.

Visual Basic 5, 13 chapters, 457 pages, **$40.00**
ISBN 1-890774-00-6

MVS JCL

MVS/ESA • MVS/XA • MVS/370   Doug Lowe

Anyone who's worked in an MVS shop knows that JCL is tough to master. You learn enough to get by...but then you stick to that. It's just too frustrating to try to put together a job using the IBM manuals. And too time-consuming to keep asking your co-workers for help...especially since they're often limping along with the JCL they know, too.

That's why you need a copy of *MVS JCL*. It zeroes in on the JCL you need for everyday jobs...so you can learn to code significant job streams in a hurry.

You'll learn how to compile, link-edit, load, and execute programs. Process all types of data sets. Code

JES2/JES3 control statements to manage job and program execution, data set allocation, and SYSOUT processing. Create and use JCL procedures. Execute general-purpose utility programs. And much more.

But that's not all this book does. Beyond teaching you JCL, it explains the basics of how MVS works so you can apply that understanding as you code JCL. That's the kind of perspective that's missing in other books and courses about MVS, even though it's background you must have if you want to bring MVS under your control.

MVS JCL, 17 chapters, 496 pages, **$49.50**
ISBN 0-911625-85-2

MVS TSO

Part 1: Concepts and ISPF   Doug Lowe

Now you can quickly master ISPF with this practical book.

Chapter 1 introduces you to MVS (both MVS/XA and MVS/ESA)...good background no matter how much MVS experience you've had. It also shows you how TSO/ISPF relates to MVS, so you'll understand how to use ISPF to control the operating system functions.

The remaining 7 chapters teach you all the specifics of using ISPF for everyday programming tasks. You'll learn how to edit and browse data sets; use the ISPF utilities to manage your data sets and libraries; compile,

link, and execute programs interactively; use the VS COBOL II or OS COBOL interactive debugger; process batch jobs in a background region; manage your background jobs more easily using the Spool Display & Search Facility (SDSF) to browse JES2 queues; use member parts lists to track the use of subprograms and COPY members within program libraries; use two library management systems that support hierarchical libraries—the Library Management Facility (LMF) and the Software Configuration and Library Manager (SCLM); and more!

MVS TSO, Part 1, 8 chapters, 467 pages, **$42.50**
ISBN 0-911625-56-9

MVS TSO

Part 2: Commands and Procedures (CLIST and REXX)   Doug Lowe

If you're ready to expand your skills beyond ISPF and become a TSO user who can write complex CLIST and REXX procedures with ease, this is the book for you. It starts by teaching you how to use TSO commands for common programming tasks like managing data sets and libraries, running programs in foreground mode, and submitting jobs for background execution. Then, it

shows you how to combine those commands into CLIST or REXX procedures for the jobs you do most often...including procedures that you can use as edit macros under the ISPF editor and procedures that use ISPF dialog functions to display full-screen panels.

MVS TSO, Part 2, 10 chapters, 450 pages, **$42.50**
ISBN 0-911625-57-7

DB2 for the COBOL Programmer

Part 1 / Second Edition (Covers Version 4.1)　　　　　**Curtis Garvin and Steve Eckols**

If you're looking for a practical DB2 book that focuses on application programming, this is the book for you. Written from the programmer's point of view, it will quickly teach you what you need to know to access and process DB2 data in your COBOL programs using embedded SQL. You'll learn:

- what DB2 is and how it works, so you'll have the background you need to program more easily and logically

- how to design and code application programs that retrieve and update DB2 data

- how to use joins and unions to combine data from two or more tables into a single table (that includes Version 4 enhancements like outer joins and the explicit syntax for inner joins that simplify your coding)

- how to use column functions and scalar functions to save COBOL coding

- how to code subqueries whenever one SQL statement depends on the results of another

- how to handle the complications caused by variable-length data and null values in DB2 tables

- how to use error handling techniques and ROLLBACK to protect DB2 data

- why program efficiency is vital under DB2...and how to use the locking features right so you don't tie up the whole system

- how to use SPUFI and QMF to create the test tables you need to debug your programs

- how to develop DB2 programs interactively (using DB2I, a TSO facility) or in batch

So if you want to learn how to write DB2 application programs, get a copy of this book today!

DB2, Part 1, 15 chapters, 431 pages, **$45.00**
ISBN 1-890774-02-2

DB2 for the COBOL Programmer

Part 2 / Second Edition (Covers Versions 4.1 and 5)　　　　　**Curtis Garvin and Anne Prince**

Once you've mastered the basics of DB2 programming, there's still plenty to learn. So this book teaches you all the advanced DB2 features that a senior programmer or programmer/analyst needs to know...and shows you when to use each one. You'll learn:

- how data sharing works on the parallel sysplex and other System/390 configurations

- advanced locking concepts that let you understand how locking and data sharing affect each other and what impact that has on program efficiency

- how to use dynamic SQL

- how to work with distributed DB2 data

- how to execute stored procedures that move SQL code off of the client and onto the database server to reduce network overhead

- how to use DB2 from CICS programs

- what you need to know about database administration to set up a quality assurance environment

- and more!

So don't wait to expand your DB2 skills. Get a copy of this book TODAY.

DB2, Part 2, 13 chapters, 395 pages, **$45.00**
ISBN 1-890774-03-0

 Call toll-free 1-800-221-5528 (Weekdays, 8-5 Pacific Time) • Fax 1-559-440-0963 • www.murach.com

CICS for the COBOL Programmer

Second Edition   **Doug Lowe**

This 2-part course is designed to help COBOL programmers become outstanding CICS programmers.

Part 1: An Introductory Course covers the basic CICS elements you'll use in just about every program you write. So you'll learn about basic mapping support (BMS), pseudo-conversational programming, basic CICS commands, sensible program design using event-driven design techniques, testing and debugging using IBM-supplied transactions (like CEMT, CECI, and CEDF) or a transaction dump, and efficiency considerations.

Part 2: An Advanced Course covers CICS features you'll use regularly, though you won't need all of them for every program. That means you'll learn about browse commands, temporary storage, transient data, data tables (including the shared data table feature of CICS 3.3), DB2 and DL/I processing considerations, distributed processing features, interval control

commands, BMS page building, and more! In addition, *Part 2* teaches you which features do similar things and when to use each one. So you won't just learn how to code new functions...you'll also learn how to choose the best CICS solution for each programming problem you face.

> **CICS, Part 1,** 12 chapters, 409 pages, **$42.50**
> ISBN 0-911625-60-7
>
> **CICS, Part 2,** 12 chapters, 352 pages, **$42.50**
> ISBN 0-911625-67-4

The CICS Programmer's Desk Reference

Second Edition   **Doug Lowe**

Ever feel buried by IBM manuals?

It seems like you need stacks of them, close at hand, if you want to be an effective CICS programmer. Because frankly, there's just too much you have to know to do your job well; you can't keep it all in your head.

That's why Doug Lowe decided to write *The CICS Programmer's Desk Reference*. In it, he's collected all the information you need to have at your fingertips, and organized it into 12 sections that make it easy for you to find what you're looking for. So there are sections on:

* BMS macro instructions—their formats (with an explanation of each parameter) and coding examples

* CICS commands—their syntax (with an explanation of each parameter), coding examples, and suggestions on how and when to use each one most effectively

* MVS and DOS/VSE JCL for CICS applications

* AMS commands for handling VSAM files

* details for MVS users on how to use ISPF

* complete model programs, including specs, design, and code

* a summary of CICS program design techniques that lead to simple, maintainable, and efficient programs

* guidelines for testing and debugging your CICS applications

* and more!

So clear the IBM manuals off your terminal table. Let the *Desk Reference* be your everyday guide to CICS instead.

> **CICS Desk Reference,** 12 sections, 507 pages, **$49.50**
> ISBN 0-911625-68-2

 Call toll-free 1-800-221-5528 (Weekdays, 8-5 Pacific Time) • Fax 1-559-440-0963 • www.murach.com

Order Form

Our Unlimited Guarantee

To our customers who order directly from us: You must be satisfied. Our books must work for you, or you can send them back for a full refund...no questions asked.

Name & Title _____

Company (if company address) _____

Street Address _____

City, State, Zip _____

Phone number (including area code) _____

Fax number (if you fax your order to us) _____

Qty	Product code and title	*Price
VB and Access development		
___ VB60	Murach's Visual Basic 6	$45.00
___ VB50	Client/Server Programming: Visual Basic 5	40.00
___ AC97	Client/Server Programming: Access 97	40.00
Mainframe database programming		
___ DB1R	DB2 for the COBOL Programmer Part 1 (Second Edition)	$45.00
___ DB2R	DB2 for the COBOL Programmer Part 2 (Second Edition)	45.00

Qty	Product code and title	*Price
Other mainframe classics		
___ CC1R	CICS for the COBOL Programmer Part 1 (Second Edition)	$42.50
___ CC2R	CICS for the COBOL Programmer Part 2 (Second Edition)	42.50
___ CRFR	The CICS Programmer's Desk Reference (Second Edition)	49.50
___ MJLR	MVS JCL (Second Edition)	49.50
___ TSO1	MVS TSO, Part 1: Concepts and ISPF	42.50
___ TSO2	MVS TSO, Part 2: Commands and Procedures (CLIST and REXX)	42.50

❑ **Save 10%**: Take 10% off the books I've ordered, then charge the books plus UPS shipping and handling (and sales tax within California) to my
___Visa ___MasterCard ___American Express:

Card number _____

Valid thru (mo/yr) _____

Cardowner's signature _____

❑ Bill my company for the full prices of the books plus shipping and handling (and sales tax within California). P.O.# _____

*Prices are subject to change. Please call for current prices.

Your opinions count

If you have any comments on this book, I'm eager to get them. Thanks for your feedback!

To comment by

E-mail: murachbooks@murach.com

Web: www.murach.com/custserv

Postal mail: **Mike Murach & Associates, Inc.**
2560 West Shaw Lane, Suite 101
Fresno, California 93711-2765

To order now,

Call toll-free 1-800-221-5528
(Weekdays, 8 am to 5 pm Pacific Time)

Fax: 1-559-440-0963

Web: www.murach.com

Mike Murach & Associates, Inc.
Practical computer books since 1974

BUSINESS REPLY MAIL

FIRST-CLASS MAIL   PERMIT NO. 3063   FRESNO, CA

POSTAGE WILL BE PAID BY ADDRESSEE

Mike Murach & Associates, Inc.

2560 W SHAW LN STE 101
FRESNO CA 93711-9866